Naked Seeing

Naked Seeing

The Great Perfection, the Wheel of Time, and Visionary Buddhism in Renaissance Tibet

CHRISTOPHER HATCHELL

OXFORD
UNIVERSITY PRESS

OXFORD
UNIVERSITY PRESS

Oxford University Press is a department of the University of Oxford.
It furthers the University's objective of excellence in research, scholarship,
and education by publishing worldwide.

Oxford New York
Auckland Cape Town Dar es Salaam Hong Kong Karachi
Kuala Lumpur Madrid Melbourne Mexico City Nairobi
New Delhi Shanghai Taipei Toronto

With offices in
Argentina Austria Brazil Chile Czech Republic France Greece
Guatemala Hungary Italy Japan Poland Portugal Singapore
South Korea Switzerland Thailand Turkey Ukraine Vietnam

Published in the United States of America by
Oxford University Press
198 Madison Avenue, New York, NY 10016

Library of Congress Cataloging-in-Publication Data
Hatchell, Christopher.
Naked Seeing : The Great Perfection, The Wheel of Time, and Visionary Buddhism in Renaissance Tibet / Christopher Hatchell.
pages cm
Includes bibliographical references and index.
ISBN 978–0–19–998291–2 (pbk. : alk. paper) — ISBN 978–0–19–998290–5 (cloth : alk. paper)
1. Tantric Buddhism–Tibet Region—Rituals. 2. Kalacakra (Tantric rite) 3. Rdzogs-chen.
I. Title.
BQ7805.H38 2013
294.3'438—dc23
2013006562

CONTENTS

Preface ix
What Can the Eyes See? ix
Literary Sources: Three Buddhist Texts on Vision x
Organization: Three Approaches to Vision xi
Acknowledgments xiii

Introduction 1

Tibetan Renaissance: An Era of Lamps 1
Literature and Life 2
Major Religious Groups: Sarma, Nyingma, and Bön 4
Philosophical Vajrayāna and the Turn to Vision 5
Three Texts: A Trio of Lamps 8
What Vision Reveals 10
Visionary Buddhism? 11
Philosophy and the Vajrayāna 12
Reading Religious Dialogue 14
Searching for the Source 15
Future Directions 16

PART ONE | Seeing Literature

CHAPTER 1 Yumo's *Lamp Illuminating Emptiness* 21

The Wheel of Time 21

Early Tibetan Kālacakra and Yumo's *Lamp Illuminating Emptiness* 22
Yumo's Argument and Style 24
Biography of Yumo Mikyo Dorjé 27
Essential Background for the *Lamp Illuminating Emptiness* 29
Kālacakra's Visualized Generation Stage 29
Kālacakra's Visionary Six Yogas 31
Guhyasamāja and the "Stage of Self-Blessing" 41
Interpretive Analysis of the *Lamp Illuminating Emptiness* 42
Yumo's Introductory Comments 42
The Root Verse of the Treatise 43
Yumo's Concluding Summation 48
Conclusion 48

CHAPTER 2 *Tantra of the Blazing Lamps* 50

The Old Ones Encountering the New 50
The Great Perfection and the Seminal Heart 51
Seventeen Tantras and the *Tantra of the Blazing Lamps* 53
Essential Background for the *Tantra of the Blazing Lamps* 55
Gnostic Monism and the Doctrine of Recognition 55
The Enlightenment of All Good 57
The Common Ground 59
The Four Visions 59
Interpretive Analysis of the *Tantra of the Blazing Lamps* 63
The Tantra's Introductory Scenes 63
The Teaching in Brief 64
The Extensive Teaching 64
Conclusion 68

CHAPTER 3 *Advice on the Six Lamps* 70

Bön and the Great Perfection 70
The Oral Tradition from Zhang Zhung, and *Advice on the Six Lamps* 72
Primordial Beginnings and Historical Ends 74
Visionary Revelations: Tapihritsa and Gyerpungpa 75

Renaissance and the Writing of an Oral Tradition 78
Essential Background for *Advice on the Six Lamps* 82
Sound, Light, and Rays 83
The Mother, the Son, and Dynamic Energy 83
Interpretive Analysis of *Advice on the Six Lamps* 84
Introductory Materials 84
Conclusion 92

PART TWO | Views

CHAPTER 4 Seeing Emptiness 97
Vision, Philosophy, and Physiology 97
Observations on Emptiness 98
Luminous Channels and Divine Eyes: Lighting Up the Body's Darkness 103
Channels of Light in the Great Perfection 104
Divine Eyes in the Wheel of Time 105
Seeing in the Dark: Charles Bonnet Syndrome and Visual Filling-In 110
Conclusion: Views of the Ultimate 113

CHAPTER 5 Seeing Light 118
Lights in the Body 118
Lights in the Eyes 119
Spontaneity and Motion 119
The Blue Field: Entoptic Light, Floaters, and Physiology 121
Letting the Light Out: Bodily Postures for Inducing Visions 124
The Matter of Light 125
Conclusion: Two-in-One 128

CHAPTER 6 Seeing through Sexuality 130
Introduction: The Many-Faced Consort 130
Etymologies and Types of *Thig-le:* Seeds, Semen, Sights, and Symbols 134
Kālacakra: Four *Thig-le* in the Body, and One in Vision 137
The Great Perfection: Five *Thig-le* 141
Conclusion: Coming Full Circle 144

CONCLUSION 147

Circles and Straight Lines 147

◎ PART THREE | Seeing Sources ◎

TRANSLATION 1 *Lamp Illuminating Emptiness,* by Yumo Mikyo Dorjé 153

TRANSLATION 2 *Tantra of the Blazing Lamps* 201

TRANSLATION 3A *Advice on the Six Lamps* 229

TRANSLATION 3B *Commentary on the Intended Meaning of the Six Lamps,* by Drugom Gyalwa Yungdrung 265

Notes 349
Bibliography 439
Abbreviations 439
Buddhist and Bön Canonical Scriptures 440
Buddhist and Bön Treatises, Commentaries, and Historical Works 442
Reference Works 446
Secondary Sources 446
Selected Works on Seeing and Blindness 457
Spelling of Tibetan Personal and Place Names 461
Index 463

PREFACE

What Can the Eyes See?

What can the eyes see? Is it only mundane objects illuminated by the ordinary light of the world? Or might the eyes themselves be sources of illumination? When the eyes are deprived of light—for instance if we stay for a long while in a completely dark room—we eventually begin to see light where there is none: abstract spots and showers of light will emerge from the darkness and eventually transform into a rich visual field, full of objects and beings. Why do the eyes respond this way to the dark? The eyes also have unusual functions when flooded with light. For instance, if we gaze up at the sky, we see objects that are not outside of us but that are within the eye itself—floaters, spots, and squiggles—and in time those can give way to full visionary experiences, realistic scenes that seem to be projected into the sky. When the eyes meet such visionary images, is this "seeing"? And what do those evanescent and ultimately "unreal" visions suggest about the objects in our more ordinary visual worlds?

This book explores these questions of seeing through a study of Buddhist yogis who dwell in dark rooms and gaze at the sky, aiming to experience luminous visions. These meditative practices rose to popularity in eleventh-century tantric Buddhism, as part of an Indian tradition called the Wheel of Time *(kālacakra),* and also in a Tibetan movement known as the Great Perfection *(rdzogs chen).* As both of these groups began experimenting with the body's sensory system, they found that complete immersion in darkness or light resulted in unusual events of seeing, and those events could then be used as methods for pursuing long-standing Buddhist questions about appearances. Vision thus became a way of inquiring into whether things in fact exist in the way that they appear, or whether objects' apparent solidity, permanence, and meaning were in fact as illusory as the fleeting visionary lights that emerge from darkness.

In what follows, I discuss two visionary practices that are commonly called "dark-retreat" and "sky-gazing." While I do present some traditional descriptions of the techniques involved in the practice of vision, my main concern is with Buddhists' intellectual and philosophical responses to vision: how Buddhists interpret visions, and what they say their ultimate significance might be. Along the way, I look at some of the provocative ideas that arose from these visionary projects, such as the claim that religious truths like "emptiness" *(śūnyatā)* do not have to be approached through an internal mental in-sight, but that they might be seen in the exterior world—realized through the gateway of the eyes.

Literary Sources: Three Buddhist Texts on Vision

This is in many ways a literary study, organized around three literary works from three different Tibetan religious traditions. The sources are:

1. The *Lamp Illuminating Emptiness (stong nyid gsal sgron),* a Kālacakra treatise by Yumo Mikyo Dorjé,
2. The *Tantra of the Blazing Lamps (sgron ma 'bar ba'i rgyud),* a Great Perfection work belonging to the Nyingma tradition, and
3. *Advice on the Six Lamps (sgron ma drug gi gdams pa),* and a detailed commentary on this by Drugom Gyalwa Yungdrung, both of which are Great Perfection works belonging to the Bön tradition.

Though these texts came from different traditions and speak in their own distinct voices, they are clearly discussing a common topic, and I suggest that in reading them together, we can learn more about them than if they are read in isolation. On the simplest level, this group of texts speaks about the historical period from which they emerged. Popularized during Tibet's renaissance period, they suggest how seeing and vision were critical themes in the religious revival of that era. These texts make no reference to one another, but placed next to each other, their common ideas clearly show how their respective traditions competed with, borrowed from, and mutually influenced each other.

Ultimately, I also want to use these sources to get at the question of why religious authors would write about vision in the first place. If we take these texts at face value, it would seem that vision is simply a matter of the body, the mind, and the eyes; but as we read, it becomes apparent that vision is also intertwined with words. Thus, in these texts, we can see a relationship between words and the eyes: a yogi sees visions and puts them into writing; those literary visions are encountered by readers, and when those readers engage in visionary practice themselves, their reading influences and adds meaning to their own experiences of seeing. In the present book, then, through our own reading, I hope that we can come to see new dimensions of vision, as being part of a process that is not simply physical or personal, but that involves literature, discussion, speculation, memory, and culture.

Organization: Three Approaches to Vision

The book that follows is organized as a sort of "tripod," inspired by this structure's simplicity and stability. Here, I take my three literary sources and discuss them in three sections, with the sections representing three different viewpoints from which to approach the literature.

Part One of the book ("Seeing Literature") contains three chapters, one devoted to each of our three visionary texts. These chapters introduce the texts' histories, provide the theoretical background necessary for understanding them, and give interpretive analyses of their content. While these chapters are in some ways the more straightforward portion of the book, they are deliberately constructed to circle around the texts' points of contact and contention. Thus, this part of the book is not intended simply as background but also represents my efforts to present the texts so that their connections can be readily seen.

Part Two ("Views") contains three interpretive essays that approach the texts comparatively rather than individually. In this part of the book I discuss the critical themes found in these sources and also connect them to broader and more well-known Buddhist intellectual movements like Prajñāpāramitā and Mādhyamika. Chapter 4 is an essay that takes up the theme of darkness. It provides a brief introduction to the techniques and physiology of dark-room meditation but then focuses mainly on the philosophical issue of emptiness and suggests ways that visionary practices using darkness were valued for inquiring into this philosophical idea. Chapter 5 turns to the theme of light; the essay discusses sky-gazing practices by reflecting on philosophical and literary discourses of light that inspired and were inspired by sky-gazing. Finally, chapter 6 investigates the relationship between seeing and sexuality and explores how visionary practice might be understood as related to the Buddhist practice of sexual yoga.

Part Three ("Seeing Sources") contains complete English translations of my Tibetan-language sources. Each translation is prefaced with bibliographic information, comments on the editions of the texts, and my reflections on some of the difficult issues in the process of translation.

ACKNOWLEDGMENTS

The research for this book was carried out over many years and took me to Tibet and India. All this would have been impossible without two generous fellowships. The Fulbright program of the Institute of International Education funded my research in Sichuan Province, PRC; thanks in particular to Keith Clemenger, Jonathan Akeley, and Professor Li Tao of Sichuan University. The American Institute of Indian Studies funded my research in India; thank you to Purnima Metha, Elise Auerbach, Mr. Arora, and all of the other members of the AIIS staff.

Thanks as well to my academic mentors, who provided me with invaluable advice and guidance on the project. First, thanks to David Germano, whose own work and teaching were my primary inspiration. Thanks as well to Paul Groner, Bob Hueckstedt, Karen Lang, and Kurtis Shaeffer, whose insightful comments and suggestions have been invaluable. Thanks also to Jeffrey Hopkins for his assistance and encouragement, and for helping to spark my interest in Tibetan studies.

During my research I was assisted by several Tibetan scholars, who inspired me with their knowledge, dedication, humor, and patience. Thank you to H. H. Lungdok Tenpai Nyima, who graciously hosted my extended stay at Menri Monastery in Dolanji and provided me with needed encouragement. My deepest gratitude goes to Lopön Trinley Nyima Rinpoche of Menri Monastery, who found time in his busy schedule to answer my endless questions, always doing so with a clarity and straightforwardness that I found nowhere else; Ponlop's keen interest in scholarly issues, his enthusiasm for his own tradition, and his willingness to discuss matters of esoteric thought revived my research and my spirits from their lowest point and made this work both possible and enjoyable. Thanks also to Khenpo Ngawang Dorjee in Charlottesville, who was enthusiastic about discussing Yumo's life and thought. Thanks as well to Geshe Namgyal and Geshe Sonam, who helped me out of many impasses as I wandered through Bön literature. And thank you to the many other teachers who helped me along the way, particularly Sherab Dorjé, Dorjé Tashi, Pema Tsultrim, and Geshe Samdup.

While my research interests are sometimes called "textual," I have never been able to accept that literature is bounded by what an individual reader sees on the page. This project has taught me how literature is mixed up with life and culture, and my reading has been both supported and influenced by my experiences with Tibetans and Tibetan communities. Because of this, I would like to dedicate this book to the people of Tibet, without whose humor, stubbornness, pride, and beauty none of the intellectual issues in this book would have ever interested me at all.

This work will always be associated in my mind with Julian Paul Green, a shooting star who fell in the Tibetan mountains that he loved, and whose memory has often inspired me to continue.

Finally, my greatest inspiration and support have come from my wife, Kimberly. Without her, the whole project would have seemed more like research and less like drinking tea.

Naked Seeing

| Introduction

Tibetan Renaissance: An Era of Lamps

In Buddhist literature, the image of a lamp is often used to indicate the illuminating presence of a buddha. Śākyamuni, for instance, is called the "Lamp of the World," signifying how his teaching pervades and lights up the universe. Tibetan authors also use lamps to mark the bright spots in their religious histories, with the term "era of lamps" *(sgron ma'i bskal pa)* used for a period in which a buddha is present to dispel the darkness of ignorance.

When Tibetan historians look back at their own past, they see two such bright periods. The first of these began in the seventh century, when Buddhism was first introduced to the Tibetan plateau. Known as the "earlier spread" *(snga dar)* of Buddhism, this is recalled as the era when Tibet was at the height of its powers, with a fearsome military presided over by a series of emperors who also sponsored Buddhist activities. Buddhism flourished under this imperial support: the Tibetan script and new Buddhist terminologies were created; the first monastery, Samyé, was constructed; networks of temples and sacred sites appeared; scholars and practitioners were invited from India; and Indian Buddhist texts were translated in large-scale projects. Yet government expenditures on religion—along with the rise of monastic landownership, and taxes that required ordinary families to support monks[1]—introduced new economic tensions. All of this may have combined to tip the empire off balance; Tibetan histories often suggest that imperial largesse ultimately led to the demise of the last major emperor, Relpachen. Though the nature of his demise is unclear, legend has it that Relpachen was assassinated, an act that was in protest of his extensive support for Buddhism.

Relpachen's successor Lang Darma, the last emperor, was also short-lived. Depending on one's perspective, Darma either attempted to rein in the power of the Buddhist clergy (according to modern historical thought), or instituted a persecution of Buddhism (according to traditional Buddhist accounts). The truth may be somewhere in between, but the result is agreed upon: Darma was assassinated in 842. This time, according to the popular Tibetan accounts, the assassin was a Buddhist monk.

Darma's death sent Tibet into its "period of fragmentation" *(sil pa'i dus),* as the empire split in a battle over succession and eventually collapsed, and political power was divided up among local clans.[2] Little is known about this period, though there are accounts of civil unrest,[3] and the near absence of religious literature from the period[4] suggests organized religion must also have broken apart. However, religion certainly survived during this time, and in the absence of central control took on forms that were distinctively local, making this a time of diversity and ferment that, when Buddhist activity re-emerged in force, would permanently influence the character of Tibetan religion. Nonetheless, when Tibetans look back at this period, they see it as their "era of darkness" *(mun pa'i bskal pa).*

The present book is set in the time of Tibet's ensuing religious renaissance, starting near the end of the tenth century when organized Buddhism began to reassert its presence. Tibetan historians call this period the "later dissemination" *(phyi dar)* of Buddhism, and also refer to it as the "era of lamps" *(sgron ma'i bskal pa).* The revival of Buddhism in this period began with small pockets of religious activity that still remained from the imperial period, and thus, in a traditional metaphor, religion is said to have sprung up like flames from the embers. Tibetans use this "embers" image to suggest how the renaissance was sparked by fragments of the past: small monastic ordination lineages that were able to survive, rituals and practices maintained by clans associated with the empire, temples and trade routes that had fallen into disuse, and the powerful memory of the once-great religious kings. But "flames" also suggests how the renaissance would consume the past, as the era's Modernists would portray the "old" traditions—no matter how vital—as broken, sometimes degenerate, and in need of reformation. One part of the renaissance, then, was a drive to remake religion rather than simply reviving it, and this prompted efforts at retranslating texts, importing previously unknown traditions and ritual systems from India, building new temples and institutions, and constructing religious lineages that would challenge and integrate the power of the old clans.

Literature and Life

One major feature of this renaissance was the appearance of new religious literature. It might seem self-evident that written texts would play a primary role in a religious revival, but in fact "reading" is not always the primary use of books in Buddhist cultures, where texts are often used as sacred objects, irrespective of the particular doctrinal details they may contain. Thus it is useful to recall that the written content of books—and not just their sacred power—can also be a motivating agent in society: literature acts as the basis of personal relationships, forms central points around which communities are organized, prompts travel and economic activity, sparks debates, defines rivalries, and even serves as a space for creative thought.

This was particularly true in Tibet's renaissance, when there were intensive efforts to import and translate new works from India, to revitalize and revise bodies of literature that already existed in Tibet, and to compose works that were completely new. In this environment, translators became cultural heroes, and their tribulations on the road to India became material for legends. Literature thus prompted an educated class of Tibetans to cross borders and form new personal relationships, as they traveled to India, worked with Indians, and brought Indian scholars back to Tibet. Literature also prompted travel within Tibet itself, as students moved between communities centered around teachers of a particular specialty, and then moved on to other centers as their needs or interests progressed.

A good example of a renaissance life-in-literature is Yumo Mikyo Dorjé, a relatively unknown author whose treatise the *Lamp Illuminating Emptiness* is central to this book. Yumo's life story is instructive because his biographies contain relatively little mythology, and though they are spare, they hit the major themes of Tibetan religious life in the mid-eleventh century. Yumo was born to a nomadic family in western Tibet, near Mt. Kailash. The youngest of four sons, as a child he became ordained along with his parents and siblings, and the family remained so for the remainder of their lives. Yumo's religious life, however, was not simply centered around wearing robes and maintaining vows; he embarked on a path of scholarship, punctuated at first by studies of the Middle Way *(madhyamaka)* and epistemology *(pramāṇa)*. He later met a teacher named Lama Sok Chenpo, famed at the time for his knowledge of monastic discipline. Yumo traveled to Sok Chenpo's community, and his relationship with this renowned *vinaya* teacher would open doors for him for the rest of his career.

Yumo gradually became interested in tantra and is said to have found instruction in several of the major tantras like Hevajra. During this period, he decided to enter into a brief retreat where he would copy texts, a practice used for making merit. A companion suggested he copy the *Vajragarbha Commentary,* an important work in the Kālacakra tradition, and one that must have only recently come to Tibet. The biographies say that "simply hearing the name" of this text changed the direction of Yumo's life. He became determined to find a teacher who could explain it, and thus traveled to central Tibet hoping to meet Somanātha, the Kaśmiri paṇḍit who helped translate the *Kālacakra Tantra* into Tibetan, and who was reportedly visiting Tibet. Yumo was successful in meeting with Somanātha, but when he requested teachings, the paṇḍit rebuffed him. Yumo did, however, find favor with members of Somanātha's inner circle and thus was able to study Kālacakra very close to one of its most important sources in Tibet.

Many of the themes in Yumo's story exemplify Tibet's religious renaissance: religious sentiment strong enough to prompt the ordination of an entire family; an enthusiasm for Mahāyāna literature (biographies mention Śāntideva); studies in exoteric topics like *pramāṇa;* a core emphasis on monasticism and the *vinaya;* a key moment of inspiration based on a written text; and all of this culminating in an interest in tantra. Yumo's religious path was not organized around sects or important institutions but by relationships with individuals and travels between their local communities. Finally—and this is perhaps his most quintessentially "renaissance" characteristic—he very consciously participated in a time of religious creativity and development. Not simply memorizing and mastering an established tradition, he sought to experiment with the freshest and most cutting-edge forms of Buddhist thought and practice, in his case the system of Kālacakra.

Major Religious Groups: Sarma, Nyingma, and Bön

In broadest terms, Yumo was part of a movement that would come to be known as Sarma: the "New Ones" or the "Modernists." This was a group of self-styled reformers who wanted to re-establish and re-authenticate Tibetan Buddhist traditions by bringing them back to their Indian roots. Their project involved learning Indian languages and collaborating with Indian scholars in an effort to retranslate Buddhist literature, all the while looking to compose, discover, and import Buddhist texts that were as yet unknown. Their success can be judged by their eventual and continuing domination of the Tibetan Buddhist world.

But the Modernists were far from dominant in the eleventh century, as they existed in a competitive dialogue with two other broad, heterogeneous movements: Nyingma and Bön. The group that Sarma would be defined against was called Nyingma, or the "Old Ones." Also undergoing a revival, this diverse group tended to cast their gaze not to India and the future but to Tibet's own past, to the literature and traditions that had been imported from India before the fall of the dynasty. Like the New Ones, Nyingma was not simply a revivalist movement. During the renaissance, Nyingma traditions would produce some of Tibet's most innovative religious writings, revealing them as "treasures" *(gter ma)* said to have been written and hidden away during the time of the dynasty.

Finally, the third major group in this period was Bön *(bon),* which in some ways is the era's least understood and most complex movement. In broadest terms, Bön is Tibet's non-Buddhist religious system,[5] which traces its own origins to western Tibet and beyond, to lands called Ölmo Lungring and Zhang Zhung[6] in the centuries before Buddhism arrived. In Bön histories, the seventh-century arrival of Buddhism in Tibet was not the beginning of an "era of lamps," but was the beginning of Bön's decline. This culminated in Zhang Zhung being annexed to Tibet by the Buddhist king Songtsen Gampo (d. 649), and Bön being persecuted and banned from central Tibet by King Trisong Detsen, perhaps in the year 785.[7] While these histories are enormously difficult to sort out, it is clear that Bön's encounter with Buddhism began a slow process of transformation, which by the end of the renaissance would leave Bön outwardly resembling Buddhism, complete with a monastic system, a pantheon of buddhas, and a doctrine oriented toward the attainment of enlightenment. Bön symbolizes its own vibrant and complicated mixture of orthodox Buddhism and indigenous Tibetan religion through the figure of their eighth-century hero Drenpa Namkha, who, given the choice to convert to Buddhism or leave central Tibet, is said to have cut off his own hair, ordained himself, and publicly practiced Buddhism in the day while secretly practicing Bön at night.

Philosophical Vajrayāna and the Turn to Vision

During the renaissance period, each of these three groups produced a great amount of new literature. While much of their writing dealt with conventional Mahāyāna issues, their core interests were unabashedly oriented toward the esoteric path, known to Buddhists as tantra, or the Vajrayāna. In the treasure trove of Vajrayāna literature that remains from this era, we find works of every imaginable pedigree: new imports from India, retranslations of Indian originals, purported retranslations, native Tibetan works revived from the imperial period, new Tibetan compositions and revelations, and Tibetan compositions purporting to be Indian. Among these writings were many related to the late Indian tantric systems that were the era's freshest materials, and that are now viewed as among the greatest and final expressions of Indian Buddhist thought. Of particular interest was the Kālacakra system, prized for its highly developed scholastic literature, and its elaborate visualization-driven rituals organized around political maṇḍalas and Buddha-kings. But equally popular were tantric materials that operated on a smaller scale: a dizzying variety of compendia dealing with physiology, herbology, sexuality, magic, astrology, and unusual yogic techniques.

With their antisocial rhetoric, horrific imagery, and transgressive sexual practices, esoteric Buddhist traditions seem completely unsuited to the concerns of community building, monasticism, and popular religious revival that must have been important during Tibet's renaissance. Nonetheless, in this period tantra attained such dominance that it became (and remains) the space in which much of Tibetan religious activity was carried out: ritual, yoga, popular religion, funerary traditions, astrology, divination, religious arts, and increasingly, philosophy.

The Vajrayāna is not often thought of as a source of great philosophical ideas in Buddhism, as its literature at first glance seems to address pragmatic rather than theoretical concerns: providing instructions for ritual performance on the social level, while on the personal level providing methods for making yogic accomplishments and attaining magical powers. There is, however, a deep philosophical strain in late Indian Vajrayāna, which speculates on topics like the nature of mind, the illusory nature of appearances, the social construction of reality, and the ultimate emptiness of all things. This speculative side of the Vajrayāna is not separate from the hallmark tantric interests in ritual and yogic techniques. Rather, it uses such pragmatic matters as starting points from which to digress into theory. The literature related to dark-retreat and sky-gazing provides a particularly good example of this trend. These works describe visionary yogic practices, but they also use the topic of vision to raise a host of intellectual issues related to knowing, appearances, and the nature of phenomena.

As groups like Kālacakra and the Great Perfection began practicing and writing about vision, they were able to draw on prominent visual themes that were already present in esoteric Buddhism. The classic practices of tantra, for instance, involve reimagining and transforming the body by regarding it with various kinds of seeing or visualization. In one of the best-known tantric techniques, the practitioner visualizes him- or herself in the transcendent form of a buddha, complete with ornaments, symbolic hand implements, and a divine retinue. The famous sexual yogas found in the tantras involve similar visualizations but turn the gaze from the surface of the body to its interior and involve envisioning and manipulating subtle energies within the body, in an effort to ultimately reconfigure the body and mind.

Tantric literature does not just describe the performance of such practices but also delves into the issues of how such transformations might be possible, what features of the subtle body allow them to take place, and what that subtle body might signify. Often these inquiries begin with discussions of the body's intrinsic purity, such that a person's five psychophysical components *(skandhas),* five elements, five limbs, and five fingers are identified with five distinct "families" of buddhas. The idea that transcendent forces larger than the individual are at work in the body then leads to a host of theoretical issues: the connection between the personal space of the inner body and the public space of the world, correspondences between the structure of the body and that of the universe, how the purity of the body might relate to its ultimate emptiness, and so forth. Still, with some exceptions (notably the *Guhyagarbha Tantra*), the philosophical content of tantras themselves can be rather mild, and unless a commentator brings it into the foreground, it tends to get lost among other esoterica: descriptions of magical symbols, secret gestures, and ritualized sexual interactions; methods for lengthening life, arranging maṇḍalas, summoning ḍākinīs, and conquering enemies; recipes for potions, poisons, and medicines; and instructions on yogic postures, breathing techniques, scripted visualizations, and ritual offerings.

Among the late Indian tantras, the *Kālacakra Tantra* stands out as having a very overt philosophical dimension, and along with its commentary *Stainless Light* stands as a compelling integration of tantric yoga and philosophical thought. Kālacakra certainly contains all of the practical esoteric details that one would expect in a tantric tradition. But it also contains a strand that speaks in provocative terms about Buddhists' central philosophical issue, emptiness.

The Kālacakra tradition's claims about emptiness are bound up with a suite of meditative techniques called the "six-limbed yoga" *(ṣaḍaṅgayoga, sbyor ba yang lag drug)*. These six yogas are visionary practices, designed to induce luminous appearances that arise before the yogi's eyes. Organized around the themes of "day and night" or "light and dark," they instruct the yogi to spend lengthy periods either gazing at the blank sky or residing in a dark room specially prepared to seal out all light. Both of these are forms of sensory deprivation and result in a series of unstructured appearances of light—like sparks, fireflies, and so forth—that ultimately coalesce into a vision of deities, or the appearance of a luminous goddess known as the Great Seal *(mahāmudrā, phyag rgya chen mo)*.

This Great Seal, however, is not a simple visionary image of a divine body; rather, she is also identified as emptiness itself, appearing in animate form. This is an unusual claim about emptiness, and so Kālacakra literature is full of details explaining what the nature of this Great Seal might be. For a typical example, we can turn to the following passage from the *Lotus Girl*,[8] Kālacakrapāda's commentary on *Stainless Light*. Kālacakrapāda here is discussing a comment in *Stainless Light* that calls the Great Seal the "woman with conventional form."[9] He takes this comment as an opportunity to discuss how the visionary Great Seal, while ultimately being emptiness itself, is still able to appear with conventional aspects:

> [In *Stainless Light*, the phrase] "woman with conventional form" indicates that [the Great Seal] is emptiness with a conventional

> nature, not a nature that is devoid of all aspects. What is the meaning of this? I will explain: The eyes of beginners—the very eyes that see pots, pillars, and so forth—see universal form in the sky, endowed with all aspects. That [form] is not ultimately existent, because it is beyond atomic structure, and because it is not produced through a process involving a "produced object" and a "producer." But still it is not non-existent, because it has the nature of the supreme and unchanging bliss, and because the yogi sees it in the sky.[10]

Here we have a kind of visionary tantric discourse that is experimenting with ways of overturning the idea that emptiness is encountered only through a contemplative insight called "higher seeing" *(vipaśyanā, lhag mthong),* which simply realizes that phenomena are "devoid of all aspects." In place of this, it makes the claim that emptiness must be encountered in the exterior world, that it must very literally be met with the eyes in vision. This project provides one of the clearest examples of the movement in late Indian tantra toward integrating esoteric meditative techniques with key issues in philosophy. In the case of Kālacakra, visionary experiences are used as gateways for bringing the issue of emptiness into one's own experience; but they are also used as starting points for traditional literary and philosophical speculation into emptiness and thus contribute new ideas (not just new practices) to the Buddhist world. This combination of visionary experience and critical thought, in which each informs the other, represents a kind of "visionary philosophy"—a tantric movement that uses the eyes and practices of seeing as alternative means for inquiring into classical Buddhist ideas.

Three Texts: A Trio of Lamps

Kālacakra is one of the most complex and sprawling of the Indian Buddhist traditions, and its introduction into Tibet was necessarily a gradual one. Though Tibetans began to translate Kālacakra literature during the first half of the eleventh century, it appears that the tradition did not rise to popularity all at once but rather as a series of subspecialties that interested different religious groups at different times. One of the earliest surviving Tibetan-authored works on Kālacakra is a set of four short treatises that Yumo Mikyo Dorjé composed, probably in the final third of the eleventh century, and which circulated under the name the *Cycle of the Four Radiant Lamps (gsal sgron skor bzhi).* Though Yumo was certainly familiar with the many facets of the Kālacakra tradition, his writing leaves aside the bulk of Kālacakra's esoterica and focuses on the theory and implications of its six visionary yogas.

With Yumo's works serving as one example, we can see that by the end of the eleventh century, Kālacakra's unique path of vision had begun to capture the imagination of tantric practitioners in the Sarma movement, and that the theory and practice of these yogas were becoming matters of serious discussion. At this same moment, visionary practice was also rising to popularity in Tibet's other chief religious movements, Nyingma and Bön. The Nyingma and Bön counterparts to the Kālacakra practices of vision are found in the Great Perfection *(rdzogs chen),* a tradition that is common to both Nyingma and Bön and is in many ways a collaborative creation of the two. While the Great Perfection contains a diversity of visionary yogas, their basic format bears many similarities to Kālacakra's six yogas: an organizing theme of dark and light, the use of dark-retreat and sky-gazing, a sequence of visions that progresses from unstructured spots of light to encounters with fully formed deities, and a tendency to use these visions as the basis for philosophical discussion.

There are certainly major differences between the visionary practices in Kālacakra and the Great Perfection. The preliminary practices that prepare the yogi for vision are different, as are the details and sequences of the main practices. The Great Perfection also presents a unique system of luminous energy channels that traverse the body's interior and give rise to vision, a feature that is absent in Kālacakra. The two also vary widely on their valuations of sexual yoga (as we will see in chapter 6). Still, the points of contact between the traditions suggest that, despite their differences, the visionary elements of Nyingma, Sarma, and Bön were once in dialogue.

What was the nature of this dialogue, and how did ideas and practices move across sectarian borders that are now much less permeable? Answers to these questions are fraught with historical problems, not the least of which is that Nyingma, Sarma, and Bön have not been in truly productive contact for centuries and have gone to great lengths to conceal or forget that they ever were. In the visionary literature examined here, these groups make no overt references to each other. Written histories also do not describe substantial exchanges and tend to look back with a sectarian eye, defining the religious landscape with the neat sectarian lines that would form in later centuries.

However, Tibet's renaissance was a time when those sectarian boundaries were only beginning to be formed, and when local traditions were actively regarding, inspiring, and imitating each other. Accounting for this process of cross-sectarian competition, emulation, and dialogue is one of the main challenges in reading the literature of this era. The issue is that when individual writings from the period are read in isolation, the connections between them tend to remain hidden. When read in groups, however, the same texts can take on very different characters, as traces of their dialogue are revealed.

The present book aims to create one model for coming to terms with renaissance literature, which is to read it thematically: picking a central theme and investigating that theme in multiple texts across sectarian lines. To that end, I offer an analysis and translation of three key works on vision—three "lamps," if we follow the titles of the texts—one each from the Sarma, Nyingma, and Bön traditions. These are:

1. Sarma: A Kālacakra treatise by Yumo Mikyo Dorjé called the *Lamp Illuminating Emptiness (stong nyid gsal sgron),*
2. Nyingma: A Great Perfection work called the *Tantra of the Blazing Lamps (sgron ma 'bar ba'i rgyud),* from the collection known as the *Seventeen Tantras,* and
3. Bön: A Great Perfection work called *Advice on the Six Lamps (sgron ma drug gi gdams pa)* and a detailed commentary on this by Drugom Gyalwa Yungdrung, both of which are part of Bön's "Oral Tradition from Zhang Zhung."

What follows is a portrait of the rise of Buddhist visionary practices and their supporting philosophical frameworks as they developed in eleventh- and twelfth-century Tibet, as Tibetans were rapidly assimilating and transforming Indian tantric traditions, and as boundaries of all kinds were being crossed: cultural, sectarian, philosophical, and practical. Like the literature on which it is based, this study is oriented much more toward the theoretical than toward details of yogic practice. While the works examined here do take pragmatic directions at times, they make no pretense of being instruction manuals. They do of course mention bodily postures, specialized "gazes," breathing techniques, and so forth, but such practicalities seem to have been conveyed more fully in the oral traditions that circulated alongside the written ones. Writing, on the other hand, was used for its abilities to record and circulate ideas. The authors investigated here use the written word very self-consciously: they ornament their claims with images and metaphors of luminosity; they play subtle word games with terms taken from classical Buddhist discourses about seeing, the eyes, and philosophical "views"; and they speak in an evocative language of light. All of this results in a style of Buddhist literature that is rewarding to read and deserving of greater recognition.

What Vision Reveals

Before embarking, I want to reflect briefly on the value of reading this visionary literature and suggest that these writings have more to offer than simply unusual details about esoteric practices. Some of what this literature reveals is particular to Buddhist intellectual history, but from a broader perspective, these works can also contribute to our understandings of religion, culture, and reading.

Visionary Buddhism?

It is not too difficult to make a case for Buddhism being a "visual" tradition, given its well-developed visual arts, its practices of visualization, its detailed epistemology that investigates the act of seeing, and its abundant literary references to light. However, Buddhism is not typically thought of as being "visionary," or as using acts of seeing that involve the physical eyes and objects in the external world. This might create the impression that Buddhists' engagement with the visual is somehow artificial, based in practices of constructed visualizations, or limited to the artistic and metaphorical realms, where "light" is always in quotation marks, a stand-in for the real issue of enlightened knowing.

But Buddhism in fact has vibrant visionary traditions that involve actual practices of seeing and actual experiences of light using the actual eyes. The visionary yogas discussed here are tied to classical Buddhist discourses of seeing and epistemology, but also need to be clearly distinguished from the other visual and ocular-centric parts of Buddhism, whether those be the "recollection of the Buddha" practices and related Pure Land techniques,[11] tantric practices of visualization and envisioning, various types of "pure vision" practices[12] used for revealing new scriptures, or even the Buddha's own visionary experiences in the dark (the visions he had during the three watches of the night that culminated in his enlightenment).

A constellation of several features will help to define what I am calling "vision" or "visionary" in the context of this book.[13] First, the "visionary" yogas examined here are not practices of visualization where an image of a deity or a divine environment is deliberately constructed in the mind's eye. Rather, they are techniques that lead to the experience of spontaneously arising visual experiences, which are said to occur without deliberate effort or conceptual imagination, and which appear before the practitioner's eyes.

Second, the traditions examined here are distinctive in presenting a developmental model of vision. These are not visions that provide instant access to alternate worlds, or that result in sudden encounters with fully formed deities. Rather, they are visions that unfold over time, beginning with an experience of unstructured bits of light, like sparks, flashes of luminosity, fireflies, radiant nets, showers of rain, or concentric circles called *thig-le*. Eventually—over days or weeks—these lights begin to take representational form and ultimately coalesce into images of deities, divine retinues, maṇḍalas, and pure environments.

Third, "visionary yoga" in this context involves practices of sensory deprivation, in which the yogi is immersed in dark or light, accomplished by staying in a dark room or gazing at the cloudless sky. While one of the most frequent claims about the resulting visions is that they arise "spontaneously," in practice these yogas involve holding the body and eyes in predefined postures and gazes. In some instances, these practical techniques are critical responses to more well-known practices of tantric yoga, particularly in cases where they attempt to reorient esoteric Buddhism away from the use of sexual yoga.

Fourth, the ultimate aim of these "visionary" practices is enlightenment. As such, they differ from (but may remain in relationship with)[14] other practices where vision is used for aims such as prognostication or textual revelation. The notion of "enlightenment" changes, however, when it is brought into the visionary context. Under the influence of these traditions' interest in the dynamics of light, the ultimate Buddhist attainment comes to involve features like dissolving or burning away the body's atoms and physical elements, such that the practitioner attains a body composed of light, much like the bodies of the divinities that a yogi sees in vision.

Finally, "vision" here is a part of Buddhism that is difficult to separate from philosophical "views" and abstract ideas. Literary accounts of these visions treat them not as fantastic or otherworldly experiences but as esoteric counterparts to traditional Buddhist epistemologies, and as alternative ways of negotiating difficult intellectual issues, such as the relationship between emptiness and appearances.

Philosophy and the Vajrayāna

One of the ways that Buddhists organize their literature is by dividing it into two genres: works that describe "methods," and those that describe "views." The first refers to prescriptive writings that lay out practical paths of action, providing instructions on ritual, yoga, esoteric sciences, the attainment of magical powers, and so forth. Works in the second category might be called philosophical, in the sense that they offer more purely theoretical reflections and ask questions about how meaning is made, how our lives can go astray, and how we imprison ourselves with our minds.

Tantric literature is normally associated with the "methods" category, an assumption that seems reasonable given Buddhists' common claim that the Vajrayāna offers no distinctive positions on emptiness or ultimate truth but instead offers distinctive practices and techniques for realizing that ultimate truth. It is thus sometimes tempting to think of Vajrayāna literature as a body of specialized writings that is intended for "practitioners only," a group who is somehow uninterested in literary, philosophical, or aesthetic matters. However, it turns out that a good deal of tantric writing is not particularly prescriptive, and many tantric authors—far from being composers of instruction manuals—are interested in theory, poetry, metaphor, and the expressive potential of words.

For a concise example of the philosophical strain that appears in esoteric literature, here are two rather cryptic lines from *Advice on the Six Lamps:*[15]

> Raise the great oceans upward—
> Focus on the dark space at the iron mountains.

This is actually one of the more "practical" passages in the *Advice,* as it is referring to a particular method of sky-gazing where the eyes (the "great oceans") are rolled back and focused on the shadowy edge of the visual field. If the *Advice* were simply a manual for practitioners, why couldn't it just be straightforward and say: "Roll the eyes up, and direct your gaze to the dark mountain-shaped area formed by the borders of your eyes"? One obvious reason is that in poetic expression, these "instructions" can have greater meaning. A key metaphor here is the "iron mountains," which in Buddhist writing often refers to the circle of mountains that surround a maṇḍala, and that represent the outermost barrier of a world system. The *Advice* here thus evokes how sky-gazing can take us to the edge of our visual world: the margins where we might overturn our ordinary assumptions about seeing and discover how objects' deepest nature is not in the dark spaces beyond our view or in ordinary appearances but in the intersection of the two.

The tendency seen here—using the practical as a starting point for the theoretical—is quite common in late Vajrayāna writing and points to how Buddhists use their esoteric traditions as places for revisiting and reinventing Buddhist philosophical issues. While not purporting to depict the philosophical dimension of the Vajrayāna in all its expansiveness, the present book does tell one of its particular stories: how ideas and problems inherent in visionary yoga spilled over into the realm of ideas, and how the treatment of those ideas—about seeing, knowing, enlightened awareness, and the self-disclosing properties of the universe—became a central function of the practices with which they are associated.

Just as the works examined here do not contain the level of detail that would allow them to be used as practical manuals, they also do not present themselves as fully formed philosophical systems. Rather, they speak in a way that sets up an exchange between vision and philosophy, so their real subject matter is somewhere in between. I call this "visionary philosophy," where "philosophy" does not refer to a kind of completely systematized speculative thought that seeks to provide closure to problematic issues but instead refers to the basic practice of asking "why," particularly in relation to matters of knowing, emptiness, and ultimate truth. In the case of the literature examined here, the aim of this kind of philosophy is not to always provide final answers. Rather, it provokes discussions and raises new types of questions that make everyday acts like seeing seem either foreign or ultimately significant, and thus loads them with new meanings that might help us puzzle our way out of the realm of theory and finally out of the ordinary ways that we perceive the world.

Reading Religious Dialogue

This book also deals with one of the difficulties of reading literature from Tibet's renaissance period, which is accounting for the complicated matrix of debates, dialogue, borrowing, development, and experimentation that underlies any given work. Our historical knowledge of the period is still quite fragmentary, so while we know that the early renaissance was a time of religious creativity and development, we do not often have a nuanced or localized picture of how new religious movements arose and achieved popularity.

Individual religious writings from the period unfortunately do not overtly provide rich historical information. Caught up as they were in the exuberance of system-building, they were not always preoccupied with attacking specific opponents, defending themselves from named rivals, citing allies who inspired them, or setting out their own positions within a defined sectarian system. My primary sources, for instance, clearly share a common set of practices and ideas about vision. Yet, at the same time, concrete information about particular moments of contact between the traditions, or specific exchanges between named historical figures, is lacking both in the sources themselves and in other historical works.

In the absence of a better historical record, we still need to find ways to see the workings of religious influence and dialogue, even if the individual people and places that were involved in them remain unknown. One method is to recognize that, because the religious traditions of the time had not yet closed themselves off from each other, traces of their contact can often be found in their writings. Seeing this contact, however, requires reading multiple works as a group, across sectarian lines, and this sort of reading can feel uncomfortable and cumbersome for those of us who are interested in Tibetan religion. In particular, we have come to feel most secure within the rigid sectarian boundaries that characterize Tibet's classical period, and so we tend to read in ways that retrace those fault lines: emphasizing isolated traditions, individual personalities, and single texts.

This can be a problematic way to read literature from the Tibetan renaissance (or from any period), but there are certainly many possible alternatives. One way of reconstructing the now-forgotten connections between renaissance movements would be through detailed philological studies: examining the language and shared terminology of different texts, and using techniques from textual criticism and historical linguistics to determine the relationships of texts and the directionality of influence between them.

Such methods would be perfectly valid but are simply not the path I take in this book. My approach reflects my own tendency to treat texts as literature rather than as data, and thus has more to do with reading in a particular way rather than applying any particular philological technique. Without ignoring linguistic approaches, a solution I propose is to select key works from across the sectarian spectrum and read them thematically, looking at a series of philosophical reflections and debates that coalesce around a single theme—in this case the theme of vision. While always trying to emphasize the broad differences and individual stories told by each of the sources here, I pay particular attention to the story that they tell as a group and in this way hope to reveal a dialogue between them that would otherwise remain hidden.

Searching for the Source

One final issue that is revealed by reading these visionary works is the problematic nature of our desire to find the "sources" of unusual religious traditions. In particular, I hope that the esoteric texts examined here will help us think about the use of Buddhist literary "sources" and how we employ texts to suggest that some traditions might be the "sources" of others.

Because the two principal religious systems discussed here—Kālacakra and the Great Perfection—are so unusual, discussions about them often speculate about where the traditions may have "come from," as if there were some more authoritative source behind them that could account for their distinctive features. This desire to point to neat sources (and the related interest in authenticity) is not just felt by outsiders to these traditions. It also haunts the Kālacakra and Great Perfection traditions themselves. A basic issue that these two groups—like all Buddhists—want to emphasize is that their ideas and practices can be traced back to a buddha and thus do not come from outside the Buddhist world.

For Kālacakra, these issues of source and authenticity are raised by the late date of the *Kālacakra Tantra,* the highly syncretic language and concepts it contains, and its idiosyncratic approaches to the philosophy of emptiness and the practice of tantric yoga, all of which have been used to suggest that the tradition might be either a fabrication or a hybrid Indian tradition that is not completely Buddhist.[16] The Great Perfection has also been subject to similar questions about its authenticity, these based on the fact that non-Tibetan textual sources for the tradition are absent and that its presentations of the body, the cosmos, and visionary yoga seem at first glance to be unique in Buddhism. Bön is then doubly plagued by issues of source; its embrace of the Great Perfection, combined with the broader problem of its own tangled histories, have caused it to be portrayed as an outsider tradition that simply copied Buddhist sources, while having no authentically Buddhist history of its own.

As readers observing these traditions, we tend to replicate these questions about "source," asking questions like: "What is the source of Bön?," "Where did the Great Perfection come from?," or "Where did Buddhists find these practices of vision?" My own feeling is that such discussions have needlessly imitated traditional anxieties about origins and authenticity and can become bogged down in searching for the "true source" of unusual religious phenomena. The problem with the quest for sources is that it ignores the very basic fact that fully developed religious traditions (like any other phenomenon enmeshed in culture) develop not through straight lines of influence but rather in circles of dialogue.

This book thus does not attempt to locate the original source of any particular motif, philosophical idea, or practice, much less its "authenticity." Instead, I am interested in how the topic of vision served as a meeting point for a discussion between three very different traditions and how that discussion eventually transformed each of those traditions in ways that cannot be reduced to directional borrowing or influence, since their mutual development was inseparable from as near their beginnings as our now distant perspectives can fathom.

Future Directions

The story that I tell here is an incomplete one, in the sense that the practices and ideas I discuss were in reality touched by traditions, both Buddhist and non-Buddhist, that are simply beyond the scope of my study. On the Buddhist side, it should be remembered that exoteric Tibetan traditions were hotly debating issues of epistemology *(pramāṇa)* at the same time that the tantric Kālacakra and Great Perfection movements were crafting their own inquiries into the relationships between seeing, knowing, and liberation. Studies of epistemology in the early Tibetan renaissance could thus add quite a bit to our understanding of tantric practices of vision. Such studies are becoming increasingly possible, due to a large collection of early Kadampa materials that has recently been published;[17] this includes works written by scholars at Sangpu Monastery, one of the centers in the development of the Tibetan *pramāṇa* tradition. Materials by two Sangpu abbots, Ngog Lotsawa (1059–1109) and Chapa Chökyi Seng-gé (1109–1169), will be important sources for broadening our understanding of Tibetan approaches to Buddhist epistemology and would complement tantric approaches by providing rich detail of contemporaneous lines of thought that were being pursued in more conservative or traditional circles.

While the Tibetan religious movements discussed in this book tend to look for inspiration to Buddhist India, or to lands west of Tibet like Zhang Zhung, this should not cause us to overlook the fact that non-Buddhist groups in both India and China have similar paths of vision. Perhaps the most relevant of these is the tradition of Kaśmiri Śaivism. Fundamental Śaivite works like the yogic anthology *Vijñānabhairava*[18] contain a host of themes that could connect them to Kālacakra and the Great Perfection: discourses of light and practices of gazing at the sun and sky;[19] practices of darkness and themes of space;[20] specific techniques like pressing the eyes and blocking the senses;[21] and common visual imagery like spots of light (*bindu* or *tilaka*) and peacock feathers.[22] A host of other affinities—a doctrine of "recognition" *(pratyabhijñā)* much like the Great Perfection's,[23] a gnostic cosmogenesis[24]—suggest how Kālacakra and the Great Perfection must have been in a wider circle of discussion that included Śaivite traditions. A study incorporating Śaivism might also provide evidence that the visionary techniques discussed here existed well before their rise to prominence in Buddhists and Bönpo literature of the eleventh century.

Next—and these points of contact will be somewhat harder to construct—there are a wealth of thematic connections between Buddhist light practices and meditative techniques found in the later schools of Daoism.[25] The medieval Daoist tradition called "Highest Clarity" (Shangqing)[26] would be one starting point, as a primary interest of this school was in formulating Daoist ideas and practice in terms of luminosity.[27] Among its light-related practices are techniques for absorbing light energy from the sun and moon, in an attempt to transform the ordinary body into a body composed of light. Several features of the tradition are echoed in the Great Perfection, such as its scriptural basis in visionary revelations, its emphasis on subtle body energetics, and its interests in embryology.[28] Its concepts of circulating *jing* ("essence" or "seminal essence") throughout the body could particularly be compared to the Buddhist concepts of *thig-le* I discuss in chapter 6 (though the relation between *jing* and *thig-le* of course would need to be explored by using a broad range of Daoist traditions).

Returning to the Great Perfection tradition, an investigation of artwork produced by proponents of the Great Perfection could move this study beyond the literary realm into disciplines related to the visual arts. In particular, a type of didactic painting, still produced today, depicts visionary experiences and the subtle-body features that give rise to them. During my research, I encountered several striking and historic images relating to the "lamps" traditions, but treating them properly in this context would have taken me too far afield.

Finally, an aspect of the Bön tradition that I was not able to address during my research is its own Kālacakra *(dus kyi 'khor lo)* tradition. An analysis of the divergent bodies of this literature, and whether the tradition moves out of the purely ritual realm and into the esoterica and vision associated with Indian Kālacakra are matters that could occupy scholars for some time to come.

PART I | Seeing Literature

CHAPTER 1 | Yumo's *Lamp Illuminating Emptiness*

The Wheel of Time

Among the esoteric Buddhist traditions from India, the one that is perhaps the greatest in scope and complexity is Kālacakra, or the "Wheel of Time." In its own narrative accounts, the Kālacakra tradition places its beginnings during the lifetime of the Buddha, who spoke Kālacakra's lengthy "root tantra" at Dhānyakaṭa, a Buddhist community centered around a monumental stūpa located in the region of modern-day Andhra Pradesh.[1] Tradition recounts that this teaching, known as the *Tantra of the Primordial Buddha,*[2] was delivered to a king named Sucandra, who then propagated it in his kingdom of Śambhala, a legendary Buddhist land said to be to the north of India. Generations later, the eighth king of Śambhala, Mañjuśrī Yaśas, propounded an abridged version of the *Tantra of the Primordial Buddha;* this shorter work, known today as the *Kālacakra Tantra,* was eventually propagated in India and became one of the most influential works in Buddhist tantra.

These traditional origin accounts, however, contradict modern academic analyses of Kālacakra's main written texts: the *Kālacakra Tantra* and *Stainless Light* (the commentary from which the tantra is virtually inseparable). Both of these texts bear marks suggesting that they emerged in the northern part of the Indian subcontinent early in the eleventh century,[3] during the final flowering of esoteric Buddhism. Unlike many tantric works, the core Kālacakra literature contains overt historical and political discussions, which put forth a bold narrative expressive of Buddhists' tenuous position in India during the eleventh century. At this time, the thirteenth-century Muslim invasions that would destroy the great Buddhist monasteries were still on the distant horizon, but Mahmud of Ghazni's campaigns in northwest India had begun, and if *Stainless Light* is any indication, Buddhists sensed that this might be the beginning of their end.

Stainless Light speaks in strident language about Buddhists' vulnerability to the "barbarian" doctrine from Mecca,[4] predicting an invasion of India that might even sweep up into Śambhala.

Kālacakra's explicit warnings about an Islamic attack are accompanied by equally strong polemics against Indian brahmins, who for reasons ranging from the astrological to the ethical are accused of making India and Śambhala vulnerable to barbarian invasion. A brief citation from *Stainless Light*[5] will help to give a sense of the tone found in this strand of Kālacakra. In this passage, Śambhala's Buddhist king Mañjuśrī Yaśas criticizes a group of brahmins in his land, equating them with Muslims because of their performance of sacrifice:

> There is no difference between the barbarian doctrine and the doctrine of the Vedas, as both engage in killing. For that reason, [brahmins,] the sons of your lineage, and your grandsons and so forth, seeing the glory of those barbarians and their demon-deity engaging in battle, will, 800 years in the future, become barbarians themselves. Once they become barbarians, then everyone dwelling in the 960,000,000 villages, the four castes and so forth, will also become barbarians!

The basic message here is the brahmins are a sort of gateway for the "barbarian" Muslim doctrine, so for the safety of the kingdom, the brahmins must either be initiated into Kālacakra—convert to the Buddhist Vajrayāna—or leave Śambhala. For Kālacakra, the final resolution to the Islamic and Vedic problems will not come until generations in the future, when king Mañjuśrī Yaśas is predicted to return as the thirty-second king of Śambhala, Raudra Cakrī. At that time, the prophecy says, there will be a cataclysmic battle, in which the Buddhists and converted brahmins finally defeat the barbarians and usher in a new era of peace.

These discourses of conversion, conquest, and time run deep in the early Kālacakra literature. They form one of the tradition's main narratives and serve as a thread that ties together Kālacakra's broad expanse of subdisciplines, which range through the sciences, technology, magic, astrology, and philosophy. Even Kālacakra's yogic practices are woven into this narrative, the idea being that the future war with the barbarians is an outer manifestation of an inner battle against the barbarians of ignorance.[6]

Early Tibetan Kālacakra and Yumo's *Lamp Illuminating Emptiness*

It seems amazing that such an idiosyncratic, polarizing, politicized, and India-centric tantra would capture the imaginations of Tibetans, but

Kālacakra ultimately came to be considered across the Sarma schools as the culmination of tantric Buddhism. Perhaps this suggests that, just as narrative threads can hold a tantric tradition together, those threads can also be untied, letting the pieces of a tradition come apart and take their own trajectories. This appears to be how Tibetans initially dealt with Kālacakra, as their early engagement with the tradition places little emphasis on barbarians, brahmins, or war. Instead, Tibetans turned to Kālacakra's other spheres and were particularly attracted to its visionary yogas and its unique philosophy of emptiness.

Thus Kālacakra did not come to Tibet in a single straight line, nor were its complex doctrines all agreed upon or assimilated right from the beginning. Rather, the tradition took hold in its new home through a process of translation, retranslation, negotiation, and interpretation. Kālacakra began moving into Tibet very soon after the *Kālacakra Tantra* appeared in India, with the first Tibetan translation of the tantra appearing around 1027.[7] The *Kālacakra Tantra* itself was then translated and retranslated into Tibetan numerous times; for the most part those variant translations are not currently available, so we do not know how they might vary. Two major translations would come to dominate, with these coming from lineages based on Tibetans' collaboration with two foreign masters: the Kaśmiri paṇḍit Somanātha, and the Newari Samantaśri.[8]

The speed with which Kālacakra moved from its inception in India to its export to Tibet meant that Tibetans did not encounter it as an antique tradition but had a chance to meet some of the major figures in its early lineage. One of these was Somanātha himself, who was active in India during Kālacakra's early spread, and who is said to have met the two towering figures in Kālacakra's Indian lineage: Kālacakrapāda and Nāropa.[9] In the mid-eleventh century, Somanātha came to Tibet, where he was renowned as a master of the *Kālacakra Tantra* and of a group of commentaries associated with it, called the "Three Bodhisattva Commentaries."[10]

The paṇḍit's fame was apparently great enough that news of his Tibetan visit was heard by an unknown young tantric from western Tibet, named Yumo Mikyo Dorjé. Yumo had become interested in Kālacakra, and on hearing about the paṇḍit's visit he decided to travel to central Tibet to receive his teachings. Though Yumo could not convince Somanātha to teach him personally, he did eventually receive teachings from the paṇḍit's students and thus became one of the early Tibetan scholars and adepts of Kālacakra.

Once he was fully drawn into the Kālacakra movement, Yumo began to write, and there are some suggestions that he did so widely.[11] Even if this is so, his only work currently available is a group of four short treatises known collectively as the *Cycle of the Four Radiant Lamps*.[12] One of those treatises is the *Lamp Illuminating Emptiness,* which serves as one of the main sources of this book.

The *Lamp Illuminating Emptiness* is a rare document from the early days of Kālacakra in Tibet. Probably composed in the final third of the eleventh century, it is among the earliest writings on Kālacakra by a Tibetan author and provides an image of the time when Kālacakra was not a dominant tradition but a new import whose esoteric practices of vision and reformulations of key Buddhist ideas must have been viewed with a mixture of suspicion and curiosity.

Yumo's Argument and Style

Yumo's *Lamp* is essentially about the visionary experiences that arise during the Kālacakra practices called the "six yogas."[13] His treatise, however, is not a prescriptive manual, and hardly even mentions the six yogas by name. Rather, it takes the topic of visionary appearances as a basis for philosophical speculation, particularly for expounding on Kālacakra's ideas about emptiness. In brief, the argument of the *Lamp Illuminating Emptiness* is this: enlightenment can only be achieved through tantra. It is well known that tantra involves sexual practices using different kinds of consorts, but for the most part those do not lead to liberation. In particular, yogas involving an "action seal" (an actual physical woman) or a "gnostic seal" (a visualized consort) are ineffective for bringing about enlightenment. Those intent on liberation must instead unite with the "Great Seal," a *visionary* consort whose image arises spontaneously and without any deliberate ritual evocation or visualization.

In the context of Kālacakra, the Great Seal is not simply an alternative kind of sexual partner, but is a spontaneous appearance that the yogi sees in the sky and within the body, and who is no different from the meditator's own gnosis. Visually, she is described in terms of luminosity: as a flame, a radiant light, or a flash of lightning. Yumo also identifies her with Kālacakra's own consort Viśvamātā and the classical Buddhist goddess Prajñāpāramitā, who is associated with insight and emptiness. This latter identification is key to understanding her import: the reason that the Great Seal can lead to liberation is that an encounter with her is nothing less than an encounter with emptiness. This is because, the Kālacakra tradition says, the Great Seal is composed of "empty-form" *(stong gzugs)*.[14] That is, she appears in a form that is empty of inherent nature and devoid of atomic structure, but that is nonetheless capable of appearing to the eyes. She thus provides an immediate and visceral experience of the unity of emptiness and appearances, and this kind of encounter, Yumo claims, is the only way to attain liberation.

For Yumo, classical descriptions of emptiness, which present it as the "abiding reality of things" or a "lack of inherent nature," are simply describing the "view" of emptiness. They are not describing an emptiness with which you can work or, in Yumo's terms, an "emptiness that is a path."[15] The "path" kind of emptiness is an observable emptiness, an emptiness that can become an object of the eyes.[16] The empty-form Great Seal is precisely this kind of emptiness, and so Yumo's treatise unfolds as a lengthy speculation on her nature, attempting to show how and why a visionary encounter with her might be a pathway out of saṃsāra.

Yumo wrote the *Lamp Illuminating Emptiness* in a style found occasionally in Buddhist literature, in which an author extracts essential portions of other works and arranges them with brief connecting comments in his own voice to articulate an overall argument. The bulk of Yumo's *Lamp* is thus citations from major pieces of tantric literature, while in comparison his own words are very few. This style does not always make for easy reading, and it would be simple to dismiss Yumo as a writer whose only method is scriptural citation. However, careful reading reveals a real breadth in his tantric erudition, and then slowly an argument begins to emerge from all the citations, like the vision articulated by an artist working in collage.

The pieces of this collage are all Indian, and almost exclusively tantric. While all of his sources would eventually make it into the Tibetan canon, it is important to remember that at Yumo's time that canon had not yet been formed. Some of his sources, particularly the Kālacakra works, were still quite new to Tibetans, and Yumo must have been among the earliest readers of these freshly minted translations. The Kālacakra corpus, however, is by no means Yumo's only concern; he quotes broadly from works related to the Hevajra, Cakrasaṃvara, and Guhyasamāja tantras and occasionally mixes in independent poetic sources like Saraha's songs of liberation.

This appeal to such a variety of sources is typical of early Kālacakra authors, who regularly adopted ideas and passages from other Buddhist (and non-Buddhist) traditions. While this might seem ecumenical, the underlying goal is more often to demonstrate how the distinctive views of the *Kālacakra Tantra* and *Stainless Light* are actually buried within earlier texts and traditions, though in forms that are difficult to discern. This perspective led the tradition to refer to the *Kālacakra Tantra* as an "illuminating tantra,"[17] meaning that it clearly reveals the Buddha's true intention, which was present but hidden in other tantras. A typical statement from *Stainless Light*[18] illustrates this attitude:

> In the root tantras and abridged tantras, the fourth wisdom-gnosis [initiation] and the meditation on the Great Seal [with its] path of smoke and so forth are totally hidden. But in some root tantras, these are completely clear. Here in the root tantra [called the]

> *Paramādibuddha,* as well as in the *Abridged [Kālacakra] Tantra,* the fourth wisdom-gnosis [initiation] is completely clear, and the meditation on the Great Seal [with its] path of smoke and so forth is also completely clear....

Here, "path of smoke and so forth" refers to the appearances that a yogi sees in Kālacakra's visionary practices, and "meditation on the Great Seal" refers to how those initial visions gradually coalesce into an appearance of the Great Seal. The concern of the Kālacakra tradition is to show how these are not recent innovations but practices and ideas that were indeed contained in other teachings, albeit hidden from view.

This is also one of the core ideas animating Yumo's own work. As we will see later, he very consciously extracts citations from non-Kālacakra works and uses them to suggest how distinctive Kālacakra views about the Great Seal have pedigrees in other tantras. Yumo's basic method of operation is to take a phrase out of the *Kālacakra Tantra,* for example, a phrase suggesting that the Great Seal is "radiating light." He then forms a collection of citations from other works containing the same words "radiating light" and arranges the citations so that they take on meanings suggested by each other. Reading all the citations collectively, and then referring back to the original piece from the *Kālacakra Tantra,* the reader is given the feeling that the Great Seal may indeed have been the real intent of discussions in earlier texts that otherwise never explicitly mentioned her.

It is legitimate to ask if this method simply treats citations out of context and claims that they are something they are not. This would be an easy criticism, but in my reading, Yumo provides us with more than just sleight of hand. Though his method may not correspond to our own accepted reading practices, it does represent one way that Buddhist authors read their own literature.[19] A saying in *Stainless Light* mentions this method, saying: "Tantra should be understood through other tantras."[20] The idea here is that a single tantric work *(rgyud)* is related to other tantras through threads *(rgyud)* or continua of ideas; tantras thus can be read broadly and in groups, so that the themes, motifs, and ideas that they share can be used to illuminate each other, even if by all accounts they are different in their own particular contexts. While my own perspective prevents me from accepting the idea that fully developed themes like Kālacakra's Great Seal are "hidden" in earlier tantras, I do admire how Yumo is able to use a wide range of Buddhist literature to create a cluster of related images—about light, the sky, seeing, and emptiness—and then to fashion those images into an argument that neatly connects Kālacakra's visionary practices with other facets of the Buddhist tradition.

It is also fair to question whether there is anything creative or interpretive about Yumo's work at all, or if it is just a collection of tantric quotations. One interpretive feature of Yumo's *Lamp* is what it leaves out. In Yumo's treatise we find no mention of Kālacakra's elaborate ritual arts, its scientific discussions of herbology, medicine, and embryology, its plans for creating flying war machines and weapons for flinging molten metal on one's enemies, its paths for attaining supernatural feats or wielding magic swords. He makes no mention of Kālacakra's detailed descriptions of magical elixirs, its elaborate cosmology, or its unusual sexology, which encourages men to offer their wives to Buddhist practitioners.[21] Constructions of maṇḍalas, ritual initiations, methods for fending off death, and ways of predicting the future are also absent.

Yumo's *Lamp* sweeps all this aside for an almost exclusive focus on matters of emptiness and vision. Yumo's Kālacakra is thus not filled with images of war but of goddesses and light. Having cleared this more pristine space, he is able to bring complicated issues about the Great Seal into the foreground, and in that context he often makes claims about the role of the eyes in enlightenment that are more forceful than they are in the *Tantra* or *Stainless Light*. In these ways, Yumo reveals his own voice, which it turns out is sometimes more idiosyncratic than the idiosyncratic tradition of Kālacakra itself.

Biography of Yumo Mikyo Dorjé

Though he is not among the founding fathers or translators of Kālacakra in Tibet, Yumo was more than a marginal figure in its early history, and he remains an important link in the Tibetan Kālacakra lineage, especially for the Jonang tradition. In his day, Yumo was apparently not identified with any organized school or sect but was rather a student of individual charismatic Sarma teachers and eventually became such a teacher himself.

Several brief biographies[22] of Yumo exist, and these are detailed enough to give an interesting, if sketchy, picture of his life and times. Yumo was born in western Tibet[23] to a nomadic family, sometime during the first third of the eleventh century.[24] The Buddhist revival was on, and when Yumo was ten, he, his three brothers, and his parents all took ordination together. Yumo took an early interest in studies and traveled to live with a series of teachers, first in southwestern Tibet,[25] and then in central Tibet.[26] When he was first ordained, he was given the name "King of Faith."[27] Later, while living at Mt. Dönmo, two of his teachers gave him the nickname "Yumo." He would also come to be known by his tantric name Mikyo Dorjé, or "Unshakeable Vajra."[28]

Yumo's early studies revolved around the works popular in the Sarma movement. It is said that he studied middle way and valid cognition during this period; Śāntideva's *Compendium of Trainings*[29] also made a lasting impression on him. He eventually studied monastic discipline with a renowned *vinaya* holder named Lama Sok Chenpo. The prestige Yumo gained from studying with this lama paid off later in his life. According to the biographies, his early association with Sok Chenpo was the one factor that convinced his tantric teachers that he was a suitable vessel for the esoteric instructions.

When Yumo's studies did turn to tantra, his initial interests were apparently in Hevajra. He was soon drawn to the Kālacakra movement by the *Vajragarbha Commentary*, which offered a Kālacakra interpretation of the *Hevajra Tantra*. A story that recurs in many of Yumo's biographies is that an intense faith arose in Yumo when he first heard the name of this text. When he asked who might be able to explain it, he was told about the Kaśmiri paṇḍit Somanātha, one of the major figures responsible for introducing Kālacakra materials into Tibet and translating them into Tibetan.

In one of the defining moments of Yumo's story, he moved to central Tibet and began studying works by Śāntideva. During this period, he heard that an Indian paṇḍit was nearby and realized that this must be Somanātha. He traveled to meet the paṇḍit and bravely approached him but was rebuffed: Somanātha pointed to a wealth of offerings that had been piling up around him and told Yumo that if he carried them to Nepal, he might be able to receive the teachings in the future. The eager Yumo agreed but before leaving learned that Somanātha had pulled this trick on others and had not given them teachings in return.

Yumo's confidant at this point, a monk named Gompa Tsüldrak, told Yumo that he would certainly be able to obtain tantric teachings from Tsüldrak's own lama, Drogön Namla-tsek, who had received all of Somanātha's teachings. With the assistance of Gompa Tsüldrak, Yumo was introduced to Drogön. Impressed that Yumo had spent time with Lama Sok Chenpo, Drogön spent four years giving Yumo empowerments, instructions, and esoteric advice. This places Yumo in the second generation of Tibetan Kālacakra practitioners: not among those who studied with Indian teachers but among those who trained under their primary disciples.

The histories tell of Yumo moving to the region of U-yuk[30] in his later life, where he spent long periods meditating in caves and eventually attained realization. It is said that he taught and wrote extensively and displayed magical feats, but unfortunately no detailed information about these activities is found in extant histories. Among his magical abilities, it is said that he had the power to emanate himself as a crow or a cuckoo, and that he appeared to one of his disciples in this form.

Yumo died at eighty with a small set of disciples. He would not leave a legacy in terms of founding a school or lineage, but his work was kept alive by Kālacakra enthusiasts. His *Lamps* cycle continued to be taught in the fourteenth century by Dolpopa,[31] whose Jonang tradition would eventually place Yumo in their own Kālacakra lineage and see him (retroactively) as advocating their distinctive position of "other-emptiness" in a tantric context.[32] In the fifteenth century, Yumo's *Lamps* were still renowned enough to gain mention in the foundational history the *Blue Annals*.[33] In the modern period, his works slipped into obscurity and were briefly lost; as they slowly resurface, interest in them is being rekindled in Tibetan circles related to Kālacakra and Jonang.

Essential Background for the *Lamp Illuminating Emptiness*

Yumo's *Lamp Illuminating Emptiness* assumes that the reader has a broad background in extremely esoteric matters concerning Buddhist tantric yoga. The treatise focuses on theory related to Kālacakra's "completion stage" meditations, but it hardly mentions these overtly. A casual reader might not even be able to discern that they are the basic subject matter of the *Lamp*. Underlying this main topic is a deep ambivalence about the importance and nature of Kālacakra's "generation stage" meditations, but this too goes mostly unstated. In order to fill in some of this essential background, in the following I make some brief comments on the generation stage, and then provide a more detailed survey of Kālacakra's completion stage practices. Finally, I discuss some issues related to the *Guhyasamāja Tantra,* in order to help illuminate an experimental line of thought in which Yumo suggests connections between this tantra and Kālacakra.

Kālacakra's Visualized Generation Stage

Buddhist tantric yogas are often divided into two broad phases: a "generation stage" *(utpatti-krama, bskyed rim)* and a "completion stage" *(niṣpanna-krama, rdzogs rim).* Generation stage yogas are typically methods through which one begins to "generate" or "give birth" to oneself as a buddha. One method of accomplishing this is to transform one's self-image: cutting off the idea that one is an ordinary, deluded, neurotic being. This ordinary self-perception is then deliberately replaced with the "divine pride" of being a buddha who is capable of performing enlightened deeds. This feeling of pride is reinforced by imagining or maintaining the "clear appearance" of dwelling in a divine environment. The core generation stage practice thus involves following a scripted sequence of visualizations that create a detailed visualized world, in which one imagines oneself as an elaborately ornamented buddha dwelling in a richly decorated, multistoried palace, surrounded by a divine retinue.

The Kālacakra tradition has four generation stage practices:[34] (1) In the first yoga, named "Supreme King of Maṇḍalas,"[35] the practitioner's body is imaginatively dissolved and then re-formed, or reborn, in the visualized image of the buddha Kālacakra residing within his elaborate maṇḍala. (2) The second yoga, "Supreme King of Actions,"[36] then involves a visualization of four goddesses arousing the practitioner/buddha to perform enlightened activities in the world. (3) "*Thig-le* Yoga"[37] shifts the focus from the royal world of maṇḍalas to the interior of the body and interactions with sexual consorts. This stage is a type of Buddhist sexual yoga, practiced with either a visualized or an actual consort. Desire for this consort causes a gnostic fire to blaze up at the yogi's navel energy-wheel and melts a reservoir of seminal nuclei *(thig le)* stored at the crown of the head. This causes the seminal nuclei to drip down his body's central energy-channel and results in a sequence of blisses as the nuclei travel to the tip of the sexual organ. (4) "Subtle Yoga"[38] is then a continuation of the previous yoga, in which the seminal nuclei are moved back up the central channel, resulting in another sequence of blisses.

Two features of the Kālacakra generation stage warrant mention here. The first is how sexualized it is. Generation stage yogas prior to Kālacakra more commonly involved the "royal-buddha" and "divine-palace" scenarios of the first two yogas, while the "blazing and dripping" sexual practices were the hallmarks of the completion stage. By the time of Kālacakra, however, the sexual model had made inroads even into the generation stage. This suggests how pervasive the sexual model of tantra was in the time of the *Kālacakra Tantra,* but it also provides an example of how those sexual practices had undergone a process of taming, whereby they were turned into scripted visualizations rather than physical encounters. As we will see later, these factors will play a part in a visionary reaction to sexual yoga.

Second, it should be noted that tantric traditions usually set up the generation stage as a practice that prepares the yogi for the completion stage, so that it has to be practiced first for the completion stage to have any effect. This is not exactly the case in Kālacakra, at least in the presentation of *Stainless Light.* In spite of its statements that the generation stage purifies the body to pave the way for the attainment of the four buddha-bodies,[39] *Stainless Light* also mentions repeatedly that the generation stage is only tangentially involved in enlightenment, as it is simply a collection of practices that lead to "mundane" attainments, not to the attainment of buddhahood. There is thus no explicit claim that the generation stage must precede the practice of the six completion stage yogas. We unfortunately have little data about the living Kālacakra tradition as it existed in India, so the text of *Stainless Light* does not necessarily indicate that the completion stage yogas (which are said to lead to buddhahood) were practiced in isolation from the generation stage. The necessity for the generation stage often is simply assumed, and indeed this necessity is generally asserted in Kālacakra to this day. At the very least, what *Stainless Light* does indicate is a strong tendency in Kālacakra to separate the completion stage from the generation stage intellectually, and to discuss the theory of the completion stage on its own, as having its own integrity that does not need support from other domains of tantra.

Yumo exemplifies this last tendency particularly well. His *Lamp Illuminating Emptiness* focuses exclusively on the completion stage and makes almost no mention of the generation stage outside of suggesting its deficiencies. Yumo's problem with the generation stage—and this is straight out of *Stainless Light*—is that, because it is uses visualization, it is a practice that involves conceptual thought *(kalpanā, rtog pa).* As such, it is not suited to bring about profound nonconceptual states, and thus, in Yumo's words, is "not the path to the accomplishment of complete enlightenment."[40]

Kālacakra's Visionary Six Yogas

The alternatives to these practices of conceptuality are practices of vision, where consorts and divinities are encountered not as predetermined, constructed visualizations but in visions that arise spontaneously, without imagination or ritual evocation. Kālacakra's visionary practices are found in its completion stage, which is composed of a sequence of practices called the "six yogas."[41] Yumo does not present these yogas systematically, but he does assume that the reader has a thorough background in them. For this reason, I give a general summation of the six yogas here.[42] This will necessarily omit details and skip over debates surrounding the particular nuances of each yoga, as my goal is simply to provide the essential information necessary for understanding Yumo's work. To keep my description grounded, however, I follow one popular summation of the six yogas, which is found in the *Vajrapāṇi Commentary.*[43] In each of the following sections, I first provide a passage from the *Vajrapāṇi Commentary* and then make my own comments on it.

Introductory Comments on the Six Yogas

The *Vajrapāṇi Commentary* begins its discussions of the six yogas with some introductory comments that it derives from the *Later Cakrasaṃvara Tantra*. The discussion begins:

> In the *Later Cakrasaṃvara [Tantra],*[44] the Transcendent Victor said:
>
> Withdrawal and meditative concentration,
> Breath control and likewise retention,
> Recollection and concentration
> Are asserted to be the six yogas.

Thus, it should be known that withdrawal is before meditative concentration, and it should be known that breath control is before mantra recitation. Here the term "mantra recitation" means "neutral recitation" or "vajra recitation," i.e., "retention" of breath. As well, it should be known that recollection is before bliss; here, the term "bliss" refers to "concentration."

In this way, through these six yogas, a yogi will attain [the state of] a buddha. Outsider yogis, via common [yogas], attain worldly accomplishments. As for the worldly accomplishments of beginner childlike yogis,[45] they are fruits [produced] by worldly truths: minds involved with conceptual meditations like mantra recitation and concentration on maṇḍala wheels, or the bliss of "action" mudrās and "gnostic" mudrās, which is defiled bliss or fluctuating bliss. Through [such] worldly truths, one's final residence is [at most] Akaniṣṭha.

Thus, the attainments [of] worldly and transcendent yogis are due to the two stages [respectively, of generation and completion].

As is evidenced in this passage from the *Vajrapāṇi Commentary*, Kālacakra literature (as well as literature of other Buddhist tantric traditions that have "six yogas" systems) delights in applying different names and organizational schemes[46] to the six yogas. So, to present them in a simpler list, Kālacakra's six yogas are:

1. Withdrawal *(pratyāhāra, sor sdud)*
2. Meditative concentration *(dhyāna, bsam gtan* or sometimes *sor gtan)*
3. Breath control *(prāṇāyāma, srog rtsol)*
4. Retention *(dhāraṇā, 'dzin pa)*
5. Recollection *(anusmṛti, rjes dran)*
6. Concentration *(samādhi, ting nge 'dzin)*

The *Vajrapāṇi Commentary* suggests how these six completion stage practices are fundamentally different from the Kālacakra's generation stage practices, which it portrays as "mantra, maṇḍala, and mudrā" practices, dominated by language, mentally constructed visualizations, sexual encounters, and other forms of dualism.[47] As such, they are said to lead to worldly accomplishments rather than transcendent ones.

1. Withdrawal Yoga

Here, I will explain the attainments that transcendent yogis make through the six-limbed yoga, just as they are. In this context, "withdrawal" means that the sense powers (the eyes and so forth) are not engaging the sense consciousnesses (the visual consciousness and so forth) with external objects (form and so forth). Rather, the divine sense powers (the divine eye and so forth) engage the divine sense consciousness (the divine visual consciousness and so forth)

> in internal objects. Inwardly, one focuses on emptiness, and thus all manner of unimputed things come to be seen in the empty [space]. This is the seeing of the reflected forms of the buddhas of the three worlds, which are seen like [objects appearing to] a young girl in a prognostic mirror. This describes the branch of withdrawal.

The practice that the *Vajrapāṇi Commentary* describes here, "withdrawal yoga," uses sensory deprivation in a process that "withdraws" the sense faculties—particularly the visual faculty—from external sense objects.[48] The practice is divided into "nighttime" and "daytime" phases, where a yogi practices in a dark room with no holes to let in the light,[49] and later stays outdoors or in a structure "with no cover,"[50] situated so that only the blue canopy of the sky can be seen. Dwelling in these controlled environments, the yogi holds the body in prescribed postures and places the eyes in specialized gazes.[51] Eventually, visionary appearances begin to arise. These appearances of light come to be perceptible, tradition suggests, because alternative visual faculties,[52] like the "divine eyes,"[53] step in and take over for the ordinary, withdrawn visual consciousness.

As Buddhist yogic techniques, these dark-room and sky-gazing practices are quite unusual. However, according to the Kālacakra tradition, precedent for them can be found in one of the most famous bodies of Mahāyāna literature: the Perfection of Wisdom scriptures. Kālacakra authors writing on the six yogas are fond of citing a passage from the *Perfection of Wisdom Sūtra in 8,000 Lines,*[54] which reads:

> Then, Śakra,[55] the lord of the gods, asked the venerable Subhūti: "Noble Subhūti! When one practices yoga in this Perfection of Wisdom, on what does one practice yoga?"
>
> Subhūti replied: "Kauśika! When one practices yoga in this Perfection of Wisdom, one practices yoga in space.[56] Kauśika! Someone wishing to train and practice yoga in this Perfection of Wisdom should practice yoga in [a place] without cover."

In the Kālacakra view, the "space" practices mentioned here refer to a dark-room technique, while the "without cover" comment refers to sky-gazing practices. In this interpretation, night-yoga and day-yoga are not inventions of Kālacakra, or practices that it adopted from non-Buddhist sources, but rather are techniques with an authentic Buddhist history that Kālacakra is now bringing into a tantric context.[57] The preceding passage is of course just a few lines from the enormous corpus of Perfection of Wisdom literature, and so it does not provide us with evidence for a fully developed tradition of dark-room and sky-gazing practice in the Indian Mahāyāna. Nonetheless, it does indicate how the Kālacakra tradition takes inspiration from the Perfection of Wisdom, a fact we can also see in the following lines from *Stainless Light,* which, without citing the *Sūtra in*

8,000 Lines, uses language that clearly echoes it. Referring to the night-yoga and day-yoga techniques, *Stainless Light*[58] says:

> Here, in the Mantra vehicle, and in the Perfection of Wisdom vehicle, there are two types of yogic meditations: in space, and [a place] without cover.

Did early Kālacakra authors actually have direct knowledge of visionary texts or practices related to the Perfection of Wisdom? More evidence is needed. At the very least, passages like this one from *Stainless Light* show that the Kālacakra tradition does not see its visionary techniques as disconnected from the Perfection of Wisdom but rather as tantric implementations of it.

In describing the visions experienced in night-yoga and day-yoga, Kālacakra texts outline a set of ten appearances, or "ten signs," that arise before the eyes of the yogi. These are smoke, mirage, lights in the clear sky, a butter lamp, blazing, the moon, the sun, vajras, the supreme form, and a seminal nucleus *(thig-le)*.[59] The precise names of these ten, and the times at which they appear, vary slightly throughout Kālacakra writings, but all agree that they arise spontaneously, without being deliberately or conceptually constructed. In a common metaphor, the ten visions are likened to images that appear during a *pratisenā* divination,[60] a ritual in which a young girl sees images arise spontaneously on the surface of a mirror. These prognostic images are not deliberately constructed by the girl who is the medium in such a divination; nonetheless, the images appear in the mirror, are seen with her eyes, and can be acted on reliably in the real world. The metaphor of the prognostic mirror suggests how Kālacakra's ten appearances are not consciously constructed by the yogi but nonetheless appear as reflections of a reality that is deep within the mind and that can be acted upon to discover that reality.

Several things are notable about these "ten signs." The first is that, as seen earlier in the *Vajrapāṇi Commentary,* writings about them commonly have philosophical overtones and suggest how vision can be used to mediate the relationship between appearance and emptiness. Kālacakra authors describe the lights seen in vision as being composed of "empty-form,"[61] and so encountering these appearances can suggest to the yogi how all phenomena are constituted of a dynamic emptiness that gives rise to appearances, and how things can have no inherent nature but still be able to appear and function. Second, as Yumo frequently states, visionary appearances are also considered to be appearances or manifestations[62] of the mind. As such they represent a practice of the mind observing the mind: an opportunity for the mind to literally see itself and discover its own nature.

Finally, as is suggested by Vajrapāṇi's comment likening visions to reflections of buddhas, some sort of transcendent character is attributed to these appearances.[63] This point is a matter of some debate among Kālacakra advocates, but the *Vajrapāṇi Commentary* here evidences a general trend toward viewing them as expressions of a transcendent dimension of the mind, or even as internal buddhas[64] that are manifesting in the external world to be seen. This idea is perhaps most evident in descriptions of the tenth vision, which is an appearance of a luminous "seed" or "seminal nucleus" *(thig-le):* a black line eventually appears in this seminal nucleus, and within the black line emerges an image of a buddha.[65] The image of a tiny buddha within a seed suggests how these spots of light are potencies that express themselves in the form of buddhas, as well as leading to the yogi's own transformation into a buddha.

2. Meditative Concentration Yoga

> In "meditative concentration," all existent things are seen as empty. With reference to them, there is (1) "insight," meaning that the mind engages with those things, (2) "comprehension," referring to the mind's apprehension of [those] things,[66] (3) "analysis" which is the understanding of [those] apprehended things, (4) "joy," meaning that the mind abides on all [those] things, and (5) "bliss," which is the excellent bliss of not wavering from all [those] things. This describes the fivefold branch of meditative concentration.

"Meditative concentration" is a continuation of withdrawal yoga. Practicing in the same settings, and with the same gazes and postures, the yogi attempts to absorb the mind in the ten visionary objects, so that mind and its objects are known to be one.[67] This phase of the six yogas is thus a kind of focusing meditation, with the empty-form appearances as its object. However, the goal is also to break down the notions of subject and object, so that the yogi becomes accustomed to visual objects as being no different than the mind that perceives them. The preceding passage describes how the ten visionary objects (1) first are engaged with mentally and viewed as being empty, then (2) are more fully apprehended as empty creations of the mind, and finally (3) one gains a full understanding or realization with respect to them. The yogi then (4) abides stably in this realization, concentrating on the empty-forms, and finally (5) the perceiving mind is unified[68] with the perceived forms,[69] resulting in a feeling of bliss.

While in their practical application Vajrapāṇi's comments refer to the "ten signs," his intent does not seem to be limited to this; as this passage states, meditative concentration is where "all existent things" are seen as being empty. Thus, the realizations brought about by an encounter with empty-form are intended to implicate all phenomena. Through seeing visionary appearances—whether they are sparks of light or empty-form visions of a Buddha—one comes to know that all things share in the nature of those visions, which are empty and yet are able to appear.

3. Breath-Control Yoga

> "Breath control" means blocking the *lalanā* and *rasanā,* the left and right pathways, so that the life-winds[70] constantly enter into the central pathway, the *avadhūtī.* Through the yogas [called] "filling," "vase," and "expelling," [the winds] exit the *avadhūtī* with the syllable OṂ, are held with the syllable HŪṂ, and enter with the syllable ĀḤ.[71] The yogi should become familiar with these, which have the nature of the moon, Rāhu, and the sun.[72]

The third yoga, called "breath control," is performed in the same settings as the preceding yogas,[73] and is begun after the appearances brought on by the previous yogas have arisen. Thus, it still involves seeing empty-forms,[74] which are considered to be of the same nature as the yogi's mind. However, this stage also marks a transition point in the six yogas, where the practitioner is not just focused on visual forms but also begins to work with the wind-energies of the subtle body.

The basic goal of breath control is to remove the winds from the body's left and right energy-channels, bring them into the central channel,[75] and unite them at the navel.[76] Withdrawing the winds from the two side channels is said to be one of the physiological bases for the arising of vision, as this process withdraws the sense faculties from their ordinary objects and opens the way for the alternative sense-powers (such as the divine eye, and so forth) to perceive objects such as empty-form. During breath control, after the winds enter the central channel, the practitioner encounters a spontaneously appearing empty-form image of Kālacakra and his consort Viśvamātā, who appear within the yogi's body, at the site of the central channel. When the focus of the practice turns to the navel region, these deities appear at the navel wheel.

Breath control uses two basic techniques. The first is called "vajra recitation,"[77] which aims to move the winds into the central channel. In this practice, the meditator places the eyes in a wrathful gaze called the "gaze of Amṛtavarta,"[78] which is directed at the central channel at the brow, the level at which the winds will enter the central channel. At the same time, a breathing practice is performed, where the breath is inhaled, abides, and is exhaled in conjunction with the three syllables ĀḤ, HŪṂ, and OṂ.[79]

The second technique is called "vase yoga,"[80] a deep-breathing exercise that in this context is used to bring the winds to the navel energy-wheel at the central channel, where they are combined into a "globe" or "ball" of wind.[81] As the concentrated mind is focused on the navel region, and the winds are brought there, the empty-form image of Kālacakra and

Viśvamātā appears there.[82] As a sign of accomplishment, a luminous halo is also said to appear around the yogi's body.[83]

The practice of breath control is also said to bring about the experience of "immutable bliss."[84] This is because the winds at the navel energy-wheel serve as the fuel for the ignition of a gnostic fire, called the *caṇḍālī,* which blazes from the navel.[85] As the *caṇḍālī* flame blazes up, it melts *thig-le* stored at the crown of the head, resulting in the *thig-le* dripping down the central channel and producing sensations of bliss. This stage of the six yogas could thus be thought of as a kind of sexualized practice, in that it involves the standard components of Buddhist sexual yogas (channels, winds, seminal nuclei, *caṇḍālī* flame,[86] bliss), but does so without the explicit presence of a consort.[87] Indeed, *Stainless Light* suggests that the winds entering the central channel (and the associated arising of the *caṇḍālī* flame) is a kind of union with Kālacakra's own consort Viśvamātā, saying that "the winds entering the central channel is an embracing of Viśvamātā, who is not an object."[88]

4. Retention Yoga

> "Retention" means that the vital energies[89] enter the maṇḍalas of "great-power,"[90] water, fire, and wind, which are at the navel, heart, throat, and forehead. As they do not go outside [of those energy-wheels], this is called the "vital energies abiding in the seminal nuclei." This describes the branch of retention.

"Retention yoga" is a continuation of the wind-related practices begun in the previous yoga. Just as before, the winds are brought into the central channel and combined at the navel, but now the defining characteristic is that the winds are "held" or "retained" in a sequence of four[91] energy-wheels that are located along the body's vertical central channel. Each of those wheels is the site of particular types of seminal nuclei,[92] so when the winds are held in the wheels, they are said to mix with the seminal nuclei.[93] As the mind and winds are focused on a particular wheel, a spontaneously arising empty-form image of Kālacakra and Viśvamātā appears there. The practice begins at the navel wheel, and then the focus moves sequentially up the wheels and then back down again, with the image of the deities appearing in each of the wheels.[94]

5. Recollection Yoga

> "Recollection" refers to seeing your desired deity, the aspects of whose form are free from conceptuality.[95] From that, many rays of light emanate, in the form of a luminous maṇḍala. From that, many forms radiate, emanating in the nature of the three realms. This describes the branch of recollection.

"Recollection yoga" marks another turning point in the six yogas. While building on the preceding practices, the focus now turns more squarely to the perception of a deity, and the production of bliss in the subtle body. According to the *Vajrapāṇi Commentary,* the defining feature of this phase of the six yogas is "seeing your desired deity." The *Kālacakra Tantra* offers a similar characterization, saying: "Recollection [yoga] is the perception of Caṇḍālī in the body and in the sky."[96] The meaning of these two statements seems to be essentially the same.[97] That is, the *caṇḍālī* flame is a gnostic fire burning at the yogi's navel and at the same time is a vision of a "desired deity"—also known as the Great Seal[98]—that shines out of the body and is seen in the sky.

Nāropa[99] is more explicit about this connection between *caṇḍālī* and the Great Seal. Discussing recollection yoga (which here he refers to under one of its alternate names, *sādhana*), he writes:

> Then, in the *sādhana,* [one sees] the form of a deity. Due to the power of [having practiced the yoga of] retention, the yogi sees Caṇḍālī, abiding at the navel, blazing up, free of all obscurations, like [an image in] a prognostic mirror—the Great Seal, radiating from a luminous maṇḍala giving off limitless clouds of buddhas' light rays.

Here Nāropa refers to the *caṇḍālī* fire using the language that Kālacakra authors apply again and again to the Great Seal: luminous and appearing like an image in a prognostic mirror. In comments like this, we can see how the "desired deity" that is seen in recollection yoga brings together the worlds of sexual and visionary yogas. That is, from one perspective, recollection yoga is clearly based on the standard paradigm of Buddhist sexual yoga, which involves the *caṇḍālī* flame, dripping seminal nuclei, the production of bliss, and so forth. During this practice, as the fire at the yogi's navel fire blazes up, it heats a reservoir of *thig-le* stored at the crown of the head. These *thig-le* melt and drip down the central channel, causing a series of blisses as they pass through the energy-wheels located on that channel.[100] Arriving at the tip of the yogi's sexual organ, they are retained there, resulting in the bliss of nonemission. *Stainless Light*[101] sums up the practice:

> Here, based on passion *(chags pa)* for the gnosis [consort], there is a melting of the moon *thig-le*—the moon [i.e., white] *thig-le* melt. That [yoga] in which, based on the gnosis [consort], the enlightened-mind *thig-le* melt and are held in the vajra-jewel, and in which there are three unchanging [moments of bliss] in the secret, navel, and heart [energy-wheels], is *sādhana* [i.e., recollection yoga].

Here *Stainless Light* describes recollection yoga using the terminology typical of sexual yogas, including mention of a "gnosis" (or "visualized") consort.

Yet, even as works like *Stainless Light* discuss the possibility of performing Kālacakra's completion stage yogas with visualized consorts, or even with physical ones,[102] this is clearly not the tradition's ideal mode of procedure. Rather, in one of the most common refrains of Kālacakra's completion stage literature, the tradition exhorts yogis to abandon both the physical consort (the "action seal") and the visualized consort (the "gnostic seal"), in favor of a superior type of consort, called the Great Seal. The *Kālacakra Tantra,*[103] for instance, advises:

> Abandon this action seal, whose heart has impurities, and the gnostic seal, who is imputed!
> For perfect, complete enlightenment, one should meditate with the Supreme Seal, the mother who is the progenitor of the supreme victors!

This Supreme Seal or Great Seal is not a flesh-and-blood woman or a deliberately imagined consort, but rather is a visionary consort, who appears spontaneously, arising before the eyes (to use the traditional metaphor) like an image in a prognostic mirror. This consort is said to be empty of any physical, atomic structure, and yet still is able to appear to the yogi. In Kālacakra terms, she is thus "empty-form," both empty and appearing. An encounter with this sort of consort is then no ordinary sexual encounter but is an "embracing"[104] of empty-form.

While it is easy to see how tantric traditions might replace physical consorts with visualized ones, the move from those types of consorts to the visionary Great Seal is not quite as simple. For one, Kālacakra authors shy away from giving simple descriptions of the Great Seal's visual form, such as depicting her with a particular number of arms, a particular color, a particular set of ornaments, and so forth.[105] In part, this is to preserve the fact that one of the Great Seal's major dimensions is that of emptiness itself, which is devoid of such appearances. However, the Great Seal is clearly not just empty but is also appearing (and it is this topic that motivates much of Yumo's treatise). When this visual dimension is described, it is commonly in terms of raw luminosity: the Great Seal as radiant light, or a flash of lightning. Rather than presenting us with particular aspects or characteristics of the Great Seal, Kālacakra authors most often tell us that she is "endowed with all aspects" or "endowed with the supreme of all aspects,"[106] as if all potential appearances are contained within her.

So, this Great Seal is no simple consort: she is empty but is also everything, is immaterial but is able to spontaneously appear to the eyes just as form does, and is within the yogi while also appearing externally, in the sky. Perhaps the most useful metaphor for understanding the Great Seal, then, is that of "union." While union of course refers to sexual embrace, it also suggests the bringing together of apparent opposites. Kālacakra's visionary practices involving the Great Seal thus can be seen as aiming to provide an experience that is beyond duality, where a perceiving subject (the yogi) and a perception (of the Great Seal) are realized to be one and the same, such that the "objects of cognition and cognition become unified."[107]

6. Concentration Yoga

> "Concentration" means that, through passion *(chags pa)* for the desired deity, one attains the unchanging bliss. In this, the mind is unified, free of the dualistic conception of "apprehender" and "apprehended." The Tathāgatas explain this as the branch of concentration.

The final of the six yogas is in many ways a culmination of them all, involving visionary appearances, the manipulation of subtle-body energies, and the presence of the Great Seal, with all of the intertwined sexual and philosophical connotations that this consort implies. According to the *Vajrapāṇi Commentary,* the defining characteristics of "concentration" yoga are the experience of unchanging bliss and a consequent unification of the mind in which dualism is transcended. In other words, "union" with the Great Seal leads to the somatic experiences of "unchanging" bliss, as well as a mental "unification" in which one realizes that the perceiving self and the perceived Great Seal are ultimately not different from each other.

Another major aim of this yoga is to divest the body of its atomic structure, burning away its physical elements so that the yogi becomes an empty-form just like the Great Seal. The mechanics of this[108] are based on the "blazing and dripping" type of sexual yoga described earlier, but use a distinctive process in which red and white *thig-le* are sequentially "stacked" in the yogi's central channel. Here, based on desire for the Great Seal, the flame at the yogi's navel begins burning. A single red *thig-le* is drawn from the tip of the male's sexual organ and moved up to the top of his central channel, at the forehead, where it stays. A single white *thig-le* then descends to the tip of his sexual organ, where it stays. This cycle is said to result in one moment of "unmoving" or "unchanging" bliss, and that blissful mind is used to cognize emptiness. Here is a good summation of the process from a later Tibetan author, the fifteenth-century exegete Khedrup Norsang Gyatso:[109]

> Practitioners with the keenest abilities, from the time they are able to generate the great unchanging bliss, rely solely on the Great Seal to generate unchanging bliss.[110] To elaborate: focusing one-pointedly on yourself in the form of Kālacakra "mother and father" with their bodies in union, you meditate with desire. Via this, the *caṇḍālī* fire blazes up, and a single red "particle" *(rdul)* travels to the crown area of one's coarse body. When it is stabilized there, the white *bodhicitta* melts from the crown area and descends down within the

> central channel, going to the tip of the vajra jewel, where it stays. Through the power of the Great Seal, it is stabilized there, resulting in one moment of unchanging bliss. That moment of unchanging bliss, which is indivisible in essence from you in the aspect of the empty-form Kālacakra "father and mother" bodies, realizes non-aspected emptiness[111] directly—emptiness [realized like] water being poured into water. That is the attainment of the first of the 21,600 [moments of] unchanging bliss, the path of seeing where emptiness is newly seen in direct perception, and the first [bodhisattva] ground, called "utter joy."

This movement of the *thig-le* is repeated until 21,600[112] red *thig-le* are stacked from the crown to the sexual organ, and 21,600 white *thig-le* are stacked from the sexual organ to the crown. The central channel in this way becomes filled with *thig-le*. The 21,600 moments of unchanging bliss experienced during this process cause the 21,600 ordinary winds to cease,[113] and destroy the 21,600 components of the yogi's physical body,[114] such that a body of gnosis[115] is obtained.

The importance of the visionary context is suggested by Vajrapāṇi's preceding comments about the elimination of the concepts of apprehending subjects and perceived objects. That is, the Great Seal, seen in the vision of the yogi, is not an "object" independent from the yogi, as she is composed of nothing other than the gnosis that dwells within him. Thus union with her is also the "unification" *(gcig tu gyur pa)* of the mind, a state where a known object and a knowing cognition are mixed together as one *(gcig tu 'dres pa)*.[116] This esoteric method of realizing emptiness,[117] with its undertones of Yogācāra, informed by visionary experience, and cast in terms of classic sexual yoga, is the context that must be kept in mind when reading Yumo's treatise.

Guhyasamāja and the "Stage of Self-Blessing"

Before turning to Yumo's *Lamp* itself, some quick comments about one of Yumo's secondary lines of thought are in order. Though the *Lamp* mainly revolves around the theory of Kālacakra's six yogas, Yumo frequently refers to two works related to the "noble tradition" of Guhyasamāja:[118] Nāgārjuna's *Five Stages*[119] and Āryadeva's *Lamp Integrating the Practices.*[120] Yumo unfortunately does not explicitly discuss his interests Guhyasamāja,[121] but his references to the tradition are a prominent feature of his *Lamp,* and they allow for a few basic conclusions.

Yumo's references to the Guhyasamāja mainly relate to that tradition's completion stage practice called the "stage of self-blessing."[122] This same term "stage of self-blessing" surfaces occasionally in Kālacakra, where it can refer to generation stage meditations on peaceful deities.[123] However,

Kālacakra works also use "self-blessing" to refer to visionary practice, particularly to encounters with the empty-form Great Seal.[124] Yumo brings up one of these passages explicitly in his *Lamp*.[125]

In the context of Guhyasamāja, "self-blessing" refers to completion stage techniques for mixing the mind with internal winds in order to transform one's body into the actual body of a deity: a body devoid of atoms[126] and produced "through mere gnosis."[127] These goals are very much like those of Kālacakra, and Yumo appears to have been experimenting with how the Guhyasamāja stage of self-blessing might be equated with Kālacakra's path of vision.[128]

As is typical of Yumo, he makes the identification not through logic or explicit statements but by bringing together similar terms, themes, and language in both systems. He seems especially interested in this section of Guhyasamāja for its language about luminous minds, immaterial bodies composed of gnosis, and deities seen in the sky.[129] We can thus read his interest in Guhyasamāja as calling on the authority of that tantra to support his larger claims about the body, particularly the idea that enlightenment involves removing the body's atomic structure and physically transforming it into a luminous buddha.

Interpretive Analysis of the *Lamp Illuminating Emptiness*

The following section is intended to be read alongside Yumo's *Lamp*, as an interpretive guide. My goal here is not to give an account of each point that Yumo makes but rather to suggest what themes and ideas emerge from Yumo's writing, particularly as they may form connections with similar ideas in the Great Perfection.

Yumo's Introductory Comments

Yumo begins his treatise by declaring what came to be one of the basic values of the Sarma movement: the supremacy of the tantric path. Calling on a host of authoritative sources—the *Nāmasaṃgiti*, Hevajra, Guhyasamāja—he makes it clear that tantric yoga is the only path to enlightenment, and that other methods will not lead there, even with millions of years of effort.

It is often said that what is distinctive about tantra is not its view of emptiness but rather the special techniques that tantra offers for the realization of emptiness. This is not exactly so for Yumo. He is careful to accept Buddhists' normative ideas about emptiness, to pay homage to Nāgārjuna, and to speak of tantra's distinctiveness in terms of "method," but in reality Yumo finds in Kālacakra a special presentation of emptiness that transcends all others. With this in mind, he proposes to discuss what "emptiness" means, specifically in the context of tantra. For this purpose, Yumo outlines two styles of dealing with emptiness: (1) the intellectually determined "view" of emptiness *(lta ba gtan la phab pa'i stong pa nyid)* and (2) emptiness that is a "path" *(lam du 'gyur pa'i stong pa nyid).*

In Yumo, the "view" of emptiness refers to a classical Buddhist philosophical presentation of emptiness. It is what many Buddhists would probably say if asked what "emptiness" means: things' lack of inherent essence; things' not being established via their own natures; or their freedom from the four extremes of existence, nonexistence, neither, and both. Yumo states in no uncertain terms that these are not a path to enlightenment.

Again, it should be stated that Yumo does not simply abandon the "view" of emptiness. This kind of philosophical emptiness, he notes, is useful for overturning clinging and attachment. The problem with the "view" type of emptiness (though he does not explicitly use these terms) is that it is simply an absence—a negative—and an absence is not something that you can do anything with, that can lead you anywhere, or that can even be perceived. In Yumo's terms, it "is not suitable to be known or experienced" *(rtog cing nyams su myong pa mi 'thad)* because it "cannot become an object of the mind" *(blo'i yul du mi 'gyur pa).*

This is the basis of Yumo's turn to vision. An "emptiness that is a path," such as a spontaneous vision of the Great Seal appearing in empty-form, is something that a yogi can experience, as it becomes an object of the eyes. It is this kind of observable emptiness *(dmigs pa dang bcas pa'i stong pa nyid)* that, for Yumo, is the final meaning of emptiness. For him, this idea is present in all the tantras but is most clear in the system of Kālacakra. He dedicates the rest of his treatise to explaining it from this perspective.

The Root Verse of the Treatise

In order to explain this "path" emptiness, Yumo selects a verse from the *Kālacakra Tantra* that he says presents it clearly. This is verse 4.198,[130] which describes the appearance of the Great Seal, seen during the practice of the six yogas:

> The *mudrā* is like an illusion, [appearing] in the sky and the mind, like a form in a mirror,
> Displaying the three worlds, emanating rays like stainless lightning.
> Indivisible in the external world and the body, [she is] not an object, and dwells in the sky, a mere appearance.
> The nature of mind and that which comes from mind, embracing all migrating beings, one in the guise of many!

The remainder of Yumo's treatise (some forty pages) is dedicated to explaining this verse. Yumo individually examines each critical phrase (first "The mudrā...," then "in the sky...," then "in the mind..."), explaining its meaning, suggesting how it contributes to the understanding of the Great Seal, providing abundant citations from related discussions in other tantric works, and answering hypothetical disputes.

The following is a brief discussion of Yumo's comments on this verse. Because the phrase-by-phrase commentary can be found in the full translation, here I have simply structured my presentation around each of the verse's four lines.

(a) The mudrā is like an illusion, [appearing] in the sky and the mind, like a form in a mirror,...

The mudrā referred to here is of course the Great Seal, the visionary "consort" that appears to the yogi, and which Yumo identifies with Viśvamātā (the consort of Kālacakra) and Prajñāpāramitā. This double identity—(1) a multiarmed tantric consort and (2) the pacific goddess associated with the philosophy of emptiness—is emblematic of the Great Seal's role in Kālacakra and in Yumo's own thought. That is, she is at once a visible divinity and an abstract, intangible principle that is the underlying nature and source of all phenomena.

All of this plays on the meaning of the term "great seal" *(mahāmudrā, phyag rgya chen mo),* which in exoteric contexts can simply refer to emptiness, the one unifying characteristic of all phenomena that is present in everything like an authenticating seal. In the tantric context, "seal" has the sense of "sexual consort," so calling the supreme kind of consort the "Great Seal" is both a way of deliberately sexualizing a classical term and of connecting Buddhist discourses of sexuality back to more normative Buddhist thought.

Yumo reminds us here of several ways that tantric terms can oscillate between these two registers. The Great Seal, for instance, can be called the *dharmadhātu,* which has the two meanings of "sphere of reality" and "vulva." She is also known as the "mother of all buddhas," meaning on the one hand that she guides beings (through the Perfection of Wisdom) to the maturity of buddhahood, or on the other hand that union with her leads to the "birth" of oneself as a buddha. These dual associations make her a key figure for uniting the worlds of Buddhist tantra and Buddhist philosophy, and Yumo uses them particularly to suggest how the sexualized visionary practices related to the Great Seal are in fact methods of encountering emptiness.

The Great Seal also serves as a bridge for the internal and external worlds, making her an embodiment of the famous Kālacakra slogan: "Just as it is in the external world, so it is within the body."[131] As Yumo describes in detail, she is a visionary appearance seen in the sky (or in the dark-retreat) with the eyes, but as that vision is itself composed of mind, it also dwells in the interior world of the body. Through a vision of her, the internal perceiving mind encounters itself in the external world, such that one encounters one's own nature, like seeing one's own face in a mirror.

Finally, Yumo uses the comparison of the Great Seal to an "illusion" and a "form in a mirror" to help develop some distinctively Kālacakra ideas about emptiness, where the term means not just "empty of inherent nature" but also "empty of atoms" or "empty of material structure." The basic claim is that the Great Seal is devoid of atomic structure and yet still appears and functions in the world; by encountering her in vision, one realizes that this is the nature of all phenomena, including oneself. The six yogas then provide methods for divesting one's own body of its material form, such that one's body transforms into the same empty-form as the Great Seal. With this as background, Yumo suggests how the Great Seal is like a mirror that reflects reality back to those that perceive her, and "union" with her becomes not so much about an esoteric and ecstatic union with a divine woman as it is about realizing that one is continually embraced by that reality.

(b) Displaying the three worlds, emanating rays like stainless lightning.

In this section, Yumo turns more fully to the issue of light and discusses the Great Seal as source of light in both the metaphorical and literal senses. Discussing her radiant nature, he suggests not only how the Great Seal gives off light but how she is a source that radiates out the universe itself. These ideas are particularly evidenced in Yumo's interpretation of the statement that the Great Seal "displays the three worlds."[132] First, this indicates that she "reveals" or helps the yogi to understand the nature of the world. That is, through encountering her in vision, the yogi gains experience with an appearance that is insubstantial and yet functioning, such that the true nature of the entire universe is displayed. Second, Yumo describes how the Great Seal "displays" the three worlds in the sense of being the source of all appearances. That is, as a dynamic emptiness, the universal form that constitutes everything, she is the source of the entire world, which lights up due to her.

In interpreting the "lightning" comment, Yumo first uses this to contrast the gnostic seal (i.e., a visualized consort) with the Great Seal. The gnostic seal, in this scheme, is like the sun, whose regular and constant rays suggest the passage of time, or a visualized deity constructed gradually and with effort. The Great Seal, in contrast, is a blaze that comes out of nowhere, instantly. Yumo then explores the content of her light, suggesting how it is a singular luminosity that can be perceived as multiplicity, like a ray of light being divided up into the five colors of the rainbow. Though Yumo does not make it explicit, the five colors of light here correlate to the five elements, so the Great Seal's ability to emanate light rays can be read as a continuation of the above argument about her being the source of the phenomenal world.

(c) Indivisible in the external world and the body, [she is] not an object, and dwells in the sky, a mere appearance.

Yumo uses "indivisible in the external world and the body" to return to the theme of how the Great Seal exemplifies the unity of the external universe and the internal world of the body. There are two ways that this can be read. First, Kālacakra literature discusses how the Great Seal appears in two different places: appearing within the body (either as a gnostic flame at the yogi's navel or as an image of Viśvamātā that appears at the central channel),[133] but also appearing in the external world. Second, and this is what Yumo is more interested in, the Great Seal is often used to suggest the link between the external world of perceived objects and the internal world of the perceiver. A monistic strain revolving around these ideas surfaces sometimes in Kālacakra, where we are told that visions of the Great Seal are not based on the ordinary perceptual model of an "internal" consciousness perceiving an "external" object, with its resulting spiral into duality, conceptuality, ignorance, and suffering. Rather, the Great Seal is both the internal consciousness and the external object, constituting and uniting both worlds. At times the Great Seal also resembles the primary "substance" of a gnostic universe, much like the one depicted in the Great Perfection. Few Buddhists propose this kind of monistic view, and Yumo seems to acknowledge the rarity of the view by declaring that the Great Seal is not the purview of "false lamas,"[134] a term he frequently uses to imply that non-Kālacakra interpretations of the tantras are counterfeit.

Commenting on "not an object,"[135] Yumo adds to his message that the Great Seal is not an "object" as defined by classical Buddhist standards. Here, he focuses again on her lack of materiality and the fact that she is not made of the five elements. While she is thus not a traditional material object, the very fact of her appearance prevents her from being a non-object, or a non-thing.[136] One of Yumo's underlying messages here is how the material can be translated into the immaterial, and then come back again: beings arise from the Great Seal, condense into form, and eventually are liberated back into their original formlessness.

The second "sky" section of Yumo's treatise follows. Here, the discussion again revolves around the idea that the Great Seal appears as a vision in the sky. The special focus here is that such visionary experiences are not supernatural occurrences but are accessible to ordinary beings[137] engaged in the practice of tantra, who see them with their "ordinary eyes" or the "eyes of beginners."[138]

Finally, Yumo uses "mere appearance" to focus on the empty nature of the appearance of the Great Seal. That is, the emphasis on "mere" indicates how she is insubstantial and, while having no aspects, somehow also contains all aspects. The section contains a lengthy (for Yumo) and pointed statement, where he criticizes others' claims about the "path," particularly the idea that it involves an emptiness that is hidden or beyond experiential contact. His description of his opponents borders on invective, at one point stating: "Let it be known that they have not met with the true path; the mantra vehicle, which is like the finest butter, is spoiled by the filthy water of all their unclean concepts."[139]

(d) The nature of mind and that which comes from mind, embracing all migrating beings, one in the guise of many!

"Mind and arisen from mind" *(sems dang sems byung, citta-caitta)* is a phrase seen occasionally in Kālacakra, which gives a tantric spin to a common epistemological term. In Buddhist discussions of minds and awareness, the phrase normally refers to a main "mind" *(sems, citta)* and the secondary "mental factors" *(sems byung, caitta)* or mental events that always accompany that main mind. In this visionary context it refers to the mind of the yogi *(sems)* and the vision of the Great Seal that arises from that mind *(sems byung)*, with the suggestion the two are indivisible. Yumo's discussion here unfolds as a type of tantric epistemology, which tries to establish the plausibility of perceptual models that do not adhere to the dualistic subject/object format. He proposes a kind of epistemology in which, because everything is constituted of the Great Seal, the objects perceived by a mind are nothing other than the mind's exteriorization of itself. In this way he suggests how visual perception—the system that provides our most visceral experiences of dualism—might be brought into the path by employing it to view "pure" objects like the Great Seal.

With "embracing all beings" Yumo returns to the connections between the classical and tantric Great Seals, suggesting how we might provide a new interpretation of the consort's "embrace." That is, the Great Seal might provide an "embrace" as a type of consort, but in reality she is a gnosis that is spread throughout the world and is localized in all beings, "embracing" them by pervading and encompassing them. This section further develops the monistic strain of Kālacakra that Yumo is attracted to and provides suggestions of how the Great Seal is present everywhere and acts as the single seed that gives rise to and constitutes the world. As Yumo notes, when Buddhists posit one thing that is shared by all beings, they are often speaking of "ignorance"; in his view, it is in fact the omnipresent Great Seal that unites all beings, encompassing even their ignorance, which is the very factor that keeps the Great Seal from being seen.

Finally, Yumo uses the "one in the guise of many" comment to develop the idea that the world of multiplicity, subjects, and objects is only a distortion that results from the ordinary mind. That is, while the Great Seal is a singularity that pervades and constitutes the world, the mind perceives the Great Seal as a multiplicity, as all of the apparently distinct objects of the saṃsāric world. Cyclic existence is thus separated from transcendence by an interpretive standpoint, such that liberation comes about by a shift in perspective as much as through a complicated series of practices. It seems notable here that Yumo does not in fact describe this shift in the very technical terms of the six yogas, but rather as a simple revolution in perception that leads to enlightenment. In this way, he comes very close to the "recognition" doctrine found in the Great Perfection, and it is possible to see in his focus the hint that technical matters of yoga might be equally as dispensable in the path to transcendence as technical matters of scholastic thought.

Yumo's Concluding Summation

In the end, Yumo circles back to the idea that the Great Seal is the hidden intent of all tantras, even if she is not explicitly mentioned in them. He provides a partial list of code words that refer to her—terms from *bhaga* to "suchness"—and emphasizes that a proper reading of the tantras relies on an understanding of the *Bodhisattva Commentaries*. One last time, he reminds us that analytical and static treatments of emptiness are not the path, as liberation only comes through "seeing emptiness with the eyes."[140]

A series of concluding verses pokes fun at inferior tantric teachers while praising his own, whom he refers to simply as Jetsün, "foremost of the venerable ones."[141] This closing section contains a verse of aspiration that is distinctively Yumo, which prays for all beings "to attain the state of vajra-holder by apprehending emptiness with the eyes."[142]

Conclusion

Yumo's comments about "seeing emptiness" are in many ways emblematic of his work as a whole, in that they show him taking an important theme from Kālacakra and then magnifying it. The relationship of seeing and emptiness is of course a fundamental concern in Kālacakra, but works like *Stainless Light* deal with this in the more measured language of seeing the "form of emptiness" rather than with Yumo's more unusual language of seeing "emptiness" itself.

Another issue magnified under Yumo's *Lamp* concerns sexual yoga. As we had an opportunity to observe earlier, the first two of Kālacakra's six yogas—"withdrawal" and "meditative concentration"—are free of the sexualized blazing-and-dripping practices. Distanced from consorts and sexual fluids, these initial visionary yogas focus on raw appearances of luminosity. The theory and philosophy related to vision then pervade the remainder of the six yogas, even as those return to the sexual model. Yumo is most interested in this trajectory away from the sexual and toward the philosophical, to the extent that, while his work does candidly discuss sexual tantra, he tends to engage with sexuality through language, images, and philosophical wordplays rather than as sticky ritual encounters with real or imagined women. This interest in using vision to move Buddhist esoteric tradition toward a different kind of sexuality, or even away from sexuality altogether, is one that, as we will see later, is shared by the Great Perfection.

Yumo's work is also remarkable in its depiction of the Great Seal. His *Lamp* repeatedly portrays the Great Seal not just as the great visionary consort but as a singular gnostic force that is the source and substance of the universe: pervading everywhere, underlying everything, and residing within all beings. While these monistic and gnostic themes are present in *Stainless Light,* they are (in my reading) difficult to pinpoint, surrounded as they are by Kālacakra's riot of multiplicity. In a more focused interpretation like Yumo's, however, they come out much more clearly.

These two features of Yumo's *Lamp*—its relative disinterest in standard consort practice and its related move toward a singular gnosis that gives rise to the world—are features of the other visionary systems rising to popularity in Tibet right at Yumo's time: the visionary systems of the Great Perfection. We thus find in Yumo a Tibetanized Kālacakra that looks slightly more like the Great Perfection, while in the Great Perfection we will see a rapidly changing system that begins to look quite a bit like Kālacakra. Turning to the Great Perfection systems, we will see them at different times mirroring Kālacakra, following their own paths, and extending some ideas suggested in Kālacakra: casting away the consort and presenting a fully gnostic universe whose origin is reenacted in practices of vision.

CHAPTER 2 | *Tantra of the Blazing Lamps*

The Old Ones Encountering the New

At the same time that the Sarma movement was ushering in a new era of Tibetan esoteric Buddhism with imported tantras like the Kālacakra, major changes were also taking place within the Nyingma. The eleventh and twelfth centuries witnessed an outpouring of previously unseen literature from the Old Ones, but these works emerged with a historical caveat: the claim that they were not in fact new. Maintaining that their lineages and traditions originated from the dynastic period, the Nyingma cast many of their renaissance texts as rediscoveries of materials that had been hidden during the eighth century, or as revivals of small but ancient oral traditions that had been continuously transmitted since that time.

Thus, in contrast to the Sarma groups—who portrayed themselves as favoring modern translations and new imports from India—Nyingma, at least outwardly, turned to Tibet and the past. We should not assume, however, that Nyingma groups isolated themselves from the interests of the Sarma or from current developments in Indian tantra. In fact, the Nyingma literature from the renaissance was often profoundly different from that of the dynastic period and often contained the same subtle-body practices, gnostic themes, and discourses of sexuality and death that were the hallmarks of late Indian tantra.[1] Nyingma tantric movements thus were aiming to remain current in the esoteric trends of the ninth to eleventh centuries, all the while maintaining that their core traditions originated in the eighth. The situation seems to leave two very reductive perspectives from which we might approach their renaissance literature. The first possibility is to defy historiographical practice and to accept as literal the claim that the Nyingma's new revelations and revivals were also present in the eighth century as fully formed traditions, even though they seem so clearly informed by later developments. The second possibility, while not as fantastic, is also unattractive: to discard completely the Nyingma's own self-representation and treat their revelations as being disingenuous.

There is, however, a middle ground, one that comes out clearly when Nyingma and Sarma renaissance materials are read together. This proposes that Nyingma did indeed engage with late Indian tantra, but did so in a very different way than Sarma, whose methods favored translating Indian works and forming their own versions of Indian traditions. The Nyingma, however, when encountering late Indian tantra, did not attempt to transplant those traditions whole but disassembled them and moved selected themes, practices, and ideas into their own existent traditions. As a result, they were mixtures of both old and new: infused with new materials, their old traditions took on new life and followed new paths, so that they cannot be viewed as being straight from India, any more than they can be viewed as having been excavated intact from the Tibetan earth. This perspective will also inform our understanding of the Sarma movements, whose claims of translation and transplantation are often as difficult to assess as those of discovery and revelation.

The Great Perfection and the Seminal Heart

One of the major events in the renaissance transformation of the Nyingma was their thorough reworking of the Great Perfection *(rdzogs chen).* The Great Perfection is a broad religious tradition shared by Nyingma and Bön, and has made some of Tibet's most imaginative contributions to Buddhist thought and practice, with its emphasis on vision, dynamic emptiness, primordial purity, and the agency of a luminous awareness in the universe. Though its origins are both obscure and contested, the Great Perfection seems to have arisen in Tibet in the late eighth century. The tradition's own histories present divergent accounts of its early lineage, but all of them trace the Great Perfection's origins to points much earlier than the eighth century and look to homelands outside of the Tibetan plateau. One popular account describes the Great Perfection as being of Indian origin, telling of how it first appeared on earth to Garab Dorjé, an obscure figure from Oḍḍiyāna who was miraculously conceived when the buddha Vajrapāṇi, disguised as a swan, delivered a series of pecks to his mother's heart as she was bathing. Garab Dorjé, in this presentation, later received the full transmission of the Great Perfection from Vajrapāṇi and passed it down through a closely held lineage that proceeded through the shadowy figures Mañjuśrīmitra, Śrīsiṃha, Jñānasūtra, and Vimalamitra.[2] In some accounts Vimalamitra brought the Great Perfection to Tibet[3] in the late eighth century, teaching it to King Trisong Detsen and a small group of disciples at the court. This initial transmission was not spread widely, and tradition maintains that it was eventually buried as treasures that would be revealed in the eleventh century.

The Indian origins and early Tibetan transmission of the Great Perfection cannot be reliably verified through available literary or historical sources, so modern historians treat the tradition primarily as a Tibetan innovation. Nonetheless, it is critical to remember that the intellectual roots of the Great Perfection are indeed deep in India, given the tradition's affinity with Indian thought on Buddha-nature, gnostic elements of Buddhist completion stage practices, the *Guhyagarbha Tantra,*[4] and forms of nondual Kaśmiri Śaivism. It is also clear that (by Tibetan standards) the tradition is genuinely old, as groups referring to themselves as "Great Perfection" indeed existed in the late eighth to early ninth centuries,[5] and their core ideas reemerged, though transformed, after Tibet's period of fragmentation.

The earliest stratum of the Great Perfection is now called the "Mind Series" *(sems sde),*[6] though it is not clear if this was a unified movement, or even if "Mind Series" was always synonymous with the Great Perfection.[7] Nonetheless, an early body of Great Perfection literature called the "eighteen texts of the Mind Series,"[8] perhaps dating from the late eighth to late tenth centuries, laid down the Great Perfection's thematic core, setting a basic format around which later iterations of the Great Perfection were built. The Mind Series literature presents a blend of radical emptiness and speculation on the agency of a luminous awareness in the universe. Presenting a state of affairs where all beings and all appearances are themselves the singular enlightened gnosis of the buddha All Good (Samantabhadra, Küntu Zangpo), it also shows a disinterest in specifying any kind of structured practices or concepts via which one could connect with that gnosis.[9] Rather, the tradition argues, there is nothing to do and nothing to strive for, so the reality of All Good will manifest in its immediacy just by relaxing and letting go. A short Mind Series poem called the "Cuckoo of Awareness"[10] exemplifies this strain of thought:

> In variety, there is no difference.
> And in parts, a freedom from elaborations.
> Things as things are, are not conceptual, but
> The shining forth of appearances is All Good.
> Since you are finished, cast off the sickness of effort!
> Resting naturally, leave things [as they are]!

In the renaissance, the themes exemplified here—equality, simplicity, nonconceptuality, letting go, the manifestation of appearances, and the buddha All Good—remain at the center of the Great Perfection but became elaborated in a variety of increasingly technical and practical ways. "Great Perfection" then became a name for a wide variety of movements, not controlled by any central authority, who shared a core commitment to the rhetoric of pristine gnosis but incorporated it into their own diverse interests in esoteric philosophy, ritual, death-related practice, sexuality, medicine, and alchemy.

As a result, during the renaissance, the Great Perfection began to take on many of the characteristics of tantra that it once seemed to reject: rituals, initiations, concrete practices, systematic thought, and sexuality. Yet even as the Great Perfection moved closer to classical tantra, it sought ways to do so while remaining true to its early rhetorical core. Exemplifying this is a set of visionary practices that rose to popularity in the eleventh century, which in many ways served to re-enact the scenario found in the "Cuckoo of Awareness": they involved letting go of conceptuality so that an inner gnosis at the heart, identified as the buddha All Good, would shine forth into appearance.

In the Nyingma Great Perfection, these visionary practices are most associated with a movement known as Seminal Heart *(snying thig).* One of many incipient Great Perfection movements and lineages competing and overlapping with each other in the renaissance,[11] the Seminal Heart would eventually attain dominance and determine the direction of the Nyingma Great Perfection as a whole. In terms of its innovations, the Seminal Heart brought to the Great Perfection a distinctive gnostic cosmogony in which a luminous awareness bursts forth from a container, bringing about the world. This creation narrative is then mirrored in visionary yogas, where light bursts from the container of the body to be seen with the eyes. In turn, these visions are accounted for with new ideas about the structure and formation of the human body, which map the body with luminous energy-channels and describe their functioning as driven by transcendent dimensions of the body's elements, winds, and seminal nuclei.

Seventeen Tantras and the *Tantra of the Blazing Lamps*

The literary foundation of the Seminal Heart is a collection of tantras called the *Seventeen Tantras (rgyud bcu bdun),* all of which are written in the voices of buddhas like Samantabhadra and Vajradhara. The Seminal Heart regards these tantras as having been brought to Tibet in the eighth century by Vimalamitra, who served both as the Seminal Heart's revealer and concealer, in the sense that he taught the tradition's core works and wrote exegetical materials about them, but eventually concealed the tradition as a treasure for later revelation. In particular, the Seminal Heart's histories suggest that Vimalamitra taught the *Seventeen Tantras* to a disciple named Nyang Tingdzin Zangpo, who concealed them in the eighth century. At some point near the beginning of the eleventh century, these materials were discovered in the "Hat Temple"[12] to the northeast of Lhasa by one Dangma Lhüngyi Gyeltsen, who was acting as the temple's caretaker. The tantras were then passed in a lineage through the figures Jetsün Seng-gé Wangchuk, Jégom Nakpo, and finally to the first datable person, Zhangtön Tashi Dorjé (1097–1127).[13]

In the early renaissance, Great Perfection authors were still concealing their own voices within those of buddhas and writing under pseudonyms of legendary figures. As such, the literature of the Seminal Heart tradition can be dated with much less precision than that of a tradition like the early Tibetan Kālacakra, which has translations made at generally agreed-upon dates, and exegetical works by known figures whose lives are attested to in independent historical sources. When it comes to the *Seventeen Tantras,* there are no such luxuries, and so the collection has to be dated by suggesting plausible authors and by working backward from known figures who cited or mentioned the tantras in their own works. Perhaps the best way of arriving at basic dates is to read the narrative of the Seminal Heart's initial teaching, concealment, and subsequent revelation as a narrative of gradual collective inscription and redaction by its group of revealers and early proponents.[14] The latest possible date for the collection of the *Seventeen Tantras* and their commentaries can be placed at 1127, the death of Zhangtön Tashi Dorjé, whose *Great Chronicles of the Seminal Heart*[15] presents one of the major accounts of the early Seminal Heart and discusses the tantras' lineage. The scholarly Zhangtön stands out as a likely candidate for having authored the tantras' commentaries, which would place them in the early twelfth century. The Tibetan-language tantras themselves may have begun circulating on paper by the mid-eleventh century, possibly inscribed by the two earlier members of Zhangtön's lineage.[16]

As a group, the *Seventeen Tantras* are stylistically quite similar, though they do not read as compositions produced from a single author or even a single historical moment. The tantras are all buddha-voiced and are cast in a traditional format where a buddha engages in a dialogue with his retinue, with the retinue posing questions and the buddha providing answers. These dialogues are set in diverse locations, from pristine space to volcanoes and charnel grounds, and their topics encompass all the Seminal Heart's concerns, from the peaceful to the horrific: cosmogony, the subtle body, speculation on the gnostic "ground" that underlies the world, buddha-nature, discussions of light-energy, practical techniques for calming the mind and producing visions, ritual empowerments, maṇḍala construction, signs of meditative accomplishment, postdeath states, attaining liberation after dying, funerary rituals, relics, prognostications for the time of death, subjugation rituals, strange recipes, and advice for dealing with zombies.

Some of the longer tantras in the collection, like the monumental *Tantra of Unimpeded Sound (sgra thal 'gyur),* seem to be synthetic anthologies, as they read like compilations and even refer to other of the *Seventeen Tantras.* On the other hand, many of the seventeen are clearly not synthetic, a prime example being the tantra that is a main source for this book: the *Tantra of the Blazing Lamps.* The *Lamps* tantra is very tightly organized, self-consciously literary, and focuses throughout on a single subject: the Seminal Heart practices of vision. Written in verse, the tantra bills itself as an Indian composition, translated by Vimalamitra and a Tibetan named Kawa Pal-dzeg.[17] The tantra describes how a luminous awareness, located at the heart, might be projected out of the eyes and into the sky, resulting in a sequence of radiant visions. Despite its esoteric subject matter, the tantra proceeds methodically and bears all the marks of Tibetan scholasticism, laying out the essence, etymology, classification, natures, and so forth of four "lamps," which together represent the bodily structures, perceptual apparatus, content, and theoretical background of vision according to the Seminal Heart.

Essential Background for the *Tantra of the Blazing Lamps*

The *Tantra of the Blazing Lamps* and its commentary *Stringing a Garland of Pearls*[18] in some ways form a self-contained unit, as they provide a detailed and structured account of the Seminal Heart's system of visionary yoga. These works are, however, heavily weighted toward the theoretical and were also written for Seminal Heart insiders who were familiar with the tradition's distinctive terminology and views. The tantra thus does not attempt to present the Seminal Heart's broadest ideas, as these are assumed to be known by the reader; nor does it fully outline practical matters about yoga, though it frequently refers to these in passing.

In the following, I supply some of this essential background in order to quickly bring the reader up to speed. Focusing on the gnostic orientation and soteriology of the Seminal Heart, I present the tradition's central narrative—the enlightenment of the buddha All Good—and discuss some ways that this narrative drives visionary theory and practice. I also provide a traditional account of the tantra's path of vision, which describes how luminous appearances unfold in a sequence called the "four visions."

Gnostic Monism and the Doctrine of Recognition

The Great Perfection, in both its Nyingma and Bön incarnations, could be described as a type of gnostic monism. These terms "gnostic" and "monism" have their own connotations in the study of religion, so it would be good to quickly clarify them here, particularly because these are not terms that traditions like the Great Perfection (or Kālacakra) apply to themselves. First, "gnostic" is not meant to imply connections to other religious traditions that have come to be termed "gnosticism," such as those arising in the Middle East in the late first century CE. Rather, "gnostic" here is intended to refer to a view, which is particularly prominent in the Great Perfection, that the primary component of the universe is a type of luminous, enlightened awareness *(rig pa).* In the Great Perfection, the apparently solid external objects that surround us are in fact a kind of solidified knowing: a high-energy gnosis that has become confused and slowed down to the point that it has entered a state of ossified dormancy.

Next, "monism" in this context refers to the Great Perfection's idea that gnosis is the primary and singular "substance" of the world. In this view, the diversity of the environment and the beings that inhabit it are all derived from a singular awareness.[19] The term "monism" is thus useful for indicating the Great Perfection's interests in unity, as well as in the singularity *(nyag gcig)* of awareness, which contrast to the proliferations *(spros pa)* of deluded thought and the ordinary world. By using the term "monism," it is not my intention to suggest that the Great Perfection reifies its "one," as in fact the tradition tends to portray awareness as ultimately being beyond the concepts of one and many. Another potential problem with the term "monism" is that Buddhist traditions often take pains to distinguish themselves from monistic Hindu traditions, so the term here should also not be taken as implying an equivalence between the two, or as suggesting that the Buddhist traditions described here are explainable simply as imports from Hinduism.

In the view of the Seminal Heart, all of the world's beings, objects, and appearances are said to rise up from the "ground" *(gzhi)* of reality, which in its primordial state is a field of pure possibility, beyond differentiation. Awareness serves as the dynamic, knowing dimension of this ground and acts as a kind of luminous vibrancy that "lights up" *(snang)* from the ground, creating appearances through its "dynamic energy" *(rtsal).* In this view, all appearances are simply the "play" *(rol pa)* or the "radiation" *(gdangs)* of awareness, with some appearances (such as visionary ones) being awareness appearing in its unclouded intensity, while others (like ordinary objects) are only its dimmed derivations.

In the Great Perfection, awareness plays a primary role in beings' enlightenment, as well as their wandering in saṃsāra, the crucial issue separating these two being whether or not awareness is "recognized" *(ngo shes pa)* for what it is. That is, if beings and their environments are in fact constituted of the same awareness, beings can either recognize that, or they can mistakenly view the world as containing external objects, absolutely separate from themselves as perceiving subjects. "Recognition," then, is the simple act that leads to enlightenment. "Nonrecognition," on the other hand, is the Seminal Heart's version of the basic ignorance that Buddhists say afflicts all beings, causing them to divide up the world into factions, split between a "self" that needs to be protected and "others" who become objects of attachment or hatred.

One of the main functions of visionary practice is to work out this issue of recognition. The practices of dark-retreat and sky-gazing are based on the idea that pure awareness is locked away in the body's core, localized at the heart. A set of luminous energy channels then run from the heart to the eyes, acting as pathways through which awareness can travel and exit the body. Based on special yogic techniques, awareness can be induced to emerge from the eyes and light up into visionary appearances. This provides an opportunity for recognition: for the yogi to realize that the visionary appearances "out there" are none other than presencings of an internal awareness, and thus to undo the basic error of ignorance.

The Enlightenment of All Good

While these issues of recognition and gnosis are often dealt with in abstract terms, the Great Perfection also puts them in more dramatic form: the story of the enlightenment of the primordial buddha named "All Good" (Samantabhadra, or Küntu Zangpo in Tibetan). As a philosophical drama, the enlightenment of All Good neatly describes and brings together several parts of the Great Perfection, including its cosmology, its visionary yogas, and its presentation of human embryology. The narrative, however, is typically found in pieces, so it is difficult to point to a definitive telling of the story in a single text.[20] To provide an overview of it here, I rely on Longchenpa's synthetic presentation, found in his fourteenth-century *Treasury of Words and Meanings.*[21]

The story of All Good's enlightenment begins as far back as the imagination allows: at a point before time, before the universe, and before sentient beings or buddhas. At this point, all of existence is depicted as a vase[22] that contains the pure possibility of the universe, which is the inexpressible source and fabric of the world called the "ground" *(gzhi).* Longchenpa describes the ground as:

> the self-emergent primordial gnosis of awareness, the original primordially empty Body of Reality, the ultimate truth of the expanse, and the abiding condition of luminously radiant reality, within which such oppositions as cyclic existence and transcendent reality, pleasure and suffering, existence and non-existence, being and non-being, freedom and straying, awareness and dimmed awareness, are not found anywhere at all.[23]

Three important ideas come together in this description of the ground: (1) it is not a substance but is a primordial awareness; (2) it is associated with the Body of Reality, the most subtle, intangible, inapprehensible, formless "body" of a Buddha; and (3) while the ground is described in negative terms (as being empty of reality/unreality and so forth), it is not an emptiness of static darkness but one that is alive with radiance and light.

The story of All Good's enlightenment thus begins with a vase containing something like a Buddha-embryo, but one whose radiance is completely interiorized, sealed away like a lamp inside a closed pot. Next, an obscure event takes place: a gnostic wind stirs in the vase. This leads to the seal of the vase bursting open, and awareness flows out into space in a graded series of lights, Buddhas, and pure lands. In Longchenpa's description:

> The encasing seal of the Youthful Body in a Vase is rent open, and the gnostic winds' impulsion raises awareness up from the ground. As its self-presencing thus dawns in the eight gateways of spontaneous presence, the originally pure Reality Body's manifestation like a cloudless sky becomes present above... and down further below are the measureless world systems of the sixfold living beings' self-manifestation through the gate of cyclic existence.[24]

This describes the primordial ground-presencing *(gzhi snang),* when awareness moves into exteriority and into historical time. Most important here is the concept of the "eight gateways," the first six of which are the essential forms that awareness takes when it first manifests: lights, Buddha-bodies, gnosis, compassion, freedom, and nonduality. The final two gateways, then, are viewpoints from which the first six are perceived, and are called the gateways to purity and impurity.

These last two gateways are in fact the two perspectives that lead to either saṃsāra or nirvāṇa. As awareness spills out of the vase and into the reaches of space, for the first time it encounters appearances of itself (i.e., the first six "gateways"). If awareness recognizes those appearances as itself, it passes through the gateway to purity, and the presencing process stops and reverses in its tracks. The awareness is not sealed away again but is optimized, "taken to its limit" *(thar phyin pa),*[25] perfectly integrated with itself in such a way that it immediately becomes a completely functional enlightened being: the buddha All Good.

The story does not end with All Good, however, as a portion of awareness does not recognize itself in the ground-presencing but mistakenly interprets its own appearances as being something other than itself. This tragic error is portrayed in the *Tantra of the Adamantine Hero's Heart-Mirror,*[26] where awareness itself wonders:

> Have I emerged from that over there, or has that over there emerged from me?

Duality begins with this thought, and awareness passes through the gateway of impurity. This process is called "straying" *('khrul pa),*[27] in the sense that awareness makes an error and strays from itself, into suffering. This strayed portion of awareness comes to constitute our ordinary universe of self-alienation, ignorance, and violence—slowing down to become beings' ordinary minds and the physical matter of the world.

The Common Ground

Because the ground-presencing provides the opportunity for All Good's moment of recognition, it gives rise to his enlightenment. But this same process also serves as the condition for nonrecognition, and thus leads to the saṃsāric world of suffering and alienation. Thus just as the ground begins to emerge from the vase into historical time, in the moment just before the drama of recognition/nonrecognition, there is a point where the ground can be called the "common ground" *(spyi gzhi),* meaning that (depending on whether it is self-recognized or not) it will serve as the basis for both transcendence and bondage. Longchenpa puts it this way:

> When the ground-presencing dawns from within the ground's range, it in turn is termed the "common ground" in light of its serving as the ground or foundation for both freedom and straying: it is referred to as the "foundation of freedom" by force of its acting as the ground for freedom, and it is referred to as the "foundation of straying" by force of its acting as the ground of sentient beings' errant straying.[28]

For Buddhists, it is rather complicated to suggest that saṃsāra and nirvāṇa have the same source,[29] as it calls into question the fundamental principles of ignorance being the "true cause" of suffering, while an opposing "true path" leads to liberation. The idea of a single cause for both, rooted in classical Buddhist theories of nonduality, had clearly gained currency in esoteric circles during the Tibetan renaissance, as it is also found in Yumo, who discusses how the Great Seal manifests as both saṃsāra and nirvāṇa.[30] In some ways, this type of "common ground" speculation is simply a consequence of these movements' monistic tendencies, but it can also be read as an idea that is associated with vision. Particularly in the *Tantra of the Blazing Lamps,* the common ground is closely associated with the eyes, which act as its instruments. The act of seeing thus determines whether the ground leads to cyclic existence or transcendence, an event that can occur at the universe's start, in visionary practice, or at points in between.

The Four Visions

Visionary practice in the Great Perfection is essentially an effort to re-enact the enlightenment of All Good by creating an opportunity where awareness can be recognized for what it is. This process starts with the idea that pure awareness is contained in the heart area of the subtle body—an analog to the pot at the beginning of the universe. Yogic techniques are then used to make awareness manifest into appearance (analogous to the ground-presencing), so that one has the chance to recognize it not as "other" but as oneself, and thus to cut off straying at its root.

In the Great Perfection, vision is not practiced independently or without preparation but rather as the culmination of a suite of meditative techniques. This broader collection of practices has come to be organized in two stages called "breakthrough" *(khregs chod)* and "direct transcendence" *(thod rgal)*.[31] "Breakthrough" refers to meditations that cultivate a stable, vivid awareness with the goal of becoming attuned to the mind's emptiness and primordial purity. Informed by poetic passages that evoke naturalness, purity, unfabricatedness, and freedom, breakthrough hearkens back to the Mind Series and in many ways is a practical re-implementation of it, modeled on the classic Buddhist practice of integrating calm-abiding *(śamatha, zhi gnas)* and special-insight *(vipaśyanā, lhag mthong)*. "Direct transcendence" is then synonymous with visionary practice itself. The two stages are intended to function sequentially, with breakthrough acting as a preparation for direct transcendence, creating a stability without which the yogi would chase after or grasp at visions instead of letting them take their own natural directions. The two stages also serve as an organizing scheme for Great Perfection thought, in that breakthrough allows classical Buddhist issues of emptiness, as well as the Great Perfection's own Mind Series material, to be integrated with their esoteric path of vision.

The terms "breakthrough" and "direct transcendence," however, do not appear at all in the *Tantra of the Blazing Lamps*. Nor do they appear in the tantra's lengthy commentary *Stringing a Garland of Pearls,* despite "direct transcendence" being virtually synonymous with the four lamps. Thus, while these two terms were certainly in use during the eleventh century, they play a relatively minor role in the *Seventeen Tantras* as a whole,[32] and as a dyad do not figure as a major organizing scheme.[33] They are also absent in the Bön tradition's *Advice on the Six Lamps* and Drugyalwa's lengthy commentary. It thus appears that this basic division, which is so dominant in the mid-fourteenth-century works of Longchenpa, was only rising to prominence at the time of the *Seventeen Tantras*.

Though the language of "breakthrough" and "direct transcendence" is absent in the source materials we are examining here, the basic relationships that they represent—dark and light, primordial purity and spontaneous presence, emptiness and luminosity—are pervasive. The "lamps" represent the side of the Great Perfection that would come to be known as "direct transcendence," which uses light to inquire into the spontaneous and self-forming nature of appearances. This inquiry, however, is carried out only against a background of reflection upon emptiness and primordial purity. In describing these practices of light, the commentary *Stringing a Garland of Pearls* often refers to a set of "four visions" *(snang ba bzhi),* which lays out ascending levels of visionary experience, from its initial onset up through liberation. Because these four visions are a major feature of the four lamps materials (and we will see a similar "five visions" scheme associated with the Bön six lamps), we should briefly explore them, as they convey how the "lamps" literature depicts its own practices of light.[34]

(1) The Vision of Awareness' Immediacy[35]

The Seminal Heart's visionary practices are essentially simple, though full accounts of their practical details can become quite elaborate. The most basic descriptions of vision advise placing the body, speech, and mind in prescribed ways, and then simply waiting for visions to arise. This involves, first, holding the body in one of three postures *('dug stangs gsum),*[36] and not speaking. The mind is then ideally placed in a state of nonconceptuality such that one's inner awareness and external environment are seamlessly integrated.[37]

These procedures can be carried out in two settings. When practiced in the light, they are performed outdoors, either sitting in the shade with the sun at one's back and a clear view of the open sky, or sitting so that the gaze can be directed a safe distance to the side of the sun. When practiced in the dark, a room is prepared by blocking off all windows and cracks that could let in light, and constructing zigzagging entryways or portals so that air and food can enter the room, but light will be kept out. A typical dark-retreat might last seven weeks.

Practitioners report that once some time has been spent in the dark, visions start to appear in the form of chaotic displays of light. This first stage is called the "vision of awareness' immediacy," indicating that this is the point at which awareness first comes directly into view. Descriptions of this initial vision usually mention a foreground and a background. The foreground is a frenzied display of lights (much like the "noise" in the eyes that can be seen if you close your eyes and press on the eyeballs). Two important forms of this light are circular appearances called *thig-le* ("seminal nuclei"), and linked chains of spots that are called the "little linked lambs of awareness."[38] The lambs appear against a radiant blue background field, called the "expanse" *(dbyings),* which also forms a boundary or "fence" *(ra ba)* around them.

In literature, these luminous appearances against their blue background are often used to bring up a recurring philosophical topic: the "indivisibility of the expanse and awareness" *(dbyings rig dbyer med).* The discussion revolves around the fact that the term "expanse" is classically used to refer to emptiness, and so its appearance in the visionary context as a field of blue serves to conceptualize emptiness as a clear blue sky. "Awareness" then refers to the appearances, composed of the meditator's own awareness, that arise out of that emptiness to be seen in the sky. This brings us back to a scenario very much like the ground-presencing and suggests how emptiness is a kind of possibility that gives rise to all appearances.

(2) The Vision of the Intensification of Experience[39]

At the next stage, visionary experience becomes more intense. The number, shape, and size of the appearances increase, and they begin to assemble together in simple configurations. *Stringing a Garland of Pearls* describes three groups of appearances that arise here: (1) shapes (like stacks of flowers, pointed spears, rows of stūpas, latticework, tents, and multi-eyed forms), (2) *thig-le* (in increasing levels of subtlety, clustering together in groups of five, and some with partial bodies beginning to take shape in them, foreshadowing the future appearance of maṇḍalas), and (3) manifestations of light (like rays, colored stripes, and hoops).

A distinguishing feature of this stage is that visionary appearances become continuous, spontaneously appearing at all times, whereas in the earlier stage they may have been stimulated by gazing at light sources or by physical means like pressing on the eyes. Now they appear without effort, and so the stage is compared to a "jackal's eyes,"[40] whose bright concentric circles appear (i.e., are kept open) without regard to day or night. This is also a period in which the chaotic motions of the lights begin to stabilize. In a process that is often described as a type of herding practice, the lambs are brought into the "fence" of the expanse, ceasing their movements. As *Stringing a Garland of Pearls* puts it:

> The adamantine linked-lambs of awareness, which move and manifest due to the propulsion of the gnostic winds, [remain] in the sky without entering into the beyond, held like captives within the expanse.[41]

(3) The Vision of Awareness' Optimization[42]

"Optimization" *(tshad la phebs pa)* here is literally "to arrive at the full measure of" or to "arrive at the limit of," so this is the vision where awareness fully discloses what it is, and where visions appear in their greatest clarity and in their most structured form. At this stage, the abstract lights begin to organize themselves, ultimately taking shape as a maṇḍala of 100 peaceful and wrathful deities: the expanse transforms into the broad environment of a buddhafield *(zhing khams),* the *thig-le* transform into inestimable mansions *(gzhal yas khang),* and the linked-lambs transform into buddha-bodies.

(4) The Vision of Exhaustion within Reality[43]

The final vision is one in which appearances are exhausted, dissolving back to the expanse from which they emerged. Though this stage is described as an experience of appearances fading away, it is still termed a "vision"—as if the absence of appearances opens up a space in which to see how things really are. *Stringing a Garland of Pearls* writes:

> Then, the intensifying experiences end: a vision shines forth of the exhaustion of the phenomena of the mind, the exhaustion of the internal elements, the exhaustion of the enumeration of the three bodies, the exhaustion of dependent phenomena. Nobody can express this by saying, "It is like this...."[44]

This concluding vision is in many ways the reverse of the ground-presencing, where instead of the ground giving off appearances, everything is instead resolved and recollected within it. The vision is also one of the Seminal Heart's main descriptions of enlightenment, and thus this tradition that is so concerned with appearances in the end portrays transcendence as appearances' dissolution. The final vision is, however, not just an image of emptiness but an image of coming home, where appearances that are the presencings of awareness finally dissolve so that their source can be seen nakedly.

Interpretive Analysis of the *Tantra of the Blazing Lamps*

With this background, we can now begin to look directly at the text of the *Tantra of the Blazing Lamps* itself. The following should provide a basic guide for readers of the tantra, though it is not indented to bring out every detail or doctrine that the tantra contains. The headings in this section are based on the topical outline found in the tantra's commentary.

The Tantra's Introductory Scenes

One standard way for a tantra to begin is with an introductory scene *(gleng gzhi)*. This is an opening statement that indicates the basis *(gzhi)* on which the discourse *(gleng)* was delivered. Typically, this introductory section lays out the basic narrative of the tantra by specifying who the teacher is, who the audience is, where the teaching was delivered, under what circumstances it was delivered, and so forth. Though it is not a requirement, the introductory scene of a tantra usually begins with the same phrase used to open a sūtra, which in Tibetan is: "Once upon a time I heard this speech...."[45] The presence of this statement indicates that the tantra is the speech of a buddha that was heard by a "compiler" who is now reporting it to us.

The *Seventeen Tantras* each begin with two introductory scenes rather than one. The first is called the "extraordinary" introductory scene and begins with "Once upon a time I *taught* this speech...,"[46] indicating that the speech is being delivered to us directly from the Teacher, rather than being a secondhand report of a compiler. In the *Tantra of the Blazing Lamps,* this first introductory scene indicates the extraordinary way that the tantra came into being. The tantra here is portrayed not as a speech that was delivered by a buddha but rather as the event of the beginning of the cosmos. That is, when primordial awareness rose up from the ground and flowed into space, it encountered itself for the first time. This encounter, the point at which awareness sees and recognizes itself, *is* the teaching of the tantra, which originally took visual rather than verbal form. Because this ground-presencing is not limited to the past, but is an ongoing process that maintains the universe in the present and propels it into the future, it is said that the tantra "was spoken, is being spoken now, and will be spoken."

The ordinary introductory scene then provides a slightly more normative narrative. Just as from the "extraordinary" perspective, the tantra was a singular awareness encountering itself, so too in the second introductory scene the tantra is shown to have a "teacher" and an "audience" that are not separate from each other. The basic scene here is the buddha Dorjé Chang (Skt. Vajradhara) posing questions to the buddha Dorjé Chang: a buddha talking to himself at the beginning of the universe. To distinguish the two Dorjé Changs, the tantra refers to the enlightened Teacher as "Teacher Dorjé Chang," or "Pure Appearance Dorjé Chang"; the student (who seems to be pretending not to be enlightened) is then called "Pure Continuum Dorjé Chang," "Causal Dorjé Chang," and "Pure Cause Dorjé Chang."[47]

The Teaching in Brief

Following the introductory scenes, the teacher Dorjé Chang makes a very brief statement about each of the four lamps. The teaching here is so succinct that the student Dorjé Chang claims not to fully understand what he has taught himself. The remainder of the tantra is then the student Dorjé Chang asking for extensive explanations of the initial brief teaching.

The Extensive Teaching

The main body of the tantra consists of four chapters in question-and-answer format, with one chapter dedicated to each of the lamps.

(1) The Far-Reaching-Lasso Water Lamp

The first chapter of the tantra discusses the "far-reaching-lasso water lamp" *(rgyang zhags chu'i sgron ma).* This is the first of the Seminal

Heart's "four lamps" and most often refers to the eyes along with a set of subtle energy-channels that connects the eyes to the heart.[48] Together, these act as the pathway through which awareness, located at the heart, shines out through the eyes and into view. The term "far-reaching-lasso water lamp," however, is also used to refer to the mundane function of the eyes: perceiving the ordinary appearances that lead to ignorance, attachment, and hatred.

The water lamp in its fullest sense thus encompasses the dual role of the eyes—their ability to perceive both liberating visions and the distorted appearances that bind beings in saṃsāra. In etymologizing "far-reaching-lasso water lamp," the tantra says that the eyes are a "lasso" in the sense that they pull in ordinary appearances from the exterior world, and are also used to rope in visionary appearances like the little-linked-lambs. "Far-reaching" means that they can draw in nirvāṇa, casting saṃsāra to a great distance, or conversely, that they can pull in saṃsāric appearances, and cast nirvāṇa far away. Finally, "water" indicates the ordinary watery composition of eyes but also suggests that the eyes are not inherently ordinary, just as water has no inherent shape.

The idea that the "lasso" of the eyes could be used on the spiritual path to "draw in nirvāṇa" is quite striking, especially when compared to discussions about seeing and the eyes found in Buddhist ethical literature. Traditionally, the eyes are regarded as the gateways of distraction, desire, and immorality, leading beings to continually take rebirth in saṃsāra.[49] Restraint of the eyes is thus an important part of moral discipline, and warnings about the eyes appear frequently in Buddhist ethics. One of the monastic vows, for instance, reads:

> When among the houses of others, I will walk with eyes not wandering, gazing [downward not more than] a yoke's length ahead. This is a training to be performed.[50]

In its practices of sensory deprivation, the Great Perfection echoes a theme seen here: that controlling input to the eyes leads to spiritual progress.[51] However, its practices come with the further suggestion that this "controlling" allows a transcendent dimension of the eyes to take over. As such, the water lamp represents an alternative moral and soteriological view of the eyes, and they become active participants in transcendence rather than simply passive receptors of the world.

(2) The Lamp of Self-Emergent Insight

While the water lamp is "lamp-like" in that it shines out luminous visions, the "lamp of self-emergent insight" *(shes rab rang byung gi sgron ma)* is a lamp in the more metaphorical sense of its ability to "illuminate" things or make them known. The term "insight" *(prajñā, shes rab)* here is literally "superior cognition," and refers to the pure, nonconceptual knowing power of the mind,[52] which contrasts to ordinary cognitions of mundane, deceptive objects.[53] In a reflection of classical assumptions about insight, the insight lamp has a special relationship with emptiness, as it is what can cognize objects as being without a concrete identity.

In general, the insight lamp is what serves as the perceiving subject in vision,[54] while the visionary objects are usually the linked-lambs, the five lights, the *thig-le* lamp, or simply awareness itself. However, the Seminal Heart deliberately resists the complete separation of subjects from objects, and so the term "insight lamp" can also refer to pure gnosis itself, residing at the heart and manifesting as visionary objects. Its roles as both subject and object can be seen in the lamp being named "self-emergent," which indicates that the lamp's knowing power arises on its own without cultivation, learning, or effort, but also indicates that this knowing power spontaneously emerges as appearances. The two are of course resolved in apperception, with the lamp being the appearances that shine forth as well as the perceiver of them. As gnosis itself, the insight lamp is in some ways the chief of all the lamps, as it is the source of them all,[55] the unfindable object that appearances point to but that is only seen nakedly when those appearances finally dissolve.

(3) The Empty Seminal Nuclei Lamp

If the first two lamps are, respectively, the mechanism that gives rise to vision and the insight that perceives vision, this third lamp, the "empty seminal nuclei lamp" *(thig le stong pa'i sgron ma),* is vision's content. That is, it refers to visionary appearances themselves, particularly to lights in the form of concentric circles, resembling the circles on a peacock's feather, or those in the eyes of a hawk, a fish, or a cat.[56] These circular forms are thematized as "seminal nuclei" *(thig-le),* a multivalent term commonly used for either regenerative fluid, or the subtle energetic potencies that are manipulated in the body during sexual yoga. The Great Perfection's visionary *thig-le* still retain a "seminal" connotation, in that they give rise to images of buddha-bodies, and eventually transform into fully formed visions of buddhas' residential palaces.

Giving these luminous seeds the name "seminal nuclei" is thus a very deliberate play on a key term from traditional Buddhist tantra; in chapter 6 we will see how these visionary *thig-le* can be seen as a critiques of the tradition of sexual yoga. Though such polemics of sexuality are an undercurrent in the *Tantra of the Blazing Lamps,* and are critical to understanding the Great Perfection's place within esoteric Buddhism, the *Tantra of the Blazing Lamps* is more interested in using seminal nuclei to suggest philosophical ideas and to provoke discussions about yogic practice.

The theme of wholeness and totality is particularly strong in this chapter, as the tantra plays on the spherical *(zlum po)* shape of seminal nuclei to suggest that their importance lies in their ability to "round up" *(zlums)* or "bring together" opposites. Seminal nuclei are thus said to "round up" nirvāṇa and saṃsāra, happiness and suffering, the singular and the multiple, stillness and movement, the external and the internal, emptiness and appearances.[57] "Round up" here does not have the sense of falsely resolving philosophical tensions but of taking issues that are perhaps irresolvable and bringing them together within a single sphere.[58] Seminal nuclei, for instance, can produce cyclic existence (by operating as semen) or transcendence (by operating as visionary appearances); they can be singular (i.e., composed of a unitary awareness) and multiple (appearing as distinct forms in vision). Echoing the role of the Great Seal in Kālacakra, they also demonstrate how something can be without inherent nature (i.e., the "empty" seminal nuclei) and yet also vividly appear and perform functions.[59]

The theoretical discussions that surround the empty seminal nuclei lamp should not create the impression that this lamp is only about philosophical abstractions. In some ways it is the most concrete of the four lamps, and its chapter is also the main place in the tantra where actual meditative techniques are discussed. In both the tantra and its commentary, these are only sketched out and usually defer to fuller descriptions found in oral traditions. Nonetheless, the eleventh section of this chapter describes several techniques for making the luminous *thig-le* appear: by stimulating energy-channels on the side of the neck, by squeezing the eyeballs with the fingers, and by using special gazes and bodily postures. The tantra also describes this lamp as creating "confidence" or "belief" *(yid ches)* in the doctrine, meaning that the immediacy and vividness with which it lights up create an interest and excitement that is not achieved by intellectual abstractions.

(4) The Lamp of the Pure Expanse

The fourth lamp, the "lamp of the pure expanse" *(dbyings rnam par dag pa'i sgron ma),* represents the background, the screen, on which visions are displayed. The expanse lamp is generally described as a deep blue appearance,[60] first experienced in the corner of the eyes, which ultimately becomes a multicolored[61] background for the seminal nuclei, linked-lambs, and other visions. The tantra's chapter devoted to this lamp plays on the term "expanse" *(dbyings)* as referring equally to emptiness (*chos dbyings,* the "expanse of reality"), to the deep blue and multicolored visionary experience produced by the body's inner channels and wheels (the "inner expanse"), and to the sky itself (the "outer expanse").[62] Thus the lamp is not intended solely as a simple background screen but represents the background of emptiness that unites the inner and outer worlds and creates a space in which their appearances can be displayed.

Themes of "home" and "rest" also fill the discussions about this lamp: the expanse is the "fence" that contains the linked-lambs and acts as "awareness' home."[63] The expanse is also called the "objective sphere" *(yul)* of awareness, where *yul* refers simply to the location or objective range in which awareness dwells, but also carries the colloquial sense of "home" or "home region." The expanse is thus the place where at the end of the day things settle down, where the chaotic motion of the lambs is finally contained, and into which visions finally dissolve.

The tantra says that without the expanse, "awareness would have no objective sphere,"[64] meaning that the expanse creates a space in which visions can be displayed and recognized. But the empty expanse is more than just an open space filled up by appearances; the expanse is an appearance itself, which arises in an event called the "lighting up of the expanse" *(dbyings snang).* The expanse lamp is thus a meditation on the role of the surrounding environment in the formation of appearances, and it speaks to how that background of emptiness is neither passive nor inherently separate from the foreground. This lighting up of the expanse in a display of its affinity with the foreground dramatizes the issue of the "inseparability of the expanse and awareness" *(dbyings rig dbyer med),* with the five colors of the expanse representing how the full spectrum of appearances are inherent within emptiness, just as they are directly evident in the visionary manifestations of awareness.

Conclusion

One of the main tensions throughout the *Tantra of the Blazing Lamps* comes from the contrast between its style and its content. In matters of style, the tantra is literary, highly intellectual, sometimes obscure, and often scholastic. Its commentary *Stringing a Garland of Pearls* magnifies these trends and stands as a full academic tour de force on vision, complete with all the structured discussions, digressions, and terminology one would expect from a scholastic treatise. Highly concerned with systems and organization, the commentary shows a love of explaining its topics through lists and enumerations: the four visions, six minds, five insights, five self-emergent primordial gnoses, three appearances, nine primordial gnoses, five karmic winds, four wheels, four channels, three obscurations, four conventional and four ultimate elements, six seminal nuclei, three unwavering states, three ways of remaining still, five paths, eighteen emptinesses, four channels, three ignorances, three expanses, and four types of change, to name only some.

In contrast to this, in terms of its content, some of the tantra's main themes are unity, spontaneity, nonconceptuality, antischolasticism, freedom, relaxation, primordiality, and letting go. The disjunction points to one of the most interesting facets of the "lamps" tradition, which is how it brings together equally strong preoccupations with structure and process. Perhaps the best example of this is the tantra's set of "four visions," which presents a path of vision that is self-arising and spontaneous but that also depends on premeditated practices, unfolds in a preplanned sequence, and culminates in a vision of a traditional set of 100 peaceful and wrathful deities. The four visions thus raise questions of why a doctrine of spontaneity would be organized with such deliberate precision, or why "spontaneous" visionary experiences would ever be expected to correspond to literary accounts at all. One way of accounting for this relationship between literature and spontaneous vision is to view works like the *Tantra of the Blazing Lamps* not just as antique records of visionary experience but as inextricable elements of the process of vision itself, where visionary practices and experiences shape and produce literature, and the literature in turn directs vision and acts as a resource for interpreting its significance.[65]

Visionary literature, whether oral or composed like the *Tantra of the Blazing Lamps,* also casts spontaneous experiences into forms that can be discussed and exchanged between individual practitioners and broader religious groups. This type of exchange of ideas clearly was taking place between the Great Perfection and Kālacakra in the eleventh century, as a new Great Perfection emerged looking quite like Kālacakra in its direct mirroring of the first two of its six yogas. But in its move away from sexuality for a focus on primordial purity and luminosity, the transformed Great Perfection also looked very much like itself. And so while its turn to vision in some ways appears to arise from nowhere, it turns out to be produced from a complex of channels: domestic, foreign, literary, yogic, and the human body itself. While from our distant perspective it may be impossible to untangle those strands or to see them as anything more than unstructured circles of dialogue, they eventually congealed in their own formations, like the *Tantra of the Blazing Lamps,* so they ceased to look like the seeds that produced them and were ultimately absorbed back into the Great Perfection itself.

CHAPTER 3 | *Advice on the Six Lamps*

Bön and the Great Perfection

During the early Tibetan renaissance, as the Buddhist Sarma and Nyingma invented and reinvented themselves, the Bön tradition also entered a transformative period. It was at this time that Bön became permanently entwined with Buddhism, sharing a complicated relationship that operated sometimes on Buddhist terms and sometimes on their own. During this time, Bön began to move much closer to Buddhism,[1] transforming itself into an organized religious system that outwardly was quite similar to that of the Buddhists.

The directions that it took in the eleventh century would eventually result in a Bön religion complete with a *vinaya;* a monastic system; a canon of sūtras, tantras, and commentaries; an organized pantheon of buddhas; and a doctrine involving karma, two truths, bodhicitta, and the path to enlightenment. Yet even as Bönpos mirrored the broad conventions of Tibetan Buddhism, they maintained distinctive histories, lineages, and traditions that prevented Buddhists from ever reciprocally accepting Bön as one of their own. Most notably, Bönpos did not look back to Śākyamuni as their founder or to India as their spiritual homeland but proclaimed their own buddha, Shenrap Miwo, who was enlightened in the distant past as a layman in the land of Ölmo Lungring,[2] a shadowy place said to be to the far west of Tibet. Before coming to Tibet, Shenrap's doctrine is said to have flourished in the kingdom of Zhang Zhung, so it is that land and its language to which Bönpos trace their history, rather than to India and Sanskrit.

By the time of the Tibetan renaissance, the doctrine of Shenrap was making what Bönpos consider to be its third spread in Tibet, having been persecuted first by the eighth Tibetan king, Trigum Tsenpo (who predates Tibetan histories), and then again by the thirty-eighth king, Trisong Detsen

(742–797).[3] Two events in the eleventh century signaled the advent of Bön's third spread, its renaissance. The first was in the literary realm: a major treasure discovery in 1017 by Shenchen Lu-ga (996–1035),[4] who revealed a large cache of texts on subjects encompassing ritual, historical narrative, tantra, and the Great Perfection. The second event was the construction of Bön's first monastery, Yeru Wensakha, founded in 1072.[5] These two events would have far-reaching consequences, as Shenchen's revelation would serve as the nucleus of the Bön canon, which would be stabilized by 1450.[6] Yeru Wensakha, an important institution in its own right until its destruction by flood around 1386,[7] would be reconfigured to become Bön's dominant monastery, Menri, established on a nearby site in 1405.[8]

Long before its canon was formalized, Bön had begun to use a variety of systems to organize its growing body of doctrines and literature. One of the most enduring of these would be the "nine vehicles,"[9] an ascending classification of the various doctrines of Bön, beginning with divination and continuing through methods of placating minor deities and demons, magical ways of defeating enemies, rituals for death, basic morality and practices of laypeople, monastic discipline, tantric practice, and culminating with the Great Perfection. In some ways, these nine vehicles can be read as a way of integrating Bön's more esoteric and noninstitutional practices with those that more closely resemble the norms of classical institutional Buddhism. Yet, we also must be careful in interpreting Bön's lower vehicles as "non-Buddhist" or "pre-Buddhist," given that practices involving prediction, exorcising demons, and so forth are popular among Tibetan Buddhists of all schools. The nine vehicles are thus in many ways a representation of the full spectrum of Tibetan religious life, in that they include the elements that are typically overlooked by more orthodox Buddhist classifications.[10]

The Great Perfection that constitutes the highest of Bön's nine vehicles is of course the mirror image of the Great Perfection in Nyingma. While the Bön Great Perfection has different lineages, histories, and literature than its Nyingma counterpart, the two traditions are thematically and practically so close that they must have arisen in a relationship of mutual influence and dialogue. The study of Bön's Great Perfection is still quite young, and so we have little understanding of its real diversity, such that our knowledge of its broader movements, histories, literary cycles,[11] and internal complexities is not much more sophisticated than the abbreviation that Bönpos use to classify their Great Perfection traditions: "the three: A, Dzogs, and Nyan" *(a rdzogs snyan gsum).*

This triad arranges the Bön Great Perfection into the three main systems: (1) Guidance in the Letter A *(a khrid),* (2) Dzogchen *(rdzogs chen),* and (3) the Oral Tradition from Zhang Zhung *(zhang zhung snyan rgyud).*[12]

The first of these, "Guidance in the Letter A," was popularized by an eleventh-century hermit from Tsang named Meü Gong Dzö (1038–1096). Possibly inspired by eleventh-century treasures, the system was elaborated in Gong Dzö's own writings, and later formalized by Drugyalwa.[13] In general, the "Guidance" presents a series of practices that begin with stabilizing meditation focusing on the Tibetan letter A, and later proceed without meditative supports. The meditations aim for a vivid tranquility, informed by contemplations on the mind's empty and unfabricated nature, and complemented by simple breathing and sky-gazing exercises. Devoid of the visionary elements most associated with the Great Perfection, the tradition is nonetheless deeply involved with the themes of relaxation, luminosity, purity, and the experience of unfabricated gnosis.

The second tradition, eponymously named "Dzogchen," is the least studied of the three. It also has an eleventh-century pedigree in the sense that it is based on treasure revelations produced in 1088 by Ngödrup Drakpa, which resulted in a major cycle called the "Great Expanse of the Highest Peak."[14] These works should prove valuable for future study, given their apparent connections with the Mind Series and the Nyingma tradition.[15]

The Oral Tradition from Zhang Zhung, and *Advice on the Six Lamps*

The third of Bön's Great Perfection traditions, called the Oral Tradition from Zhang Zhung, is the dominant one. Unlike its counterparts, the Oral Tradition is not based on treasure revelations or works of human authorship but rather on a doctrine said to have originated with the primordial buddha All Good, which was then passed down through a series of enlightened beings until making its way to the human realm in the eighth century. Tradition maintains that during the period of fragmentation after the fall of the empire, these teachings were never hidden as treasures but continued to be transmitted orally in an unbroken lineage until they reemerged in the eleventh century.

In content, the Oral Tradition from Zhang Zhung is closely related to the Seminal Heart. The broadest features of the two traditions seem nearly identical, from their cosmogony described in the narrative of All Good, to their concerns with death and their practices of vision. To be sure, the two traditions diverge in terms of style, lineage, narrative, and history, but their practices of vision, in particular, both arranged around a series of gnostic "lamps," leave no question that they shared close relations.

Histories of the Oral Tradition depict it as a movement that was not always unitary and describe how its lineage split and came back together at key junctures. The Oral Tradition has also favored different literary works at different periods in its development, but by far the most important has been the *Four Cycles of the Oral Transmission (bka' rgyud skor bzhi),*[16] a collection of works so synonymous with the tradition that it is colloquially referred to simply as the *Oral Tradition from Zhang Zhung.*

The collection centers around a series of revelations received by the Zhang Zhung yogi and magician Gyerpung Nangzher Löpo, to whom an enlightened being named Tapihritsa appeared in the form of a "little luminous boy"[17] floating in space. The basic works in the cycle are concerned with the Great Perfection views of awareness and the universal ground, but they also delve into more practical matters about vision, bardo practices, the subtle body, signs of death, and yogic exercises. The collection also contains later works like lineage histories and lengthy academic commentaries, which gradually came to be included in the group. The essential works, however, are the shorter ones attributed to Tapihritsa, which have come to be known for their pithy and colloquial language, and for their ability to convey abstract matters of the Great Perfection with a characteristic earthiness and charm.

The first of Tapihritsa's revelations is known as *Advice on the Six Lamps (sgron ma drug gi gdams pa)* and presents a path of vision organized around six gnostic "lamps":

1. The lamp of the abiding ground
2. The lamp of the fleshy heart
3. The lamp of the smooth white channel
4. The far-reaching-lasso water lamp
5. The lamp that introduces the buddhafields
6. The lamp of the bardo period

The first four represent (1) the primordial ground dwelling within beings, (2) the ground's residence at the heart, (3) the main pathway in which awareness is contained, and (4) the gateways through which awareness emerges in vision. (5) The fifth lamp presents a series of brief introductions, aimed at recognizing that the fields of the five buddhas dwell within the body. (6) The bardo lamp then presents methods for attaining liberation in the postdeath state, should it not be attained during life.

This system of lamps is analogous to the group of four lamps found in the *Tantra of the Blazing Lamps,* and reading the two together provides evidence of the relationship and shared concerns of the Seminal Heart and the Oral Tradition from Zhang Zhung. If the similarities of their views and yogic programs are not enough, their sharing of the unusual term "far-reaching-lasso water lamp" leaves little doubt about the continuity between the two. Indeed, their exchange is broad enough that, while the "six lamps" and "four lamps" are, respectively, characteristic of Bön and

Nyingma, Bön works can be found using the system of four lamps,[18] and Nyingma works occasionally present six.[19]

Primordial Beginnings and Historical Ends

Bön literature contains several histories that lay out the origins and lineage of the Oral Tradition from Zhang Zhung, but as we will see, these histories are still quite difficult to assess. The most popular lineage history is Patsün Tengyal's fifteenth-century *Biographies of the Lineage Lamas,*[20] which now circulates with the *Four Cycles of the Oral Transmission* collection. Drugyalwa (1242–1290) also wrote an influential history,[21] and he also sketches out the Oral Tradition's basic lineage in his commentary to *Advice on the Six Lamps.*[22] The difficulty with all these sources is that they provide very brief biographies of a series of lineage holders, beginning with divinities (like the buddha All Good) and ending with figures who are clearly historical (like Drugyalwa), but there is no clear boundary separating the two. Of the lineage holders between these two poles, some seem semidivine, some seem semihistorical, and others seem plausibly historical but are so obscure that they are not attested in independent historical works. As a consequence, the first identifiable humans in the lineage do not appear until the eleventh century.

This has put the Oral Tradition and academic historiography at an impasse, with the Oral Tradition having its own sources that trace its history back to the eighth century and beyond, but with academic historians protesting that there is no verifiable evidence for the tradition before the eleventh century. The present book does not propose a way out of the impasse. I do not want to evade the difficult issue of locating the beginning point of the Oral Tradition, but because that problem seems insoluble with the available sources, at least we can use the impasse to come to a more sensitive understanding of some of the basic issues that have led to it. The first issue is that in the Tibetan tradition, revealed literature—whether coming from visionary sources, rediscovered treasures, or secret oral transmissions that become public—tends to first emerge as small cryptic seeds that over time grow into larger works. This is not a hidden part of these literary traditions but is simply one way that the process works: some texts are discovered as treasures written on tiny "scrolls" that are gradually translated into full book-length treatises;[23] some originate as oral "dictations" that become expanded;[24] other discoveries may incorporate preexisting manuscripts in the production of a new work;[25] others still may be pithy remarks received in vision, which are written down and gradually expanded.[26] While this adds no evidence for the Oral Tradition's existence as a mature system in the imperial period, it does help to clarify that the traditional claim for its eighth-century pedigree is not the same as a claim that its existent written literature dates to that same period.[27] Thus there is some room for common ground, namely, to identify a basic period when the Oral Tradition began to appear *in writing* and started to resemble the collection that we have today.

A second issue is that, from my perspective as a reader, we do need to take seriously the claim that the Oral Tradition was indeed once "oral." Reading broadly in its literature, one often comes upon particularly pithy or colloquial turns of phrase that appear in multiple works and that also continue to be used in modern oral explanations and conversations. This kind of repetitive phrasing is quite characteristic of oral literature, and while its uses in the Oral Tradition are not as prevalent as, for instance, the oral formulaic tags found in the Greek epics, they do stand out as phrases that are more widespread than the text at hand, and as a colloquial diction that contrasts with their literary surroundings.

All this is to say that I find no reason to deny that the Oral Tradition from Zhang Zhung could have continuity with some oral tradition that predates the eleventh century, but nor do I see any need to claim that today's text of *Advice on the Six Lamps* is an unmodified piece of eighth-century Tibetan literature. While it would be presumptuous to speculate on the nature of such an oral tradition, the histories do point to a period when the Oral Tradition began to take concrete form in writing. As might be expected, the date coincides with the moment that the *Seventeen Tantras* were also being inscribed on paper.

Visionary Revelations: Tapihritsa and Gyerpungpa

Before turning to the eleventh century, however, we need to quickly pass through the Oral Tradition's divine prehistory and the accounts of its 8th-century visionary revelation on earth. This will set up the narrative context for *Advice on the Six Lamps* (which depicts the tradition's revelation) and also is important background for the Oral Tradition's spread during the renaissance.

In accounts like those of Drugyalwa and Patsün Tengyal, the first phase in the Oral Tradition's descent to earth involved a series of nine buddhas, beginning with the "Primordial Teacher" (i.e., All Good); these buddhas passed the teaching down to each other in a sequence of mind-to-mind transmissions.[28] The last of the nine buddhas, Sangwa Düpa,[29] passed it to a "person" *(gang zag)* named Lhabön Yongsu Dakpa; this began a second phase in the descent called the "oral transmission of the twenty-four men,"[30] in which the doctrine was transmitted orally and through miraculous means. Despite being called "men," these twenty-four beings possess magical powers and show all the marks of divinity, though the last among them do begin to resemble humans.

The last of the twenty-four men, Tsepung Dawa Gyaltsen,[31] then conveyed the doctrine to one of the Oral Tradition's most famous figures, a yogi from Zhang Zhung named Tapihritsa. The lineage-histories do not contain detailed accounts of Tapihritsa's life, but in the brief sketches that they do offer, Tapihritsa is presented as a historical figure: a human being who had a mother, father, and teacher, and who used meditative practice to divest himself of his material body and attain buddhahood.[32] On the whole, however, Tapihritsa seems more divine than human, particularly given his ability to manifest at will to help whatever beings are in need. He is thus something of a transitional figure, part human and part divine, who bridges the gap between transcendent buddhas and the ordinary beings on earth.

In a foundational moment for the Oral Tradition, Tapihritsa used his powers of emanation to appear to the Zhang Zhung yogi Gyerpungpa, and in a visionary exchange taught him the doctrine of the Oral Tradition. When Bön texts describe this meeting, Tapihritsa is likened to the primordial buddha himself, so Gyerpungpa receives the teaching straight from its source, without it having to pass through a long series of masters. In this sense, the transmission from Tapihritsa to Gyerpungpa bypasses the "long lineage" of nine buddhas and twenty-four men and is traditionally described as its own special two-member "short lineage." Gyerpungpa is thus in many ways the Oral Tradition's first fully human figure, and while his life stories depict him as possessing yogic attainments and mundane magical powers, he is also portrayed as an imperfect being, with an arrogance and spiritual ignorance that were not tamed until he finally met Tapihritsa.

Accounts of this meeting can be found in several works in the *Four Cycles* collection,[33] including *Advice on the Six Lamps*. Gyerpungpa's significance for Bön is, however, broader than the part he plays in the transmission of the Great Perfection. Traditional Bön histories depict him as a magician who was able to dispatch ritually prepared magical missiles against his enemies, and who used them to defend Zhang Zhung against the aggression of the Buddhist king Trisong Detsen (742–797).[34] While Gyerpungpa's life story may indeed be based on that of a historical person, it is difficult to discern what his "real" character may have been. Narratives of his life do make for fantastic reading: they credit him with having lived 573 years,[35] and they are unhesitating in their descriptions of the scope of his magical powers, particularly in vanquishing the enemies of Bön. Patsün Tengyal writes:

> Performing the *spu* [ritual], if he were to recite mantras on a full measure *(srang)* of gold for three years, it could destroy Tibet; performing the *khyung* [ritual], if he were to recite mantras over half a measure for three months, it could destroy the king and his retinue.[36]

In a narrative that is obviously not repeated in Buddhist sources, Bön histories describe how Gyerpungpa hurled such ritually prepared gold toward Tibet, whereupon Trisong Detsen was seized by illness.[37] Fearing for his life, the king sent envoys to Gyerpungpa, submitted to his demands, and protected the doctrine so that it remained as a living oral tradition *(snyan rgyud)* and never had to go underground or be hidden away as a treasure. Given these deeds, Gyerpungpa is obviously much more than the human source of the Oral Tradition from Zhang Zhung—he is its defender, an image of the once-great power of Zhang Zhung, and a symbol of the complicated relationship between Bönpos and the orthodox Buddhists.

Accounts of Gyerpungpa generally suggest that before he encountered the Great Perfection, his powers had gone to his head, and he was so proud of his status and magical abilities that he was unable to reach the ultimate attainment of enlightenment. Enter Tapihritsa, who appeared to him several times and revealed to him the Oral Tradition from Zhang Zhung. In their first encounter,[38] Tapihritsa appeared disguised as a precocious wood-carrier boy, who subtly teased the powerful magician. In a famous exchange, Gyerpungpa realized there was something unusual about the servant boy, and asked him with some hostility:

> "Your mind seems to have been affected by religious tenets....Who is your teacher? What experiences have you had? What meditations do you perform? What is your burden? What is it that you are doing [by acting as a wood carrier]?"
>
> The little boy replied: "My teacher is ordinary appearances! I have had the experience of non-conceptuality. My meditation is all the appearances of the three realms. My burden is discursive thought. What I am doing is serving beings!"[39]

The boy eventually ascends in the sky in a blaze of light, revealing himself as Tapihritsa.

Their second meeting occurred five years after the first, when Gyerpungpa was meditating on an island in the middle of Darok lake, in northwestern Tibet.[40] Tapihritsa appeared in a vision to Gyerpungpa, emerging in the sky as a young boy, naked and blazing with white light. Filled with faith, Gyerpungpa prostrated to him, and Tapihritsa proceeded to reveal the tradition of the Oral Tradition from Zhang Zhung. Among Tapihritsa's revelations, *Advice on the Six Lamps* is said to have been delivered first. This short work on vision thus has a certain pride of place in the Oral Tradition and over time grew in importance, such that it would eventually be circulated and studied along with two commentaries.

Renaissance and the Writing of an Oral Tradition

The two commentaries to *Advice on the Six Lamps* date from the thirteenth century: one written by Uri Sogyal, and then one by Drugom Gyalwa Yungdrung (1242–1290). The editions of the *Advice* that these two authors used were practically identical (as are many of their comments), and so the commentaries provide evidence that the *Advice*—and presumably the other core works of the *Four Cycles* collection—was stable and on paper by the mid-thirteenth century.[41] This still leaves a large gap between the Oral Tradition's legendary beginnings and the point at which we know for certain that it had been written down. Fortunately, the tradition's lineage-histories like those by Patsün Tengyal and Drugyalwa allow us to narrow that gap somewhat. Since their descriptions of the tradition's oral lineage proceed straight back to the beginning of time, it is difficult to use them as sources on the history of the tradition's oral dimensions. They are, however, much more focused when it comes to matters of writing, and they suggest that the Oral Tradition started to take form on paper in the late eleventh century.

Advice on the Six Lamps[42] relates that, after his visionary revelation, Tapihritsa gave Gyerpungpa permission to spread the Oral Tradition widely. This ended a prior restriction that the doctrine could only be taught by one master to one student. Gyerpungpa, however, was not very successful in propagating it and found only two suitable candidates, one of whom was just three years old, and the other seventy-three.[43] He conveyed the Oral Tradition only to the elderly student, and so after Gyerpungpa, the lineage remained in a single line through five masters, until reaching a figure named Pönchen Tsenpo.

Pönchen Tsenpo is a transformational figure in the lineage-histories, as he passed the Oral Tradition from Zhang Zhung to two students in two different versions, one of which came to be called the Transmission of the Word *(bka' rgyud),* while the other is known as the Experiential Transmission *(nyams rgyud).* The Transmission of the Word is also called the Upper Tradition (*stod lugs,* referring to its spreading in the highlands, not to its importance) and is associated with the materials transmitted from Tapihritsa to Gyerpungpa, which were eventually codified in the *Four Cycles* collection. The second version then came to be known as the Lower Tradition *(smad lugs).*[44] These two lineages proceeded in their own separate directions until being reunited in the person of Yangtön Chenpo. Their relationship is perhaps easier to see in Figure 3.1.[45]

Yangtön Chenpo is the Oral Tradition's first datable figure. His activities are recorded in some short biographical sketches, which are particularly interesting because they portray him collecting and writing down important

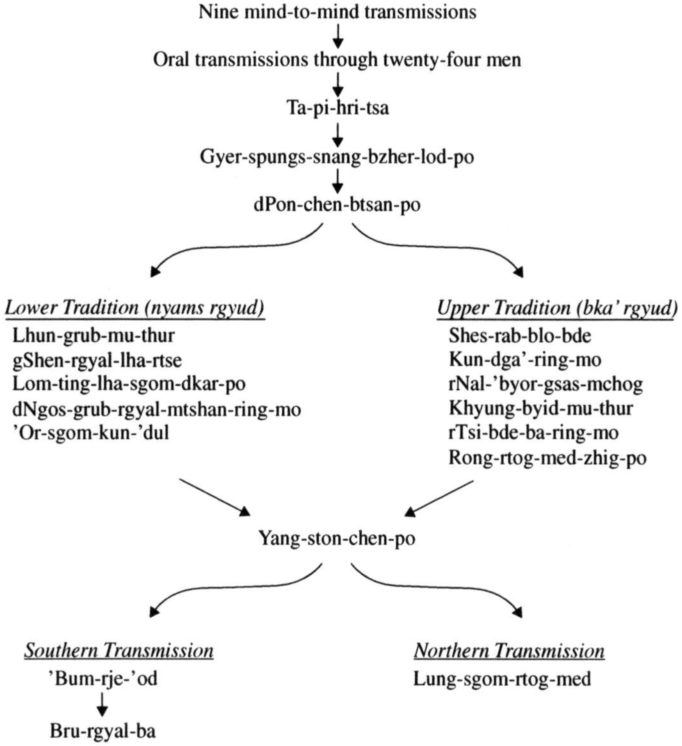

FIGURE 3.1 Lineage of the Oral Tradition from Zhang Zhung

teachings. These biographies thus help to establish a general period when the Oral Tradition began to make its way into written texts. Though we do not have precise dates for Yangtön, he is said to have studied with the translator Ba-ri Lotsawa (1040–1111),[46] as well as with Dru-chen, who founded Yeru Wensakha Monastery in 1072;[47] both of these suggest that Yangtön was active in the late eleventh century. Yangtön is remembered as having a broad religious background. First and foremost, he was a scholarly and institutional figure with literary interests, who studied at Yeru Wensakha, was versed in exoteric philosophy, debated with Buddhists,[48] and eventually founded a monastery[49] himself. Yet Yangtön also did extensive retreat practice, exhibited the behavior of a madman, and had numerous visionary experiences, including encounters with Pönchen Tsenpo.[50]

Yangtön was also an energetic collector of the Oral Tradition's diverse teachings. Through his active searching, he was apparently able to receive and thus reunite the full scope of materials from both of the Oral Tradition's lineages. Thus it came to be that, in Drugyalwa's words, "all the scriptures *(lung),* underlying meanings *(dgongs pa),* and permissions *(rjes gnang)* of the Upper and Lower versions of the Oral Tradition were complete in Yangtön."[51] Not satisfied with simply receiving them in oral form, Yangtön also began putting some of these in writing.

In the accounts of Yangtön's inner circle written by historian Patsün Tengyal, acts of writing are mentioned several times, and Yangtön is portrayed as a voracious collector of Great Perfection teachings and transmissions. In this passage, Yangtön hears of a particular doctrine and immediately seeks out its teacher, Orgom Kündül;[52] this results in him receiving and writing down the Experiential Transmission:[53]

> Sebön Trogyal[54] mentioned [to Yangtön] a doctrine involving thirteen chapters and important points. [Yangtön asked him:] "You know such topics? Who did you receive them from?"
>
> "From my lama Orbön Kündül, who holds the divine lineage."
>
> Thinking, "Now, this [lama] might be able to elaborate on what I am missing," [Yangtön] went to meet Orgom and made a request.
>
> [Orgom responded:] "Not satisfied with the whole ocean, [you are asking for] my little fish-eye?"
>
> "That is what I am requesting!" he replied. In two and a half months, he set down in writing the words and meanings of the extensive and condensed versions of the Experiential Transmission, without exception.

Here, Orgom chides Yangtön for being someone who already possesses a vast number of teachings (the "whole ocean") but still wants more (the "fish-eye"). In this account, Yangtön also has an unusual concern for preserving the doctrine on paper, as he is careful to write the teachings down completely.

Mentions of writing can also be found in Patsün Tengyal's record of the life of Orgom Kündül. Here, the inscriptions produced during Orgom's meeting with Yangtön are referred to simply as "notes," but we also see some unnamed "men from Kham" who are also collectors of texts, and who write down more than a hundred pages of Orgom's teachings:[55]

> Late in his life, two men from Kham asked him for texts. The lama swore: "In this lineage whose aim is to cut off superimpositions, there is not the adulteration of even a single letter, so I have not written anything down.[56] But because Yangtön requested me, we two made some notes so that we would not forget. Except for those, I have nothing in writing, not even [the size of] a dog's tongue!" The men from Kham believed him. The three wrote from the lama's heart, and within twenty days the three had...one hundred twenty pages.

Though both these accounts mention how parts of the Oral Tradition from Zhang Zhung were written down, they do not refer to the *Four*

Cycles collection in which our six lamps text is included.[57] But Yangtön did actively seek out the *Four Cycles* and finally assembled it from different sources, in a process that bears some suggestions of redaction. In Patsün Tengyal's account,[58] after meeting Orgom Kündül, Yangtön heard of a hermit named Rong Tokmé Zhikpo who had attained realization through practicing the Oral Tradition from Zhang Zhung. Faith sprang up in Yangtön, and he went to meet Tokmé Zhikpo, who meanwhile had been dreaming about Yangtön. Yangtön told Tokmé about the Oral Tradition materials he had collected, and Tokmé replied that there were still more available:[59]

> What you have is the Experiential Transmission and [secret] mantra.[60] I have the cycles of the "Word Transmission" that Pönchen Tsenpo spoke to Gu-gé Sherap [Lo-de],[61] known as the *[Four] Cycles of the Oral Transmission.* I have already explained the "External [Cycle], a General Delineation of the View"[62] to Lung-gom [Tokmé],[63] so you should request that from Lung-gom. As this is a single transmission, it is not acceptable for me to explain it [to you also]." He then offered him the esoteric instructions on the other three cycles.

As the story goes, Yangtön then went to meet Lung-gom, and the two exchanged their respective parts of the *Four Cycles,* completing the set of four for both of them.[64]

While none of these brief histories points directly to the writing down of the *Four Cycles,* Yangtön is a likely candidate for having redacted the collection. In him, we have a scholarly and institutional figure whose life project is finding and collecting esoteric Bön materials. He is also—according to both Drugyalwa and Patsün Tengyal—actively interested in putting Oral Tradition materials on paper. The story of him collecting the *Four Cycles* from different sources (though admittedly a later account) portrays him as someone who is engaged in the assembly and organization of his sources, and whose encounters with diverse traditions are not left up to fortune and circumstance, but are based on his own efforts and interests.

It thus seems that the beginnings of the Bön monastic tradition in the late eleventh century, and the consequential drives for systematization and codification that come with institutional religion, set the context for the inscription of the *Four Cycles*. The activities of Yangtön and his circle of students and teachers in the late eleventh to early twelfth centuries also place this event at the same time that the *Seventeen Tantras* were being redacted. From this perspective, Yangtön's role is very much like that of his Seminal Heart counterpart Zhangtön Tashi Dorjé, both of whom guided their traditions into new eras through their literary projects: assembling materials from shadowy masters of the past and crafting those materials into organized packages that could then spread more widely as coherent movements.

Essential Background for *Advice on the Six Lamps*

While *Advice on the Six Lamps* differs from the *Tantra of the Blazing Lamps* in terms of emphasis, style, and presentation, it is difficult to point to substantial doctrinal differences between the two. Thus, the background from the previous chapter—about the ground, the ground-presencing, the enlightenment of All Good, and the stages of vision—all applies to Bön's six lamps tradition as well.[65] In comparing the lamp traditions of Bön and Nyingma, it is natural to look for something "distinctively Bön" about the six lamps, or "distinctively Nyingma" about the four lamps, but the problem with this approach is that whatever differences one finds are usually not sustained throughout the broader traditions. So, while it does seem important that the critical term "little linked-lambs" does not appear in the Bön *Advice on the Six Lamps,* the term is easily found in other Bön Great Perfection works outside of the Oral Tradition.[66] Likewise, it might be noted that the *Tantra of the Blazing Lamps* does not discuss a "bardo" lamp, but the bardo is clearly a feature of Nyingma's Great Perfection traditions in general.

Nonetheless, it does seem appropriate to think of the "six lamps" and "four lamps" as being the major statements on the lamps by Bön and Nyingma, respectively, given that these are the enumerations found in their most definitive works. In these two works, what we have is not so much two different doctrines but two different pieces of literary expression, and so the primary distinction between them is found in their use of language.

Much of what is distinctive about *Advice on the Six Lamps* comes from the unusual terms and metaphors that give the work its character: its reference to the heart as "a deep-red tent with a crystal roof" *(mchong gur smug po shel gyi kha bad can)*; its terms for the gnosis located at the heart, such as "king of awareness" *(rig pa'i rgyal po)* or "thumb-sized primordial gnosis" *(ye shes tshon gang)*; its use of the term "enlightened mind" *(byang chub sems, bodhicitta)* to indicate the primordial ground; its various names for the visual faculties like the "great oceans" *(rgya mtsho chen po),* the "lamps" *(sgron ma),* or the "queens of the eyes" *(mig gi rgyal mo)*; and its occasional use of Zhang Zhung language, such as when it terms the heart-to-eyes channel the *tsang-ri bur-lang*.

Some of the terms used in the *Advice* do provide new conceptual structures or mini-narratives that are not as explicit as in the *Tantra of the Blazing Lamps.* Two of these deserve further explanation here: the triads "sound, light, and rays" and the "mother, son, and dynamic energy."

Sound, Light, and Rays

Perhaps the most characteristic set of terms found in *Advice on the Six Lamps* is the triad "sound, light, and rays" *(sgra 'od zer gsum).* Also referred to as the "three great appearances" or the "three great presencings,"[67] these are the three basic appearances that arise in visionary practice. At the same time, "sound, light, and rays" are also the first manifestations that appear in the gnostic "big bang" that, for the Great Perfection, begins the universe. Broadly speaking, then, the triad serves to connect the Great Perfection's visionary practice and its cosmogenesis.

In terms of the cosmos, descriptions of the "ground-presencing"[68] relate how awareness rises up from the ground and first manifests in three basic forms: a resounding but empty sound, a five-colored light, and a host of rays radiating outward from that light. These appearances are then mirrored in visionary practice, when awareness rises up from the yogi's heart, to take the form of "three visionary objects" or "three appearing objects."[69] In this context, "sound" is a roaring noise that appears at the center of one's head. "Light" then refers to rainbow light or semistructured patches of light, which contrast to "rays" that streak across the visual field like flying spears. Great Perfection writings often mention how simple experiences of sound, light, and rays can be produced by techniques like blocking the ears (which produces a roaring sound) or manually stimulating the eyes (which results in appearances of spots and streaks of light). In full-fledged visionary experience, however, the three are said to arise of their own accord and act as the building blocks of vision, in the sense that they combine into more structured forms as the meditator continues in visionary practice.

In essence, "sound, light, and rays" are the most basic forms in which awareness can express itself; in this capacity, *Advice on the Six Lamps* refers to them variously as the "expressive energy," "radiation," or "magical displays" of awareness.[70] While not being different from awareness, they are the energy of awareness that allows it to be seen, and that serves as its objective dimension.[71] As objects of perception, they are also the conditions through which one becomes enlightened or trapped in cyclic existence.[72] As the *Advice* describes it, "sound, light, and rays" have effects, respectively, on a yogi's speech, body, and mind. If "light," for instance, is not recognized as awareness' own self-presencing, one strays into an ordinary body; but when realized for what it is, "light" becomes a condition for the body becoming completely transformed into that of a buddha.

The Mother, the Son, and Dynamic Energy

Another triad found throughout *Advice on the Six Lamps* is "the mother, the son, and dynamic energy" *(ma bu rtsal gsum).* These three are used to explain one of the Great Perfection's central mysteries: how an undefiled awareness could be the source of the ordinary mind, and how that ordinary mind might then reconnect with its source, like a wandering son returning to his mother.

The "mother" here refers to the fertile and creative ground. Her "son" is awareness, which is born from the ground and appears to separate from it. "Dynamic energy" in the context of *Advice on the Six Lamps* often has the sense of a productive energy that exists between two things that are in fact a unity.[73] Thus it indicates the dynamic tension of their relationship, an energy that propels the son away from the mother, and that leads him to take on an apparently separate identity and grow into something only faintly resembling what he was at birth. At the same time, this energy is also a pathway back to its source, and so lets the son trace his way back to the mother, resolving their separation in a flash of recognition.

A son reuniting with his mother is thus one of the Oral Tradition's main metaphors for enlightenment. Underlying the notion of enlightenment as "reunion" is the idea that, even in a gnostic universe where everything is primordially pure, enlightenment can only come about through a process of straying and realization. That is, though the mother-ground and son-awareness are at all times indivisible, they must experience separation, even if that separation is only a delusion. Thus the indivisibility of a mother and son while the son is in the womb is different from their indivisibility after they have gone separate ways and been reunited. As a consequence, the primordial purity of awareness is not a kind of "enlightenment" because it has neither lost its way nor finally walked down a path that returns it home.

Interpretive Analysis of *Advice on the Six Lamps*

As in the previous two chapters, this section is intended to provide a basic interpretive framework for the *Advice,* but it is not intended to be a substitute for the text and Drugyalwa's commentary, which are translated in full in the third part of this book. Rather than giving a full account of every idea and section of the *Advice,* what follows will focus on its main themes, and on explaining the basic meaning of the six lamps, with the intention of making clear the similarity between the *Advice* and the *Tantra of the Blazing Lamps,* as well as the concerns it shares with Kālacakra.

Introductory Materials

Advice on the Six Lamps begins with a basic scene-setting, which provides the narrative of Gyerpungpa's two visionary encounters with Tapihritsa, the second of which resulted in the teaching of the *Advice.* Some brief praises and a summation of the six lamps follow. The summation presents the six lamps in terms of "six important points of the enlightened mind," a popular formula that may derive from oral traditions, given how frequently it comes up in discussions of the lamps.[74] Finally, there is a brief section in which Tapihritsa gives Gyerpungpa permission to spread the teaching more widely than its one-to-one lineage.

The remainder of the *Advice* is composed of six chapters, with one dedicated to each of the six lamps.

(1) The Lamp of the Abiding Ground

The "lamp of the abiding ground" *(gnas pa gzhi'i sgron ma)* simply refers to the primordial ground, which is described as a lamp because it "lights up" into appearances. The chapter devoted to this lamp is not so much about vision as it is about the Oral Tradition's basic philosophical view, though it uses the narrative of All Good to integrate that view with cosmology and yogic practice. The central question in this section of the *Advice* is the same problem of singularity and diversity that is addressed in the *Tantra of the Blazing Lamps* and in Yumo's discussions of the Great Seal: how a pure, unitary, all-pervasive gnosis could give rise to the impure, diverse world of suffering.

The *Advice* addresses the issue of diversity by laying out a continuum that leads from the ground, to awareness arising from the ground, and finally to the ordinary mind arising from awareness. This triad is one of the basic touchstones that appears throughout the *Advice;* it begins with the ground itself, which is the "common ancestor"[75] of cyclic existence and transcendence, and which contains the potential of the three bodies of the buddhas, but which is still ultimately singular. From this unitary ground, awareness emerges; though apparently separate from the ground, awareness is still described in pure terms, as being the ground's pure knowing capacity, composed of five primordial gnoses. Awareness, however, also contains an energy that impels it to take perceptible form, and thus to become an object of awareness as well as a knower. This "expressive energy"[76] manifests as the "triad of sound, light, and rays," which, as we have seen, forms the conditions for straying and realization.

The ordinary mind is thus a kind of efflorescence of awareness, the dimmer rays compared to its sun. The mind becomes ordinary when these rays look back and see themselves as separate from that sun. Once this basic duality occurs, the rest of the manifest world follows, and so after discussing the mind, the *Advice* turns to a lengthy description of the ordinary universe. This is the most exoteric section of the *Advice;* framed by the Great Perfection narrative of All Good, it provides a basic image of the world drawn from classical Buddhism, with discussions of karma, saṃsāra, and suffering, and complete with all the requisite enumerations: six types of birth, three realms, five poisons, twelve links, six consciousnesses, eight consciousnesses,[77] and so forth. The "ground" that constitutes this lamp is at once the most esoteric idea of the Great Perfection but also the place where the tradition presents its most normative Buddhist face. Serving as a backdrop for visionary practice, it puts out the Great Perfection's message of unity, in the sense both of a unitary fabric of the universe, and of the Great Perfection's unified integration with more traditional forms of Buddhist thought.

(2) The Lamp of the Fleshy Heart

The "lamp of the fleshy heart" *(tsi ta sha'i sgron ma)* refers to the primary residence of awareness within the body. This residence is unusual because maps of the subtle body are usually based on an idealized symmetry, so that mentions of the "heart" typically indicate the "heart center," the energy-wheel that is at the level of the heart, but which is on the body's vertical center line. The "lamp of the fleshy heart" breaks with these models and, in an acknowledgment of the universe's essential asymmetry, places the core of the subtle body off-center, within the muscle of the actual fleshy heart.[78] Inside the heart there is said to be a tiny chamber in which awareness—often referred to in these contexts as the "thumb-sized primordial gnosis"[79]—dwells inseparably from the ground. This pure gnosis is also called the "primordially present nucleus of the universal ground and awareness";[80] because this represents the inseparable mixture of the "mother" ground and the "son" awareness, it is the analog of the "body in a vase" that begins the narrative of All Good.

In one of the memorable images of the *Advice,* awareness is said to reside in "a deep-red tent with a crystal roof, inside a tent of radiant light."[81] The "deep-red tent" is the muscle of the fleshy heart, with the "roof" being an enveloping cover of fat. Hidden inside this, however, is a luminous mansion, shaped like an eight-petaled lotus. Though inspired by the body, the image of awareness' residence is also recognizable as one of the most iconic of Tibetan images: a dark brown tent covered in glittering snow and lit by an internal fire. This presents the main theme of the chapter, which is inner luminosity, or how the body and the surrounding environment might contain light where externally there appears to be none. Philosophically, the heart is thus used to explore how gnosis and material form contain and constitute one another, a problem that is also at the heart of Kālacakra's visionary system. Chapter 2 of the *Advice* presents this in a series of three extended metaphors that depict the ensnaring of a bird, a horse, and a fish. The "bird" metaphor is:

> The universal ground is like the sky, completely pervasive. Awareness is like a bird, dwelling there in its own place. The intellect is like

> the bird's wings, which propel it everywhere. The body is like a trap, and the winged creature is caught in the trap. So, the bird and the trap can come together and separate, but they do not come together with or separate from the expanse of the sky.[82]

Here physical reality (in the form of the body) is cast as a trap that captures awareness, with the twist that the trap is composed of nothing but awareness itself. The image is thus one of awareness becoming entangled in itself, becoming knotted up and inactive so that it loses its radiance. While it is enmeshed in the physical world, there are still some key locations where awareness "shines out from the depths,"[83] the chief of these being the body, whose internal darkness hides vivid colors and whose solidity is infused with motion. The heart thus becomes a residence in which to carry out meditations on the relationship between mind and matter. These inquiries in turn are modeled on classic Buddhist ideas about dependent arising, where reality is seen as being constituted not by solid identities but by a net of things coming together and separating, here with the additional idea that these relationships are formed and broken in the larger field of the unitary ground.

(3) The Lamp of the Smooth White Channel

The "lamp of the smooth white channel" *(dkar 'jam rtsa'i sgron ma)* refers to the body's central energy channel,[84] which in the Oral Tradition is a sort of reservoir of pure gnostic energy. The channel is called a "lamp" because the "originally pure awareness shines within it, like the sun shining in the cloudless sky."[85] The luminosity of the channel forms a deliberate contrast with the opaque deep red of the fleshy heart (to which the central channel connects). While both serve as containers of awareness, within the heart, awareness' radiance remains interiorized, like a lamp hidden in a pot, while in the central channel its glow is fully evident.

It should be made clear that this "smooth white channel" is not the special heart-to-eyes channel that is operative in vision. Rather, it is the main channel of the subtle body, which runs from the crown of the head down to the base of the spine and projects to the energy-wheel in the genital region. While awareness is technically spread throughout the body, this channel is where it is most intense and active, and so the channel serves as the central area from which awareness performs its broad functions of energizing and maintaining the body and mind.[86]

The functions of the "lamp of the smooth white channel" are thus not limited strictly to the visionary sphere; rather, this chapter of the *Advice* serves to illuminate the larger role of awareness in the formation and development of the body. In particular, the *Advice* here gives a Great Perfection description of the formation of the human embryo. This embryology begins when three elements—the consciousness of the child, and the regenerative fluids of the father and mother—come together for the first time in the womb. The embryo's heart forms first, an area that serves as the "seat"[87] of the "space" elemental energy. Awareness' creative energy, conceptualized as "light,"[88] then causes a "space wind" to blow, which begins to structure the body by opening up a central channel in the upward and downward directions from the heart. Two channels then split off from the bottom of the central channel and return upward, crossing over the top of the brain and connecting to the two nostrils; these are the (red) left channel and the (white) right channel. Together with the central channel, they form the body's main "trunk."[89]

As the *Advice* describes it, the remainder of the body is then formed by wind energies related to the elements earth, water, fire, and wind. These winds open up four channels that project to the spleen, kidneys, liver, and lungs, and thus establish those organs. Secondary elemental winds then arise at all the organs, opening up channels to the five limbs (the head is considered a limb), causing them to project from the body, perhaps like balloons being inflated. Subsidiary elemental winds arise in the limbs, separating out the five fingers of each hand, the five toes of the feet, and the five senses (from the head). Finally, vibrant *(dwangs ma)* versions of all the winds cause the five sense-powers to function, while coarse *(snyig ma)* versions of the winds form the body's five sets of entrails.

Far from being a digression, the embryology described here in the *Advice* is one of the core topics of the Oral Tradition (and as might be expected is also a feature of the Seminal Heart).[90] In this context, embryology is not so much aimed at creating models useful for medical diagnosis as it is in illuminating the broader concepts of "birth" and "development," and how these might be integrated with Great Perfection concepts of the birth and development of the universe. The *Advice* is not as overt as it could be, but the preponderance of fives in its embryology is a claim about how the fives of the body (its fingers, toes, limbs, organs, and vessels) are derivatives of five buddhas and five primordial gnoses. This sets up the notion that the body is in fact the residence or buddhafield of the five buddhas, a point that is made more fully in the context of the "introduction" lamp. In this way, discussions of embryology act as sequels to the story of All Good, providing detailed explanations of how enlightened gnosis actually takes shape as the organs and entrails of a human being.

Finally (and this is more evident when comparing it to accounts of the subtle body like those in Kālacakra), this chapter on the "lamp of the smooth white channel" forms a real contrast with the sexualized central channel found in the tantric completion stage. In those contexts, the central channel is imagined as a pathway down which seminal fluid drips, passing through energy-wheels that result in orgasmic joys. Here in the

Advice, this "smooth" channel is free of such peaks of bliss, while its "white" light suggests the cool of the moon rather than the heat of the *caṇḍālī* fire.

(4) The Far-Reaching-Lasso Water Lamp

The "far-reaching-lasso water lamp" *(rgyang zhags chu'i sgron ma)* is the one lamp that is found in both the "six lamps" and "four lamps" traditions, and it has the same basic function in both. The lamp serves as the "gateway" through which awareness shines out of the body and consists of the eyes along with a special channel that connects them to the heart. The *Advice* identifies this channel with a Zhang Zhung name, *tsang-ri bur-lang,*[91] which means "head channel," referring to the fact that the channel splits off from the central channel at the top of the brain.[92] From this point, the channel turns into two channels with narrow stems and wide openings, like flowers, that open up into the eyes.

The chapter dedicated to the water lamp is the briefest of the six chapters of the *Advice,* perhaps because the issues associated with it are discussed fully in the lamps of the "channel" and the "fleshy heart." Nonetheless, this luminous channel is one of the most recognizable elements of both the Oral Tradition from Zhang Zhung and Seminal Heart traditions. As a feature of the body whose chief function is for liberation-through-vision, it is symbolic of how the Great Perfection traditions redraw the map of the subtle body, bringing to light new structures to serve their own philosophical and yogic programs.

(5) The Lamp That Introduces the Buddhafields

The "lamp that introduces the buddhafields" *(zhing khams ngo sprod kyi sgron ma)* describes how one's own body can be recognized as containing the residences or "buddhafields" of the buddhas' three spiritual bodies. This recognition is made not through ritual activity or logical deduction but by being "introduced" to the nature of the three bodies, so that they can then be fully recognized. This chapter of the *Advice* provides introductions in two ways, first by evocative verbal descriptions of the three bodies, and then by explanations of how the bodies might be recognized during visionary experience. The "lamp that introduces the buddhafields" is thus a "lamp" in the sense of something that "illuminates" a topic, but it also deals explicitly with sources of light and provides detailed descriptions of how the awareness that constitutes the three bodies appears in vision. The chapter consequently has a very experiential tone, as sections of it serve as repositories of details on the experience of vision. It is here also that some of the tradition's richest and most enigmatic language is found.

The *Advice* describes the process of recognizing the three bodies in two basic phases: (1) first one is introduced to them, after which (2) one uncovers their hidden reality, or comes to a final decisive conclusion about their nature. The "introduction"[93] is a fundamental feature of the Great Perfection tradition, as it serves as the point of entry into yogic practice. Introductions here often supplant the tantric model in which a ritual initiation serves as a gateway into a tradition. They thus exchange a scripted ritual in favor of a personalized and contextualized interaction between a teacher and student. In a typical introduction, a spiritual mentor uses a variety of techniques—ranging from symbolic, to verbal, to physical—to introduce a student to the nature of his or her own mind. The flash of experience gained through that introduction (like being briefly introduced to a person) is then carried into visionary practice (likened to coming to know an introduced person more deeply). In the case of the *Advice,* the verbal introductions to the three bodies point them out so that their qualities can ultimately be recognized in visionary experience, and within oneself.

This second step is called "discovery" or "reaching a final conclusion,"[94] and represents a step in which one comes to have visceral experience about what the three bodies really are. As is typical of the Great Perfection, the *Advice* presents a way that this can be accomplished without any structured practice, suggesting that it is possible for those of high abilities to identify the Reality Body directly. Hearkening back to the Mind Series type of Great Perfection, this simply involves letting the mind rest naturally without modification, so that it settles into a state of nonduality where there is no unenlightened "self" separate from an "other" Reality Body. As the *Advice* says:

> Set primordial gnosis nakedly, not clothed in the "animal skin" of conceptuality. Set awareness in its bareness, not spoiling it with minds of clinging and desire. Not creating or altering anything in the mind, set it in an untouched manner. Not following after memories or concepts, set it without chasing or grasping.... No longer led astray by distortion, buddhahood is now manifest![95]

The more practical method for "reaching a final conclusion" is the path of vision, which the *Advice* also terms "higher seeing" (Tib. *lhag mthong;* Skt. *vipaśyanā*). In a play on the classical use of this term (which refers to the moment when emptiness is encountered in direct perception), "higher seeing" here does not refer to a meditation on a formless emptiness but takes on the sense of "higher sights," referring specifically to the three basic expressions of awareness: sound, light, and rays. Drugyalwa's commentary details how these three develop into visions of buddhafields and aims to suggest how visual means can convey religious truths with an impact that at least equals that of reasoning. In making this argument, the *Advice* continually works with classical Buddhist templates like the three bodies but rearranges them to suit its needs. The "introduction" lamp thus suggests how emptiness, normally a discussion associated with the Reality Body, might be moved into the purview of the form bodies, such that light, appearance, and manifestation become appropriate fields in which to investigate the absence of inherent identity.

(6) The Lamp of the Bardo Period

Advice on the Six Lamps ends with a discussion of death. This final chapter focuses on the "bardo," the transitional period when a dying person leaves behind the old body but has not yet taken birth in a new one. As the body separates from the mind during the process of dying, the sequential failure of the body's internal faculties is said to result in a series of visions of light, which represent the luminous mind emerging from behind the body that once obscured it. It is because of these appearances that the bardo period is called a "lamp." Much as in visionary practice, the lights experienced at death create the chance for the dying person to recognize them as self-presencings (and thus to become enlightened), or to be terrified and confused by them, and to seek refuge in another body, continuing the cycle of existence.

The bardo lamp is thus representative of the Great Perfection's interests in death, a side of the tradition famously represented in the *Tibetan Book of the Dead*.[96] Dying here is presented not so much as a transition between rebirths but as a point at which the relationships between dying, disembodiment, and transcendence can be explored. Instead of being a simple ending or beginning, death here is the "border at which straying and realization meet,"[97] a sort of crossroads where the broader dynamics of the universe, its continual death and rebirth, are put on display and can be investigated through visual means. Because this bardo period is so critical for determining the future paths that a dying person will take, the *Advice* says that a person's thoughts and reactions here have a greater "propulsive force"[98] than they do during life. In recognition of this, the Great Perfection has developed a widespread tradition of preparing for death, which involves introductions and instructions about dying, as well as directly guiding a person during the process of death.

Many of these instructions are of course about the thought processes, emotions, and physiology of death, but they also provide advice on interpreting the visual images that arise during the experience of dying. The bardo lamp chapter of the *Advice* presents these materials in the form of a lecture delivered by Tapihritsa to Gyerpungpa, which lays out the stages and physical details of dying, as well as the kinds of light that are experienced as death progresses.

The chapter, in brief form, simply lays out three ways of dealing with death, based on the acumen of the dying person. The method for people of high acumen, predictably, simply involves relaxing and doing nothing; at the time of death such people can instantly recognize their own awareness and become enlightened, just like a garuḍa bird hatching from its egg and instantly being able to fly. Beings of intermediate capacity take the visionary path: viewing and recognizing the appearances of light that arise before the eyes at death. Finally, lesser beings are not able to become enlightened while dying but are able to take a fortunate rebirth (based on the power of simply hearing the advice on the lamps) and then make their attainment in that next lifetime.

The bardo lamp comes at the end of the *Advice,* and while it is well integrated with the other lamps, it does not necessarily fit in the broader program of organized, retreat-based yogic practice. On first glance, the bardo lamp might be read as an afterthought, tacked on to the main group of lamps due to its affinity with them. It is possible, however, to see the entire "lamps" tradition as informed by a broader tantric speculation on the process of dying. The idea that luminous signs of death (resembling sparks, fireflies, and so forth) manifest themselves in the vision of a dying person appears widely throughout Buddhist tantra.[99] These same appearances, which circulate in lists like the "five signs," the "eight signs," and the "ten signs," also appear as elements of tantric yogic practice, where they are typically noted as "signs of success," external indications that a yogi has accomplished some inner feat like drawing the winds into the central channel. The bardo lamp in some ways amalgamates both of these trends: it views the "sparks and fireflies" appearances as signs of death, but then uses those signs not just as epiphenomena of internal events but as the focal points of a visionary yogic practice.[100] Looked at this way, phenomena of death are not footnotes to the lamps tradition but are at its center, the cultivated spontaneity of visionary practice resembling a formalization of the utterly spontaneous visions that occur at death.

Conclusion

When looking back at the religious dialogue of the Tibetan renaissance, it is easy to assume that there were only two basic spheres of cross-sectarian exchange, the most prominent being a competitive interaction between Sarma and Nyingma, and the other being the complicated relationship between Nyingma and Bön. The Bön tradition of vision investigated here complicates this picture because in its connections with Kālacakra, it suggests how the dialogue among Tibetan traditions was more of a circle, which included the participation of Bön.[101]

The dialogue between Bön and Nyingma is well illustrated by *Advice on the Six Lamps* and the *Tantra of the Blazing Lamps,* which appear to have simultaneous histories and share nearly identical doctrines. Both of them, however, are mature, original expressions in their own rights. With their distinct lineages and languages, they do not appear to have "copied" each other directly, though they do show every indication of having arisen in an interdependent relationship. The Bön Great Perfection's interaction with Sarma tantric movements is more difficult to assess. Their interconnections are quite difficult to see in written histories of the period, though glimmers do come through in figures like Yangtön, who studied philosophy under the Buddhist translator Ba-ri, possibly at Sakya Monastery.[102] Reading the Oral Tradition's visionary literature next to Tibetan works from the Kālacakra tradition, however, the connections become more clear. The influx of Kālacakra into Tibet during the early and mid-eleventh century came at a time when the Oral Tradition was probably still in vital but uncodified oral form. In the late eleventh century, when Kālacakra attained a firm foothold and began to inspire experimental writings like Yumo's, the Oral Tradition itself was also in the process of being written down. If writings on the Great Perfection's "lamps" can be seen in part as responding to the Kālacakra visionary "yogas of day and night," Bön must have been just as aware of Kālacakra as the Nyingma traditions were, as it is difficult to imagine that their knowledge of Kālacakra would have been filtered through Nyingma in every instance.

In the "six lamps" and "four lamps" traditions it thus appears that Bön and Nyingma were developing their own narrative frameworks and traditions of vision, as well as trading ideas extensively between one another, reacting to Kālacakra, and reacting to each other's reactions to Kālacakra. At the same time, even when we see clear evidence for such complex dialogue, given the state of the historical record, it remains difficult to identify what particular persons, specific places, precise dates, or particular media may have been involved.

Nonetheless, looking at the Nyingma, Sarma, and Bön sources investigated here along with their surrounding histories, several broad conclusions can be drawn about the exchange in visionary ideas that took place during the Tibetan renaissance. First, the regional touchstones are almost always central and western Tibet, and the broad context is within the rise of Buddhist institutions, at a period when institutional values provided direction but not utter control. Buddhist institutions—whether organized lay communities or monastic establishments—are important here because the literary forms of our visionary works all suggest the institutional concern for systems, organization, and writing, as they are each found within recently crafted literary collections and cycles, which themselves form elements in the architecture of larger traditions.

Reading into biographies of figures from the period, it is apparent that the trends toward organization, collection, and system building—while contained within an environment of budding institutions—were still driven by individual inspiration and singular charismatic teachers. The biographical sketches of Yumo and Yangtön are instructive because their subjects' critical moments of inspiration came simply from hearing the names of teachers and hearing the names of texts. The possibility of meeting with individual masters and doctrines—not the reputation of great monasteries or organized movements—was very much a motivating force for Tibetan advocates of vision during this period, and it was those sources of inspiration combined with individual initiative that prompted their travels and fieldwork. That travel, in turn, was marked by moments where doctrines and texts were exchanged, and this occurred through processes as diverse as teaching, discovery, collection, and recording of esoteric traditions.

While it is easy to find copying and direct influence between Nyingma, Sarma, and Bön in general, none of the Kālacakra or "lamps" works investigated here are directly derived from one another on the level of sentences or paragraphs.[103] Rather, their common ground is on the level of structures, ideas, narrative backgrounds, and key terms, all of which suggests a deep conversational interaction rather than covert reading and hasty plagiarizing of texts. It appears that this common ground emerged as individuals crossed paths while traveling in an increasingly stable society, and as lineages crossed each other in a diverse religious environment. These crisscrossing paths then gradually grew into nets of influence. Yangtön's philosophical studies with Buddhists also provide a reminder of how exoteric topics may serve more readily as points of contact than topics in the highly charged world of tantra, and thus it should be acknowledged how wider dialogue on more normative topics may have built relationships and pathways that were later used for the exchange of esoteric concepts about vision.

PART II | Views

CHAPTER 4 | Seeing Emptiness

Vision, Philosophy, and Physiology

Surely the most striking features of the Kālacakra and Great Perfection texts are the descriptions of practices, which involve fantastic visions encountered during weeks-long retreats in total darkness. Yet these texts are not simply accounts of esoteric yogic practices, as they also contain nuanced and poetic reflections on some of the major issues in Buddhist thought. As they turn from practices of seeing to matters of philosophy and insight, these writings play on the Buddhist term "view" *(darśana, lta ba),* a word commonly used to mean "philosophy" or "school of thought," but which can also mean "to look" or "to see." Generally speaking, Buddhist philosophical "views" rarely involve actual practices of seeing at all, and sometimes go so far as to portray the eyes—along with the senses and the body—as being of little value in the pursuit of religious truths. Yet in Kālacakra, and perhaps even more so in the Great Perfection, philosophical views are closely related to acts of seeing, and intellectual discussions often take directions that are suggested by visual experience, the eyes, and human physiology. This chapter explores one of these discussions: speculations about seeing in the dark.

In the literature of Kālacakra and the Great Perfection, the dark room becomes more than just a logistical detail and takes on a metaphorical power. The image of lights emerging from its darkness becomes a homology for appearances arising from emptiness *(śūnyatā, stong pa nyid),*[1] and so the dark-retreat comes to be a way of immersing oneself in this philosophical topic. The association of emptiness with acts of seeing then leads the Kālacakra and Great Perfection traditions to invest themselves in visual form in a way that is atypical for Buddhists. They start to search for ultimate significance in the details of the visual world and use emptiness as a way to describe how appearances might reveal themselves, instead of using it as a way to tear appearances apart. One inspiration for these ideas must have been Buddhist writings like the *tathāgatagarbha* scriptures, which cast the ultimate as more of a "fullness" than an emptiness. But at the same time, our tantric works also evoke more conservative approaches to emptiness and play with using terminology from Buddhist epistemological traditions—terms like "direct perception" and "higher seeing"—to describe their paths of vision. Below, we will explore some of these connections between seeing and emptiness, in which esoteric discussions of dark rooms and visionary practices tend to digress into very recognizable discourses about emptiness and the ultimate, all the while adding to our notion of what "emptiness" and "seeing" might mean.

Observations on Emptiness

To begin, let us turn to two Kālacakra passages which claim that the ultimate can be encountered by using the eyes. First, here is *Stainless Light* describing the practice of visionary yoga:[2]

> [The yogi] sees emptiness with all aspects[3] everywhere in the sphere of the sky: unproduced phenomena that are like prognostic images in a mirror. He considers these as dream objects, distinct appearances elaborated by his own mind. This casts away (a) the emptiness [that follows from] the analysis of phenomena as being aggregates of atomic particles, and (b) the nihilistic emptiness. He desires the phenomenon of internal bliss that is an object of his own awareness.

Similarly, Kālacakrapāda's *Lotus Girl*[4] says:

> [By continually meditating on the six-limbed yoga, the yogi] will see empty-forms, endowed with all aspects, appearing externally in the sky. Similarly, they will be seen internally, using the mental sense-faculty. Moreover, those things that appear on the exterior and interior are not existent, as they transcend the relationship of produced-and-producer. But they are also not nonexistent, as they are objects of engagement of the sense faculties.

The passages here weigh in on a classic Buddhist debate about ultimate truth, which is whether the ultimate is something that can be observed and expressed, or whether it simply indicates an openness or absence that cannot be described in positive terms, and that is beyond the reach of the mind. Mahāyāna authors have tended to approach this issue in two general ways, neither of which is quite as radical as the suggestions in the preceding passages that the ultimate might be encountered with the eyes. The first approach is rooted in the idea of no-self and casts the ultimate in negative terms, as things' emptiness of identity, essence, or concrete nature. In the second, there is something left when those false superimpositions of identity are cleared away: something positive that is deep within beings, or some transcendent qualities that become manifest once they are uncovered. Mahāyāna writers often put these two approaches in competition with each other, with some declaring the positive approach to be the superior and final view, and others depicting it as a type of interpretable teaching that does not represent the Buddha's ultimate intent, or even depicting it as heretical.

It seems best, however, to treat these two approaches as being in a symbiotic relationship, or as representing the boundaries that define investigations into the ultimate, and between which one can shift when any single line of thought threatens to lock the ultimate into an easy or concrete position. The Kālacakra and Great Perfection traditions often use this dual approach: they are interested in emptiness, absence, and so forth, but are also wary of claims that would make the ultimate truth completely ineffable and unobservable. The problem for these visionary traditions is that the idea of an unobservable or unfindable ultimate is quite prominent in important Mahāyāna literary works, and so it is not easy to dismiss. The Perfection of Wisdom scriptures contain some of the most famous examples, which are memorable for their rhetoric of negativity in which "finding" the ultimate is really a nonfinding where nothing is found, in an act that is performed by nobody. This passage from the sūtra in 25,000 lines[5] gives a typical example:

> Subhūti said: "Kauśika, it is like this—here is how it is! Apart from [his] nature that is devoid of basis, the Tathāgata is not observed to exist; and apart from [his] thatness, the Tathāgata is not observed to exist. Yet the Tathāgata also is not observed in a nature that is devoid of basis, and a nature devoid of basis is not observed in the Tathāgata. The Tathāgata is also not observed in thatness, and thatness is not observed in the Tathāgata. The Tathāgata is also not observed in the suchness of form, and the suchness of form is not observed in the Tathāgata. The Tathāgata is also not observed in the nature of form, and the nature of form is not observed in the Tathāgata...."

Here, contacting or "observing" *(dmigs pa)* emptiness (or "thatness") is equated with contacting the Buddha himself, but with the caveat that this observation really means to observe nothing at all. Similar ideas appear in the treatises of Nāgārjuna,[6] as in this verse that casts nirvāṇa as a state of peace in which nothing is observed:

> Completely pacifying all observations,
> And completely pacifying elaborations, is peace.

The Buddha nowhere taught
Any dharma to anyone.

And for one more notable example, here is the famous statement by Śāntideva, whose plain language is often cited as evidence of how the ultimate is beyond the senses or the ordinary mind:

> This truth is recognized as being of two kinds: conventional and ultimate. Ultimate reality is beyond the scope of the intellect....[7]

Dealing carefully with this complex of issues that presents the ultimate as beyond observation, expression, and contact is one of the major concerns of the visionary branches of Kālacakra and the Great Perfection. While they try in various ways to honor their Mahāyāna heritage, they also try to make the ultimate more observable by working with it in the visual sphere. Yumo is particularly direct in promoting this kind of path, and he openly ridicules the idea that enlightenment could be brought about by "a hidden phenomenon that is beyond being an object of engagement of the mind."[8] Here he is dispelling an objector who brings up the idea of an unobservable emptiness:[9]

> You might object: "It is said that 'not seeing anything at all, suchness is seen'; thus, nonunderstanding is itself the supreme understanding." Although [the supreme understanding] has been given that name, there is no such experience. The path-emptiness is something that can be experienced, and this is an absolute necessity.

In Yumo's response, "path-emptiness"[10] refers to empty-form, or emptiness that manifests in vision. Thus, as Yumo makes clear, vision is not a call to abandon the Buddhist philosophical project of emptiness. His comments about the necessity for experience are rooted in a broader view that emptiness is not just a kind of spaciousness that passively allows for the world to function, but rather is a dynamism that actively generates the world and creates experiences of itself.

This kind of energetic emptiness is also a hallmark of the Great Perfection, which speaks of a "dynamic energy"[11] through which the empty ground expresses itself and allows itself to be experienced. The position is illustrated well by the *Tantra of the Blazing Lamps,*[12] in a description of the "empty seminal nuclei lamp":

Naturally the reverse of emptiness,
It is a radiant appearance that creates experience,
In which a fivefold primordial radiation
Is present as a natural flow.

The "empty seminal nuclei" described here are visionary experiences; as their name implies, they are viewed as empty but are also the "reverse" of emptiness in their ability to manifest in five-colored light, and thus to give rise to experiences.

Such attempts to coax the ultimate out of the sphere of pure negativity are of course reminiscent of important Mahāyāna scriptures that speak about the ultimate in more positive terms,[13] and posit a "buddha nature" *(tathāgatagarbha),* a "sphere of reality" *(dharmadhātu),* a "luminous" *(prabhāsvara)* mind, or even a "reality body" *(dharma-kāya)* as a transcendent element that remains present when everything mundane is cleared away. Indeed, many of the themes important in visionary literature are readily apparent in such works.[14] Here, for instance, is a passage from Nāgārjuna's *Praise of Dharmadhātu,*[15] which associates the ultimate with images of light and uses the metaphor of a lamp in a vase (an image often used by the Great Perfection):[16]

> Just as a lamp dwelling in a vase
> Does not shine forth at all,
> When dwelling in the vase of the afflictions,
> The *dharmadhātu* also is not seen.
>
> From whichever of its sides
> A hole is punched in the pot,
> From those very sides
> The nature of light will emerge.
>
> When the vase [of the afflictions] is broken
> By the vajra of *samādhi,*
> At that time, [the *dharmadhātu*] shines forth
> Throughout the limits of the sky.

One way of distinguishing these positive treatments of the ultimate from those found in Kālacakra and the Great Perfection is to note how the tantric sources are much less shy about using the term "emptiness." Works like Nāgārjuna's *Praise* commonly cast emptiness as something that removes attachment and afflictions, but when it comes to making positive descriptions about the ultimate, they refer not to emptiness but to entities like the *tathāgatagarbha,* the *dharmadhātu,* and so forth. Nāgārjuna's *In Praise of the Dharmadhātu,*[17] for instance, says:

> However many sūtras teaching emptiness
> Were spoken by the victors,
> They all turn back the afflictions,
> But do not diminish this *dhātu.*

Here, the negative sort of emptiness is simply the remover, while the entity of ultimate significance is something (at least terminologically) different: the *dharmadhātu.* When Yumo, in contrast, begins a similar line of thought, he says that the ordinary "view" of emptiness "overturns the craving for concrete things [and] in dependence on it the afflictions are controlled."[18] But when speaking in positive terms, he does not turn to a buddha-nature or a *dharmadhātu* but instead returns to emptiness itself and lays out in detail his ideas about the "path" emptiness. Kālacakra literature in particular abounds with new terms for emptiness that point to its energetic and observable qualities: empty-form, animate emptiness, observable emptiness, emptiness endowed with all aspects,[19] (in Yumo) path-emptiness, and (later in the Jonang tradition) other-empty.[20] These ideas attempt to describe how emptiness itself might have positive dimensions that would allow it to appear, or that would allow it to serve as an animate matrix that generates the world.

We even find in these sources a tendency to deify emptiness, so that it becomes associated with a buddha like Viśvamātā or All Good. These discussions frequently use a kind of "mother" imagery reminiscent of that found in the Perfection of Wisdom sūtras, where the goddess Prajñāpāramitā is portrayed as the "mother of the buddhas" (in an indication of how the emptiness she represents gives birth to enlightenment). In the Great Perfection, the "mother" *(ma)* becomes the empty ground itself, which gives rise not just to the Buddhas but to the entire world. For Kālacakra, in turn, it is the Great Seal who is the creator of all. In the following passage from *Stainless Light,*[21] the Great Seal is described in the guises of both emptiness and goddess, giving birth to the buddhas and acting as the source of the world:

> The Great Seal is the defining characteristic of all phenomena, their lack of inherent nature. It is [also] endowed with all supreme aspects, and is [the goddess] Prajñāpāramitā, the mother who gives birth to all the buddhas. It is also expressed by the term "source of phenomena." "Source of phenomena" should be understood as meaning "that from which all phenomena arise without having any inherent nature."

The mixture of terminology is instructive here. It indicates how such tantric explorations of emptiness look partially to the past for authority (with Prajñāpāramitā and the language like "lack of inherent nature" evoking the classic Mahāyāna). Yet we also have a very tantric play on words in the term "source of phenomena,"[22] which can be taken literally as "source," but in tantra also has the sexualized meaning of "vulva." The passage thus in some ways sexualizes emptiness itself[23] and portrays the activity of emptiness as a goddess giving birth to the world and producing buddhahood through her embrace. Characteristically, the Great Perfection does not employ as much overtly sexual imagery but rather tends toward mini-narratives like the "mother meeting with the son," or "how the world arises from the ground,"[24] or the "enlightenment of All Good." These nonetheless have a similar intention, in that they portray emptiness as a constructive force that impels the world together rather than demanding that it be torn apart.

Though these observable, creative versions of emptiness provide examples of how tantra contributes to Buddhist theories of the ultimate, it is worth noting that such contributions often go unmentioned even by tantrics themselves. Yumo, for example, openly suggests that the Vajrayāna is only a system of "method" (meaning that it offers distinctive yogic methods for attaining enlightenment) but has no distinctive "view" of emptiness beyond referencing things' emptiness of inherent nature.[25] On the other hand, he is somewhat disdainful about that view, in the sense that he subordinates it to the type of emptiness associated with tantric practices of vision:

> In this context [of tantra], what is "emptiness"? Arrogant scholars mostly say: "It is the abiding reality of phenomena," or "It is the reality of phenomena," or "It is things being empty of inherent nature," or "not being established by way of their own entity," or "being unproduced from the beginning," or "being free from the extremes of existence, nonexistence, both, or neither," or that it is the "complete pacification of all elaborations." And they claim that understanding things in this way is the path! But I do not accept that. That is an [intellectual] determination of the abiding reality of things, and thus is the "view," an explanation of tenets. But it is not the object of meditation on the "path," [which is described in] the stages of the oral instructions.[26]

What is notable about this passage is the amount of exoteric philosophical language being used by this thoroughly tantric author—the message being that the tantric path of vision is an inquiry into emptiness that is equally sophisticated and ultimately more powerful than those in the writings of authors like Nāgārjuna.[27] Yumo is of course an eccentric and outspoken figure, so the directness of his statements here is not always matched in more tradition-bound literature of Kālacakra or the Great Perfection. The underlying message, however, is very much the same: that outside of the classical, textual tradition, there are oral traditions and esoteric instructions relating to vision that, while not invalidating classical approaches, offer alternative and superior ways for attaining the "higher seeing" that comes about when directly encountering emptiness.

Luminous Channels and Divine Eyes: Lighting Up the Body's Darkness

In addition to speculating about the ultimate significance of the dark-room lights, our authors also spend time explaining what makes vision possible. This leads them into descriptions of the features of the body that contribute to vision: channels of light that traverse the interior of the body, or transcendent types of "eyes" that can be attained and that allow for the perception of visions. As we will see, these practical discussions characteristically circle back to the philosophical realm, and in their own ways make comments on matters of emptiness and ultimate truth. One way of thinking about these physiological materials is that, on top of their basic descriptive functions, they operate as literary ways of inquiring into emptiness. The Great Perfection's network of "light channels," for instance, is certainly intended to explain the bodily basis of vision. But at the same time, the language that those explanations use suggests how the channels participate in explorations of the ultimate: acting as conduits for "empty" seminal nuclei, and having a "suchness" dimension that allows them to intuitively grasp emptiness. Further, the imagery of light appearing in the body's darkness also evokes, reinforces, and comments on the Great Perfection's core ideas about how appearances arise from the ground of emptiness.

Channels of Light in the Great Perfection

In the Great Perfection, the ordinary body contains a subtle "adamantine body"[28] that manages its growth, development, and functioning. The tradition describes this subtle body in terms of three basic components: channels, winds, and seminal nuclei.[29] The energy channels here are much like those found in other Buddhist and Hindu tantric traditions, consisting of a set of three vertical tubes that run from the genital area to the cranium, passing through a series of horizontal "wheels." The three basic channels then branch out and spread throughout the body, creating a system of pathways much like the body's ordinary circulatory system. Propelled by the energy "winds," seminal nuclei then circulate throughout the body using these pathways and act as tiny organizing centers and matrices, producing the energy for the body's motion, guiding and organizing its growth and development, contributing the energy for ordinary and transcendent mental functioning, and serving as the basic seeds operative in conception.

In addition to this set of conventional channels, the Great Perfection describes a set of luminous channels *('od rtsa)* that branch out from the heart and also spread throughout the body, like a circulation system that carries not blood or seminal nuclei but light. Canonical texts do not all agree on the names and functions of the luminous channels,[30] but one standard way of presenting them is this set from the Nyingma *Tantra of the Blazing Lamps:*[31]

> At the center of all sentient beings' bodies
> Emerging from the immeasurable mansion of their precious *citta*-heart
> There are many thousands of channels.

> But in particular, there are four great channels:
> (1) The great golden *kati* channel,
> (2) The one that is like a silk thread,
> (3) The slender coil, and (4) the crystal tube.

These four "great" channels serve as the main pathways for awareness' radiant energy, directing it around the body where it serves as the deepest source of our vitality. The light channels are generally correlated with (or even located within) the ordinary channels, so in this way they can be seen as the high-energy foundations and sources of the ordinary channels.[32]

The luminous channels, however, are more than simple reduplications of the ordinary energy channels. One major innovation here is the "slender coil" and "crystal tube" channels, which run from the heart, vertically up the spine, over the crown of the head, and connect to the eyes. The main function of these is visionary: they serve as the pathway for luminous awareness, which resides in the heart, to travel upward and project out of the eyes, and be seen in vision. These heart-to-eye channels are also described in Bön sources, though they appear under different names.[33] Thus despite slight variations in their descriptions of the light channels,[34] both the Bön and Nyingma traditions make the same claim: that the body is literally wired for vision. So, while these traditions acknowledge that part of the human condition is being imprisoned in a body, they also suggest how the body has physical structures that provide a way out of that trap. If the heart-to-eyes channels are a kind of soteriological dimension of the body, it should come as no surprise that discussions of them frequently turn back to matters of ultimate truth and emptiness. As we will see in more detail later, the Great Perfection's light channels are described as the "suchness" dimension of the visual system, indicating how their function is to visually intuit, or self-recognize, the ultimate, much as if they are composed of a dynamic emptiness whose nature it is to see itself.

Divine Eyes in the Wheel of Time

While this system of light channels is not found in Kālacakra, the tradition does have its own distinctive notions of human physiology, including some features that are used to account for the perception of visions. Among these is a group of "five eyes" that can be attained through yogic practice, and which allow for the perception of Kālacakra's luminous empty-forms. *Stainless Light*[35] contains several mentions of these, such as its suggestion that:

> In sequence, the (1) fleshy eyes, (2) divine eyes, (3) buddha eyes, (4) insight eyes, and (5) gnosis eyes will arise through the power of meditation.

These form the alternative visual system that becomes operative in the practice of Kālacakra's six yogas, as the meditator withdraws from the ordinary sensory system. The idea here is that during the six yogas, the practitioner's winds enter the body's central channel, and this causes the withdrawal of ordinary senses as well as the production of visionary appearances, which are encountered with transcendent (rather than mundane) eyes.

These "eyes" are actually not unique to the Kālacakra system, as references to them can be found throughout Buddhist literature: in the *nikāyas,* in the *abhidharma,* in the Perfection of Wisdom scriptures, and even in the Great Perfection.[36] Characteristically, Kālacakra's adoption of these eyes seems to come from the tradition's reflections on its Buddhist literary heritage, in which it found inspiration in references to esoteric eyes and modes of seeing and then reimagined them and worked them neatly into its own visionary project.

The full set of five eyes is perhaps most characteristic of the Perfection of Wisdom scriptures, and given how Kālacakra uses those scriptures as a touchstone, it seems reasonable to think that they served as a primary source of inspiration. Passages like the following, from the *Perfection of Wisdom Sūtra in 25,000 Lines,*[37] are particularly helpful in understanding Kālacakra's interest in the five eyes:

> Śāriputra! Because bodhisattva-mahāsattvas are endowed with that kind of gnosis,... when they meditate on the Tathāgata's ten powers, his four fearlessnesses, his four individual correct knowledges, his great love, his great compassion, and his eighteen unique buddha-qualities, they do not observe those eighteen unique buddha-qualities [and so forth]....
>
> Śāriputra! This is the gnosis of the bodhisattva-mahāsattvas: bodhisattva-mahāsattvas endowed with this gnosis thoroughly perfect all the qualities of a buddha, but they do not see all those buddha qualities at all.
>
> Śāriputra! Moreover, when the bodhisattva-mahāsattvas engage in the Perfection of Wisdom, they attain the five eyes, and completely purify them. What are those five? They are: (1) the fleshy eyes, (2) the divine eyes, (3) the eyes of insight, (4) the dharma eyes, and (5) the buddha eyes.

The "eyes" in this context are essentially a way of describing the attainments of bodhisattvas and buddhas. As would be expected from the Perfection of Wisdom genre, the eyes here are prefaced by the core message of emptiness for which the Perfection of Wisdom literature is famous. Nothing, we are told, not even the qualities of a buddha, has any sort of intrinsic or observable existence when regarded with the gnosis of a bodhisattva. It seems remarkable that, following this, the five eyes are mentioned in a positive light. That is, instead of saying "no fleshy eye, no divine eye, no eye of insight...," the five eyes are mentioned as actual attainments that arise from the realization of emptiness (through the Perfection of Wisdom). As we will see, the sūtra then goes on at length to describe what *can* be seen with each of the eyes. This in turn suggests how discourses of seeing and light are one way of turning discussions of emptiness to more positive matters. To get a better idea of what kind of "seeing" the five eyes provide, it will be helpful to quickly outline the *Sūtra*'s description of the five eyes.[38]

(1) "Fleshy eyes" is a term that is sometimes used to refer to the ordinary mundane eyes, but in this context is a sort of super-sight, a purified physical eye that can see for hundreds or thousands of leagues across space, and can see thousands of other world systems. (2) The "divine eyes" or "god's eyes" allow one to "see" the specific effects of karma, so that one knows the details of the birth, death, and rebirth of other beings.[39] (3) The "eyes of insight" are the bodhisattva's insight[40] into emptiness conceptualized as eyes. Focused as it is on things' emptiness of true existence, this is an eye that does not have an object; in the words of the sūtra, it "does not see any phenomenon at all." (4) The "dharma eyes," then, are related to compassionate activities, as they allow the bodhisattva to see others' level of spiritual development, see their personal histories, and see what might best assist them. Finally, (5) the "buddha eyes" are a buddha's ultimate realization, thematized as a set of eyes. As the *25,000 Line Sūtra*[41] puts it:

> After the bodhisattva [generates] bodhicitta, he sets [himself] in equipoise in the vajra-like *samādhi,* and then attains the state of an omniscient one: being endowed with the ten powers of a tathāgata, having the four fearlessnesses, four individual correct knowledges, the eighteen unique buddha-qualities, great love, great compassion, great joy, great equanimity, and the unobscured liberated qualities of a buddha. That is the [buddha] eye. When a bodhisattva mahāsattva is endowed with that eye, with respect to aspects, there is none that he does not see, none that he does not hear of, none that he does not know, none that he does not understand.

Taken together, the eyes in the *25,000 Line Sūtra* fluctuate between being metaphorical "eyes" and actual instruments of sight. On the whole, they read more as instruments that lead to particular types of knowledge or insight rather than organs that allow for visual experience. Yet the references to visual abilities such as seeing across vast distances suggest how the eyes are able to function in discussions of both metaphorical and actual seeing.

Much later in Buddhist history, as the visionary Kālacakra tradition adopts these kinds of transcendent eyes, we find a set of five eyes that is much more instrumental in acts of seeing. *Stainless Light,* for instance, goes so far as to claim that the five eyes are the instruments through which a yogi perceives visions of empty-form. This is a provocative claim, and it is tempting to dismiss it as a rhetorical one, or perhaps as an example of tantric excess. Yet these comments come in the context of a discussion where we can see the tradition deliberately trying to work out, in epistemological terms, the mechanics and ultimate benefits of visionary practice.

To understand what *Stainless Light* might be up to here, we can turn to a verse from the *Kālacakra Tantra,*[42] which states how yogic encounters with deities can be understood as employing two very different types of valid cognition *(pramāṇa, tshad ma),* these being direct perception *(pratyakṣa, mngon sum)* and inference *(anumāna, rjes dpag). Stainless Light* will go on to claim that it is only visionary practices (like those in Kālacakra's completion stage) that provide a kind of direct perception of buddhas. In contrast, deity-meditations that involve the use of static reference points like drawings and statues[43] provide only inferential encounters with the divine:

> When deities are taken as meditative objects, there are two kinds: those that are directly perceived, and those that are [perceived through] inference.
> The ones that are directly perceived are manifold complete-enjoyment bodies, [seen] like stars in the sky, via the union of the principles [of emptiness and compassion].[44]
> Those not directly perceived, but inferred, are like lifeless bodies; they are not in accordance with reality, and are imputed;
> Yogis whose minds are not completely ripened take such [objects]—like drawings and so forth—[as] objects of observation for the sake of [their] meditation.

Here the language of "direct perception" and "inference" might be read as a simple appeal to the authority of *pramāṇa*-type language,[45] but the distinction between mediated and direct encounters with buddhas is actually basic to visionary completion stage yogas, where the direct path of vision is contrasted to the conceptual artifice of visualization. In his *Stainless Light*[46] commentary, Puṇḍarīka goes on to explain this verse and is rather direct in promoting a path where a yogi encounters deities—and the ultimate—in a direct perception that is made possible through the five eyes:

> Here, in accordance with the [varied] mental abilities of sentient beings, the deities that yogis take as their meditative objects are [said to be] of two kinds: those that are directly perceived, and

those that are [perceived] through inference. From among those that are directly perceived and those that are [perceived] through inference, the ones perceived directly are the manifold complete enjoyment bodies, which come to be [perceived] like stars in the sky, like constellations, via the union of the principles [of emptiness and compassion]. [These] are objects apprehended by the fleshy eyes and so forth, [and are like] the three worlds and three times, which resemble dreams and illusions.

Here, (1) at first, a beginner yogi, without having higher perception, sees various forms[47] using the fleshy eyes.[48] (2) Then[49] through the power of [having reached] the point of higher perception,[50] they are seen with the divine eyes.[51] (3) Then through the power of [having reached] the point of being separated from attachment,[52] they are seen with the buddha eyes.[53] (4) Then,[54] through the power of [having reached] the level of a bodhisattva,[55] they are seen with the eyes of insight. (5) And then,[56] through the power of the [enlightened] mind [attained at] the stage of a complete buddha,[57] they are seen with the eyes of gnosis,[58] freed from remainder.

In that way, all five eyes of the tathāgatas—the fleshy eyes and so forth—are for the purpose of seeing emptiness. Other sentient beings are blind to the observable object of emptiness *(stong nyid lta ba'i yul).*

Ideas like these continued to resonate with Kālacakra advocates as they looked for ways to explain the path of vision in distinctively Buddhist terms like the five eyes. Here, for instance, is fifteenth-century Tibetan exegete Khedrup Norsang Gyatso[59] discussing the same passage, but mapping the five eyes onto Kālacakra's six yogas:

During the stages of (1) withdrawal and (2) meditative concentration, empty-forms are seen with the fleshy eye consciousness. After completing meditative concentration, higher perception *(mngon shes)* is attained; then, until one has completed (3) breath control, (4) retention, and (5) recollection, and as long as one has not separated from desire for the union of the two [sexual] organs, [the empty-forms] are seen with the higher perception of the divine eyes. After attaining the completion of the stage of recollection, when one creates an actual Great Seal consort and separates from desire for the "action" and "gnostic" consorts, [i.e., during (6) concentration,] then [the empty-forms] are seen with the buddha eyes. Then, at the point of [becoming] a bodhisattva—from the first moment when one attains the unchanging bliss of the first of the twelve bodhisattva grounds—[empty-forms] are seen with the eyes of gnosis.

Clearly, in passages like these, the five eyes are instruments in transcendent forms of seeing and are not simply metaphors for knowing. Yet even in these contexts the five eyes still retain their long-standing associations with insight. Indeed, keeping both sides of the metaphor active seems to be critical, especially here in the Kālacakra context, where, as Norsang Gyatso remind us, the visual object is empty-form, something that is at once luminous and empty. It is this unique set of circumstances that helps us to understand both Kālacakra's turn to the eyes and its unusual statements about the ultimate, reflected in *Stainless Light*'s comments that the five eyes "are for the purpose of seeing emptiness."

Seeing in the Dark: Charles Bonnet Syndrome and Visual Filling-In

When reading Buddhist descriptions of "nighttime yoga" and "dark-retreat," one cannot help but wonder about the science of lights appearing in the dark. Are there basic neurological explanations for these visionary appearances? If so, what implications would the scientific descriptions have for the religious ones? Or vice versa? Below, I would like to begin to make some of these connections by taking a brief look at some scientific literature on spontaneous visual phenomena and sensory deprivation. In so doing, I do not pretend that any differences will be resolved between, say, contemporary neurology and the Great Perfection. Nor do I have any desire to present the religious material as "scientific," though I do not think enough attention is paid to scientific and medical dimensions of tantric traditions.[60] Though there may be some hazards in exploring this territory, there are as well many relevant connections between the two sides, and they often proceed in parallel directions.

Scientists have for some time been interested in the mind's ability to create visual imagery when it is deprived of actual input from the eyes. The phenomenon made its way into scientific literature as early as the mid-eighteenth century, when a Swiss naturalist named Charles Bonnet began to write observations of the visual experiences of his grandfather, Charles Lullin, who suffered from cataracts and had undergone an early form of cataract surgery to have them removed. Years after the operation, Lullin began to report realistic visionary experiences; though he was otherwise cognitively unimpaired, his visual world was filled with fantastic faces and animals, which would appear suddenly, growing and shrinking in size. Now known as Charles Bonnet syndrome,[61] such visual experiences are common among people suffering from cataracts and macular degeneration; similar appearances are also seen by patients with brain injuries that partially impair the visual system. Patients report seeing images that are vivid, realistic, and mobile, often taking the form of cartoon-like creatures that mix into and interact with the ordinary environment. In some cases, patients with a large visual scotoma (a blank spot in the visual field, which can be brought on by a brain injury) may see the scotoma filled with images, like a television screen, while the remainder of their visual field remains normal.[62]

The experience of Charles Bonnet–type imagery is generally thought to be related to a diminishing of visual stimulation, brought on by disorders of the eye or by brain injuries. Some studies have focused on inducing similar imagery in subjects with intact visual systems by placing them in total visual deprivation, a context that would mimic that of dark-retreat. A blindfolding experiment conducted at Harvard Medical School,[63] for instance, placed thirteen subjects in specially constructed blindfolds that allowed the eyes to move freely but blocked out all light. The subjects remained blindfolded for five days and were given tape recorders to allow them to document their experiences. Unsurprisingly, the reports by the blindfolded subjects correlate closely with literary accounts of visionary experiences in dark-retreat: the onset of visual experiences as unstructured spots and patches of light (called "phosphenes"), which for many subjects eventually turned into complex, realistic experiences like peacock feathers, faces, architecture, and landscapes.

The precise processes that lead to such visual experiences are not yet completely understood but are usually approached as a type of visual "filling-in," similar to how the visual system conceals the eyes' blind spot. The blind spot, however, is a case of "perceptual" completion performed by the visual neurons, which conceal the blind spot by filling it in with patterns and colors taken from the parts of the visual field that surround the blind spot.[64] Images produced by this kind of perceptual completion are simple and not subject to change once they are formed. The visual system, however, is capable of a much more complex type of completion, "conceptual" completion,[65] in which gaps are filled in with rich imagery drawn, it seems, not from the external environment but from within the mind, particularly from memory.[66] Neurologist V. S. Ramachandran suggests this as a model for beginning to explore Charles Bonnet–type imagery:

> In Bonnet syndrome, the images are based on a sort of "conceptual completion" rather than perceptual completion; the images being "filled in" are coming from memory (top down)—not from the outside (bottom up).[67]

The idea that memory might spill out into visual experience points to a connection between our "actual" external visual worlds and the "visual" experiences that are seen in the mind's eye. Indeed, it seems that Charles Bonnet–type imagery, and even visual imagination, may involve "running our visual machinery in reverse."[68] In other words, in normal visual perception, information enters the eyes and is transmitted to the visual cortex, a processing area where it is sorted and relayed into two higher visual pathways responsible for the perception of (1) depth and motion, and (2) shape, color, and recognition.[69] The visual cortex, however, does not just relay sensory input to more specialized visual areas of the brain but also receives information back from those specialized areas. Thus, in recalling an object in the mind's eye, information seems to flow from the higher visual centers back to the visual cortex, such that in imagining an object the visual cortex becomes active, almost as if the object was actually being seen.[70]

This kind of back-projection is speculated to cause the realistic visual imagery seen in both Bonnet syndrome and sensory deprivation. Ramachandran has suggested that, in ordinary circumstances, input from the eyes keeps the visual system working in the bottom-up direction, "vetoing" the process whereby memories and cognitive images break into the visual field.[71] Even when the eyes are closed, or when one walks into a dark room, the functioning eyes contain a kind of "spontaneous activity," producing a low-level baseline signal sufficient to maintain bottom-up functioning.[72] However, if the visual pathways are impaired, "this baseline signal is removed, and so you hallucinate."[73]

In interpreting the significance of the appearances that result from sensory deprivation, contemporary neurologists obviously come with a very different set of assumptions than those held by Buddhists. Nonetheless, when it comes to the basic nature of these appearances, there is little in the neurological reports that in fact conflicts with the Buddhist accounts. It is important to remember that the descriptions of vision found in both Kālacakra and the Great Perfection do not generally treat dark-retreat appearances as "mystical" or otherworldly experiences. Rather, those visions are said to be based on the structures of the ordinary body, and as such are accessible to anyone. In addition, Buddhists explain them as involving a reversal of the visual system's ordinary direction and repeatedly describe them as being nothing more than mere appearances of the mind,[74] both of which seem compatible with ideas in the neurological reports.

Many of the scientific reports also help to reinforce our understanding of why these particular sorts of visions might be used in religious contexts. In particular, (1) they represent a type of vision that is different from a true "hallucination," in that the subject who experiences them remains "insightful as to their unreal nature."[75] Patients have reported them as being more-real-than-reality, this kind of hypervividness causing them to stand out and be realized as ultimately unreal.[76] (2) Second, these visual appearances tend to be somewhat malleable, disappearing when directly scrutinized.[77] They may thus be useful, as Buddhists suggest, for cultivating a kind of soft focus, which does not analyze, grasp at, or follow after motion and appearances. In a similar vein, these are also types of appearance that are easily reinterpreted based on advice given by others, as when a patient is told by a companion that the cows she is seeing in a nearby field are not actually real.[78] Advice on interpreting and reinterpreting visions, of course, is one of the key elements in retreat practice, where one's spiritual teacher provides oral instructions on how to deal with vision. (3) Finally, unlike dreams or fantasies, these appearances are often "context appropriate, reflecting the subject's psychologic state and changing in content and frequency as a function of the subject's daily activities."[79] That is, they do not typically play out as dreamlike narrative fantasies unrelated to a person's history but take form based on one's experience, learning, and immediate surroundings. In this vein, some of the reports of subjects in the Harvard study are similar to those found in religious literature: the ability (without light) to see objects that one is holding, or to see (and see within) one's own body.[80] So, "context appropriate" here could also be read as "culturally appropriate," such that a contemporary Westerner might experience an encounter with Elvis,[81] while a Buddhist monk might instead encounter beings from his own particular pantheon. This cultural dimension of vision then suggests how learning, literature, and even philosophical thought might direct and influence the content of the visionary world.

Perhaps the most significant point of contact between the neurological and religious speculations on seeing in the dark is that they both treat these appearances as windows into the nature of the mind that produces them. Neurologists may take them as an opportunity to see into the dynamic relationship between memory, imagination, and the visual system. Buddhists, in contrast, use them as ways of implicating all appearances as being like visions: evanescent, deeply related to mind, luminous structures that arise from a dynamic matrix of darkness.

Conclusion: Views of the Ultimate

While the practice of dark-retreat readily evokes so many issues related to emptiness, it is troublesome for its advocates to say in an unqualified way that dark-retreat is a path to encountering the ultimate. This is because Buddhists usually place a divide between consciousness (and thus acts of perception like seeing) and the ultimate. Suggestions of this divide can be found in classical works like the ones we looked at earlier—the Perfection of Wisdom scriptures, Nāgārjuna's "Collections of Reasonings," and so forth. As a formal doctrine the position is associated with Prāsaṅgika, an Indian-inspired philosophical movement that began gaining currency in Tibet in the twelfth century. This school would eventually become the central exoteric viewpoint of the major Tibetan schools. Its assertion that emptiness is beyond the ordinary mind was stated perhaps most iconically by Candrakīrti, in his claim that the ultimate "cannot be taught directly, as it is inexpressible and just not an object of consciousness."[82]

Histories of Prāsaṅgika are difficult to assess, but Tibetans' own religious historiography places it as the principal movement in Indian Mahāyāna thought and traces its beginnings to around the sixth century, in the figures of Buddhapālita and then Candrakīrti. The ideas of these figures are then said to have been passed through a series of luminaries like the eighth-century Śāntideva, and Atiśa (ca. 982–1054), who is credited with bringing them to Tibet. Given this lineage of its now dominant ideology, it would indeed seem strange to find two of Tibet's renaissance tantric traditions advancing claims that were completely contrary to Prāsaṅgika, in their suggestions about how emptiness might be approached with the eyes.

There is, however, a growing consensus among modern scholars that the historical record does not confirm the Tibetan depiction of Prāsaṅgika. The foundational Candrakīrti in fact seems to have been virtually ignored in India until some 300 years after his death; his works, further, were not fully translated in Tibet until the eleventh century, and it was not until the twelfth century that a Prāsaṅgika movement was constructed around him.[83] So, it seems that we should not assume that any of our visionary authors necessarily framed their own thought in terms of an established Prāsaṅgika view, or restricted themselves to stay within its boundaries. Indeed, none of the visionary works examined in this book make mention of Prāsaṅgika or a figure named Candrakīrti, despite their deep involvement in the philosophy of emptiness. Their authors were, on the other hand, certainly aware of more broadly accepted versions of emptiness that acted as foils to their own. In the case of Yumo, for instance, these ideas about the ultimate derive from widely accepted sources like the Perfection of Wisdom and Nāgārjuna, rather than from any Prāsaṅgika doctrine.[84]

It is in fact a testament to how contested and open to interpretation matters about perception and the ultimate were that, at the very same time that Prāsaṅgika began its rise in Tibet, movements within Nyingma, Sarma, and Bön were each experimenting with doctrines that, when it comes to appearances, were precisely its opposite.[85] That is, instead of embracing a formalized doctrine about a remote ultimate, esoteric groups were experimenting with ways to portray emptiness as perceptible and as being continually present in front of our very eyes, but unseen due to the blindness of ignorance.

While these attempts to reconcile the senses and emptiness in some ways appear to be on the fringes of Buddhist thought,[86] they can also be read as variations on the mainstream Buddhist project of finding ways to see or encounter the Buddha. That is, while their descriptions of a perceptible ultimate do speak of it as an abstract emptiness, they also tend to personify that emptiness as an enlightened being like the Great Seal or All Good. A fine example of this is in the fifth chapter of the *Lotus Girl,*[87] Kālacakrapāda's commentary to *Stainless Light*. In the following extract, Kālacakrapāda is looking at a verse of praise from *Stainless Light*'s fifth chapter, in which the deity Kālacakra is described as "one whose atomless emptiness can be observed, and whose kind compassion is not observed."[88] In the course of explaining this line, Kālacakrapāda discusses what is meant by "emptiness"; compare his comments with the Prāsaṅgika emptiness that is "just not an object of consciousness":

> What is this emptiness? This is indicated by the term "observable." That is, it is an object of engagement of the eye sense-power and so forth; it is not a nature that is devoid of all aspects. You might ask: "Since it is not a nonexistent nature, then wouldn't it be an existent nature?" This is dealt with by the term "atomless." Because it is beyond atomic structure, it is not existent. For instance, the things [that are seen] in the dream-period are not nonexistent, as they are experienced directly; but they are also not existent, as they transcend the relationships of "producer and produced" and "apprehender and apprehended." In the same way, the form of emptiness is not nonexistent, because the yogi sees it in direct perception, via the eye sense-power; but it is also not existent, as it does not arise from earth, water, fire, wind, and so forth.

Passages like this demonstrate that advocates of tantric visionary practices are not just making minor alterations or adding formal qualifications to existing theories of emptiness, but are using vision to make their own claims about what emptiness is and trying to find ways to bring it within the boundaries of perception.

Is it legitimate to read these works as actually saying that emptiness can be seen? In the case of Yumo, the answer is clearly yes. His *Lamp* contains repeated claims about a "path" emptiness being an object of the eyes, as well as statements like his concluding prayer that aspires for all beings to "attain the state of a vajra-holder by apprehending emptiness with the eyes."[89] Such direct and iconoclastic statements can perhaps only be made by someone in Yumo's position: an individual who is not representing any institution or sect, who is participating in a diverse and vibrant religious revival, and who can also claim access to esoteric oral instructions. In contrast, works like the *Kālacakra Tantra* and *Stainless Light,* which form the foundations of a major tantric tradition, are somewhat more muted, at least in their language.

Where more traditional presentations of Kālacakra differ from Yumo is that they typically describe how a yogi sees "empty-form" or the "form of emptiness" rather than simply "emptiness." That is, a visionary object is not simply "emptiness" but is emptiness' dimension of form. Empty-form, then, is a type of object that reveals rather than conceals its lack of inherent identity, and that thus provides a visceral experience of emptiness rather than simply providing an absence.

The same general position applies to the Great Perfection, which, in the works examined here, does not claim that a yogi sees "emptiness." Rather, visionary appearances are constituted of an empty awareness, and the dynamic qualities of this awareness result in a luminous display that discloses awareness' own emptiness at the same time that it lights up into appearance. On the other hand, Great Perfection literature very self-consciously refers to such visionary practices with classical Buddhist terms that usually refer to meditation on emptiness. The experience of visionary appearances, for instance, is often called "higher seeing" *(lhag mthong, vipaśyanā),*[90] a term for the Buddhist practice of contemplating no-self or emptiness. The *Twenty-One Nails,* one of the key works in the Bön *Four Cycles* collection, also refers to its four visionary lamps as the "path of seeing" *(mthong lam, darśana-mārga),*[91] a term widely used by Buddhists to refer to the point in "higher seeing" meditation when emptiness is first experienced directly. Echoing this, the commentary to the *Tantra of the Blazing Lamps* often refers to the lamps as the "path of direct perception" *(mngon sum lam).*[92] And it is not uncommon to find passages like the one below, also from the commentary to the *Tantra of the Blazing Lamps,*[93] which describe how a "suchness factor"[94] of the eyes is responsible for perceiving emptiness, much as if the eyes are constituted of a dynamic, knowing emptiness whose duty is to perceive itself:

> Moreover, there is "saṃsāric form," which refers to different shapes, but there is also the "form of reality," which refers to the different [visionary appearances] like latticework, pendants, and so forth. As for the colors of these two: white, red, yellow, green, and blue, as well as the colors of crystal, dust, and so forth, are the different colors pertaining to the side of cyclic existence. The "colors" of reality are its distinct dynamic energies, enlightened qualities, and so forth. Relative to these, the factor of the saṃsāric eye-consciousness collects in aspects of existence and coarse qualities. But the suchness factor of the eyes collects in emptiness, naturelessness, the expanse, awareness, and primordial gnosis.

Comments like these are some of the most memorable features of visionary literature and leave little question that these traditions are intent on encountering emptiness, and doing so in ways that truly involve looking with the eyes. In some ways, the problem of "seeing" emptiness here is mitigated by the use of transcendent faculties of sight (the "suchness factor" here, or the "five eyes"), and also by setting the act of seeing in a monistic context, where empty visionary appearances are not separate from the perceiver and thus not properly "objects." However, more broadly it could also be said that these presentations of emptiness, which favor disclosure over deconstruction and appearance over absence, are influenced by an ethos of vision: they claim that the ultimate is not the purview of an internal insight, and that it can only be correctly and fully encountered by being seen.

CHAPTER 5 | Seeing Light

Lights in the Body

One of the great legacies of the Vajrayāna is its incorporation of the body into the Buddhist path. Esoteric Buddhist groups rejected the ideas that the body was an obstruction, or an object of disgust, or something that necessarily led away from Buddhist ideals. Instead, they championed the use of the body in spiritual practice. In so doing, they helped to promote a group of specialized studies related to the body, including medicine, embryology, yoga, sexuality, and investigations into the process of dying. While Kālacakra and the Great Perfection contain all of these traditional tantric discourses about the body, their interests in luminosity and vision lead them in other directions as well, and result in some distinctive ideas about the body being filled with light.

Writings on dark-retreat and sky-gazing are thus not just about light in dark rooms or in the distant sky but also about luminosity within the body: in its subtle channels, in its energy-wheels, and at its heart. These works even describe the body as lighting up in front of the eyes, a display of its interior accompanying the visions that are seen in the sky. Kālacakra's Great Seal, for instance, is "indivisible in the external world and the body,"[1] her light illuminating the inside of the body just as she manifests in the sky. The Bön commentator Drugyalwa also writes vividly about visions that light up the body:

> Practicing unwaveringly and continuously, the luminosity of awareness manifests directly: ... [externally] wheels of light—their natural glow brilliant and lustrous—become clearly visible without obscuration. As for the body, its inside and outside—the flesh and blood, channels and muscles, the sense faculties and their seats, the vital organs and vessels—become clearly visible without obstruction.[2]

What is happening in these visionary discussions that bring light into the body? Below, we will explore the issue in several ways. First, we will examine an interrelated group of discourses about light shining out of the body and into the sky. These discussions about the externalization of internal lights will allow us to explore some of the traditional claims about sky-gazing, along with some scientific perspectives on the visual appearances that are seen while looking at fields of blue light. Second, we will turn to images of bodies that are composed of light and will look at the idea that light energy is the primary "matter" of both ordinary and transcendent bodies.

Lights in the Eyes

Spontaneity and Motion

Some of the most memorable passages from our texts on dark-retreat and sky-gazing are the descriptions of vision, written from the perspective of practitioners. The Great Perfection literature is especially rich in this regard, with its accounts of lights that (in the traditional description) shine out from the heart, through the eyes, and into the sky. Here is one example from Drugyalwa's work,[3] which describes the initial chaos of light experienced during the stage called the "onset of vision":

> At that time, those visions tumble like water falling from the face of the mountains, or like mercury scattering and beading together: they are unstable, arising and stopping, scattering and coming back together, wavering and quivering. Internally, your experience of one-pointedness is insubstantial, and temporary. As they wax and wane, doubts appear.

Visionary texts are of course not alone in containing these sorts of evocative visual descriptions; classical tantric works in particular are well known for their accounts of visualized Buddhas and divine environments, and sūtras like the *Avataṃsaka* are filled with visual and visionary imagery. One thing that stands out about Drugyalwa's passage is how it depicts objects in motion. Reading works from the Great Perfection and Kālacakra, one sees a difference from the relatively static visualizations and *sādhana*-based practices, in which a practitioner sticks to a script that lays out how to mentally construct a visualization. The alternative offered by visionary yoga is a visual field that is organic, spontaneous, asymmetrical, and filled with movement. The "doubts" that Drugyalwa mentions hint of a sense of chaos that is initially felt, almost as if the showers of light are out of the bounds of what is safe.

The *Vajrapāṇi Commentary,* one of the Kālacakra-inspired "Bodhisattva Commentaries," contains an instructive passage on these intertwined themes of motion, light, the body, and the eyes. Though complicated and written in the typically technical language of a Kālacakra treatise, the passage is worth reading, especially for the ways that it uses moving lights to introduce philosophical concepts. To briefly set up this discussion: in the Kālacakra tradition, visionary appearances are sometimes termed the "moving and unmoving";[4] this term can refer collectively to living beings and their inanimate environment, but here is used to distinguish between abstract visions of light and those that take anthropomorphic form, like deities. In the following passage, the *Vajrapāṇi Commentary* is in the midst of discussing a group of verses from the *Litany of Names of Mañjuśrī,* a work that is a favorite touchstone for the Kālacakra tradition; the verses describe Mañjuśrī as both "having all aspects" and "having no aspects."[5] In its typical way, the *Commentary* takes the *Litany of Names* as an opportunity to digress into the world of Kālacakra theory, in this case applying the language of the *Litany of Names* to Kālacakra's "moving and unmoving" visions, with the underlying intent of revealing how the *Litany*'s language (which does not at all reference Kālacakra) has hidden content related to vision. The *Vajrapāṇi Commentary* reads:

> Vajra-words like [the *Litany*'s phrase] "Having all aspects, having no aspects" [express] the definitive meaning. Here, "Having all aspects, having no aspects" refers to the "unmoving," i.e., that which is seen via withdrawal [yoga]: things like pots, friezes, and so forth that appear in the manner of [the images that arise in] a mirror divination. "Having all aspects" refers to their being known through being seen via direct perception, which is free from conceptuality and unmistaken. "Having no aspects" refers to them as transcending atomic nature, [and thus being known] through that same freedom from conceptuality. Because they are objects realized by [both] covered and uncovered eyes, they are not form, but they are also not something that is other than form. They are not objects realized by the eyes, but they are also not objects that are realized without the eyes.
>
> In that way, "Having all aspects, having no aspects" [also] refers to the "moving," i.e., to the great [goddess] Prajñāpāramitā, emptiness endowed with all supreme aspects.[6]

Here "moving" and "unmoving" both refer to appearances of empty-form (and both technically "move" across the visual field), but the "moving" refers at the same time to a dynamic being (the Great Seal) and to an energetic force that moves the entire universe. That this "moving" entity is also a type of emptiness indicates how useful visionary imagery is in esoteric thought: the emptiness described here is far from being a static absence, but it also is not even bounded by or relative to yogic practice; rather, it is an all-pervasive motivating force that appears and takes shape on its own, just as visions do.

The use of epistemological language here (the definition of "direct perception" as "free from conceptuality and unmistaken"[7] being one of the most recognizable phrases from the Buddhist *pramāṇa* tradition) brings the esoteric matters of vision back to earth, portraying them in the terms of classical Buddhist inquiries into knowing. Technically speaking, neither Kālacakra nor the Great Perfection offers a fully developed visionary epistemology, in the sense they do not make detailed, organized presentations of what types of minds see what types of visions, and so forth.[8] The comment in the *Vajrapāṇi Commentary* about "covered and uncovered eyes,"[9] however, is typical of how both these traditions deal with the role of the eyes in visionary experience. Though the comment is from an Indian Kālacakra work, it resembles a claim frequently made by the Great Perfection, that visionary phenomena can be perceived in darkness or with the eyes closed just as well as they can in the light or with the eyes open. Thus in strict terms, the experience of visions is not dependent on the ordinary eyes (which function while open and in relation to external sources of light), but at the same these experiences would be impossible without the eyes, which serve as its gateways.

The Blue Field: Entoptic Light, Floaters, and Physiology

As the *Vajrapāṇi Commentary* has just suggested, there is a complicated back-and-forth in both these traditions about how "ordinary" the experience of vision is. While it is common to read that vision is an extraordinary sort of seeing, both Kālacakra and the Great Perfection are also careful to maintain a kind of egalitarian stance about vision. That is, the visions they describe can be seen by anyone with an intact sensory system. Vision (at least in its initial stages) does not arise due to skill, blessings, or transcendent realization but simply happens due to the internal dynamics and properties of the ordinary body. Indeed, the basic visionary experiences described by these traditions are prosaic enough that they would not be called into question by ophthalmologists or neurologists, though of course such specialists would give very different explanations of the sources and implications of the visions.

In chapter 4, we looked at some scientific ideas about sensory deprivation that were relevant to practice in the dark. It seems in order here to continue that discussion in terms of light. While the practice of sky-gazing might not seem to be a kind of sensory deprivation, in fact long periods of staring at uniform scenes or fields of light can produce visionary experiences much in the same way as immersion in the dark. The brain appears to need a dynamic, changing input, and when confronted with monotony such as that produced by the empty sky, it can eventually begin to create its own visual imagery.[10] The phenomenon has been reported not just by yogis but also by sailors and airplane pilots, who may spend long periods staring at the sea or the sky.[11]

A few other scientific issues about seeing light are helpful in interpreting the practice of sky-gazing. In particular, it is useful to understand the phenomenon of entoptic ("within the eye") lights that occur when one gazes at a field of blue, like the sky. If you gaze at the open sky, not necessarily in a religious context, you can encounter a previously unseen world of light and motion. The uniform field of blue provides a background against which the internal dynamics of the eyes are projected, and so you are confronted with a blue screen filled with darting streaks of light, slowly drifting blobs, and chains of spots that appear to race along winding pathways. These entoptic appearances are of two basic kinds. The slowly drifting blobs, threads, and concentric circles are "floaters," caused by debris floating in the vitreous humor of the eye.[12] The more quickly moving lights arise from what is called the "blue-field entoptic effect," in which leukocytes (white blood cells) moving through the capillaries of the eyes are perceived as luminous spots.[13] The blue light of the sky creates an environment in which these lights are easily seen, though any uniformly blue field (like a computer screen) will do. The effect is produced when the particular blue light of the sky (at a wavelength of around 430 nanometers) passes through the capillaries in the eye.[14] This blue light tends to be absorbed by the red blood cells that make up most of our blood, and the portion of the retina behind the capillary compensates by becoming slightly more sensitive to blue. When the occasional white cell makes its way through a capillary, it acts as a tiny window, allowing a greater intensity of light to reach the retina behind the capillary. These extra bits of light are perceived as round dots with dark tails, squiggling in series across the sky.

The visionary phenomena that arise in the course of Buddhist sky-gazing are of course more complex and distinctive in their visual character and semantic import than floaters and buzzing lights. Nonetheless, simple entoptic phenomena are among the first appearances encountered by a sky-gazer, and descriptions reminiscent of them appear in Great Perfection works. Here, for instance, is Drugyalwa's account of the "onset of vision," where the concentric circles, squiggles, and linked chains are described in terms of "seminal nuclei" *(thig-le):*

> [Now] crystal-colored *thig-le* of awareness, like little peas, appear within the luminosity. And, there are appearances of larger formations, with two or three [*thig-le*] connected together, or with many

> connected together, and so forth. As well, there are nuclei of awareness called "necklaces of seminal nuclei," which are like silver threads or white silk cords, on which *thig-le,* like peas or grains, are strung in the manner of garlands.[15]

Part of the sky-gazer's task is to deal with the mind's tendency to chase after such objects as they move across the sky. While not forcefully ignoring them, the challenge is to prevent them from becoming focal points that would constrict the basic spaciousness of the mind. Here, much as in dark-retreat, the Great Perfection takes basic features of the body and uses them in the service of its doctrines—in this case their ideal of letting appearances be rather than obsessively chasing after them.

It is of course important not to simply equate sky-gazing appearances with simple entoptic phenomena, even though these may be some of the initial appearances that yogis encounter. Indeed, the full visionary experience brought on by sky-gazing is said to be just as realistic and complex as that brought on by dark-retreat. (Scientists also point to direct connections between visions experienced in dark and light settings, suggesting how the "visual monotony" of a blue field like the sky can act as a kind of sensory deprivation, much like a dark room.)[16] As well, we should not ignore the interpretive perspective of the viewer when considering the significance of the lights he or she sees in the sky. Authors like Drugyalwa indeed do not speak of these appearances in simple physiological terms, but this does not mean that they are unaware that entoptic phenomena are rooted in the body. Rather, in their texts we find images like floating circles that contain subtle or incipient forms of deities[17]—images that resemble entoptic phenomena, but that are said to have divine dimensions. This might be best understood by recalling how Great Perfection texts very commonly describe natural phenomena in terms of underlying transcendent processes. The body's five fingers, five limbs, five internal organs, and so forth, for instance, are often attributed to the agency of the five buddhas (but the five fingers are clearly not asserted as being the five buddhas).

Entoptic phenomena are also described as "gateways" into or "introductions" to the processes that underlie visions. The act of pressing on the eyes[18] is a common example. This manually stimulates the retinas and produces a shower of entoptic light that is easy for anyone to experience. These sorts of visual appearances are referred to as "involving effort" *(rtsol ba can),* meaning that they do not occur spontaneously like dark-retreat or sky-gazing visions but arise based on deliberate activities like squeezing the eye, manually stimulating particular channels, and so forth. They are thus viewed not as marks of accomplishment in yogic practice but as simple ways to introduce a person to the luminous possibilities of the body, or to see sparks from the radiant awareness within.

In a similar way, we might also think of entoptic phenomena as openings for some of the philosophical discussions that surround the practice of sky-gazing. They thus provide an introduction to several of the distinctive ways that these visionary traditions think about light. First, while they are clearly located within the container of the body, they appear as objects in the distant field of the sky, and thus create for the viewer a dissonance between external objects and the inner world. These lights thus serve as an intermediary that brings together the fragmented worlds of "self" and "other," as well as the personal space of the body and the public world. Second, the motion of these lights creates the sense that there is an unseen vibrant dimension behind the objective sphere, or a background energy that underlies appearances. Finally, encountering motion where one expects stasis sets up discussion of the solidity of appearances themselves, in which light is used as a model for explaining how our environment could be devoid of the solidity and concreteness that we attribute to it, but in that absence is still able to appear and function.

Letting the Light Out: Bodily Postures for Inducing Visions

In the Buddhist presentations, vision occurs when the body and eyes are placed in special postures designed to create the optimum conditions for bringing out visions. Drugyalwa describes the necessity for these physical means in a famous line that says:

> A snake has arms and legs, but unless you squeeze it they can't be seen.[19]

The joke here is that if you wring a snake's body, hidden arms and legs might pop out and become evident. The "snake" represents the body of the yogi, with its internal energy channels holding concealed lights; the "squeezing" is the application of physical postures that configure the channels in a way that promotes the flow of internal winds and energies, thus giving rise to visionary experiences that would not otherwise arise.

The various Great Perfection traditions advocate different sets of yogic postures and gazes—the three gazes, the five gazes, and so forth[20]—many with evocative names like the "gaze of the majestic lion"[21] (a crouching posture where the yogi is on all fours, with a straight back and an upward gaze). Facial postures are also applied in vision; Drugyalwa describes several aspects of these, such as rolling the eyes upward and frowning to bring the brow over the eyes, creating a kind of dark horizon at the top of the visual field.[22] In the Kālacakra tradition, instructions on the six yogas call for postures like the "wrathful gaze of Uṣṇīṣa":[23] an upward gaze where the eyelids partly cover the eyes, performed while sitting in the lotus position with hands bound into fists and clenched into the abdomen.[24]

While this focus on physical postures is certainly representative of the general esoteric Buddhist focus on the body, there are some notable departures from the norm. The postures here are relatively simple, and they tend (at least in the Great Perfection and in the first two of Kālacakra's six yogas) to forgo dramatic scenarios like blazing-and-dripping in favor of simply placing the body in a particular configuration and letting it function. The body is thus the foundation of the simplicity and spontaneity of vision, and emphasizes the "ordinariness" of vision, which is not held to be a transcendent peak experience accessible only to advanced yogis but to anyone with a body who applies the proper techniques. Yumo is careful to remind his readers of this aspect of vision. Arguing with an objector who suggests that vision might not be possible for "ordinary beings," he states in no uncertain terms that such beings can indeed see empty-form with the "ordinary eyes."[25] In support of this position he brings up a passage from the *Lotus Girl:*

> The eyes of beginners—the very eyes that see pots, pillars, and so forth—see universal form in the sky, endowed with all aspects. That [form] is not ultimately existent, because it is beyond atomic structure, and because it is not produced through a process involving a "produced object" and a "producer." But still it is not non-existent, because it has the nature of the supreme and unchanging bliss, and because the yogi sees it in the sky.[26]

The comments here exemplify the absence of otherworldly rhetoric that often characterizes these visionary writings. Also notable, the passage uses the ordinary body to return the discussion to matters of exoteric philosophy. Through connecting the body and light, Kālacakra and the Great Perfection both find a way to pursue philosophical thought in a particularly "visionary" way: inspired by standard Buddhist topics (here the issues of subject and object, existence and nonexistence), but treating them in ways that are informed by visual encounters with light. Their methods of course influence their conclusions and lead them away from a dull world of pots and pillars and a rhetorically moderate Middle Way, and into new discussions about inner luminosity and all-pervasive light-energy.

The Matter of Light

The relationship between the immaterial and material worlds is a particular problem for Kālacakra and the Great Perfection, as they propose a transcendent world that is ultimately immaterial or composed of gnosis, but they still want to be able to account for the ordinary world that appears to be made of physical elements and atoms. For both these traditions, light becomes an ideal way to bridge the material and immaterial: it has no solid structure but is still able to take on shape, color, and visible form. In the Great Perfection, light is used to depict the continuum between gnosis and matter, where the full spectrum represents pure awareness, and the five individual colors of the rainbow represent the five elements, or the diversity that arises as awareness passes through the prism of ignorance. Kālacakra has similar concerns, though it leans more toward discussions of atoms than elements, its main project being how to burn those physical atoms away so that the body can be revealed as a luminous empty-form. In both of these cases, light is not just something contained in the body or the physical world but can also represent the fabric of the material world itself; it is not the other side of material or somatic being but is what can move across the registers of the material and immaterial, and thus negotiate between them.

Buddhist uses of light are often marked by a tension between the analogical (e.g., the mind as "illuminating") and the phenomenological (i.e., pointing to actual experiences of light).[27] On the whole, scholars have noted, quite rightly, that the theme of "light" in Buddhist writings tends toward the metaphorical side of this spectrum. Matthew Kapstein, for instance, calls our attention to the fact that even when Buddhist authors describe experiences of light, those experiences ultimately point elsewhere, so that "it is not the experience of light per se that is enlightening, but rather the manner in which that, or for that matter any other experience, is itself understood."[28]

Visionary traditions like Kālacakra and the Great Perfection, however, push back. Very consciously reversing this tendency, their literature abounds with discussions of lights that are experienced with the eyes, and that clearly move out of the metaphorical realm. While carefully maintaining light's metaphorical power, they use light in ways that would lose their main force if they were interpreted only as literary imagery. As an example, take the comment in the *Kālacakra Tantra* that depicts the visionary Great Seal as "displaying the three worlds."[29] One way of reading this is to treat it as a metaphor (and this is indeed an interpretation that Yumo advances).[30] Such a reading plays on the notion that visionary objects point away from themselves and provide examples of the nature of appearances in general: immaterial, insubstantial, fleeting, empty, and intimately related to mind. So, the Great Seal's capacity for "displaying the three worlds" can mean that, by encountering her empty-form, one intimately experiences an object that is empty and yet appears, that is composed of mind and yet seen in the external world. In this way, all the other appearances of the three worlds are "illuminated," or come to be seen in her light.

But what Yumo really relishes, and where he speaks in his fullest voice, is when light actually becomes visible, where the Great Seal *is* the appearances of the three worlds, where she is seen in the sky, and where she literally illuminates the world with her light.[31] Yumo is particularly interested in a strain of thought that deifies such visible light, equating it with radiant goddesses—Viśvamātā, Prajñāpāramitā, the Great Seal—whose empty-form is not just localized in visionary appearances but is said to pervade everywhere and constitute everything. "Displaying the three worlds" thus can also refer to the Great Seal shining forth in the form of beings and their environments, acting as the "creator of appearances"[32] and the source of all phenomena.[33] In this view (and this is not the only model of the universe presented in Kālacakra), the world is ultimately composed of a luminous gnosis that gives rise to the five elements as derivatives of it. Gnosis here comes to be classified as an element (the tradition calls it the "sixth element"); though it is not physical like the other elements, it is the primary building block of the world in the sense that it is the source of all the other elements and pervades everything.[34]

The continuum between gnosis, light, and the elements is also a key concept in the Great Perfection and in many ways is much more developed and explicit there. Both the Seminal Heart and the Oral Tradition from Zhang Zhung contain extensive discussion of the "five lights,"[35] which are the five colors of the rainbow (white, yellow, red, green, and blue) and represent the basic energy of the primordial ground. In the Great Perfection's cosmogony, awareness rises up from the ground and becomes present as these five, splitting up like pure light passing through a prism. The lights thus represent the most basic energy of awareness, which is its fivefold power to take form in appearances.[36]

As the five lights stray from the ground, they dim and become solidified, eventually coalescing into the five elements (earth, water, fire, wind, and space). When cast in the form of the ordinary elements, the luminosity of the five lights is muted, but their basic energy still remains active, resulting in each element having a distinctive power: fire's power to burn, water's power to collect things together, and so on. Based on these powers, the light elements act almost like little bureaucrats, each performing a particular duty in the production and functioning of the body and the material world. *Advice on the Six Lamps* here describes how the lights, which take the form of elements and operate through the power of winds, assist in the assembly of the embryo:

> Then, from the center of the heart, through the creative energy of light and awareness, the winds of the four elements arise, and open up the hollows of the [secondary] channels in the four directions, like tightening the ropes of a tent. Then the four vital organs develop, establishing the "seats" of the four elements. Next, the five elemental limb-winds arise from the five vital organs. They open

up the hollows of channels, and cause the body's five "elemental" limbs to project out.[37]

As they create the body during gestation, the energies of the five lights also add functioning to the sensory system:

> Within the hollows of those five channels is the radiation of the five lights, from which the five vibrant[38] elemental energies respectively arise. This produces the consciousnesses' "powers" *(rtsal)* of discerning their five objects.[39]

As one might suspect, the lights also dwell in potent form at the heart as the somatic incarnation of that originary ground and, given the proper circumstances, shine out of the body to form the multicolored appearances of vision in an echo of the cosmogonic expansion.

Conclusion: Two-in-One

Both Kālacakra and the Great Perfection place emphasis on the experience of vision and thus are traditions where light is not just encountered as a metaphor or as words on the page. Yet because part of the import of these visible experiences is in how they are interpreted, light inevitably circles back to become a matter of writing, theory, and speculation. So while experiences of light are important for these visionary traditions, they also need to cast those esoteric visionary experiences into approved Buddhist frameworks, and this draws them back into the world of texts, writing, and metaphor. Yumo, for instance, is an author intent on moving the issues of light off of the page and into the eyes and the sky, but in order to defend vision as an authentic Buddhist path, he ranges widely through tantric literature and composes a treatise containing textual citations whose words vastly outnumber his own.

When these visionary traditions use light specifically as a literary device, two images often recur: the "moon in water" (seen more frequently here in the Kālacakra sources) and the "sun and its rays" (more typical of our Great Perfection sources). The "moon" image suggests how a single source of illumination can become manifold, like the singular moon shining into multiple vessels of water; the "sun and its rays" covers a similar theme, indicating how countless rays shine from the singular sun but remain connected to their source even in their separation from it. These images get at their authors' primary written uses of light: to suggest how multiplicity and singularity might ultimately be connected.

Theories about how "two" might actually be "one" are of course at the heart of late Buddhist tantra, with its central image of two deities sexually united as one, a "mother" and a "father" who are ultimately indistinguishable. Metaphor is thus a fundamental issue in tantra, if you take metaphor as a way of expressing and experiencing two different things at once, without forcing them into a false conflict or a false resolution. It is in these terms that it is best to think about visionary uses of light, both the written ones and those that take place before the eyes.

Visions of light take the logically senseless ("empty" and "appearing") and make it sensible: they allow opposites to be active at once or to appear at the same time. Light, with its inherent ambiguity—its ability to be both singular and multiple, to be an experience and a metaphor—is thus used to deal with opposites in a way that prevents them from canceling each other out, or having to neatly resolve. This is quite a contrast to the typical exegetical tendency to use metaphor to simplify and domesticate tantric thought, by locking its paradoxical and shocking images into fixed and accepted meanings: "the male deity is compassion," "the female deity is wisdom," and so forth. When these same issues are put in complex, shifting, and mobile experiences of light, the tendency toward closure is averted, so that "two" and "one" can be present at the same time.

CHAPTER 6 | Seeing through Sexuality

Introduction: The Many-Faced Consort

The two preceding chapters focused on the common ground between Kālacakra and the Great Perfection, with the goal of exploring the remarkable similarities of their visionary practices. This may have created the impression of a great consonance between these two traditions, but in fact Kālacakra and the Great Perfection are in other ways quite different. This chapter turns to one of the central points from which they diverge: their values regarding sexuality and the Buddhist tradition of sexual yoga.

The sexual dimensions of Kālacakra and the Great Perfection could be examined from many perspectives, but the one I choose here is to follow the images of *thig-le* ("seminal nuclei") that appear in the literature of these traditions. The term *thig-le* is quite multivalent, so it is revealing to see different ways in which each tradition uses it. *Thig-le,* for instance, commonly refers to coarse sexual fluids or, alternatively, to sexualized energetic components of the subtle body. In visionary contexts, however, *thig-le* are a type of visual appearance: spots or circles of light that appear in the darkness or in the sky. These two types of *thig-le*—the bodily *thig-le* and the visionary *thig-le*—point to a relationship between tantra's sexual practices and its practices of vision, and suggest how Buddhist visionary practices are related to, and sometimes provide alternatives to, Buddhist practices of sexuality.

To understand the relationship between these two types of *thig-le,* it is easiest to start with the more common (and earlier) notion of "bodily" *thig-le* and review the types of sexual practices in which they appear. While esoteric Buddhism contains a real variety of sexual techniques, for our purposes here we can focus on three types: "sacramental," "yogic," and "visualized" sex.[1] The first, "sacramental" sex, is perhaps the most basic of the three. This refers to ritual acts of sex that are not directly associated with yogic physiology (such as inner winds, energies, and so forth). The focus of these practices is on external activities that are performed with the goal of attaining worldly powers and benefits. Scholars like Ronald Davidson have suggested that this appears to be one of the earliest strata of Buddhist sexual practice.[2] Though we have little knowledge about the living traditions that may have used these practices, the surviving literature[3] describes how Buddhist adepts would travel to a secluded area and try to lure a divine female consort for the purposes of sexual union. The consort might be a nonhuman (such as a *yakṣī*) summoned for the event by special mantras, or a human to whom divine qualities were attributed through means such as ritual or visualization. When the couple united, the result was a kind of union with the divine, thought to confer powers or divine properties on the adept. There was also an important product of this union: the resulting *thig-le* were thought to contain potent qualities and were viewed as a sort of divine seed.[4]

For the most part, purely sacramental sex did not become a major part of later esoteric Buddhism. In another form, however, sexuality indeed became a central feature of Buddhist tantric traditions. Particularly in the literature of the "Highest Yoga" *(anuttara-yoga)* tantras, we see descriptions of how sexual arousal causes a gnostic fire (called *caṇḍālī*) to ignite within the body, leading to the motion of internal winds and *thig-le* and ultimately resulting in experiences of bliss and nonconceptuality. This is "yogic" sex, where sexual union is a method for arousing energies within the body and bringing about profound mental states. Even in literature that advocates yogic sex, we can still see fragments of the earlier idea of sex as a sacramental act. These are particularly visible in discussions of initiation ceremonies, which describe sexual rituals that provide purification and power, and which involve exchanges of *thig-le* thought to be infused with divine potency. A passage here from the Kālacakra treatise *Stainless Light*[5] provides an example of how such rituals looked in late tantric literature. In this passage we are told about a suite of four tantric initiations in which a Buddhist teacher has intercourse with a consort, his student drinks the resulting *thig-le,* and the student then unites with the consort:

> First, for this empowerment, the student should offer the teacher a mature girl, who is twelve years old and so forth, and who is free from the flaws of fear, confusion, and so forth. Then, having made supplications and so forth, the student should supplicate the lama with praises of the teaching. Then, the lama, pleased with this, should have the student touch the breasts of his own, worldly, conventional consort. Via this, the vase empowerment [is conferred].
>
> Then, having made the secret offering, the "nectar" is given to the student, and the consort's *bhaga* is revealed to him. Through

> this—experiencing and gazing at the "moon"—the secret empowerment [is conferred].
>
> Next are the insight and gnosis empowerments: with the seed-syllables OṂ and so forth, [she is] endowed with factors [representing] the five [buddha] families.... Then the lama, with the conqueror Vajrasattva acting as a witness, should give the consort to the student, for the purpose of them holding hands and embracing each other. When the student first engages thus, the empowerment is definitively conferred.

Initially, sacramental and yogic uses of sexuality seem to have been driven by cultures of *siddhas* who were either outside of or on the very fringes of normative Buddhism. However, in a process that is still poorly understood, their practices not only found acceptance among esoterically inclined Buddhists but even found their way into literature used at Buddhist monastic institutions despite clashing with the paradigm of celibacy. Buddhists often exhibit a type of conservatism in which, once an idea or practice proves itself, it is granted a sort of tenure and can no longer be completely dismissed. Thus, when it became clear that sexual yoga was a permanent fixture of esoteric Buddhism, the conservative, monastic, and institution-based forms of Buddhism could only develop methods for coping with it. One major coping strategy was rhetorical. Explicitly sexual passages in Vajrayāna texts were treated as referring to metaphorical rather than actual sex or were explained as representing the "union" of classical Buddhist concepts like wisdom and compassion. Alternatively, they might be explained away as special uses of language that were intended to be shocking or revealing, or to appeal to beings in a desirous world.

On the practical level, sexual yoga was often recast as a visualized practice. This marked the turn to a third type of sexuality: "visualized" sex. This practice, which would be more tolerable for monastic Buddhists, no longer required an actual flesh-and-blood consort. Rather, sexual yoga could be an imagined scenario where one visualized oneself as an enlightened buddha in union with an equally divine partner.

A related type of sexualized practice, and the type that I would like to focus on here, becomes evident in late Indian tantric literature, particularly that surrounding the *Three Bodhisattva Commentaries.* Reading these works, we see authors who are interested in abandoning the physical consort but who want more than just an imagination of her as a replacement. It is here that they turn to the Great Seal (or the "Great Consort") who is neither physical nor visualized but who appears spontaneously in vision. A hierarchy that progresses from ordinary consort practice, through visualization and ultimately to vision, is mentioned again and again in Kālacakra literature, in a formula that urges yogis to give up *both* the flesh-and-blood consort (the "action seal") and the visualized consort (the "gnostic seal") in favor of the visionary Great Seal. The *Kālacakra Tantra*[6] urges:

> Abandon the action seal, whose mind has impurities, as well as the gnostic seal, who is imputed.
> To bring about complete enlightenment, meditate [with] the Supreme Seal, the supreme mother who gives birth to the victors!
> The unclothed, unchanging, conqueror of all darkness, as pervasive as the sky—unite [with her] through yoga!
> She is the resplendent primordial gnosis dwelling within the body, which steals away the impurities of ordinary existence, and is realized in Kālacakra.

Characteristically, this passage from the *Kālacakra Tantra* begins to move in a philosophical direction at the very moment that it abandons the traditional consorts. The visionary Great Seal is neither a coarse consort nor an imagined partner but is the great "mother" Prajñāpāramitā, whose embrace is none other than the embrace of all things by emptiness.

There are some suggestions in Kālacakra completion stage writings that the tradition would like to use this visionary Great Seal material in ways that would bypass the traditional sexual paradigm altogether. The first two of Kālacakra's completion stage yogas ("withdrawal" and "meditative concentration") present this possibility: they deal with abstract visionary appearances rather than female consorts and bear little trace of sexuality. As the sequence of six yogas progresses, however, the blazing-and-dripping model of yoga returns, and withdrawal and meditative concentration become incorporated into a more standard sexualized practice, albeit carried out in a visionary (rather than visualized) environment.

Despite the persistent comments about abandoning consorts, and the presence of these two light-based completion stage yogas, it is not clear that the Indian Kālacakra tradition was contemplating tantric yoga devoid of a consort. Even though the alternative Great Seal is not a traditional "consort," she is incorporated seamlessly into the tradition's sexualized practices and is discussed using sexual language and metaphors. Still, it does appear that when Kālacakra began moving into Tibet, some of its new converts were inspired to think about tantra in ways that put the consort far in the background. Yumo, for instance, treats Kālacakra's completion stage, consorts, and its sexualized language in highly abstract terms, discussing the soteriology and philosophical implications of the Great Seal, while leaving aside practices involving the lower consorts and the mechanics of sexual embrace.

But it is the Great Perfection traditions that truly define a tantric path away from the consort. In their works on dark-retreat and sky-gazing, we see visionary practices that look quite like the initial yogas of the

Kālacakra completion stage but that dispense with the consort altogether.[7] Rather than heading for the ordered world of retention, sequential blisses, and stacking *thig-le,* the Great Perfection sets out for a more organic world where *thig-le* are released from the eyes and take their own directions in the sky.

One way of exploring how Kālacakra and the Great Perfection relate practices of "sexuality" and "seeing" is by tracing how "seminal nuclei" are used in their writings and in their practices. In the following, I take up this project, first providing some of the basic meanings and classifications of the Tibetan term *thig-le,* with the goal of suggesting why the term was so attractive to advocates of visionary practice. With this background, we can then explore some specific uses of *thig-le* in the Kālacakra and Great Perfection and see what they might reveal about the relationships between sexual yoga and vision.

Etymologies and Types of *Thig-le:* Seeds, Semen, Sights, and Symbols

Just as Buddhist sexual practices range from the physical to the visionary, so the Tibetan term *thig-le* ("seminal nuclei") has also two sides to it. In many cases, the term references physical "semen" or "seeds," but at other times *thig-le* are simply circular patterns, drops, or spots, such as those seen in vision. I have not encountered any sources that give a historical etymology of the term, but it is possible that these two connotations are actually independent of each other and come together only in the contexts of tantric practices of vision. Creative etymologies of the term *thig-le* do, however, appear frequently in the literature of the Great Perfection. Typically, these state that the first syllable, *thig* (which colloquially means "line"), means "straight" and "unchanging."[8] This is a bit cryptic, given the usual association of *thig-le* with circles rather than straightness. However, it appears to indicate how *thig-le* "emerge straight from within [the body] via the channels,"[9] and suggests how the line forming a *thig-le*'s circling rim is perfect and without variation, such that a smaller circle is a replica of a larger one. The syllable also calls to mind the straight lines *(thig)* that are used to lay out the internal structure of a maṇḍala; this latter sense evokes how *thig-le* are organized circles, providing the lines that organize the world, or acting as blueprints that define things' boundaries.[10] The syllable *le,* then, is etymologized as "spread out" or "pervasive,"[11] indicating how *thig-le* can pervade the body or the sky. There is also the sense here that *thig-le* are applicable everywhere and represent a kind of omnipervasive outline that encompasses and structures the world.

Alongside these speculative ideas that are particular to the Great Perfection are a variety of more broadly used meanings and associations for the Tibetan word *thig-le*. The term thus has a rich multivalence, but it is also difficult to translate because selecting just one of those meanings (as with the popular translation "drop") can be deceptive, as other semantic associations are then elided. Yet, as the following list will suggest, one important feature of *thig-le* is their ability to evoke many of these meanings at a single time.

1. *Nonsexual uses. Thig-le* has a number of meanings that have no sexual overtones. Many of these come from its use as a translation-equivalent for the Sanskrit *bindu,* meaning "a spot," "a drop," "a particle," or "a bit."[12] In this sense, it is also used as the Tibetan word for *anusvāra* (the circular dot that hovers above a Sanskrit syllable, used to indicate a nasal). In a separate usage, Tibetans also use *thig-le* to refer to the "inner essence"[13] of something, indicating the potent part of something, or the "heart essence"[14] of a topic.[15] An additional meaning important to keep in mind for visionary thought is the use of *thig-le* to indicate the number zero; it thus has a symbolic connection with the concepts of emptiness[16] and the sky,[17] both of which are also used as code words for "zero."[18]

2. *Seminal fluid. Thig-le* is the common term, used in ordinary colloquial speech, to refer to "sperm," the male regenerative fluid. The term can also be used more broadly in reference to the father's and mother's respective "white and red" contributions to the production of a fetus; here, the male's "white" contribution is sperm, while the woman's contribution is conceptualized as red uterine blood.[19]

3. *Tantric "seminal potencies." Thig-le* are one element in the triad of "channels, winds, and *thig-le,*" the three main components of the subtle body that constitute the crucial physiological framework for sexual yoga. Here, *thig-le* represent a kind of seminal potency analogous to the ordinary "red and white" regenerative fluids, but which come together to produce an "embryo" that matures into a buddha. In Buddhists' classic sexual yoga paradigm, a subtle wind is used to fan an inner fire burning at the (male) yogi's navel. As the fire blazes up, it melts a reservoir of white *thig-le* stored at his crown, which then drip down his central channel, causing a series of "four joys" as they pass through the forehead, throat, heart, and navel wheels. In union with a consort, the yogi moves the dripping *thig-le* to the tip of his sexual organ, and holds them there; in a process that is rarely described, he then extracts the consort's red *thig-le,* and moves the "fertilized" mixture of red and white back through his urethra. The *thig-le* then ascend the central channel, resulting in another sequence of four joys (this time in reverse), and finally the *thig-le* are distributed throughout the body.

4. *Circular visionary appearances.* In the visionary yogas of Kālacakra and the Great Perfection, *thig-le* are spontaneous visionary appearances experienced with the eyes, which take the form of spots of light. The literature and visual art of the Great Perfection classically presents them as concentric circles that form rainbow-colored halos, often containing the image of a buddha or other iconography.[20] Individual *thig-le* can appear in any number of sizes, numbers, and colors, and also collect together in groups to make geometric formations. Arising independently of any sexual context, these *thig-le* nonetheless retain their "seminal" associations, in that they are seeds of the more structured visions to come. More technically, they are seeds in the sense of being tiny potential residences of Buddhas; in the Great Perfection tradition, visionary *thig-le* ultimately transform into the inestimable mansions[21] of buddhas, a function also suggested by Kālacakra's visionary *thig-le,* which houses a tiny buddha.

5. *Symbolic representations.* Finally, it should be mentioned that the concept of *thig-le* as "circular potencies" or "centers of power" results in a great deal of circle imagery in visionary tantric literature. This is particularly so in the Great Perfection, where a wide array of images—concentric circles, eyes, irises and pupils, peacock feathers, lassos, rings, dishes, beads of mercury, corrals, fences, walled cities, maṇḍalas—often serve to invoke the concept of the *thig-le* and to suggest how a single enlightened awareness operates in spheres large and small.

Ultimately, the function of *thig-le* is to bring together—or, in the language of the Great Perfection, "to round up"[22]—collections of meanings, and thus they are perhaps best seen as circles in which esoteric Buddhists organize or bring together their ideas. A traditional expression of this is found in the *Tantra of the Blazing Lamps,*[23] in a set of verses that classifies the different types of *thig-le,* grouping them into five types:

> The seminal nuclei themselves abiding in the ground
> Round up appearances and fictive beings, cyclic existence and transcendence, into one.
> The seminal nuclei abiding in the channels of the body
> Round up happiness and suffering into one.
> The conventional "causal" seminal nuclei
> Are the cause and conditions for the production of the body and mind,
> Rounding up the aggregates, the [eighteen] sensory spheres, and so forth into one.
> The ultimate unelaborated seminal nuclei
> Round up the expanse and awareness into one.
> The seminal nuclei of the self-emergent fruit
> Round up the wisdom-energy of all the buddhas
> Into the expanse that is free from exertion.

If we think of *thig-le* as circular patterns used to group or organize ideas, they then have a close analog in the form of the maṇḍala. Yet as seen here, *thig-le* function on a more local level, not representing vast structures in which to map out universes, buddhafields, hosts of deities, and divine environments, but as circles that function organically in a given context to bring together sets of opposing issues—the internal and external, emptiness and appearances, cyclic existence and appearance, the body and the universe.

Below I turn to particular instances of these organizing circles, examining the uses of *thig-le* in Kālacakra and then in the Great Perfection. Examining how they are used to organize and address new philosophical concerns in their own particular systems, we will see how these *thig-le* both evoke and evade their own sexual associations. In this way, perhaps we can start to think of them as "rounding up" the seemingly opposed worlds of tantric sexuality and tantric practices of vision.

Kālacakra: Four *Thig-le* in the Body, and One in Vision

In Kālacakra literature, one prominent way of classifying *thig-le* is with a set of four distinct types, which the tradition calls the (1) body, (2) speech, (3) mind, and (4) gnosis *thig-le*.[24] We will have the chance to examine the idiosyncrasies of these below, but to start off we can think of them simply as divisions of the "bodily" *thig-le* commonly found in tantric traditions. That is, they are features of the subtle body and are also manipulated in yoga, using a process that involves moving them into the central energy-channel. Kālacakra's unique project here is to sequentially bring thousands of *thig-le* into the central channel and to "purify" them so that they lose their materiality. In this way, they become the components of a divine body rather than components of an ordinary physical body.

Given this tradition's many complex discussions about thousands of these "bodily" *thig-le,* it is easy to overlook a singular "visionary" *thig-le* that also appears in its literature. Free of any overt sexual connotations, this *thig-le* is not a potency or seed inside the body but is a visual appearance that is seen with the eyes. This *thig-le* is found in descriptions of "withdrawal" and "meditative concentration," the first two stages of Kālacakra's six-limbed yogas. These two stages—to review—are the ones that lay out Kālacakra's basic visionary program of "day" and "night" yogas. As well, they constitute the initial stages of vision where (just as in the Great Perfection) a practitioner sees unstructured appearances of light that in later stages will take form as images of divinities. These abstract visions are the "ten signs," the last of which is a *thig-le:* a "spot" or "seed" of light. The classic description of this sequence of visions is this rather cryptic passage from the *Kālacakra Tantra:*[25]

> With the mind fixed in space and unclosed eyes, the vajra path is entered.[26]
> And thus from the emptiness (1) smoke, (2) a mirage, (3) lights in the clear sky, (4) a butter-lamp flame,
> (5) Blazing, (6) the moon, (7) the sun, (8) vajras, (9) the supreme form, and (10) a *thig-le* come to be seen.
> In the center of that [*thig-le*], is the form of a Buddha, not an object, the Complete Enjoyment Body.
>
> With eyes wide, the yogi should gaze in the cloudless sky
> Until a black line, radiating stainless light, comes to be seen in the channel of time.
> There, the Omniscient Form is seen, [like] the sun [shining] in water, transparent and multi-colored,
> Endowed with all aspects, but not an object—one's own mind, not the mind of another.

These verses are generally interpreted as indicating that the *thig-le*—while technically classified as a "daytime" appearance that is seen in the sky—is also seen in the body, in the central channel.[27] Eventually, a line comes to be seen in the *thig-le,* black and yet blazing with light; within the line, a buddha image then appears.

This visionary appearance is quite different from the *thig-le* that are parts of the subtle body: this one is not deliberately retained in the body, it can appear in the external world, and is luminous rather than substantial. However, it is not an accident that this vision shares a name with the various types of bodily *thig-le,* as it freely borrows associations from them. The visionary *thig-le,* for instance, is clearly a type of seed that contains an incipient buddha. The vision is thus useful for seeing how Kālacakra experimented with the *thig-le* concept outside of an explicitly sexual context. Still, despite the presence of this visionary *thig-le,* it is fair to say that Kālacakra's main uses of the *thig-le* concept are within its more conventionally tantric sexualized practices and involve the interior of the subtle body rather than the exterior visual sphere.

If the *thig-le* in the sky is the most exceptional of Kālacakra's many seminal nuclei, the tradition's most pervasive typology would then be the four *thig-le* (of body, speech, mind, and gnosis). These four are developments on an idea that is common to many Buddhist tantric systems, which is that "red" and "white" *thig-le* (originating, respectively, from one's own mother and father) pervade the entire body, with white *thig-le* particularly concentrated at the head, and red at the navel. The four *thig-le* are then special subsets of these basic *thig-le;* they are material, mustard seed–sized mixtures of the red and white constituents, which contain subtle mind and wind,[28] and are concentrated respectively at the forehead, heart, throat, and navel wheels.[29]

One of the basic ways that Kālacakra uses these *thig-le* is to help explain how ritual and yogic practice could transform the ordinary body into a divine one. That is, ritual initiations and practices like the six-limbed yoga function to purify or transform one's *thig-le,* and it is through that process that a practitioner can become a buddha. As Norsang Gyatso[30] describes:

> Generally, the position of Highest Yoga Tantra is that a basis—a phenomenon within one's own continuum—is transformed into a buddha's enlightened qualities via the path of skillful means. In particular, the *Great Commentary* describes [this basis as] the four *thig-le* of enlightened body, speech, mind, and gnosis. In addition, it explains that these four *thig-le,* in that order, possess the capacities to produce (1) the Nirmāṇakāya and so forth, the form bodies, (2) the Saṃbhogakāya, which possesses all aspects of enlightened speech, (3) the Dharmakāya, the non-conceptual enlightened mind, and (4) the Svabhāvikakāya, the body of great bliss.

In some ways, such explanations of the four *thig-le* read as a physiological version of the buddha-nature theory,[31] where the *thig-le* are seminal forms of a buddha, dwelling in one's body. The Kālacakra tradition does often discuss a sort of dual functioning to these *thig-le,* in which each type of *thig-le* has an ordinary function that it carries out in saṃsāric contexts, and a transcendent function that becomes active when the *thig-le* are acted upon by ritual and yoga. For instance, under ordinary circumstances, the "body" *thig-le* are said to be the potencies that give rise to everyday appearances (and, one would assume, would also give rise to the ordinary body); when transformed, they generate pure appearances, such as the visionary appearances of empty-form.[32] Likewise, the "speech" *thig-le* are said to produce the dyad of impure and pure speech, the "mind" *thig-le* produce the dyad of "unclear"[33] and transcendent nonconceptuality, and the "gnosis" *thig-le* produce ordinary and supreme bliss.

Kālacakra also tends to map the four *thig-le* on to all sorts of fourfold psychophysical functions, where the *thig-le* act like little bureaucrats whose duties are to keep the body and mind running. For instance, each of the four *thig-le* are given responsibility for producing one of the "four periods"[34] of consciousness: the four basic states of waking, dream, deep sleep, and bliss.[35] Thus the "body" *thig-le,* which predominate at the forehead energy-wheel, are said to give rise to the waking state when the wind energies (and the minds that they carry) are concentrated at the forehead. Similarly, when the wind energies concentrate at the throat, heart, and navel energy-wheels, the respective states of dream, deep sleep, and bliss arise due to the speech, mind, and gnosis *thig-le.*

Kālacakra also uses the four *thig-le* as major features of its ritual and yogic practices. The tradition's seven lower initiations, for instance, are each designed to purify one of the four classes of *thig-le* (see table 6.1). Similarly, the four "higher" initiations, as well as the four "highest" initiations (which have the same names as the "higher" ones), are also specifically directed at purifying the four *thig-le*.

In these fourfold initiations, as well as in key Kālacakra yogic practices, the basic method of transforming the four *thig-le* is by employing "bliss" or "joy." This bliss is produced through the classic blazing-and-dripping type of yoga, in which a reservoir of *thig-le* at the crown is melted, drips down through four energy wheels, and produces a corresponding experience of four types of bliss. The four types of bliss serve to purify or activate the four *thig-le,* with the process of blazing-and-dripping taking on the special significance of burning away the material aspects of *thig-le* so they become less substantial. The ultimate transformation of the four *thig-le* takes place in "concentration" yoga, the last of the six yogas, where 21,600 moments of bliss finally destroy the material aspect of the *thig-le.* With their destruction, the four states of the ordinary mind (waking, dream, deep sleep, and bliss) vanish, as do the ordinary winds and karmic potencies that they contain. This marks the attainment of buddhahood.

TABLE 6.1 Concepts Associated with the Four *Thig-le*

	BODY *THIG-LE*	SPEECH *THIG-LE*	MIND *THIG-LE*	GNOSIS *THIG-LE*
Location	forehead wheel	throat wheel	heart wheel	navel wheel
Period	waking	dream	deep sleep	fourth/bliss
Impure function	impure appearances	impure speech	unclear non-conceptuality	sexual bliss
Pure function	pure appearances	buddha-speech	non-conceptuality	supreme bliss
Resulting body	Nirmāṇakāya	Saṃbhogakāya	Dharmakāya	Svabhāvikakāya
Lower initiations	water, crown	crown pendant, vajra-and-bell	vajra-conduct, name	permission
Higher/Highest Initiations	vase	secret	insight	gnosis
Four joys	joy	supreme joy	extraordinary joy	innate joy

This table is based on VP 5.120 (Bu vol. 3, VP ch. 5, p. 48a.1ff.); the *Vajrapāṇi Commentary* (D1402, p. 127a.3ff.); Norsang Gyatso, *Ornament of Stainless Light* (trans. Kilty), 183ff., 395ff.; Gyatso, Tenzin, and Jeffrey Hopkins, *The Kālacakra Tantra: Rite of Initiation for the Stage of Generation* (London: Wisdom Publications, 1989), 120, 260; and Wallace *Inner Kālacakra,* 158, 189ff, 201ff.

The multiple roles in which the Kālacakra tradition casts its *thig-le*—as producers of appearances, dreams, speech, babies, bliss, confused minds, buddha-bodies, and so forth—suggest how *thig-le* are not simply "seeds" but are also central points around which ideas, rituals, and contemplative practices are organized. Seen in this way, we might think of them as containers for a tradition's central values. In the case of Kālacakra, it is possible to see how the tradition contains two different centers, represented by its two contrasting types of *thig-le*: one bodily and one visionary. It might seem that these two would have to remain as separate spheres, but in the case of Kālacakra, the two grow together, forming concentric circles. Rather than simply competing with tantric practices of sexuality, the tradition's visionary values transform the sexual paradigm. Sexualized yoga thus comes to be entwined with visionary encounters, so that in ideal circumstances it is free of physical or imagined consorts, who are abandoned in favor of a luminous Great Seal. It is this circle of visionary ideals that Yumo addresses as Kālacakra moves into Tibet.

The Great Perfection: Five *Thig-le*

Great Perfection authors show a true exuberance for the concept of *thig-le,* and their writings contain a host of classification schemes, functions, and typologies of *thig-le*.[36] Many of these types of *thig-le* are related to vision, luminosity, or the pristine dynamics of the ground, and bring with them a polemic suggesting that the Great Perfection was superior to more conventional tantric movements, whose sexualized *thig-le* kept them stuck in the realm of bodily substances and consorts.

At the center of the Great Perfection's varied notions of *thig-le* is a simple idea that would have also been familiar to proponents of Kālacakra: ordinary "seminal" *thig-le* are simply the coarse correlates of higher-level, transcendent *thig-le,* the latter being energetic potencies contained in the body that can develop into the qualities of a buddha. The Seminal Heart tradition refers to these two types of *thig-le* as "conventional" and "ultimate" *thig-le*; the same dyad is found in the Oral Tradition of Zhang Zhung, under the names "bodily" and "mental" *thig-le*.[37]

The term "conventional" *thig-le* refers partially to the ordinary red and white regenerative constituents, but mainly references the subtle-body correlates of those, the *thig-le* that are used in the Buddhist blazing-and-dripping practices involving sexual consorts. Great Perfection traditions declare again and again that this kind of sexualized tantra is not the true spiritual path, saying that those practices are simply a kind of efficacious means, designed to gradually lead beings of lower abilities to the distinctive techniques of the Great Perfection.[38] The Great Perfection then casts itself as oriented toward the "ultimate" *thig-le,* as in this classic passage from the *Tantra of Unimpeded Sound:*[39]

> By relying on the ultimate *thig-le,*
> You discover the objects of the empty Reality Body.
> Stimulating the "lamp of the empty seminal nuclei"
> You train in the dynamics of awareness.
> If you practice meditation day and night,
> These [*thig-le*] manifest directly without any effort.

The *thig-le* described here are of course the nuclei of buddhas hidden within the human body. What distinguishes them from other such "buddha-nature" theories is that these seeds tend to grow into luminous visions, projecting images of themselves into the sky as concentric circles.

An expansive treatment of *thig-le* in the Great Perfection tradition is found in our *Tantra of the Blazing Lamps,*[40] whose presentation of the "empty seminal nuclei lamp" discusses a fivefold typology of *thig-le:*

> The seminal nuclei *(thig-le)* themselves abiding in the ground
> Round up appearances and fictive beings, cyclic existence and transcendence, into one.
> The seminal nuclei abiding in the channels of the body
> Round up happiness and suffering into one.
> The conventional "causal" seminal nuclei
> Are the cause and conditions for the production of the body and mind,
> Rounding up the aggregates, the [eighteen] sensory spheres, and so forth into one.
> The ultimate unelaborated seminal nuclei
> Round up the expanse and awareness into one.
> The seminal nuclei of the self-emergent fruit
> Round up the wisdom-energy of all the buddhas
> Into the expanse that is free from exertion.

This provides a succinct list of the different ways that the Great Perfection thinks of *thig-le.* The first of these, (1) the "*thig-le* abiding in the ground," refers to the ground itself, cast as *thig-le,* and represents the ambiguous, energetic potential within every individual that can manifest itself as either the enlightened qualities of a buddha or the various types of ignorance. (2) The "*thig-le* abiding in the channels of the body" are the subtle-body *thig-le,* which course through the energy channels, and which are the focal points of tantric yogas. (3) The "conventional 'causal' *thig-le*" are the basic white-and-red constituents that a male and female contribute to the formation of an embryo. (4) The "ultimate unelaborated *thig-le*" are the transcendent *thig-le,* differing from the "ground" *thig-le* in that they are not an indeterminate energy but the exclusively pure potential for beings to recognize and reconnect with awareness. Finally, (5) the "*thig-le* of the self-emergent fruit" are the *thig-le* operative in vision, which light up in the sky as circles of light and serve as the seeds of more elaborate visions and of one's own ultimate recognition.

These final visionary *thig-le* are one of the most distinctive features of the Great Perfection, emblems of what the tradition views as its triumph over the sexual paradigm, and at the same time evidence of its deep debt to it. Descriptions of these visionary lights are also some of the most evocative features of Great Perfection literature; this passage from Drugyalwa's *Six Lamps* commentary[41] describes a yogic encounter with a chaos of light and *thig-le* and hints at the fears and uncertainties it brings on:

> Having unwaveringly trained awareness on those earlier visions and brought them into your meditative experience, [now] crystal-colored *thig-le* of awareness, like little peas, appear within the luminosity. And, there are appearances of larger formations, with two or three [*thig-le*] connected together, or with many connected together, and so forth. As well, there are nuclei of awareness called "necklaces of *thig-le,*" which are like silver threads or white silk cords, on which *thig-le,* like peas or grains, are strung in the manner of garlands. At the center of each of those *thig-le* dwells the tiny forms of a deity-body, just slightly bulging out of its hollow.
>
> At that time, those visions tumble like water falling from the face of the mountains, or like mercury scattering and beading together: they are unstable, arising and stopping, scattering and coming back together, wavering and quivering. Internally, your experience of one-pointedness is insubstantial, and temporary. As they wax and wane, doubts appear....

As these visions progress, the movement of the *thig-le* is said to calm, and they appear in a variety of forms and aspects: clustering together in patterns, forming strings,[42] congregating in abstract maṇḍalas, appearing in varied colors, and containing abstract images or the forms of deities. As is seen here, they often house buddhas, and thus are incipient maṇḍalas or divine mansions, but are also described as "seeds of the Form Bodies and the source of the buddhafields."[43]

In the Great Perfection, one of the underlying functions of these visionary *thig-le* is to recenter esoteric Buddhism, moving its focal point away from the tactile to the visual, from the experience of bliss to the experience of recognition. In so doing, the luminous *thig-le* make an implicit critique of sexualized tantric practices, equating them with deliberate effort and conceptuality. The visionary *thig-le* transgress the chief tantric regulation about *thig-le,* which is to guard stringently against "losing" them, that is, to hold them in the body even at moments of intense bliss. *Stainless*

Light repeatedly reminds us of the importance of non-emission, accusing those who lose their *thig-le* of being animals or, as here,[44] ridiculing them for their fruitless practice:

> What will increase the bliss of one who loses his white [semen]
> When meeting with his insight[-woman]?
> From what will the mango's fruit arise
> If its buds fall when meeting with the spring?

In one of the Great Perfection's more subtle critiques of tantra, the tradition advocates the precise opposite of the doctrine of retention: relaxing and letting the *thig-le* go, releasing them from the eyes into the sky. The move from the inside to the outside is in fact one of the main features of these visionary *thig-le,* which not only function as containers—of bodies, buddhas, ideas, energies, and so forth—but also put those contents on display so they can be seen, recognized, and function in the external world. This seems to be the suggestion behind one final etymology of *thig-le,* here from Vimalamitra's commentary to the *Tantra of Unimpeded Sound:*[45]

> *Thig* means "to create arrays," [a function] that arises in conventional and ultimate ways. *Le* means "to conceive and uphold." Via the conventional [*thig-le*], cyclic existence is perceived, and via the ultimate [*thig-le*], perceptions of transcendence are brought about.

Here the syllable *thig* (again playing on the meaning "line") is said to indicate that *thig-le* are entities that create patterns, organizations, or arrays[46]: they array themselves in geometric forms in the sky but also act as the deep organizing principles of the universe. The syllable *le* is treated with a complex wordplay, which points to *thig-le* as functioning to "create perception" *('dzin par byed),* putting their contents on display so they can be apprehended in the world. By the same token, they are not just displays waiting to be perceived but are the very forces that "actively uphold" or "actively maintain" *('dzin par byed)* the world, indicating how they are fragments of the very awareness that underlies both cyclic existence and transcendence.

Conclusion: Coming Full Circle

One of the distinguishing features of the Great Perfection's visionary practices is their ability to stay in contact with tantric ideas, all the while distancing themselves from tantra's hallmark practices of sexuality. Yet even as the dark-retreat and sky-gazing bypass the consort, the Great Perfection still keeps the concept of *thig-le.* Why retain this most sexualized of images? A similar question could be asked about the Kālacakra tradition: Why does its completion stage initially set a course that seems to head away from sexual practices, only to return to the consort's embrace?

In the Tibetan sources we have been examining here, it turns out that sexuality is not so much about a physical, erotic encounter between two beings as it is about the concepts and ideas that such encounters evoke, along with the results that they ultimately bring about. Yumo, for instance, writes his lengthy *Lamp* as a description of a "Great Consort" but hardly mentions the mechanics that an encounter with her (sexual or otherwise) might entail. Yumo's approach remains thoroughly tantric, but there is a great distance between him and the early Indian "sacramental" approaches to sexuality, which were more focused on the power of physical union itself. In Yumo, much as in the Great Perfection, we find a kind of intellectualized sexuality that takes precedence over esoteric sexual behavior.[47]

This approach to sex also allows them to think through ideas that are more difficult to contemplate in other contexts, as if sexuality provides a key set of metaphors or creates a radical backdrop in front of which controversial topics look more plain. For an example of this, we could think about the issue of the creation of the world, a topic that Buddhists in most other contexts try to avoid. In the Vajrayāna, however, the issues inherent in sexuality and its related *thig-le* become circles in which Buddhists are able to imagine the possibility of creation, as they begin to speculate on how the cosmos might be conceived in and arise from various fertile wombs: the Great Seal, Prajñāpāramitā, or the Great Perfection's motherly "ground." These issues of conception, gestation, and birth also allow these traditions to develop their abiding interests in embodiment, leading to new ideas about how bodies, both mundane and transcendent, are produced and grow. Circling all of these topics are *thig-le,* which act as forces that create and maintain the body, and which can also unleash the potential for it to be transformed or transcended.

Again, here it is not so much the act of sex as its language that is important, and this points to one final way of understanding the staying power of sexuality in the visionary systems that would seem to want to abandon it. Buddhists often use literature to think with, such that creative development is inspired by concepts inscribed in their past, even if those creative developments take different directions than the ones suggested in their sources. Sexual language and practice dominated the esoteric traditions from which these visionary systems arose. For Kālacakra, whose broader tradition was so steeped in the sexualized body, it seems natural that its "withdrawal" and "meditative concentration" yogas would be incorporated into the larger discourse, so that its final attainment would involve seeing but be accomplished via sexuality. For the Great Perfection, however, sexuality was not just something to see with but to see past; though they may have been able to see beyond consort practice, the language of union, seeds, birth, and nakedness was too productive to be abandoned, and it was via these ideas, rooted in sexuality, that they saw into their own future.

Conclusion

Circles and Straight Lines

I began this study with the idea of dialogue and set out to portray three groups—Sarma, Nyingma, and Bön—in a way that reveals a conversation they once had over the topic of vision. As we have seen, this interaction is not recorded overtly in their literature but is discernible through the interconnected themes, ideas, and yogic techniques that collect around their practices of seeing. History, unfortunately, prevents us from knowing the particular moments, places, and people involved in this dialogue, and this in turn complicates our ability to judge whether their meetings were direct or indirect, open or deliberately concealed, and whether these meetings later were purposefully hidden or simply forgotten.

Certainly their dialogue remains hidden today. During my research I traveled through Tibet, Nepal, India, and the United States, speaking to heirs of each of these visionary traditions; some of these scholars were vibrant and open, others reticent and secret; some were engaged with and in full command of their traditions, and for others ideas and practices of vision were antiquities whose relevance and lineages had faded. Nonetheless, I became convinced that these traditions are very much alive. However, I also realized the ways that they remain isolated from each other. While the broader traditions in which my informants participated—Sarma, Nyingma, and Bön—are currently in broad social and intellectual contact, when it comes to esoteric matters of vision, in my personal experience I found none of them to be in active dialogue.

In my study here, it has thus been up to the literature of these traditions to reveal the nature of their former conversations. As a way of concluding, I would like to experiment with taking two final images from this literature—the images of the "common ground" and of Kālacakra's *thig-le* bisected by a black line—and seeing if these images can illuminate their traditions' connection, or if they further conceal it.

As we have seen, the Great Perfection's concept called the "common ground" is the idea that a single matrix or "ground" produces both saṃsāra and nirvāṇa, and so indicates how a single source might give rise to worlds that diverge and become alienated, even as they may remain right next to each other. In some ways I have found this "common ground" to be a useful image for thinking about the divergence and spread of these three very different visionary traditions, even as they hold to a common central core. Using this model, Kālacakra's "six yogas" tradition could be seen as the source and inspiration for the Great Perfection traditions of vision: entering Tibet during the renaissance, the yogas were broken apart, reinterpreted to suit different settings, and those reinterpretations eventually became distant enough from their source that their former associations were forgotten. I certainly think this view is valid for understanding some aspects of these traditions' relations, particularly for their most concrete common ground, which is their unusual set of yogas involving the sky and the dark-room. But ultimately I find this approach dissatisfying because it searches not for connections but for a final source, and in so doing puts that source beyond scrutiny, in a place where it cannot be observed: the eleventh-century Indian Kālacakra movement, about whose living tradition virtually nothing is known. In so doing, it evades the complicated fact that traditions like Bön and Nyingma have histories of their own, that are not simply derived from others, even if those histories are fragmentary or beyond recovery.

Still, it does appear that Kālacakra was the first major tradition to integrate these yogas of light and dark into a widespread, written Buddhist program, though given Kālacakra's breadth it is important to remember that vision is simply a fragment of the tradition rather than the whole, and that fragment itself came from parts that are presently unknown. It is this image, of a fragment of a tradition that escapes—crossing a "black line" or a boundary—and is then absorbed by others in fragments, that to me better fits the complex interaction of the visionary sources examined here. Rather than being transmitted or copied as a concrete tradition or doctrine, the visionary model found in Kālacakra and the Great Perfection instead seems to have spread as a coherent group of experiences and themes, which are both organized into and actively reorganize the traditions that adopt them. Thought of as the seeds of traditions, or as circles of concepts with the potential to organize themselves into different forms depending on the perspective from which they are regarded, the visionary exchanges between these traditions begin to resemble *thig-le*. And just as visionary *thig-le* are at once internal and external, so these visionary religious traditions can be seen to develop from internal and external inspirations, all the while being moved by visionary experiences that rise up from a source that they all share, which is the ground of the human body.

My hope now is that readers will be able to turn to the translations of primary sources from the Kālacakra, Nyingma, and Bön traditions, prepared with an understanding of their main ideas, and also with an interest in listening to the voices of these compelling writers.

PART III | Seeing Sources

TRANSLATION 1 | *Lamp Illuminating Emptiness* by Yumo Mikyo Dorjé

Bibliographic Information and Notes on Editions

At present, I know of only one published manuscript of Yumo's complete *Cycle of the Four Radiant Lamps.* This is a copy of a handwritten manuscript, published by Palace Monastery in Gangtok, Sikkim. I refer to this edition of Yumo as YM-SG, in reference to its publisher Sherab Gyaltsen. Though it is now widely available in libraries, the author is misidentified, so it appears in catalogs under the name A-wa-dhū-ti-pa Btsun-pa Bsod-nams. This manuscript is quite a rare document, but it is very prone to errors; to complicate matters, printing imperfections result in a few illegible sections. Fortunately, another manuscript of the *Lamp Illuminating Emptiness* has recently surfaced (this does not include Yumo's other three Lamps). The provenance of this is currently unknown,[1] but it may be several centuries old and could possibly have been from the library at Drepung. This manuscript (which I simply call YM) corrects many of the errors of the Gangtok edition, and having a second source to confirm unusual and difficult passages has removed many questions from the task of translation. Yumo's *Cycle of the Four Illuminating Lamps* has also been published in book format;[2] this edition appears to be based on the above manuscripts and contains a number of annotations that will be useful to readers.

Textual Problems and Translation Practices

The state of Yumo's *Lamp* is in many ways typical of Tibet's religious literature, which at times is fragmentary and damaged. If both editions are used, the text becomes quite readable, but questions still remain, and the work poses some serious challenges that need to be briefly noted here. The main issue is simply the large number of errors that have crept into the manuscripts, presumably from centuries of imperfect copying. These are more than just the occasional misspelling: the sources of citations are sometimes misidentified, whole lines are occasionally missing from verse quotations, and so forth. The common scribal errors themselves can easily send the reader down the wrong path, in what is already a difficult work.

The good news is that, because the bulk of Yumo's work is citations taken from translations of Indian works that would later become canonical, many of the problems can be cleared up by the (laborious) process of locating the citations in the Tibetan Kangyur and Tengyur. One problem with this method, however, is that Yumo lived at a time of intense translation activity, so the translations that he personally worked from often differ from the ones that eventually made it into the canon. A good example of this can be seen in Yumo's citations from the *Kālacakra Tantra,* his most important source. The Tibetan translation of the tantra that Yumo worked from is no longer available,[3] so when citations of the tantra in the manuscript are questionable (which is frequently), the reader is forced to refer to one of the available translations of the tantra, which may be slightly different in meaning from the one that Yumo used.

The problems with the manuscripts make it difficult to construct a critical edition (a process I do not attempt), but, more important, they occasionally thwart the reader's desire to know precisely what Yumo understood from his sources. My own efforts at navigating these problems have been guided by the following methods. First, I compiled the two available versions of the *Lamp* into a single edition, so that I could easily read them together. I then sourced Yumo's voluminous citations in the Dergé edition of the Tibetan canon and put the Dergé rendering of those passages in my edition as well.

This clears up many of the problems, but two issues remain. First is how to deal with citations where Yumo's text seems mistaken, but where his source translation differs from the available ones. In these cases, my main assumption has been that Yumo understood the sources that he read, and that he worked from materials that were clear to him. Thus, translating a nonsensical passage just because it is there on the page in Yumo's extant manuscripts is clearly more misleading than translating from a source that varies in minor ways from the one that Yumo originally used. Where I have made translations based on outside sources (usually the Dergé canon), I have explained this in the endnotes and tried to produce a clear translation influenced by what is in Yumo's work, but referring primarily to the more reliable edition.

The second issue is with Yumo's own words, which cannot be independently verified in other texts. Most of the problems with these are cleared up by comparing the two editions and deciding between variants based on an overall understanding of Yumo's text. For these, my intention has been to follow YM wherever possible, as it is simply more reliable. Yumo's words still do occasionally remain obscure, and the occasional interlinear notes *(mchan 'grel)* in YM are evidence that his text was occasionally cryptic even for his target audience; in these cases, I provide a literal translation, give the Tibetan in the notes, and offer my own interpretive comments.

Conventions and Translation Practices

Use of editions: Aside from the issues noted above, the translation is based on YM. When I read from YM-SG this is mentioned in the notes.

Subheads: Yumo's text contains basic headings that specify which words from the *Kālacakra Tantra* he is discussing. I have used these, but I have also added a few other headings, which should be understood as my additions to the text.

Page numbers: Page numbers supplied in [brackets] refer to the pagination of the YM edition.

The *Lamp Illuminating Emptiness*

by Yumo Mikyo Dorjé

[614] *Homage to Mañjughoṣa! Homage to Kurukullā!*

I constantly bow with respect at the lotus feet of the Jetsün,[4]
Who removes the great poison of bad views through the nectar of his advice,
Who cuts away the vines of conceptuality at their roots,
Who clears away the dense darkness of ignorance, and brings the hidden meaning of the tantras to light.

I bow to the Reality Body, completely pure of the stains of conceptuality, like the sky;
To the Enjoyment Body, which teaches the doctrine in all languages at once, with a single voice;
To the Emanation Body, which teaches whatever is needed for the sake of beings with different inclinations;
And to the Essential Body, the identity of the four bodies:[5] to Kālacakra!

Statement of Intent: The Path of Secret Mantra

The path of secret mantra is what the Able Ones concealed in the tantras. Sealed with the "six parameters,"[6] it is the Word of the lamas that contains profound [language] and the definitive meaning. Its meaning remained obscure to beings like those born in Magadha—to people who attained fame as scholars—even as they focused their minds on it. So, what need to mention those people from borderlands, with their weaker minds and made-up views, which are outside of the true ones [that appear] via the kindness of the true lamas? Here, in dependence on [citations from] tantras and on [my] understanding, I will thoroughly analyze this object of investigation,[7] using an understanding that has abandoned its afflictions. [615]

Characteristics of the Mantra Vehicle

The mantra vehicle (1) has clearly been taught as being the supreme path, (2) is the ultimate vehicle, (3) is the essence of the teachings of the Transcendent Victor, and (4) brings about complete liberation through its distinctive methods.

(1) You might ask: How is it clearly taught to be the supreme path? As the *Supplement to the Guhyasamāja Tantra*[8] says:

> Having understood its classifications,[9]
> The supreme *siddhi* will be accomplished.

Through other [methods], even the protector Buddhas
Could not give rise
To peace, the supreme attainment,
In ten million eons [of effort].

This expresses the definitive meaning: buddhahood will not be attained, even in ten-thousand million years, through other systems that do not understand this great secret of the Supreme Yoga.

(2) Why is it the ultimate of all the vehicles? It is the one that makes the Gnosis Body of all the buddhas become manifest. This is stated in the *Litany of Names of Mañjuśrī,* in the fifteenth verse of the "Praise of the Gnosis [of Equality]":[10]

Through the methods of the various vehicles,
He realizes the aims of beings. [616]
Though his renunciation is from the three vehicles,
He abides in the fruit of the single vehicle.

That is, only this vehicle leads to the fruit of the attainment of buddhahood.

(3) Is it really the essence of the teachings? As Nāgārjuna[11] himself said:

Of the 84,000 heaps of dharma
Taught by the Great Muni,
The characteristic of manifest enlightenment
Was taught as the essence that comes from the essence.

And:[12]

For one who does not discover
The stage of self-blessing,[13]
His [other] efforts, at sūtra, tantra,
And conceptual thought, will be senseless.

That is, among the teachings of the Transcendent Victor, the secret-mantra vehicle is like *ghee,* which is the essence of butter.

(4) And how is it a distinctive method for bringing about liberation? As was stated in the glorious *Guhyasamāja Tantra:*[14]

Outcastes, flutemakers,[15] and so forth,
People who have committed the five heinous crimes—
By following the practices of mantra,
Will become buddhas in this life.

This explains that [tantra] is a method that can bring about liberation, even for someone who has committed the five heinous crimes. [617]

Nāgārjuna says:[16]

> At the stage of self-blessing,
> The identity of the chief of all buddhas is attained.
> In this very life, a Buddha [body]
> Will undoubtedly be attained.

This describes it as a method for making quick progress.

Approaching the Ultimate[17] says:

> Like fire coming from wood, and water from pure water-crystal,
> Like butter from yogurt, and metals from ore,
> So undefiled bliss comes from uniting with the genitals of a woman.
> Take up that activity of union, the method of the fortunate ones!

And the glorious *Hevajra Tantra*[18] also states:

> Just like fire is applied
> To the body of someone burned by fire,[19]
> In the same way, desire itself
> Can completely heal the burns of desire.
>
> The wild activities of beings
> Are the things that bind them.
> But when combined with skillful means,
> They bring liberation from the bonds of existence.

Here, it is said that [tantra is] a superior method because it turns the afflictions themselves into the path. In other tantras, it is said to have the most methods, to be free of difficulties, to be quick, and so forth. There are unfathomable numbers of such explanations, [618] and though I could elaborate on them, for now I will just leave it here.

◎ ◎ ◎

You might ask: "What does 'mantra' refer to?" It refers to emptiness and compassion. As the *Supplement to the Guhyasamāja Tantra*[20] asks:

> What is adamantine mantra?

It gives the answer:[21]

> The syllable *man* means "mind," and
> The syllable *tra* means "protector."

Through this statement, "mantra" should be understood as something that "protects the mind." This explanation is an etymology;[22] as for the meaning, the same tantra says:[23]

> "Adamantine protector of all"
> Explains the activity of mantra.

Here "adamantine" refer to emptiness, while "protector of all" refers to compassion. Thus, "emptiness and compassion" explain the term "mantra."

Further, regarding this topic, the Transcendent Victor[24] said:

> Tantra should be understood through other tantras.

To continue, the *Hevajra Tantra*[25] asks:

> What does *He* mean?
> And what does *vajra* mean?

It answers:

> *He* means "great compassion,"
> And *vajra* refers to "insight."

Thus, *vajra* refers to "emptiness," while *He* is a way of calling out. *He* indicates the "protector of all," and so refers to "great compassion."[26] [619]

With respect to those, emptiness and compassion are the "basis of explanation" *(gleng gzhi)*[27] of all the tantras. "Explanation" *(gleng)* means to "express" *(smra),* and "basis" *(gzhi)* is a type of "cause" *(rgyu).* Thus "basis of explanation" *(gleng gzhi)* means "cause for which something is expressed" *(smra rgyu).*

Further, here [in the *Hevajra Tantra*] it is said that the basis of explanation of the tantras is the syllables *E-VAM. Hevajra's* chapter on the "Basis of Explanation"[28] also describes the basis of explanation as being "union" *(sdom pa),* explaining that this union is indicated in the syllables *E-VAM:*

> The union of all the Buddhas
> Is renowned as the syllables *E-VAM.*

You might wonder: "Since the subject matter is explained as being *E-VAM,* does that mean it is not explained as being 'emptiness and compassion'?" In fact, it is explained [that way]. *Stainless Light*[29] says:

> The syllable *E* and the syllable *VAM* indicate the essence of the enlightened mind, in which (1) emptiness endowed with all aspects, and (2) compassion that is not prejudiced in favor of any particular object[30] are indivisible. The syllables *E* and *VAM* are Vajrasattva, the enlightened mind, Kālacakra, the Ādibuddha, the beings possessing method and insight, the yogis for whom the nature of knowledge and objects of knowledge are indivisible, peace without beginning or end, [620] Māyajala,[31] and Saṃvara. The yogi should understand all of these, and similar terms, as indicating the "uncaused" yoga in which the identity of method and insight are nondual.

Accordingly, *E-VAM* is the cause leading to the expression of the tantras, and *E-VAM* is emptiness and compassion.

This is how "mantra" should be understood!

An Exposition of Emptiness

In this context, what is "emptiness"? Arrogant scholars mostly say: "It is the abiding reality *(gnas lugs)* of phenomena," or "It is the reality *(chos nyid)* of phenomena," or "It is things being empty of inherent nature," or "not being established by way of their own entity," or "being unproduced from the beginning," or "being free from the extremes of existence, non-existence, both, or neither," or that it is the "complete pacification of all elaborations." And they claim that understanding things in this way is the path! But I do not accept that. That is an [intellectual] determination[32] of the abiding reality of things, and thus is the "view," an explanation of tenets. But it is not the object of meditation on the "path," [which is described in] the stages of the oral instructions.

You might object: "This contradicts the teachings of all of the Middle Way treatises, like Nāgārjuna's 'Collections of Reasoning,' and so forth, [which state] that enlightenment is attained by determining that things are empty of inherent nature, and then familiarizing oneself with that." [621] [I reply:] The determination of things as being empty of inherent nature is a truth; indeed, that determination is the "view."

You might object: "Does this mean that [emptiness] is not the object of meditation?" That is not the case. If that were so, it would be [like] the three tenets of the hearers, which assert existence and consequently involve meditation on atomic particles.[33] If you accept this, it would contradict the path involving meditation on four noble truths.[34]

Further, you might object: "This contradicts the *Entry into Suchness,*[35] which says:

> The view of emptiness leads to liberation:
> The various meditations are all for the sake of that.

[I reply:] That is [referring to] the "view," the intellectually determined emptiness,[36] and one is not liberated by meditatively becoming familiar with that. This should be understood from the statement that "through meditating on the emptiness that is a path, liberation comes about."[37]

Well then, what is the problem with meditating on that intellectually determined view? This [type of meditation] has been repudiated in the tantras. As it is said:[38]

> Śākyamuni, the Tathāgata,
> Wishing to attain manifest enlightenment,
> Gave rise to the thought: "Through great emptiness
> I will attain buddhahood!"
> He then sat on the banks of the Nairañjana River,
> Dwelling in the unwavering *samādhi*. [622]

At that time, the Conquerors[39] dwelling in the sky's expanse
[Appeared,] like seeds filling a sesame pod.
Snapping their fingers, in a single voice
They said to the Conquerors' Son:

"This [unwavering] concentration is not the pure one;
And through it you will not attain the final goal!
Contemplate the supreme 'brilliance,'[40]
Which is like the canopy of the sky!"

This refutation is also found in the *Tathāgata Saṃgra Tantra.* Thus, it should be clear that determining a view and then merely adhering to it without letting the mind waver, is not the path! When Lokeśvara[41] uses the term "emptiness," [however,] he is referring to this ["path" emptiness], as can be understood in detail through the Gnosis chapter [of *Stainless Light*].

Further, something that is a "path" must be understood *and* experienced. It is not acceptable to say that the "emptiness of inherent nature" is understood and experienced, because it doesn't become an object of the mind.[42] A buddha's gnosis is conventional truth.[43] If something is to become an object of that, it is unsuitable for it to be intrinsically established, because it is established as the object of gnosis.[44] Anything formulated with conceptual thought is an elaboration; because of being conceptual, they do not become objects [of the mind].

You might object: "It is said that 'not seeing anything at all, suchness is seen'; [623] thus, non-understanding is itself the supreme understanding." [I reply:] Although [the supreme understanding] has been given that name, there is no such experience. The path-emptiness is something that can be experienced, and this is an absolute necessity. Below, I will explain this.

You may ask: "Well then, if things' abiding reality as expressed in the 'view'—their emptiness of inherent nature—is [simply] an intellectual determination, then what is the necessity for the [Buddha's] teaching that things are empty of inherent nature?" There is a great necessity for it, as explained in the *Vajra Tent:*[45]

If emptiness is your method,
Then you will not become a buddha.
Because effects are not separate from causes,
Method is not emptiness!

Because it overturns wrong views and
The self-grasping of those
Who follow the view of self,
The conquerors taught emptiness.

That is, because [the teaching of emptiness] overturns the craving for concrete things, the afflictions are controlled by depending on it, and so forth. Thus it should be understood as having unfathomable benefit. For this reason, the Transcendent Victor[46] said:

> Whoever understands this doctrine of "nothing at all,"
> Will not become attached to any phenomena. [624]

Further, if all phenomena were not empty of inherent nature, how could the attainment of complete enlightenment ever come about, as one's inherent essence could not turn into something else?[47] This was also stated by Ārya Nāgārjuna[48] himself:

> Wherever there is emptiness, there all worldly and otherworldly aims will come about.

The point was also made by the Transcendent Victor in the *Perfection of Wisdom*[49] scriptures:

> Subhūti! If all phenomena were not empty of inherent nature, then the bodhisattva-mahāsattvas could not attain manifest complete buddhahood through training in and accomplishing the Perfection of Wisdom that leads to unsurpassed, perfect, complete enlightenment. But because all phenomena are empty of inherent nature, the bodhisattva-mahāsattvas can attain manifest complete buddhahood through training in and accomplishing the Perfection of Wisdom that leads to unsurpassed, perfect, complete enlightenment.

Here, it should be understood that "all phenomena being empty of inherent nature" indicates the "view," while "training in the Perfection of Wisdom" correlates to the esoteric instructions. [625]

You may ask: "What then is the underlying intention of saying that enlightenment is attained if things are realized as being empty of inherent nature—devoid of production or cessation, permanence or nihilism, going or coming?" The intention [is to refer to] the emptiness that is a path.[50] Ārya Nāgārjuna[51] said:

> The vajra-like *samādhi,*
> The completion stage itself, and
> The illusion-like *samādhi*
> Are said to be without duality.[52]
>
> The terms like "unproduced" and so forth
> Indicate the nondual gnosis:[53]
> They are all its "expressers."
> This is not explained elsewhere!

> The buddhas of the three times,
> As numerous as the sands of the Ganges,
> Accomplished the identity of the Great Seal [via] this very [*samādhi*],[54]
> Which abandons the positions of "existence" and "non-existence."

Further, Kālacakrapāda[55] stated:

> Here, "emptiness" is referring to "observable emptiness" *(dmigs pa dang bcas pa'i stong pa nyid)*. Because this creates the cognition of the nature of all things, it is called "gnosis" *(ye shes)*. Through this gnosis whose nature is emptiness, a saṃsāric cognition becomes pure, one which is non-conceptual in nature. Because this is unmoving, undiminishing, [626] and at all times dwells in the nature of self-awareness, it is called "unchanging." This is then known as the Co-emergent Body *(lhan cig skyes pa'i sku)*.

This point is also made in the *Vajrapāṇi Commentary:*[56]

> Because they are objects realized by both closed and un-closed eyes, they are not form, [and they are also not something other than form]. They are not objects engaged by the eyes, and they are not realized by something else. In that way, ["Having all aspects, having no aspects" also] refers to the "moving," i.e., to Prajñāpāramitā and the great emptiness endowed with the supreme of all aspects.

On this same topic, *Stainless Light*[57] says:

> [The yogi] sees emptiness with all aspects *(rnam pa thams cad pa'i stong pa nyid)* everywhere in the sphere of sky: unproduced phenomena that are like prognostic images in a mirror. He considers these as dream objects, distinct appearances elaborated by his own mind. This casts away (a) the emptiness [that follows from] the analysis of phenomena as being aggregates of atomic particles, and (b) the nihilistic emptiness. He desires the phenomenon of internal bliss, which is his own awareness.

Thus, it should be understood that (a) the emptiness that follows from logical analysis, and (b) the nihilistic emptiness [627] are not the path!

A Commentary on the *Kālacakra Tantra,* Verse 4.198

What then is this "emptiness that is a path"? Other sources will not clarify it, but it is spoken of clearly in verse 198 of the "Methods of Accomplishment" chapter of the *Śrī Kālacakra Tantra,*[58] the condensed King of Tantras, in which insight and method are nondual:

> The *mudrā* is like an illusion, [appearing] in the sky and the mind, like a form in a mirror,

Displaying the three worlds, emanating rays like stainless lightning.
Indivisible in the external world and the body, [she is] not an object, and dwells in the sky, a mere appearance.
The nature of mind and that which comes from mind, embracing all migrating beings, one in the guise of many!

That is its meaning in brief. [Below,] I will unravel it fully.

Comments on "The *mudrā*..."

Here, a *mudrā* is something that performs the action of applying a seal. [The Great Seal is so called] because she applies the seal of unchanging bliss, uncontaminated joy, and unreferenced compassion.[59] [628] The *Root Kālacakra Tantra*[60] says, further:

> The forms that emerge from emptiness are the cause;
> The effect is the bliss produced from the "unchanging."
> The effect seals the cause,
> And the cause seals the effect.
>
> The apprehension of empty-forms is the cause.
> The effect is apprehending [with] unchanging compassion.
> Emptiness and compassion are indivisible.
> This is what is meant by "enlightened mind."

The characteristics of this *mudrā* were described by Kālacakrapāda.[61] As he said:

> The *mudrā* who "seals" unsurpassed enlightenment is beyond existence and non-existence, and is thus said to be "like an illusion." Take the example of a singular form that is [reflected in] a mirror: it is seen in the mirror, appearing [there] while remaining in its former place. The external concrete thing is not what appears in the mirror, because that stays in its place. Still, [the reflection] is nothing but that [physical object], because that [reflection] appears like that [physical object]. In the same way, a yogi, through the power of continually meditating on the six-limbed yoga, [629] will see the form of emptiness,[62] endowed with all aspects, appearing externally in the sky, and, similarly, will see them internally via the mind sense-faculty.

That same [*mudrā*] is [the goddess] Prajñāpāramitā. As the *Lotus Girl* says:[63]

> The *mudrā* is Prajñāpāramitā, the one who gives birth to all the tathāgatas of the past, future, and present. Because she seals the utterly non-located nirvāṇa, or the bliss of non-emission, she is called "Seal." Because she is more distinguished than the Action

and Gnostic *mudrās,* and because she is free of any karmic predispositions related to cyclic existence, she is called "Great."

The one who gives birth to the buddhas was spoken of in the *Kālacakra Tantra:*[64]

> Through desire for the Great Seal,
> Bliss arises, which is produced from the "similar cause."
> Thus, that [bliss] that is similar to [its] cause
> Is the empowerment conferred by the Great Seal.
>
> [She] should be known as the mother who gives birth to all Protectors,
> The mistress of the nine types of beings.

Stainless Light[65] also says:

> I bow to Viśvamātā, [630]
> Who gives birth to all the buddhas,
> Who has abandoned birth and destruction,
> Whose conduct is all good!

The *Perfection of Wisdom*[66] scriptures also state:

> Subhūti! The bodhisattvas' [activities of] giving and so forth involve elaborations, so be aware that they are [just] ornaments. Ultimately, the *dharmadhātu* is the mother of the victors!

You may ask: "Doesn't that [term "Great Seal" actually] refer to the *dharmadhātu,* to freedom from elaborations, to the abiding reality of things?"[67] That is not the case. This is explained in the "Accomplishment of Supreme and Unchanging Gnosis" section [of *Stainless Light*],[68] where it is described by way of an enumeration of its names:

> The Great Seal is the defining characteristic of all phenomena, their lack of inherent nature. It is [also] endowed with all supreme aspects, and is Prajñāpāramitā, the mother who gives birth to all the buddhas. It is also expressed by the term "source of phenomena" *(chos 'byung).* "Source of phenomena" should be understood as meaning "that from which all phenomena arise without having any inherent nature." Natureless phenomena [include] the ten powers, the four fearlessnesses, and so forth, and the heap of [the Buddha's] 84,000 doctrines. [631] Because those arise [from the Great Seal, she is] the source of phenomena, the buddhafield, the residence of the bodhisattvas, the abode of bliss, and the site of birth.

Elsewhere, *Stainless Light*[69] says:

> For example, among [the terms] "woman," "young lady," and so forth, the name "woman" is not the chief one, as all [the other

synonyms] also indicate "an existent that has hair and breasts." In the same way, from among the secret names such as the "syllable *E*,"[70] "great secret," "lotus," "source of phenomena," the "space element," "abode of great bliss," "lion throne," and "*bhaga*," the "syllable *E*" is not the chief one, as all of them also refer to emptiness of the omniscient ones.

The *Gnosis Vajra Compendium Tantra*[71] also says:

> As for "lotus," [it refers to] the "*bhaga*." Vajra terms like "insight," "*mudrā*," and "royal concubine" are [its] definitive meaning.

The same source[72] also says:

> Conventionally, it becomes clearly present as the symbols of a woman, a lotus, a *bhaga*, and hosts of goddesses.

The *Vajrapāṇi Commentary*[73] also enumerates the names of this [*mudrā*]. [632] As it says:

> This also has many names: "*E*," "*bhaga*," "lotus," "abode of bliss," "blissful realm," "lion-throne," "without reference," "thatness," and "Prajñāpāramitā." Those are the basis.

The same source[74] also states:

> The basis is Prajñāpāramitā,
> Called the "source of all aspects."

Further, the emptiness that is the "abiding reality of things" is not something that can become an object that is seen with the eyes. But this [*mudrā*] who has universal form and arises from the mind can become an object of engagement of the eyes, just like a form does. As the *Root Kālacakra Tantra*[75] says:

> With the two eyes not opened, not closed,
> The one who, in the emptiness, does not make imputations
> Will see forms, like images in a dream.
> Meditate continually on those forms!

The same source[76] states:

> In a young girl's prognostic mirror,
> A previously unseen thief is seen.
> Having gone there, the officiant can see [him]
> With his two ordinary eyes.[77]
>
> If [the girl] sees an existent form [in the mirror],
> Why doesn't she see her own face?

If she sees a non-existent form,
Why isn't it the horns of a rabbit?[78] [633]

She doesn't see with "other" eyes,
But she also doesn't see with her own.
What she sees is unborn,
Just like the son of a virgin.

Elsewhere it mentions:[79]

Liberated [from] form and non-form,
Like a prognostic image in a mirror.

Further, the *Glorious Thig-le of the Great Seal Tantra*[80] says:

Listen you Great Seal goddesses,
Who have the supreme aspect of intense bliss!
The Great Seal is the supreme secret,
Inexpressible, inexhaustible, unborn.
Having all forms and free of form,
The supreme identity: formless form!
Free of being fat, being thin, and the like,
In nature [she] is indestructible.

For those reasons, [the *mudrā*] is not "form" because of not being composed of atoms, but also is not formless, because of being seen with the eyes. This is also stated in *Stainless Light:*[81]

I bow to the Great Seal,
Who is beyond atomic reality,
Whose nature is like an image in a prognostic mirror,
Who is endowed with all supreme aspects! [634]

And *Thig-le of the Great Seal*[82] clearly states that this same Great Seal—not composed of atoms, yet still visible to the eyes like a prognostic image—is Prajñāpāramitā:[83]

[The *mudrā*'s] six symbolic ornaments—
Earrings, bracelets, wheels,
Necklaces, ashes, and Brahma's thread—
Are reminders of the six perfections:
Giving, morality, patience, effort,
Concentration, and insight.

Giving is teaching the doctrine.
Morality is being mindful of karma.
Patience is remembering the commitments.
Effort should be known as [referring to] *samādhi*.

Concentration is being mindful of gnosis, and
Insight *(prajñā)* is the Great Seal.
Ultimately, that is how they should be understood.

When that Prajñāpāramitā becomes an object of the eyes, it is called an "observable emptiness."[84] As the *Lotus Girl*[85] says:

Here, "conquerors" refers to the transcendent victors Vairocana and so forth. The transcendent victor Vajrasattva is their "lord," so he is called the "supreme" one. His "consort" is the Great Seal, [635] whose nature is that of an observable emptiness. Because she is more distinguished than the "action" consort and so forth, and because she confers unsurpassed enlightenment, she is known as the "excellent consort."

You might object: "If something were to be 'observable,' wouldn't that make it conceptual? It is unacceptable to say that non-conceptual gnosis arises from conceptuality." That is not the case. As chapter 4, verse 199, of the *Condensed Kālacakra Tantra*[86] explains:

Abandon the action seal, whose mind has impurities, as well as the gnostic seal, who is imputed.
To bring about complete enlightenment, meditate [with] the Supreme Seal, the supreme mother who gives birth to the victors!
The unclothed, unchanging, conqueror of all darkness, as pervasive as the sky—unite [with her] through yoga!
She is the resplendent primordial gnosis dwelling within the body, which steals away the impurities of ordinary existence, and is realized in Kālacakra.

Based on this, [it is evident that] the conceptual imputations of the generation stage, the [energy] wheels, the threads,[87] the mystic fire, the channels and winds, the *nādas,* [636] the classes of sounds, the lights, hand-implements, and seed-syllables, *thig-le* and subtle yoga, and so forth—are not the path to the accomplishment of complete enlightenment. Rather, seeing while making no conceptual imputations should be understood as the path.[88] *Stainless Light*[89] adds:

Likewise, this apparition *(snang ba)* of the mind
Will not be seen through conceptual meditative techniques.

This same source states:[90]

Having cast away the "action" seal,
And abandoned the "gnostic" seal,
Pure [bliss] arises from the Great Seal!
It is innate, not associated with others.

The unchanging bliss of the Great Seal,
Is beyond conceptual meditations,
And has no need for subjects, objects,
Shapes, thoughts, or expressions.

[She] has the aspect of a city of gandharvas,
The nature of an image in a prognostic mirror!

And the *Ādibuddha Tantra*[91] also says:

Meditation on the formless
Is not the meditation performed by [true] yogis.
In the emptiness, they see without imputation,
And so [the objects that appear] are not thought of as things or non-things.

Based on those [citations], [637] it should be understood that this [*mudrā*] is a non-conceptual path.

You might wonder: "What is attained via the 'action' seal and the 'gnostic' seal?" This is explained in *Stainless Light:*[92]

> The "action" seal is one who has breasts and hair. The "gnostic" seal is one that is imputed by your mind. The "Great" Seal is separate from all conceptuality, a woman whose form is like a prognostic image. The siddhis related to them are threefold: the siddhi of the "action" seal is an experience of the desire [realm]; the siddhi of the "gnostic" seal has the characteristic of the form existence; the siddhi of the Great Seal is separate from things and non-things, and is endowed with all supreme aspects.

These are the siddhis that are attained.

You may object: "This contradicts what is said in the tantras, that the siddhi of the Great Seal will be attained even through the 'action' seal and so forth." [638] Those [tantras] speak in consideration of other topics, and in other contexts, so I will not go into them in detail here.

Then you might wonder: "If it is the case that [the "action" and "gnostic" seals] are not causes for complete enlightenment, then it is not suitable for them to be [included] among the Buddha's teachings at all." There is no such problem. This is just like the *Expression of Auspiciousness Sūtra* that was taught to the merchants Trapuṣa and Bhallika,[93] or like bodhisattvas engaging in all of the worldly arts, crafts, and conventions, but doing so for the sake of accomplishing the temporary happiness of sentient beings. Thus, in accordance with the levels of minds of sentient beings, [the lower consorts] were also taught in order to accomplish the worldly happiness of beings. This is also similar to explanations found in the *Avatamsaka Sūtra.*

To continue, in saṃsāra this Great Seal appears as subjects and objects, but in nirvāṇa is the maṇḍala circle, the five gnoses, and so forth. This is explained in the fourth chapter of the latter part of the *Hevajra Tantra:*[94]

In the completion stage yogas [639]
She is the bhagavatī, the "insight-woman."

Not long or short,
Not square or round,
Beyond smell, taste, and flavor—
She is the creator of the innate joy!

The yogi who arises through her,
Savors her bliss.
With her, the siddhi that bestows
The bliss of the Great Seal comes about.

Form, sound, and also smell,
Taste, as well as touch,
And the nature of the *dharmadhātu*—
They are analyzed with this "insight."[95]

She is the form of the innate,
The excellent yoginī of great bliss.
She is the maṇḍala circle,
And has the nature of the five gnoses:

She is the form of the mirror-like gnosis,
The actuality of the gnosis of equality,
The true individually discriminating [gnosis],
The [gnosis] that is effacious,

And the pure [gnosis] of the *dharmadhātu*.
She is me, the Lord of the Maṇḍala,
And she is Nairātmyā, the Yoginī.[96]
She possesses the nature of the *dharmadhātu*.

In that way, this [*mudrā*] is Prajñāpāramitā, appearing in the form of emptiness, beyond atomic structure, and symbolized by the letter *A*. In saṃsāra [she] is known as "ignorance,"[97] [640] while in nirvāṇa she is known as the "Mother of all the Conquerors." This very [*mudrā*] is mentioned in the *Litany of the Names of Mañjuśrī,*[98] in [the verses] praising the *vajradhātu* [*maṇḍala*]:

The Buddha, the Transcendent Victor,
The Complete Buddha, arisen from the letter *A*.

Enough with elaborations![99]

Again, because [the *mudrā*] pervades the limits of the 10 million world systems and creates their appearances, [she] "seals" them, and thus is called the "Great Seal." As the yoginī tantra *Thig-le of the Great Seal*[100] says:

> Goddess! When you dwell
> In the petals of the "emanation" wheel at the navel,
> Then you are known as "insight."
> What a delight! How supreme! What a wonder!
>
> You dwell in union, nondually, with me:
> O Heroine! What a delight!
> From the realm of Brahma, the limits of the 10 million [worlds]
> Are sealed by you. What a wonder!
>
> Sealing countless numbers [of beings],
> You are renowned as the Great Seal! [641]

If all those [citations] were to be summarized, it would indicate the following: Because of sealing the fruit, because of sealing unsurpassed enlightenment, and because of sealing the external and internal, [this *mudrā*] is called the "Great Seal." Because of producing the buddhas and all their enlightened qualities, [she] is called "Mother of the Conquerors."

Comments on "Like an illusion..."

This means "similar to" an illusion. To expand on this, the mahāyoga tantra *Gnosis Vajra Compendium*[101] says:

> Accordingly, the tathāgatas [in] buddhafields as numerous as the sands of the river Ganges are like illusions, like the moon reflected in water, like reflections, like mirages, like dreams, like echoes, like gandharvas' cities, like optical illusions, like rainbows, like lightning, like water bubbles, and like reflections in a mirror. These twelve analogies for illusions illustrate the *samādhi* of great bliss.

You might ask: "Aren't those [simply referring to] the seeing of some particular enlightened qualities via a particular *samādhi*?"[102] This is not the case. *Stainless Light*[103] explains:

> [The Great Seal] is the object that completely destroys the obscurations of the five aggregates [642] and so forth. [She] is like the eight prognostic images.[104]

You may wonder: "How do you know that this [term "illusion"] refers to the form of emptiness, Prajñāpāramitā?" It should be known through the detailed explanations in the bodhisattva Vajragarbha's *Commentary [to the Hevajra Tantra]:*[105]

> [Her] individual appearances are established through nine examples. These are: a reflection, a magical image, an echo, a dream, the illusion of a wheel, a mirage, a reflection in a mirror, the moon reflected in water, and the sky. She is "insight" *(prajñā)* and the letter *E.*[106]

To continue, *Ultimate Letters*[107] says:

> Friends! What appears to the mind
> Is external, apprehended in the mind via colors.
> The illusory yogi is beyond examples,
> And reflects well only on this!

You might ask: "How do you know that this [term "illusion"] also refers to the Great Seal?" The bodhisattva Vajrapāṇi[108] has said:

> The Transcendent Victor said that [in] meditation, the Great Seal appears in the cloudless sky, like an image cast in a prognostic mirror, or an illusion. [643]

Nāgārjuna also makes this point in the *Five Stages:*[109]

> Here in this vajra vehicle, much is explained,
> But what is [truly] necessary?
> Whatever [phenomena] the yogi observes,
> Those he should think of as illusions.
>
> Whoever sees things as reflections in a mirror,
> Dreams, illusions, water bubbles,
> And optical illusions,
> He is said to be "chief."
>
> Whatever is seen and touched—
> The world—is like an illusion.
> Conventionalities devoid of reference points
> Are said to be "like illusions."

The same source[110] also says:

> The characteristics demonstrated as "illusions"
> Precisely illustrate this:
> The illusion of conventional truth
> And also the Complete Enjoyment Body.
>
> That itself is a gandharva being.
> The Vajra Body is also that.

[The term "illusion" also refers to] things that are not composed of atoms but are still able to be seen, like the moon reflected in water. *Thig-le of the Great Seal*[111] says:

The *dharmadhātu* is renowned as the "*bhaga*"!
The *bhaga* is the precious vessel,
Containing the good qualities of Iśvara and so forth.
That is renowned as the *bhaga* everywhere.

Dharma [644] indicates "*bhaga,*"
And *dhātu* should be understood as "mind."
[Everything] in the limitless realms of sentient beings,
Has "mind" as its cause.

In its conventional forms, it is seen
Like the moon reflected in water.

You might object: "What the twelve examples of illusion illustrate is how things appear to cognition during 'post attainment,' or how one believes things to be during the 'yoga of activity,' after arising from *samādhi*."[112] That is not the case. Rather, they are what constitutes the equipoise-phase of *samādhi*.[113] As Āryadeva said in the *Lamp Integrating the Practices:*[114]

> When one is perfectly familiar with the radiances and prototypes, classified by the winds upon which they ride, just as they are, then at that time one arrives at the *samādhi* of the mind[-vajra]. Dwelling in complete knowledge of the mind, pure and just as it is, one enters [the stage of] "conventional truth," via the twelve examples of illusion. When one is equipoised in the "illusion-like" *samādhi,* at that time one attains the empowerment of the buddhas.

You may wonder: "Isn't the intention of that [illusion-like] *samādhi* comparable to (a) training in [645] a conceptual deity-body, or (b) [considering] objects of the mental consciousness as being 'like illusions,' as arising in the aspect of generic images?"[115] This is not the case. As Āryadeva's *On Purifying Mental Obscurations*[116] says:

In a stainless mirror,
A stainless eye perceives forms,
Pure in nature and stainless,
With complete clarity.

It is the same for a yogi:
In the stainless mirror of gnosis,
In a virtuous mind cleared of the net of conceptuality,
Gnosis is clearly evident.

Here it is indicated that [gnosis] shines forth clearly when not cloaked in conceptuality, [so the *samādhi*] is not conceptual.[117]

Comments on "In the sky..."

This refers to seeing that form of emptiness, equal in extent to the sky. This should be understood as indicating that, once stability is obtained, the Great Seal is seen pervading to the limits that the sky pervades. The sādhana chapter of the *Condensed [Kālacakra] Tantra* says:[118]

> Abandon the action seal, whose mind has impurities, as well as the gnostic seal, who is imputed.
> To bring about complete enlightenment, meditate [with] the Supreme Seal, the supreme mother who gives birth to the victors! [646]
> The unclothed, unchanging, conqueror of all darkness, as pervasive as the sky—unite [with her] through yoga!
> She is the resplendent primordial gnosis dwelling within the body, which steals away the impurities of ordinary existence, and is realized in Kālacakra.

This point is also made by Saraha in his *Ultimate Letters:*[119]

> Forms predisposed by a great bliss that is aware of itself,
> At that time all become equal with the sky.

This refers to empty-forms, purified of karmic predispositions, born from the great bliss in which one is aware of one's own mind. Those are what is equal in extent with the sky! Moreover, the *Accomplishment of Primordial Gnosis*[120] says:

> The Great Vajra pervades all,
> Dwells in all of the sky,
> Pervades the mind of all beings,
> And is the great source of all merit.
>
> Pervading here and there, the Vajra Possessor,
> The all-knowing guide of the world:
> This is the conqueror Vajradhara,
> Spoken of in all the tantras.
>
> Whoever has the kindness of the lama,
> He will attain the best of those.

The enlightened qualities should also be understood as they are stated in that scripture.

You may ask: "If the Transcendent Victor said that understanding all phenomena to be like the sky [647] leads to the attainments of liberation and omniscience, is that Great Seal similar in characteristics to the sky?"[121] [She] is completely similar. As it says in the *Later Hevajra Tantra:*[122]

> Without you, all the three realms
> Would be like a person without a head.
>
> You shine the light of gnosis
> In countless world systems.
> Everything, every nature
> Of all things, all occurrences, and
>
> All phenomena, are thoroughly known by you.
> And so you are renowned as the Omniscient One.
> Moreover, Goddess, your kindness
> Is inexpressible, the authentic truth.
>
> Through your kindness, you acquire
> The state of countless Tathāgatas.
> You come from the state of the sky,
> And you return to the state of that supreme sky:
>
> The supreme sky is your own condition!
> You rest in the ease of the supreme sky!
> You always dwell in the supreme sky!
> Your conventional [form], supreme in aspect,
> Is like a garland of lotuses.[123]

Here, it is stated with perfect clarity: the cause of omniscience is nothing but this.[124]

Comments on "In the mind..."

This refers to the Great Seal appearing in the form of emptiness; further, this is your mind-itself, manifesting as the cause, the path, and the fruit. [648] The condensed king of tantras, the *Kālacakra Tantra,*[125] elaborates:

> There, the Omniscient Form is seen, [like] the sun [shining] in water, transparent and multicolored,
> Endowed with all aspects, but not an object—one's own mind, not the mind of another.

Regarding the meaning of this, the bodhisattva Lokanātha says "not the mind of another" means that "one does not know via the mind of another."[126]

To continue, *Stainless Light*[127] says:

> The apprehended objects are like appearances in a mirror, like prognostic images: those are "gnosis," the mind as an object of apprehension. That is the meaning.

Further, the *Litany of Names of Mañjuśrī,*[128] in the third verse praising the individually discriminating gnosis, says:

> He is profound: formless but [with] excellent form,
> Endowed with universal form arisen from the mind.
> He is the glory of all forms' appearance, and
> Bears all illusions, without exception.

The glorious *Ādibuddha Tantra*[129] also says:

> An unproduced and unceasing
> Object of knowledge is seen here.
> While classified as an external object of knowledge, [649]
> It is from your own mind, not elsewhere.

You may object: "Doesn't this just mean: 'While the unproduced and unceasing *dharmadhātu* is ultimately devoid of inherent establishment, conventionally it appears as subjects and objects, which are [simply] manifestations of your mind'?"[130] That is not the case. The same source[131] states:

> Uniting with the daughter of a barren woman
> In a dream indeed produces bliss.
> So too, intimacy with the one
> Who is a form arisen from the sky.

The *dohās*[132] also say:

> Meeting with a beautiful lady that never existed,
> Your dreaming mind is elated without a ground.
> Don't see your body and mind as different,
> And at that time, the buddha will be at hand.

Approaching the Ultimate[133] says:

> Through the power of mental carelessness, the sufferings of hell,
> And through mental kindness, the bliss of liberation.
> Dream images—who made them?
> Happiness and suffering—through whose kindness does one attain them?
> Demons are your own mind, there are no other demons.
> So too with the tathāgatas: tathāgatas [650] are nowhere else!

The *Lotus Girl*[134] also states:

> For instance, in a mirror your eyes see the eyes' reflection. In the same way, the appearance of your mind is seen with your mind. That is the ultimate insight-gnosis, not the proper union of the *bhaga* and *liṅga.*

Further, this same source[135] mentions:

> The Great Seal, whose nature is the form of emptiness, is merely a manifestation of your mind, not an external, concrete thing; this is because [she] is yourself appearing to yourself. Thanks to emptiness, she arises from your mind. This is like your own face appearing [to you] as a reflection in a mirror.

Lopön Āryadeva[136] also says:

> I will explain the emergence of the deity-reality *(lha'i de kho na nyid),* the esoteric instruction of all the buddhas, which has passed through the succession of the lineage lamas, and is not the domain even of the lords of the tenth ground. What is called "thoroughly knowing your mind, truly and just as it is"[137] [651] is not [found] within the aggregates, elements, or even in the sensory fields. It is taking on a deity-body, endowed with all the characteristics [of a buddha], simply through the thorough radiances of mere gnosis.[138] This is a body whose nature is that of the mind of all the buddhas; it is also illustrated by the twelve examples of illusion (illusions, dreams, and so forth).

Thus, your mind is the path, and moreover, is present as an apprehended-object of the eyes.[139] All the buddhas spoke of this in all of the tantras—it was not spoken of in the other vehicles. This is not the domain of false lamas, and it is sealed by the "six parameters"!

Comments on "Like a form in a mirror..."

This refers to your mind itself, arising in the form of emptiness, just like a reflection arising in a mirror. That form, further, is not composed of atoms. *Stainless Light*[140] elaborates:

> It is like how, through the power of mantras and the blessings of a deity, immaterial appearances of past, future, [652] and present phenomena arise to a young girl in a prognostic mirror. The material phenomena from the past, future, and present are not facing the mirror. But even in the absence of those material objects, it is not the case that there are no immaterial appearances in the mirror. And further, those events are not thoughts created by the young girl. In the same way, the yogi, through the force of his mind having been blessed, sees immaterial appearances in the sphere of the sky, [despite] their absence in the material triple-world.

The *Ādibuddha Tantra*[141] also mentions this:

> This host of essences [that emerges] from emptiness,
> Is devoid of any conceptual essence.

> It is like the immaterial images
> A young girl sees in a prognostic mirror.

The *Lotus Girl*[142] also says:

> Further, it is like a young girl seeing previously unseen things in a mirror and so forth, without involving any objects. In the same way, universal form, based on co-emergent bliss, [653] is seen by the yogi, who doesn't impute it [with his mind].

Considering this topic, Ārya Nāgārjuna[143] also stated:

> Understand that the illusory body
> Is like a reflection in a mirror.
> Its colors are like a rainbow, and
> Its pervasion is like the moon reflected in water.
>
> Liberated from form and non-form,
> Vajrasattva is completely resplendent,
> Appearing clearly
> Like a reflection in a stainless mirror.

This indicates that all [of his] features, endowed with radiant light, are clearly seen.[144]

Comments on "Displaying the three worlds..."

This indicates that the appearances of the impure world systems are also the appearances of this [Great Seal], which appear as saṃsāric due to the condition of ignorance. The *Condensed [Kālacakra] Tantra*[145] elaborates:

> Merely mind, the essence of mantra, surrounded by deities, having the nature of suffering and happiness—
> To the holy ones [you appear in] peaceful form, an experience resulting from their own actions; to the cruel ones [you appear] cruel.
> Whoever [654] fully performs a complete action, the effect of that arises in his mind, [invariably,] like a ritual.
> Lord of the world, having universal form, producer of the three existences: Vajrasattva, homage to you!

This "mere mind"[146] is endowed with the "ten powers" [of a bodhisattva], has the nature of a great being, and maintains the thirty-one realms [of saṃsāra]. Those who experience [it as] either happiness or suffering are experiencing their own karma. When emptiness is ignorantly apprehended,[147] the three worlds are produced in that way.

You might wonder: "If that form of emptiness was to appear as the Great Seal, then what would the three worlds' appearance be like?"[148] It would appear as Prajñāpāramitā, the form of emptiness, mental form, and universal form. As *Stainless Light*[149] says:

> The self-blessing is this: in emptiness
> The three worlds are displayed.

The *Lotus Girl*[150] explains the meaning of this:

> "Self-blessing" is what is seen in the sky, the three worlds having the nature of universal form. [Those] are seen as having the nature of your own [internal] three worlds. [655] That is the meaning.[151]

That is, everything included in the animate and inanimate worlds would be seen as being no different than illusions.

The condensed *Śrī Hevajra Tantra*[152] says:

> This is the great gnosis,
> Abiding in everyone's body,
> In a manner both dual and nondual—
> The supreme self, both concrete and immaterial.
>
> Pervading and abiding in the animate and inanimate world,
> Said to be the "one having illusory form...."

This indicates that in the bodies of sentient beings, [gnosis or great bliss[153]] is neither dual nor nondual,[154] and is beyond being a thing or a non-thing. It explains that everything animate and inanimate, without exception, is pervaded by illusory form.[155] This same topic was also clearly explained by Ārya Nāgārjuna:[156]

> Thus, in this way, all beings
> Are explained here as being like illusions.
> Resting in the illusion-like *samādhi*
> Everything is seen to be like that.
>
> The quintet of form, feeling,
> Cognitions, formatives,
> And consciousness,
> Along with all four elements, [656]
>
> The eyes and so forth, the objects,
> And all five consciousnesses—
> [Every] part of the external and internal worlds—
> All are illusions. There is nothing else.

This means that, while resting in the "illusory" *samādhi,* the *skandhas,* the elements, the sense fields, and everything connected with the external and internal worlds, are seen to be like illusions. Thus it is said:[157]

For instance, skillful magicians
Make effort at creating illusions;
Thus, they understand their reality,
And are not are attached to the illusions.
It is the same with the skillful complete-buddhas,
Who know the three existences as being like illusions.

The meaning of this should be understood through the above [citation by Nāgārjuna].

The *Sūtra of the Illusion-like Samādhi*[158] says:

> Bodhisattva Excellent Lotus-Heart! If a bodhisattva is endowed with one single doctrine, then he will not turn back from complete enlightenment, and will attain the five superknowledges. What is it? It is the illusion-like *samādhi*! And what is that? It is not dwelling in any of the three realms at all.

"Not dwelling in the three realms" should be understood as meaning: although the three realms are clearly visible, not grasping at them as concrete things or signs. [657] In this way, although you "dwell" in the three realms, you will not be covered in the faults of the three realms. In *On Purifying Mental Obscurations,*[159] Lopön Āryadeva says:

For instance, although a lotus grows from the mud,
It is not covered by the mud's faults.
In the same way, the yogi is not covered in
The faults of the various karmic predispositions.

For instance, when the moon is reflected in water,
It is not actually covered in water;
Like a variegated reflection
It is not covered in the flaws of being seen.

Though it is suitable to say that [the yogi] is not touched by the flaws of the external three realms, this is because [his] inner three realms are not touched by flaws.[160]

Further, the *Condensed Cakrasaṃvara Tantra*[161] says:

Through seeing and touching
And hearing and thinking,
You will be liberated from all sin.
Have no doubt in this.

The bodhisattva Vajrapāṇi[162] discusses the meaning of this [in his passage beginning]:

> The three internal spheres, without exception, are seen in the form of buddhas. Their great bliss [658] is also touched....

And continuing through:

> One will be liberated from all the sins created by body, speech, and mind: the five crimes of immediate retribution, the ten non-virtues, and so forth.

Thus, it should be known that in the inner three realms' freedom from defects, the external three realms come to be untouched by stains.

Comments on "Emanating rays like stainless lightning. . . ."

That which is "like the sphere of the sun" and that which is "like lightning" are all totally complete.[163] This one[164] is called the *dharmadhātu*. The Gnosis chapter of the *Condensed [Kālacakra] Tantra*[165] expands on this:

> At first, in order to increase the co-emergent bliss of the conquerors, one is intimate with an "action" *mudrā*;
> Later, with one of sunlike form, her body, face, legs, crown protuberance, and limbs all complete;
> [And finally] with the one like a bolt of lightning, who gives birth to unmoving bliss, [her] characteristics totally complete:
> [She] arises [due to] the vajras, dwells in the three existences [and] the bodies [of those who live there], and is the *dharmadhātu*!

Elsewhere[166] it states:

> Homage to the giver of birth, youthful in form, like stainless lightning, who is [endowed with] the splendor [of the] twelve suns, [659]
> Who dwells in the state of the gnosis vajra, [and is symbolized by] a *visarga*.

Still, you might ask: "What establishes that this[167] is referring to the Great Seal?" The bodhisattva Vajrapāṇi states this in [his commentary to] the *Glorious Dechog:*[168]

> The Great Seal—free of all obscurations, like an image in a prognostic mirror—blazes up and, ornamented with maṇḍalas of light, emanates clouds of light rays in infinite buddhafields.

Further, this emanation of light rays is in five [colors]. The *Enlightenment of Vairocana Tantra*[169] says:

> A pure body like a rainbow
> Will be seen by meditating on reality.

Āryadeva himself[170] explains the meaning of this [passage]:

> "Rainbow" refers to the bow of Indra. And what is that? It is a manifest display of five [colored] light. Just as a rainbow in the canopy of the sky is clearly visible with its five distinct colors, so

too the body [that is seen] is also displayed like that. Thus, it is called "a pure body like a rainbow."

On Purifying Mental Obscurations[171] also mentions:

> The sun of the mind becomes clearly visible, [660]
> Liberated from the clouds of bad views.

[Thus, to the phrase from the *Kālacakra Tantra*] "emanating rays," one should join "like the rays of the sun, containing all colors."

Comments on "Indivisible in the external world and the body..."

This indicates that the Great Seal is seen externally in the sky, and will also be seen internally, in your body. The *Kālacakra Tantra*[172] elaborates:

> The atoms of [her] original body have dissolved, and it is equal to the sky; its marks are totally complete;
> The variety of the original three worlds arises like a dream, free of obscurations.
> [Her] speech is never interrupted, and enters the minds of others through [being cast in] different languages.
> [Her] mind, full of profound bliss, unwavering and innate, embraces all bodies.

This indicates that [her] original body,[173] which is not atomic, is seen in the exterior world, to the limits of the sky's pervasion. Moreover, with all signs[174] complete, [she] acts to remove the obscurations of the three worlds. This universal form, which is like a dream, is a presencing of your own mind in the form of an external appearance. [661]

As for [her] internal manifestation, the *Kālacakra Tantra* says:[175]

> The one who originally is empty-form dwells [in] the [three] qualities and [five] objects, [so their] nature is pure.
> Thoroughly dwelling in the elements and the aggregates, and likewise in the faculties of the eyes and so forth, they are [also of] equal [taste].
> Dwelling in [the periods of] waking, dreaming, and so forth, [they are] equal [in] great bliss, which is indestructibly present.[176]
> This is the knowledge-woman, the mother of the buddhas, present in the state of the vajra[177]—the yogi should search [for her]!

> Chiefly through the force of the body, the divine eyes come about in the yogi's supreme body.[178]
> The [divine] ears [arise] through the force of speech, and through mind the ability to enter [others'] minds.
> Through the power of an insight-body, [comes] the power to recollect past lives in the residences of the three worlds.

Through the power of insight-speech, you gain the power to create magical displays at any time, equal [in extent] to the sky, and all-pervading.

Through the power of insight-gnosis comes the bliss that is equal, always indestructible.[179]

The three existences are not seen with the ordinary eyes, but are seen through the power of the divine eyes.

Through the power of divine hearing, the expressions of living beings' minds and mouths are heard.

O Lord of Men! In this way, touch and so forth are all transformed through the yogas of body, speech, and mind.[180]

These matters are also discussed in [662] the *Lotus Girl:*[181]

> [By continually meditating on the six-limbed yoga, the yogi] will see empty-forms, endowed with all aspects, appearing externally in the sky. Similarly, they will be seen internally, using the mental sense-faculty. Moreover, those things that appear on the exterior and interior are not existent, as they transcend the relationship of produced-and-producer. But they are also not non-existent, as they are objects of engagement of the sense faculties.

The *Lotus Girl* also clearly states:[182]

> "Variety" refers to animate and inanimate things. Because she illuminates the nature of those things, she is called "Mother of Variety."

Ārya Nāgārjuna[183] also says:

> Everything is seen to be like that.

This and the lines associated with it were explained earlier.[184]

The *Lotus Girl*[185] says:

> At night, thanks to the emptiness of the eye sense-faculty and so forth, the sense objects—form and so forth—are cast away. At that time, [the Great Seal] is seen by the yogi in the exterior and in the body, due to their indivisible nature, like the sun and the sun's rays. Until [the dualistic notions of] "perceiver" and "perceived" are eliminated, this does not occur.

This is not the purview of false lamas!

Comments on "Not an object..."[186]

[663] This indicates that the Great Seal, though seen with the eyes, is beyond atomic structure, and thus "is not an object like form and so forth." The *Kālacakra Tantra,*[187] in the section presenting the purity of the four bodies, states:

> There, the Omniscient Form is seen, [like] the sun [shining] in water, transparent and multicolored,
> Endowed with all aspects, but not an object—one's own mind, not the mind of another.[188]

You may object: "Something 'endowed with all aspects' isn't a 'non-object'; if something has [visible] form, then certainly it can only be composed of atoms." This is not the case. The atomic particles are the earth, water, fire, and wind particles; it might seem that everything is either a collection of these, or is suitable to be one of them. But not everything is one of those. The "Gnosis" chapter of the *Kālacakra Tantra*[189] states:

> Though the aspect of earth appears, it isn't solid; as for water, it [has the] form of liquid but is not wet, because it isn't water.
> Though the aspect of fire appears, it isn't fire; and that which [appears] like wind isn't wind.
> Empty in aspect and yet seen, [their] intense and varied hues—white, green, and so forth—[664] are not colors.
> Although endowed with all aspects, [these] are not [ordinarily] seen, due to the power of the demonic stains and afflictions of your mind.

Here, form is empty of concrete reality, and thus is not a thing. But because of being established in sensory direct-perception, it is not a non-thing. To provide an example, it is like a dream. This is discussed further in *Approaching the Ultimate:*[190]

> In pure direct perception, forms are empty-things,
> So those things and non-things have no [true] causes.
> They are like illusions, dreams, and magical displays:
> There are effects there, but no concrete reality.

The *Lotus Girl*[191] says:

> ["Atomic particles" refers to] the atomic particles of earth, water, fire, and wind, which are in nature firm, wet, warm, and moving. Because of being free of the characteristics of these, [the Great Seal] is said to be "beyond the nature" of atomic particles.

It continues:

> Though free of the natures of earth, water, fire, wind, and so forth, [the Great Seal] is still an object of engagement for yogis.

Further, this source[192] states:

> [The Reality Body is "not a thing"] because it is not a concrete thing whose entity is earth, water, fire, or wind. [665] This is because it is unfabricated, and arises self-emergently from space.

Then wouldn't it be a non-existent thing? [This objection is refuted in] the phrase "not a non-thing." In its [possession of] all aspects, it is not a non-existent thing, like sky-flowers and so forth. This is because its entity can be experienced, and because it gives rise to all of the enlightened qualities of the buddhas, who are endowed with all aspects.

This one who is an object of the eyes but has no atomic structure, who is emptiness and also manifests in form, is spoken of clearly in all of the tantras. But those who rely on inferior lamas do not know it, as they do not have the esoteric instructions, and so it is as if they are following deceptive words.

Comments on "Dwells in the sky..."

This indicates [that the Great Seal is] initially seen in the sky. As the *Jñānatilaka Tantra*[193] says:

You dwell in the residence of the supreme sky.
As for your conventional form....

The bodhisattva Lokanātha[194] has also stated:

This causeless Vajra-yoga[195] [666] is free of permanence and nihilism, is beyond worldly examples, and casts away thoughts of "existence" and "non-existence." It is seeing in direct perception, without imputations created by your mind: like a prognostic image in a young girl's mirror. It is a motivating object,[196] endowed with all aspects, emerging in the sky.

Elsewhere[197] he has said:

[The root verse means:] In [accordance with] ultimate truth, [please] also [explain the maṇḍala] that doesn't involve striking a chalk-line; that doesn't involve laying out colored powders; that doesn't involve a mind conceptually meditating on such things as deities' colors, hand implements, and shapes; that is all aspects [arising] in the sphere of the sky, like a prognostic image.

The tantra called *Emanation of Blessings*[198] says:

The doctrine is free of conceptuality—
It is the abandoning of all conceptual thought.
In it, the concepts of "mind" and "arisen from mind"
Will be completely cast away.

My doctrine is manifest buddhahood,
And that comes from the sky.
[But] the childish—those who engage with
Conceptual objects—are not aware of it.

Approaching the Ultimate[199] says:

> Just as an unproduced prognostic image
> Appears in a young girl's mirror,
> In the same way, [667] events of the past, future, and present,
> Are seen by the vidyā-yogi, in the sky.

This describes cognitions of [events of] the three times appearing in empty-form.

You may object: "That is how the Buddha, the Transcendent Victor, sees. It isn't referring to objects of ordinary people like us, is it?"[200] It *is* an object of ordinary beings. The *Lotus Girl*[201] explains:

> The eyes of beginners—the very eyes that see pots, pillars, and so forth—see universal form in the sky, endowed with all aspects. That [form] is not ultimately existent, because it is beyond atomic structure, and because it is not produced through a process involving a "produced object" and a "producer." But still it is not non-existent, because it has the nature of the supreme and unchanging bliss, and because the yogi sees it in the sky.

Thus, it should be understood that [the Great Seal] is seen in the sky with these same ordinary eyes.

The *Ādibuddha Tantra*[202] says:

> So too, intimacy with the one
> Who is a form arisen from the sky.

Elsewhere[203] it is said: [668]

> It is just like a butter lamp resting in a pot:
> Because of this, [its light] will not appear.
> [But] if that pot is broken,
> The lamp's light comes shining out.
>
> In the same way, the pot is your body
> And reality is like the lamp.
> When broken by the lama's advice,
> The buddhas' gnosis bursts out.
>
> The sky arises from the sky,
> And the sky sees the sky.
> [Such] practices are taught well
> In the oral advice of the lamas.

Similarly, the *Glorious Profound Primordial Tantra*[204] says:

> The sky emerges from the sky.
> Everything is empty—the great sky!

You might think: "In asserting what is the characteristic of all phenomena—of pure [and] impure natures, of the totally afflicted and the completely purified—the Transcendent Victor said: 'If all phenomena are seen as being like the sky, then suchness is seen.' This is explaining a characteristic [of all phenomena]; so 'seeing in the sky' is not indicating a location or a residence *(gnas).*"[205] That is not the case. It *is* indicating a residence; as explained earlier, it is also associated with a characteristic.[206] *Stainless Light*[207] says: [669]

> As for the "residence *(gnas)* of great bliss," it is the *dharmadhātu,* whose characteristic is like the sky. It is the unmixed source of phenomena, beyond worldly examples; it is all good, the residence of great bliss.

The *Ultimate Letters*[208] also says:

> The mind should be apprehended like the sky,
> View all phenomena, too, as equal to the sky.
> When you consider that mind to be unfathomable,
> Then the unsurpassed will be attained.

This was explained at length earlier.[209]

Comments on "A mere appearance..."

This refers to [the Great Seal as] an entity that you experience.[210] That is the path. Beyond being a hidden object of the mind, it is not space.[211] The tantra *Thig-le of the Great Seal*[212] says:

> Turned away from "perception" and "perceiver,"
> Separated from all aspects:
> The supreme yoga, unproduced and pure,
> A direct experience of natural bliss.
> That is explained as its nature.

This explains that, in being empty, [this path] is free from all aspects, has the characteristics of the sky, is unproduced, and has abandoned "perception" and "perceiver." And yet, it is still experienced. The third chapter of this same source[213] says: [670]

> A form in the shape of a half-moon arises,
> Dwelling within the wind *cakra.*
> Neither divided nor whole,
> It is seen like the moon reflected in water.
>
> Mahamāya, the Mother of Beings,
> Singular, though countless keep [her] company;
> Subtle, supreme and other than supreme,
> Unproduced, nondual, unthinkable.

> The "mother" of the maṇḍalas of wind,
> Hard to realize, except by the buddhas.

This describes the indestructible wind, which produces all the maṇḍalas of winds without exception;[214] called a "mother" because beings are born from it, it is unborn and nondual, and is seen [like] the moon reflected in water.[215]

Chapter five of the king of tantras, the *Śrī Kālacakra Tantra*[216] says:

> [The Great Seal is] a mere appearance in your mind, arising in your intellect, like a reflection in a mirror.
> The conqueror's sons and the buddhas keep company with her, as should the powerful yogis.
> As the gnostic visions increase, they burn away completely the hosts of demons, along with objects,[217]
> Attachment, and so forth, [and] convey the bliss of equality in the yogi's body—this is the function of the yogas.[218]

Thus, the path is something that appears to the mind, that is seen with the eyes like a reflection. [671] It is not formulations like the "abiding reality of things" or "things' emptiness of essence," which are determined through scripture and reasoning. Understand this: the path is not something that you have conviction for in thought.[219] As Lopön Āryadeva[220] himself said:

> Those who engage in the methods of the sūtra school and so forth, and even those meditators who dwell in the stage of generation, they declare: "All phenomena are like illusions! Like dreams!" And though they have great conviction, through their examples they are unable to understand the production of a deity body, through mere gnosis, through the nature of the mind, [as explained in] the esoteric instructions of the stage of self-blessing.

Here you might ask: "The esoteric instructions on the stage of self-blessing do say 'in reality your mind is like the sky.' But what establishes this as [referring to] an illusion-like 'mere appearance'[221] [of a deity body] in the sky, endowed with lights and apprehended by the eyes?" Āryadeva[222] has said:

> In truth, the mind is free of shape and color. A mere radiance *(snang ba tsam),* its essence is like the sky. Like ultimate truth, it is difficult to contact. Even so, [672] the three radiances *(snang ba gsum)* are a mere shining-forth *(snang ba tsam),* and are supported by wind. Because they are co-mingled, they are light.[223] Thus consciousness is bound in wind. Then, an illusion-like deity body arises, which has the dual luminosity *(snang ba gnyis)* of insight

and method as well as the five[-colored] lights, and is endowed with all the various enlightened qualities.

This is called the "esoteric instructions on [the stage of] self-blessing" because your own mind blesses your mind. It involves a manifestation of the conventional form of emptiness, and thus should be understood through its explanations in the context of [the stage of] conventional truth.[224]

You may object: "If this [appearance] is your mind, then it would be suitable for anyone to see."[225] [That is not the case.] Empty-form will not be seen through conceptual minds. Saṃsāric minds are conceptual, and thus are polluted minds. It is only thanks to non-conceptual minds that such empty reflections[226] come to be seen. Therefore, that ["mind" of which the Great Seal is a "mere appearance"] should be understood as being a "mind that is not a conceptual mind."[227] As is said in the *Perfection of Wisdom* scriptures:[228]

> That mind [673] is a mind that is not a mind.

Further, Saraha himself said:[229]

> Nothing can be said about *kālakūṭa:*[230]
> The intellect grasps at its skylike nature.
> [But if] that intellect is made into non-intellect,
> It becomes the supreme beauty of the innate nature.
> In house upon house it is spoken of,
> [But] the residence of great bliss is not completely understood.

As well as:[231]

> Gye Ma! [In] yoga you should question things.
> Abandon the head, heart, navel, the secret area, the hands and feet—they are unseen.
> Thought constructs objects, and
> By considering other things, the winds become blocked.
> But if the mind is made known by the mind,
> Then the winds and mind are unfluctuating and stable.

The *Lotus Girl*[232] says:

> "Empty body" refers to one that transcends all worldly conceptual thought, and has the nature of emptiness. It is not [perceived by] worldly apperceptive cognitions, which involve "objects of awareness" and "awareness."

In this same source, it is also stated:[233]

> Seeing universal form endowed with all aspects [674] is not [seeing] something that in nature is devoid of all aspects.

Furthermore, the *Explanation of the Accomplishment of Supreme and Unchanging Gnosis*[234] says:

> Whoever, through the power of karmic predispositions from another life, and through the power of the esoteric instructions of a true lama, at all times, day and night, manifestly embraces [the Great Seal]—who has abandoned all imputed phenomena, is a mere appearance of your mind, is the great emptiness endowed with all supreme aspects, and who gives rise to the innate joy—that one is called "Attainer of the Siddhi of the Great Seal," "Transcendent Victor," "All-Knower."

That "mere appearance" is your mind, becoming directly manifest to the sense faculties.

Though the path is indeed like this, there are some who say that [the path] is "a mere mental conviction that 'the nature of all phenomena is emptiness,'" or is "analyzing with the individually discriminating insight, leading to the arising of a conviction that one meditatively familiarizes oneself with," or that it is "a hidden phenomenon that is beyond being an object of engagement of the mind," or that it is "simply refuting other's assertions," or "with respect to exaggerations and denigrations in your [675] cognition, a simple cessation of [those] exaggerations and denigrations via a reasoning mind and on the basis of some special reasonings," or that "everything included in the external and internal is taught as being your mind, and that which, upon searching, is not found to be mind is the Reality Body," and so forth. Those proponents of the path have not met with a real spiritual friend, and are outside of the intent of the word of the Transcendent Victor. Such stupid, counterfeit "experts" have not yet amassed any collections [of method or insight], and are like blind people serving as leaders of the blind. Let it be known that they have not met with the true path. The mantra vehicle, which is like the finest butter, is spoiled by the filthy water of all their unclean concepts.

Comments on "The nature of mind and that which comes from mind..."

This refers to your mind as (1) an empty object, and (2) the subjective mind that apprehends it. *Stainless Light*[235] elaborates:

> Through the power of meditating on the form of emptiness, the apprehending mind [676] is brought together with the appearance of the mind as an apprehended object.

You might object: "If your mind appears as an 'object' and a 'subject,' that is subject/object-based conceptuality, which is the cause of saṃsāra—it is not the path." This is not the case. Impure objects and subjects are the cause of saṃsāra. Pure objects and subjects are the path to liberation! Though a singular mind appears as multiple—as objects and a subject—it is due to their impurity or purity that they become the seeds for either cyclic existence or transcendence. As Saraha[236] says:

> The mind-itself alone is the seed of all,
> From which ordinary existence and transcendence rise.
> Homage to that mind, which, like a wish-fulfilling jewel
> Provides whatever fruit one desires.
>
> If the mind is bound, you are bound.
> If it is let go, liberation is definite!
> By that which binds a fool,
> A skillful one is quickly liberated.

Āryadeva[237] said:

> Likewise, this precious mind
> Is colored by the hues of conceptuality.
>
> If the precious mind is isolated
> From the hues of ordinary conceptuality,
> It [will be seen as] pure from the beginning, unproduced,
> The innate [677] nature, stainless.

The *Gnosis Vajra Compendium Tantra*[238] explains that the path is the pure phenomenon of "mind" and "that which comes from mind":

> The great yoga of "mind" and "that which comes from mind" is the *samādhi* of great bliss. That [*samādhi*] is illustrated by the examples of illusion....

The 500,000[-line] *Śrī Hevajra Root-Tantra*[239] also says:

> Through the union of emptiness and form,
> The elements are consumed, and in that way there is bliss.
> When stainless enlightenment comes about,
> [One can] bless the minds of others.

This tantra establishes that when your mind manifests in the form of emptiness, then the six superknowledges—knowing the minds of others, and so forth—will arise completely.

Comments on "Embracing all migrating beings..."

The one who naturally dwells in sentient beings should be understood as being the path. This is also stated in the *Glorious Thig-le of the Great Seal Tantra:*[240]

"Self" is everywhere, in everything,
Forever dwelling as everyone's identity.
As the nature of all things,
It is present [678] as what pervades them.
Without this "self," all migrating beings
Would be like trees whose roots are cut.

This same chapter[241] explains the use of that term "self" through [discussing] what is symbolized by the letter *A*:[242]

Listen, and I will explain
The ultimate meaning of the term "self":
A is the syllable with the supreme form
Dwelling within everyone's body,
With all supreme aspects perfectly complete.
Present [in] all, unproduced, all-knowing,
Always empty, all-pervasive,
The cause that makes everything one.

You might object: "How do we know that what is described there [in that tantra] is that very one [who dwells in all beings], emptiness appearing in form?" The same source, in the "Chapter Explaining the *Dharmadhātu*"[243] says:

Further, listen and I will explain
That which is renowned as the *dharmadhātu*.
Space is the *dharmadhātu*.
Dhātu indicates "seed,"
[And this] is within every *dharma*.
It is the cause and the supreme residence.
Just like oil is in a sesame seed,
And just as fire is [latent] in firewood,
So, it is in all phenomena.
In this way, it exists in all phenomena
But still is not seen.
The *dharmadhātu* is renowned as the *bhaga*.
The *bhaga* is the vessel for the precious [jewel]. [679]

Here, it can be understood with perfect clarity.[244]

The *Glorious Jñānatilaka Tantra*[245] also says:

Without you, all the three realms
Are like a man without a head.
You are the gnosis creating the light
In the countless world systems.

This describes something that, via its very essence, abides in all sentient beings. From the impure perspective, this comes to be called "ignorance."[246] Only in the pure tantras is it explained as being the "one symbolized by the letter *A*." The true intention of the tantras is difficult to determine, can only be understood through the esoteric instructions of a true lama, and is sealed with the "six parameters." It is not something that will become evident through the explanations of ordinary beings. As *Stainless Light*[247] says:

> [The object arising from vajra-yoga] emerges from the sky, is all good, has all the faculties, and abides as the nature of all sentient beings...unconnected to reasonings and examples.

The *Ultimate Letters*[248] also says:

> What it is and where it abides:
> That is not seen right here!
> All the experts, though skilled in their treatises,
> Don't sense the buddha present in their bodies.

You may ask: "Isn't this just saying that we are unaware of the very nature of the mind or the very nature of the knowing luminosity, which exists within all sentient beings?"[249] This is not the case. As the *Śrī Vajra Maṇḍala Ornament Tantra*[250] says:

> [She] is everywhere: in all realms and
> In all sentient beings, in all places;
> Dwelling equally in all bodies,
> Present equally as the mind and the elements.

Though the mind and the elements may resemble it, they are not the very nature of the mind.[251] And further, though it is explained as something that exists in sentient beings, it is not the [ordinary] mind. To say that what dwells in all "sentient beings" *(sems can)* is the "mind" *(sems)* would be completely senseless, because it would be like saying "fire exists in fire," and there is no need to establish that. The point that this[252] "dwells within" beings is explained again and again in the authentic tantras. As the *Ornament of the Vajra [Maṇḍala] Tantra*[253] says:

> Like all the potential for fire
> Dwells in firewood,
> Like sesame oil in a sesame seed, and
> Sugar cane permeated by juice,
> Like fragrance in a flower,
> And like butter in yogurt,
> The Great Seal dwells completely in everything:

In all sentient beings,
In the animate and inanimate,
In form and in formless concepts.

How could the Great Seal [681] dwell within all sentient beings? This passage indicates that the Great Seal abides such that we are not aware of [her] causal agency.[254] Otherwise, though it indeed does not need to be established that all sentient beings are the residence of the mind, one might still ask how the name "sentient being" also came to be applied to the residence of the Great Seal.[255] This profound intention is hidden in the pure tantras, and is difficult to understand. *Approaching the Ultimate*[256] elaborates:

This is an effect that accords with [the system of] cause-and-effect:
Unproduced phenomena being produced and seen,
Endowed with all aspects, completely and utterly pure,
Possessing all the faculties, dwelling at the heart of all.

That one [who "embraces all beings"] is also symbolized by the letter *A*. As the *Glorious Ornament of the Vajra Maṇḍala Tantra*[257] says:

In the center of the heart, indestructible,
Blazing, like a pure butter lamp,
Unchanging and extremely subtle:
The letter *A*, supreme and holy!

This "one symbolized by the letter *A*" is the main cause of the attainment of buddhahood. Regarding this, the *Litany of the Names of Mañjuśrī*[258] refers to:

The complete buddha, arisen from the letter *A* … .

And:[259]

The glorious buddha, born from a lotus… .

This is stated clearly here and in other sources. [682] This profound intention is the domain only of the *Bodhisattva Commentaries*. Other [sources] are like blind people that act as leaders for the blind. Though I have expressed briefly and with confidence [here], it is extremely profound, and one should abandon verbal expressions, so these elaborations should suffice [until] the time it is pointed out by a lama.

Comments on "One in the guise of many…"

Though singular, to saṃsāric cognitions [the Great Seal] appears as multiple, as subjects and objects. In pure vision, [she is] seen everywhere like the moon [reflected in multiple vessels of] water. This is explained in the later supplement to the *Glorious Thig-le of the Great Seal Tantra:*[260]

> While having a singular nature, [the Great Seal]
> Always appears divided: in variety, multiplicity, and the like.
> How is it claimed that [she] is multiple?
> This one whose nature is everywhere,
> Is seen via a form with conventional aspects,
> Like the moon reflected in water.

The king of tantras, the glorious *Cakra of Time*[261] says:

> Though singular and multiple, you are one! You are equal and unequal, right and left, front and back,
> Above and below—everywhere. A variegated form in green, white, and gold;
> Having but not having length and shortness, a body and enlightened qualities; and neither man nor woman. [683]
> You who are the singular basis of all, the excellent *bhaga,* the supreme *bhaga:* I bow to you!

In that way, though singular [the Great Seal] appears in multiplicity, as both cyclic existence and transcendence. If [her] singularity is pure, then all [of her] multiple appearances are pure; ignorance of this is the basic doctrine.[262]

Here you might assert: "If that [Great Seal] exists in everything, then it would be suitable for all sentient beings to see [her]; this is because [she] would exist as a part of you, like your own hand." [I reply:] There is no contradiction in not seeing something that exists within you. As the *Ādibuddha Tantra*[263] says:

> Having gone there, the officiant can see
> With his two ordinary eyes.
>
> If he sees an existent form,
> Why doesn't he see his own face?
> If he is sees a non-existent form,
> Why isn't it the horns of a rabbit?

Here, the practitioner sees due to being endowed with the advice of an authentic lama. But this does not cause him to see something that is a part of him,[264] or that never existed.[265] How is this? As *Stainless Light*[266] says:

> ...This is because [empty-form] is not substantial. *"Though empty in aspect it comes to be seen"* [684] indicates that it is like an illusory city: although it has colors like white and so forth, because

it is not composed of matter, it is not "colored." And though it is endowed with all aspects, the childish never see it.

Concluding Summation

Thus, there are different terms in various languages that express this [Great Seal]: "Prajñāpāramitā, the complete purification of ignorance," the "form of emptiness," "Great Seal," the "secret," "*bhaga,*" "vajra-seat," "source of phenomena," "lion's throne," the "letter *E,*" the "letter *A,*" the "first letter," "Nairātmyā," "Vajravārāhī," "Viśvamātā," "Viśvamūrti," "Vajravārāhī,"[267] "site of great bliss," the "space element," "suchness," and so forth. This is due to the kindness of all the bodhisattvas and the true lamas, and is the domain only of myself and a few others like me.

You might wonder: "Was such a Great Seal seen in former times?"[268] Here is a statement from the Buddha[269] [himself]:

> Having abandoned all activity, and
> Thoroughly investigated [for] one day,
> If the signs do not arise there, [685]
> Then at that time my words are false.

This should be understood as meaning: After a single day and night, the first factor [of success] on the path [to abandoning] ignorance will be seen with the eyes. If one is not on the path, signs like these are not quick [to arise]. As it is said, "By meditating with your conceptual mind, [there is] desire, anguish, fear, and madness."[270]

Explaining "this speech," it is said:[271]

> Accordingly, "determining insight" and "non-objectifying compassion" are called "protectors of cognition"; insight and compassion are [thus] the mantra of the buddhas.

Furthermore, this path is something that comes from all the tantras—it is their definitive intention. It doesn't come from just one tantra, as should be fully understood through the statement: "One endowed with the *Three Bodhisattva Ornaments* will attain complete enlightenment."

Accordingly, the emptiness that involves analyzing with reasoning, and the emptiness of no-mental-activity,[272] are not the ones that are the path. Rather, this seeing of emptiness with the eyes, and the "co-emergent, equal, nondual primordial gnosis" [are the path].

Those who propound the "single taste of bliss and emptiness," the "single taste of appearance and emptiness," the "single taste of objects and subjects," [686] and so forth—they are only following after words and making meaningless assertions. What does this "co-emergent primordial gnosis"[273] refer to? I could lay this out in detail, but citing so many scriptures would create suspicion, so for now I will leave it here!

Concluding Verses

Here I have clearly distinguished and explained the "path" of emptiness, which is difficult to realize.
May whatever merit arises from that, like the moon freed from the clouds,
Cause all beings to enter this supreme path of nondual tantra,
And attain the state of vajra-holder by apprehending emptiness with the eyes.

The profound meaning of the vehicle of secret mantra, a meaning that is difficult to understand, is expressed in other places and by other people.
This path, which among the six seals is the one of definitive meaning, is hidden, and clarified [only] by relying on the advice of lamas.
Thus ordinary beings will not understand it; what need to mention the understandings of arrogant scholars with their intellectual treatises?
For these reasons, my assertions here accord with the word of the Able Ones, not with the systems of common beings.

Some in former lives have not purified their mindstreams,
And have not established the collections of merit in their continuum. [687]
Being of lesser discriminating insight,
They will denigrate the profound meaning, and develop no interest.

Some have not met with a true spiritual friend, and
Follow after whoever has the most fame and fortune.
One looked after by such a sinful "friend"
Will not find the hidden definitive meaning of the tantras.

Some, not having found the profound meaning of the tantras,
Follow after the words of others
Who propound many meaningless systems.
What keeps them from becoming insane?

Some people, born alone, without tenet systems,
Do not properly distinguish faults and good qualities,
And become firmly attached to whatever system they hear first.
How are they not deceiving themselves?

Some, through the power of their afflictions,
Automatically become firmly attached to the lower systems.[274]
They are like a servant girls attached to leftover food,
And don't develop interest in the marvelous doctrine.

Some attain a wealth of fame and so forth in this world,
And preach primordial liberation.
Compounding their afflictions and behaving so badly,
Don't they bind themselves with primordial liberation?

If the Reality Body doesn't decrease the afflictions [688] for even a moment,
What does it do for anyone?
Realizing a Reality Body that can't help your insignificant sufferings—
Isn't that a complete falsehood?

Some say "buddhahood will be attained in the bardo,"
And indicate the path to the student after death.
But after death, experiences will not recur,
So doesn't this make the student stupid?

Though a doctrine doesn't accord with their minds,
Some say to the people "Have faith in this!"
And although it appears mistaken, they take it up assiduously,
Devotedly accepting its written volumes,

Oral instructions, and its words.
What do bad tenets do for anyone?
Doesn't this just plant the thorn of [wanting] fame,
A following, and possessions in their hearts?

Some give explanations of secret mantra
Via words, logic, and the vehicle of characteristics.
While their discriminating insight is great,
Aren't they mixing in glue with the cooking oil?

Some, without a lama's esoteric instructions to fully establish
The unfathomable underlying intent of the tantras,
Impute it via their own conceptual minds, and propound this.
Aren't they just repeating idle gossip that spreads wrong views?

Some write books on the spiritual bodies, hand implements, [689] seed syllables,
The wheels, threads, mystic fire, blazing and dripping,
The classes of sounds, subtle [yoga], the channels and winds, and so forth:
The hundreds of methods of accomplishment, and the thousands of esoteric explanations.

They act with the conceit of scholars—
Who is served by such conceptual yogas?
For sustaining others [who need] basic food and clothing,[275]
Trifling merchandise is of no benefit, is it?

Thus, [giving] this vajra vehicle, the essence of the teachings,
Which is difficult to find in tens of millions of eons,
To those having little faith and no commitments,
Is like pouring gold dust in a manure pit—it is not suitable!

In this world I have not had the fortune
To attain renown as a scholar.
But due to the eminent kindness of the Jetsün,[276]
[I have found] fortune equal in greatness to Mt. Meru:

Through [his] explanation of the *Bodhisattva Commentaries,*
I journeyed to the profound meaning of the tantras.
Thus, due to the Jetsün's kindness,
I have taken hold of all the weapons.[277]

Using explanations from the tantras, oral transmissions, and treatises,
And through the eminent kindness of the Jetsün,
I, the teacher Yumo, have composed this,
[Revealing] what the path of emptiness is.

Colophon

The single path of all the buddhas of the three times, [690] the final among all the vehicles, the clear explanation of the preeminent path to liberation, is known as "Kālacakra." A king of tantra in which method and insight are nondual, it is a knot of vajra words; as it is stamped with the seal of the "six parameters," it is by its very nature difficult to understand. The *Lamp Illuminating Emptiness,* which illuminates its underlying intention, is now finished!

Closing Invocation

May the six types of beings attain buddhahood! Virtue! It is good!

TRANSLATION 2 | *Tantra of the Blazing Lamps*

Bibliographic Information and Notes on the Various Editions

In preparing this translation of the *Tantra of the Blazing Lamps,* I have consulted four editions of the *Seventeen Tantras:* the Tsamdrak edition (TB), the Tingkye edition (TK), the Dergé edition (DG), and the Adzom Drukpa edition (AD).[1] I have also made extensive use of the commentary *Stringing a Garland of Pearls* (MTP). My goal has been to make a translation that reflects the meaning of this commentary. For reasons discussed below, TB is the edition that to me most closely resembles the root text that the commentary is based on. I have thus used TB as the basis for the translation, though TB certainly contains numerous variants and errors that I do not follow.

Below are brief notes on all the editions I have used, as well as on the tantra's commentary. These focus on my preferences among the editions, and issues that may have affected my interpretation of the tantra.

TB edition: TB represents what I suspect is an older version of the tantra, before it went through some minor revisions and additions. Those revisions are evident in the DG and AD editions, which contain lines that are not present in TB, TK, or the commentary. The extra lines are not so numerous (representing around 19 lines of verse and some other minor additions), but nonetheless they appear to me to be later additions. TB is certainly not without its flaws and (like all the other editions) frequently provides different readings than those in the commentary *Stringing a Garland of Pearls,* but overall I have preferred it as it is reasonably accurate and most closely reflects the spirit of the commentary.

TK edition: TK is similar in form to TB and does not contain the additions found in DG and AD. It is, however, full of errors. For me, it is most important as a good witness to the earlier form of the tantra. It frequently agrees with MTP where other editions do not, and its variants sometimes provide ways out of interpretive impasses, but because of its errors, it is the edition that I have preferred least.

DG and AD editions: These are virtually identical to each other. Both are very clean and reliable editions of the tantra, with AD having perhaps a few more errors. As noted above, these two contain a small amount of material not found in other editions, and they also contain expanded colophons. DG and AD also sometimes contain less difficult readings than the others; my overall impression of them is that they represent a later cleaning-up of the tantra, performed by an educated and careful hand. One example of this can be found in the opening colophons, where the "Indian language" title of the tantra (which in the other editions is in an unknown language) has been rendered in Sanskrit.

Stringing a Garland of Pearls: Until recently, the commentaries to the *Seventeen Tantras* were thought to have been lost. In 1992, however, several of them appeared in a newly revised edition of the Nyingma canonical collection the *Continuously Transmitted Precepts (bKa' ma).*[2] Among these is a copy of the very rare commentary to the *Tantra of the Blazing Lamps,* called *Stringing a Garland of Pearls (Mu tig phreng ba brgyus pa).*[3] The published commentary is not in ideal condition, as it is based on an incomplete manuscript (less than 10 percent is missing), and the process of copying from this manuscript introduced frequent errors; the original manuscript is currently not available, though there are plans for its republication.[4] Still, the commentary is quite readable and almost always illuminating; at more than 300 pages, it provides more than ample information about the twenty-five-page tantra. I have used it as my main source for interpreting the *Tantra of the Blazing Lamps.*

Conventions and Translation Practices

Use of various editions: My basic practice in reading the tantra was to compile all the editions into a single diplomatic edition and to read that alongside the commentary MTP. My preference has been to try to follow TB or MTP, except where they seem unreasonable or mistaken.

Form and subheads: The subheads in the translation are from the commentary MTP, which organizes the tantra using a neat topical outline. These headings do not appear in the Tibetan root text itself. In my translation, each subhead contains an enumeration to remind the reader of the current level of the outline.

With the exception of the introductory scenes, the tantra is written in seven-syllable verse; I have thus arranged the text in stanzas, placing breaks between them where I feel it makes the text more understandable; the stanza breaks are not in the actual text but are often based on changes of topic that appear in MTP.

Indented verses represent the speech of one of the two interlocutors; verses that are not indented are narration, or are textual apparatus (such as prefatory material and colophons).

Page numbers: Page numbers supplied in brackets refer to the pagination of the TB edition.

The *Tantra of the Blazing Lamps*

[1] Prefatory Material

[1.1] The Name of the Tantra

[467] In Sanskrit, the title is *Svarṇa-puṣpa-kānti-ratna-āloka-jvala-tantra;*[5] in Tibetan it is *The Beautiful Precious Golden Flower—The Tantra of the Blazing Lamps.*

[1.2] Homage

I prostrate to the transcendent victor Glorious Naturally Arising Manifestation![6]

[2] Main Body of the Tantra

[2.1] CHAPTER ONE: The Far-Reaching-Lasso Water Lamp[7]

[2.1.1] Introductory Scenes

[2.1.1.1] The Extraordinary Introductory Scene

> Once upon a time, I taught this:[8] From the ground of emptiness, a maṇḍala of unbounded radiance, a great manifestation was arrayed without distinction or differentiation—a process for training in the great non-differentiation. [In the buddhafield] Ground of Great Primordial Self-Illumination, unimpeded awareness self-manifested from the matrix of the naturally dawning unimpeded activity of the great self-presencing. [468] Thus, this inexpressible meaning[9] was spoken, is being spoken now, and will be spoken.

[2.1.1.2] Profound Syllables Intervening between the Two Introductory Scenes

SARVA A SA MA MA DHA THEM BHAI TA A LO KE. A NAM PA LAM KE. A SARVA MA NI SHA. A AA AAA AAAA MMA E KA SA RĀ TYA NYA TA MA![10]

[2.1.1.3] The Ordinary Introductory Scene

> Once upon a time, I heard this, the *Illuminator of the Lamps*, on the grounds [of a palace, filled with] a variety of precious objects, ornamented with "eyes" of the fivefold primordial gnoses, and intensely radiant in color. [This was] the unfathomable lighting up of the ground, vast but with a spacious

center,[11] cleansed of all boundaries, its summit utterly transparent, shining forth unobstructedly in all the ten directions. On this site devoid of inside or outside, was an array [of deities] and a Perfectly Complete One,[12] made beautiful by all [those] ornaments.

In a palace of reality that is wholly transparent from whichever of the ten directions it is viewed, Pure-Appearance Dorjé Chang looked at Pure-Continuum Dorjé Chang[13] with the naturally manifesting great activity of his compassion. [469] Then from his heart—the unified matrix of nondual gnosis—[he took] this extraordinary secret of the great unsurpassed nucleus. Enclosing it in the vase of his spacious throat, he arranged it on the faculty of his tongue, which was an extraordinary efficacious means. Then, he proclaimed these [topics] in words that illuminated the adamantine lamps.

[2.1.2] A Brief Explanation of the Meaning of the Tantra's Four Chapters

[2.1.2.1] An Explanation of How the Tantra's Core Meaning was Caused to Emerge

Naturally-Pure-in-Lineage Dorjé Chang!
Through my unimpeded attentiveness,
I enabled the analytical intellect to arise everywhere.

Out of my dimension that is devoid of appearances,
In order to eliminate ordinary intellect, thought, and memory,
And to clear away the doubts of the [lower] vehicles,
I elaborated this. So you listen!

Although awareness unceasingly appears to itself
In all of the world systems,
Nobody at all sees it!

As for that unseen great primordial gnosis,
Whoever sees [this] beautiful flower[14]
Will see the gnosis that was previously unseen.

Then, in the primordial gnosis of the lamps,
The adamantine nucleus itself will dawn,
Presencing naturally, as it has been from the very beginning.

It is a mere dawning devoid of setting, and
This unsetting primordial gnosis [is like] a great treasury:
Whoever practices it will have good fortune.

Possessing good fortune and a virtuous nature,
There is not even an atom of non-virtue here.
[It leads to] the atomless self-awareness itself,
Which is devoid of the conventions of words.

[2.1.2.2] The Actual Summation of the Tantra's Four Chapters

All of this [concerns] the four lamps, through which
The radiance within all sentient beings is apprehended.

(1) The "far-reaching-lasso water lamp," in its very essence, [470]
Collects in form and so forth.

(2) The "self-emergent insight lamp"
Eliminates the doubts of the [lower] vehicles.

(3) The "empty seminal nuclei lamp"
Brings together and integrates cyclic existence and transcendence.

(4) The "lamp of the pure expanse"
Plants the seeds for yogic experiences.

All these are their distinctive manifestations.

[2.1.3] An Extensive Explanation of the Far-Reaching-Lasso Water Lamp

[2.1.3.1] A Brief Questioning

Then, Pure-Continuum Dorjé Chang
Experienced joy, delight, and faith,
And supplicated Pure-Appearance Dorjé Chang,
Speaking these words of request:

Hey! Hey![15] The Teacher Dorjé Chang,
The self-manifesting Teacher of all the buddhas,
Mentioned a "far-reaching-lasso water lamp"
In his speech on the four lamps.
When the Teacher spoke these words earlier,
I did not understand—please explain them to me [now]!

[2.1.3.2] A Brief Answer

Then Dorjé Chang the Great
Gave a complete narration, speaking these words:

E-ma! Pure-Continuum Dorjé Chang!
I have viewed the visions of the four lamps
Lighting up in the exterior,
All of them sequentially appearing as objects of [my] mind.

As for the far-reaching-lasso water lamp,
It supports three types of appearance,[16] and
It apprehends three types of appearance.
Thus it is at the heart of all vision.

Because all those [three] are viewed with this [lamp],
It maintains the ground of vision, [471] in which
It abides like a seed that gives rise to a fruit.

[2.1.3.3] An Extensive Questioning

Causal Dorjé Chang [then] supplicated
The Teacher, Dorjé Chang the Great,
Speaking these words:

Hey! Hey! Teacher Dorjé Chang!
Regarding that "far-reaching-lasso water lamp":

(1) What is its essence?
(2) What did you say its etymology was?
(3) What classifications does it have?
(4) What are its characteristics, the ways that it exists?
(5) And its residence—where does it reside?
(6) By what was it first produced?
(7) The appearances coming from its gateways of shining-forth, what are they like?
(8) What examples illustrate it?
(9) And through what [signs] can the experiential measure of all these be ascertained?

O Teacher—please explain all this to me!

[2.1.3.4] An Extensive Presentation of Answers

[2.1.3.4.1] The Essence of the Far-Reaching-Lasso Water Lamp

Then, the Teacher spoke again:

Hey! Ma![17] Causal Dorjé Chang—
I will teach, and you should unerringly
Grasp it all, Dorjé Chang!

Through its essence, the far-reaching-lasso water lamp
Collects in both [types of] appearance.[18]
Because its factors of apprehension[19] that create seeing are unobstructed,
One apprehends [via] both [its] dimensions.[20] Through sight,
One [thus] sees in accordance with saṃsāra and nirvāṇa.

[2.1.3.4.2] The Etymology of "Far-Reaching-Lasso Water Lamp" *(rgyang zhags chu'i sgron ma)*

Its etymology is like this:

(1) "Far-reaching" *(rgyang)* means that it takes hold of distant continua:[21]

Grasping appearances as "form," and
Collecting in colors and so forth.
Yet it also creates the seeing and apprehension
Of the body [of] awareness, from a great distance.
Thus from the realized perspective, [472] it propels
Cyclic existence to a great distance, and thus is "far-reaching."
And from the unrealized perspective, it propels
Transcendence to a great distance, and thus is "far-reaching."

(2) Similarly, since this [lamp] ensnares saṃsāric appearances—
Form and [the other of] the five sense-objects—
It is called a "lasso" *(zhags).*
Due to it,[22] appearances in the objective fields of the senses
Are recalled, considered, and grasped as self-existent;
Thus it is a "lasso," [as it] grasps from a distance.
[But] in the same way, it takes hold of awareness
Manifesting in the cloudless sky as "bodies devoid of self";[23]
Not letting [those] appearances escape into the beyond,
It is called a "lasso."

(3) As for "water" *(chu):* Having reversed attachment
For those appearances in its own place, and
Devoid of minds attached to everything,
Appearances are left alone, in their own places.[24]
Then, there is no adhering to a self; thus it is called "water."[25]

(4) As for "lamp" *(sgron):* Because it causes your visions
To become greater and greater,
It makes the gnostic energy of awareness radiantly apparent, and thus is called a "lamp."
Because all the appearances of the coarse elements
Are unimpededly discerned by your cognition, and
Become radiantly apparent in your sensory gateways, it is called a "lamp."

(5) By placing awareness in the outer expanse,
The inner expanse lights up, purified in its own place.
Because it gives birth to this visionary experience,

Through which the expanse and awareness are mixed, it is also called a "mother" (*ma).*

And because the eyes are also the gateway of shining-forth
For the vibrant energy of all the sense faculties,
They are called the ground of all, the "mother."

[2.1.3.4.3] The Classifications of the Far-Reaching-Lasso Water Lamp

Its classifications are threefold: [473]
(1) The far-reaching-lasso water lamp
Composed of the vibrant elemental energies,
(2) The far-reaching lasso composed of primordial gnosis, and
(3) The far-reaching lasso comprised of the sense faculties.

[2.1.3.4.4] The Characteristics of the Far-Reaching-Lasso Water Lamp

The characteristics of this [lamp] are as follows:
It is an unceasing shining-forth, which [matures][26]
The vibrant essence of the sense faculties in the gateway of the eyes.
Produced [at the navel, it now] abides in the lotus-eyes.[27]
Its specific character being to maintain the sense faculties.[28]

The activities of its elements[29] are: propelling,
Collecting, apprehending, and increasing appearances.

The activity of its primordial gnosis is to gaze,
And apprehend [in] the residence and above.[30]

It is the faculty that naturally apprehends
Objects, subjects, and non-objects.[31]

[2.1.3.4.5] The Residence of the Far-Reaching-Lasso Water Lamp

The abode of this [lamp] is the eyes.
Because its ability to create visual perception is unobstructed,
It is that which apprehends objects.

※[32]

From the white conch-shell house of the brain,
Taking three curls to the right,
Is a channel shaped like a buffalo horn.
This [lamp] abides in that channel,

Which gathers together the vibrant essence of all the sense faculties
And shines the faculties forth to objects.

[2.1.3.4.6] What Establishes the Far-Reaching-Lasso Water Lamp

Initially, when entering the womb
Of the mother who will give birth to your body,
The beginnings of the entire body [take form]
At the great knot of the navel channel
From which [emerges] the triangular central [channel].
[There,] the fruits of the eyes develop
From the vibrant cause and condition provided by your father and mother. [474]
Further, due to the dual contributions of the father and mother,
[Those eyes] are a mixture of black and white.[33]

[2.1.3.4.7] The Gateways through Which the Far-Reaching-Lasso Water Lamp Shines[34]

The gateway through which it shines is the eyes themselves.
It arises into all appearances
Through the channel that shines forth the sense faculties to the objects.

[2.1.3.4.8] Analogies for the Far-Reaching-Lasso Water Lamp

Just like an iron grappling hook
Can hold any [animal] by the nose,
This [lamp] holds the two "noses"
Of cyclic existence and transcendence.

[2.1.3.4.9] The Experiential Measure of the Far-Reaching-Lasso Water Lamp

Through this lamp, and its function of creating appearances,
Objective forms appear, but so does awareness.
Its experiential measure is the appearance of the little linked-lambs.

[2.1.3.5] Chapter Colophon

This has been the first chapter of the *Tantra of the Blazing Lamps,* an explanation of the far-reaching-lasso water lamp.

[2.2] CHAPTER TWO: The Self-Emergent Insight Lamp

[2.2.1] A Brief Questioning

Then Pure-Lineage Dorjé Chang,
Having understood that explanation
Again supplicated [the Teacher] in a speech using these words:

> Hey! Hey! Transcendent Victor Dorjé Chang!
> Through the Teacher's earlier explanation
> I found the profound definitive truth!
>
> Earlier you mentioned
> The "self-emergent insight lamp."
> Just as with the water lamp,
> I seek to listen to an explanation of its meaning.
>
> (1) What is its essence?
> (2) What is its etymology?
> (3) Could you explain its classifications?
> (4) What are its characteristics?
> (5) Through what gateways does it shine forth and appear?
> (x) And, into what aspects can it be divided?[35]
> (6) Also, what is its residence?
> (7) What are the measures of [having experienced] its underlying intent? [475]
> (8) And through what examples can it be expressed?
>
> Great compassionate Teacher
> I seek to listen to all of these!

[2.2.2] An Extensive Presentation of Answers

[2.2.2.1] The Essence of the Self-Emergent Insight Lamp

Then the Teacher spoke again:

> Hey! Ma! Causal Dorjé Chang!
> I will teach! So you
> Grasp all of this without straying!
>
> This lamp of self-emergent insight
> Is present as the cognizing power
> Of all the [four] lamps,
> And so it is a dimension in all of them:
> The "differentiating insight" [and so forth],
> Through which one abides in a state of non-differentiation.

As the essence that gives rise to [those] subtle dimensions,
It has been present from the primordial beginning.

[2.2.2.2] The Etymology of the Self-Emergent Insight Lamp *(shes rab rang byung sgron ma)*

Through cognition *(shes)*, you completely engage
All the appearances of things and non-things,
And know their overarching reality.
Finding confidence in letting-be without seeking
You know the measures of your own primordial gnosis.

The naturally pure Reality Body
That cannot be found by anyone, [is found] via self-awareness.
Thus it is supremely *(rab)* illuminating, and superior to all others.

Devoid of analytical points made by others,[36]
It arises on its own, a primordially pure object
That is not the object of others:[37] thus it is termed "self" *(rang)*.

Its reality has never be found through activity,
Because it is not something that anyone can wish for.
It has been self-manifesting since the primordial beginning, and thus is named "emergent" *(byung)*.

It is called a "lamp" *(sgron)* because it illuminates
Reality-itself and all [phenomena] without duality.

It is termed "mother" *(ma)* because its own state [476] is pervasive.

[2.2.2.3] The Classifications of the Self-Emergent Insight Lamp

It has five classifications:

(1) The "self-emergent insight that dwells in the ground"
Serves as the basis for phenomena like the body.

(2) The "insight that nakedly apprehends appearances"
Apprehends the expanse and awareness in front of oneself.

(3) The "insight of unobstructed mindfulness"
Gathers in the objects of one-pointed cognition.

(4) The "individually discriminating insight"
Distinguishes general and specific characteristics.

(5) The "insight of the three types of engagement"
Settles matters in the natural bardo [of this life].

[2.2.2.4] The Characteristic of the Self-Emergent Insight Lamp

It is what cognizes all phenomena,
Appearing and non-appearing, as being devoid of nature.
This is its characteristic.

[2.2.2.5] The Gateways through which the Self-Emergent Insight Lamp Shines

Its gateways of shining-forth are the five sense-faculties.
In particular, it shines forth through the nose.
The signs [of its existence] are that at night
When one yawns, sneezes forcefully,
Or coughs with great force,
Lucent red light radiates [from the nose]
In the form of sparks.
Due to those measures and signs,
The gateway of its shining forth is identified [as the nose].

[2.2.2.6] The Residence of the Self-Emergent Insight Lamp

The pure essences of cognition
Are within the four productive[38] channels.
In a nature that is moving, quivering, pulsating,
Light, and propelling,
They encircle the maṇḍala of the *citta,*
In the character of rising sparks.

These five-in-four,[39] [when] accompanied by the karmic winds
Are a cognitive energy that is extremely clear and aware.
[477]

In the flavor, solitary, all-pervasive,
And empty-crystal-tube channels,
The insights dwell in the nature of
A great self-knowing clarity.

As the primordial radiation composed of the four "names,"[40]
As the essence that distinguishes everything,
It primordially resides in the body.

When it is itself held back by the winds,
Cognition becomes a fog of forgetfulness.

When insight's energies are caught in the trap [of the elements],
It becomes foggy, without its dimension of radiance.

When wind propels the insight's energies,
Then teachings that you have heard earlier,
Can be brought to mind and clearly explained.

The clarity or unclarity of these energies
Arises from the motion and vibration of the winds,
Which abide in the channels, at the center of the body.

[2.2.2.7] The Experiential Measure of the Self-Emergent Insight Lamp

(1) The measure of the "self-emergent insight dwelling in the ground"
Is the experience of the equality of all phenomena.
When this arises, it is the attainment of the assurance of stable cognition.
When that is unchanging,
And always abides in your continuum,
One apprehends [via] the insight that dwells in the ground.
One's body will then feel light
And cognitions will be radiantly clear.

(2) The measure of the "insight that nakedly apprehends appearances"
Is that you let [appearances] be.
The sign of having experienced this is the five colored lights at the center of the body
Shining forth into the exterior without any effort.
Then, cognizing them, [478] you take hold of your own place.
Your body, too, will not touch the ground,
And you will be able to move
Whatever you direct your cognition to, even if it is inert matter.
This is the sign of having mastered the powers [of this insight]!

(3) The measure of the "insight of unobstructed mindfulness"
Is that your cognition doesn't engage with others
So you delight in dwelling alone,
Always preferring isolated places.
Not desiring friends and close companions,

Your cognition becomes one-pointed and unwavering.
Even when others speak to you,
You are free from perceptions of "subject" and "object."
Finding certainty in this unchanging view,
You feel like you are flying in the sky.
Wherever you direct your mind, there [your straying] stops.
How could the influence of others
Have the power to alter this?
Devoid of anxiety, this cognition is blissful and spacious;
Whoever gives rise to it
Has taken hold of the insight of unobstructed mindfulness.

(4) Now for the measures of the individually discriminating insight.
(a) You can distinguish the universal ground from the reality body,
And in this way there are the following signs:
You are freed from the mind that clings to the body,
So your awareness remains wherever you put it,
And your body becomes like inert matter.
(b) You can distinguish the mind from primordial gnosis
And thus your gateways of movement are blocked.[41]
(c) You can distinguish the vibrant and coarse dimensions of the elements;
For whoever does this, coarse appearances naturally cease
And the linked-lambs are easily experienced.
(d) In the same way, for whoever distinguishes cyclic existence from transcendence, [479]
It is impossible for erroneous minds to arise,
And even if they do, they are of no harm or benefit.
(e) Others,[42] through their own insight,
Will intellectually determine [the characteristics of] cyclic existence and nirvāṇa.
This is the individually discerning insight!

(5) The measure of the "insight of the three types of engagement" is as follows:
(a) If only one word [of] a whole teaching is spoken,
You will understand the whole body of that teaching:
This is the sign of arriving at the measure of the "insight derived from hearing."
(b) The power *(zungs)* to critically think about anything
Arises easily in your continuum,
And so "thinking" is mastered as well.

(c) Nothing that happens can harm you, and
Deluded thoughts and attachments naturally cease:
Through this, you attain the "insight arisen from meditation."

[2.2.2.8] Analogies for the Self-Emergent Insight Lamp

It is, for example, like dried tinder:
If tinder comes in contact with even a tiny spark,
Fire flares up and burns it all.
Likewise, insight burns up karmic predispositions.

All of these are the lamp of insight!

[2.2.3] Chapter Colophon

This has been chapter two of the *Tantra of the Blazing Lamps*, an explanation of the self-emergent insight lamp.

[2.3] CHAPTER THREE: The Empty Seminal Nuclei Lamp

[2.3.1] A Brief Questioning

Then, those convincing words having arisen
To the Causal Dorjé Chang,
He became a great equanimity, free of conceptuality.
Great insight having naturally arisen,
He got to the root of all phenomena—the single taste.
Realizing objects to be free of concrete reality and empty,
For the sake of all future sentient beings
He made this request to Dorjé Chang: [480]

Hey! Hey! Buddha Dorjé Chang!
Having attained the stainless eye[43]
That naturally brings all phenomena to light,
I have gotten to the root of all phenomena:
Their freedom from elaborations, their great primordial purity.
For the sake of all future sentient beings,
Whom I hold in [my] heart with compassion,
[I ask:] Just as with the insight lamp,
Regarding the term you mentioned earlier,[44]
The "empty seminal nuclei lamp":

(1) What is its essence?
(2) What is its etymology?
(3) And, what classifications does it have?
(4) What are its characteristics, its underlying intention?
(5) As for its residence, where does it abide?

(6) What are its gateways of shining forth?
(7) And what is its nature?
(8) How does it appear in the objective sphere?
(9) Through what can the experiential measure of all of this be apprehended?
(10) What is its actuality?
(11) What are the esoteric instructions related to its methods?
(12) And how can it be illustrated through examples?

Dorjé Chang, I seek to listen to all these
For the sake of all sentient beings.

[2.3.2] An Extensive Presentation of Answers

[2.3.2.1] The Essence of the Empty Seminal Nuclei Lamp

Then Dorjé Chang,
The great natural purity,
Again spoke in words, delivering this speech:

Hey! Ma! Pure-Lineage Dorjé Chang!
What you have asked is excellent,
I will explain it to you!
For the sake of future [beings]
Remember these words that I teach.

The empty seminal nuclei lamp [481]
[Creates] confidence in all phenomena.
Whoever cognizes it
Experientially enjoys the spiritual body of the [singular][45] *bindu*.
And those who become familiar with it will attain it [as] an object of engagement.[46]

Thus, in essence it is
A singularity, free of subtle parts,
A great natural radiance, free from the darkness of emptiness.

In nature it is present as a naturally luminous equality,
A sphere devoid of conceptuality and elaborations.

In it the four self-empowerments are complete without being conferred
So it has a natural primordial red radiance.[47]

Because it is stainless and pure from the beginning,
It is devoid of the fetters of self and the afflictions,
Radiant of its own accord, and empty by its very essence.

This is how its nature is asserted!

[2.3.2.2] The Etymology of the Empty Seminal Nuclei Lamp *(thig le stong pa'i sgron ma)*

"Thig" means unchanging and straight,[48]
Primordially free from any fabrication.

"Le" refers to its great expansive display,
In which appearances are perfectly complete in their
own place.

Because it is "empty" *(stong pa)*, minds that
Apprehend concrete things and cling to objects are stopped.
Due to the great emptiness of its nature,
Minds that cling to self do not arise [in its] radiance.

Being a "lamp" *(sgron ma),* it lights up as the five lights,
Its own state radiant and aware.

These are its etymologies.

[2.3.2.3] The Classifications of the Empty Seminal Nuclei Lamp

Its classifications are fivefold:

(1) The seminal nuclei themselves abiding in the ground
Round up appearances and fictive beings, cyclic existence and
transcendence, into one.

(2) The seminal nuclei abiding in the channels of the body
Round up happiness and suffering into one.

(3) The conventional "causal" seminal nuclei
Are the cause and conditions for the production of the body
and mind, [482]
Rounding up the aggregates, the [eighteen] sensory spheres,
and so forth into one.

(4) The ultimate unelaborated seminal nuclei
Round up the expanse and awareness into one.

(5) The seminal nuclei of the self-emergent fruit
Round up the wisdom-energy of all the buddhas
Into the expanse that is free from exertion.

All of these are the classifications of that [lamp].
The unfluctuating empty seminal nuclei illuminate
The important point of rounding up
The fivefold aspects of appearing objects into one.

This radiance does not set [like the sun],
But from the beginning has been a great self-emergence,
Free of all these words and elaborations, abiding as one.
When you see it, that is it—
There is no other place to seek!

[2.3.2.4] The Characteristics of the Empty Seminal Nuclei Lamp

Dwelling in itself, it is a singular wisdom energy
[In which] the conventions of enumerations are exhausted:
Beyond the clinging that would apprehend it as "one,"
How would it be possible to apprehend it as "two"?

Its distinctive character is its empty essence
Through which attachment to concrete things is blocked.
In nature, it is an unchanging, non-conceptual purity:
The nucleus without companion,
Not [produced by] meditation, and without limits.

It is the wisdom energy of a great natural abiding,
In which you continually abide without activity.

Its characteristic is emptiness pervaded by radiance, and
In its own condition, the limits of the body are exhausted.

In brief, it is liberated from being an object of self-grasping.
Through the primordial glow of [its] great emptiness
Whose natural presence [483] was not created by anyone,
It primordially abides as a great equality.

[2.3.2.5] The Residence of the Empty Seminal Nuclei Lamp

At the center of all sentient beings' bodies
Emerging from the immeasurable mansion of their precious
citta-heart
There are many thousands of channels.
But in particular, there are four great channels:

(1) The great golden *kati* channel,
(2) The one that is like a silk thread,
(3) The slender coil, and (4) the crystal tube.

In these four in particular,
[This lamp] abides and rides on the horses of wind.
It has the nature of emerging,
Entering, naturally shining, and presencing—
Primordially free from elaborations.

As (1) the excellent *thig-le* of the ground,
(2) The excellent *thig-le* of the path,
(3) The peak of excellences *thig-le*,
And (4) the *thig-le* ornamented with excellences,
It is present in the channels.

The nature of the signs of [accomplishment related to] all of these [*thig-le*]
[Emerges from] within the channels [based on] the important points of the body.[49]
It has been present from the primordial beginning
In the "support" of the body of all sentient beings.

[2.3.2.6] The Gateways through which the Empty Seminal Nuclei Lamp Shines

As for its lighting up: the activity of its shining forth [takes place]
Through the gateway known as the *cakṣu*,
Which is the gateway of sentient beings' eyes, unobscured by [any negative] conditions.
Inherently illuminating,
Their light and rays
Are like the maṇḍala of the sun.

Its method of shining forth is unceasing.
Thus, in conjunction with the sense faculties,
And in the objective sphere of appearance, luminosity [484]
[Shines forth] from anyone's eyes.

[2.3.2.7] The Nature of the Empty Seminal Nuclei Lamp

Naturally the reverse of emptiness,[50]
It is a radiant appearance that creates experience,
In which a fivefold primordial radiation
Is present as a natural flow.

It is the essence of these illuminating processes,
And abides as something other than things:
Not as emptiness,
But as something primordially self-characterized
At the beginning of intrinsically radiant cognition.

Since the [time of the] great original purity at the beginning,
Its nature has been like this:

Uncreated by anyone, naturally radiant,
Its nature primordially so.

[2.3.2.8] How the Empty Seminal Nuclei Lamp Appears in the Objective Sphere

In the space before you, empty but appearing,
Its own-essence unimpeded,
It is present as a great self-emergent *thig-le*.
Inexpressible, dwelling within you, its essence also
Primordially appears in the sphere of the sky.

[2.3.2.9] The Experiential Measure of the Empty Seminal Nuclei Lamp

Whoever takes hold of the seminal nuclei
In the intermediate space, without giving off or holding back,[51]
There comes to its measure.
The signs of liberation appear without effort;
Using effort, there is [a similar] measure.[52]

[2.3.2.10] How the Empty Seminal Nuclei Lamp Appears to the Six Types of Beings

To gods, the *thig-le* composed of the five lights
Are the size of their full hand-span,
Existing as great, naturally luminous globes.
For demigods, they are a full hand-width,
And for humans, the size of their thumb,
Existing as uncontaminated globes.
For animals, they don't appear externally;
For hungry ghosts their essence is extremely tiny;
And for hell beings they are simply an [internal] natural radiance.

To gods, [485] they appear as predominantly white.
To demigods, then, green is greater.
To humans, they are a luminous red, naturally beyond clinging.
For animals, blue predominates.
For hungry ghosts, then, they are yellow.
And to hell beings, they are in five colors.

The actuality of the lamp is like that:
Present as a factor of naturally radiant knowing.

[2.3.2.11] The Esoteric Instructions on Becoming Familiar with the Empty Seminal Nuclei Lamp

Squeezing the bulb and corner of the eye
With your thumb and index finger,
[This lamp] lights up manifestly. Have faith in that!

Using the important points on becoming familiar with it,
It lights up in the sky,
And comes to have the five colors, though weaker in red.
Through this, the autonomy of awareness is attained.
That is the natural liberation without effort.

The methods involving effort are as follows:
With your index and [other] fingers, repeatedly stimulate
The channel on the outer side of your neck,
Which forcefully pulses and beats.
Then, with skill in the methods of placing the eyes,
Light radiates out the length of an arrow.
Then it blazes up, at which point a variety [of bodies, etc.]
are apprehended.
Through [following] the oral instructions on these methods,
All of this will come about as [it is described] here.

[2.3.2.12] Analogies of the Empty Seminal Nuclei Lamp

It is, for example, like the spots of a peacock;
In the same way, it is like the eyes of a hawk;
Or, further, like the eyes of a fish;
In the same way, it is like the eyes of a thieving animal.[53]
It is present like all of these.

[2.3.3] Chapter Colophon

This has been chapter three of the *Tantra of the Radiant Lamps*, [486] an explanation of the empty seminal nuclei lamp.

[2.4] CHAPTER FOUR: The Lamp of the Pure Expanse

[2.4.1] A Brief Questioning

Then Pure-Lineage Dorjé Chang,
Having opened the gateway [of] the non-abiding primordial gnosis,
Again supplicated [the Teacher] in this way:

Hey! Hey! Transcendent Victor Dorjé Chang!
Just as [you] the Teacher mentioned
The empty seminal nuclei lamp,

Earlier you [also] spoke of
The "pure lamp of the expanse."
Regarding this term that you mentioned before:

(1) What is its essence?
(2) What is its etymology?
(3) What are its classifications?
(4) What is its nature?
(5) What are its characteristics, its underlying intent?
(6) How does one become familiar with it?
(7) By what [signs] is its experiential measure known?
(8) Where is its abode?
(9) And, from what gateways does it shine forth?
(10) What is its actuality?
(11) What examples illustrate it?

Although I understood[54] all of these earlier,
For the sake of future sentient beings
I seek to listen to them from Dorjé Chang.

[2.4.2] An Extensive Presentation of Answers

[2.4.2.1] The Essence of the Lamp of the Pure Expanse

Then Dorjé Chang the Great
Replied, speaking these words:

Listen, Pure-Lineage Dorjé Chang!
My teaching is flawless—
Take hold of it with your flawless mind!

Lighting up as the corral of the little linked-lambs,
The lamp of the completely pure expanse
Collects in the essence of awareness.[55]

For whoever is familiar with it, [487] its reality
Is deep blue, unchanging, and naturally radiant,
An encircling aura that abides as the corral [of awareness].
Naturally luminous, it lights up as the external sphere,
Unfabricated in its very essence.

[2.4.2.2] The Etymology of the Lamp of the Pure Expanse *(dbyings rnam par dag pa'i sgron ma)*

It lights up in the "aspect" *(rnam pa)* of the objective sphere,
And is a "purity" *(dag pa)* in which the stains are exhausted
to their limit.

The "expanse" *(dbyings)* acts as awareness' own domain:
It is into this that one should drive
The adamantine little linked-lambs,
Whose own essence is devoid of conceptuality.
Within the containing walls of the internal expanse
You don't have to hold them back[56] or [forcibly]
stabilize them.
Without separating [from you], they appear continually.[57]

As a "lamp" *(sgron)*, it nakedly displays
The adamantine linked-lambs, in the sky,
Causing them to appear, but without inherent nature.

As an etymology of its nature,
"Mother" *(ma)* indicates that by apprehending its reality
One primordially abides in an inseparable union.[58]

[2.4.2.3] The Classifications of the Lamp of the Pure Expanse

Its classifications are threefold:

(1) The pure expanse dwelling in the ground, through which
The gnostic energy of awareness is apprehended as the spiritual bodies.

(2) The expanse that lights up in the pathways, through which
The radiance of awareness' *thig-le* are gathered in.

(3) The expanse that lights up in the objective sphere, through which
The little linked-lambs are held in prison.

All of these are its classifications.

[2.4.2.4] The Nature of the Lamp of the Pure Expanse

Its nature is as follows: through its unceasing manifestation
Ordinary minds, concrete things, and memory-driven thought are all exhausted.

In the intrinsically pure appearance of the expanse,
The unwavering equality is cognized
Within non-conceptual awareness.
Thus, in the expanse where everything [488] is equal,
There is the primordial exhaustion of conceptuality,
Abiding in the expanse, which is pure in its own nature.

Devoid of dualistic terms [creating] signifiers and signified,
There is no internal or external in the expanse, and
[Everything] is present in the range of this great natural pervasion.

[2.4.2.5] The Characteristics of the Lamp of the Pure Expanse

It is a transparency with no outside or inside
And thus is unobscured and stainless—
A great, primordial, original purity!

Because it is pure in aspect,
It is present primordially as the characteristics of the expanse.

Without it, awareness would have no objective sphere,
So the unimpeded shining forth of its lighting up
Is the lamp of the expanse.

[2.4.2.6] The Esoteric Instructions on Becoming Familiar with the Lamp of the Pure Expanse

Through differentiating saṃsāra and nirvāṇa,
Body and speech settle into a natural state of rest.

Then, after discerning the lighting-up of the expanse and awareness,
And attaining the measure of becoming familiar with it,
The visions that appear in the exterior
Increase one upon another
As, in stages, you attain the great natural familiarization.
When you attain the measure of stability in this,
All phenomena become exhausted.

Here I have explained how one should become familiar with it
In [terms of two] branches.[59]

[2.4.2.7] The Experiential Measure of the Lamp of the Pure Expanse

From the lighting up of an unchanging dark blue
Emerge five lights of radiant colors.
Then, as this becomes completely clear,
It rises up in the space above and in front of you,
Separated from your body
By four finger-widths or one hand.
That comes about as the experiential measure of this [lamp].

[2.4.2.8] The Residence of the Lamp of the Pure Expanse

It resides in the eyes, unconditioned by the elements, [489]
And thus causes your own awareness itself,
Lighting up as the linked-lambs,
To be apprehended in the cloudless sky.

While your cognition is internally radiant
It abides in the maṇḍala of the *citta,*[60]
[And later] radiates outward into the cloudless sky.

[2.4.2.9] The Gateways through which the Lamp of the Pure Expanse Emerges

Abiding in the pure eye consciousness[61]
Are the illuminating and blazing five lights—
Unchanging and pervasive,
Present as a great, blue, natural radiation.

Unobstructedly shining forth in vision,
It lights up in the external objective sphere.

While its gateway of shining forth is the eyes,
It presences in an unchanging and pervasive way.

Its manifestations are naturally pure:
As an indivisible union of the expanse and awareness,
They have been present from the very beginning; let go and
They naturally manifest as objects of your experience.
[These] visions are intimately related to the eyes,
And thus without conditions they shine forth in the sky.
In that way, the gateway of shining forth [of this lamp] is unobstructed.

[2.4.2.10] The Actuality of the Lamp of the Pure Expanse

In this way, whatever person
Has the three points[62] of the oral instructions,
And becomes familiar with the expanse, [the following] will manifest.

From the upper portion[63] of the body,
This [lamp] is encountered [with] the two [eyes, as] a pair [of arcs],[64]
Which have the natures [respectively] of method and insight.
The two coil together, and as one
Are a finger's width [away], not touching you.

By virtue of possessing the conditions for its emergence,
It will manifest at noontime, and also at night, [490]
The deep blue correlated to its own essence.

In nature, the expanse is a house of light.
As an unchanging great primordial glow,
It is within all buddhas and sentient beings
Without anyone having created it,
Primordially dwelling as a nondual equality.

From its subtle great pervasion,
It shines forth in your cognitive dimension,
And is perceived directly—this is completely secret!

Whoever desires to practice
This great secret
Will reawaken into buddhahood from the primordial awakening.

Viewed from the perspective of concrete things,
[Its] illumination [instead] appears like night.
[But] by becoming familiar with emptiness,
It is a natural radiance, and devoid of apprehendable
objects, thus
An emptiness that no one apprehends!

This is radiance and emptiness
Primordially pervasive and present—
A self-manifesting emptiness,[65] a radiant object.

Here, grasping the measures of its wisdom energy,
It is present as the great natural purity itself,
Timelessly dwelling in the illuminated sky,
An unchanging expanse containing everything.

In this, there are no conditions [needed] for its emergence,
So there is no one at all that does not attain buddhahood,
And saṃsāric appearances are not possible.

[2.4.2.11] Analogies of the Lamp of the Pure Expanse

It is, for example, like the letter *na-ro* (ནོ),
Whose two arcs combine into one,
[And whose] blackness is not liable to change.

Having attained confidence from becoming familiar with
it, [491]
Its colors become distinct and completely present,
Like a rainbow in the space before you.

Then, through the power of further meditation,
[You come] to possess its signs, and
The space before you also becomes like this![66]

[2.4.3] The Benefits of Understanding the Tantra

Whoever desires to understand this tantra,
Should they be excellent and endowed with fortune,
Will understand the tantra themselves,
And attain unimaginable great enlightened qualities.[67]

The tantra's characteristics are threefold:
Its essence, its practice, and its objects to be known.
In this way, through these characteristics of the tantra,
One will realize one's own essence!

[2.4.4] Chapter Colophon

This has been chapter four of the *Tantra of the Blazing Lamps*, an explanation of the lamp of the pure expanse.

[2.4.5] Rejoicing that the Tantra has Been Spoken

Through the Teacher giving this speech,
Pure-Lineage Dorjé Chang and the others
Became joyous and full of delight,
And praised what had been said.

[3] Closing Material

[3.1] Colophon

The Beautiful Precious Golden Flower—The Tantra of the Blazing Lamps, which emerged as the essence of the 164,000 [verses] of the Great Perfection, is finished!

TRANSLATION 3A | *Advice on the Six Lamps*

Bibliographic Information and Notes on Various Editions

Advice on the Six Lamps is an important work for the living Bön tradition and continues to be taught in modern monasteries. As a text, it is thus not difficult to find. Nonetheless, there are numerous editions of the *Advice* and its commentaries, and new ones continue to emerge, so here I briefly describe the various editions that I used in this translation.

Advice on the Six Lamps and Drugyalwa's commentary are both found in a major anthology called the *Four Cycles of the Oral Transmission.*[1] The collection is somewhat loosely defined, as some works (like Drugyalwa's *Lamps* commentary) may appear in one edition of the *Four Cycles* but not in others. The *Four Cycles* collection appears in the catalog of the Bön canon written by Nyima Tenzin (b. 1813), the twenty-second abbot of Menri Monastery.[2] *Advice on the Six Lamps* appears in Nyima Tenzin's listing and thus is considered to be canonical.[3]

For my translations, I had the luxury of working with four editions of the *Four Cycles* collection:

1. Menri edition. This is the most popular edition, and comes from blockprints carved in the 1950s[4] at Menri Monastery in Tibet. In 1960, Lopön Tenzin Namdak carried a copy of this edition out of Tibet, narrowly escaping the violence of that period. Reproductions of this, in traditional *pecha* format, are used in Bön monasteries today. Tenzin Namdak also published the blockprints in Delhi;[5] these reproductions, bound in book format, have become the main source for the study of the *Four Cycles* in the West. On the whole, this edition is quite clean and reliable; though it does contain occasional errors, most of these are easily resolved. Because it is currently considered the authoritative edition, I have used it as the primary source for my translation.

2. Nyag-rong edition. This is a blockprint edition from Nyag-rong, consisting of new prints made from old woodblocks; H. H. Menri Trizin acquired these prints during my stay at Menri Monastery. The appearance of this edition is the kind of coincidence that every researcher hopes for; thanks to H. H. Menri Trizin for informing me of these, and for allowing me access to them. In the years to come, this will become an edition of major interest, especially because it contains some materials not included in the Menri edition, and also because it may have been edited by the Bönpo luminary Shardza Tashi Gyaltsen (1859–1934).

The collection comes with a catalog written by Shardza, in which he mentions editing the *Four Cycles* at the time of its carving.[6] If Shardza's catalog belongs with Nyag-rong blockprints,[7] then this edition could date from the lifetime of Shardza, perhaps the first decades of the twentieth century. The colophons to the individual works, many mentioning Shardza and his circle, will be of great interest to historians, though I have not made a detailed study of them here.

The Nyag-rong edition is exceedingly clear. Handling prints from these old blocks and reading them alongside the Menri edition is a great pleasure. It corrects many of the errors in the Menri edition but of course introduces a few minor errors of its own. The edition is particularly helpful due to the editor's liberal use of punctuation and his tendency to break up complex sentences into shorter elements. The result is that even when the words and spellings are identical between the editions, the two still may read very differently because of the punctuation.

I have not made a detailed investigation of the provenance, dating, and so forth of the Nyag-rong edition, and so have only used it to inform my reading of Menri. My impression is that while the Menri blocks themselves appear to be younger, they may preserve an older stratum of the *Four Cycles* texts, and I expect traditional scholars may continue to prefer them. Still, serious readers will want to consult both editions, especially if Nyag-rong's clarity indeed turns out to be the product of Shardza Tashi Gyaltsen.

3. Dolpo edition. This is a very handsome manuscript on small pages collected by David Snellgrove on a trip to Dolpo.[8] It is an extremely valuable manuscript that, while not ancient, does preserve an older form of the collection (Drugyalwa's *Lamps* commentary, for instance, is not included). Though the texts in the manuscript are almost identical in form to the Menri edition, the spelling used in the manuscript is not standard (*dka' dag* for *ka dag, brtsal* for *rtsal,* and so forth). The orthography contributes a real flavor to the texts and will be useful to those studying the language of the Great Perfection traditions in Dolpo. These interests, however, are beyond the scope of my study, and so I have referred to this edition only occasionally.

4. Nangtha Tenzin Nyima edition. This is a modern edition, published in Western book format.[9] It does not specify the edition on which it is based but appears to be the Menri edition, entered into a computer and then revised to correct some spelling errors. This will not replace the Menri edition, but it is handy to use and is becoming more available inside Tibet, and its corrections are sometimes illuminating.

5. Kanjur editions. Because *Advice on the Six Lamps* was included among the primary works *(bka')* in the Tibetan canon, copies of it can be found in the published editions[10] of the Bön "Kanjur." I did not have consistent access to these during my research, and so have not made use of them.

Commentaries to *Advice on the Six Lamps*

Two major commentaries to *Advice on the Six Lamps* circulate with the Oral Tradition from Zhang Zhung literature.[11] The first, by Uri Sogyal, is called *Ornament of Sunlight: A Commentary on the Lamps.*[12] I have found little more information on Uri than that offered by Patsün Tengyal,[13] who provides only the basic sketch so typical of Tibetan histories: a member of the Northern Lineage *(byang rgyud)* of the Oral Tradition; born in the Dong *(ldong)* clan; became ordained at thirteen; received the Oral Tradition from Riwa Shertsul; and was renowned as a great meditator and author.

Much more is known about the second commentator: the famous thirteenth-century author Drugom Gyalwa Yungdrung.[14] Born in 1242, Drugyalwa became one of Bön's chief exegetes, a towering commentator and systematizer, his role in some ways comparable to that of Longchenpa in the Nyingma tradition. Drugyalwa grew up in one of Bön's first families, the Dru (Bru), so named because they trace their ancestry back to Gilgit *(bru sha).*[15] In 1072 his ancestor Druchen Namkha Yungdrung founded the first Bön monastery, Wensakha, located in Yeru.[16] This is the location where Drugyalwa was born. By all accounts he was a precocious child, able to discuss the massive treatise *mDzod phug* by his eighth year.[17] Drugyalwa came to be known for his broad education and eventually became a major repository of Bön lineages and oral traditions. In his later life, he seems to have ascended to the abbacy of Yeru Wensakha.[18] Bön monasteries today still actively study his writings.

Among Drugyalwa's literary works is *A Commentary on the Intended Meaning of the Six Lamps.*[19] Typical of his style, this is a straightforward, lucid, and not overtly polemical text. It methodically cites a line or two from *Advice on the Six Lamps,* and then proceeds to explain the meaning. It should be noted here that Drugyalwa's commentary is closely related to

Uri's: the two are in fact so similar that it seems certain that one was written with the use of the other. The commentaries each organize the *Advice* by breaking it up into their own distinctive topical outlines (*sa bcad),* which is itself an important way of interpreting a root text. But other than this, their expositions are often very close and sometimes identical. The commentaries sometimes have an inverse relationship in which passages on which Uri comments briefly will be heavily commented upon by Drugyalwa; where Drugyalwa skims over a verse, Uri often will fill in more details.

In this book I have not undertaken a detailed philological study to try to determine which of the commentaries is earlier, though if I were to hazard a guess, I would place Uri as the older author.[20] Still, there are numerous sections in Uri where he cites lengthy passages of the *Advice* and leaves them with little or no comment, giving the impression that his work might be amplifying Drugyalwa's, whose comments to those sections were sufficient. Another possibility is that Uri's comments were annotations *(mchan 'grel)* to the root text, which were later assembled into a separate work and then expanded by Drugyalwa.

At any rate, the important point is not "who is first" but what the relationship of these commentaries tells us about Tibetan literary practices. That is, while one commentary appears to be based on (and occasionally copied from) the other, in this literary culture these practices are not looked upon as a kind of plagiarism, and the copying is not secret or shameful: the two commentaries in fact sit side by side in the Menri and Nyag-rong editions of the *Four Cycles.*

There is of course no reason to deny that large-scale copying has been a part of Tibetan Buddhist traditions and that it contributes to sectarian tensions.[21] Typically when academics discuss "copying" as it relates to the Bön tradition, the discussion revolves around what Bön may have copied Nyingma (or vice versa), as part of the competitive relationship between the two traditions. One problem with this approach is that (as our two commentaries suggest) copying also happens within traditions, and so is not simply a matter of how traditions relate to one another but is part of the broader methods through which religious literature and ideas are developed.

Conventions and Translation Practices

As a final note, I would like to list a few of my basic conventions and practices, in order to help the reader in using my translations of *Advice on the Six Lamps* and Drugyalwa's *Commentary.*

1. Use of editions: My goal has been to provide a translation based on the Menri edition (ZZNG), but I have often relied on the Nyag-rong edition (NR) to help interpret difficult passages. In some cases, I do prefer readings found in NR, and use this edition for the translation. In these cases, I mention the issue in the endnotes.

2. *Subheads*: These are based on the topical outline *(sa bcad)* that Drugyalwa uses to organize his commentary. Often I translate his subject headings literally, but at times I simplify them or make them less cryptic, hoping that a less technical outline will make the translation easier to navigate. Though the root text itself does not contain an outline, I have placed Drugyalwa's headings there as well, in order to facilitate comparison between it and the commentary.

3. *Page numbers*: Page numbers supplied in brackets refer to the pagination of the Menri edition.

4. *Formatting of root text and commentary*: The root text is written in a mixture of verse and prose; this is reflected in the layout of the translation, where verse is set in the form of stanzas. I first present the *Advice* in its entirety, so that it can be read more easily on its own, free of any overt commentarial perspective (except for the topical outline). Here in the root text, indented verses represent the speech of Tapihritsa; verses that are not indented are narration, or textual apparatus. Note also that I save my own footnotes for the commentary, so discussions of difficult elements in the root text are located in the commentary.

The root text is also repeated in the commentary, as Drugyalwa typically cites a few lines of it before providing his comments. On a few occasions, Drugyalwa does not cite the lines on which he comments but breaks them up and intersperses his own comments among the words of the root text. In these cases, I place the words of the root text in bold, but I also go ahead and supply the full root text just before his comments. There are also a few instances where Drugyalwa cites only a few words of a passage, followed by "and so forth," to indicate a longer passage. In these cases, I also go ahead and supply the entire passage. Finally, it should be noted that Drugyalwa's version of the root text occasionally differs slightly from the version in ZZNG; I mention these discrepancies in the footnotes.

Advice on the Six Lamps

[1] Introductory Material

[1.1] Title Page

[269] This is *Advice on the Six Lamps,* from the Great Perfection's Oral Tradition from Zhang Zhung.

[1.2] Homage

[270] *Homage to the self-aware, all-knowing Küntu Zangpo!*

[1.3] How Tapihritsa Spoke to and Advised Gyerpungpa

[1.3.1] Their First Encounter

Once the great Gyerpung Nangzher Löpo was staying on the west side of the Drachê valley, in the hermitage of Deer Face Rock. At that time, an emanation of the master Tapihritsa came to him, conquered his arrogant pride, and taught him how awareness really is. Releasing him from all the ties that bound him, he sent him out to the open plain, his awareness taking hold of its own place.

[1.3.2] Their Second Encounter

Then, some five years later, the great Gyerpung was living on an island in the middle of a lake, doing ascetic practices. In the daytime of the fifteenth day of the first summer month, Gyerpungpa was dwelling in thought, when in the sky in front of him he saw an emanation of Tapihritsa: an immaculate body with a color like white crystal, a self-arisen body with no ornaments at all, a body free of any obscurations or coverings, just sitting there nakedly. Full of faith and yearning, [Gyerpungpa] made circumambulations and prostrations. The Lord himself [Tapihritsa] then responded:

> Fortunate son of the family, you whose karma was purified in your previous lives, focus yourself and listen to me teach the ultimate meaning! So that you can lead future generations of fortunate beings onto the unerring [271] path, I will teach you three pieces of my profound, innermost advice!

[1.4] Praise of this Teaching for Explaining Things the Way They Really Are

[1.4.1] How these Uncommon Instructions are Supreme among all Others

> [Tapihritsa continued:] This is the final of the 84,000 types of Bön—the Great Perfection—the innermost essence of Bön.

It is the esoteric instructions passed through the "mind transmission" of the nine Sugatas, and is the "oral transmission" of the twenty-four men.

[1.4.2] How Common Instructions Distort the True Meaning

A lama who gives the esoteric instructions without understanding these "six important points on the enlightened mind" is like someone showing an object to a blind man. Even though he explains the many tantras and scriptures of the Great Perfection, in the absence of these esoteric instructions they will be like a body without a heart, or the senses without the eyes. Whichever of the 84,000 gateways of Bön he explains will be no more than the interpretable meaning, a partial expression, and will be nothing that could bring you to the heart of things.

[1.4.3] Praise of the Good Qualities of this Advice

[1.4.3.1] The Distinctive Good Qualities of this Advice

Son of the family! For those reasons, this advice is said to be the mirror that allows you to identify the face of the universal ground, the lamp that brings out the hidden primordial gnosis, the esoteric instructions that strip awareness naked, the advice that allows you to cut off straying from the depths, the essential advice that points a finger to the way things really are!

[1.4.3.2] The Topics Explained in this Advice

Here I will teach you six things: (1) How the essence of the "lamp of the abiding ground" is present: this is the important point of identifying the universal ground. (2) The "lamp of the fleshy heart," which is where the ground dwells: this is the important point of self-awareness shining out from the depths. (3) How the "lamp of the smooth white channel" is the path from which [primordial gnosis] emerges: [272] this is the important point of transparent primordial gnosis. (4) How the "far-reaching lasso water lamp" is the gateway in which [awareness] shines: this is the important point of seeing awareness nakedly. (5) The "lamp that introduces the buddhafields," which is how the path is brought into your experience: this is the important point of discovering the three bodies. (6) The "lamp of the bardo period," which is the border where straying and realization meet: this is the important point of how cyclic existence separates from transcendence.

[1.4.3.3] An Explanation of Who to Teach and Who Not to Teach

> Son of the family! To faithless, selfish beings who have wrong views; to uncertain, insincere people who are distracted and lazy; or to vulgar, childish people who follow the lower vehicles, do not speak even a word of this advice!
>
> Those who from their depths fear birth and death, who seek enlightenment, who have faith and nothing to regret, who carry the lama on the crown of their head, who abandon worldly activities to accomplish profound aims—to those suitable vessels for this advice, you may teach it!

After saying this, he gave him the esoteric instructions on the six lamps, advising him in the "six important points on the enlightened mind."

May this not decline until the end of time! May the aims of sentient beings be accomplished! Sa-Ma-Ya!

[2] Main Body of the Teaching

[2.1] CHAPTER ONE: The Lamp of the Abiding Ground

[2.1.1] A Brief Explanation of the Lamp of the Abiding Ground

> *Homage to Küntu Zangpo, the self-aware primordial buddha!*
>
> Son of the family! This is the lamp of the abiding ground.

[2.1.2] An Extensive Explanation of the Lamp of the Abiding Ground

> Here I will teach you (1) the essential abiding reality of the ground,
> And (2) how cyclic existence parted from transcendence.

[2.1.2.1] The Essential Abiding Reality of the Ground

[2.1.2.1.1] An Extensive Explanation of the Abiding Reality of the Ground

> Now to explain the abiding reality of the ground,
> Which should be understood through three aspects:
> The universal ground, awareness, and the ordinary mind.

[2.1.2.1.1.1] An Explanation of the Universal Ground

[2.1.2.1.1.1.1] A Brief Indication of the Universal Ground

> The universal ground is the enlightened mind itself!

[2.1.2.1.1.1.2] An Extensive Explanation of the Universal Ground

Luminous, empty, unmodified and unspoiled:
It is the great original purity, the Bön Body,
Free of any stains and untouched by limitations.

Spontaneously present in nature, it is the Complete Body:
Totally complete, utterly complete, everything [273] complete!

Undefined, it is the indeterminate Emanation Body:
Impartial, its miraculous appearances can shine forth in any form.

But still, [the ground] is not individuated or separated:
Extending through beings and their apparent worlds, like space,
It is spread throughout all cyclic existence and transcendence.

It is the single radiant "sky," covering everything;
The sky of radiance devoid of parts or divisions.

It is the single great "space" from which everything shines forth,
An empty space that has no dimensions.

It is the single great "expanse" in which everything resides,
The expanse of equality, in which there is no high or low.

That is called the "enlightened mind"!

[2.1.2.1.1.1.3] Summation of the Explanation of the Universal Ground

Provisionally, [the ground] is explained in these three ways.
But from the definitive perspective, it has no divisions:
It abides as the single great sphere.

Sa-Ma-Ya!

[2.1.2.1.1.2] An Explanation of Awareness

[2.1.2.1.1.2.1] Awareness' "Subjective" Dimension: Its Gnostic Energy

Awareness arises from the space of the universal ground
Like the sun shining from the space of the sky.
Luminous in essence, but empty in nature,
It is knowing awareness, devoid of conceptuality.
This is called the "gnostic energy" of awareness.

[2.1.2.1.1.2.2] Awareness' "Objective" Dimension: Sound, Light, and Rays

In that [space], its three expressive energies shine forth:
The triad of sound, lights, and rays.
Light dawns in the radiant sky,
Sound emerges spontaneously from empty space,
And nondual awareness radiates outward as rays.
These are called the visionary "objects."

[2.1.2.1.1.2.3] The Indivisibility of Awareness and those Objects

The objects and awareness are not different;
Not divided up, they are an integrated union.

[2.1.2.1.1.2.4] An Enumeration of Awareness' Different Aspects

It is called the "gnostic energy of awareness,"
The "universal ground of embodied knowing awareness,"
The "mirror-like primordial gnosis, the ground of good qualities," and
The "universal ground consciousness, the ground of karmic pre-dispositions."
Distinct and yet wholly complete,
Awareness shines individually in the mindstreams of beings.

[2.1.2.1.1.2.5] How Cyclic Existence and Transcendence Arise from that Indivisible Unity

The universal ground is nonconceptual and neutral,
Its essence originally pure and immaculate.
But it is still the basis of both cyclic existence and transcendence, of faults and good qualities.

Through awareness' connection with light,
It serves as the ground of the spiritual and ordinary bodies.
Through awareness' connection with sound,
It serves as the ground of enlightened and ordinary speech.
And through awareness' connection with rays, [274]
It serves as the ground of the realized mind and the intellect.

Sa-Ma-Ya!

[2.1.2.1.1.3] An Explanation of the Ordinary Mind

[2.1.2.1.1.3.1] How the Ordinary Mind Arises

Now to describe the ordinary mind:
Though the "king of knowing awareness" is non-conceptual,

It is the ground from which the variety of memory-driven
thought shines forth.

Like the sun's energy gives off rays of light,
The energy of awareness gives off the ordinary mind:
The hosts of memory-driven awareness that engage with
objects.
The six consciousnesses and six objects [thus] shine forth as
its energy.

[2.1.2.1.1.3.2] An Enumeration of the Aspects of the Ordinary Mind

It is known as the "thinking mind,"
And called "memory-driven" because it remembers and
is aware,
Or called the "mind" because it experiences objects.

Sa-Ma-Ya!

[2.1.2.1.2] A Summation of the Abiding Reality of the Ground

[2.1.2.1.2.1] A Summation of the Mother, Son, and Dynamic Energy

In brief, it is like this:
The universal ground, awareness, and the ordinary mind;
The ground, the nucleus, and the magical displays;
The mother, the son, and dynamic energy;
These are also the "mind" and the "mind-itself"!

[2.1.2.1.2.2] How Those Three Are Present within Sentient Beings

Here is how they are present as a seamless union
Within the continuum of a single being:

The universal ground is like the plane of the sky,
Awareness is like the orb of the sun,
And the mind is like the sun's rays.

Sound appears as self-emergent dynamic energy,
Light is like a house of luminous rainbows,
And rays are like a net of sunbeams.

This is its primordial abiding character!

Sa-Ma-Ya!

[2.1.2.2] How Cyclic Existence and Transcendence Parted

Here is how cyclic existence and transcendence parted:

[2.1.2.2.1] A Brief Explanation of the Separation of Cyclic Existence and Transcendence

How did Küntu Zangpo become the primordial buddha?
And how did sentient beings begin their karmic wanderings?
Küntu Zangpo became the primordial buddha through realization,
And through non-realization, sentient beings began to revolve, impelled by karma.

The universal ground and awareness are the "basis" of realization and straying.
The three visionary objects are the "condition" of realization and straying.
And memory-driven cognition is the "cause" of realization and straying.

The universal ground and awareness possess neither realization nor straying,
And in them there is no separation of cyclic existence and transcendence.
So, the memory-driven mind is where realization and straying emerge,
And where cyclic existence and transcendence appear to be two.

[2.1.2.2.2] An Extensive Explanation of How Cyclic Existence and Transcendence Parted

[2.1.2.2.2.1] How Transcendence Came About

[2.1.2.2.2.1.1] How Things were Realized the Way they Really Are

Here are the reasons that realization came about:
When the three visionary objects shone forth as [the ground's] expressive energy,
The cognition of memory-driven awareness
Saw them in the supreme way, as self-presencing illusions. [275]

With the three self-presencing objects serving as conditions
Awareness arose in its nakedness, bare.
And the unobscured universal ground was vividly realized.

Through this realization, awareness took hold of its
own place,
And not following after objective appearances,
At that time attained autonomy.

[2.1.2.2.2.1.2] How That Realization Led to Transcendence

Nirvāṇa's magical emanations
Shone forth of their own power, without being created.

Through awareness' connection with light,
Emanations of bodies shone forth everywhere.
Through awareness' connection with sound,
Emanations of speech shone forth everywhere.
And from awareness' connection with rays,
Emanations of mind shone forth everywhere.

All the enlightened qualities and activities arose automatically
From the threefold dynamism of body, speech, and mind.
This didn't happen because of amassing the two collections,
Rather, it occurred automatically through the force of
realization!

Sa-Ma-Ya!

[2.1.2.2.2.2] How Cyclic Existence Came About

[2.1.2.2.2.2.1] How Straying Occurred

[2.1.2.2.2.2.1.1] How the Co-emergent Ignorance Arose

Here are the reasons that sentient beings strayed:
When the three visionary objects manifested,
The cognitive power of the memory-driven mind
mistook them.
Not knowing them as illusory self-presencings, it saw them as
appearances of another, as real.
Seeing them as other, the mind obscured the reality of
awareness.
Not understood as its own awareness, the reality of the
universal ground was not realized.
That is the co-emergent ignorance!

[2.1.2.2.2.2.1.2] How the Completely Reifying Ignorance Arose

Through the force of ignorance, cognition moved toward
objects;

Reifying the appearing objects, it grasped at them.
This is called the "mental consciousness."

As cognition moved after objects, it couldn't hold its place;
With cognition not holding its place, the three appearing objects became chaotic.
From that turmoil in the three appearing objects, the five causes—the elements—arose.
Once the five causal elements appeared, the five objects' appearances arose.
When the appearances of the five objects arose, then the five gateways of consciousness came about.
The six consciousnesses then reified the objects, breaking them up into diversity.
That is the ignorance that reifies everything!

[2.1.2.2.2.2.1.3] How the Self-Grasping Mind Arose

Through the power of the ignorance that reifies everything, [276] things became apprehended as "self" and "other."
Through this grasping at self and other, the afflictions of the five poisons arose.
That is the afflicted mental consciousness!

[2.1.2.2.2.2.1.4] How Karmic Predispositions Accumulate in the Ground

Through the power of the five poisons, the performance of formative action began.
Then through the power of action and the afflictions, karmic predispositions were collected in the ground.
So the universal ground, devoid of conceptuality, [is also] the ground where karmic predispositions collect.

The group of six consciousnesses amasses them,
Hoarding up the karma and the various afflictive predispositions.
The afflicted intellect then holds them, not letting them go.

[2.1.2.2.2.2.2] Having Strayed, the Various Ways That Beings Wander in Cyclic Existence

[2.1.2.2.2.2.2.1] Various Ways of Classifying Cyclic Existence

When the power of those karmic predispositions grew strong,
Bodies composed of conceptual mind took form.
Influenced by delusion, they strayed into the formless realm.

When the power of the predispositions grew even more coarse,
Bodies of radiant light took form.
Influenced by anger, they strayed into the cycles of the form realm.

When the power of the predispositions grew even greater than that,
Physical bodies of flesh and blood took form.
Influenced by attachment, they strayed into the desire realm.

Through awareness' connection with sound, light, and rays,
The triad of body, speech, and mind took form.

The six consciousnesses amassed karmic predispositions, resulting in straying into the appearances of the six classes of beings.
The afflictions of the five poisons resulted in straying into the five paths of cyclic existence.
Through the major causes of the four elements, the four types of birth were established.
And from flesh, blood, heat, and breath, the four illnesses of the body's constituents arose.

[2.1.2.2.2.2.2.2] The Essence of Cyclic Existence

The container world, its contained beings, the body, and the mind arose due to awareness' connection with light.

[2.1.2.2.2.2.2.2.1] How the External World Arose from the Ground

Here is how the external container world shone forth from the "mind":
From the connection between the light of space and awareness,
The fluttering winds emerged, gusting and wavering.
Impelled by their motion, fire emerged with its quality of heat.
Then from the discord between fire's heat and wind's coolness, wetness emerged, as water.
From the essence of water, the grounding of earth was produced. [277]

All of the container world developed from this process,
As the appearances of the five objects shone forth from the essence of the causal elements.

That is how the external container world shone forth from the "mind"!

[2.1.2.2.2.2.2.2] How Sentient Beings Arose from the Ground

Here is how the internal contents [of the world]—sentient beings—shone forth from the "mind":
From the connection between the light of space and awareness,
The memory-driven mind and the moving winds emerged.
From the connection between winds and mind, the fluttering of breath emerged.
Through the power of breath, heat emerged, the domain of fire.
When heat and breath came together, blood emerged, the domain of water.
From the essence of blood, flesh emerged, the domain of earth.
From the connection between the body and mind, the five vital organs developed,
Forming the "seats" of the five elements.

The "energy" of the five elements shone through the five limbs,
The "essence" of the five elements collected in the five interior cavities,
And the "gateways" of the five elements projected to the five sense faculties.
Then the perceiving powers of the five consciousnesses each arose,
Experiencing and apprehending their respective five objects.

That is how beings shone forth from the "mind"!

[2.1.2.2.2.2.2.3] How We Continually Revolve in Cyclic Existence

The five elements' connection with the mind produces the afflictions of the five poisons:
The connection between space and mind produces anger.
The connection between breath and mind produces pride.
The connection between heat and mind produces jealousy.
The connection between blood and mind produces desire.
And the connection between flesh and mind produces ignorance.

The connection between those five poisons and the five elements produces the five aggregates:
The connection between anger and space produces the consciousness aggregate.
The connection between pride and breath produces the formatives aggregate.
The connection between jealousy and heat produces the cognitions aggregate.
The connection between desire and blood produces the feeling aggregate.
The connection between ignorance and flesh produces the form aggregate.

Through the relationship of the five aggregates and five poisons, [278]
Come formative actions, and the various types of behavior.
Through their cause-and-condition relationship with action and the afflictions,
The general and specific sufferings of cyclic existence emerge.

[2.1.2.2.2.2.3] A Summation of the Topic of Straying

Since beginningless time, we have cycled limitlessly,
Circling through all the three realms, and taking up bodies of the six migrations,
As the twelve links of dependent-arising spin the wheel of cyclic existence.
This is not caused by evil: it arises through the power of ignorance!

[2.1.2.2.3] A Conclusion to the Topic of the Separation of Cyclic Existence and Transcendence

Though cyclic existence and transcendence may seem distinct,
They are simply perspectives of realized and non-realized minds.
In reality, cyclic existence and transcendence are not divided in two.
They abide as a great equality, as the single sphere!

[2.1.3] Conclusion of the Chapter

This completes the lamp of the abiding ground. Sa-Ma-Ya!

[2.2] CHAPTER TWO: The Lamp of the Fleshy Heart

[2.2.1] A Brief Explanation of the Lamp of the Fleshy Heart

Homage to Küntu Zangpo, self-awareness shining out from the depths!

Son of the family! The lamp of the fleshy heart is where the ground dwells. This is called the "important point of self-awareness shining out from the depths."

[2.2.2] An Extensive Explanation of the Lamp of the Fleshy Heart

[2.2.2.1] What this Lamp is, and How it is Present

[2.2.2.1.1] How this Lamp Abides: The Essence of the Universal Ground

When the duality of realization and straying emerged in the memory-driven mind, then the duality of cyclic existence and transcendence arose. But the universal ground and awareness do not experience straying or realization—not in the past, future, or present. They have never experienced the split between cyclic existence and transcendence!

Well, then, with regard to that primordially present nucleus: the universal ground that has never experienced obscuration and the awareness that has never experienced straying....

[2.2.2.1.2] Where this Lamp Dwells: The Nature of the Heart

Where does [this] ground dwell right now? It dwells in the luminous vault within the cavity of space: in a deep-red tent with a crystal roof, inside a tent of lamplight. This is called the "heart that holds the channel." From the outside it looks like an eight-cornered jewel, but from the inside like an eight-petaled lotus. At its center are the five lights, present like a tent of rainbows.

[2.2.2.1.3] How this Lamp Abides: Its Characteristic of Primordial Gnosis

[2.2.2.1.3.1] The Inseparability of the Mother and Son—The Universal Ground and Awareness

In the space of that [luminous tent], the universal ground and awareness are unmixed with anything, immaculate, present as the great original purity. The universal ground completely pervades the body, [279] just like the sky. But obscured by the clouds of confusion, its radiance is absent. In the center of the heart, primordial gnosis dwells as the "great depth luminosity," like the sky free of clouds.

Awareness is present in the body, spreading throughout it like the shining sun. But obscured by the darkness of conceptuality, its radiance is absent. In the center of the heart, however, self-awareness dwells as the "great depth dawning," like the sun devoid of darkness.

Like the sun shining in the cloudless sky, [these two] dwell at the center of the heart—inseparable like a mother and son.

[2.2.2.1.3.2] How the Ordinary Memory-Driven Mind Arises

The memory-driven mind is like the rays of the sun.
From its seat at the heart, it is drawn into the channels;
Through the sensory gateways, it experiences objects and takes hold of them.

[2.2.2.2] The Coming Together and Separation of the Mind and Body

How is it that the illusory body and the mind come together and separate?

The universal ground is like the sky, completely pervasive. Awareness is like a bird, present there in its own place. The intellect is like the bird's wings, which propel it everywhere. The body is like a trap, and the winged creature is caught in the trap. So, the bird and the trap can come together and separate, but they do not come together with or separate from the expanse of the sky. It is not situated in any particular place, but is completely present everywhere.

The universal ground is like the earth, which reaches everywhere. Awareness is like a man, dwelling there in his own place. The intellect is like a horse, which can take him anywhere. The body is like a hobble, with which the man holds the horse captive. So, the rope, the man, and the horse can come together and separate, but they do not come together with or separate from the expanse of the earth. It is not situated in any particular place, but is completely present everywhere.

The universal ground is like an ocean, spread far and wide. Awareness is like a fish, dwelling there in its own place. The intellect is like the fish's fins, which move it everywhere. The body is like a net, and the fish is captured in the net. [280] So, the net and the fish can come together and separate, but they do not come together with or separate from the expanse of the ocean. It is not situated in any particular place, but is completely present everywhere.

So he spoke.

[2.2.3] Conclusion of the Chapter

This completes the lamp of the fleshy heart. Sa-Ma-Ya!

[2.3] CHAPTER THREE: The Lamp of the Smooth White Channel

[2.3.1] A Brief Explanation of the Lamp of the Smooth White Channel

Homage to Küntu Zangpo, the body of transparent primordial gnosis!

Son of the family! The lamp of the smooth white channel is the pathway into which [primordial gnosis] emerges. This is called the "important point of transparent primordial gnosis."

[2.3.2] An Extensive Explanation of the Lamp of the Smooth White Channel

[2.3.2.1] The Essence of this Lamp: What it is that Shines Forth

That primordially present nucleus of the universal ground and awareness abides at its residence in the center of the heart, but its pathway is the "path of the channel," into which it shines self-emergently.

[2.3.2.2] The Pathway of this Lamp: Where it Shines

[2.3.2.2.1] The Support: How the Body and Mind Emerge

Now, to explain how the body and mind shine forth from the "enlightened mind." When the body and mind come together in the mother's womb, space creates an opening, earth develops and firms up [the embryo], and water brings it together as one and sustains it. The heat of fire then ripens the body and mind, and wind separates out its vibrant energies from its solid parts and defines the hollows of its channels. So, the life-energy of the body comes from outside, developing via the navel, while the life-energy of the mind comes from inside, shining forth from the heart.

[2.3.2.2.2] The Supported: How the Winds and Channels Develop

[2.3.2.2.2.1] How the Main "Trunk" Develops

In the mixture of the white and red constituents, first the [child's] heart forms, and that serves as the seat of the space element. Then, from the center of the heart, through the creative energy of light and awareness, the wind of the space-element arises, and that opens up the gateway of the heart-channel. Then, the upward-moving wind opens the hollow of the central channel in the upward direction. That goes through the center of the "enjoyment" wheel at the throat, pierces the "great bliss" wheel at the crown, and projects to the gateway at the Brahma's aperture at the crown of the head. That is the path of transcendence!

The downward-voiding wind opens the hollow of the central channel in the downward direction. It goes through the center of the "emanation" wheel at the navel, pierces the lowest vertebra, and projects to the "method and wisdom" wheel at the secret [281] place. That is the pathway of cyclic existence!

From the lowest vertebra, two channels—of cyclic existence and transcendence—branch off from the central channel. One on the right and one on the left, they exit the upper vertebra, go over the brain's membrane, and bend downward at the level of the two eyelids, piercing the nasal cavities.

The right one is the channel of cyclic existence, where the solidified "bodily" *thig-le* and the afflicted winds flow, causing the hosts of problems to arise. The left one is the channel of transcendence, where the vibrant "mental" *thig-le* and the winds of primordial gnosis flow, causing the hosts of enlightened qualities to arise. None of these faults or enlightened qualities flow from the central channel—from it, awareness shines forth as a great primordial purity.

Those three channels are the "space channels that are the ground of all." The heart is like a pitched tent, in which the three channels are present like its tent pole.

[2.3.2.2.2.2] How the Secondary Winds and Limbs Develop

Then, from the center of the heart, through the creative energy of light and awareness, the winds of the four elements arise, and open up the hollows of the channels in the four directions, like tightening the ropes of a tent. Then the four vital organs develop, establishing the "seats" of the four elements. Next, the five elemental limb-winds arise from the five vital organs. They open up the hollows of channels, and cause the body's five "elemental" limbs to project out.

[2.3.2.2.2.3] How the Subsidiary Winds and Limbs Develop

Then, the subsidiary elemental winds emerge, splitting into groups of five. These separate out the five sense faculties from the head, and the five fingers and toes from the four limbs.

[2.3.2.2.2.4] How the Vibrant Channels and Winds, and the Seats of the Sense Faculties Develop

Then the five vibrant elemental-winds arise from the five vital organs. Opening up hollow channels in the upward direction, they project to and establish the five elemental gateways, the five seats of the sense powers. These are the five elemental gateways in which the five objects appear.

Within the hollows of those five channels [282] is the radiation of the five lights, from which the five vibrant elemental-energies respectively arise. This produces the consciousnesses' "powers" of discerning their five objects; for this reason they are called the five sense "powers."

[2.3.2.2.2.5] How the Coarse Channels and Winds, Internal Cavities, and Substances Develop

Then, the five coarse elemental-winds emerge from the five vital organs. Opening up hollow channels in the downward direction, they lead to the formation of the five entrails. These are the "vessels" of the elements: the essences of the five elements—the five "samaya substances"—flow inside of them.

[2.3.2.2.3] The Divisions of the "Supported" Channels

In that way, the three channels form the "trunk," and the elemental channels are the branches. Those split into 360 limbs. And those are split into 21,000 subsidiary limbs, which in turn split into 84,000 leaves. The various powers of cognition arise through these. But though the channels emerge in such variety, the central channel is the one that is the "lamp."

[2.3.2.3] The Mode of this Lamp: How it Shines Forth

The universal ground is completely pervasive in the channels, like the sky. But obscured by the clouds of confusion, its radiance is absent. In the pathway of the central channel, primordial gnosis shines forth as an utter transparency, like the sky when it is free of clouds.

Awareness is present in the channels, spreading throughout them like the sun. But enveloped in the darkness of conceptual thought, its radiance is absent. In the pathway of the central channel, self-awareness shines forth as a great original purity, like the sun, which is devoid of darkness.

Like the sun shining in a cloudless sky, the mother and son shine indivisibly in the pathway of the central channel.

So he spoke.

[2.3.3] Conclusion to the Chapter

This completes the lamp of the smooth white channel. Sa-Ma-Ya!

[2.4] CHAPTER FOUR: The Far-Reaching Lasso Water Lamp

[2.4.1] A Brief Explanation of the Far-Reaching Lasso Water Lamp

Homage to Küntu Zangpo, the body of self-arisen primordial gnosis!

Son of the family! The far-reaching lasso water lamp is the gateway in which [awareness] shines. This is called the "important point of seeing awareness nakedly."

[2.4.2] An Extensive Explanation of the Far-Reaching Lasso Water Lamp

[2.4.2.1] What Shines Forth: The Essence of the Universal Ground

The nucleus of the universal ground and awareness, present since the primordial beginning—that is it!

[2.4.2.2] Where it Shines from: The Gateways of this Lamp

The ground dwells at the center of the heart. [283] When drawn into the pathway of the channel, it shines in the gateways of the water lamp. At the center of the conch-shell house of the brain, coming from the central channel, is a channel called the *tsang-ri bur-lang*. A single channel that splits into two tips, it connects to the eyes. The gateways of the channel appear like an opened *zer-ma* flower, projecting to the gateways through which awareness is seen. From the hollow of that channel, the five lights shine forth, like the concentric spots on a peacock.

[2.4.2.3] How it Shines Forth: Its Fundamental Abiding Character

In the gateway through which those lights are seen is the mother—the universal ground, like the sky, without exterior or interior—its primordial gnosis shining forth everywhere. Awareness dawns in these gateways of seeing, devoid of conceptuality, shining like the orb of the sun. The mind is like the rays of the sun, discerning objects with its multitudes of memory-driven awareness.

Light, awareness' own light, rises in the sky like a house of rainbows. Rays, awareness' own rays, shine in the canopy above you, like a net of sunbeams. In that way, that primordially present nucleus appears directly, vividly, in the gateway of the sense faculty, without waxing or waning, without being something that the mind creates in the gateway of the lamp. This is the important point of seeing awareness nakedly!

So he spoke.

[2.4.3] Conclusion to the Chapter

This completes the far-reaching lasso water lamp. Sa-Ma-Ya!

[2.5] CHAPTER FIVE: The Lamp That Introduces the Buddhafields

[2.5.1] A Brief Explanation of the Lamp That Introduces the Buddhafields

Homage to Küntu Zangpo, self-awareness arising into manifestation!

Son of the family! The lamp that introduces the buddhafields is how the path is brought into your experience. This is called the "important point of discovering the three bodies."

[2.5.2] An Extensive Explanation of the Lamp That Introduces the Buddhafields

There are two issues here: (1) introducing the three bodies, and (2) finally discovering them.

[2.5.2.1] An Introduction to the Three Bodies

[2.5.2.1.1] An Introduction to the Reality Body

As for the introduction:

Son of the family! Its residence is the universal ground, the enlightened mind itself pervading everywhere without partiality.

This is the expanse of Bön-itself, and in that residence, dwelling as this self-aware great original purity, is the Bön [284] Body shining forth to itself. And so the buddhafield of the Bön Body is present within you, accompanying you always, but you don't recognize it!

[2.5.2.1.2] An Introduction to the Complete Body

Son of the family! Its residence is a deep-red tent with a crystal roof. This inestimable mansion of lamplight is Akaniṣṭha, the buddhafield that nothing surpasses! In that residence—within self-awareness' gnostic energy—sound, light, and rays are spontaneously present. Through this, all of cyclic existence and transcendence are spontaneously complete. This is the Complete Body shining forth to itself, and so the buddhafields of the Complete Body dwell within you! But if you don't realize this, they appear as ordinary deluded realms.

[2.5.2.1.3] An Introduction to the Emanation Body

Son of the family! Its residence is complete with three roots, six wheels, a trunk, branches, limbs, and secondary limbs. This is the buddhafield where the lettered-retinue is complete. In that residence—in the gnostic energy of self-awareness—dynamic energy manifests as six consciousnesses and six objects, and then carries out the various activities of body, speech, and mind. This is the natural shining forth of the Emanation Body, and so the buddhafields of the Emanation Body dwell within you! But due to lack of realization, appearances appropriate to the six classes of beings arise.

[2.5.2.2] Discovering the Three Bodies

As for the discovery of the three bodies: in the introduction to the "essential awareness," you discover the Reality Body, and in the introduction to the "awareness of higher seeing" you discover the Form Bodies.

[2.5.2.2.1] Discovering the Reality Body in the Introduction to the Essential Awareness

[2.5.2.2.1.1] The Introduction

Three lamps provide introductions to the "essential awareness": (1) through the "lamp of the abiding ground" you identify the ground, (2) through the "lamp that illustrates with examples" it is represented in examples, and (3) through the "lamp of the signs of primordial gnosis" you are introduced to it in terms of signs.

[2.5.2.2.1.1.1] Identifying the Ground through the Lamp of the Abiding Ground

Son of the family! To identify the ground....

[2.5.2.2.1.1.1.1] Introduction to the Mother

...Set the lamps in their own place, and then cognition will not reify objects. When it is left in its own place, cognition will not engage with objects, [285] and abides without being covered by the objective sphere. At that time, in the universal ground—empty and luminous, devoid of shadows or coverings, completely clear, really radiant—objective appearances arise, like reflections in a mirror. That complete clearness, that real radiance—that is it!

[2.5.2.2.1.1.1.2] Introduction to the Son

As for awareness, at that time make it empty of memory or concept; make it without aim. Rest spaciously without grasping, nakedly without concept; in that state, objective appearances shine forth like reflections arising in a crystal ball. That intense vividness, that is it!

[2.5.2.2.1.1.1.3] Introduction to Their Dynamic Energy

The ordinary mind, with its varieties of memory-driven awareness, individually discriminates and differentiates objects. That is it!

[2.5.2.2.1.1.2] Illustrating the Reality Body through the "Lamp of Examples"

Son of the family! To illustrate its meaning with examples: (1) a butter lamp illustrates how primordial gnosis is naturally luminous, (2) a lotus illustrates its immaculate original purity, (3) the orb of the sun illustrates the spontaneous presence of its luminosity, (4) a mirror illustrates its being unobscured and naturally clear, (5) a crystal ball illustrates its naked transparency, and (6) the sky illustrates how primordial gnosis is completely present everywhere.

[2.5.2.2.1.1.3] An Introduction to the Reality Body through the "Lamp of the Signs of Primordial Gnosis"

Son of the family! To introduce you to it in terms of signs, there are two introductions: (1) to the universal ground, and (2) to awareness.

[2.5.2.2.1.1.3.1] An Introduction to the Universal Ground

To introduce you to the reality of universal ground: it is like a butter lamp that, free of the shadows of enveloping darkness, is starkly evident in its natural radiance. In the gateways of the lamp, the universal ground is free from every trace of darkness, and the natural radiance of primordial gnosis stands out starkly.

It is like a lotus living in the mud but bearing none of its stains, immaculate and nakedly present. In the gateways of the lamp, the universal ground bears no stains whatsoever, and is nakedly present as an original purity.

It is like sun, which was never created by anyone, its intense luminosity shining in full view since the primordial beginning. In the gateways of the lamp, the universal ground, which has never been created by anyone, [286] shines forth into full view as the great self-emergent primordial gnosis, which has been spontaneously present as an intense luminosity since the very beginning.

It is like a mirror without obscurations or coverings, in whose clarity everything can be reflected and appear without obscurations. In the gateways of the lamp, the universal ground is not obscured or covered by anything at all, and is present as the self-arising primordial gnosis, in whose clarity all the appearances of external objects arise without obscuration.

It is like a crystal ball which, free of coverings, is a transparency, bare and naked. In the gateways of the lamp, the universal ground is not cloaked in any obscurations or coverings whatsoever, and so is present as the bare, naked, transparent primordial gnosis.

It is like space, which is not external or internal, but pervades everywhere. In the gateways of the lamp, the universal ground is not internal or external, but pervades everywhere as the great transparent primordial gnosis.

[2.5.2.2.1.1.3.2] Introduction to the Reality of Awareness

Son of the family! Now, to introduce you to the reality of awareness: Just as the universal ground abides, awareness too abides in that way!

[2.5.2.2.1.2] Discovering the Reality Body

Now, to discover the reality of that:

[2.5.2.2.1.2.1] How to Make the Discovery

Set primordial gnosis nakedly, not clothed in the "animal skin" of conceptuality. Set awareness in its bareness, not spoiling it with minds of clinging and desire. Not creating or altering anything in the mind, set it in an untouched manner. Not following after memories or concepts, set it without chasing or grasping. With little motion in the mind, set it in the great equality. Not stopping the flow of awareness, extend the rope of the innate state.

[2.5.2.2.1.2.2] Where This Discovery Is Made

External and internal, container and contents, cyclic existence
and transcendence,
All are fake, "false caves" contained in the mind,
But all are without exception discovered as the
enlightened mind.

[2.5.2.2.1.2.3] The Good Qualities Resulting from This Discovery

No longer led astray by distortion, buddhahood is now manifest!

[2.5.2.2.2] Discovering the Form Bodies in the Introduction to the Awareness of Higher Seeing

Son of the family! Through the introduction to the "awareness of higher seeing," the Form Bodies are discovered.

[2.5.2.2.2.1] The Introduction to the Awareness of Higher Seeing

[2.5.2.2.2.1.1] The Method through which Higher Seeing Arises

Raise the great oceans upward—[287]
Focus on the dark space at the iron mountains.

[2.5.2.2.2.1.2] An Introduction to its Manifestations as Self-Presencings

In the visual canopy, a brightness laden with light,
You see a net of magical rays,
Like a spider's web or a tangled necklace.

Within the blackness, a darkness laden with rays,
You see immeasurable [environments] of lamplight,
Appearing in the sky like rainbows.

The gateway of the sound of empty space appears
At the center of the pool of the conch-lake.
From sound's secret tubes at the "half moons,"
Self-emergent sound rings forth,
Sounding continuously: U, Ru, Ru!

[2.5.2.2.2.2] The Discovery of the Form Bodies

[2.5.2.2.2.2.1] A General Explanation

[2.5.2.2.2.2.1.1] How to Meditatively Take Them into Your Experience

The moving intellect is tamed in sound.
The memory-driven mind is held in light.
The three powers of awareness are refined in rays.

[2.5.2.2.2.2.1.2] How Experiences and Visions of Luminosity Arise

The three powers having been refined in rays,
The maṇḍalas of the three bodies appear to you:
In the mind-itself, empty and selfless,
Empty magical apparitions shine forth in vision.

Self-aware primordial gnosis has no concrete form,
But awareness' efflorescence is the "higher sights" and the
Form Bodies.

Like a rainbow drawn in the sky,
Like an unfurled roll of brocade,
Like a reflection appearing in a mirror!

[2.5.2.2.2.2.2] A Detailed Explanation

[2.5.2.2.2.2.2.1] How to Practice

Here are the methods for training:

Catch the wriggling goldfish
In the dark-room, with a net of light!

Face the completely clear mirrors of awareness
Toward the canopy of the brilliant sky!

Aim the spear of the attentive mind
At the shields of radiant light!

[2.5.2.2.2.2.2.2] How Experiences and Visions of Luminosity Shine Forth

[2.5.2.2.2.2.2.2.1] How Luminosity Arises

At that time, you see the "seeds" of the Form Bodies
Shining in the sky like a constellation of stars.

[2.5.2.2.2.2.2.2.2] How Meditative Experiences Arise

Through becoming familiar and involved with those,
Five particular meditative experiences arise:

[2.5.2.2.2.2.2.2.2.1] The Experience of the Onset of Vision

First, at the onset of vision, you see
Something like mercury, scattering and beading together.

[2.5.2.2.2.2.2.2.2.2] The Experience of the Flaring Up of Vision

Then, vision flares up: in the sky
You see the sun and the moon come into full view.
You see awareness as wheels of light.
You see *thig-le* forming luminous tents!

[2.5.2.2.2.2.2.2.2.3] The Experience of Abundant Vision

Then vision becomes abundant,
And you see the maṇḍalas of the Complete Bodies of the five families.

[2.5.2.2.2.2.2.2.2.4] The Experience of the Completion of Vision

Then vision becomes complete:
You see the maṇḍalas of the spontaneously present seals;
You see buddhafields [288] of illuminating light;
You see miraculous appearances, devoid of fluctuating motion.

[2.5.2.2.2.2.2.2.2.5] The Final Experience

Then the final visions appear:
Lights, awareness' own light—
The natural light of emptiness, like a rainbow.
Sounds, awareness' own sounds—
The natural sound of emptiness, like an echo.

Rays, awareness' own rays—
The magical emanations of emptiness, like an apparition.
Bodies, awareness' own form—
The reflections of emptiness, like the moon reflected in water.

[2.5.2.2.2.2.2.3] How the Discovery Is Made

The "false cave" of appearances is exhausted in the mind,
And the Form Bodies are discovered as being the mind.

[2.5.2.2.2.2.2.4] The Enlightened Qualities That Ultimately Manifest

When straying is eliminated from its depths, it is impossible to stray again,
And the three bodies become manifest, right then.
The power of karmic cause and effect is a great falsehood—
This is the buddhas' forceful method!

[2.5.2.2.2.3] Advice on Keeping These Esoteric Instructions Secret

This is [my] final and ultimate advice!
It is medicine for those who are pure,
But for those who are ignorant, it will turn into poison.
So, don't teach it to everyone, but keep it secret and hidden.

This [advice] is [like] the milk of the white lion—
Pour it into the vessels of the fortunate!
But from unsuitable vessels, who have no fortune,
Keep it for a thousand eons,
Like the jewel in the throat of the water dragon!

This is the advice he gave.

[2.5.3] Conclusion to the Chapter

This completes the lamp that introduces the buddhafields. Sa-Ma-Ya!

[2.6] CHAPTER SIX: The Lamp of the Bardo Period

[2.6.1] A Brief Explanation of the Lamp of the Bardo Period

Homage to Küntu Zangpo, the self-aware manifest buddha!

Son of the family! The lamp of the bardo period is the border at which straying and realization meet. This is called the "important point of cyclic existence separating from transcendence."

[2.6.2] An Extensive Explanation of the Lamp of the Bardo Period

Here I will teach you how the body and mind separate,
How realization leads to liberation,
And how non-realization leads to straying.

[2.6.2.1] How the Body and Mind Separate

There are two points about the separation of the body and mind: (1) how the elements disintegrate, and (2) how they contract back into one another.

[2.6.2.1.1] How the Elements Disintegrate

To explain how the elements disintegrate, it is like this: (1) The spleen, which is earth's [289] domain, weakens and your body can't feel touch. You are unable to raise your left arm, and your nine openings fill with secretions. (2) The kidneys, which are water's domain, weaken and your ears can't hear sound. You are unable to raise your left leg, and you can't hold back your urine. (3) The liver, which is fire's domain, weakens and your tongue can't sense taste. You are unable to raise your right arm, and blood emerges from your nose. (4) The lungs, which are wind's domain, weaken and your nose can't sense smell. You are unable to raise your right leg, and you lose your feces, though you try to hold it back. (5) The heart, which is the domain of space, weakens and your eyes can't see forms. You are unable to hold up your head, and the *thig-le* slip out from your secret place.

[2.6.2.1.2] How the Elements Contract Back into One Another

And to explain how the elements contract, it is like this: (1) earth sinks into water, and your body's strength is lost. (2) Water then sinks into fire, and your body's luster is lost. (3) Fire sinks into wind, and your body's heat is lost. (4) Wind sinks into mind, and though you try to retain your breath, you lose it. (5) Mind then sinks into the universal ground; the breath stops, and the body and mind separate.

This time of death is the border between happiness and suffering. Positive and negative thoughts have a great propulsive force here, so advice on how not to err [in the bardo] should be given in accordance with [the dying person's] abilities.

[2.6.2.2] How Realization Leads to Liberation

Son of the family! There are three ways that realization leads to liberation: supreme, medium, and low.

[2.6.2.2.1] How Beings of the Highest Ability Attain Liberation

Those of highest ability are like garuḍa chicks, or lion cubs—their three powers are already complete, so as soon as the body and mind separate, the vibrant and coarse dimensions of their elements are distinguished, cyclic existence is shaken out from the depths, and straying is purified right in its own place: the gnostic energy of awareness dawns like the sun, spreading throughout the sky of the universal ground whose expanse has no parts or divisions. The magical displays of the three bodies then shine forth without ceasing, like the rays of the sun, [290] and continuously carry out the aims of beings.

[2.6.2.2.2] How Beings of Intermediate Ability Attain Liberation

For those of medium ability, at that time, the external appearances of fire, water, earth, and wind cease and the manifestations of sound, light, and rays shine forth. Separated from the physical body of flesh and blood, awareness is now without a basis, and is present in its nakedness. The hosts of karma, afflictions, and distorted conceptual thought cease, and the universal ground becomes present without obscurations or coverings.

At that time, through the power of having been introduced to the "essence" and the "higher sights," and having become familiar with them, the six superknowledges and the six recollections arise, and buddhahood is attained.

The six superknowledges are these: (1) Because awareness now abides without a physical basis, you can know past and future lives. (2) Because the universal ground is present without obscurations, you can know the workings of karmic cause and effect. (3) Through the pure divine eye you can know pure buddhafields and impure realms. (4) When the three appearances of sound, light, and rays shine forth, you know they are the luminous bardo of Bön-itself. (5) From having been introduced to its essential nature, you know that the three bodies are spontaneously present within your mind. (6) And through having been introduced to the "higher sights," you know the self-presencings of sound, light, and rays to be the lighting up of the three bodies.

And the six recollections are these: (1) first, remembering that you are moving between lives, (2) then remembering that this is the bardo, (3) then remembering that awareness is abiding without any physical support, (4) then remembering the lama's advice, (5) then remembering that the sound, light, and rays are self-presencings, and (6) then remembering that your mind is the Buddha.

Awareness is seen via its bare nakedness, and the unobscured universal ground is vividly realized. Through that realization, awareness takes hold of its own place, no longer following after appearances. Not following after appearances, those appearances are liberated as self-presencing illusions. With appearances liberated as self-presencings, [291] straying clears away naturally, of its own accord. When straying naturally clears away, the three bodies shine forth naturally. When the three bodies shine forth naturally, the ability to accomplish the aims of beings arises of its own accord.

[2.6.2.2.3] How Beings of the Lowest Ability Attain Liberation

Those of lowest ability have entered the gateway of this advice, but having little understanding or realization, they don't recognize the luminous bardo of Bön-itself, and stray into the karmic bardo of existence. But through the power of the oral instructions, they attain a body in a fortunate rebirth. And there, due to their pure karmic fortune, their previous karmic predispositions will be awakened, and they will attain liberation in one more life.

[2.6.2.3] How Non-Realization Leads to Straying

Son of the family! Here is how those who don't realize go astray. For the lowest of beings, who haven't entered into the gateway of this advice:

Through the negative power of karma, you do not recognize the abiding reality.
The moving winds rise up, blowing the ocean of awareness,
Stirring up ripples of predispositions and waves of conceptuality.
The sky of the universal ground is obscured by the clouds of confusion,
And the sun of awareness is cloaked in the darkness of the afflictions.

Sound, light, and rays are seen as extrinsic appearances that are truly real.
And visual appearances arise in two ways, driven by virtuous or non-virtuous karma.

You have a mental body, which you see as your previous form;
Your faculties are complete, and via mind you move without obstruction.
But with no stable place to stay and no protector
You are like a child abandoned by its mother.
Enveloped in the darkness of straying, an ocean of suffering overflows,
And you writhe about like a fish cast on the hot sands.

The winds of the karmic dispositions rise up, and you wander in the lands of the six types of beings,
Circling continually like a water wheel, or the wheel of a chariot.
You have no source of protection in the three worlds—how sad!
The time of liberation never arrives, and you despair, exhausted.

Keep in mind the terrible nature of straying, [292] and turn your back on this disintegrating world! Make effort on the path, fortunate son of the family!

[2.6.3] Concluding Summation of the Lamp of the Bardo Period

In these ways, realization leads to buddhahood, while non-realization leads to wandering in cyclic existence. The bardo is where you reach the border between those two, so this is the "important point of how cyclic existence separates from transcendence."

[3] Concluding Material

[3.1] The Great Good Qualities of This Advice

Son of the family! These six points on the enlightened mind are the esoteric instructions that bring about realization of the mind, for those who haven't realized it. They are like lamps for those who think there is no such mind, mirrors for those who cannot see it, and iron hooks for those from whom it escapes. They are nails for minds that fall apart, refreshment for minds that are foggy, enhancement for minds that are shallow, yokes for minds that are stubborn, and keys for minds that are imprisoned.

[3.2] When and How It Should Be Taught

Son of the family! In the future, you determine who to give this to and who to keep it from, doing so in accordance with their abilities. If people have the karmic fortune, then lead them on the unerring path!

[3.3] How Tapihritsa's Emanation Departed

Having taught this, the Emanation Body [of Tapihritsa] ceased to appear, like a rainbow dissolving in the sky.

[3.4] How Gyerpungpa Attained His Enlightened Qualities

And Gurub Nangzher Löpo, having discovered what awareness really is, made all of the supreme and ordinary attainments.

[3.5] Conclusion

This concludes the Great Perfection's *Advice on the Six Lamps*—an oral transmission unembellished by human words. *Sarva Maṅgalam!*

TRANSLATION 3B | *Commentary on the Intended Meaning of the Six Lamps*

by Drugom Gyalwa Yungdrung

[1] Introductory Material

[1.1] Title Page

[355] This is the *Commentary on the Intended Meaning of the Six Lamps*, from the Great Perfection's Oral Tradition from Zhang Zhung.

[1.2] Homage

[356] *Homage to Küntu Zangpo—self-awareness appearing to itself!*

[2] Main Body of Drugyalwa's Commentary

Here is the final of all the tantras, scriptures, and esoteric instructions; the supreme essence of all vehicles, gateways, and advice; the quintessence of the heart of Küntu Zangpo! This is the esoteric instructions passed down through the mind-transmission of the Nine Conquerors; it is the oral transmission passed through the Twenty-Four Knowledge-Holders, and is the accomplishment of Gyerpung Nangzher Löpo.

This advice on the "Six Points on the Enlightened Mind"[1] contains three sections: (1) the introductory material, (2) the main body, and (3) the conclusion.

[2.1] Drugyalwa's Explanation of the Introductory Material in *Advice on the Six Lamps*

Here there are three topics: (1) an explanation of the homage, (2) an explanation of the way that [Tapihritsa] spoke to and advised [Gyerpungpa], and (3) an explanation of the praise, where the essential characteristics of the advice are also described.

[2.1.1] Comments on the Homage from *Advice on the Six Lamps*

Homage to the self-aware, all-knowing Küntu Zangpo!

Here, in the name Küntu Zangpo, ***Kün*** ("all") means "everything," not wavering from the nature of primordial buddhahood.[2] ***Zang*** ("kind") means that all the realms where there are beings to be trained, without exception, are the objects of his compassion. Those [realms] are all the playful expression of his Gnosis Body. The nature of his enlightened qualities is such that they shine forth indiscriminately, and offer protection impartially, without being close to some and far from others.

"**Self-aware**" means that his mind is the self-emergent primordial gnosis, just as it is: naturally shining forth to itself, and illuminating the objects on which it shines. All things to be known—both as they are, and in their full extent—are his domain, so he is called "**all knowing**."

If you were to classify him, there would be [the Küntu Zangpo] with attributes and without attributes. [357] Both of these are the object of homage. Here, "**homage**" indicates paying respect to them[3] with the three gateways, particularly by bowing down with one-pointed body, speech, and mind, or [with the attitude that] you are inseparably connected.[4]

[2.1.2] How Tapihritsa Spoke to and Advised Gyerpungpa

Here there are two topics: (1) how he spoke at their first meeting, and (2) how he spoke at their second meeting.

[2.1.2.1] The First Encounter

Once the great Gyerpung Nangzher Löpo was staying on the west side of the Draché valley, in the hermitage of Deer Face Rock. At that time, an emanation of the Lord Tapihritsa came to him, conquered his arrogant pride, and taught him how awareness really is. Releasing him from all the ties that bound him, he sent him out to the open plain, his awareness taking hold of its own place.

This passage answers four questions: (1) To whom was [the advice] spoken? It was spoken to that great suitable vessel for the teachings known as "**the great Gyerpung Nangzher Löpo**." (2) Where did this take place? He was taught "**on the west side of the Draché valley,[5] when he was staying in the hermitage of Deer Face Rock**," an isolated place where one's virtues increase. (3) By whom was it spoken? It was spoken by "**an emanation of the Lord Tapihritsa**," who came when the time for [Gyerpungpa's] training, or teaching, had come. (4) Why was it spoken? This is answered in the line "**conquered his arrogant pride, and taught him how awareness really is**." The great Gyerpungpa had become filled with arrogance, thinking how great he was, and this was preventing him [from obtaining] the supreme goal. To clear this away, [Tapihritsa] taught him to nakedly see the way things really are. Then, "**releasing him from all the ties that bound him, he sent him out to the open plain**."[6] This means that [Gyerpungpa] was in an ordinary state,[7] on top which was an oppressive conceit in his own outlook; [Tapihritsa] released him from this, and endowed him with the wisdom energy of the nondual great equality, such that "**his awareness took hold of its own place**." [358] The additional details can be filled in by the more extensive histories.[8]

[2.1.2.2] The Second Encounter

> **Then, some five years later, the great Gyerpung was living on an island in the middle of a lake, doing ascetic practices. In the daytime of the fifteenth day of the first summer month, Gyerpungpa was dwelling in thought, when in the sky in front of him he saw an emanation of Tapihritsa: an immaculate body with a color like white crystal, a self-arisen body with no ornaments at all, a body free of any obscurations or coverings, just sitting there nakedly. Full of faith and yearning, [Gyerpung] made circumambulations and prostrations. The Lord himself [Tapihritsa] then responded: "Fortunate son of the family, you whose karma was purified in your previous lives, focus yourself and listen to me teach the ultimate meaning! So that you can lead future generations of fortunate beings onto the unerring path, I will teach you three pieces of my profound, innermost advice!"**

Here, six questions are answered.

(1) First, at what time was [the advice] spoken? "**Then, some five years later, the great Gyerpung was living on an island in the middle of a lake, doing ascetic practices. In the daytime of the fifteenth day of the first summer month....**" This recounts the particulars of the year, month, day, and place.[9]

(2) Second, to whom was it spoken? It was taught to the great "**Gyerpungpa [who] was dwelling in thought....**" This indicates [that he was resting in] his own unelaborated wisdom-energy.

(3) Third, by whom was it spoken? "**When in the sky in front of him he saw an emanation of Tapihritsa: an immaculate body with a color like white crystal....**" This explains that the Teacher[10] was a pure, transparent vision. "**A self-arisen body with no ornaments at all...**" means that he was not tainted by the faults of conceptuality. "**A body free of any obscurations or coverings, just sitting there nakedly**"; this is symbolic of him being naturally luminous and bare.

(4) Fourth, how was it spoken? It was spoken as a response to a request. "**Full of faith and yearning,**" the great Gyerpung himself had "**made circumambulations and prostrations**" with his body. "**The Lord then responded: 'Fortunate son of the family. . . .'**" After giving him this sign, [Tapihritsa] continued: "**'You whose karma was purified in your previous lives . . .'**"; this distinguishes him as being a suitable vessel for the teachings. "**'Focus yourself and listen to me teach the ultimate meaning!'**" expresses the promise to speak, and [the student's] commitment to listen.

(5) For what purpose was it spoken? This is answered in the line: "**'So that you can lead future generations of fortunate beings onto the unerring path. . . .'**" This explains that this is the chief of all entryways to the path.

(6) What was spoken? This is indicated by: "**'I will teach you three pieces of my profound, innermost advice!'**"[11] This indicates that he taught internal, secret, and supremely secret advice—the ultimate advice in the form of profound essential points.

[2.1.3] Praise of the Teaching, and Its Essential Characteristics

There are three topics here: (1) explaining that these uncommon instructions are supreme among all others, [359] (2) explaining how the common classes of instructions teach the true meaning in a distorted manner, and (3) a praise, demonstrating that [this teaching] possesses excellent qualities.

[2.1.3.1] How these Uncommon Instructions are Supreme Among all Others

> **"This is the final of the 84,000 types of Bön—the Great Perfection—the innermost essence of Bön. It is the esoteric instructions passed through the 'mind transmission' of the nine Sugatas, and is the 'oral transmission' of the twenty-four men."**

First, this mentions the abandonments and their corresponding antidotes,[12] saying: "**This is the final of the 84,000 types of Bön.**" Because all of those are found in this [advice], "**the Great Perfection**" is said to be the "**innermost essence of Bön.**" Thus, while those [84,000] are said to be like butter, this [present advice] is explained to be the most refined, the quintessence.[13] It is also "**the esoteric instructions passed through the 'mind transmission' of the nine Sugatas,**" referring to the lineage from the Primordial Teacher down through Sangdu,[14] who transmitted their state and their natural wisdom-energy in a self-arising fashion.[15] Following this, there was the "**'oral transmission' of the twenty-four men,**" in which it was passed from the Priest of the Gods[16] through Tsepung Dawa Gyaltsen;

they transmitted it from one ear to the next, through [various] methods and miraculous displays. These represent the "long lineage."[17]

There is also a "short lineage," which refers to Tapihritsa, an emanation of Küntu Zangpo, speaking it to Gyerpungpa.[18] From him it was then passed sequentially to the others in the lineage.

In the "ultimate lineage,"[19] all are equal in Küntu Zangpo, the mind-itself. This is Küntu Zangpo teaching to Küntu Zangpo, in a lineage that is primordially perfect and contains no adulteration.[20]

[2.1.3.2] How Common Instructions Distort the True Meaning

> **"A lama who gives the esoteric instructions without understanding these 'six important points on the enlightened mind' is like someone showing an object to a blind man. Even though he explains the many tantras and scriptures of the Great Perfection, in the absence of these esoteric instructions they will be like a body without a heart, or the senses without the eyes. Whichever of the 84,000 gateways of Bön he explains will be no more than the interpretable meaning, a partial expression, and will be nothing that could bring you to the heart of things."**

This passage explains five things. (1) What is explained but not understood [by common teachers]: This is indicated by "**without understanding these 'six important points on the enlightened mind'....**" (2) By whom [such instructions are given]: "**a lama who gives the esoteric instructions....**" (3) An example: "**is like someone showing an object to a blind man...,**" that is, [the student] will be unable to determine what it is. (4) A reason: "**Even though he explains the many tantras and scriptures of the Great Perfection, in the absence of these esoteric instructions they will be like a body without a heart, or the senses without the eyes.**" This explains that they will have no essence, and their meaning will not be realized. (5) How [such teachers teach]: "**Whichever of the 84,000 gateways of Bön he explains will be no more than the interpretable meaning, a partial expression, and will be nothing that could bring you to the heart of things.**"[21] All of their hosts of words are provisional, and teach in a distorted manner. Thus they make it difficult to arrive at the real meaning [360] and bring it into your experience.

[2.1.3.3] A Praise, Demonstrating That This Teaching is Endowed with Excellent Qualities

Three topics are covered here: (1) an explanation of the distinctive good qualities of this advice, (2) a statement of the topics that it contains, and finally (3) an explanation of who to keep the teaching from and who to give it to.

[2.1.3.3.1] The Distinctive Good Qualities of This Advice

> **"Son of the family! For those reasons, this advice is said to be the mirror that allows you to identify the face of the universal ground,"**

Just like your face becomes visible when it is displayed on the surface of a mirror, this advice lets you see the ground, which is otherwise unseen.

> **"...the lamp that brings out the hidden primordial gnosis,"**

Just as an object becomes visible if you hold up a lamp, so this advice brings out the hidden primordial gnosis and makes it evident.

> **"...the esoteric instructions that strip awareness naked,"**

Just like stripping off someone's clothes until they are bare and naked, this advice puts awareness on display transparently, with nothing obscuring it.

> **"...the advice that allows you to cut off straying from the depths,"**

If water is diverted from an irrigation channel at its head, it won't come down [in the channel]; in the same way, if you cut off straying at its source, from then on it will not be possible to stray.

> **"...the essential advice that points a finger to the way things really are!"**

Just as an object is seen nakedly when it is indicated by a pointing finger, so awareness comes to be displayed in naked seeing when its abiding reality is introduced through the "pointing of a finger."

[2.1.3.3.2] The Topics Contained in This Advice

> **"Here I will teach you six things: (1) How the essence of the 'lamp of the abiding ground' is present: this is the important point of identifying the universal ground. (2) The 'lamp of the fleshy heart,' which is where the ground dwells: this is the important point of self-awareness shining out from the depths. (3) How the 'lamp of the smooth white channel' is the path from which [primordial gnosis] emerges: this is the important point of transparent primordial gnosis. (4) How the 'far-reaching lasso water lamp' is the gateway in which [awareness] shines: this is the important point of seeing awareness nakedly. (5) The 'lamp that introduces the buddhafields,' which is how the path**

is brought into your experience: this is the important point of discovering the three bodies. (6) The 'lamp of the bardo period,' which is the border where straying and realization meet: this is the important point of how cyclic existence separates from transcendence."

The six topics are listed in the passage "**The lamp of the abiding ground...**" and following. The subject matter here is clear.

[2.1.3.3.3] An Explanation of Who to Teach and Who Not to Teach

This contains two sections: (1) the actual explanation, and (2) a concluding summation of the topic.[22]

[2.1.3.3.3.1] The Actual Explanation

"Son of the family! To faithless, selfish beings who have wrong views; to uncertain, insincere people who are distracted and lazy; or to vulgar, childish people who follow the lower vehicles, do not speak even a word of this advice!"

The passage from "**Son of the family...**" through "**...do not speak**" explains that the advice should be kept secret from those who are unworthy vessels. The reason is that [through teaching such people,] the advice would lose its power, the blessings of the lineage would disappear, and your commitments would become contaminated. Thus it should be kept completely and utterly secret!

"Those who from their depths fear birth and death, who seek enlightenment, who have faith and nothing to regret, who carry the lama on the crown of their head, who abandon worldly activities to accomplish profound aims—to those suitable vessels for this advice, you may teach it!"

Then, the passage from "**Those who from their depths fear birth and death...**" through "**...you may teach it!**" explains that the advice can be taught to those who have a karmic connection with it. The reason is that they are suited to be the representatives[23] of the Teacher, it will accomplish the aims of beings, and it will serve the great purpose of preventing this advice from ever coming to an end. [361]

[2.1.3.3.3.2] Concluding Summation

After saying this, he gave him the esoteric instructions on the six lamps, advising him in the "six important points on the enlightened mind."

Having given this basic overview, next there is a prayer of aspiration:

> **May this not decline until the end of time! May the aims of sentient beings be accomplished!**

And finally, syllables indicating secrecy:

> **Sa-Ma-Ya!**

[2.2] Drugyalwa's Explanation of the Main Body of *Advice on the Six Lamps*

Here, there are six sections, [corresponding to each of the lamps].

[2.2.1] CHAPTER ONE: The Lamp of the Abiding Ground

First is the "lamp of the abiding ground." There are three sections here: (1) a brief explanation, (2) an extensive explanation, and (3) a conclusion.

[2.2.1.1] A Brief Explanation of the Lamp of the Abiding Ground

> ***Homage to Küntu Zangpo, the self-aware primordial buddha!***

"**Küntu Zangpo**" has the same meaning as before.[24] "**Self-aware primordial buddha**"[25] refers to the gnostic energy of self-emergent awareness, which since the primordial beginning has been present as the actual buddha.

> **"Son of the family! This is the lamp of the abiding ground."**

This indicates that the [following] instructions will explain the essence of the universal ground, just as it is.

[2.2.1.2] An Extensive Explanation of the Lamp of the Abiding Ground

> **"Here I will teach you the essential abiding reality of the ground,**
> **And how cyclic existence parted from transcendence."**

The extensive explanation has two topics, in accordance with the [root] scripture: "**(1) the essential abiding reality of the ground, and (2) how cyclic existence parted from transcendence.**"

[2.2.1.2.1] The Essential Abiding Reality of the Ground

Here there are two topics: (1) an extensive explanation, and (2) a summation.

[2.2.1.2.1.1] An Extensive Explanation of the Abiding Reality of the Ground

> **"Now to explain the abiding reality of the ground,**
> **Which should be understood through three aspects:**
> **The universal ground, awareness, and the ordinary mind."**

In accordance with this, three topics are explained here.

[2.2.1.2.1.1.1] An Explanation of the Universal Ground

First is an explanation of the universal ground. This has three sections: (1) a brief explanation, (2) an extensive explanation, and (3) a summation.

[2.2.1.2.1.1.1.1] A Brief Explanation of the Universal Ground

> **"The universal ground is the enlightened mind itself!"**

This means that it is the fundamental ground of both cyclic existence and transcendence, the ground from which they emerge, their great common ancestor.

[2.2.1.2.1.1.1.2] An Extensive Explanation of the Universal Ground

> **"Luminous, empty, unmodified and unspoiled:**
> **It is the great original purity, the Bön Body,**
> **Free of any stains and untouched by limitations."**

The universal ground, since the very beginning, has been present as the "Great Being" of the three bodies: "**luminous**" in its lack of obscurations or coverings, devoid of any marks of concrete reality, and thus "**empty**." "**Unmodified**" by causes and conditions and "**unspoiled**," it is thus "**originally pure**." Since the primordial beginning, it has dwelled nakedly, not clothed in anything at all, and unobscured. This is the "**Bön Body**,"[26] which is "**free of any stains**" like happiness or suffering, faults or good qualities, virtue or non-virtue, cyclic existence or transcendence, objects or consciousnesses. It is a transparent purity, "**untouched by limitations**." [362]

> **"Spontaneously present in nature, it is the Complete Body:**
> **Totally complete, utterly complete, everything complete!"**

"**Spontaneously present in nature**" means that in its state, there is nothing like cyclic existence or transcendence, happiness or suffering, afflictions or primordial gnosis. Those arise spontaneously from it—they are not created for a purpose, and are not established through exertion, but arise in a self-emergent fashion. Thus [the universal ground] is the "**Complete Body**," in the sense that everything is "**totally complete**" in it: external and internal, objects and consciousnesses, everything without exception. Everything is "**utterly complete**" there: all of cyclic existence and transcendence. And it is "**everything complete**," comprising all things knowable, everything with nothing left out: the condensed super-perfection![27]

"Undefined, it is the indeterminate Emanation Body:"

Its essence is not established as anything in particular, yet it takes form as any variety of magical emanations.[28] Its activities arise in any form whatsoever, but there is nothing about which one can say: "This is its defining characteristic."

"Impartial, its miraculous appearances can shine forth in any form."

Though its nature is to abide as the great equality of all sides and divisions, due to realization or non-realization, its aspects, or its activities[29]—mistaken appearances, the expanse of Bön,[30] happiness, suffering, and so forth—arise in manifold variety.

"But still, it is not individuated or separated:
Extending through beings and their apparent worlds, like space,"

The universal ground is a singularity that pervades all of cyclic existence and transcendence. So does it dwell individually in each being? Indeed, it is the single sphere *(thig le)* that completely pervades everything, dwelling individually and variously as the natures of the appearing worlds and the life forms [that they contain]. Yet it does so like space, which is not individuated or multiple.

"It is spread throughout all cyclic existence and transcendence."

The "universal ground of embodied knowing awareness"[31] is in the continuum of all buddhas and sentient beings, primordially distinct, naturally manifesting in each of them. But the "singular essential ground"[32] pervasively spreads throughout everything.

Next is an explanation of [the ground in terms of the "three spaces":] the sky, space, and the expanse.

"It is the single radiant 'sky,' covering everything;"

(1) Devoid of obscurations or coverings, [the ground] is an intense radiant luminosity, able to pervade all of cyclic existence and transcendence, without having to be big or small, many or few, fine or coarse, thick or thin—just like oil pervades a sesame seed.

"The sky of radiance devoid of parts or divisions." [363]

In it, there are no cardinal directions or intermediate directions, no above or below, no center or boundaries, no outside or inside, no surface or depths, no beginning or end. Devoid of those, it is present throughout the entire apparent world, throughout all life forms, through all of cyclic existence and transcendence, as a great equality with no parts or divisions.

"It is the single great 'space' from which everything shines forth,"

(2) [The ground is also] the great "space," empty and devoid of self. There is nothing knowable, no phenomenon of cyclic existence or transcendence, that does not emerge from it, that is not possible in it, that does not shine forth from it.

"An empty space that has no dimensions."

There is nothing that will not fit within its range, nothing that is not included in it. But it is still never obstructed or confined, never depleted or filled.[33]

"It is the single great 'expanse' in which everything resides,"

(3) In the nondual great equality of its expanse abides everything knowable, all of cyclic existence and transcendence, with nothing cast out, without union or separation, with nothing being near or far.

"The expanse of equality, in which there is no high or low."

Abiding in that way, it is the "great universal heap,"[34] devoid of good or bad, large or small, high or low, waning or waxing, without separation or mixing.

"That is called the 'enlightened mind'!"

Named this in order to identify it, it is also called the "universal ground of primordial presence," the "common ground of cyclic existence and transcendence," and the "essential ground."

[2.2.1.2.1.1.1.3] Summation of the Universal Ground

"Provisionally, it is explained in these three ways."

When represented in language, with names and words, [the ground] is said to be threefold: space, Bön-itself,[35] and the mind-itself. These represent it, respectively, through an example, a meaning, and a sign.[36]

"But from the definitive perspective, it has no divisions:"

In reality, it is beyond the expressions of speech or thought.

"It abides as the single great sphere."

It is subtle and uncountable, and it transcends expression in signs. From this perspective, the example, meaning, and sign are all drawn together indivisibly, as a single taste. But in order to present it systematically, and to provide an introduction to it, it has been cast into these divisions, as they help to create a special conviction about it.

"Sa-Ma-Ya!"

This applies a seal of secrecy.

[2.2.1.2.1.1.2] An Explanation of Awareness

The explanation of awareness' gnostic energy [364] has five topics: (1) The abiding nature of the "subject" (i.e., awareness' gnostic energy); (2) how the three "objects" (i.e., sound, light, and rays) shine forth; (3) an explanation of those objects and awareness as an indivisible unity; (4) a detailed explanation enumerating awareness' different aspects; and (5) how cyclic existence and transcendence arise from that indivisible unity.

[2.2.1.2.1.1.2.1] Awareness' "Subjective" Dimension: Its Gnostic Energy

"The so-called 'gnostic energy of awareness' is as follows."

The innate universal ground that shines forth within you is known as the "universal ground of embodied knowing awareness." Like the orb of the sun shining onto everything individually from the singular space of the sky, [awareness] comes to reside in the continuum of each and every being.

"Awareness arises from the space of the universal ground
Like the sun shining from the space of the sky."

This refers to the "ultimate abiding universal ground"[37] (exemplified by the sky) from whose singular space shines the "universal ground of embodied knowing awareness" (exemplified by the orb of the sun). This is how the gnostic energy of awareness shines forth individually, into the continuum of each and every being.

"Luminous in essence, but empty in nature,
It is knowing awareness, devoid of conceptuality."

Further, that awareness is radiant because it has no obscurations or coverings; but in nature it is also empty, devoid of self. It is beyond being an object engaged by the ordinary mind, and dwells as the non-conceptual "king of knowing awareness."[38]

[2.2.1.2.1.1.2.2] Awareness' "Objective" Dimension: Sound, Light, and Rays

"In that [space], its three expressive energies shine forth:"

This refers to the self-presencing of the unimpeded radiation of the nondual ground and awareness, in which the three great visionary objects shine forth.

"The triad of sound, lights, and rays.
Light dawns in the radiant sky,
Sound emerges spontaneously from empty space,
And nondual awareness radiates outward as rays.
These are called the visionary 'objects.'"

What shines forth? "**The triad of sound, light, and rays**." Explaining this further, the verse says that awareness "**dawns**" as "**light**" in the unstained and naturally "**radiant sky**." "**Sound emerges spontaneously from empty space**" refers to sound emerging from its empty and selfless dynamic energy. "**Nondual awareness radiates outward as rays**" means that rays shine forth from its expressive energy, in which emptiness and radiance are nondual. Finally, it says that "**these**," meaning the triad of sound, light, and rays, i.e., the visionary objects, are called "**objects**" because they shine forth as self-presencings. In fact, all external objects shine forth from that [ground]. [365]

Here, the gnostic energy of awareness is known as a "subjective knower."[39]

[2.2.1.2.1.1.2.3] The Indivisibility of Awareness and Those Objects

"The objects and awareness are not different;"

Those two are not individuated; they are not things that are subject to coming together and parting.

"Not divided up, they are an integrated union."

The objects arise from awareness' dynamic energy, and it is in the objective expanse that awareness appears. Thus, not distinguished by divisions, not mingled by mixing, [awareness and the objects] abide as an indivisible unity.

[2.2.1.2.1.1.2.4] An Enumeration of Awareness' Different Aspects

"It is called the 'gnostic energy of awareness,'"

The awareness that shines forth nakedly from the space of the universal ground—naturally radiant, non-conceptual, unobscured—is known as the "gnostic energy of awareness."

"The 'universal ground of embodied knowing awareness,'"

This is the source-potential of all memory-driven thought and knowing awareness, its essence continuous through the three times.

"The 'mirror-like primordial gnosis, the ground of good qualities,' and..."

Radiant in essence but without true nature, the function of this is to be the ground from which all the enlightened-bodies and the primordial gnoses shine forth, and the ground into which they are set free.[40]

"The 'universal ground consciousness, the ground of karmic predispositions.'"

In essence morally neutral, the function of this is to be the ground in which the afflictions accumulate.

"Distinct and yet wholly complete,"

The apparent worlds and their life forms appear individually, with distinct characteristics. But, just as everything is wholly complete within the range of the sky, they are wholly complete within the single sphere (*thig le*).

"Awareness[41] shines individually in the mindstreams of beings."

In the state of the enlightened mind, each and every thing in cyclic existence and transcendence is complete, while in the mindstream of a single being, awareness arises individually.

[2.2.1.2.1.1.2.5] How Cyclic Existence and Transcendence Arise from That Indivisible Unity

"The universal ground is non-conceptual and neutral,"

In essence [the ground] abides as a great original purity, transcending the domains of illustration or expression where you could say "this thing is it." Its activities [366] do not fall to any partiality or bias whatsoever.

"Its essence originally pure and immaculate."

It is not touched by any limitations at all, but is present as a pure transparency, naked and bare, naturally radiant, and without stains.

"But it is still the basis of both cyclic existence and transcendence, of faults and good qualities."

In the absence of realization, it is the ground of the faults and shortcomings of cyclic existence; with realization present, it is the ground of the enlightened qualities of transcendence.

"Through awareness' connection with light,
It serves as the ground of the spiritual and ordinary bodies."

With realization present, all the emanations of the buddha-bodies emerge; in the absence of realization, what emerges is all of the aggregates that constitute the ordinary bodies of sentient beings.

"Through awareness' connection with sound,
It serves as the ground of enlightened and ordinary speech."

The magical emanations of buddha-speech emerge from the dynamic energy [of their connection], as does the ordinary linguistic speech of sentient beings.

"And through awareness' connection with rays,
It serves as the ground of the realized mind and the intellect."

The knowing primordial gnosis of the buddhas emerges from the dynamic energy [of their connection], as does all the memory-driven conceptuality of sentient beings.

"Sa-Ma-Ya!"

This indicates profundity and secrecy.

[2.2.1.2.1.1.3] An Explanation of the Ordinary Mind

Here there are two topics: (1) how the ordinary mind *(blo)* arises in the ground, and (2) an enumeration of its different aspects, once it has emerged.

[2.2.1.2.1.1.3.1] How the Ordinary Mind Emerges

"Now to describe the ordinary mind:"

This is what grasps at an essence of things, even though there is not even an atom of one there. It is called the "thinking mind."[42]

"Though the 'king of knowing awareness' is non-conceptual,
It is the ground from which the variety of memory-driven thought shines forth."

Although in its essence there is not even an atom of conceptuality, it is the ground from which the thinking mind and the various memory-driven minds shine forth, as its magical apparitions and expressive energy.

"Like the sun's energy gives off rays of light,
The energy of awareness gives off the ordinary mind:"

Just as light rays emerge through the energy of the sun, the various thought- and memory-driven minds emerge from the gnostic energy of awareness.

"The hosts of memory-driven awareness that engage with objects. [367]
The six consciousnesses and six objects [thus] shine forth as its energy."

This refers to the arising of the six consciousnesses, and [the six objects of those consciousnesses] form, sound, smell, taste, touch, and *bön*.[43]

[2.2.1.2.1.1.3.2] An Enumeration of the Aspects of the Ordinary Mind

"It is known as the 'thinking mind' *(bsam pa'i blo)*,"

When it considers objects using thought *(bsam)*, it is called the "mind" *(blo)*.

"And called 'memory-driven' because it remembers and is aware,"

Due to its thought, there is memory and awareness, so is called "memory-driven."[44]

"Or called the 'mind' *(sems)* because it experiences objects."

This memory-driven mind is what engages with objects.

[2.2.1.2.1.2] A Summation of the Abiding Reality of the Ground

Two topics are explained here: (1) an enumeration of the "sources": mother, son, and dynamic energy,[45] and (2) how those are present in the continua of beings.

[2.2.1.2.1.2.1] A Summation of the Mother, Son, and Dynamic Energy

"In brief, it is like this:"

To present the esoteric instructions in brief, it is like this:

"The universal ground, awareness, and the ordinary mind;"

These represent the enlightened mind, the gnostic energy of awareness, and the ordinary memory-driven mind.

"The ground, the nucleus, and the magical displays;"

The enlightened mind is called the "ground"; the gnostic energy of awareness is called the "nucleus," and the ordinary mind is called the "magical displays."[46]

"The mother, the son, and dynamic energy;"

The "mother" is the enlightened mind, the "son" is the gnostic energy of awareness, and the "dynamic energy" of their indivisible relationship is the ordinary mind.

"These are also the 'mind' and the 'mind-itself'!"

Here, "mind" refers to the ordinary memory-driven mind. The enlightened mind is the "mind itself," whose essence pervades everything. The gnostic energy of awareness is the "mind itself" that is innate, that dwells within you.

[2.2.1.2.1.2.2] How Those Three Are Present within Sentient Beings

"Here is how they are present as a seamless union
Within the continuum of a single being:"

How do those three dwell within the continuum of a single being? The "mother" of the universal ground and the "son" [of awareness] are indivisible, and are present [within beings] as the abiding reality of the actual Buddha.

"The universal ground is like the plane of the sky,
Awareness is like the orb of the sun,
And the mind is like the sun's rays."

The mother, or the "**universal ground**," is empty, abiding like "**the sky**." The son, or the gnostic energy of "**awareness**," is present like "**the orb of the sun**." Those two are inseparable, dwelling as emptiness and radiance without duality, like the sun shining in the sky. [368] All the memory-driven thought of the "**mind**" is present such that it naturally arises and naturally disappears, like "**the sun's rays**."

"Sound appears as self-emergent dynamic energy,
Light is like a house of luminous rainbows,
And rays are like a net of sunbeams.
This is its primordial abiding character!"[47]

From within the range of that,[48] the objects, luminously radiant, presence naturally [in] the empty expanse, shining forth like illusions: (1) "**sound**," awareness' own sound, arises like an echo "**as the dynamic energy**" of awareness; (2) "**light**," awareness' own light, rises in the sky like "**a house of rainbows**"; and (3) "**rays**," awareness' own rays, shine in the sky like "**sunbeams**."

Furthermore, those objects and their perceiving cognition are without duality, indivisible. The great luminosity has, from the very beginning, been present as the nature of the enlightened bodies, primordial gnoses, ornaments, maṇḍalas, and buddhafields. As the "ground" luminosity, it dwells as the primordial buddha. When its reality arises in the mindstreams [of beings] and becomes manifest, it is the "path" luminosity, the manifest buddha. And, when it is completely perfected and reaches its final limit, then it is the "fruit" luminosity, the perfectly complete buddha.

[2.2.1.2.2] How Cyclic Existence and Transcendence Parted

> **"Here is how cyclic existence and transcendence parted:"**

There are three sections here: (1) a brief explanation, (2) an extensive explanation, and (3) a conclusion.

[2.2.1.2.2.1] A Brief Explanation of the Separation of Cyclic Existence and Transcendence

> **"How did Küntu Zangpo become the primordial buddha?**
> **And how did sentient beings begin their karmic wanderings?**
> **Küntu Zangpo became the primordial buddha through realization,**
> **And through non-realization, sentient beings began to revolve, impelled by karma."**

You may ask: "**How did Küntu Zangpo become the primordial buddha?**" The answer is that "**Küntu Zangpo became the primordial buddha through realization.**" And you may ask: "**How did sentient beings begin their karmic wanderings?**" The answer is that "**Through non-realization, sentient beings began to revolve, impelled by karma**."

> **"The universal ground and awareness are the "basis" of realization and straying."**

Although in their essence they possess not even the slightest trace of realization or straying, they are the ground from which both realization and straying arise.

> **"The three visionary objects are the 'condition' of realization and straying."**

When sound, light, and rays are not understood as self-presencings, that serves as the condition for realization and straying to emerge.

> **"And memory-driven cognition is the 'cause' of realization and straying."**

This refers to the duality of realization and non-realization arising in the ordinary mind.

> **"The universal ground and awareness possess neither realization nor straying,"**

Although the universal ground and awareness are the ground of realization and straying, those two have no stains whatsoever.

> **"And in them there is no separation of cyclic existence and transcendence." [369]**

In the abiding reality of the ground, there is no separation of those into two.

"So, the memory-driven mind is where realization and straying emerge,"

In accordance with there being memory and negative memory,[49] those emerge as a duality.

"And where cyclic existence and transcendence appear to be two."

Thus, transcendence arises due to realization, while cyclic existence arises due to non-realization.

[2.2.1.2.2.2] An Extensive Explanation of How Cyclic Existence and Transcendence Parted

This has two sections: the way that (1) transcendence and (2) cyclic existence parted.

[2.2.1.2.2.2.1] How Transcendence Came About

There are two sections here: (1) how things were realized the way they really are, and (2) how that realization led to the attainment of transcendence.

[2.2.1.2.2.2.1.1] How Things Were Realized the Way They Really Are

"Here are the reasons that realization came about:"

You may ask: "How did Küntu Zangpo make his realization?" The answer is:

"When the three visionary objects shone forth as [the ground's] expressive energy,"

This refers to the time when sound, lights, and rays [first] manifested.

"The cognition of memory-driven awareness
Saw them in the supreme way,[50] as self-presencing illusions."

Via the memory-driven mind *(dran pa'i blo),* he saw the lights as his own lights, like a rainbow; the sounds as his own sounds, like echoes; and the rays as his own rays, like a mirage.

"With the three self-presencing objects serving as conditions
Awareness arose in its nakedness, bare."

Just as you see your face when you look in a mirror, via the condition of the [three] objects, awareness came to be seen. At that time, awareness, which had never worn the "animal skin" of the conceptual mind, arose in its nakedness.

"And the unobscured[51] universal ground was realized vividly."

This means that the universal ground, which had never been cloaked in karmic predispositions or obscurations, came to be vividly realized.

"Through this realization, awareness took hold of its own place."

This refers to Küntu Zangpo taking hold of his kingdom.

"And not following after objective appearances,"

Awareness, having taken hold of its kingdom, no longer followed after the "populace"[52] of appearances.

"At that time attained autonomy."

When the awareness of objects[53] gained autonomy, it no longer followed after objects of cognition.

[2.2.1.2.2.2.1.2] How That Realization Led to Transcendence

"Nirvāṇa's magical emanations [370]
Shone forth of their own power, without being created."

At the time of that realization, the spiritual bodies, primordial gnoses, and so forth—the hosts of good qualities—shone forth through their own power, without the necessity of any intention to do so.

"Through awareness' connection with light,
Emanations of bodies shone forth everywhere."

Through the expressive energy of that [connection], enlightened bodies and apparitions shone forth: the buddha's three bodies, five bodies,[54] the five deities,[55] inestimable mansions, buddhafields, ornaments, maṇḍalas, bodily colors, implements, and light rays.

"Through awareness' connection with sound,
Emanations of speech shone forth everywhere."

Through the expressive energy of that [connection], a multitude of true speech emerged: melodious brahmā's speech,[56] the gateways of Bön, and the vehicles.

"And from awareness' connection with rays,
Emanations of mind shone forth everywhere."

Through the expressive energy of that [connection], the five all-knowing primordial gnoses arose. From those, all the ways that they divide up—in 61, in 84,000, in multiples of tens of thousands and hundreds of thousands—arose.

"All the enlightened qualities and activities arose automatically
From the threefold dynamism of body, speech, and mind."

The qualities of greatness and the enlightened activities arose from the energy of that indivisible triad, appearing of their own accord, without relying on any type of effort.

"This didn't happen because of amassing the two collections,
Rather, it occurred automatically through the force of realization!"

This didn't come about from amassing the collections of merit and wisdom, as is the case in the lower [vehicles]. Rather, through the force of [Küntu Zangpo's] realization, it occurred effortlessly and spontaneously.

[2.2.1.2.2.2.2] How Cyclic Existence Came About

"Here are the reasons that sentient beings strayed:"

There are three topics here: (1) how straying actually occurred, (2) having strayed, the ways [that beings] wander in cyclic existence, and (3) a summation of this topic.

[2.2.1.2.2.2.2.1] How Straying Occurred

This has four sections: (1) how the "co-emergent ignorance" arose, (2) how the "completely-reifying ignorance" arose, (3) how the self-grasping afflicted mind arose, and (4) how karmic predispositions accumulated in the ground. [371]

[2.2.1.2.2.2.2.1.1] How the "Co-emergent Ignorance"[57] Arose

Now, for the first topic:

"When the three visionary objects manifested,"

This refers to the time when the triad of sound, light, and rays shone forth into actuality.

"The cognitive power of the memory-driven mind[58] mistook them."

This means that it did not know the objects' actual character.

"Not knowing them as illusory self-presencings, it saw them as appearances of another, as real."

Not knowing the sound, light, and rays as the expressive energy of awareness, it saw them as autonomous appearances on the other side. This is like your own form appearing on the surface of water, and not seeing it as your own form but as that of another.

"Seeing them as other, the mind obscured the reality of awareness."

The conceptual mind clothes naked awareness, like clouds covering up the sun.

"Not understood as its own awareness, the reality of the universal ground was not realized."

Not recognizing its own sun-like awareness, it became clouded over with ignorance, like an enveloping darkness. Thus the reality of the sky-like universal ground became obscured, like the sun setting and leaving an obscuring darkness.

"That is the co-emergent ignorance!"

This refers to the non-recognition of the abiding reality, even though it is right there as a part of you.

[2.2.1.2.2.2.2.1.2] How the "Completely-Reifying Ignorance" Arose

The second topic is how the "completely-reifying ignorance"[59] arose:

"Through the force of ignorance, cognition moved toward objects;"

This is the "moving mind," emerging due to non-recognition.

"Reifying the appearing objects, it grasped at them.
This is called the 'mental consciousness.'"[60]

This means that it clung to sound, lights, and rays as having true aspects.

"As cognition moved after objects, it couldn't hold its place;"

This refers to awareness not holding its own place.

"With cognition[61] not holding its place, the three appearing objects became chaotic."

This is like wind entering the clouds, stirring them into turmoil.

"From that turmoil in the three appearing objects, the five causes—the elements—arose."

This is fire, water, earth, wind, space, [372] and so forth arising from sound, light, and rays.

"Once the five causal elements appeared, the five objects' appearances arose."

Form, sound, smell, taste, and touch emerged from the essence of the five elements.

"When the appearances of the five objects arose, then the five gateways of consciousness came about."

Then each of the five consciousnesses related to those objects emerged: the eye, ear, nose, tongue, and body consciousness.

"The six consciousnesses then reified the objects, breaking them up into diversity."

Now, things became apprehended as good and bad, big and small, high and low, self and other, enemy and friend, god and demon, and so forth.

"That is the ignorance that reifies everything!"

This is the cognition that apprehends things as being separate, and is called the "separately apprehending consciousness."

[2.2.1.2.2.2.2.1.3] How the Self-Grasping Afflicted Mind Arose

The third topic is how the afflicted mind[62] arose.

"Through the power of the ignorance that reifies everything, things became apprehended as 'self' and 'other.'"

Apprehending in that way, the apprehender apprehended itself as an object.[63]

"Through this grasping at self and other, the afflictions of the five poisons arose."

This refers to coming to have desirous attachment for attractive objects, aversion for unattractive ones, delusion toward ones that are neither [attractive nor unattractive], pride in one's own greatness, and jealousy of others' good qualities.

"That is the afflicted mental consciousness!"

That afflicted mind, which reifies things as being separate, and apprehends self as other, is a deluded cognition.

[2.2.1.2.2.2.2.1.4] How Karmic Predispositions Accumulated in the Ground

The fourth topic discusses how karmic predispositions accumulate.

"Through the power of the five poisons, the performance of formative action[64] began."

This is the emergence of the various kinds of action that involve effort.

"Then through the power of action and the afflictions, karmic predispositions were collected in the ground."

This means that actions and the afflictions piled up karmic predispositions in the universal ground.

Where are these predispositions collected?

"So the universal ground, devoid of conceptuality, [is also] the ground where karmic predispositions collect."

If they are indeed stored there, what piled them up there in the first place?

"The group of six consciousnesses amasses them," [373]

That is it! And as for what is held there:

"Hoarding up the karma and the various afflictive predispositions."

That is it! And who holds on to what is stored there?

"The afflicted intellect then holds them, not letting them go."

That is it!

[2.2.1.2.2.2.2.2] Having Strayed, the Various Ways That Beings Wander in Cyclic Existence

Now, to explain how we wander in cyclic existence. This has three sections: (1) various ways that cyclic existence can be classified, (2) its essence, and (3) how [beings] continually revolve there.

[2.2.1.2.2.2.2.2.1] Various Ways of Classifying Cyclic Existence

There are six divisions here: the different (1) realms, (2) bases, (3) classes of beings, (4) paths leading to it, (5) ways of being born there, and (6) types of suffering.

[2.2.1.2.2.2.2.2.1.1] The Realms of Cyclic Existence

First, "three cyclic existences" corresponding to the three realms are described.

"When the power of those karmic predispositions grew strong,
Bodies composed of conceptual mind took form.
Influenced by ignorance, they strayed into the formless realm."

"**When the power of those karmic predispositions grew strong**" means that those karmic predispositions became well developed. "**Bodies composed of conceptual mind took form**" refers to being based in bodies of mental form.[65] "**Influenced by delusion, they strayed into the**

formless realm" means that, based on that cause, they wandered into the formless realm.

> **"When the power of the predispositions grew even more coarse,**
> **Bodies of radiant light took form.**
> **Influenced by anger, they wandered[66] into the cycles of the form realm."**

"**When the power of the predispositions grew even more coarse**" means that the karmic predispositions had become even greater [than before]. "**Bodies like apparitions of shining light took form**" refers to being in bodies of light. "**Influenced by anger, they wandered into the cycles of the form realm**" means that, based on that cause, they wandered into the form realm.

> **"When the power of the predispositions grew even greater than that,**
> **Physical bodies of flesh and blood took form.**
> **Influenced by attachment, they strayed into the desire realm."**

"**When the power of the predispositions grew even greater than that**" refers to the karmic predispositions becoming still more powerful, with manifest attachment. "**Physical bodies of flesh and blood took form**" refers to bodies that possess physical flesh and blood. "**Influenced by attachment, they strayed into the desire realm**" means that, based on that cause, they wandered into the desire realm.

[2.2.1.2.2.2.2.2.1.2] The Bases of Cyclic Existence

> **"Through awareness' connection with sound, light, and rays,**
> **The triad of body, speech, and mind took form."**

If you divide [cyclic existence] by means of its "bases," there are three: **body, speech, and mind**.

[2.2.1.2.2.2.2.2.1.3] The Beings in Cyclic Existence

> **"The six consciousnesses amassed karmic predispositions, resulting in straying into the appearances of the six classes of beings."**

If you divide it by its types of inhabitants, there are "six cyclic existences," corresponding to the **six classes of beings**.[67]

[2.2.1.2.2.2.2.2.1.4] The Paths Leading to Cyclic Existence

> **"The afflictions of the five poisons resulted in straying into the five paths of cyclic existence."**

Divided up according to paths, there are "five cyclic existences," corresponding to the **five** causal **paths**.[68]

[2.2.1.2.2.2.2.2.1.5] The Ways Beings Are Born in Cyclic Existence

> **"Through the major causes of the four elements, the four types of birth were established."**

Divided according to the gateways through which beings are born, there are "four cyclic existences": miraculous birth, birth from heat, birth from an egg, and birth from a womb. [374]

[2.2.1.2.2.2.2.2.1.6] The Types of Suffering in Cyclic Existence

> **"And from flesh, blood, heat, and breath, the four illnesses of the body's constituents arose."**

Its particular types of suffering are: wind illness, which comes from breath; bile illness, which comes from heat; phlegm illness, which comes from blood; and disorders in [wind, bile, and phlegm] combined, which come from flesh.

[2.2.1.2.2.2.2.2.2] The Essence of Cyclic Existence

> **"The container world, its contained beings, the body, and the mind arose due to awareness' connection with light."**

There are two topics here: (1) how the external container world arose from the "mind,"[69] and (2) how the internal contained-beings arose from the "mind."

[2.2.1.2.2.2.2.2.2.1] How the External World Arose from the Ground

> **"Here is how the external container world shone forth from the 'mind':**
> **From the connection between the light of space and awareness,**
> **The fluttering winds emerged, gusting and wavering.**
> **Impelled by their motion, fire emerged with its quality of heat.**
> **Then from the discord between fire's heat and wind's coolness, wetness emerged, as water.**
> **From the essence of water, the solid ground of earth was produced.**
>
> **All of the container world developed from this process,**
> **As the appearances of the five objects shone forth from the essence of the causal elements.**
> **That is how the external container world shone forth from the 'mind'!"**

This is the maṇḍalas of wind, fire, water, and earth taking form from the basic state[70] of space.

[2.2.1.2.2.2.2.2.2.2] How Sentient Beings Arose from the Ground

"Here is how the internal contents [of the world]—sentient beings—shone forth from the 'mind':
From the connection between the light of space and awareness,[71]
The memory-driven mind and the moving winds emerged.
From the connection between winds and mind, the fluttering of breath emerged.
Through the power of breath, heat emerged, the domain of fire.
When heat and breath came together, blood emerged, the domain of water.
From the essence of blood, flesh emerged, the domain of earth.
From the connection between the body and mind, the five vital organs developed,
Forming the 'seats' of the five elements.

The 'energy' of the five elements shone through the five limbs,
The 'essence' of the five elements collected in the five interior cavities,
And the 'gateways' of the five elements projected to the five sense faculties.
Then the perceiving powers of the five consciousnesses each arose,
Experiencing and apprehending their respective five objects.

That is how beings shone forth from the 'mind'![72]"

These topics come up in greater detail in [the explanation of] the lamp of the smooth white channel.[73]

[2.2.1.2.2.2.2.2.3] How Beings Continually Revolve in Cyclic Existence

There are three topics here: (1) the causes in dependence on which we revolve, (2) the essential form in which we revolve, and (3) what effects this produces.

[2.2.1.2.2.2.2.2.3.1] The Causes in Dependence on Which We Revolve

We revolve in cyclic existence due to the five poisons:

"The five elements' connection with the mind produces the afflictions of the five poisons:
The connection between space and mind produces anger.
The connection between breath and mind produces pride.
The connection between heat and mind produces jealousy.

The connection between blood and mind produces desire.
And the connection between flesh and mind produces ignorance."

The subject matter here is clear.

[2.2.1.2.2.2.2.2.3.2] The Essential Form in Which We Revolve

We revolve in the form of the five aggregates:

"The connection between those five poisons and the five elements produces the five aggregates:
The connection between anger and space produces the consciousness aggregate.
The connection between pride and breath produces the formatives aggregate.
The connection between jealousy and heat produces the cognitions aggregate.
The connection between desire and blood produces the feeling aggregate.
The connection between ignorance and flesh produces the form aggregate."

The subject matter here is clear. [375]

[2.2.1.2.2.2.2.2.3.3] The Effects of Revolving in Cyclic Existence

"Through the relationship of the five aggregates and five poisons,"

These are related as cause and condition.[74]

"Come formative actions, and virtuous, non-virtuous, and neutral behavior."[75]

As the mind moves toward objects, then karmic predispositions are piled up [by] formatives.[76] When they are acted upon, [their results] are experienced. If they lead to a pleasing result, they are virtuous; if they lead to an unpleasant result, they are non-virtuous; and if they provide a result that is neither, they are morally neutral.

"Through their cause-and-condition relationship with action and the afflictions,
The general and specific sufferings of cyclic existence emerge."

Action and the afflictions [bring about] "general" suffering: birth, old age, sickness, and death. "Specific" suffering refers to the heat and cold experienced by hell beings, the hunger and thirst of hungry ghosts, the stupidity of animals, the change experienced by humans, the conflict and fighting of demigods, and the gods' suffering of dying and falling to lower realms.

[2.2.1.2.2.2.2.3] A Summation of the Topic of Straying

"Since beginningless time, we have cycled limitlessly,"

This means that we have been revolving [in cyclic existence] for a time without beginning or end.

"Circling through all the three realms, and taking up bodies of the six migrations,"

Our residence is the three realms, where we take birth in the bodies of the six types of beings.

"As the twelve links of dependent-arising spin the wheel of cyclic existence."

For a time without beginning or end, we have revolved in cyclic existence. Due to the system of the twelve links of dependent-origination, we spin continually, like the wheel of a chariot.

"This is not caused by evil: it arises through the power of ignorance!"

As for [the reason that] beings revolve in cyclic existence and wander about: they wander in cyclic existence due to not realizing the way things really are!

[2.2.1.2.2.3] Conclusion to the Topic of the Parting of Cyclic Existence and Transcendence

"Though cyclic existence and transcendence may seem distinct,
They are simply perspectives of realized and non-realized minds."

From the viewpoint of realization, transcendence appears. From the viewpoint of non-realization, cyclic existence [376] appears.

"In reality, cyclic existence and transcendence are not divided in two."

In the essence of the universal ground and awareness, there has never been this separation of cyclic existence and transcendence!

"They abide as a great equality, as the single sphere!"

This is the ground, dwelling as the inseparable mother and son.

[2.2.1.3] Conclusion of the Chapter[77]

That concludes the lamp of the abiding ground.

This means that there is nothing else left.

Sa-Ma-Ya!

This applies a seal of secrecy, ordering [the advice] to be kept from those who are unsuitable vessels.

[2.2.2] CHAPTER TWO: The Lamp of the Fleshy Heart

Second is the explanation of the "lamp of the fleshy heart." There are three sections here: (1) a brief explanation, (2) an extensive explanation, and (3) a conclusion.

[2.2.2.1] A Brief Explanation of the Lamp of the Fleshy Heart

> ***Homage to Küntu Zangpo, self-awareness shining out from the depths!***

To explain the homage: The universal ground is present at the center of your heart as an immaculate, utterly pure, self-illuminating self-awareness. And that is Küntu Zangpo, so he is indicated as the object of homage.

> **"Son of the family! The lamp of the fleshy heart is where the ground dwells. This is called the 'important point of self-awareness shining out from the depths.'"**

The universal ground at the center of the heart is not obscured by anything at all. Because it is present as a great natural radiance, it is called a "lamp."

[2.2.2.2] An Extensive Explanation of the Lamp of the Fleshy Heart

The extensive explanation contains two sections: (1) an explanation of what this lamp is and how it is present, and (2) an explanation of how the mind and body come together and separate.

[2.2.2.2.1] What this Lamp is, and How it is Present

Three topics are explained here: (1) what is present: the "essence" of the universal ground, (2) where this dwells: the "nature" of the heart, and (3) how this dwells: the "characteristic" of primordial gnosis.

[2.2.2.2.1.1] How this Lamp Abides: The Essence of the Universal Ground

> **"When the duality of realization and straying emerged in the memory-driven mind, then the duality of cyclic existence and transcendence arose."**

When "realization" and "non-realization" arose in the memory-driven mind, cyclic existence and transcendence split into two.

> **"But the universal ground and awareness do not experience straying or realization—not in the past, future, or present. They have never experienced the split between cyclic existence and transcendence!" [377]**

Although cyclic existence, transcendence, and so forth, arise from the basic state of the universal ground and awareness, they have never been covered by the stains of cyclic existence, transcendence, or anything else. From the very beginning, they have dwelled as a great primordial purity.

> **"Well, then, the universal ground that has never experienced obscuration,"**

Unobscured by anything at all, the universal ground dwells as a natural luminosity.

> **"...and the awareness that has never experienced straying,"**

Never having been covered by "straying" or "realization," awareness remains immaculate.

> **"...with regard to that primordially present nucleus...."**

This refers to the ultimate buddha, which has been intrinsically present[78] since the primordial beginning.

[2.2.2.2.1.2] Where this Lamp Dwells: The Nature of the Heart

> **"Where does [this] ground dwell right now?"**

This [section] explains where it dwells.

> **"It dwells in the luminous vault within the cavity of space:"[79]**

As it is the heart that supports the elemental energy of space,[80] it dwells within that.

> **"...in a deep-red tent with a crystal roof,"[81]**

This indicates the "heart," in which it resides.

> **"...inside a tent of lamplight."**

Inside the heart is a tent composed of the five lights; it dwells in the middle of that, like a butter lamp inside a vase.

What, then, are its characteristics?

"This is called the 'heart that holds the channel.'[82] From the outside it looks like an eight-cornered jewel,"

This describes its external shape.

"...but from the inside like an eight-petaled lotus."

This is its internal aspect.

"At its center are the five lights, present like a tent of rainbows."[83]

This is the shape of the "heart of radiant light."

[2.2.2.2.1.3] How This Lamp Abides: Its Characteristic of Primordial Gnosis

There are two topics here: (1) an explanation of the universal ground [and awareness] as inseparable, like a mother and son, and (2) the way that the ordinary memory-driven mind arises.

[2.2.2.2.1.3.1] The Universal Ground and Awareness, Inseparable Like a Mother and Son

"In the space of that [luminous tent], the universal ground and awareness are unmixed with anything, immaculate, present as the great original purity."

That Bön Body,[84] in which the expanse and [378] primordial gnosis are without duality, is not adulterated by anything—not by straying, conceptuality, afflictions, or anything else. Immaculate and originally pure, it dwells as the actual buddha. The intended meaning here is to say that all sentient beings are buddhas—this is concealed and hidden in other tantras and scriptures.

Now, this topic is explained in detail:

"The universal ground completely pervades the body, just like the sky. But obscured by the clouds of confusion, its radiance is absent."

Although its presence completely pervades the exterior and interior of the body, it is obscured by confusion, and isn't radiant, like the sky when it is covered by clouds.

"In the center of the heart, primordial gnosis dwells as the 'great depth luminosity,'[85] like the sky free of clouds."

The universal ground dwells in that way at the center of the heart, so when you look inward at its actuality, you recognize yourself. This is like the cloudless sky, or like opening the door of a treasure-house and looking inside.

"Awareness is present in the body, spreading throughout it like the shining sun. But obscured by the darkness of conceptuality, its radiance is absent."

Although awareness dwells in the body like this, it is dimmed by conceptuality, and isn't luminous.

"In the center of the heart, however, self-awareness dwells as the 'great depth dawning,'[86] like the sun devoid of darkness."

Awareness abides like that in the center of the heart, so by looking into its essence, awareness is realized nakedly. This is like looking at the sun, which is free of darkness.

"Like the sun shining in the cloudless sky, [these two] dwell at the center of the heart—inseparable like a mother and son."

Just as the empty sky and the rays of the sun are inseparable, the mother (the empty universal ground), and the son (awareness' luminous gnostic energy), dwell without duality at the center of the heart. Thus, by looking inward, the essence of the Bön Body [379] will be seen nakedly, and realization will occur.

[2.2.2.2.1.3.2] How the Ordinary Memory-Driven Mind Arises

"The memory-driven mind is like the rays of the sun.
From its seat at the heart, it is drawn into the channels;
Through the sensory gateways, it experiences objects and takes hold of them."

The seat of the memory-driven mind is situated in the heart; [from there] it is drawn into the pathways of the channels. Then, from the gateways of the sense faculties, it builds up attachment and aversion for objects, and grasps at them.

[2.2.2.2.2] The Coming Together and Separation of the Mind and Body

"How is it that the illusory body and the mind come together and separate?"

This poses a question. The answer is as follows:

"The universal ground is like the sky, completely pervasive. Awareness is like a bird, present there in its own place. The intellect is like the bird's wings, which propel it everywhere. The body is like a trap, and the winged creature is caught in the trap. So, the bird and the trap can come together and

separate, but they do not come together with or separate from the expanse of the sky. It is not situated in any particular place, but is completely present everywhere.

The universal ground is like the earth, which reaches everywhere. Awareness is like a man, dwelling there in his own place. The intellect is like a horse, which can take him anywhere. The body is like a hobble, with which the man holds the horse captive. So, the rope, the man, and the horse can come together and separate, but they do not come together with or separate from the expanse of the earth. It is not situated in any particular place, but is completely present everywhere.

The universal ground is like an ocean, spread far and wide. Awareness is like a fish, dwelling there in its own place. The intellect is like the fish's fins, which move it everywhere. The body is like a net, and the fish is captured in the net. So, the net and the fish can come together and separate, but they do not come together with or separate from the expanse of the ocean. It is not situated in any particular place, but is completely present everywhere."

"**The universal ground is like the sky**," the earth, or the ocean, which are present everywhere, "**completely pervasive. Awareness is like a bird**," a person, or a fish, which are "**present there**," each in its "**own place. The intellect is like wings**," a horse, or fins, "**which propel**" them "**everywhere. The body is like a trap**," a hobble, or a net, which serve to hold something so it can't leave. But although the body and mind come together and are separated, there is no coming together or separation [from] the universal ground.

"**It is not situated in any particular place, but is completely present everywhere**" means that, unlike the mind, which is supported by the body, the universal ground is not something that you come together with or separate from at all. Rather, it is present throughout the body and mind, totally pervading them.

[2.2.2.3] Conclusion of the Chapter

This completes the lamp of the fleshy heart.

This means that there is nothing left.

Sa-Ma-Ya!

This applies a seal of secrecy, ordering [the advice] to be kept from those who are unsuitable vessels.

[2.2.3] CHAPTER THREE: The Lamp of the Smooth White Channel

Third is the explanation of the "lamp of the smooth white channel." There are three sections here: (1) a brief explanation, (2) an extensive explanation, and (3) a conclusion.

[2.2.3.1] A Brief Explanation of the Lamp of the Smooth White Channel

> ***Homage to Küntu Zangpo, the body of transparent primordial gnosis!***

"**Küntu Zangpo**" has the usual meaning [explained in the previous chapters]. "**Transparent primordial gnosis**" refers to the universal ground, not obscured by anything at all—a "luminous" transparency from within the pathway of the [smooth white] channel. Having no concrete nature or features, it is also an "empty" transparency. And because this luminosity and emptiness are nondual, it shines forth as a "nondual" transparency. This "transparent primordial gnosis" [380] is the object of homage.

> **"Son of the family! The lamp of the smooth white channel..."**

This refers to the central channel, so-called because the originally pure awareness shines within it, like the sun shining in the cloudless sky.

> **"...is the pathway into which [primordial gnosis] emerges. This is called the 'important point of transparent primordial gnosis.'"**

While the channels in general are the pathways of awareness, the central channel specifically is the pathway in which primordial gnosis shines as a transparency.

[2.2.3.2] An Extensive Explanation of the Lamp of the Smooth White Channel

Here, there are three topics: (1) the essence [of this lamp]: what it is that shines forth, (2) its pathway: where it shines, and (3) its mode: how it shines forth.

[2.2.3.2.1] The Essence of this Lamp: What it is that Shines Forth

> **"That primordially present nucleus of the universal ground and awareness abides at its residence in the center of the heart, but its pathway is the 'path of the channel,' into which it shines self-emergently."**

That is it!

[2.2.3.2.2] The Pathway of this Lamp: Where it Shines

This has three sections: (1) the "support" or the way that the body and mind come into being, (2) the "supported" or the way that the channels and winds develop, and (3) the classifications of those "supported" channels.

[2.2.3.2.2.1] The Support: How the Body and Mind Emerge

> **"Now, to explain how the body and mind are related to[87] the 'enlightened mind.'"**

Awareness, through its connection with light, arises as the body; through its connection with rays, it arises as the mind.

> **"When the body and mind come together in the mother's womb,"**

This refers to the time when the body and mind first meet.[88]

> **"...space creates an opening, earth develops and firms up [the embryo], and water brings it together as one and sustains it. The heat of fire then ripens the body and mind, and wind separates out its vibrant energies from its solid parts and defines the hollows of its channels."**

In that way, the four elemental energies give rise to and develop the body.

> **"So, the life-energy of the body comes from outside, developing via the navel,"**

Through the dynamic energy of light and awareness,[89] the child's life-rope at its navel, and the mother's heart-rope become connected. In this way, the nutrition of the food that the mother eats is moved through the hollow of the navel-channel, and the [child's] body is nurtured.

> **"...while the life-energy of the mind comes from inside, shining forth from the heart."**

The universal ground and awareness abide at the heart, [381] and it is there that the various powers of knowing[90] arise.

[2.2.3.2.2.2] The Supported: How the Winds and Channels Develop

There are five topics here: (1) how the main "trunk"[91] develops, and (2–5)[92] how the body's solidified dimensions, channels and winds, vital organs and interior cavities, and "samaya substances" develop.

[2.2.3.2.2.2.1] How the Main "Trunk" Develops

> **"In the mixture of the white and red constituents, first the heart forms,"**

Within that, the heart forms initially.

> **"...and that serves as the seat of the space element."**

On it, the domain of space is supported.

> **"Then, from the center of the heart, through the creative energy of light and awareness, the wind of the space-element arises, and that opens up the gateway of the heart."**[93]

Through the dynamic energy of light and the "thumb-sized primordial gnosis," the space-wind arises from the center of the heart, and opens up the tube of the central channel. Recall that the heart (from among the five vital organs), the space wind (from among the five winds), and the central channel (from among the channels) have already been formed.

> **"Then, the upward-moving wind opens the hollow of the central channel in the upward direction."**

From among the five major winds, the one called the "upward-moving wind" opens up the tube of the central channel in the upward direction.

> **"That goes through the center of the "enjoyment" wheel at the throat,"**

It exits from there....

> **"...pierces the "great bliss" wheel at the crown,"**

Then it pierces the wheel located at the top [of the head], the wheel from which the blissful flow of *thig-le* descends.

> **"...and projects to the gateway of the Brahma's aperture at the crown of the head. That is the path of transcendence!"**

When awareness exits from the central channel at the Brahma's aperture, one attains buddhahood, whether their karma is pure or impure.[94] All the important points of the profound transfer of consciousness are met with here.

> **"The downward-voiding wind defines**[95] **the hollow of the central channel in the downward direction."**

That wind opens the hollow of the central channel in the downward direction.

> **"It goes through the center of the 'emanation' wheel at the navel,"**

It goes down through the "emanation" wheel, the wheel responsible for the production and "emanation" of the entire body.

"...pierces the lowest vertebra,"[96] [382]

The channel pierces through that location.

"...and projects to the 'method and wisdom' wheel at the secret place."

It projects to the gateway at the wheel where bliss arises based on method and wisdom, meaning the red and white *thig-le.*

"That is the pathway of cyclic existence!"

When awareness exits from there, one wanders in cyclic existence.

"From the lowest vertebra, two channels—of cyclic existence and transcendence—branch off from the central channel,"

From that lower point,[97] two channels split from the central channel; the right one is white and the left one is red, their shape being like the base of the letter *cha.*[98]

"One on the right and one on the left, they exit the upper vertebra,"[99]

Those two are located at the right and left of the central channel, and exit the upper vertebra together with the two "pulsing veins" on the sides of the neck.[100]

"...go over the brain's membrane, and bend downward at the level of the two eyelids, piercing the two nasal cavities."[101]

Because these exit through the gateways of the nostrils, through the practice of [respectively] inhaling and exhaling the smooth and coarse winds,[102] wind and mind can be brought into the central channel, causing many luminous experiences and realizations to arise.[103]

"The right one is the channel of cyclic existence,"

The white channel on the right side, and all the right channels that separate off from it, are where awareness flows when it is accompanied by the negative dynamic energies.[104]

"...where the solidified 'bodily' *thig-le*[105] and the afflicted winds flow,"

This refers to the flow of the bodily *thig-le* and the coarse afflictive winds.

"...causing the hosts of problems to arise."

Flowing in that way, they lead primarily to the arising of our deficiencies.

"The left one is the channel of transcendence,"

The red channel on the left side, and all the left channels that split off from it, are where awareness flows when it is accompanied by positive dynamic energies.[106]

"...where the vibrant 'mental' thig-le[107] and the winds of primordial gnosis [383] flow, causing the hosts of enlightened qualities to arise."

This refers to the flow of primordial gnosis and the blissful winds of primordial gnosis, which leads primarily to the arising of enlightened qualities.

"None of these faults or enlightened qualities flow from the central channel—from it, awareness shines forth as a great primordial purity."

None of the stains of "faults" or "enlightened qualities" flow from the central channel; rather it is where awareness shines forth as an intense original purity.

"Those three channels are the 'space channels that are the ground of all.'"

The right, left, and central channels are the main channels, the "space channels that are the ground of all."[108]

"The heart is like a pitched tent, in which the three channels are present like its tent pole."[109]

This is how the channels and the heart are shaped.

[2.2.3.2.2.2.2] How the Surrounding Limbs[110] Develop

"Then, from the center of the heart, through the creative energy of light and awareness,"

Through the creative energy of light and the "thumb-sized primordial gnosis," all the "limb" channels and winds arise, along with the internal organs and vessels.

"...the winds of the four elements arise,"

This refers to the arising of the wind-wind, the fire-wind, the water-wind, and the earth-wind.

"...and open up the hollows of the channels in the four directions, like tightening the ropes of a tent."

Now, the four winds open up the hollows of the channels in the four directions, and the four "limb" channels take form.

"Then the four[111] vital organs develop, establishing the 'seats' of the four elements."

The seat of wind is situated at the lungs, the seat of fire at the liver, the seat of water at the kidneys, and the seat of earth at the spleen.

"Next, the five elemental limb-winds[112] arise from the five vital organs. They open up the hollows of channels, and cause the body's five 'elemental' limbs to project out."

From the heart the space limb-wind emerges, opens up the hollow of a channel, and causes the "space limb" (the head) to extend. From the lungs, the wind limb-wind emerges, and causes the right leg to extend. From the liver, the fire limb-wind [384] arises, and causes the right arm to extend. From the kidneys, the water limb-wind emerges, causing the left leg to extend. From the spleen, the earth limb-wind emerges, causing the left arm to extend.

[2.2.3.2.2.2.3] How the Elemental Subsidiary Limbs Develop

"Then, the subsidiary elemental limb-winds[113] emerge, splitting into groups of five. These separate out the five sense faculties from the head, and the five fingers and toes from the four limbs."

(1) From the head, the space wind separates into a set of five: the space wind's [wind-]wind, the space wind's fire-wind, the space wind's water-wind, the space wind's earth-wind, and the space wind's space-wind. These separate out the five seats for the sense faculties from the head. (2) Wind's [wind-]wind, wind's fire-wind, wind's water-wind, wind's earth-wind, and wind's space-wind separate out the five toes from the right leg. (3) The fire wind's [wind-]wind, the fire wind's fire-wind, the fire wind's water-wind, the fire wind's earth-wind, and the fire wind's space-wind separate out the five fingers from the right arm. (4) The water wind's [wind-]wind, the water wind's fire-wind, the water wind's water-wind, the water wind's earth-wind, and the water wind's space-wind separate out the five toes from the left leg. (5) The earth wind's [wind-]wind, the earth wind's fire-wind, the earth wind's water-wind, the earth wind's earth-wind, and the earth wind's space-wind separate out the five fingers from the left arm.

[2.2.3.2.2.2.4] How the Vibrant Channels and Winds, and the Seats of the Sense Faculties Develop

"Then the five vibrant elemental-winds[114] arise from the five vital organs. Opening up hollow channels in the upward direction, they project to and establish the five elemental gateways: the

> **five gateways that are the seats of the sensory faculties. These are the five elemental gateways in which the five objects appear.**"

(1) The vibrant space-wind[115] opens a hollow channel upward from the heart, projecting to and establishing the gateway that is the seat of the eye sense-power, the "space gateway" that engages with forms. (2) The vibrant wind-wind [385] opens a hollow channel upward from the lungs, projecting to and establishing the gateway that is the seat of the nose sense-power, the "wind gateway" that engages with smells. (3) The vibrant fire-wind opens a hollow channel upward from the liver, projecting to and establishing the gateway that is the seat of the tongue sense-power, the "fire gateway" that engages with tastes. (4) The vibrant water-wind opens a hollow channel upward from the kidneys, projecting to and establishing the gateway that is the seat of the ear sense-power, the "water gateway" that engages with sounds. (5) The vibrant earth-wind opens a hollow channel upward from the spleen, projecting to and establishing the gateway that is the seat of the body sense-power, the "earth gateway" that engages with physical sensations.

> "**Within the hollows of those five channels is the vibrant quintessence**[116] **of the five lights, from which the five vibrant elemental-energies**[117] **respectively arise. This produces the consciousnesses' 'powers' *(rtsal)* of discerning their five objects; for this reason they are called the five sense 'powers' *(dbang po)*.**"

(1) From the hollow of the eye-channel,[118] the vibrant space-energy arises from the radiation of the white light, producing the eye-consciousness' power to discern form. This becomes known as the "eye sense-power." (2) From the hollow of the nose-channel, the vibrant wind-energy arises from the radiation of the green light, producing the nose-consciousness' power to discern smells. This becomes known as the "nose sense-power." (3) From the hollow of the tongue-channel, the vibrant fire-energy arises from the radiation of the red light, producing the tongue-consciousness' power to discern tastes. This becomes known as the "tongue sense-power." (4) From the hollow of the ear-channel, the vibrant water-energy arises from the radiation of the blue light, producing the ear-consciousness' power to discern sounds. This becomes known as the "ear sense-power." (5) From the hollow of the body-channel, the vibrant earth-energy arises from the radiation of the yellow light, producing the body-consciousness' power to discern touch. This becomes known as the "body sense-power."

[2.2.3.2.2.2.5] How the Coarse Channels and Winds, Internal Cavities, and Substances Develop

> "**Then, the five coarse elemental-winds**[119] **emerge from the five vital organs. Opening up hollow channels in the downward**

direction, they lead to the formation of the five entrails. These are the 'vessels' of the five[120] elements: [386] the essences of the five elements—the five 'samaya substances'—flow inside of them."

(1) The coarse space-wind opens up a hollow channel that proceeds downward from the heart, leading to the formation of the "space vessel," the seminal vesicle. Space's "*citta* essence,"[121] the "nectar" of the "enlightened mind," i.e., the *thig-le*, flow from within there. (2) The coarse wind-wind opens up a hollow channel that proceeds downward from the lungs, leading to the formation of the "wind vessel," the small and large intestines. Wind's essence, the "nectar" of feces, flows from within there. (3) The coarse fire-wind opens up a hollow channel that proceeds downward from the liver, leading to the formation of the "fire vessel," the gall-bladder. Fire's essence, the "nectar" of bile, flows from within there. (4) The coarse water-wind opens up a hollow channel that proceeds downward from the kidneys, leading to the formation of the "water vessel," the bladder. The "nectar" of urine flows from within there. (5) The coarse earth-wind opens up a hollow channel that proceeds downward from the spleen, leading to the formation of the "earth vessel," the stomach. Earth's essence, the "nectar" of the "great meat,"[122] flows in there.

[2.2.3.2.2.3] The Divisions of the "Supported" Channels

"In that way, the three channels form the 'trunk,' and the elemental channels are the branches. Those split into 360 limbs. And those are split into 21,000 subsidiary limbs, which in turn split into 84,000 leaves. The various powers of cognition arise through these. But though the channels emerge in such variety, the central channel is the one that is the 'lamp.'"

In the other channels, the gnostic energy of awareness is dimmed by the clouds of distorted conceptual thought, so its radiance is absent. But in the pathway of the central channel, it shines forth in all its radiance, without being obscured by anything whatsoever. For this reason, [the central channel] is called a "lamp."

[2.2.3.2.3] The Mode of this Lamp: How it Shines Forth

"The universal ground is completely pervasive in the channels, like the sky. But obscured by the clouds of confusion, its radiance is absent."

Although the universal [387] ground completely pervades the channels, due to the stains of confusion, its radiance is absent.

"In the pathway of the central channel, primordial gnosis shines forth as an utter transparency, like the sky when it is free of clouds."

The universal ground—empty, luminous, unobscured—appears in the central channel, completely pervading it.

"Awareness is present in the channels, spreading throughout them like the sun. But enveloped in the darkness of conceptual thought, its radiance is absent."

Awareness has no radiance when it is in the [other] channels, because it is dimmed by the powers of conceptuality.

"In the pathway of the central channel, self-awareness shines forth as a great original purity, like the sun, which is devoid of darkness."

In the pathway of the central channel, awareness shines forth nakedly, not clothed by conceptual thought.

"Like the sun shining in a cloudless sky, the mother and son shine indivisibly in the pathway of the central channel."

"**Like the sun shining in a cloudless sky**," the universal ground and awareness "**shine forth**" self-emergently as an "**indivisible**" emptiness and luminosity "**in the pathway of the central channel**."

[2.2.3.3] Conclusion to the Chapter

This completes the lamp of the smooth white channel.

The subject matter here is clear.

Sa-Ma-Ya!

This is as explained above.

[2.2.4] CHAPTER FOUR: The Far-Reaching Lasso Water Lamp

Fourth is the "far-reaching lasso water lamp." There are three sections here: (1) a brief explanation, (2) an extensive explanation, and (3) a conclusion.

[2.2.4.1] A Brief Explanation of the Far-Reaching Lasso Water Lamp

Homage to Küntu Zangpo, the body of self-arisen primordial gnosis!

"**Küntu Zangpo**" has the usual meaning [explained in the previous chapters]. "**Self-arisen primordial gnosis**" refers to the universal ground and awareness, the actual buddha, who appears in the gateway of this lamp in a self-arising fashion, without being created by anyone at all. Because this is the "**body**" of Küntu Zangpo, it is the object of "**homage**."

> **"Son of the family! The far-reaching lasso water lamp is the gateway to which [awareness] projects.[123] This is called the 'important point of seeing awareness nakedly.'"**

From the eyes—the gateways of the water lamp—the universal ground and awareness shine forth as all the enlightened bodies and buddhafields, not obscured by anything at all. Gazing at that and seeing it directly is called the "important point of seeing nakedly."

[2.2.4.2] An Extensive Explanation of the Far-Reaching Lasso Water Lamp

There are three topics here: (1) what shines forth: the essence of the universal ground, (2) where it shines from: the gateways of the lamp, and (3) how it shines [388] forth: its fundamental abiding character.

[2.2.4.2.1] What Shines Forth: The Essence of the Universal Ground

> **"The nucleus of the universal ground and awareness, present since the primordial beginning—that is it!"**

The nucleus *(snying po)*, unproduced, primordially pure, spontaneously present in nature, luminously radiant, and uncomposed—that is it!

[2.2.4.2.2] Where it Shines From: The Gateways of this Lamp

> **"The ground dwells at the center of the heart. [283] When drawn into the pathway of the channel, it shines in the gateways of the water lamp."**

The residence of awareness is the heart, its pathway is the channel, and the gateways through which it shines are the eyes.

> **"At the center of the conch-shell house of the brain, coming from the central channel, is a channel called the *tsang-ri bur-lang*."[124]**

This means that the "eye channel"—the *bur-lang*—splits off from the central channel at the center of the brain.

> **"A single channel that splits into two tips, it connects to the eyes."**

Dividing in that way, it connects to the two eyes.

> **"The gateways of the channel appear like an opened *zer-ma* flower,"**

The openings of this channel are the seats of the eye sense-faculty, and have the shape of an opened *zer-ma* flower.[125]

> **"...projecting to the gateways through which awareness is seen."**

They project to the gateways through which consciousness perceives forms.

> **"From the hollow of that channel, the five lights shine forth, like the concentric spots on a peacock."**

From the cavity of that channel, awareness' own light shines forth, appearing like the concentric spots on a peacock. Based on this, the gateway for the seeing of awareness is opened.

[2.2.4.2.3] How it Shines Forth: Its Fundamental Abiding Character

> **"In the gateway through which those lights are seen is the mother—the universal ground, like the sky, without exterior or interior—its primordial gnosis shining forth everywhere."**

It shines forth, empty and luminous, spread out everywhere like the range of the sky.

> **"Awareness dawns in these gateways of seeing, devoid of conceptuality, shining like the orb of the sun."**

In those gateways, the gnostic energy of awareness shines forth nakedly, without conceptuality, like the orb of the sun.

> **"The mind is like the rays of the sun, discerning objects with its multitudes of memory-driven awareness."**

From this gnostic energy of awareness, the creative display of the memory-driven conceptual mind shines forth in all its variety, and then discerns objects. [389]

> **"Light, awareness' own light, rises in the sky like a house of rainbows."**

From the gateways of this lamp, awareness' own natural light shines forth in vivid luminous colors, like a house of rainbows.

> **"Rays, awareness' own rays, shine in the canopy above you, like a net of sunbeams."**

Rays, which are awareness' own rays, arise as a natural radiation in the gateway of the eye sense-faculty,[126] like the rays of the sun shining in the canopy of the sky.[127]

> **"In that way, that primordially present nucleus..."**

Sound, light, and rays are called awareness' "creative energy," or its "radiation," or its "magical displays," or the "dawning of the essential nucleus."[128]

> **"...appears vividly in the direct perception of the sense-faculty,[129] without waxing or waning, without being something that the mind creates in the gateway of the lamp."**

In the gateway of this lamp, your own natural radiation—just as it is, without being increased or diminished, without the causes and conditions of mental effort that would intend for it to do so—shines forth vividly in the direct perception of the [eye] sense-faculty.

> **"This is the important point of seeing awareness nakedly!"**

In dependence on those manifestations—practicing, training, and taking them on the path—you will come to see the way things are, just as they are. Thus, this is called the "important point of seeing nakedly."

[2.2.4.3] Conclusion to the Chapter

> **This completes the far-reaching lasso water lamp.**

The subject matter here is clear.

> **Sa-Ma-Ya!**

This is just as explained above.

[2.2.5] CHAPTER FIVE: The Lamp that Introduces the Buddhafields

Fifth is the "lamp that introduces the buddhafields." There are three sections here: (1) a brief explanation, (2) an extensive explanation, and (3) a conclusion.

[2.2.5.1] A Brief Explanation of the Lamp that Introduces the Buddhafields

> ***Homage to Küntu Zangpo, self-awareness arising into manifestation!***

Here, [in the name Küntu Zangpo,] ***Kün*** ("all") refers to the "ground of all," the foundation of all the ways that the mind arises: as positive conceptual thoughts, destructive conceptual thoughts,[130] and so forth. ***Zangpo*** ("good") indicates that all of those come from the range of the mind itself, appearing from it and disappearing back into it of their own accord. Arising as the expressive energy of primordial gnosis, they are not to be embraced or abandoned.[131] "**Self-awareness**" refers to the mind itself, the essential primordial gnosis. "**Arising into manifestation**" indicates that when self-awareness arises into manifestation, it results in realization, in the buddha becoming actualized. [390] "**Homage**" refers to paying homage with [a mind] naturally purified of memory-driven conceptuality.

> **"Son of the family! The lamp that introduces the buddhafields..."**

The buddhafields of the three bodies exist as a part of you.[132] In dependence on the methods of the "six important points," they become manifest, and this lamp introduces them to you in naked seeing.

> **"...is how the path is brought into your experience. This is called the 'important point of discovering the three bodies.'"**

What is explained here is the important point of the ground's three bodies becoming manifest, taking hold of their own places once they have arisen, and the ensuing discovery that everything is the mind itself.

[2.2.5.2] An Extensive Explanation of the Lamp that Introduces the Buddhafields

> **"There are two issues here: (1) introducing to the three bodies, and (2) finally discovering them."**

The extensive explanation has two sections: (1) being introduced to the three bodies, and (2) finally discovering them.[133]

[2.2.5.2.1] An Introduction to the Three Bodies

There are three sections here [corresponding to the three bodies].

[2.2.5.2.1.1] An Introduction to the Reality Body

First is the introduction to the Bön Body[134]:

> **"As for the introduction: Son of the family! Its abiding nature[135] is the universal ground, the enlightened mind itself pervading everywhere without partiality. This is the expanse of Bön-itself,"[136]**

The mind-itself, empty and luminous, completely pervasive, is the expanse of Bön.[137]

> **"...and in that residence, dwelling as this self-aware great original purity, is the Bön Body shining forth naturally."[138]**

From the range of the universal ground, which is like the pure sky, the gnostic energy of awareness shines forth nakedly like the sun, bearing no flaws, immaculate. That is the natural shining forth of the Bön Body!

> **"And so the buddhafield of the Bön Body is present within you, accompanying you always, but you don't recognize it!"**

The buddhafield of the Bön Body exists within you primordially. But not recognizing it, you wander in cyclic existence. This is like a person who is so close to their face that they cannot see it. It is like a poor person beneath whose house there is a jewel, but who doesn't recognize it and is racked with hunger.

[2.2.5.2.1.2] An Introduction to the Complete Body

Now, to introduce the buddhafield of the Complete Body:

> **"Son of the family! Its residence is a deep-red tent with a crystal roof. [391] This inestimable mansion of lamplight is Akaniṣṭha, the buddhafield that nothing surpasses!"**

This refers to the heart, which on the outside is shaped like an eight-sided jewel, but from the inside appears like a luminous eight-petaled lotus. In the center of this is a tent composed of the five lights. What is being defined here is the actual Akaniṣṭha.

> **"In that residence—within self-awareness' gnostic energy—"**

Inside of that dwells immaculate awareness, Küntu Zangpo, who is devoid of identity.

> **"sound, light, and rays are spontaneously present."**

This refers to the three great presencings,[139] awareness' own dynamic energy shining forth without obstruction.

> **"Through this, all of cyclic existence and transcendence are spontaneously complete."**

The gnostic energy of awareness has a fivefold energy through which it appears[140]—the five lights—which is intrinsically complete within it. Due to that completeness, all the appearances of cyclic existence and transcendence, without exception, are also complete [in it].[141] To elaborate, the appearances of "transcendence" are the inestimable mansions, buddhafields, ornaments, maṇḍalas, the enlightened bodies' colors and hand implements and illustrative marks, the main deities and their retinues and their emanations, the five bodies, five deities,[142] five families,[143] and so forth. All these pure appearances are complete there, spontaneously and without requiring effort. The appearances of "cyclic existence" are the external container world, the beings it contains, the eons, existence,[144] the environments of the six classes of beings, the maṇḍalas of the three realms, the five elements, five *skandhas,* five poisons, five vital organs, five internal vessels, five limbs, five sense-powers, the seats of the five sense-powers, the five objects, and so forth. All these impure appearances are complete there, spontaneously and without requiring effort.

In the gnostic energy of awareness, the root of sonic expression—"sound"—is intrinsically complete. Thus externally arising sounds, the internal sounds of awareness, the magical speech of the buddhas, the sign-based languages that are the speech of sentient beings, and so forth, in all their variety—every possible type of resounding sound—are complete there, spontaneously and without requiring effort.

In the gnostic energy of awareness, the root of mental activity—"rays"—is intrinsically complete. Because of that completeness, [392] all the different kinds of perceiving cognition, as many as there are—the tens of thousands and hundreds of thousands of types of the buddhas' knowing primordial-gnosis, the 84,000 types of sentient beings' ordinary minds, and so forth—are complete there, spontaneously and without requiring effort.

> **"This is the Complete Body shining forth to itself, and so the buddhafields of the Complete Body dwell within you!"**

In this way, all of cyclic existence and transcendence are spontaneously complete in the gnostic energy of awareness, without requiring any effort. And so the buddhafields of the Complete Body are present within you. Further, all the appearances related to cyclic existence (the *skandhas,* the constituents,[145] the sense spheres[146]), as well as [the transcendent appearances of] the five bodies, the five deities, the five families, and so forth, dwell in this buddhafield of the Complete [Body].

[To describe how these buddhafields arise:] (1) Awareness' gnostic energy being empty in essence is the "empty primordial gnosis," which glows with a radiant white light. From its core, the tathāgata of the central direction emerges: he is from the Tathāgata family, and his body is white. (2) Awareness being radiant but without nature is the "mirrorlike primordial gnosis," which glows with a yellow light. From its core, the tathāgata of the eastern direction emerges: he is from the Swastika family, has a yellow body, and holds a swastika in his hand. (3) Awareness being undivided and even is the "equality primordial gnosis," which glows with a green light. From its core, the tathāgata of the northern direction emerges: he is from the Wheel family, has a green body, and holds a wheel in his hand. (4) Awareness being distinct but totally complete[147] is the "individually discerning primordial gnosis," which glows with a red light. From its core, the tathāgata of the western direction emerges: he is from the Lotus family, has a red body, and holds a lotus in his hand. (5) Awareness being effortless and spontaneous is the "effacious primordial gnosis," which glows with a blue light. From its core, the tathāgata of the southern direction emerges: he is from the Jewel family, has a blue body, and holds a precious jewel in his hand.

In that way, through the "glow" of the five families, [393] the Bön Body is present as if it were a deity-body.[148]

> **"But if you don't realize this, they appear as ordinary deluded realms."**

Although the buddhafields of the Complete Body have dwelled within you since the primordial beginning, through not realizing that, they shine forth as the host of impure appearances: the five demons,[149] the five poisons, the five elements, the five *skandhas,* and so forth—as distorted, subjective appearances and so forth.

[2.2.5.2.1.3] An Introduction to the Emanation Body

> **"Son of the family! Its residence is complete with three roots, six wheels, a trunk, branches, limbs, and secondary limbs. This is the buddhafield where the lettered-retinue is complete."**[150]

The "three roots" are the right, left, and central channels. The "six wheels" are the great-bliss wheel at the crown, the enjoyment wheel at the throat, the Bön[151] wheel at the heart, the emanation wheel at the navel, the method-and-insight wheel at the secret area, and the wind wheel at the soles of the feet. "Trunk" refers to the life-channel.[152] The "branches" are the channels related to the vital organs, internal vessels, and sense faculties. The "limbs" are the channels related to the head, and to the body's legs and arms. The "secondary limbs" are the 21,000 or 84,000 [channels] that branch off from their insides, outsides, and middles. All of these are the buddhafield of the Emanation Body! The five lights, seed-syllables, *thig-le*, and so forth are the foundational "seeds" of the deities.

> **"In that residence—in the gnostic energy of self-awareness—dynamic energy manifests as six consciousnesses and six objects, and then carries out the various activities of body, speech, and mind. This is the shining forth[153] of the Emanation Body,"**

The six consciousnesses and the six objects arise from the expressive energy of awareness. This energetic knowing capacity shines forth without regard to direction, and performs the various activities of body, speech, and mind—the ones marked by deliberate effort. These appearing impartially and wherever [is necessary] is the shining forth of the Emanation Body.

"...and so the buddhafields of the Emanation Body dwell within you!"

All these buddhafields of wheels and channels [394] are filled with Emanation Bodies: (1) the Shen[154] who trains the gods, Yeshen Tsugphü, dwells at the center of the crown's "great bliss" [wheel], (2) the Shen who trains the demigods, Jégyal, dwells at the throat wheel, (3) the Shen who trains humans, Sangdu, dwells at the heart wheel, (4) the Shen who trains animals, Ti-sang, dwells at the navel wheel, (5) the Shen who trains hungry-ghosts, Mucho Demdruk, dwells at the secret wheel, and (6) the Shen who trains hell-beings, Sangwa and Ngang-ring, dwells at the wheel at the soles of the feet.

Similarly, the buddhas of the five families, along with their consorts,[155] dwell in the five internal organs. The eight primordial Shen[156] and their eight primordial ladies[157] dwell in the [eight] channels associated with the eight consciousnesses. In the head, feet, eyes, and tongue are the four flower goddesses.[158] In the body, speech, and mind are the three gods that clear away poison. In the channels related to the limbs[159] are the queens of the four times,[160] and so forth.

The forty-five peaceful deities and the thirty-four gnostic wrathful deities that are their transformations (or from a more expansive perspective the hosts of one hundred twenty-eight deities, and so forth), as well as the three hosts of inner, outer, and secret deities—as many as there are—can be related to the body, mind, and *skandhas,* such that your body is a "maṇḍala of seals." In reality, there is no place in all the residences of the channels that the Emanation Bodies do not pervade.

"But due to lack of realization, appearances appropriate to the six classes of beings arise."

Although they are present in that way, due to lack of realization, wind and mind collect into six letters located at the channels' six wheels,[161] and the appearances of the six types of beings shine forth. In particular, now wind and mind collect predominantly in our heart wheel, so appearances appropriate to the busy, frenzied human existence arise. When they collect in the channels related to the five organs, the five poisons arise. When they collect in the 84,000 minor channels, the hosts of 84,000 types of conceptual thought emerge as their expressive energy.

[2.2.5.2.2] Discovering the Three Bodies

"As for the discovery of the three bodies: in the introduction to the 'essential awareness,' you discover the Reality Body, and in the introduction to the 'awareness of higher seeing' you discover the Form Bodies."

The topic of the "**discovery**" has two sections: (1) "**discovering the Reality Body in the introduction to 'essential awareness,'**" and [395] (2) "**discovering the Form Bodies in the introduction to 'the awareness of higher seeing.'**"

[2.2.5.2.2.1] Discovering the Reality Body in the Introduction to the Essential Awareness

This has two sections: (1) the introduction, and (2) the discovery.

[2.2.5.2.2.1.1] The Introduction

There are three topics here, as indicated by the passage:

> **"Three lamps provide introductions to the 'essential awareness': (1) through the 'lamp of the abiding ground' you identify the ground, (2) through the 'lamp that illustrates with examples' it is represented in examples, and (3) through the 'lamp of the signs of primordial gnosis' you are introduced to it in terms of signs."**

[2.2.5.2.2.1.1.1] Identifying the Ground through the Lamp of the Abiding Ground

> **"Son of the family! To identify the ground…"**

This has three parts: the introductions to (1) the mother, (2) the son, and (3) their dynamic energy.

[2.2.5.2.2.1.1.1.1] Introduction to the Mother

This is the important point of clarifying your awareness: Using the gazes, the important points regarding the body, and so forth, place your mind in equipoise, so that the non-conceptual awareness will shine forth nakedly.

> **"…set the lamps[162] in their own place,"**

This refers to the particulars of the gazes: because the eyes are the location of the gateway through which awareness is seen, do not move the eyes, and don't squint or flutter the eyelashes, just set [the eyes] in their own place.

> **"…and then cognition will not reify objects. When it is left in its own place,"**

This describes the method of placing the mind: it should be placed on a single point, with the cognition not following after the past or the future, not analyzing exterior objects, and not conceptually analyzing your interior awareness.

> **"...cognition will not engage with objects, and abides without being covered by the objective sphere."**

When awareness is free of subjective grasping at subjects and objects—unspoiled by them, its complexion left alone[163]—it is present, cleansed of and unobscured by "objects" and "cognitions."

> **"At that time, in the universal ground—empty and luminous, devoid of shadows or coverings, completely clear, really radiant—"**

By gazing through the gateways of the lamps, the universal ground—insubstantial, empty, cleansed—shines forth pervasively. This is an introduction to the practice.

> **"objective appearances arise, like reflections in a mirror.[164] That complete clearness, that real radiance[165]—that is it!"**

When the universal ground manifests,[166] objective appearances shine forth, but without having any inherent nature.

[2.2.5.2.2.1.1.1.2] Introduction to the Son

> **"As for awareness, at that time make it empty of memory or concept;"**

This refers to being free from memories of the past or thoughts about the future, and thus not remembering, but [396] not forgetting.

> **"...make it without aim."**

Without aim, completely content, without an object of apprehension, it is freed from its indecisive movements.

> **"Rest spaciously without grasping,"**

This means not resting inside or outside or anywhere at all, not thinking, and not grasping at anything.

> **"...nakedly without concept;"**

Not obscured by anything, [awareness] shines forth nakedly, uncovered, without conceptuality.

> **"...in that state, objective appearances shine forth like reflections arising in a crystal ball. That intense vividness, that is it!"**

When your subjective [cognition] arises in that way, all the appearances of external objects are [encountered as] empty appearances—insubstantial, naturally radiant, naked—without grasping. Arising naturally, they are like a crystal placed on brocade, or a reflection in a mirror: appearing, but having no inherent nature.

[2.2.5.2.2.1.1.1.3] Introduction to Their Dynamic Energy

> **"The ordinary mind, with its varieties of memory-driven awareness, individually discriminates and differentiates objects. That is it!"**

In accordance with this, the "ordinary mind" is what apprehends things with thought, and makes all discriminations. To introduce it: it is moving but empty like a breeze through space; or it is like the waves of an ocean, which appear and disappear of their own accord. It should be understood as being the expressive energy of primordial gnosis.

[2.2.5.2.2.1.1.2] Illustrating the Reality Body through the "Lamp of Examples"

> **"Son of the family! To illustrate its[167] meaning with examples: (1) a butter lamp illustrates how primordial gnosis is naturally luminous, (2) a lotus illustrates its immaculate original purity, (3) the orb of the sun illustrates the spontaneous presence of its luminosity, (4) a mirror illustrates its being unobscured and naturally clear, (5) a crystal ball illustrates its naked transparency, and (6) the sky illustrates how primordial gnosis is completely present everywhere."**

Here, its six dimensions are illustrated through six examples. Exemplifying things in this way produces belief, confidence, and certainty, and leads to realization of the true meaning. The subject matter here is clear.

[2.2.5.2.2.1.1.3] An Introduction to the Reality Body through the "Lamp of the Signs of Primordial Gnosis"

This has two sections, as indicated in the passage:

> **"Son of the family! To introduce you to it in terms of signs, there are two introductions: (1) to the universal ground, and (2) to awareness."**

[2.2.5.2.2.1.1.3.1] An Introduction to the Universal Ground

> **"To introduce you to the reality of universal ground: it is like a butter lamp that, free of the shadows of enveloping darkness, is starkly evident in its natural radiance."**

This is an example. Its meaning is as follows:

> **"In the gateways of the lamp, the universal ground is free from every trace of darkness, and the natural radiance of primordial gnosis stands out starkly." [397]**

It is not obscured by anything at all—not the illusory body, appearing objects, the conceptual mind, the afflictions, or objects of cognition—and is nakedly present, so radiant! That joins the meaning [to the example].

> **"It is like a lotus living in the mud but bearing none of its stains, immaculate and nakedly present. In the gateways of the lamp, the universal ground bears no stains whatsoever, and is nakedly present as an original purity."**

The universal ground is like a lotus; not bearing any of the stains of cyclic existence, transcendence, the afflictions, objects of cognition, and so forth, it shines forth naked in its original purity, in the gateways of the lamp.

> **"It is like sun, which was never created by anyone, its intense luminosity shining in full view since the primordial beginning. In the gateways of the lamp, the universal ground, which has never been created by anyone, shines forth into full view as the great self-emergent primordial gnosis, which has been spontaneously present as an intense luminosity since the very beginning."**

The universal ground is like the sun, [its appearance] in the gateways of the lamp not created by any causes, conditions, effort, and so forth. Since the primordial beginning it has been spontaneously present as a great luminosity, shining forth into view as the great self-emergent primordial gnosis.

> **"It is like a mirror without obscurations or coverings, in whose clarity everything can be reflected and appear without obscurations. In the gateways of the lamp, the universal ground is not obscured or covered by anything at all, and is present as the self-arising primordial gnosis, in whose clarity all the appearances of external objects arise without obscuration."**

The universal ground is like a mirror; in the gateways of the lamp it is unobscured by anything that would possibly obscure it, and does not emerge due to any causes or conditions. Primordial gnosis's clarity being a natural clarity, all the appearances of external objects arise [in it] without obstruction.

> **"It is like a crystal ball which, free of coverings, is a transparency, bare and naked. In the gateways of the lamp, the universal**

ground is not cloaked in any obscurations or coverings whatsoever, and so is present as the bare, naked, transparent primordial gnosis."

The universal ground is like a crystal ball; in the gateways of the lamp it is free of coverings such as the afflictions, conceptuality, subject-object duality, and so forth, and shines forth nakedly as the transparent primordial gnosis.

"It is like space, which is not external or internal, but pervades everywhere. In the gateways of the lamp, the universal ground is not internal or external, but pervades everywhere as the great transparent primordial gnosis."

The universal ground is like space, appearing in the gateway of the lamp as pervasive primordial gnosis, without inside or outside, spreading everywhere.

[2.2.5.2.2.1.1.3.2] An Introduction to Awareness

"Son of the family! Now, to introduce you to the reality of awareness. Just as the universal ground abides, awareness too abides in that way!"

Because the universal ground and awareness are indivisible, the above [examples also] provide an introduction to the reality of awareness.

[2.2.5.2.2.1.2] Discovering the Reality Body

"Now, to discover the reality of that:"

The "**discovery**" has three topics: (1) how the discovery is made, (2) where it is made, and (3) the good qualities that result from having made it.

[2.2.5.2.2.1.2.1] How to Make the Discovery

"Set primordial gnosis nakedly, not clothed in the 'animal skin' of conceptuality."

Place the gnostic energy of awareness in its bare nakedness, free from the "clothes" of conceptuality.

"Set awareness in its bareness, not spoiling it with minds of clinging and desire."

Place awareness so that it is vibrant in its bareness, [398] with the gnostic energy of awareness free from the "clothes" of conceptuality.

"Not creating or altering anything in the mind, set it in an untouched manner."

Not creating mental contrivances like "appearance" or "emptiness," "permanence" or "nihilism," place it leisurely, without fabrication, in an untouched state.

"Not following after memories or concepts, set it without chasing or grasping."

At that time, whatever memories or concepts arise, place it without following them, so they disappear naturally.

"With little motion in the mind, set it in the great equality."

Without chasing after the past or the future, place it in equality, in the innate state.

"Not stopping the flow of awareness, extend the rope of the innate state."[168]

Continually refresh the state of mindfulness, where awareness is unobscured and naturally luminous.

[2.2.5.2.2.1.2.2] Where this Discovery is Made

"External and internal, container and contents, cyclic existence and transcendence,"

Objects and consciousnesses, the external and the internal, the container world and its contained-beings, the cycle of existence that arises due to non-realization, the transcendence that arises due to realization, and so forth—all of these arise as [awareness'] unimpeded dynamic energy.

"All are fake, 'false caves'[169] contained in the mind,"

From the ultimate or completely pure point of view, they are without reality, false appearances—they appear but have no essence at all, other than being magical apparitions of the mind. These appearances, further, are aspects of the "mind," and do not waver from the reality of awareness.

"But are[170] discovered as the enlightened mind."

All of those shine forth from the state of the enlightened mind, dwell in its state, and are liberated into its state. Thus they are determined to be the "mind."[171]

[2.2.5.2.2.1.2.3] The Good Qualities Resulting from this Discovery

"Not longer led astray by distortion, buddhahood is now manifest!"

Understanding distorted appearances[172] as false, those false appearances are liberated in the mind, and will not deceive you. This is like understanding an illusion as being an illusion, so it no longer deceives you; though it may present a deceptive appearance, you realize and understand this. When this is the case, [you realize] whatever appears as the shining forth of the expanse. Your awareness takes hold of its own place, [399] you resolve straying from the depths, and your "mind" is actualized: now buddhahood is manifest!

[2.2.5.2.2.2] Discovering the Form Bodies through the Introduction to the "Awareness of Higher Seeing"

"Son of the family! Through the introduction to the 'awareness of higher seeing,' the Form Bodies are discovered."

There are three topics here: (1) the "**introduction to 'the awareness of higher seeing,'**" (2) the "**discovery of the Form Bodies,**" and (3) advice regarding the seal of secrecy[173] that is applied to these esoteric instructions.

[2.2.5.2.2.2.1] The Introduction to the Awareness of Higher Seeing

This has two sections: (1) the method through which higher seeing[174] arises, and (2) an introduction to its manifestations as self-presencings.

[2.2.5.2.2.2.1.1] The Method through Which Higher Seeing Arises

"Raise the great oceans upward—"

The external "oceans" are the eyes, while the inner one is awareness. These two are connected, so "raise upward" means to roll the eyes up, moving awareness to the sky [and focusing it] like you are pointing a spear.

"Focus on the dark space at the iron mountains."[175]

By moving the flesh above your eyes[176] downward, the "queens of the eyes" dwell beneath, and the eyes, below, focus on the clouds, above, at the upper brows.[177] This is what is explained in the line "Focus on the space at the dark iron mountains." Further, [the "higher sights"] arise by (1) focusing [the eyes] upward, to the "externally existing lamp," (2) concentrated gazing with the "internal lamp of the sense faculties," and

(3) striking the important points of the "secret lamp of awareness."[178] This can be understood in greater detail through the oral instructions.

[2.2.5.2.2.2.1.2] An Introduction to its Manifestations as Self-Presencings

"In the visual canopy,[179] a brightness laden with light,"

This refers to seeing the open space of the sky's expanse, and to seeing the visionary objects.

"You see a net of magical rays,"

Through using the important points of the body, the gazes, the ways of conjoining wind and mind, and so forth, you come to see awareness' own rays, manifold, in all directions.

"Like a spider's web or a tangled necklace."

You see a variety [of appearances] like this, or like formations of sunbeams, or the spokes of an umbrella, or strings of flags.

"Within the blackness, a darkness laden with rays,"

This has an external sense, meaning "in a place where there are no appearances," and an internal sense, meaning "within the covering of the eyelids."[180] [400]

"You see immeasurable [environments][181] of lamplight,"

This refers to awareness' own light, which is seen in various and indeterminate ways: as tents of the five lights, or as clusters, as *thig-le*, or as buddhafields, and so forth.

"Appearing in the sky like rainbows."

This means that you will see it like that.

"The gateway of the sound of empty space appears
At the center of the pool of the conch-lake."

At the center of the conch-shell house of the brain, within the site of the central channel, awareness' own sound—the empty sound of Bön-itself, the empty tone of the universal ground—arises as an echo.[182]

"From sound's secret tubes at the 'half moons,'
Self-emergent sound rings forth,"

A tube projects [from] the central channel [to] the gateway of the ear-sense power, twisting like birch-bark; in that, awareness' own sound resounds, self-emergent and continuous.[183]

What is this like?

"Sounding continuously: U, Ru, Ru!"

Though this is always resounding, by following the advice relating to the methods of using the hands [to stimulate it], it becomes directly manifest. Further, there are three ways that [sound] is introduced to you as an illusory self-presencing: (1) an introduction to "external" empty-sound that disappears of its own accord,[184] (2) an introduction to "internal" [sound], using a technique that involves an extrinsic condition,[185] and (3) an introduction to "secret" [sound], which is self-awareness' own sound. These can be understood in greater detail through the oral instructions.

[2.2.5.2.2.2.2] The Discovery of the Form Bodies

The discovery of the Form Bodies has two topics: (1) a general explanation, and (2) a detailed explanation.

[2.2.5.2.2.2.2.1] A General Explanation

This has two sections: (1) how to meditatively take them into your experience, and (2) how experiences and visions of luminosity arise.

[2.2.5.2.2.2.2.1.1] How to Meditatively Take Them into Your Experience

"The moving intellect is tamed in sound."

This refers to the important points regarding sound, light, and rays, which are familiarizing yourself with them as self-presencings by (a) training in them simultaneously[186] and (b) meditatively taking them into your experience.

To that end, the moving, conceptual intellect is tamed by focusing it one-pointedly on your [mind's] own sound, which resounds self-emergently and continuously.

"The memory-driven mind is held in light."

The memory-driven mind is the mind that proliferates in thoughts about the past and the future. In focusing one-pointedly and [401] unwaveringly on the various presencings of your [mind's] own light, that mind is held still.

"The three powers of awareness are refined in rays."[187]

The expressive energies of unobscured, naturally luminous awareness are refined in the rays of your [mind's] own light, which shines forth in various forms, as whatever there is. When [refining[188]] these three, use the important points of the body along with those of the hands, which cause luminosity to be produced temporarily. Then, familiarize yourself with it as a self-presencing illusion.

[2.2.5.2.2.2.2.1.2] How Experiences and Visions of Luminosity Arise

> **"The three powers having been refined in rays,**
> **The maṇḍalas of the three bodies appear to you:"**

Having practiced in that way, the three bodies, which exist as a part of you, shine forth directly. Three maṇḍala appear as well: in "light" the visible body-maṇḍala appears, in "sound" the resounding speech-maṇḍala appears, and in "rays" the knowing mind-maṇḍala appears.

> **"From the mind-itself, empty and selfless,**
> **Empty magical apparitions shine forth in vision."**

Luminous appearances, the various magical emanations of the empty mind-itself, shine forth in multiplicity.

> **"Self-aware primordial gnosis has no concrete form,**
> **But awareness' efflorescence *(rtsal)* is the 'higher sights' and the Form Bodies."**

Self-aware primordial gnosis is not established with concrete features like color, shape, or form; but through its "efflorescence," or its "glow," or its "miraculous displays," an unfathomable variety of higher sights shine forth, apparitions in the aspect of empty-forms *(stong gzugs),* as well as hosts of Complete Bodies and Emanation Bodies.

How do these appear?

> **"Like a rainbow drawn in the sky,"**

They are luminous but distinctly defined, brilliant, laden with light, indeterminate, manifold, and shine forth as anything whatsoever.

> **"Like an unfurled roll of brocade,"**

They are beautiful and shimmering, luminous and vibrant, shining forth as anything whatsoever.

> **"Like a reflection appearing in a mirror!"**

They shine forth, appearing but without real nature; [402] visible but without concrete reality.[189]

[2.2.5.2.2.2.2.2] A Detailed Explanation

There are four topics here: (1) how to practice, (2) how experiences and visions of luminosity shine forth, (3) how the discovery is made, and (4) the enlightened qualities that ultimately manifest.

[2.2.5.2.2.2.2.2.1] How to Practice[190]

> **"Here are the methods for training:**
>
> **Catch the wriggling goldfish[191]**
> **In the dark-room, with a net of light!"**

A fish, for example, moves about in every direction in the water, but by using a fish net, it can be held still, right there in the water. It is the same with the movements of the memory-driven mind: when it is situated within the body and the sense faculties, it follows after awareness' rays, moving about in every direction in the objective sphere.

Based on the "external" important points (i.e., the techniques of the dark-room), the "internal" important points of the sense faculties via which darkness is cleared away (i.e. the gazes), and the "secret" [important points of] your own natural radiation (i.e., the net of light-rays), [the memory-driven mind] is held firm, the luminous "higher sights" are produced in your continuum, and self-awareness is displayed to you directly. Here, luminosity [arises via] practical meditative techniques based on the "six important points"; this should be understood in accordance with the "general descriptions of the practice."[192]

> **"Face the completely clear mirrors of mind[193]**
> **Toward the canopy of the brilliant sky!"**

If, for example, you face a mirror to the sky, reflections of the sun, the moon, the planets, the stars, and so forth will become distinctly visible in it. In the same way, awareness accords with [how you direct] the eyes. By using the "gaze of the majestic lion" and staring into the clear sky, the "external" process of the shining forth of visions, and the "internal" process of the arising of experiences will come about temporarily. This involves the practices of "uniting the three skies"[194] and so forth, which should be understood in accordance with the essential instructions on the "meditative stabilization on the brilliant sky."[195]

> **"Aim the spear of the attentive mind[196]**
> **At the shields of radiant light!"**

A powerful man, for example, can raise aloft a sharp, straight spear, [403] and focus it upon a shield. In the same way, focus the king of awareness into a single point and, like you are aiming a spear, focus on the externally existing light-wheel, and the internal light-wheel of the sense faculties.[197] Here, based on the practices related to the "union of the three lamps,"[198] the "higher sights" are produced through forceful means; this should be understood in accordance with [the instructions on] the "meditative stabilization on the naturally luminous lamp."[199]

[2.2.5.2.2.2.2.2.2] How Experiences and Visions of Luminosity Shine Forth

There are two topics here: (1) how luminosity arises, and (2) how meditative experiences arise.

[2.2.5.2.2.2.2.2.2.1] How Luminosity Arises

> **"At that time, you see the 'seeds' of the Form Bodies**
> **Shining in the sky like a constellation of stars."**

By practicing in that way, numerous visionary forms are seen: crystal *thig-le* of awareness that are the seeds of the Form Bodies and the source of the buddhafields, as well as daytime appearances of *thig-le* tents of five-colored light. These arise like constellations of stars appearing in the sky, in unfathomable sizes, numbers, and levels of subtlety and coarseness.

[2.2.5.2.2.2.2.2.2.2] How Meditative Experiences Arise

> **"Through becoming familiar and involved with those,**
> **Five particular meditative experiences arise:"**

Through unwaveringly taking those visions into your meditative experience, through constantly familiarizing yourself with them, and through involving yourself with them, you will distinguish awareness' dynamic dimensions from its coarse ones. Through that, externally, experiences and visions of luminosity will light up, while internally originally pure awareness will manifest more and more clearly. The signs of this appear in five stages: (1) the experience of the onset of vision, (2) the experience of the flaring up of vision, (3) the experience of abundant vision, (4) the experience of the completion of vision, and (5) the experience of the final vision.

[2.2.5.2.2.2.2.2.2.2.1] The Experience of the Onset of Vision

> **"First, at the onset of vision, you see**
> **Something like mercury, scattering and beading together."**

Having unwaveringly trained awareness on those earlier visions and brought them into your meditative experience, [now] crystal-colored *thig-le* of awareness, [404] like little peas, appear within the luminosity. And, there are appearances of larger formations, with two or three [*thig-le*] connected together, or with many connected together, and so forth. As well, there are nuclei of awareness[200] called "necklaces of seminal nuclei,"[201] which are like silver threads or white silk cords, on which *thig-le*, like peas or grains, are strung in the manner of garlands. At the center of each of those *thig-le* dwells the tiny form of a deity body, just slightly bulging out of its hollow.

At that time, those visions tumble like water falling from the face of the mountains, or like mercury scattering and beading together: they are unstable, arising and stopping, scattering and coming back together, wavering and quivering. Internally, your experience of one-pointedness is insubstantial, and temporary. As they wax and wane, doubts appear.[202]

[2.2.5.2.2.2.2.2.2.2] The Experience of the Flaring Up of Vision

> **"Then, vision flares up: in the sky**
> **You see the sun and the moon come into full view.**[203]
> **You see awareness as wheels of light.**[204]
> **You see *thig-le* forming luminous tents!"**

As before, by practicing unwaveringly and continuously, the luminosity of awareness manifests directly: the essence of self-awareness,[205] wheels of light—their natural glow brilliant and lustrous—become clearly visible without obscuration. As for the body, its exterior and interior—the flesh and blood, channels and muscles, the sense faculties and their seats, the vital organs and vessels—become clearly visible without obstruction.

Externally, luminous appearances shine forth in every direction,[206] without being obscured or covered up. Within those, appearances of white *thig-le*, five-colored tents of *thig-le* with five encircling halos, blazes of light in pure lustrous radiance, triads of bronze plates,[207] *thig-le* tents, peacock eggs, and so forth arise. Spreading out slower and less chaotically than before, they are able to stay still momentarily. In their centers a tiny enlightened body, [405] the size of a seed, bulges out, just a little clearer than before. Also, white chains of *thig-le*, and multicolored ones, shine forth in the fashion of rays.

Internally, your practice[208] is free of elaborations, as they dissolve naturally, and is accompanied by the arising of intensely clear realizations.

[2.2.5.2.2.2.2.2.2.3] The Experience of Abundant Vision

> **"Then vision becomes abundant,**
> **And you see the maṇḍalas of the Complete Bodies of the five families."**

This is the supreme luminosity, just as it is, arising manifestly. As awareness is made more familiar and involved with that [luminosity], impure distorted appearances (appearances of fire, water, earth, wind) cease. Then pure appearances (the enlightened bodies and buddhafields) shine forth. *Thig-le* composed of the five lights—like little tents, mustard-seeds, and so forth—shine forth in unfathomable different sizes, their manifestation slow and tame. Then, within each of them, fivefold groups [of *thig-le*] separate out into vertical rows. Within those [larger *thig-le*], at each of their cardinal directions, a luminous lotus or wheel[209] becomes visible. Or, their circumferences become encircled by halos or felt [patterns] of five-colored light. Doors with door-ornaments—strings of rays—emanate in variety and link up, shining forth in unfathomable different sizes. In the middle of those [fivefold clusters], the deities of the five families appear, their bodies, colors, and ornaments either complete or incomplete, according to circumstances.[210]

Internally, through one-pointed meditation, external and internal, objects and consciousnesses, cyclic existence and transcendence, all become of a single taste in the enlightened mind.

[2.2.5.2.2.2.2.2.2.4] The Experience of the Completion of Vision

> **"Then vision becomes complete:**
> **You see the maṇḍalas of the spontaneously present seals;**
> **You see buddhafields of illuminating light;**
> **You see miraculous appearances, devoid of fluctuating motion."**

When pure appearances arise in that way, through training the gnostic energy of awareness with respect to them, [406] the five aggregates are purified right in their own place—without abandoning them[211]—and the five deities appear. As the vibrant energies of the elements are distinguished from their solidified dimensions, the tendency to grasp at appearances as concrete is purified in its own place, and all the buddha-bodies and buddhafields, which are spontaneously present within you, become manifest. Thus, the pure self-manifesting external, internal, and secret maṇḍalas[212] shine forth without measure and without regard to direction. On the thrones within their deity-palaces, manifold appearances of the external, internal, and secret fivefold families—the main deities along with their retinues and secondary emanations—shine forth.

Further, whatever appears—the Enjoyment Bodies, Emanations Bodies, and so forth—are all endowed with the three "certainties": (1) the ornaments, (2) thrones, and (3) the major and minor marks. Light rays, unwavering and radiant, radiate in the ten directions, and this is seen in an unwavering fashion.[213]

Internally, the mental effort [that conceives of] a "meditator" and "object of meditation" is liberated into the [enlightened] mind, and a state of "no-meditation no-wavering" begins.

[2.2.5.2.2.2.2.2.2.5] The Final Experience

> **"Then the final visions appear:**
> **Lights, awareness' own light—**
> **An appearance of emptiness,[214] like a rainbow.**
> **Sounds, awareness' own sounds—**
> **The natural sound of emptiness, like an echo.**
> **Rays, awareness' own rays—**
> **The magical emanations of emptiness, like an apparition.**
> **Bodies, awareness' own form—**
> **The reflections of emptiness, like the moon reflected in water."[215]**

In this way, the contaminated body appears as the uncontaminated enlightened bodies and buddhafields, but this should be understood as the expressive energy of self-aware primordial gnosis shining forth, or magical displays that are your own pure self-presencings: the light is your own natural light, arising like a rainbow; the sound is your own natural sound, emerging like an echo; the rays are your own natural rays, shining like the rays of the sun; and the bodies are your own natural form, appearing like reflections.

Here you plumb the depths of the three visionary appearances, discover what they really are, abandon what is to be abandoned, realize what is to be realized, and your body and mind are liberated as the deity-bodies and primordial gnoses. The originally pure, immaculate, self-aware primordial gnosis is the manifestation of the Essential Body. Awareness taking hold of its own place is the Reality Body. And the shining forth of the unimpeded enlightened qualities—the bodies and buddhafields—is the attainment of [407] the two Form Bodies. Thus, this is the manifestation of the three bodies.

This is awareness taking hold of its own place, distorted appearances being purified in the [enlightened] mind, and straying being cut off at its source. Memory-driven conceptuality is liberated right in its own place, and the afflictions manifest as the primordial gnoses. The attainment of buddhahood is at hand, so you remain continually in a state where your meditation does not wander, devoid of conceptual apprehensions, and the final fruit of the path becomes manifest. For this reason it is called the "final vision."

[2.2.5.2.2.2.2.2.3] How the Discovery is Made

> **"The 'false cave' of appearances is exhausted in the mind,"**

When the magical appearances of the mind—sound, light, and rays—arise, they are definitively determined to be the [enlightened] mind.

"And the Form Bodies are discovered as being the mind."

Though the buddhafields of the Enjoyment and Emanation bodies shine forth in all their variety, they do so as the dynamic energy of self-aware primordial gnosis, and thus are discovered to be the [enlightened] mind.

[2.2.5.2.2.2.2.2.4] The Enlightened Qualities that Ultimately Manifest

"When straying is resolved from the depths, it is impossible to stray again,"

This explains that when the conditions for straying—sound, light, and rays—are determined from the depths to be self-presencings, then it is impossible to stray again.

"And the three bodies become manifest, right then."

Through self-awareness recognizing itself, the Bön Body becomes manifest. The buddhafields also become manifest, and emanations [go to] the varieties of places where there are beings to be trained; thus the two Form Bodies are manifest.[216] At this time, the three grounds are actualized,[217] as the three bodies take hold of their own places.

"The power of karmic cause and effect is a great falsehood—
This is the buddhas' forceful method!"

The lower [vehicles] assert that after amassing the collections for uncountable eons, you train on the path and thus become a buddha. But this is simply a provisional teaching, the indirect intent. Here [in the Great Perfection], you purify your karmic obstructions all at once, letting go of "cause and effect" as a false method. The three bodies of the buddha exist as a part of you,[218] and when you recognize them [408] as yourself, they manifest right at that moment, and buddhahood is attained. This is an explanation of the final, definitive meaning, the buddhas' forceful method.[219]

[2.2.5.2.2.2.3] An Explanation of the Seal of Secrecy Attached to These Esoteric Instructions

"This is my final, ultimate advice!"

These are the profound essential points, drawn from the final vehicle among them all.

"It is medicine for those who are pure,"

If you teach this to beings who possess karmic fortune, their realization and attainment will come about at the same time,[220] so it is like medicine.

"But for those who are ignorant, it will turn into poison."

If you teach it to these types of beings, there will be no realization, and due to their misunderstandings it will become a poison that binds them again.

"So, don't teach it to everyone, but keep it secret and hidden.
This [advice] is [like] the milk of the white lion—
Pour it into the vessels of the fortunate!
But from unsuitable vessels, who have no fortune
Keep it for a thousand eons,
Like the jewel that the king of the water-dragons holds in his throat!"[221]

Thus he taught.

This is the order of secrecy that accompanies the advice.

[2.2.5.3] Conclusion to the Chapter

This completes the lamp that introduces the buddhafields.

Sa-Ma-Ya!

This applies a seal of secrecy, ordering [the advice] to be kept from those who are unsuitable vessels.

The explanation of the fifth chapter is complete!

[2.2.6] CHAPTER SIX: The Lamp of the Bardo Period

Sixth is the "lamp of the bardo period." There are three sections here: (1) a brief explanation, (2) an extensive explanation, and (3) a conclusion.

[2.2.6.1] A Brief Explanation of the Lamp of the Bardo Period

Homage to Küntu Zangpo, the self-aware manifest buddha!

This indicates that if you recognize your mind as Küntu Zangpo with decisiveness and assurance, you will attain buddhahood without passing into the bardo.

"Son of the family! The lamp of the bardo period..."

When the body and mind separate, you are at once freed from all obscurations and coverings: the illusory body,[222] the conceptual mind, and the appearances of objects. Then, the universal ground and awareness shine forth without obscurations or coverings, like the sun freed from darkness, or the sky freed from clouds. For this reason, this period is called a "lamp." [409]

"...is the border at which straying and realization meet."

The bardo is where the border between straying (i.e., wandering in cyclic existence) and realization (i.e., buddhahood) is met.

"This is called the 'important point of cyclic existence separating from transcendence.'"

The bardo is the point from which cyclic existence and transcendence diverge, caused by realization or non-realization.

[2.2.6.2] An Extensive Explanation of the Lamp of the Bardo Period

There are three topics here:

"Here I will teach you (1) how the body and mind separate,
(2) How realization leads to liberation,
And (3) how non-realization leads to straying."

[2.2.6.2.1] How the Body and Mind Separate

This first topic has two sections:

"There are two points about the separation of the body and mind: (1) how the elements disintegrate, and (2) how they contract back into one another."[223]

[2.2.6.2.1.1] How the Elements Disintegrate

"To explain how the elements disintegrate, it is like this:"

When the physical body composed of the four [elements][224] initially takes form, it is built up from the space element. From space, wind emerges; from wind, fire; from fire, water; and from water earth takes form. At the time of disintegration, these disintegrate back downward: first earth, then water, then fire, then wind, and then space disintegrates.

The disintegration of the five elements results in the following: (a) internally the five vital organs that are the "seats" [of those elements] weaken; (b) externally the sensory gateways become unclear with respect to their five objects; (c) the five related limbs[225] wane and lose their strength; and (d) the five internal vessels wane, leading to the visible effect of their five respective excretions slipping out of their own accord.

To break these up in detail:

"(1) The spleen, which is earth's domain, weakens and your body can't feel touch."

Internally, the spleen, which is the seat of the earth element, weakens. Due to this, externally, its gateway, the body sense-power, can no longer feel smooth or rough tactile sensations.

> **"You are unable to raise your left arm, and your nine openings fill with secretions."**

Its related limb, the left arm, can no longer bear weight[226] (this is because a channel from the spleen splits off to the left arm). As a visible effect, the sense gateways of the mouth and nose drip their respective excretions, saliva and snot.

> **"(2) The kidneys, which are water's domain, weaken and your ears can't hear sound. You are unable to raise your left leg, and you can't hold back your urine." [410]**

Internally, the kidneys, which are the seat of the water element, weaken. Due to this, externally, the ear sense-power cannot hear sound. Its related limb, the left leg, can no longer bear weight (this is because the kidneys' "water channel" branches off to the left leg). As a visible effect, urine emerges under its own power.

> **"(3) The liver, which is fire's domain, weakens and your tongue can't sense taste. You are unable to raise your right arm, and blood emerges from your nose."**

Internally, the liver, which is the seat of the fire element, weakens. Due to this, externally, the gateway of the tongue loses its ability to experience taste. Its related limb, the right arm, can no longer bear weight (this is because the liver's "fire channel" branches off to the right arm). As a visible effect, blood emerges from the nose.

> **"(4) The lungs, which are wind's domain, weaken and your nose can't sense smell. You are unable to raise your right leg, and you lose your feces, though you try to hold it back."**

Internally the lungs, which are the seat of the wind element, weaken. Due to this, externally, the gateway of the nose can no longer experience smells. Its related limb, the right leg, can no longer bear weight (this is because the lungs' "wind channel" branches off to the right leg).[227] As a visible effect, feces emerges of its own power.

> **"(5) The heart, which is the domain of space, weakens and your eyes can't see forms. You are unable to hold up your head, and the *thig-le* slip out from your secret place."**

Internally, the heart, which is the seat of the space element, weakens. Due to this, externally, the gateways of the eyes lose the ability to see forms. Its related limb, the head, can no longer bear weight (this is because the heart's "space channel" branches off to the head). As a visible effect, the *thig-le* emerge from the secret place under their own power.

[2.2.6.2.1.2] How the Elements Contract Back into One Another

"And to explain how the elements contract, it is like this: (1) earth sinks into water, and your body's strength is lost."

As a sign of the earth-wheel at the navel having disintegrated, and its power having dissolved into water, your physical strength is lost, and your body becomes heavy. You have the sensation that you are sinking into the earth. A yellow light, the vibrant energy of the earth element, arises in your vision, dazzling yellow in appearance, like a mirage.

"(2) Water then sinks into fire, [411] and your body's luster is lost."

As a sign of the water-wheel at the secret-area having disintegrated, and its power having dissolved into fire, the mouth and nose become dry, and the body loses its luster. A dazzling blue light appears in your vision, like daybreak.

"(3) Fire sinks into wind, and your body's heat is lost."

The body's heat collapses, your speech becomes unclear, and you can't express yourself. A dazzling red light appears in your vision, like fireflies.

"(4) Wind sinks into mind, and though you try to retain your breath, you lose it."

Panicked, you look for something to hold onto; you can't catch your breath, and your eyes roll back. A dazzling reddish-green light appears in your vision, like lightning.

"(5) Mind then sinks into the universal ground; the breath stops, and the body and mind separate."

Blackness wipes out everything, your eyes open wide and bulge out, and your breath is cut off in a gasp. A white light, the vibrant quintessence of space, appears in your vision, dazzling white like the rising moon. Then, your external breath ceases, your six external consciousnesses stop, and your sense faculties move inward.

At this point, your internal winds have not ceased, and your cognition is seven times more radiant and clear than before, shining forth radiant and empty, with no obscurations or coverings. This is called the "bardo of primordial gnosis." At this point, those of superior acumen will give rise to the "assurance" of realizing the correct view. Those of middling capacity will give rise to the "glow" of recalling what they should meditate on. Those of lower capacity hit the important points of the visualization-based deity-*samādhis,* the methods of devotion and compassion, and so forth. Thus they introduce themselves and take hold of their own places; this is the mother meeting with the son in the bardo of birth and death.

> **"This time of death is the border between happiness and suffering."**

This is the border between either going upward to attain a favorable state, or falling down to a bad migration. [412] This period where the body and mind separate is the only time that this happens.

> **"Positive and negative thoughts have a great propulsive force here,"**

At this time, the quality of your thoughts—whether they are positive or negative—has great power to propel you to either a high or low state. So, [when someone is dying] it is important to give this advice in accordance with their mental abilities.

> **"...so advice[228] should be given in accordance with [the dying person's] abilities."**

Give the advice to people based on their acumen, whether they are of high, middling, or low. This can be understood[229] from the "nails"[230] and the esoteric instructions.

[2.2.6.2.2] How Realization Leads to Liberation

> **"Son of the family! There are three ways that realization leads to liberation: (1) supreme, (2) medium, and (3) low."**

In accordance with this, there are three topics here.

[2.2.6.2.2.1] How Beings of the Highest Ability Attain Liberation

> **"Those of highest ability are like garuḍa chicks, or lion cubs—"**

A garuḍa chick's three powers are complete when it is in the belly of its mother, so as soon as it breaks free of the seal of its egg, it can fly. Similarly, a tiger cub's three powers are complete when it is in its mother's belly, so as soon as it is free from the seal of the womb, it can jump.[231]

> **"...their three powers are already complete,"**

At this time [of dying], the seal of the yogi's body, speech, and mind is rent open, and self-awareness becomes manifest. The previously buried buddha, whose three powers of body, speech, and mind are complete, now takes human form.

> **"...so as soon as the body and mind separate,"**

As soon as the body and mind separate, buddhahood is attained in the manner of the sun united with the moon, like dawn on the sixteenth day.[232] As for how this buddhahood is attained,[233] at that time:

> **"...the vibrant and coarse dimensions of their elements are distinguished, cyclic existence is shaken out from the depths, and straying is purified right in its own place: the gnostic energy of awareness dawns like the sun, spreading throughout the sky of the universal ground whose expanse has no parts or divisions. The magical displays of the three bodies then shine forth without ceasing, like the rays of the sun, and continuously carry out the aims of beings." [413]**

[2.2.6.2.2.2] How Beings of Intermediate Ability Attain Liberation

> **"For those of medium ability, at that time..."**

Although beings of intermediate ability are not liberated in the first bardo,[234] they will be liberated in the "luminous bardo of Bön-itself."[235] There are two topics related to this: (1) how [that bardo] arises, and (2) how liberation is attained there.

[2.2.6.2.2.2.1] How the Reality Bardo Arises

> **"...the external appearances of fire, water, earth, and wind cease and manifestations of the internal[236] sound, light, and rays shine forth."**

The seemingly autonomous appearances that we are seeing now—of fire, water, earth, and wind; of external and internal; of the container world and its contained beings—will cease. Then the three appearances of sound, light, and rays shine forth. Here "light" is appearances of the five lights, shining forth above and below, in all the cardinal and intermediate directions, in front of and behind you, near and far away, without center or boundary. "Sound" is the sound of Bön-itself, emptiness' own sound,[237] emerging naturally from the space of the mind-itself, resounding continuously. "Rays" are the magical displays of awareness,[238] shining forth in all possible forms, such that there is no way to say "this is shining forth" or "this is not shining forth."

> **"Separated from the physical body of flesh and blood, awareness is now without a basis, and is present in its nakedness."**

Free of the appearing objects that obscure it, and free of the physical body that obscures it, awareness' vibrant essence is separated from its coarse dimensions. Devoid of a physical basis, awareness then shines forth nakedly.

> **"The hosts of karma, afflictions, and distorted conceptual thought cease, and the universal ground becomes present without obscurations or coverings."**

The hosts of karma, afflictions, and distorted conceptual thought are not abandoned—rather, they are purified right in their own place. Then, the universal ground shines forth, devoid of obscurations, like the sky freed from clouds.

[2.2.6.2.2.2.2] How Liberation is Attained in the Reality Bardo

> **"At that time, through the power of having been introduced to the 'essence' and the 'higher sights,'[239] and having become familiar with them, the six superknowledges and the six recollections arise, and buddhahood is attained."**

At this time, just as before,[240] you are introduced to the essential ground and the reality of awareness. As well, you are introduced to the "higher sights" of sound, light, and rays as being self-presencings. As you have become familiar with that fact, [now] during the luminous bardo of [414] Bön-itself, the six superknowledges and the six recollections arise, and you attain buddhahood.

> **"The six superknowledges are these: (1) Because awareness now abides without a physical basis, you can know your past and future lives."**

Free from the physical body that obscures it, your disembodied awareness can know the locations of its past and future lives.

> **"(2) Because the universal ground is present without obscurations, you can know the workings of karmic cause and effect."**

The reflections of karmic cause and effect appear in the mirror of the universal ground, so now you can know every aspect of an action's effect.

> **"(3) Through the pure divine eye you can know pure buddhafields and impure realms."**

Having attained the divine eye, which surpasses the fleshy eye, you can know the attributes of the buddhafields of the five pure families, as well as those of the impure realms of the six classes of beings.

"(4) When the three appearances of sound, light, and rays shine forth, you know they are the luminous bardo of Bön-itself."

Through the condition of the arising of the three great appearances, you know the luminous bardo of Bön-itself has begun.

"(5) From having been introduced to its essential nature, you know that the three bodies are spontaneously present within your mind."

At this time, from having been introduced to the mind-itself,[241] you attain buddhahood in the bardo, recognizing that the three bodies dwell intrinsically within you.

"(6) And through having been introduced to the "higher sights," you know the self-presencings of sound, light, and rays to be the lighting up of the three bodies."

At this time, from having been introduced to the luminous appearances of the higher sights as being self-presencings, now in the bardo you recognize the three self-presencings of sound, light, and rays to be the expressive energy of the three bodies, and it is like meeting with a person that you were familiar with before.

"And the six recollections are these: (1) first, remembering that you are moving between lives...,"

At this time, with your introduction and the arising of the three visionary appearances acting as conditions, you recall that you are moving between lives.

"(2) then remembering that this is the bardo...,"

This means that you recognize the bardo as the bardo.

"(3) then [415] remembering that awareness is abiding without any physical support...,"

Then, at this time, due to the introductions, you recall that awareness is abiding nakedly, without a physical basis.

"(4) then remembering the lama's advice...,"

Due to your previous introduction to it, you now recall the oral instructions for cutting off the bardo.

"(5) then you remember that the sound, light, and rays are self-presencings, and..."

As you have previously been introduced to the three visionary appearances as self-presencings, you now recall that fact.

"(6) then remembering that your mind is the Buddha."

Due to your previous introduction to the "subjective" mother, son, and dynamic energy[242] as being the actual Buddha, you now recall that fact.

In that way, the six superknowledges and the six recollections are the cause and condition[243] through which you become liberated in the luminous bardo of Bön-itself. Next is a description of how you become liberated based on that condition:

"Awareness is realized[244] via its bare nakedness,"

Through the condition of realizing [the three appearances[245]] as self-presencings, the gnostic energy of awareness is realized in its bare nakedness, free of the clothing of conceptuality.

"...and the unobscured universal ground is vividly realized."

The universal ground, which has never been obscured by straying, is vividly realized as a transparency, like the cloudless sky in which the sun has risen.

"Through that realization, awareness takes hold of its own place, no longer following after appearances."

Realizing in that way, the "king of awareness" takes hold of his own place, and no longer follows after the "populace" of appearances.

"Not following after appearances, those appearances are liberated as self-presencing illusions."

By not following after the three visionary objects, appearances are naturally liberated, like things that have no reality.

"With appearances liberated as self-presencings, straying clears away naturally, of its own accord."

When appearances are liberated, straying is naturally cleared away. This is like knowing a multicolored rope as a multicolored rope, through which the cognition that apprehends it as a snake will no longer arise.

"When straying naturally clears away, the three bodies [416] shine forth naturally."

When straying dissipates, the three bodies shine forth as you.[246] This is like the moment when the clouds obscuring the sun are cleared away, and the sun shines forth directly and immediately.

"When the three bodies shine forth naturally, the ability to accomplish the aims of beings arises of its own accord."

When the three bodies shine forth like the orb of the sun, the enlightened activities, like the sun's rays, radiate in all directions, and one becomes able to continuously fulfill the aims of all beings.

[2.2.6.2.2.3] How Beings of the Lowest Ability Attain Liberation

> **"Those of lowest ability have entered the gateway of this advice, but having little understanding or realization, they don't recognize the luminous bardo of Bön-itself,"**

Although they have been taught this advice, those whose minds are smaller and whose meditative familiarity with it is weaker do not recognize the luminous bardo of Bön-itself even though it appears, and at that time are they are not liberated.

> **"....and stray into the karmic bardo of existence."**

Now, appearances of the "karmic bardo of birth and death" arise. You still experience a little straying, so appearances are normal. Later, the three visionary appearances shine forth in an exclusively pure fashion: radiant light shines forth; the fortunate abodes are seen; the *yidam* deities are clearly present; and the lama's transmissions, teachings, and so forth arise.

> **"But through the power of the oral instructions, they attain a body in a fortunate rebirth."**

Due to their good qualities resulting simply from having heard the oral instructions,[247] they will recall them at that time. By practicing them [in the bardo], they will attain an excellent rebirth characterized by freedoms, that is, a favorable rebirth in a body of either a human or a god.[248]

> **"And there, due to their pure karmic fortune, their previous karmic predispositions will be awakened,"**

Due to the good karmic fortune of having received this pure advice [in their previous life], the karmic predispositions related to that will be awakened [in the next life]. Due to that condition, they will reflect on it continually, and will begin to implement this advice.[249]

> **"...and they will attain liberation in one more life."**

Such people will attain buddhahood in one life, or will attain it in the first bardo: At the age of twenty-five or thirty-five, they will develop a distinctive insight. [417] At thirty-five or forty-five, they will develop distinctive experiences and realizations. At fifty-five or sixty-five or afterward, their body will dissolve into a rainbow.

[2.2.6.2.3] How Non-realization Leads to Straying

"Here is how those who don't realize go astray.[250] For the lowest of beings, who haven't entered into the gateway of this advice:"

After the body and mind separate, at the time when awareness is dwelling in the state of luminosity,[251] [such people experience the following]:

"Through the negative power of karma, you do not recognize the abiding reality."[252]

This happens even though it is clearly evident, without any obscurations or coverings.

"The moving winds rise up, blowing the ocean of awareness,
Stirring up ripples of predispositions and waves of conceptuality."

At that time, the moving winds of conceptuality rise up, creating motion in the ocean of awareness: stirring up ripples of karmic predispositions, and stirring up waves of conceptuality.

"The sky of the universal ground is obscured by the clouds of confusion,"

The universal ground, which is like the sky, becomes obscured by the clouds of confusion, which are like an imprisoning darkness. In this way, it loses its radiance.

"And awareness[253] is cloaked in the darkness of the afflictions."

The gnostic energy of awareness, which is like the sun, becomes cloaked in the afflictions, which are like an enveloping darkness. In this way, it ceases to appear.

"Sound, light, and rays are seen erroneously, as extrinsic appearances."[254]

The expressive energy of awareness shines forth as the three great visionary appearances, which are self-presencing objects, like illusions. Although they arise in a self-emergent fashion, they come to be seen as extrinsic appearances, as if they were truly real.

"And visual appearances[255] arise in two ways, driven by virtuous or non-virtuous karma."

Impelled by virtuous karma, the sources[256]—the sound, light, and rays—will shine forth as pure visual appearances: lights, immeasurable environments, buddhafields, enlightened bodies, and so forth. Impelled by non-virtuous karma, they will shine forth as impure visual appearances: black holes, graves, roaring sounds, terrifying forms, and so forth.

"You have a mental body, [418] which you see as your previous form;"

You have no physical form, no actual form that is capable of appearing [to others]. Rather, you have [a body of] mental form, of dreamlike karmic predispositions.[257] It is said that this appears like the body you had in your former life, and that however long you stay in the bardo, for one third of that, you will appear as if in your future body.

"Your faculties are complete, and via your karma[258] you move without obstruction."

Your sense faculties have no physical support but are completely functional, and you view and experience things in accordance with your karmic predispositions. With the exception of a womb that accords with your karmic heritage,[259] you can go anywhere else, without obstruction, just by thinking about it: [through] earth, stone, rocky mountains, houses, and so forth. Through the miraculous power of your karma,[260] you travel about the realms of all the six types of beings. Now as you migrate about, no one else can see you, except for other beings in the bardo and beings who have attained the pure divine eye.

Here is the measure of suffering of those bardos:

"But with no stable place to stay and no protector
You are like a child abandoned by its mother."

There is the suffering of your awareness having no stable basis, and you are like a bee at the end of autumn, unable to find any of the moisture on which it depends. There is also the suffering of searching for the basis of a new body, and the suffering of having no guardian to protect you. The oceans of suffering overflow!

"Enveloped in the darkness of straying, an ocean of suffering overflows,
And you writhe about like a fish cast on the hot sands."

This indicates how you become like a fish writhing about on the hot sand.[261]

"The winds of the karmic dispositions rise up, and you wander in the lands of the six types of beings,
Circling continually like a water wheel, or the wheel of a chariot."

Driven by the winds of karmic predispositions, you pass through the lands of the six classes of beings, one after another, like the continual motion of a water-wheel, or the wheel of a chariot.

"You have no source of protection in the three worlds—how sad!"

In that way, the vastness of your suffering is unfathomable, but this is your own karma ripening on yourself; [419] a being[262] that cannot possibly be helped, you become an object of pity.

> **"The time of liberation never arrives, and you despair,[263] exhausted."**

Since beginningless time you have wandered limitlessly in cyclic existence, and are exhausted by your experience of unfathomable suffering.

> **"Keep in mind the terrible nature of straying, and turn your back on the appearances of[264] this disintegrating world!"**

By thinking of the terrible nature of straying and cyclic existence, the time of punishment in suffering, how difficult it is to be liberated from there, and so forth, you will turn your back on the appearances of the world.

> **"Make effort on the path, fortunate son of the family!"**

This urges and advises [Gyerpungpa] to make effort at practicing the profound path that is the method for reversing cyclic existence.

[2.2.6.3] Concluding Summation of the Lamp of the Bardo Period

> **"In these ways, realization leads to buddhahood, while non-realization leads to wandering in cyclic existence. The bardo is where you reach the border between those two, so this is the 'important point of how cyclic existence separates from transcendence.'"**

This has been an extensive presentation of the "lamp of the bardo period."

[2.3] Drugyalwa's Explanation of the Conclusion to *Advice on the Six Lamps*

This has five sections: (1) the great good qualities of this advice, (2) where and how it should be taught [in the future], (3) how the Emanation Body of the teacher departed, (4) how after that [Gyerpungpa] attained enlightened qualities, and (5) a conclusion that ends the main body of the text.

[2.3.1] The Great Good Qualities of this Advice

> **"Son of the family! These six points on the enlightened mind are the esoteric instructions that bring about realization of the mind, for those who haven't realized it.[265] They are like lamps for those who think there is no such mind,"[266]**

If you raise up a lamp, you immediately see that nothing is there.[267] In the same way, this lamp displays your mind which has no concrete reality, showing you its essential nature just as it is, directly and nakedly.

> **"...mirrors for those who cannot see it,"**

You cannot see your face, but if you look into a mirror, it can be seen. In the same way, this advice lets you directly see your mind, which you could not see before.

> **"...and iron hooks for those from whom it escapes."**

Just like an iron hook can hold anything, [420] this advice will hold the mind that will not rest, that races off to objects.

> **"They are nails for minds that fall apart,"**

A nail fixes something so it does not slip away or separate; in the same way, this advice plants the nail that keeps the mind from slipping to the side of proliferations or separating from reality.

> **"...refreshment for minds that are foggy,"**

Through its explanations of awareness' direct manifestation, [the mind's] sinking and fogginess dissipate right in their own places, and [awareness] is displayed without obscuration, in its natural luminosity.

> **"...enhancement for minds that are shallow,"**

It makes you recognize what was not recognized before, so that awareness is brought to the ground—the son, right then, is brought to meet with the mother.

> **"...yokes for minds that are stubborn,"**

It tames and settles down those whose minds are wild, making them peaceful at their core.

> **"...and keys for minds that are imprisoned."**

It liberates you from the fetters of suffering that bind you, bringing about the great naturally arising natural liberation.

[2.3.2] Where and How it Should Be Taught in the Future

> **"In the future, you determine who to give this to and who to keep it from,"**[268]

This means [for Gyerpungpa] to ascertain whether the time to teach this advice has come or not, whether to order it to be kept sealed, or to grant permission.

"...doing so in accordance with their abilities."

Beings are of superior, medium, and low capacity, so the advice should also be taught in accordance with that, [selecting] what to place in their minds, and what to apply to their continuums.

"If people have the karmic fortune, then lead them on the unerring path!"

[The advice] was spoken along with a statement of permission: "For beings who are suitable vessels, lead them on the path—lead them quickly to liberation!"

[2.3.3] How the Emanation of the Teacher Departed

Having taught this, the Emanation Body [of Tapihritsa] ceased to appear, like a rainbow dissolving in the sky.

Having spoken this advice to the fortunate being whose time to be trained had come, [421] that Emanation Body, having accomplished the aims of beings, went back into the expanse, like a rainbow disappearing into the sky.

[2.3.4] How Gyerpungpa Attained His Enlightened Qualities

And Gurub Nangzher Löpo, having discovered what awareness really is,[269]

That Shen-po endowed with good karma was liberated from the full extent of the ties that bound him. Freed from his selfish arrogance, he found belief, certainty, and decisiveness, realizing and making his attainment right at the same time.

...made all of the supreme and ordinary attainments.

He mastered[270] **"all the supreme and ordinary [attainments],"** the enlightened qualities and magical powers. As for the supreme enlightened qualities: his understanding of the view and his experiential realizations were all brought to perfection, and his self-aware primordial gnosis became manifest. He also became endowed with ordinary good qualities, like the ability to make magical displays, wield powers, and give blessings. Thus, he became endowed with many distinctive great qualities, signs of accomplishment like the superknowledges and so forth.

[2.3.5] Conclusion to the Main Body of the Text

This concludes the Great Perfection's *Lamps*[271]—an oral transmission unembellished by human words.

"Oral transmission" refers to [this] final advice on the profound meaning being transmitted from one ear to the next. "Unembellished by human words" indicates that it was transmitted orally, without interruption, by the realized ones; that the "mist" of its blessings will not disappear; that it has not become something that is just transmitted through examples or words; that its transmission contains no errors; that it is unmixed. Because its words have not gone under the earth,[272] it is particularly excellent! "Great Perfection" refers to the supreme peak of views, which is connected with the unsurpassed meaning. Through its oral advice, sentient beings are indicated as being ultimately endowed with the enlightened qualities of the buddhas, possessing them spontaneously and completely. "Lamps" indicates that this is special advice that illuminates objects that are not clear. "Concludes" indicates that there are no remaining words, that this is the conclusion of [this expression of the] ultimate intention.

[3] The Commentary's Concluding Material

From among the advice in the Great Perfection's Oral Tradition from Zhang Zhung, this explanation is part of the "inner" cycle, the "essential esoteric instructions."[273] [422] Explaining well the intended meaning of the *Six Lamps,* and without contradicting the teachings of the past siddhas or the practices of the true realized ones, it was composed and written out by Drugom Gyalwa Yungdrung, following a request by the practitioner Öglun Gomchen Tashi Sherab, who with faith and devotion, and full of respect, urged him greatly.[274] Now it is complete!

NOTES

Introduction

1. For these issues, see Ronald Davidson, *Tibetan Renaissance: Tantric Buddhism in the Rebirth of Tibetan Culture* (New York: Columbia University Press, 2005), 64. See also Tsepon W. D. Shakabpa, *Tibet: A Political History* (New York: Potala Publications, 1984), 50.

2. For a survey of the sources and issues surrounding the fall of the Tibetan empire, see Davidson, *Tibetan Renaissance*, 61ff. For a traditional Tibetan history of the period, see Shakabpa, *Political History*, 50ff.

3. See Davidson's description of "three popular uprisings" *(kheng log gsum)* in *Tibetan Renaissance*, 67ff.

4. For an account of at least one work produced in this period, see Jacob P. Dalton, "The Uses of the Dgongs Pa 'Dus Pa'i Mdo in the Development of the Rnying-Ma School of Tibetan Buddhism" (PhD diss., University of Michigan, 2002). See also Dalton's studies in *The Taming of the Demons: Violence and Liberation in Tibetan Buddhism* (New Haven, CT: Yale University Press, 2011).

5. For the varied referents of the term *bon,* and the ways that those may or may not relate to Tibetan pre-Buddhist religion, see Per Kværne, *The Tibetan Bon Religion: Iconography of a Living Tradition* (Boston: Shambala Publications, 1996), 9.

6. For a discussion of the locations of Ölmo Lung-ring and Zhang Zhung, see Samten Karmay, *The Treasury of Good Sayings: A Tibetan History of Bon* (London: Oxford University Press, 1972), xxvii. See also Samten Karmay, *The Arrow and the Spindle* (Kathmandu: Mandala Book Point, 1998), 104ff.

7. The date here is suggested by Karmay in his discussion of the confused histories surrounding the persecutions of Bön. See Karmay, *Arrow and the Spindle*, 114ff.

8. *Pad ma can,* D1350, literally the "Lotus Possessor" or "One Endowed with the Lotus."

9. *kun rdzob gzugs can ma.* See Bu vol. 1, VP ch. 1, 6a.7.

10. D1350, 102a.6.

11. See Paul Harrison's works, listed in the bibliography.

12. *dag snang*. For comments on this topic, see Tulku Thondup, *Hidden Teachings of Tibet: An Explanation of the Terma Tradition of the Nyingma School of Buddhism* (London: Wisdom Publications, 1986), 90. See also Janet Gyatso, "Genre, Authorship, and Transmission in Visionary Buddhism: The Literary Traditions of Thang-stong rGyal-Po," in *Tibetan Buddhism: Reason and Revelation*, ed. Steven Goodman and Ronald Davidson (Albany: State University of New York Press, 1992), 95-106.

13. When the term "vision" appears in the translations, this is usually rendering the Tibetan word *snang ba,* a multivalent term that can also mean "appearance," "to appear," "to presence," "to light up," and so forth. The term *lta ba* ("view" or "to look") also has some idiosyncratic uses that mean "vision."

14. These soteriological uses of vision are practiced right alongside other types of vision, in particular those that result in the revelation of new texts. Indeed, much of the literature examined in this book is related in one way or another to such revelations, and one of the works (*Advice on the Six Lamps*) provides a narrative of its own visionary revelation.

15. GDD, 286–287: *rgya mtsho chen po gyen du skyod/ lcags ri mun pa'i klong du gtad/.*

16. For an account of some of these polemics, see John Newman, "The Outer Wheel of Time: Vajrāyana Buddhist Cosmology in the Kālacakra Tantra" (Ph.D. diss., University of Wisconsin, 1987), 108. For a broader discussion of syncretism in Kālacakra, see Vesna Wallace, *The Inner Kālacakratantra: A Buddhist View of the Tantric Individual* (Oxford: Oxford University Press, 2001), ch. 3.

17. See the *bKa' gdams gsung 'bum,* which was released in thirty volumes in 2006, and followed by another thirty volumes in 2007. Consisting mainly of reproductions of manuscripts from the Drepung library, these have been published as *bKa' gdams gsung 'bum phyogs bsgrigs thengs dang po/gnyis pa,* ed. dPal-brtsegs-bod-yig-dpe-rnying-zhib-'jug-khang (Chengdu: Si-khron-mi-rigs-dpe-skrun-khang, 2006 [vols. 1–30] and 2007 [vols. 31–60]).

18. See Jaideva Singh's English translation: *Vijñānabhairava or Divine Consciousness: A Treasury of 112 Types of Yoga* (Delhi: Moltilal Banarsidass, 1979). Singh speculates that this work may date from the eighth century (see x).

19. See verses 76, 84, 85.

20. See verses 88, 89, 115, 128. Professor Shaman Hatley has also called my attention to the Śaivite work *Gartā-bhairava-sādhana* (*Sādhana of the Hole Bhairava*), located in chapter 47 of the *Brahmayāmala,* which involves digging an underground chamber and practicing in the darkness.

21. See verses 36, 37, 89. Note especially the *mudrā* described in Singh's annotations to verse 36 (33 n. 1) in which a yogi uses his fingers in a complex manner to block his sensory gateways; the technique here is quite like one used in the Bön tradition (see its mention on GDGG, 400, as "simultaneous" training).

22. See verses 32, 37.

23. See Alexis Sanderson, "Purity and Power among the Brahmans of Kashmir," in *The Category of the Person: Anthropology, Philosophy, History*, ed. Michael Carrithers, Steven Collins, and Steven Lukes (Cambridge: Cambridge University Press, 1985), 203. See also Alexis Sanderson, "The Doctrine of the Mālinīvijayottaratantra," in *Ritual and*

Speculation in Early Tantrism: Studies in Honour of André Padoux, ed. Teun Goudriaan (Albany: State University of New York Press, 1992), 287. See as well Mark S. G. Dyczkowski, *The Doctrine of Vibration: An Analysis of the Doctrines and Practices of Kashmir Shaivism* (Albany: State University of New York Press, 1987), 17.

24. See, for instance, the opening verses of Vasgupta's *Spandakārikās,* in which the world is created and destroyed by the opening and closing of Śiva's eyes; this is translated by Jaideva Singh in *Spanda-Kārikās: The Divine Creative Pulsation* (Delhi: Moltilal Banarsidass, 1980).

25. For an overview of light practices in Daoism, see James Miller's "Light," in *Daoism: A Beginner's Guide* (Oxford: Oneworld Publications, 2003), 114–130.

26. The Highest Clarity tradition was popularized under Tao Hongjing (456–536) but places its own scriptural beginnings in an earlier revelation to Yang Xi (330–386). For two studies of the tradition, see Isabelle Robinet, *Taoist Meditation: The Mao-Shan Tradition of Great Purity* (Albany: State University of New York Press, 1993); and James Miller, *The Way of Highest Clarity: Nature, Vision and Revelation in Medieval China* (Magdalena, NM: Three Pines Press, 2008).

27. It is also worth noting that one contemporary Daoist group practices a form of dark-retreat. This is the "Universal Healing Tao" group, led by the Thai monk Mantak Chia, who teaches a practice called "Dark Room Enlightenment." See his website (universal-tao.com) for several publications, including *Darkness Technology: Darkness Techniques for Enlightenment* (Chiang Mai: Universal Tao Publications, n.d.). There seems to be no precedent for this practice in other Daoist traditions.

28. For embryology, see Robinet's *Taoist Meditation,* 139ff.

Chapter 1

1. On this location, see Newman, "Outer Wheel of Time," 71.

2. *Paramādibuddhatantra (dpal dang po'i sangs rgyas kyi rgyud).* No longer extant, a portion of this work is thought to have been preserved as *A Brief Explication of Initiations (sekoddeśa, dbang mdor bstan pa),* D0361. See John Newman, "The Paramādibuddha and Its Relation to the Early Kālacakra Literature," *Indo-Iranian Journal* 30 (1987): 93–102. Also see Orofino's works in the bibliography.

3. For the dating of these works, see Newman's analysis in "Outer Wheel of Time," 75ff. and 110ff. As for the place of their production, Newman suggests eastern India (see "Outer Wheel of Time," 102). Orofino suggests northwest India; see her *Sekoddeśa: A Critical Edition of the Tibetan Translations* (Rome: Istituto Italiano per il Medio ed Estremeo Oriente, 1994), 24. Andrensen suggests Bengal; see "Kālacakra: Textual and Ritual Perspectives" (PhD diss., Harvard, 1997), 96.

4. See, for instance, the comments of *Stainless Light* on KCT 1.26 (Bu vol. 1, VP ch. 1, 89a.5), which speak of the "barbarian doctrine in the land of Mecca" *(ma kha'i yul du kla klo'i chos),* and the "demonic doctrine of the barbarian Tajiks" *(kla klo stag gzig rnams kyi lha ma yin gyi chos).*

5. Bu vol. 1, VP ch. 1, 28b.7.

6. VP on KCT 2.48–49. See Vesna Wallace, *The Kālacakratantra: The Chapter on the Individual Together with the Vimalaprabhā* (New York: American Institute of Buddhist Studies, 2004), 59.

7. The first translations of the *Kālacakra Tantra* and the *Vimalaprabhā* are said to have been by Gyi-jo Dawé Özer, in 1027. For this date, see Ko-zhul-grags-pa-'byung-gnas and rGyal-ba-blo-bzang-mkhas-grub, *Gangs can mkhas grub rim byon ming mdzod* (Lanzhou, Kan su'u mi rigs dpe skrun khang, 1992), 263.

8. The translation by Dro Gelong Sherap Drak and Somanātha is the basis for the version that appears in the Dergé canon and in Butön's collected works; Somanātha was apparently in Tibet ca. 1064 (for this date, see Newman, "Outer Wheel of Time," 92). The second major translation was by Ra Chö-rap and Samantaśri; Ra was active in the middle of the eleventh century (see Ko-zhul-grags-pa-'byung-gnas and rGyal-ba-blo-bzang-mkhas-grub, *Gangs can mkhas grub rim byon ming mdzod*, 1644).

9. See Newman's discussion of the Indian Kālacakra lineage in "Outer Wheel of Time," 70ff.

10. These three are (1) *Stainless Light,* Puṇḍarīka's commentary to the *Kālacakra Tantra,* (2) Vajrapāṇi's commentary to the *Cakrasaṃvara Tantra,* and (3) Vajragarbha's commentary to the *Hevajra Tantra.* The latter two of these commentaries (D1402 and D1180) interpret their root tantras from the perspective of *Stainless Light* and so are attempts to locate Kālacakra ideas and values in the tantric systems associated with Hevajra and Cakrasaṃvara.

11. Yumo's biographies in Khedrup Jé and MS (see notes below) both mention multiple writings; MS reads: "He also wrote many instructional treatises, like the *Four Radiant Lamps,* the *Treasured Collection,* and so forth" *(gsal sgron bzhi dang gces bsdus la sogs pa'i gdams pa'i bstan bcos yang mang du mdzad).*

12. *gSal sgron skor bzhi.* The four individual treatises are the *Lamp Illuminating Unification (zung 'jug gsal sgron),* the *Lamp Illuminating the Great Seal (phyag rgya chen po gsal sgron),* the *Lamp Illuminating Luminosity ('od gsal gsal sgron),* and the *Lamp Illuminating Emptiness (stong nyid gsal sgron).* In this book, the short reference to Yumo's *Lamp* refers to the *Lamp Illuminating Emptiness.*

13. *Ṣaḍaṅgayoga, sbyor ba yan lag drug.*

14. The term also appears as *stong pa nyid kyi gzugs,* the "form of emptiness"; this variation is a more direct reflection of the Sanskrit *sūnyatā-bimba.*

15. *lam du 'gyur pa'i stong pa nyid.* See YM, 625.

16. *mig gi mthong ba'i yul du 'gyur ba.* See YM, 632.

17. *gsal rgyud.*

18. Bu vol. 1, VP ch. 1, 59b.7.

19. Yumo's method of forming arguments through quotations is in some ways reminiscent of anthologies like Nāgārjuna's *Sūtra-samuccaya,* or Śāntideva's *Śikṣā-samuccaya.*

20. *rgyud ni/ rgyud gzhan dag gi rtogs par bya/.* This is the VP on KCT 1.2 (Bu vol. 1, VP ch. 1, 19b.3). Yumo cites this on YM, 618.

21. "Secret giving" *(gsang ba'i sbyin pa)* or "sensual giving" *('dod pa'i sbyin pa)* is mentioned several times in KCT; see, for instance, verses 4.204ff. Wallace also makes a brief mention of the practice in *Inner Kālacakratantra,* 122.

22. The earliest biography I know of is by Gyalwa Yeshé (b. 1257), a Jonang scholar who wrote a collection of short biographies of Kālacakra adepts; a manuscript of this is held by Drepung Gomang Monastery. The collection was recently

published as *dPal ldan dus kyi 'khor lo jo nang pa'i lugs kyi bla ma brgyud pa'i rnam thar* (Mi rigs dpe skrun khang, 2004). (Note that the Yumo section of this publication contains some typographical errors.)

In his *Buddha from Dolpo* (Albany: State University of New York Press, 1999), 199 n. 10, Cyrus Stearns mentions an incomplete manuscript from 1360, which contains a version of Yumo's biography. The author of this work, titled *bCom ldan 'das dpal dus kyi 'khor lo'i chos 'byung ngo mtshar rtogs brjod,* is unknown, and the manuscript is now in the Musée Guimet in Paris (no. 54588). Many thanks to Dr. Dan Martin for providing me an electronic transcription of the Yumo section. This biography closely follows the movements of the one written by Gyalwa Yeshé but is more elaborate and helps with many of the details. This work is also clearly related to (and possibly a main source of) Khedrup Jé's account.

Khedrup Jé's (b. 1385) monumental commentary on *Stainless Light, dPal dus kyi 'khor lo'i 'grel chen dri med 'od kyi rgya cher bshad pa de kho na nyid snang bar byed pa,* contains the most detailed biography of Yumo that I have seen. Closely related to the above manuscript, it adds some interesting details related to Yumo's later life. The Yumo section can be found in Khedrup Jé's collected works (New Delhi: Mongolian Lama Gurudeva, 1980), vol. kha, 176.5.

The *Blue Annals,* the foundational history completed in 1476 by Gölo Zhönnupel, contains several mentions of Yumo, including the narrative of his meeting with Somanātha. See Roerich's translation in *The Blue Annals* (Delhi: Motilal Banarsidass, 1996, reprint), 179, 186, 636, 640, 755, and 765ff.

Tāranātha (b. 1575) has a short historical work *(dPal dus kyi 'khor lo'i chos bskor kyi byung khungs nyer mkho)* containing information on Yumo. This is just a brief sketch, but, as Stearns has pointed out, it contains an important comment suggesting that Yumo established the tantric tradition of other-emptiness. The biography can be found in Tāranātha's collected works, vol. 2, 16.

Yumo also appears in Lodrö Donyod Rinpoche's *Dus 'khor chos 'byung rgyan indra nI la'i phra tshom* (Darjeeling: Bokar Ngedon Chokhor Ling, 2005), 441; and in Ngawang Lodrö Drakpa's *Jo nang chos 'byung zla ba'i sgron me* (Krung go'i bod kyi shes rig dpe skrun khang, 1990), 18. Other sources are mentioned in D. S. Ruegg, "The Jo Nan Pas: A School of Buddhist Ontologists According to the Grub Mtha' Sel Gyi Me Lon," *Journal of the American Oriental Society* 83, no. 1 (1963): 80 n. 20.

23. La-stod.

24. Yumo's histories do not provide a birth date, but by combining their details it is possible to establish a very basic time period. Combining such sources can often be a questionable practice, but it is a line of thought worth briefly pursuing because it helps to arrive at a plausible date for Yumo. First, we might consider the following statements: (1) Ngawang Lodrö Drakpa notes that Yumo was born in the first calendrical cycle (1027–1087). (2) Gyalwa Yeshé mentions that he was ordained in a tiger year; tiger years in the first calendrical cycle are 1038, 1050, 1062, 1074, or 1086. (3) Khedrup Jé mentions that he was ten at his ordination, which would make his birth date (theoretically of course) 1028, 1040, 1052, 1064, or 1076.

I would hazard the guess that the earliest date here is the most likely. Again, this may be pressing the sources beyond the point of reliability, but it is still instructive to note the following facts. (1) the *Blue Annals* (Roerich, 186) notes that Yumo's disciple Hap Jo-sé Jampel was born in 1036. (2) It also suggests (179) that a certain Dzeng, aka Dharmabodhi, born in 1051 (186), met Yumo in "U-yog," which must refer to the period following Yumo's own empowerment, when he lived in U-yug. Assuming that Yumo is older than those two figures, this points to the earlier birth date.

Continuing, the sources agree that Yumo finished receiving his tantric teachings around the age of fifty. Those teachings lasted around four years and thus may have begun around age forty-six. Just prior to those teachings, Yumo met the paṇḍit Somanātha (let us guess he was forty-five at this point). The *Great Tibetan Chinese Dictionary (tshig mdzod chen mo)* places Somanātha's entry into Tibet at 1064 (see 3216). The number 1064 minus a hypothetical forty-five years would be 1019, which is generally in the range of the earliest proposed birth date.

25. sTod-lho.

26. dBus-gtsang.

27. Dad-pa-rgyal-po.

28. Mi-bskyod-rdo-rje.

29. *bslab bsdus.*

30. 'U-yug, in gTsang.

31. Stearns notes this in *Buddha from Dolpo,* 200 n. 11.

32. Tāranātha's biographical sketch states: "He began the tradition of the tenet system of tantric other-emptiness" *(sngags kyi gzhan stong grub mtha'i srol ka phye).*

33. See Roerich's translation, 640.

34. My summary here is based on KCT 4.8–4.134, VP's comments on those verses, and discussions of these found in Wallace, *Inner Kālacakra,* 182ff., and Khedrup Norsang Gyatso's *Ornament of Stainless Light* (trans. Kilty), 277ff.

35. *maṇḍala-rājāgrī, dkyil 'khor rgyal mchog.*

36. *karma-rājāgrī, las rgyal mchog.*

37. *bindu-yoga, thig le'i rnal 'byor.*

38. *sūkṣma-yoga, phra ma'i rnal 'byor.*

39. The four generation stage yogas are said to purify four types of "seminal nuclei" *(bindu, thig-le)* related to the practitioner's body, speech, mind, and gnosis. This process of purifying the four seminal nuclei allows them to then act as seeds for the production of the four bodies of a buddha.

40. YM, 636.

41. For a survey of other Indian "six yoga" traditions, see Wallace, *Inner Kālacakra,* 25ff.

42. My summary is based on the *Vajrapāṇi Commentary,* as well as KCT 4.115–4.120, 4.193–199, and 5.115–5.127, and comments on these verses found in *Stainless Light* and the *Lotus Girl.* However, these sources are often terse, so I have used a number of other secondary sources as well. Wallace also has a presentation of Kālacakra's six yogas on *Inner Kālacakratantra,* 201ff. Kilty's translation of Norsang Gyatso's *Ornament of Stainless Light* is also extremely helpful (see 398ff.), though the comments of this later Tibetan exegete should of course not be equated with those of the early Indian

tradition. Also useful is Giacomella Orofino's "On the Ṣaḍaṅgayoga and the Realization of Ultimate Gnosis in the Kalacakratantra," *East and West* 46 (1996): 127–143.

43. D1402, 130a.3ff. The *Vajrapāṇi Commentary* is an extended commentary on the first 10.5 verses of the *Cakrasaṃvara Tantra* and is attributed to Vajrapāṇi. One of the "three bodhisattva commentaries," it interprets the Cakrasaṃvara from a Kālacakra perspective. Butön often uses this presentation of the six yogas in his interlineal comments to the VP's discussion of the six yogas (see Bu vol. 2, VP ch. 4, 49a.7, commenting on verses 4.116ff.). Note that this passage (beginning with the comments on "withdrawal") is cited in Nāropa's *Sekoddesaṭīkā* (D1351, 251b). For an extended translation and discussion of Nāropa's comments, see Vesna Wallace, "The Six-Phased Yoga of the *Abbreviated Wheel of Time Tantra (Laghukālacakratantra)* According to Vajrapāṇi," in *Yoga in Practice,* ed. David Gordon White (Princeton: Princeton University Press, 2012), 204–222.

44. D0443, 154a.6.

45. This seems to refer to those holding the lower initiations, i.e., the "seven empowerments of entering like a child" *(byis pa ltar 'jug pa'i dbang bdun).*

46. Some of these are the three purities, the four branches of approximation and accomplishment, the four vajras, and the four yogas. The most pervasive of these is the "four vajras" which classifies the yogas according to the groups of "body vajra" (yogas 1–2), "speech vajra" (yogas 3–4), "mind vajra" (yoga 5), and "gnosis vajra" (yoga 6). The *Vimalaprabhā* also refers to the six yogas as the "*sādhana* of gnosis" (*ye shes kyi sgrub thabs,* see VP on KCT 4.120, Bu vol. 2, VP ch. 4, 52a.2); this has four branches: "worship" (*bsnyen pa,* corresponding to yogas 1–2), auxiliary *sādhana* or "near accomplishment" (*nye ba'i sgrub pa,* yogas 3–4), *sādhana* or "accomplishment" (*sgrub pa,* yoga 5), and supreme *sādhana* or "great accomplishment" (*sgrub pa chen po,* yoga 6). For a summation of various other classification schemes, see Khedrup Norsang Gyatso *Ornament of Stainless Light* (trans. Kilty), 398; see also Wallace, *Inner Kālacakra,* 203.

47. See similar comments in VP 4.120.

48. Some advocates of the Kālacakra describe how the withdrawal of the sense faculties technically occurs due to meditative practice, rather than simple immersion in darkness. For a Geluk presentation, see Khedrup Norsang Gyatso's account in *Ornament of Stainless Light* (trans. Kilty), 394, 402. Here, the yogi practices penetrative-focusing, directed at the upper portion of the central channel. This causes the winds to "withdraw" from the two side channels and enter into the central channel; as a consequence, the sense faculties cease to engage with their respective objects. See also Norsang Gyatso's discussions of alternate views, on 408, 421. Note that in Vajrapāṇi's description, the blocking of the two side channels is not mentioned until the third yoga, "breath control."

49. The construction of a dark house is mentioned briefly in Avadhūtipa's *Opening the Eyes to What Is Hidden (sbas pa mig 'byed),* D1373, 240a.7; see also *Stainless Light* on KCT 5.115 (Bu vol. 3, VP ch. 5, 46a.1).

50. See VP 5.115 (Bu vol. 3, VP ch. 5, 45b.7).

51. Descriptions of withdrawal typically mention clenched fists held against the abdomen and an upward gaze called the "wrathful gaze of Uṣṇīṣa." See KCT and VP 4.120 (Bu vol. 2, VP ch. 4, 51a.7). The Tibetan commentator Khedrup Norsang

Gyatso provides an overview of the subtle-body theory underlying the postures. In general, the yogi uses a process called "penetrative focusing" *(gnad du bsnun pa),* in which attention is focused on particular points of the subtle body, especially on the central channel. This results in the winds (which normally drive sensory experience) entering the central channel at those points; the ordinary senses are thus quieted, opening the doorway for the divine senses. See Kilty (trans.), *Ornament of Stainless Light,* 391ff.

52. KCT 4.116.

53. VP 4.118. The divine eye *(lha'i mig)* is a member of a larger set of "five eyes": (1) the fleshy eye, (2) the "god's eye" or divine eye, (3) the eye of insight, (4) the dharma eye, and (5) the buddha eye. Discussions of these appear in works like the *Perfection of Wisdom Sūtra in 25,000 Lines* (D0009, vol. ka; see 71a.1).

54. D12, 111a.2: *de nas tshe dang ldan pa rab 'byor la lha rnams kyi dbang po brgya byin gyis 'di skad ces smras so/ /'phags pa rab 'byor gang shes rab kyi pha rol tu phyin pa 'di la de ltar rnal 'byor du byed pa de ci la rnal 'byor du byed par 'gyur/ rab 'byor gyis smras pa/ kau shi ka gang shes rab kyi pha rol tu phyin pa 'di la rnal 'byor du byed pa de ni nam mkha' la rnal 'byor du byed par 'gyur ro/ /kau shi ka gang shes rab kyi pha rol tu phyin pa 'di la slob cing rnal 'byor du byed par sems pa de ni bla gab med pa la rnal 'byor du byed par 'gyur ro/ /.*

For citations of this passage in Kālacakra literature, see the *Vajrapāṇi Commentary* (D.1402, 132b.6), Nāropa's *Sekoddesaṭīkā* (D1351, 254a.4), and Norsang Gyatso's *Ornament of Stainless Light* (trans. Kilty), 409. See also Wallace, "The Six-Phased Yoga of the *Abbreviated Wheel of Time Tantra* (*Laghukālacakratantra*) According to Vajrapāṇi," 208, 214; and Edward Henning, "The Six Vajra-Yogas of Kālacakra," in *As Long as Space Endures: Essays on the Kālacakra Tantra in Honor of H.H. The Dalai Lama,* ed. Edward A. Arnold (Ithaca, NY: Snow Lion Publications, 2009), 241.

55. This refers to Indra, the lord of the gods, also known as Kauśika.

56. Here, "space" *(nam mkha')* could equally be translated as "sky," so the passage could also be read as referring to a single sky-gazing-type practice, rather than as referring to a dark practice and a sky-gazing practice.

57. Norsang Gyatso, for instance, is concerned enough about this issue to mention: "do not take this ... to mean that the day and night yogas of withdrawal are taught in the perfection of wisdom sutras. If that were the case, it would mean that becoming a suitable vessel for receiving the perfection of wisdom sutras would entail receiving all four initiations." See *Ornament of Stainless Light* (trans. Kilty), 410.

58. VP 5.115 (Bu vol. 3, VP ch. 5, 45b.7).

59. This list is from KCT 5.115. Generally the first four are said to appear in night-yoga, and the remaining six appear in day-yoga; see, for example, a variant presentation in the *Supplement to the Kālacakra Tantra* (D0363, 132a.6).

60. In the *pratisenā* divination, a young girl is empowered by a deity, resulting in the ability to see images of the past, present, or future appearing in a mirror. For a full treatment of this type of divination, see Giacomella Orofino, "Divination with Mirrors: Observations on a Simile Found in the Kālacakra Literature," in *Tibetan*

Studies: Proceedings of the 6th Seminar of the International Association for Tibetan Studies, Fagernes 1992, ed. Per Kværne (Oslo: Institute for Comparative Research in Human Culture, 1994), 612–628. For broader discussion of the theme of mirrors in Buddhism, see Paul Demiéville, "The Mirror of the Mind," in *Sudden and Gradual: Approaches to Enlightenment in Chinese Thought*, ed. Peter N. Gregory (Honolulu: University of Hawai'i Press, 1987), 13–40.

61. *stong gzugs.* See, for instance, the VP's comments on KCT 4.116 (Bu vol. 2, VP ch. 4, 49b.1), and Nāropa's *Sekoddesaṭīkā* (D1351, 249b.2).

62. *snang ba.*

63. Note, for instance, a quotation from the Kālacakra *Root Tantra,* provided in VP 4.110 (Bu vol. 2, VP ch. 4, 44b.6): "In withdrawal [yoga] there is the Great Seal, who has the characteristics of empty space." On the one hand, this simply indicates that the withdrawal visions are characterized by emptiness, but it also suggests how they are fragments of the Great Seal, the supreme consort who becomes more fully present later in the six yogas. Generally speaking, when the Great Seal is associated with the ten signs, it is only the final sign (the *thig-le*), that is pointed to as being the Great Seal.

64. Edward Henning has noted how the ten signs are sometimes identified with a set of goddesses who are found in the Kālacakra maṇḍala. Henning also discusses how, for some Kālacakra authors, empty-forms are seen as evidence for an internal Buddha-nature; he notes, for instance, Tāranātha's claim that "an empty-form should be understood as a genuine expression of reality and a sign of the existence of that reality, tathāgatagarbha..." (trans. Henning). See Henning, "Six Vajra-Yogas of Kālacakra," 240–241.

65. See KCT 5.115–116, and the VP on these (Bu vol. 3, VP ch. 5, 46b.4). The VP does not explicitly discuss the nature of this buddha image in its comments to these verses. The later commentator Norsang Gyatso identifies it as Vajrasattva, as well as Kālacakra and Viśvamātā; see his *Ornament of Stainless Light* (trans. Kilty), 448, 468.

66. *sems kyi dngos po 'dzin pa.* This might also be read as "apprehending mental phenomena" or even "apprehending them as mental phenomena." The VP describes "comprehension" *(rtog pa)* as the "apprehension of [those phenomena]" *(dngos po 'dzin pa).* Butön annotates this as *sems kyi dngos po 'dzin pa* ("apprehending mental phenomena"), suggesting the common Kālacakra notion that empty-forms are merely expressions of the mind.

67. See the VP on KCT 4.115 (Bu vol. 2, VP ch. 4, 49b.2).

68. The idea of the mind's unification with the objects is from the VP's comments on KCT 4.116. Bu vol. 2, VP ch. 4, 49b.3 reads: *gzugs dang lhan cig ngo bo gcig tu dbye ba'o.* The edition found in the Dergé Kangyur (D, vol. 102, 237a.7) is more explicit, however: *gzugs dang lhan cig sems gcig tu byed pa'o* ("the mind is made one with forms"). These ideas of unification and bliss are also discussed in the final of the six yogas, concentration yoga.

69. In some more technical presentations of "meditative concentration" yoga, the yogi's concentration is specifically focused on the final sign, the *thig-le* that gives rise to a "black line" in which the image of a buddha appears; see, for instance, Khedrup Norsang Gyatso's *Ornament of Stainless Light* (trans. Kilty), 469–470. This

appearance is also referred to as the "all-knowing form" (*kun mkhyen gzugs;* see VP on KCT 5.116, Bu vol. 3, VP ch. 5, 46b.5).

70. *srog gi rlung.*

71. In other Kālacakra works, OṂ is associated with filling the lungs and ĀḤ with expelling air from the lungs. The presentation here (D0443, 130b.5) is also used by Butön in his interlinear notes to the VP (Bu vol. 2, VP ch. 4, 49b.4). However, note that the *Vajrapāṇi Commentary* passage is quoted in Nāropa's *Sekoddesaṭīkā* (D1351, 252a.3), where OṂ and ĀḤ are associated with filling and expelling.

72. These three refer, respectively, to the left, center, and right channels.

73. See Norsang Gyatso, *Ornament of Stainless Light* (trans. Kilty), 484.

74. VP on KCT 4.121 (Bu vol. 2, VP ch. 4, 52a.5): "Here, while empty-form has come to be seen, the yogi [practices] breath control, which is as follows..." *('dir stong pa nyid kyi gzugs mthong bar gyur pa na/ rnal 'byor pas srog gi rtsol ba bya ba gang yin pa de ni).*

75. KCT 4.116.

76. The winds here are often described in two categories: the "upper winds" or "life winds" *(srog rlung)* in the half of the central channel above the navel, and the "lower winds" or "downward voiding winds" *(thur sel gyi rlung)* in the half of the central channel below the navel. These two groups are moved to the navel wheel, where they are brought together or unified.

77. *rdo rje bzlas pa.* Note that the above quote from the *Vajrapāṇi Commentary* does not use the term "vajra recitation," although it does refer to the three syllables; I am using the term here based on the later Tibetan commentary of Norsang Gyatso.

78. *bgegs mthar byed pa'i lta ba.* See VP and KCT 4.120; Wallace, *Inner Kālacakra,* 205; Norsang Gyatso, *Ornament of Stainless Light* (trans. Kilty), 426.

79. As noted earlier, the order of these particular syllables is not consistent in the different commentaries. Here I am using the presentation found in the Dergé edition of the *Vajrapāṇi Commentary.* While the name "vajra recitation" suggests that the syllables are recited, note Norsang Gyatso's discussions of the syllables as being the "innate tones" *(rang gi gdangs)* of the breath, or being visualized along with the breath (see *Ornament of Stainless Light,* trans. Kilty, 485, 490).

80. *bum pa can,* VP on KCT 5.117.

81. *gong bu'i gzugs.* See discussions of this in the *Vajrapāṇi Commentary* (D1402, 133a.6), and Nāropa's *Sekoddesaṭīkā* (D1351, 246b.5, 254b.3).

82. See Norsang Gyatso's description of this in *Ornament of Stainless Light* (trans. Kilty), 502.

83. KCT 5.117.

84. KCT 4.121.

85. See Norsang Gyatso's description of this in *Ornament of Stainless Light* (trans. Kilty), 504.

86. See VP 4.110 for discussion of the *caṇḍālī* flame as representing lust or sexual desire.

87. *Stainless Light* does also suggest an alternate "forceful method" (*btsan thabs,* KCT 4.119) for practitioners who experience visions of empty-forms, but who are still unable to bring the winds into the central channel and bind them at the navel energy-wheel. This method does involve a consort; as *Stainless Light* says, the meditator

can perform a practice involving "holding back the enlightened-mind *thig-le* in the 'vajra' as it dwells in the 'lotus' of wisdom" (VP on KCT 4.119, see Bu vol. 2, ch. 4, 51a.4), which is code for practicing emissionless sexual yoga in conjunction with a consort.

88. KCT 4.122 (Bu vol. 1, 84b.5). "Not an object" here is literally "devoid of objects" *(yul dang rnam par bral ba),* the same phrase that occurs in KCT 4.198, the root verse in Yumo's treatise. Butön's comments to KCT 4.122 interpret the phrase as meaning that Viśvamātā here is not composed of atoms (and is thus not a visual object in the ordinary sense), but rather is an empty-form, arisen due to the practice of withdrawal and meditative concentration.

89. *srog,* referring to the winds.

90. *dbang chen,* here referring to the "earth" wheel.

91. According to the VP's comments on KCT 4.115, the practice involves five wheels (adding the wheel at the *uṣṇīṣa* or "crown" to those listed earlier). Norsang Gyatso's presentation adds the "secret" wheel at the genital region to make six; see *Ornament of Stainless Light* (trans. Kilty), 515.

92. These are the seminal nuclei *(thig-le)* of body, speech, mind, and gnosis, which are located, respectively, at the forehead, throat, heart, and navel wheels.

93. KCT 4.116.

94. The energy-wheels are each associated with a particular element: navel (earth), heart (water), throat (fire), forehead (wind), crown (space). After focusing at the navel wheel, the earth element is said to dissolve into the water element, at which point the focus of the practice moves up to the heart wheel. For a description of this, see Norsang Gyatso, *Ornament of Stainless Light* (trans. Kilty), 517.

95. *gzugs kyi rnam pa rnam par rtog pa dang bral ba'o/.* This passage is cited in Nāropa's *Sekoddesaṭīkā* (D1351, 252a.5) and changes "form" *(gzugs)* to "reflection" *(gzugs brnyan):* "... your desired deity, who appears in the aspect of a reflection...." In either case, this is referring to an empty-form image that is not deliberately visualized or conceptualized.

96. KCT 4.117 (Bu, vol. 1, 84a.4).

97. In his interlineal comments to *Stainless Light,* Butön equates the two; where *Stainless Light* refers to the "perception of Caṇḍālī," he adds the annotation "seeing your desired deity...." (It is clear that Butön here is quoting the *Vajrapāṇi Commentary.*)

98. For the identification of Caṇḍālī and the Great Seal, see also a quote from the Kālacakra *Root Tantra* that appears in VP 4.110 (Bu vol. 2, VP ch. 4, 44b.2): "Śaṅkhinī *(dung can ma),* the Great Seal, is called Caṇḍālī."

99. This is from the *Sekoddesaṭīkā* (D1351, 254b.7), discussing the presentation of the six yogas in the *Vajrapāṇi Commentary.*

100. The *Vajrapāṇi Commentary* describes this in the context of recollection-yoga on D1402, 133b.3ff. This description adds the throat energy-wheel to the following list of three from *Stainless Light,* resulting in a series of "four joys." In these sequences of bliss, note how "bliss" or "joys" are produced at sites other than the navel or genital region (i.e., at the throat and heart); looked at from this perspective, it could be said that the bliss involved in the six yogas is not strictly "sexual."

101. VP 4.120 (Bu vol. 2, VP ch. 4, 51b.5).

102. KCT and VP 4.117. The later, Tibetan commentator Norsang Gyatso goes so far as to state that relying on a physical consort is necessary in the initial stages of practice; see *Ornament of Stainless Light* (trans. Kilty), 529.

103. KCT 4.199 (Bu vol. 1, 97a.6).

104. *'khyud pa.* See VP 4.119, and Butön's comments (Bu vol. 2, VP ch. 4, 50b.4).

105. Yumo, on the other hand, frequently identifies the Great Seal with the goddesses Viśvamātā and Prajñāpāramitā, both of whom have standard visual representations.

106. *rnam pa thams bcad kyi mchog dang ldan pa.*

107. VP 4.117 (Bu. vol. 2, VP ch. 4, 50a.1).

108. The classic source for the subtle-body transformations enacted in "concentration" yoga is the VP on KCT 5.117d (Bu vol. 3, 47a.4). Because this is itself quite cryptic, Khedrup Norsang Gyatso's comments are very helpful; see Kilty (trans.) *Ornament of Stainless Light,* 560ff., as well as the summation on 581. See also Wallace's summation on *Inner Kālacakra,* 206, as well as Orofino's on "Ṣaḍaṅgayoga," 137.

109. mKhas-grub-nor-bzang-rgya-mtsho, *Phyi nang gzhan gsum gsal bar byed pa dri med 'od kyi rgyan* (New Delhi: bod kyi gtsug lag zhib dpyod khang, 2004), 489. See also *Ornament of Stainless Light* (trans. Kilty), 579.

110. As Norsang Gyatso discusses just before this passage, it is also possible to generate unchanging bliss by using a "gnostic" (i.e., visualized) consort. This is characteristic of practitioners with "middling" ability.

111. *rnam med kyi stong nyid.* Note how Norsang Gyatso's outlook here differs from that of Yumo, who typically emphasizes the experience of "emptiness endowed with all aspects" *(rnam pa thams cad dang ldan pa'i stong pa nyid).*

112. The number 21,600 represents the number of breaths that a person makes in one day. Because such breaths maintain the ordinary physical body, and because winds are the "mounts" bringing about the movements of the ordinary mind, the number here has the sense of the totality of the ordinary body and mind.

113. VP on KCT 5.117 (Bu vol. 3, VP ch. 5, 47a.6).

114. See Khedrup Norsang Gyatso, *Ornament of Stainless Light* (trans. Kilty), 556 and 560.

115. *ye shes lus;* see VP on KCT 4.119 (Bu vol. 2, VP ch. 4, 50b.7).

116. VP on KCT 4.117 (Bu vol. 2, VP ch. 4, 50a.1).

117. Note, for instance, Khedrup Norsang Gyatso's comment that the first moment of unchanging bliss experienced in this yoga is "the attainment of the path of seeing—wherein emptiness is newly seen with direct perception"; see *Ornament of Stainless Light* (trans. Kilty), 579.

118. For sources on this tradition, see the bibliography for Wedemeyer's dissertation, and his translation and analysis of *Lamp Integrating the Practices.* Also note Tomabechi's French translation of the *Five Stages;* his and Mimaki's edition of the *Five Stages* is listed under Nāgārjuna in the bibliography.

119. *Pañcakrama, rim pa lnga pa* (D1802).

120. *Caryāmelāpakapradīpa, spyod pa bsdus pa'i sgron ma* (D1803). Note that Yumo also cites Āryadeva's *On Purifying Mental Obscurations (cittavisuddhiprakaraṇa, sems kyi sgrib pa rnam par sbyong ba)* (D1804).

121. Yumo's biographies indicate that he studied the *Illuminating Lamp* (*pradīpodyotana-nāma-ṭīkā, sgron ma gsal bar byed pa zhes bya ba'i rgya cher bshad pa,* D1785), a Guhyasamāja commentary by the tantric Candrakīrti, while staying with his main teacher Dro-gön (see Gyalwa Yeshé's biographical sketch of Yumo, p. 16a). It thus appears that Yumo studied at least some Guhyasamāja right alongside Kālacakra, and it seems plausible that the title of his own *Illuminating Lamps (gsal sgron)* may pay homage to Candrakīrti's *Illuminating Lamp* by inverting its name *(sgron gsal).*

122. The "stage of self-blessing" *(svādhiṣṭhāna, bdag la byin gyis brlab pa'i rim)* is also known as the "[stage of] conventional truth" *(saṃvṛtisatya, kun rdzob kyi bden pa)* and the "illusion-like *samādhi*" *(māyopama-samādhi, sgyu ma lta bu'i ting nge 'dzin).* Yumo frequently brings up passages containing this latter term, from both Guhyasamāja and non-Guhyasamāja works.

The stage of self-blessing is discussed in chapter 3 of the *Five Stages,* and chapter 6 of Āryadeva's *Lamp.* Six out of eight of Yumo's *Five Stages* citations, and four out of five of his *Lamp* citations are from these chapters. For the stage of "conventional truth" in the Guhyasamāja context, see Christian Wedemeyer, *Aryadeva's Lamp That Integrates the Practices* (New York: Columbia University Press, 2007), 50, 73, 103, 243.

123. This "stage of self-blessing" contrasts to meditations on fierce deities, which are called the "hero stage" *(dpa' bo'i rim pa).* For mention of these, see the *Lotus Girl* (D1350, 99b.5), and Khedrup Jé's *Illuminating Reality* (vol. kha, 293.2).

124. The *Lotus Girl* (D1350, 100b.2) says that "self-blessing" also refers to visions of empty-form, to seeing "various forms in the sky that have the nature of the three worlds." Khedrup Jé (vol. kha, 293.2ff.) states similarly that "self-blessing" refers to seeing a visionary appearance of the Great Seal.

The *Vajra Tent Tantra* (D0419, a tantra in the Hevajra cycle) also mentions a "self-blessing" *(rang byin brlab pa)* as one of a set of six yogas (p. 39a.1); the *Vajrapāṇi Commentary* (D1402) comments briefly on this passage, saying "here, 'self-blessing' refers to withdrawal [yoga], through which conventional emptiness is seen" (p. 132a.2). Note that this citation from the *Vajrapāṇi Commentary* also appears in Norsang Gyatso's *Ornament of Stainless Light;* see Kilty's translation, 442. These connections between "self-blessing" and withdrawal yoga also appear in Nāropa's *Sekoddeśa* (D1351, 253a.1).

125. The passage from chapter 1 of *Stainless Light* (Bu vol. 1, VP ch. 1, 6a.3) is cited on YM, 654.

126. See the comments in Āryadeva's *Lamp* (D1803, 84a.6) contrasting this body with the body used in the generation stage, which is a "a mere collection of atoms" *(rdul phra rab bsags pa tsam).*

127. *ye shes tsam gyis lha nyid du bskyed pa,* Āryadeva's *Lamp* (D1803, 84a.6).

128. For instance, note Yumo's line of thought on YM, 616 and 645.

129. The "sky" theme is not particularly prominent in this portion of Āryadeva's works, but note his comparison of the deity body attained through self-blessing with a five-colored rainbow that is "distinctly visible in the vault of the sky" (D1803, 85b.5); see Wedemeyer, *Aryadeva's Lamp*, 248.

130. KCT 4.198 (Bu vol. 1, 96b.7).

131. Skt. *yathā bhāye tathā dehe,* Tib. *ji ltar phyi rol de bzhin lus.*

132. *'jig rten gsum.* The term has the basic sense of the "entire universe," which is constituted of (1) the god realms above the earth, (2) the human realm on the earth, and (3) the nāga realms below the earth. It is also used in the sense of "three realms" of the universe *(khams gsum):* (1) the desire realm, (2) the form realm, and (3) the formless realm; importantly for Yumo, these three external realms are often correlated with the three "internal" realms of a being's (1) body, (2) speech, and (3) mind.

133. See, for instance, Norsang Gyatso, *Ornament of Stainless Light* (trans. Kilty), 528–529.

134. *bla ma ldar snang.*

135. *yul bral.* Literally "free of objects," Yumo and the tantric works he cites make it clear that this means that the Great Seal is free of atoms, and thus is not an ordinary "object."

136. *dngos med.*

137. *so so skye bo.*

138. *nyi tshe ba'i mig* and *las dang po'i mig.*

139. YM, 675.

140. YM, 685: *stong pa nyid mig gis mthong pa.*

141. *rje btsun,* most likely referring to his principal teacher, Drogön Namla-tsek.

142. YM, 686: *stong pa nyid mig gis 'dzin gyis rdo rje 'dzin gyi gnas thob shog.* Note that this statement appears only in the YM edition.

Chapter 2

1. Germano makes this argument at length in chapter 10 of his *Secret Tibetan History of Buddhist Tantra in the Great Perfection* (unpublished manuscript, 1988), 476ff.

2. For a brief, traditional presentation of these figures and their relation to Padmasambhava, see Patrul Rinpoche, *Words of My Perfect Teacher,* trans. Padmakara Translation Group (London: AltaMira Press, 1994), 338ff. Germano discusses the Indian lineage and early Tibetan transmission in detail in chapter 10 of his *Secret Tibetan History,* 481ff. For the early lineages involving Padmasambhava and Vairocana, see Karmay, *Arrow and the Spindle,* 96ff.

3. Other accounts credit Padmasambhava with bringing the tradition to Tibet.

4. See David Germano, "Architecture and Absence in the Secret Tantric History of the Great Perfection," *Journal of the International Association of Buddhist Studies* 17, n. 2 (1994): 211ff.

5. For discussions of early Great Perfection manuscripts, see Samten Karmay, *The Great Perfection: A Philosophical and Meditative Teaching of Tibetan Buddhism* (London: Brill, 1988). Note in particular chapter 2, "The Ancient Documents on rDzogs chen from Tun-huang." See also Karmay's "rDzogs chen in Its Earliest Text: A Manuscript from Dunhuang," in *Arrow and the Spindle*, 98ff.

6. For this early strata of the Great Perfection, see Germano, "Architecture and Absence," 211ff. and 34ff. See also Karmay's *Great Perfection,* 22ff.

7. Germano pursues these lines of thought in "Architecture and Absence," 215.

8. *sems sde bco brgyad.* On these eighteen works, see Karmay, *Great Perfection,* 23ff. See also Germano, "Architecture and Absence," 234ff.; Germano also discusses these in detail in "Mysticism and Rhetoric in the Great Perfection" (unpublished manuscript, 2006), ch. 3, 24ff.

9. Here it is not at all clear to what extent advocates of this early form of the Great Perfection distanced themselves from tantric ritual and structured practice, or if this was simply one of their rhetorical or interpretive perspectives from which to view tantra.

10. *Rig pa'i khu byug.* See Karmay, *The Great Perfection,* 41ff., for lengthy comments on this work. My translation here is based on his edition of the Dunhuang document IOL 647.

11. For mention of some of these, see Germano's "Architecture and Absence," 267–268; Germano makes more detailed comments on these in his *Secret Tibetan History,* 396ff., 412ff.

12. *zhwa'i lha khang.*

13. For the members of this lineage, see Karmay, *The Great Perfection,* 210ff. Germano discusses this group in "Architecture and Absence," 272ff., and also gives an extensive treatment of this early lineage in chapter 10 of his *Secret Tibetan History,* 481ff.

14. Germano discusses this possibility in detail in chapter 10 of his *Secret Tibetan History.* The proposition (of which he is careful to note that we have no final, concrete proof) is that Dangma penned formative but unknown Seminal Heart texts, which inspired buddha-voiced compositions by Jetsün and later Jégom, who redacted them as the *Seventeen Tantras.* This left the scholarly Zhangtön to finalize the collection and to produce its commentaries under the name Vimalamitra.

15. *sNying thig lo rgyus chen mo,* located in the *Bi ma snying thig* portion of the *Seminal Heart in Four Parts (sNying thig ya bzhi)* (New Delhi: Trulku Tsewang, Jamyang and L. Tashi, 1971), vol. 7, pt. 3 (tha).

16. As noted earlier, this line of reasoning is Germano's and is worked out in chapter 10 of his *Secret Tibetan History.*

17. The colophon of the AD edition has: *rgya gar gyi mkhan po bi ma la mi tra dang/ /lo ts+tsha ba ska ba dpal brtsegs gnyis kyis bsgyur cing zhus te gtan la phab pa'o/.*

18. *Mu tig phreng ba brgyus pa* (MTP), attributed to Vimalamitra (mKhas-pa-bye-ma). Found in the "Lhasa" edition of the Nyingma bKa'-ma, published by Tsering Gyatso, volume Be (105), 15–325.

19. As we will see later, one way that the Great Perfection accounts for the universe's apparent multiplicity is by turning to metaphor: just as the manifold rays of the sun are inseparable from the singular sun itself, so the ignorant mind and the apparently solid objects of the world are all the dimmed efflorescence of awareness that has strayed far from its source.

20. For the enlightenment of All Good in the Bön context, see GDGG, 368.

21. *Tshig don mdzod* (Gangtok, Sikkim: Sherab Gyaltsen and Khyentse Labrang, 1983). The translations in this section are by David Germano, from his unpublished translation of Longchenpa's *The Treasury of Words and Meanings*, 1998.

22. This unusual image, also referred to as the "youthful body in a vase" *(gzhon nu bum pa'i sku),* is related to the metaphor of a lamp inside a vase (an image portraying an internal radiance that cannot be seen from the outside) that appears often in Indian literature. See it on GDGG, 377, and YM, 668.

23. Germano, trans., *Treasury of Words and Meanings,* 15.

24. Germano, trans., *Treasury of Words and Meanings,* 23.

25. TDD, 108.

26. *rDo rje sems dpa' snying gi me long gi rgyud,* one of *The Seventeen Tantras.* The passage here is cited in Longchenpa, *Treasury of Words and Meanings* (trans. Germano), 36.

27. This term is used frequently in Great Perfection literature to refer to ordinary conceptual thought *(rtog pa),* with the connotation that conceptuality is the way that we reenact or continue this original act of straying. The *Six Lamps* materials, for instance, often speak of the sunlike awareness being obscured by the "clouds of straying" *('krul pa'i sprin pa),* which obscure its basic luminosity. In these cases, *'khrul pa* might also be translated as "confusion," "deluded thought," or "distorted thought."

28. Germano, trans., *Treasury of Words and Meanings,* 14.

29. Similar ideas—that saṃsāra and nirvāṇa are one, or that emptiness is form and form is emptiness, or that a single mind might have transcendent and mundane aspects—are common in the Mahāyāna, made famous in works like *The Heart Sūtra (Prajñāpāramitā-hṛdaya)* and Aśvaghoṣa's *Awakening of Faith (*Mahāyāna-sraddhotpāda-sāstra, Ta-ch'eng ch'i-hsin lun).* Stating the equivalence of saṃsāra and nirvāṇa, however, does seem to be different than saying that the two arise from the same source.

30. See YM, 683.

31. For a discussion of these two, see Germano's "Poetic Thought, the Intelligent Universe, and the Mystery of Self: The Tantric Synthesis of rDzogs Chen in Fourteenth Century Tibet" (PhD diss., University of Wisconsin, 1992), 114ff. For the preliminary practices, see Germano's two articles "Food, Clothes, Dreams, and Karmic Propensities" and "The Elements, Insanity, and Lettered Subjectivity," in *Religions of Tibet in Practice*, ed. Donald Lopez (Princeton, NJ: Princeton University Press, 1997), 293–312 and 313–334. For a traditional presentation, see Lopon Tenzin Namdak, *Heart Drops of Dharmakaya: Dzogchen Practice of the Bön Tradition* (Ithaca, NY: Snow Lion Publications, 1993).

32. In the almost 2,000 folio sides of *The Seventeen Tantras,* the term *khregs chod* appears only four times (twice in *rDzogs pa rang byung,* and once in *Ngo sprod rin po che* and *Mu tig phreng ba*), and the term *thod rgal* appears only six times (twice in *rDzogs pa rang byung,* and once in *Ngo sprod rin po che, Klong drug, Rin chen spungs ba,* and *Mu tig phreng ba*).

33. In all of *The Seventeen Tantras,* the terms appear together only four times: *rDzogs pa rang byung,* 544, 546; *Ngo sprod rin po che,* 100; and *Mu tik phreng ba,* 536. In the two-volume, 1,600 folio-side commentary to the *sGra thal 'gyur,* the term *thod rgal* appears five times, and the term *khregs chod* is absent.

34. Presentations of the four visions differ slightly among different sources; here I rely mainly on MTP, 136ff, but have also consulted Germano's translation of Longchenpa's *Treasury of Words and Meanings,* ch. 8, 264ff.

35. *rig pa mngon sum gyi snang ba.* This is also called the "vision of reality's immediacy" *(chos nyid mngon sum gyi snang ba).* The wording "awareness'" is from MTP, 136, which is MTP's main description of the four visions.

36. The three postures are those resembling a lion *(seng ge),* an elephant *(glang chen),* and a sage *(drang srong),* which are typically correlated with the three bodies of the buddha. See *Thal 'gyur,* 310; MTP, 309ff.; and TDD, 375ff. The first posture involves crouching with the palms and soles of the feet on the floor and the gaze focused upward; the second is more bent over, with the elbows rather than the palms on the floor, the chin resting in the palm of the hands, and the gaze straight ahead; the final is a squatting posture with only the feet on the floor, the arms clasping the knees, and the gaze directed downward.

37. See MTP, 310; TDD, 375.

38. *rig pa lu gu rgyud.* See MTP, 121, where *lu gu rgyud* are synonymous with *rig pa mngon sum.* The name "linked-lambs" refers to how the luminous chains resemble a string of lambs traversing a mountainside. For a similar concept in the Kālacakra context, see KCT 4.195, which mentions "garlands of *thig-le*" *(thig le'i phreng ba)* appearing during sky-gazing.

39. *nyams gong nas gong du 'phel ba'i snang ba.*

40. MTP, 293.

41. MTP, 295.

42. *rig pa tshad la phebs pa'i snang ba.*

43. *chos nyid zad pa'i snang ba.*

44. MTP, 312.

45. *'di skad bdag gis thos pa'i dus gcig na.*

46. *'di skad bdag gis bstan pa'i dus gcig na.*

47. The name "Pure Appearance" *(snang ba rnam par dag pa'i rdo rje 'chang)* indicates how the Teacher is an embodied appearance but still does not waver from his primordial, pure, nonappearing state. As for the name of the Student, "Pure Continuum" *(rgyud dag pa'i rdo rje 'chang)* suggests that though he is ultimately not separate from the primordial buddha, he is derived from him and thus has a continuum *(rgyud)* and a family lineage *(rgyud)* within historical time that is traceable back to a pure source. "Pure Cause" *(rgyu dag pa'i rdo rje 'chang)* indicates that he is pure of the causes of the three types of ignorance (see MTP, 102–103); "Causal" *(rgyu'i rdo rje 'chang)* suggests how he acts in the world as a cause, particularly as the cause that prompted the teaching of this tantra; this last name could also be interpreted as "Animate" Dorjé Chang, i.e., the one who moves *(rgyu ba)* into the world rather than being a remote primordial purity.

48. For more on these channels, see chapter 4.

49. One classic source for such discussions is the *Discourse on the Foundations of Mindfulness* (*Satipaṭṭhāna Sutta,* MN, 10). See, for example, section 40 (153 in Ñāṇamoli and Bodhi's *Middle Length Discourses*): "Here a bhikku understands the eye, he understands forms, and he understands the fetter that arises dependent on both...."

50. *So sor thar ba'i mdo* (*Prātimokṣa-sūtra*), D2, 18a.6.

51. For a narrative example of this theme, see Ranjini Obeyesekere, "The Monk Cakkhupāla (Guardian of the Eyes)," in *Jewels of the Doctrine: Stories of the Saddharma Ratnāvaliya* (Albany: State University of New York Press, 1991), 9-35.

52. MTP, 177: The "self-emergent insight lamp" is the vibrant essence *(dwangs ma)* of cognition *(shes pa)*. It abides as the cognizing power *(shes byed nyid)* of all the four lamps, and so without it, real understanding would not arise. Therefore, it is present as a dimension of all the lamps, abiding in the channels as the four insights—the differentiating insight and so forth.

53. This is discussed on MTP, 178.

54. See MTP, 185: "the object of that insight is the directly perceived awareness" *(shes rab de'i yul rig pa mngon sum)*.

55. See TB, 475.

56. See MTP, 286.

57. See TB, 225.

58. Discussions of wholeness often play off another *thig-le* related term, "single-sphere" *(thig le nyag gcig)*; for instance, the multiplicity of *thig-le* in vision is said to be ultimately undifferentiable from the "single sphere" of reality. See MTP, 248, 267.

59. See TDD 265, which uses the distinctive Kālacakra term "empty-form" to describe visionary appearances.

60. See MTP, 291, 313.

61. See MTP, 313–314.

62. See TB, 487, and MTP, 291, 294–295.

63. *rig pa'i khyim,* MTP, 291.

64. TB, 488.

65. Here I do not mean to suggest that spontaneous "experience" necessarily precedes conceptual elaboration, abstract thought, and so forth. Indeed, before engaging in visionary practice, many will have a broad background in Buddhist thought and literature, and this frames and in some ways prefigures their subsequent "spontaneous" experiences of vision. I simply mean to suggest that in my source literature, yogic experiences often provide a leaping-off place for theoretical discussion.

Chapter 3

1. Bönpos say that they began adopting Buddhist elements as early as the royal period, when the conqueror Trisong Detsen offered three choices to Bön priests: suicide, banishment, or conversion to Buddhism. For a late account of this by Shardza Tashi Gyaltsen, see Karmay, trans., *Treasury of Good Sayings,* 90ff.

2. For this location, see Karmay's discussions in *Arrow and the Spindle,* 104ff., and *Treasury of Good Sayings,* xxx.

3. Karmay, *Treasury of Good Sayings,* xxxi, discusses the confused history of these two persecutions and suggests "the possibility that later Bon-po historians have made two persecutions out of what was in fact only one." See also Per Kværne, "The Canon of the Tibetan Bonpos," *Indo-Iranian Journal* 16 (1974): 28.

4. The dates here are from STNN, 229. For the life of Shenchen and a list of his revelations, see Daniel Martin, "The Emergence of Bon and the Tibetan Polemical Tradition" (PhD diss., Indiana University, 1991). Note that Shenchen's revelation was not the first revelation of Bön's later spread *(phyi dar)*; for earlier treasure revelations, see Kværne, "Canon," 32ff.

5. For this date, see STNN, 230. The monastery was founded by Druchen Gyalwa Yungdrung, an ancestor of Drugyalwa.

6. For this date, see Kværne, "Canon," 38. Kværne notes that the latest texts to be included in the canon seem to predate 1386.

7. Karmay, *Treasury of Good Sayings,* 139 n. 1.

8. For the date, see STNN, 232.

9. *theg pa dgu.* For a lengthy treatment of these, see David Snellgrove, *The Nine Ways of Bon: Excerpts from Gzi-Brjid Edited and Translated* (Boulder, co: Prajna Press, 1980). For alternate organizational schemes, see Snellgrove, *Nine Ways,* 16; Karmay, *Arrow and the Spindle,* 111; and Daniel Martin, *Unearthing Bon Treasures: Life and Contested Legacy of a Tibetan Scripture Revealer, with a General Bibliography of Bon* (London: Brill, 2001), 217. See also Namkhai Norbu, *Drung, Deu, and Bön: Narrations, Symbolic Languages, and the Bön Tradition in Ancient Tibet* (Dharamsala: Library of Tibetan Works and Archives, 1995).

10. These cautions are expressed well by Snellgrove; see his *Nine Ways*, 11, 20.

11. A good source for the basic literary collections of the Bön Great Perfection is in Samten Karmay, *A Catalogue of Bonpo Publications* (Tokyo: Toyo Bunko, 1977), 94ff.

12. For brief presentations of these three, see Karmay, *Arrow and the Spindle,* 155; and Per Kværne's introduction to Drugyalwa, *The Stages of a-Khrid Meditation: Dzogchen Practice of the Bon Tradition,* ed. Per Kværne and Thupten Rikey, trans. Per Kværne and Thubten K. Rikey (Dharamsala: Library of Tibetan Works and Archives, 1996), x.

13. For studies of *a khrid,* see Per Kværne, "Bonpo Studies: The A-Khrid System of Meditation," *Kailash* 1, nos. 1 and 4 (1973): 19–50 and 247–332; its relationship to the 1038 *Khro rgyud* treasure is discussed on 24; Kværne provides Meü Gong Dzö's biography on 29ff.

14. *yang rtse'i klong chen.*

15. This association is noted in Karmay, *Arrow and the Spindle,* 156.

16. The name derives from the collection dividing up its constituent texts into four groups: outer, inner, secret, and extremely secret (the various versions of the collection differ somewhat on which texts are included in which division). For catalogs listing the works in the collection, see STNN no. K108, and Shardza's catalog that circulates with NR. See also Karmay, *Catalogue of Bonpo Publications*, 94. The Tibetan-Himalayan Library (thlib.org) has a catalog available online. Reynolds also provides a brief summary of each of the texts in his *Oral Tradition from Zhang Zhung* (Kathmandu: Vajra Publications, 2005), 193.

17. *'od kyi khye'u chung.*

18. See, for instance, *dGos 'dod gsal byed bshad gzhi'i mchong,* which is in the Bön Great Perfection collection *Ye khri mtha' sel.* This work is similar in form to (though shorter than) Longchenpa's *Tshig don mdzod.*

19. For instance, in the *Zab mo yang tig.*

20. *brGyud pa'i bla ma'i rnam thar* (ZZNG, 1–130). For a brief biography of the author, see Samten Karmay, *The Little Luminous Boy: The Oral Tradition from the Land of Zhang Zhung Depicted on Two Tibetan Paintings* (Bangkok: Orchid Press, 1998), 83. The colophon of the *Biographies* specifies that it was composed in an "earth pig" year; Karmay places this at 1419 (see *Little Luminous Boy,* 77). Martin and Bentor tentatively place it at 1479; see *Tibetan*

Histories (London: Serindia Publications, 1997), entry 143. See also Daniel Martin, "Unearthing Bon Treasures: A Study of Tibetan Sources on the Earlier Years in the Life of Gshen-Chen-Klu-Dga'," *Journal of the American Oriental Society* 116, no. 4 (1996): 622.

21. *A History of the Great Perfection's Oral Tradition from Zhang Zhung, Containing Biographies [of Its Lineage Holders] (rDzogs pa chen po zhang zhung snyan rgyud kyi lo rgyus rnam thar dang bcas pa),* published in the collection *Sñan rgyud nam mkha' 'phrul mdzod draṅ ṅes skor źaṅ źuṅ sñan rgyud skor* (Dolanji: Tibetan Bonpo Monastic Centre, 1972), 539ff.

22. See GDGG, 359.

23. See Janet Gyatso's discussion of treasures encoded on "yellow papers" *(ser shog)*, or "paper scrolls" *(shog dril)*: "Signs, Memory and History: A Tantric Buddhist Theory of Scriptural Transmission," *Journal of the International Association of Buddhist Studies* 9, no. 2 (1986): 17ff.

24. This appears to be the case with the *gZi brjid,* the massive twelve-volume biography of Shenrab Miwo, which tradition maintains was dictated to the fourteenth-century treasure revealer Loden Nyingpo. See Karmay's comments on this in *Arrow and the Spindle,* 110, 124.

25. Note here the *gZer mig,* the biography of Shenrab Miwo discovered by Drangjé Tsünpa Sermig. Karmay has noted how this expands on materials similar to those found in Dunhuang manuscripts; see his *Arrow and the Spindle,* 123, 181.

26. Our present *Advice on the Six Lamps* appears to be an example of this.

27. Indeed, *Advice on the Six Lamps* does not present itself as an exact transcript of an eighth-century revelation, as it begins with a narrative describing that revelation as a past event.

28. *bde gshegs dgongs rgyud dgu.*

29. This name is also used to translate "Guhyasamāja" (gSang-ba-'dus-pa), though the connection between this buddha in Bön and his namesake associated with the famous Indian *Guhyasamāja Tantra* remains unexplored.

30. *gang zag nyi shu rtsa bzhi'i snyan rgyud.*

31. See BN, 27.1. Note that Tsepung is also the teacher of Gyerpungpa, though he does not grant Gyerpungpa the critical teachings from the Oral Tradition from Zhang Zhung.

32. See BN, 26.6ff.

33. See, for instance, these works from ZZNG: (da) *rDzogs pa chen po zhang zhung snyan rgyud las rje ta pi hri tsa'i lung bstan,* (na) *Zhe sa dgu phrug,* and (pa) *mJel thebs bar ma.* Brief biographies of Tapihritsa and Gyerpungpa are in (ka) *rDzogs pa chen po zhang zhung snyan rgyud kyi brgyud pa'i bla ma'i rnam thar* (26.6ff.). A more lengthy account of Gyerpungpa's life is found in (pha) *rDzogs pa chen po zhang zhung snyan rgyud gyi bon ma nub pa'i gtan tshigs.*

34. See Shardza's account of this in Karmay, trans., *Treasury of Good Sayings,* 97.

35. BN, 29.5.

36. BN, 29.6. I read *spu bya ba* instead of *spu byang,* in accordance with *Bon ma nub pa'i gtan tshigs,* ZZNG, 264.6.

37. BN, 30.2. These exploits are magnified in Bön *ma nub pa'i gtan tshigs* (ZZNG, *pa*).

38. The classic accounts of this first encounter are described in *rJe ta pi hri tsa'i lung bstan* (ZZNG da), and *Zhe sa dgu phrug* (ZZNG na).

39. This is from *rJe ta pi hri tsa'i lung bstan*, ZZNG, 250.2. "My teacher is ordinary appearances" is *slob dpon 'di ltar snang ba yin*, literally "My master is appearances like this. . . ."

40. For this site in contemporary gShis-ka-rtse prefecture, see John Vincent Bellezza, "A Preliminary Archaeological Survey of Da Rog mTsho," *Tibet Journal* 24 (Spring 1999): 55–91.

41. Both of these commentaries appear in the Menri edition of ZZNG. My translation of Drugyalwa's commentary appears in part 3 of this book. The precise dates of the thirteenth-century author Uri Sogyal are unknown, though in catalogs his works precede those of Drugyalwa, hinting at his temporal precedence.

42. ZZNG, 292.

43. BN, 32.1.

44. Key works from this lineage have been published in: *Zhang zhung snyan rgyud kyi bla ma'i nyams rgyud 'bring po sor bzhag pa dang bsdus pa 'thor bu bcas kyi gsung pod* (New Thobgyal, H.P.: Tibetan Bonpo Monastic Centre, 1973); and *Zhang zhung snyan rgyud bla ma'i nyams rgyud rgyas pa skya smug gnyis kyi gsung pod* (New Thobgyal, H.P.: Tibetan Bonpo Monastic Centre, 1973).

45. This is little more than a revised form of Karmay's lineage diagram in *Little Luminous Boy,* xviii.

46. Karmay mentions Yangtön's relationship with Ba-ri in *Little Luminous Boy,* xvii, but does not specify a source. See Drugyalwa's history *sNyan rgyud kyi lo rgyus rnam thar dang bcas pa*, 575.2, which specifies that Yangtön "skillfully studied the topics of *pramāṇa,* Middle Way, and the Perfection of Wisdom with Ba-ri-lo-tsa-ba" *(ba ri lo tsa ba la tshad ma dbu ma sher gsum gyi rig pa mkhas par bslabs).* Ba-ri was a translator associated with Sakya Monastery and also served as its abbot; for his dates, see Roerich, trans., *Blue Annals*, 405; and Ko-zhul-grags-pa-'byung-gnas, *mKhas grub rim byon ming mdzod,* 1075.

47. *Lo rgyus rnam thar dang bcas pa,* 575.2, lists one of Yangtön's associations as g.Yas-ru-bru-ston-rje-btsun.

48. BN, 61.1 mentions that he debated with Buddhists *(ben).* Yangtön's association with Ba-ri makes one wonder if this could have been at Sakya Monastery.

49. BN, 62.2 names it *stod skya ru ru dgon.*

50. BN, 61.4; correct *bsnyon pa* to *smyon pa* based on *Lo rgyus rnam thar dang bcas pa,* 575.4.

51. *Lo rgyus rnam thar dang bcas pa,* 577.3.

52. Orgom Kündül, no. 71 in the lineage chart above, is here called Orbön Kündül.

53. BN, 61.5. Karmay also summarizes this in *Little Luminous Boy,* 29.

54. Sebön's identity is unknown.

55. BN, 54.5. Karmay also summarizes this in *Little Luminous Boy,* 72.

56. BN here appears to read *bla yi ge 'bri ru med pa la.* I correct *bla* to *nga la,* based on Drugyalwa's rendering (574): *nga la yi ge ka tsam zhig yod re gsungs.*

57. The passages mentioned here are concerned with the Experiential Transmission rather than the Transmission of the Word (to which the *Four Cycles* is related); see the above lineage chart.

58. Note that Patsün Tengyal's version of these events is more elaborate than Drugyalwa's. Drugyalwa simply mentions that Yangtön met Rong Tokmé Zhikpo, and thus attained the materials of the Upper Tradition.

59. BN, 63.4. Karmay also summarizes this in *Little Luminous Boy,* 30.

60. *khyod kyi de rnams nyams rgyud dang sngags su 'jug.* It is not clear here what "mantra" *(sngags)* refers to, though Drugyalwa's history (576.2) mentions Yangtön's skill in "secret mantra like Me-ri and so forth" *(gsang sngags ltar na me ri las sogs pa).*

61. These are nos. 41 and 42 in the lineage chart above.

62. *phyi lta ba spyi gcod,* the first of the four cycles.

63. This is no. 49 in the lineage chart above.

64. BN, 64.5.

65. Though note the Oral Tradition's set of five rather than four visions; Drugyalwa gives a presentation of these on GDGG, 403.

66. For instance, in the *Ye khri mtha' sel.*

67. *snang ba chen po gsum.*

68. See the section "Essential Background for the *Tantra of the Blazing Lamps*" in chapter 2 for more on the ground-presencing.

69. *snang ba'i yul gsum.*

70. These are, respectively, *rtsal, gdangs,* and *cho 'phrul.*

71. *yul sgra 'od zer gsum.*

72. *rtogs 'khrul rkyen.*

73. A common reference to *rtsal* is in the phrase "the dynamic energy of the inseparable mother and son" (*ma bu dbyer med kyi rtsal;* see GDGG, 367). For *rtsal* being an energy that animates relationships, see also GDGG, 370ff., which describes the *rtsal* of awareness/sound, awareness/light, awareness/rays, the *rtsal* of the three bodies, and so forth.

74. Note that the ZZNG contains a short work on the six lamps called *Byang chub sems kyi gnad drug.*

75. *spyi mes.*

76. *rtsal*

77. The Yogācāra set of eight consciousnesses seems especially significant here. These are the normative six consciousnesses, plus an "afflicted mental consciousness" *(nyon mongs pa can gyi yid kyi rnam par shes pa)* and a "universal ground consciousness" *(kun gzhi'i rnam par shes pa),* the latter of which clearly influenced the Great Perfection's concept of the "ground" *(gzhi).* See the first chapter of *Advice on the Six Lamps,* in the section "How Karmic Predispositions Accumulate in the Ground" (ZZNG, 276) for a direct reference to the eight consciousnesses. See also David Germano and William Waldron, "A Comparison of Ālaya-Vijñāna in Yogācāra and Dzogchen," in *Buddhist Thought and Applied Psychological Research: Transcending the Boundaries*, ed. D. K. Nauriyal, Michael S. Drummond, and Y. B. Lal, 36–68 (New York: Routledge, 2006).

78. The Oral Tradition also maintains more conventional maps of the subtle body, which contain a straight central channel, divided by energy-wheels, that runs down the center of the body. The Oral Tradition thus has two competing ways of thinking about the body's channels. The first is called "the channels for meditation" *(sgom gyi rtsa),* which refers to the way the channels are thought of conceptually and how they are visualized in meditation: straight, organized, symmetrical, with distinctive colors and dimensions. The second is "the channels as they actually are" *(gnas kyi rtsa);* this refers to the channels' abiding reality *(gnas lugs),* which is as incredibly fine, subtle corridors of energy that do not necessarily conform to straight lines of imagination but follow the organic contours of the actual body.

79. *ye shes tshon gang.* For the sake of comparison, note the *Kaṭha Upaniṣad* 6.17 (trans. Olivelle): "A person the size of a thumb in the body, always resides in the hearts of men; One should draw him out of the body...; One should know him as immortal and bright." See Patrick Olivelle, trans., *Upaniṣads* (New York: Oxford University Press, 1996), 246.

80. GDGG, 380: *kun gzhi dang rig pa gdod nas gnas pa'i snying po.*

81. GDD, 278: *mchong gur smug po shel gyi kha bad can/ snang gsal 'od gyi gur khang na bzhugs so/.*

82. GDD, 279.

83. *khong shar.*

84. *rtsa dbu ma.*

85. GDGG, 380.

86. Awareness' dimension of "light" is generally held responsible for maintaining the body's physical functioning, while its dimension of "rays" allows it to serve as the basis for the mind's ordinary capacities to know. See GDGG, 381.

87. The body's five main organs (the heart, lungs, liver, kidneys, and spleen) are each said to be a seat *(rten)* of one of the elemental energies (respectively, the energies of space, wind, fire, water, and earth). The elements thus use their particular organs as a type of base of operations, where they are most concentrated, and from which they perform their particular functions in the formation of the body. The heart being the seat of "space" suggests how the body arises from a kind of dynamic emptiness. It is also an explicit reference to cosmological accounts (found in both Buddhism and Bön), which typically portray the universe as arising from the maṇḍala of space.

88. *'od.* This contrasts with the energy of its "rays" *(zer),* which forms the mind.

89. *sdong po.*

90. For a full treatment of Buddhist embryology, see Frances Garrett, *Embryology in the History of Tibetan Medicine: Becoming Human* (Abingdon: Routledge, 2008).

91. Various spellings of this occur: *rtsang ri pur langs* (GDGG), *tsang ri pur lang* (GDD), *tsang ri bur lang* (NR), *tsang ri pu lang* (MS). The spelling in GDD is perhaps best. *Tsang ri* means "channel," and *pur lang* means "head." The channel is said to take a crisscrossing path as it traverses the top of the brain, crossing itself twice before connecting with the eyes.

92. GDGG, 388. The channel actually connects to the heart, where it is inside the central channel; the top of the brain is the area where it becomes independent from the central channel.

93. *ngo sprod pa.*

94. *dmar thag bcad pa.* The sense of this term is difficult to convey in translation. Its elements mean "red" *(dmar)* and "decision" or "resolution" *(thag bcad pa);* even more literally, they are "red" *(dmar),* "rope" *(thag),* and "cutting" *(bcad pa),* where "cutting the rope" is the common Tibetan verbal phrase meaning "to decide" or "to resolve." The term "red" here has the sense of something important or arresting, such as the visceral reaction one has when seeing blood. The idea is of encountering something critically important in such a way that one knows exactly what it is, and will not forget it. It is, for example, like opening up a body and seeing the red heart, pointing at it and saying "that is the heart."

95. GDD, 286.

96. See Gyurme Dorje, trans., *The Tibetan Book of the Dead: The Great Liberation by Hearing in the Intermediate States* (New York: Viking, 2006).

97. GDD, 288.

98. *'phen pa'i stobs.*

99. For an eighteenth-century presentation of these signs, which is very close to the one that appears in Drugyalwa's commentary (GDGG, 410), see Lati Rinbochay and Jeffrey Hopkins, *Death, Intermediate State and Rebirth* (Ithaca, NY: Snow Lion Publications, 1985), 29ff.

100. See GDGG, 410. These appearances of course are also found in visionary contexts not directly related to dying, the most relevant example here being the "ten signs" of the Kālacakra completion stage yogas.

101. Bön's connections with Sarma are also evident in Bön's literary fields like logic, medicine, and the Perfection of Wisdom.

102. As noted earlier, Ba-ri served as an abbot of Sakya. Karmay notes that in later periods, Bönpos were known to travel from Menri Monastery to Sakya for studies; see Samten Karmay and Yasuhiko Nagano, eds., *A Survey of Bonpo Monasteries and Temples in Tibet and the Himalaya (Bon Studies 7)* (Osaka: National Museum of Ethnology, 2003), 4.

103. It is important to note that, on the contrary, it is common to find identical sentences and paragraphs shared by works *within* a particular tradition, such as between Drugyalwa's and Uri's commentaries, or between the *Three Bodhisattva Commentaries.*

Chapter 4

1. *Stainless Light,* for instance, associates the dark room with emptiness itself, saying: "'In the emptiness, smoke, a mirage, lights in the clear stainless sky, and a butter lamp [come to be seen].' This indicates what is seen in night-yoga." VP commenting on KCT 5.115 (Bu vol. 3, VP ch. 5, 46a.3): *stong pa la ni du ba rmig rgyu rab gsal dri ma med pa'i mkha' snang nyid dang mar me dang/ /zhes pa ni/ mtshan mo'i rnal 'byor gyis mthong ngo/ /.* Material in quotation marks is the root text from KCT.

2. Bu vol. 3, VP ch. 5, 54b.2 (commenting on KCT 5.127).

3. *rnam pa thams cad pa'i stong pa nyid.*

4. D1350, 191a.4 (commenting on KCT 4.198).

5. *Perfection of Wisdom Sūtra in 25,000 Lines (Shes rab kyi pha rol tu phyin pa stong phrag nyi shu lnga pa, Pañcaviṃśatisāhasrikā-prajñāpāramitā),* D0009, vol. kha, 46a.3.

6. MMK, verse XXIV.24, 17a.4: *dmigs pa thams cad nyer zhi zhing/ /spros pa nyer zhi zhi ba ste/ /sangs rgyas kyis ni gang du yang/ /su la'ang chos 'ga' ma bstan to/ /.*

7. *Bodhicaryāvatāra,* IX.2. The translation here is from Vesna and Alan Wallace, *A Guide to the Bodhisattva Way of Life* (Ithaca, NY: Snow Lion Publications, 1997), 115.

8. YM, 674: *blo yi spyod yul las 'das pa lkog tu gyur pa;* see also YM, 669.

9. YM, 622–623.

10. *lam du 'gyur pa'i stong pa nyid.*

11. *rtsal.*

12. TB, 484: *stong pa nyid las rang log pa'i/ /myong byed gsal ba'i snang bar ni/ /ye gdangs lnga dang bcas par yang/ /rang bzhin babs kyis gnas pa la/ /.*

13. A few of the most popular being the *Śrīmālādevī-sūtra,* the *Tathāgatagarbha-sūtra,* the *Aṅgulimālīya-sūtra,* and the *Uttaratantra-shastra.*

14. The Kālacakra and Great Perfection materials from the early Tibetan renaissance do not make overt references to these materials. Sill, by the thirteenth century, as the Tibetan commentarial traditions surrounding Kālacakra and the Great Perfection grew, they begin openly reflecting on these connections and explicitly stating them as sources.

15. *Chos dbyings bstod pa (Dharmadhātustava),* verses 5–7 (D1118, 64a.1). See also Brunnhölzl's study of this work; his translation of this verse is on 119.

16. For this metaphor, see GDGG, 377; see also YM, 668.

17. *Chos dbyings bstod pa (Dharmadhātustava),* verse 22 (D1118, 64b.2). See also Brunnhölzl's translation in *In Praise of Dharmadhātu* (Ithaca, NY: Snow Lion Publications, 2007), 117.

18. YM, 623.

19. In order, these are *stong gzugs (śūnyatā-bimba), blun pa ma yin stong pa nyid (ajaḍā-śūnyatā), dmigs pa dang bcas pa'i stong pa nyid (śālambana-sūnyatā), rnam pa thams cad dang ldan pa'i stong pa nyid (śūnyatā-sarvākārairūpetā).*

20. *lam du 'gyur pa'i stong pa nyid* and *gzhan stong.*

21. VP on KCT 5.127; the citation can be found in Bu vol. 3, VP ch. 5, 72b.5, but the translation here is based on YM, 630.

22. *dharmodaya, chos 'byung.*

23. The term "sphere of reality" *(dharmadhātu, chos dbyings)* is also given similar associations.

24. See, for instance, GDGG, 374, 420.

25. See YM, 615–617, 620.

26. YM, 620.

27. Note that Yumo tends to view Nāgārjuna from the perspective of his "Collections of Reasoning" (*rigs pa'i tshogs;* see Yumo's reference to this on YM, 620) rather than his more positive "Collections of Praises," such as the one cited above.

28. *rdo rje'i lus.*

29. *rtsa rlung thig le.*

30. For discussion on the various presentations of these channels, see Germano, "Poetic Thought," 706, n. 512 and following.

31. TB, 483.

32. For instance, in its discussion of the above passage from the *Tantra of the Blazing Lamps,* the commentary *Stringing a Garland of Pearls* maps the four luminous channels onto a basic set of four (rather than three) conventional energy channels (see MTP, 273). In this presentation, the golden *kati* and silk thread channels are said to extend from the right and left sides of the heart, and are the "actual nature" (*rang ngo*) of the ordinary right and left channels, whose conventional natures are imputed upon them. The luminous "slender coil," which extends from the center of the heart, then is similarly related to the ordinary central channel. Finally, the "crystal tube" channel is said to spiral upward from the top of the heart and is related to an otherwise unknown channel that the commentary refers to as the *sidharma (sid d+harma).*

Stringing a Garland of Pearls contains more than its fair share of mistakes, so it is possible that the name of this *sidharma* channel may simply be an error. Looking beyond its curious name, it seems worthwhile to try and puzzle out what this channel might be. It is clear that the *Garland* commentary sees a relationship between the four luminous channels and four ordinary channels in the body; the ordinary channels are typically only enumerated as threefold, so this *sidharma* is the additional "fourth" channel. Elsewhere in the *Garland* (see MTP, 189ff., which comments on the root tantra section 2.2.2.6), we do find an extended discussion of four ordinary channels: the right, left, and central channels, plus a "crystal tube" channel *(shel gyi sbu gu can,* or *shel sbug can).* There are some precedents for this term "crystal tube" or "*kati* crystal tube" being used to refer to the entire system of luminous channels (see Germano, "Poetic Thought," 706 n. 512), in which case references to this set of four channels might be read as referring to the three ordinary channels, plus the system of light channels. However, *Stringing a Garland of Pearls* clearly presents the (ordinary) "crystal tube" as having conventional functions and participating in the conventional channel system: it has defined conventional functions like managing the body's warmth; it has conventional effects in the mental realm, such as giving rise to dualistic perception and conceptuality; and it has conventional colors, being white on the outside and red on the inside. It seems plausible, then, in correlating four conventional channels to the four luminous channels, that the *sidharma* channel is the same as this conventional "crystal tube" channel, in which case you would have an ordinary and extraordinary channel called by the same name.

33. In the ZZNG, the heart-to-eyes channels are together referred to with the name *tsang-ri bur-lang*. Several different spellings occur: *rtsang ri pur langs* (GDGG), *tsang ri pur lang* (GDD), *tsang ri bur lang* (NR); the spelling in GDD is perhaps best. In Zhang Zhung language, *tsang ri* means "channel," and *pur lang* means "head," so this is simply the "head channel."

34. Note in particular that in the Bön six lamps text, the central channel (the "smooth white channel") is depicted as a pure, white, luminous channel where awareness is exclusively pure; see discussion of this on GDD, 387. The Nyingma sources investigated here tend to allow the central channel to be involved in more mundane functions; see MTP, 194ff.

35. VP on KCT 5.116 (Bu vol. 3, VP ch. 5, 46b.7).

36. For the divine eye *(dibbacakkhu)* in the Pāli *nikayās,* see particularly MN 39.19 and 77.35. See below for some references to the eyes in *abhidharma* and *prajñāpāramitā.* For the five eyes in the Great Perfection context, see MTP, 154.

37. *Shes rab kyi pha rol tu phyin pa stong phrag nyi shu lnga pa,* D0009, vol. ka, 71a.1. Note slight differences between these five eyes and the above list from the Kālacakra tradition.

38. The outline below is based on a lengthy description that follows the above passage from the *Perfection of Wisdom in 25,000 Lines.* See D0009, vol. ka, 72a.3.

39. References to the divine eye, or "god's eye," are also found in the *nikāyas* and in the *abhidharma* literature and tend to resemble the description seen here. The *Perfection of Wisdom Sūtra in 25,000 Lines,* however, does note that this eye is a property only of bodhisattvas. It is also careful to distinguish it from the "god's eyes" possessed by the four classes of great kings that live around Mt. Sumeru *(rgyal po chen po bzhi'i ris kyi lha rnams kyi lha'i mig),* and from the eyes of the other types of gods in the heavens reaching up to the realm of None Higher *('og min).* It is said that bodhisattvas can possess the eyes that characterize those types of gods, but those gods conversely cannot possess the "god's eye" that is one of the "five eyes," as these five eyes are attained only by bodhisattvas who successfully practice the six perfections.

40. *prajñā, shes rab.*

41. D0009, vol. ka, 75b.1 ff.

42. KCT 4.232 (Bu vol. 1, 105b.3): *lha yi dmigs pa gang yin mngon sum dang ni rjes su dpag pa rnam pa gnyis su 'gyur ba ste/ /mngon sum dag ni de nyid sbyor bas mkha' la skar ma bzhin du du ma longs spyod rdzogs pa'i sku/ /mngon sum min na rjes su dpag pa shi ba'i lus bzhin de nyid min pa yis ni brtags pa gang/ /de ni ri mo sogs la blta bya yongs su ma smin blo can rnal 'byor rnams kyi bsgom pa'i don/ /.*

43. Neither the *Kālacakra Tantra* nor *Stainless Light* mentions it, but it seems reasonable that visualization, and the broader category of the generation stage, could also be included here.

44. The VP's explanation of the following verse (4.233) specifies the reference of *de nyid sbyor bas* as being the "union of emptiness and compassion." This is Wallace's observation, found in her translation of chapter 4 of the VP, 259 n. 526.

45. I am thinking here of discourses like those examined by Ronald Davidson in "Masquerading as Pramāṇa: Esoteric Buddhism and Epistemological Nomenclature," in *Dharmakīrti's Thought and Its Impact on Indian and Tibetan Philosophy: Proceedings of the Third International Conference on Dharmakīrti and Pramāṇa* (Vienna: Österreichischen Akademie der Wissenschaften, 1999).

46. Bu vol. 3, VP ch. 4, 73a.3. See also Norsang Gyatso's discussion of the passage in *Ornament of Stainless Light* (trans. Kilty), 491ff.

47. Butön's interlineal comments on this passage are instructive, so I will include them here. At this point, Butön notes: "which are the forms of emptiness."

48. Butön notes: "That is like the eye possessed by dogs and so forth, and is inferior to the other four eyes." The comment here suggests how in Kālacakra the "fleshy eye" usually refers to the ordinary eye; in the classical system of the five

eyes, it refers to a kind of super-sight. (Though notice how it is still said to perceive empty-forms.)

49. Butön notes: "i.e., after training with those objects...."

50. Butön notes: "i.e., having attained [higher perception *(mngon shes)*]."

51. Butön notes: "For example, via the divine eyes, things that are subtle, inaccessible, and hidden to humans are also seen."

52. Butön notes: "i.e., having trained in that, and attained [freedom from] grasping at the three realms...."

53. For instance, within the three realms, hearers and solitary realizers, who are free from desirous attachment, see [both] ordinary phenomena *(chos can)* and reality itself *(chos nyid)*.

54. Butön notes: "i.e., having trained in that...."

55. Butön notes: "i.e., having attained the bodhisattva grounds...."

56. Butön notes: "i.e., having trained in that...."

57. Butön notes: "i.e., having attained the [buddha's] ground...."

58. Butön notes: "These are the eyes with which the buddhas (because they possess the four gnoses) see gnosis, [or see] two things: objects of cognition and cognition. This is what Vajragarbha says."

59. Khedrup Norsang Gyatso (mKhas-grub-nor-bzang-rgya-mtsho), *Phyi nang gzhan gsum gsal bar byed pa dri med 'od kyi rgyan* (New Delhi: Bod kyi gtsug lag zhib dpyod khang, 2004), 414. See also *Ornament of Stainless Light* (trans. Kilty), 491.

60. For several sources related to science and medicine in the Kālacakra tradition, see Wallace's works in the bibliography.

61. For sources on Charles Bonnet syndrome, see Kenneth Gold and Peter V. Rabins, "Isolated Visual Hallucinations and the Charles Bonnet Syndrome: A Review of the Literature and Presentation of Six Cases," *Comprehensive Psychiatry 30*, no. 1 (1989): 90–98, as well as Lauren O'Farrel, et al., "Charles Bonnet Syndrome: A Review of the Literature," *Journal of Visual Impairment and Blindness* 104 (May 2010): 261–274. For descriptions of several interesting cases, see V. S. Ramachandran, *Phantoms in the Brain: Probing the Mysteries of the Human Mind* (New York: William Morrow, 1998), 87–88, 104–112, as well as Oliver Sacks, "Silent Multitudes: Charles Bonnet Syndrome," in *Hallucinations* (New York: Knopf, 2012), 3–33. For more on Bonnet and Lullin, see Douwe Draaisma, "Towards Dusk the Images Appear: Bonnet Syndrome," in *Disturbances of the Mind*, trans. Barbara Fasting (New York: Cambridge University Press, 2009), 11–39.

62. See Ramachandran, *Phantoms in the Brain,* 107–108.

63. See Alvaro Pascual-Leone, et al., "Visual Hallucinations During Prolonged Blindfolding in Sighted Subjects," *Journal of Neuro-Ophthalmology* 24 (2004): 109–113.

64. See Ramachandran, *Phantoms in the Brain*, 88ff. for discussions of the blind spot.

65. The language of "perceptual" and "conceptual" completion and the descriptions here are from Ramachandran, *Phantoms in the Brain,* 103.

66. See Ramachandran, *Phantoms in the Brain,* 110, 274 n. 14. Ramachandran's broad comments about memory here differ from, but are not necessarily contradictory to, the observations of Pascual-Leone, et al., whose blindfolded subjects reported that

their visual experiences "were always novel and had no relation to past experiences"; see "Visual Hallucinations During Prolonged Blindfolding," 110.

67. Ramachandran, *Phantoms in the Brain,* 110; see also 274 n. 14.

68. Ramachandran, *Phantoms in the Brain,* 110.

69. For a more nuanced view of this system, and descriptions of alternate pathways of visual information, see Ramachandran, *Phantoms in the Brain,* 70ff. and 109ff.

70. See Ramachandran, *Phantoms in the Brain*, 110.

71. Ramachandran, *Phantoms in the Brain*, 111. See also Pascual-Leone, et al., "Visual Hallucinations During Prolonged Blindfolding," 112.

72. Ramachandran, *Phantoms in the Brain,* 110–111, and 275 n. 15.

73. Ramachandran, *Phantoms in the Brain*, 111. This theory does not directly address sensory deprivation brought on by blindfolding or a dark room, and in these cases would need to be extended to suggest how prolonged complete deprivation of light (in the absence of any damage to the visual pathways) also produces the same effect. Pascual-Leone, et al., discuss this "release mechanism" in the context of visual deprivation in "Visual Hallucinations During Prolonged Blindfolding," 112.

The mind's tendency to create visions of light where there is darkness suggests a deep relation between visual perception and conceptual thought. In particular, if Ramachandran's speculations are correct, the visionary experiences reported in dark-retreats would be produced by the same processes that underlie ordinary memory and imagination (see *Phantoms in the Brain,* 111–112). This would also suggest a connection between the experience of spontaneous vision and the act of deliberate visualization.

74. *sems kyi snang ba tsam.*

75. Pascual-Leone, et al., "Visual Hallucinations During Prolonged Blindfolding," 109. See also Sacks, "Silent Multitudes," 27–28.

76. Ramachandran, *Phantoms in the Brain*, 88.

77. Ramachandran, *Phantoms in the Brain*, 98.

78. Ramachandran, *Phantoms in the Brain*, 105.

79. Pascual-Leone, et al., "Visual Hallucinations During Prolonged Blindfolding," 113.

80. Pascual-Leone, et al., "Visual Hallucinations During Prolonged Blindfolding," 111.

81. As did subject 3 in Pascual-Leone, et al., "Visual Hallucinations During Prolonged Blindfolding," 110.

82. *Commentary on the "Supplement to [Nāgārjuna's] 'Treatise on the Middle Way.'" dBu ma la 'jug pa'i bshad pa (Madhyamakāvatārabhāṣya),* D3862, 255a.6: *don dam pa'i bden pa bstan par 'dod pas de ni brjod du med pa'i phyir dang shes pa'i phyir yul ma yin pa nyid kyi phyir dngos su bstan par mi nus pas/.* For a discussion of this passage, see Kevin Vose, *Resurrecting Candrakīrti: Disputes in the Tibetan Creation of Prāsaṅgika* (Boston: Wisdom Publications, 2009), 88ff.

83. See Vose, *Resurrecting Candrakīrti,* 17ff.

84. As seen above, a Prāsaṅgika-like unobservable emptiness can be found in these works as well, but it is also cast in a rich and malleable language that lends itself to reinterpretation. See, for instance, YM, 624, where Yumo interprets a portion

of a rather ordinary Perfection of Wisdom passage as referring to tantric "esoteric instructions."

85. Again, the recently published *bKa' gdams gsung 'bum* will in the coming years provide us with a much more nuanced view of the currents in philosophy and epistemology in this time period.

86. Note, however, verses 38ff. of Nāgārjuna's *Dharmadhātustava,* which make some cryptic suggestions about the five senses contacting the *dharmadhātu;* see Brunnhölzl, trans., *In Praise of Dharmadhātu,* 121ff.

87. D1350, 200a.4.

88. The verse, as stated in the *Lotus Girl* (D1350, 200a.3), is *gang la dmigs pa dang bcas rdul med stong pa nyid dang snying rje bzang po dmigs med pa.* This presents one of the classic Kālacakra dyads, which more literally could be an emptiness "with reference points" *(dmigs bcas)* and a compassion "with no reference points" *(dmigs med).* An inside joke here is that now it is "compassion" rather than "emptiness" that cannot be observed. This has the dual sense that compassion is really a type of omnipresent bliss that does not arise out of conceptual activity and thus is not a discrete object to be observed (see PC, 200a.7); there is also the sense that a buddha's compassion itself does not reference anyone or anything in particular but is impartial and all-pervasive.

89. YM, 686: *stong nyid mig gis 'dzin gyis rdo rje 'dzin gyi gnas thob shog.* Note that this reading differs from YM-SG.

90. This usage is found throughout the Bön "six lamps" literature, for instance, on ZZNG, 395. Note that the term technically refers to the "three great appearances" of sound, light, and rays. In context, it may thus be better translated as a noun, "higher sights."

91. See the *Twenty-One Nails (gZer bu nyi shu rtsa gcig gi gzhung)* ZZNG, 511, and Gyerpungpa's commentary *(gZer bu nyer gcig gi 'grel pa)* ZZNG, 554ff.

92. MTP, 54.

93. MTP, 129–130.

94. *de kho na nyid kyi cha.*

Chapter 5

1. KCT 4.198 (Bu vol. 1, 96b.7).

2. GDGG, 404.

3. GDGG, 403.

4. *rgyu mi rgyu,* or *rgyu ma rgyu.* See this usage in a quote from the *Root Tantra,* which appears in *Stainless Light* 4.110 (Bu vol. 2, VP ch. 4, 45a.1); see also the *Vajrapāṇi Commentary* passage discussed just below.

5. D0360, 7b.7, verse 145: *rnam pa thams cad rnam pa med.*

6. D1402, 136b.5; cited in YM, 626.

7. *rtog pa dang bral ba ma 'khrul ba.*

8. Though note the above discussions of the five eyes in Kālacakra, and the "gnostic eyes" *(ye shes kyi mig)* in the Great Perfection.

9. *bkab pa dang ma bkab pa'i mig.*

10. As Oliver Sacks puts it, "The brain needs not only perceptual input but perceptual *change,* and the absence of change may cause not only lapses of arousal and

attention but perceptual aberrations as well." See his "Prisoner's Cinema: Sensory Deprivation," in *Hallucinations* (New York: Knopf, 2012), 34.

11. Oliver Sacks discusses these types of "visual monotony" in "Prisoner's Cinema," 33–34.

12. For a primer on floaters, see H. E. White and P. Levatin, "Floaters in the Eye," *Scientific American* 206 (1962): 119–127. White and Levatin (p. 125) note how concentric circular patterns are formed by light refracting around circular debris in the eye, such as stray red blood cells.

13. See S. H. Sinclair et al., "Investigation of the Source of the Blue Field Entoptic Phenomenon," *Investigative Ophthalmology and Visual Science* 30, no. 4 (1989): 668–673. See also C. E. Riva and B. Petrig, "Blue Field Entoptic Phenomenon and Blood Velocity in the Retinal Capillaries," *Journal of the Optical Society of America* 70, no. 10 (1980): 1234–1238.

14. In their "Investigation of the Source of the Blue Field Entoptic Phenomenon," Sinclair et al. note that "the entoptic phenomenon is optimally perceived in the deep blue light spectrum at 430 nm, perhaps because hemoglobin has an absorption peak at this wavelength, which may produce relative dark adaptation of the photoreceptors lying beneath capillaries filled with red blood cells" (pp. 668–669).

15. For the full context, see the translation of Drugyalwa's *Lamps* commentary below, in the description of the "onset of vision," located in chapter 5 (GDGG, 404).

16. See Sacks, "Prisoner's Cinema," 33–34.

17. GDGG, 404.

18. See section 2.3.2.11 in the *Tantra of the Blazing Lamps.* For this type of introduction in a contemporary Hindu context, see Kirin Narayan, *Storytellers, Saints, and Scoundrels: Folk Narrative in Hindu Religious Teaching* (Philadelphia: University of Pennsylvania Press, 1989), 54.

19. *sbrul la rkang lag yod kyang ma gcun na mi gsal ba yin.* See Drugyalwa's *Zhang zhung snyan rgyud kyi khrid rim lag len pa,* in his *Phyag khrid* collection, 618.1. For this saying in a Nyingma context, see MTP, 310: "Without squeezing it, a snake's arms and legs are not evident; if you squeeze it, they come out" *(sbrul gyi rkang lag ma bcus par mi mngon/ gcus pas mngon pa dang 'dra'o/).*

20. For illustrations of the five gazes, see Ian Baker and Thomas Laird, *The Dalai Lama's Secret Temple: Tantric Wall Paintings from Tibet* (New York: Thames and Hudson, 2000), 138ff. See also Tenzin Wangyal, *Nyam Gyü: The Experiential Transmission of Drugyalwa Yungdrung* (Landshut, Germany: Naldjor Institute, 1996), 73ff. For the three gazes, see Namdak, *Heart Drops of Dharmakaya,* 86.

21. *seng ge 'gying ba'i lta stangs;* see GDGG 402.

22. See GDGG, 399.

23. Kālacakra's gazes are discussed in KCT and VP 4.120 (Bu vol. 2, VP ch. 4, 51a.7). See also Norsang Gyatso, *Ornament of Stainless Light* (trans. Kilty), 412, for a discussion of the effects of bodily postures and gazes in the six yogas. In general, in the Kālacakra tradition, such postures are designed to bind the winds in the central channel; when the winds remain in the central channel, they are not coursing through the other channels and propelling ordinary thoughts and sense perceptions.

As one thus withdraws from ordinary sensory and mental activity, visionary experience can begin.

24. For the "wrathful gaze of Uṣṇīṣa" *(gtsug tor gyi kro bo'i lta ba),* see KCT 4.120, and VP (Bu vol. 2, VP ch. 4, 51a.7). For more lengthy comments, see Norsang Gyatso, *Ornament of Stainless Light* (trans. Kilty), 414ff.

25. YM, 667, *nyi tshe ba'i mig.*

26. D1350, 102b.1, cited on YM, 667.

27. This language of the "analogical" and "phenomenological" uses of light is from Matthew Kapstein, "The Strange Death of Pema the Demon Tamer," in *The Presence of Light: Divine Radiance and Religious Experience*, ed. Matthew Kapstein (Chicago: University of Chicago Press, 2004), 127ff.

28. Kapstein, "The Strange Death of Pema the Demon Tamer," 126.

29. *'jig rten gsum ston byed;* KCT 4.118, cited on YM, 653.

30. See in particular his comments about the implication that the world is "like" an illusion, YM, 655.

31. YM, 653, 654, 655.

32. *snang bar byed pa.* See YM, 640 and 646, for the all-pervading Great Seal; see YM, 655, for this all-pervading entity as gnosis.

33. *chos byung.* See YM, 630.

34. See Wallace, *Inner Kālacakra,* 153. For a presentation of the six elements, see Norsang Gyatso, *Ornament of Stainless Light* (trans. Kilty), 173.

35. *'od lnga.*

36. *snang ba'i rtsal lnga.*

37. GDD, 280.

38. These are dimensions of the elements that are "vibrant" in the sense that they are responsible for creating the powers of perception; they contrast with the "solidified" or "coarse" dimensions of the elements that result in the substances (feces, urine, etc.) contained in the body's cavities.

39. GDGG, 282.

Chapter 6

1. The language of "sacramental" versus "yogic" sexuality is from Ronald Davidson; see his discussion in *Indian Esoteric Buddhism: A Social History of the Tantric Movement* (New York: Columbia University Press, 2002), 198, where he also reflects on their domestication and their relationship to visualization.

2. See Davidson's *Indian Esoteric Buddhism,* 198.

3. "Sacramental" sex appears, for instance, in works associated with *Guhyasamāja (gsang ba 'dus pa),* and the *Sarva-buddha-samāyoga (sangs rgyas thams cad dang mnyam par sbyor ba).* See Davidson, *Indian Esoteric Buddhism,* 198.

4. See Davidson's *Indian Esoteric Buddhism,* 198.

5. Bu vol. 2, VP ch. 3, 91b.7ff. (commenting on KCT 3.119).

6. KCT 4.199; note that the translation is based on Yumo (YM, 635) and PC (D1350, 192a.4).

7. My claim here is not that schools identifying themselves as Great Perfection do not practice sexualized yogas in other contexts. Indeed, these groups advocate sexual yogas as a gateway that ultimately may lead to higher practices; further, they are used in the revelation and interpretation of treasures *(gter ma),* and they also may be

used by Great Perfection yogis who simultaneously engage in other forms of tantric practice.

As well, the Great Perfection's path of vision bears the mark of its more conventionally tantric roots, as it contains imagery characteristic of more overtly sexual tantra. That is, while the Great Perfection does not directly represent a sort of visionary consort practice, the maṇḍalas of buddhas that appear in the course of its visions may be based on the tantric two-in-one model, in which a "father and mother" pair of deities appear in union.

8. See the *Tantra of the Blazing Lamps* (TB, 481): *thig ni mi 'gyur drang po la/;* see also MTP, 253, and GN, 492.

9. GN, 492: *thig le rtsa rnams kyis nang nas dran por byung la/.*

10. Note that *thig pa* can be used as a verb, to mean "knowing the measure of things" or "able to apprehend the extent of things" (TDCM: *tshad shes pa'am tshad 'dzin thub pa*), where this has the sense of being able to know or accurately predict how things are.

11. *brdal ba, spyi la khyab pa.* See the *Tantra of the Blazing Lamps* (TB, 481); see also MTP, 254, and GN, 492.

12. See entries for these in Monier-Williams, *A Sanskrit-English Dictionary* (London: Oxford University Press, 1899; Delhi: Motilal Banarsidass, 1990). Note also that *thig-le* is also used to translate similar meanings of the Sanskrit *tilaka,* as in the title of the *Jñānatilaka Tantra (ye shes thig le),* which Yumo frequently cites.

13. *snying khu.*

14. *snying gi thig le.*

15. TDCM, 1159.

16. *stong pa.*

17. *nam mkha'.*

18. See TDCM, 1159.

19. *rdul.*

20. For paintings containing *thig-le,* see Samten Karmay and Jeff Watt, eds., *Bon: The Magic Word* (New York: Rubin Museum of Art, 2007), 69, 181, 89. See also Baker and Laird, *Dalai Lama's Secret Temple,* 138ff. Note that graphic representations of concentric circles called *thig-le* may precede the use of *thig-le* as yogic visionary forms, so that the innovation in the Great Perfection would be the valorization of such visions, their associations with spontaneity, and so forth, rather than the use of the term per se.

21. *zhal yas khang.*

22. *zlum pa.*

23. TB edition, 483.

24. *lus ngag sems ye shes kyi thig le.* Note that these four are also called the "enlightened body, speech, mind, and gnosis *thig-le*" *(sku gsung thugs ye shes kyi thig le),* as well as the "*thig-le* that produce the four periods [of waking, dream, deep sleep, and bliss]" *(gnas skabs rigs bzhi skyed pa'i thig le).* For traditional presentations of the four *thig-le,* see Norsang Gyatso, *Ornament of Stainless Light* (trans. Kilty), 183ff., 395ff.; see also Tenzin Gyatso and Jeffrey Hopkins, *The Kālacakra Tantra,* 120ff., 260ff.

25. KCT 5.115–116 (Bu vol. 1, 127b.1).

26. The VP interprets this last phrase as meaning the "winds enter the central channel" *(dbu mar srog rab tu zhugs pas).*

27. As the VP notes, "channel of time" *(dus kyi rtsa)* simply refers to the central channel, and the black line appears within the *thig-le*, which itself is seen within the central channel. The VP here is not explicit about the relationship between the black line and the buddha image; Norsang Gyatso's summary of these verses suggests that the buddha image appears within the black line, and identifies the buddha as "Vajrasattva and consort in embrace," though other descriptions refer to it as Kālacakra and Viśvamātā; see *Ornament of Stainless Light* (trans. Kilty), 448.

28. See Norsang Gyatso, *Ornament of Stainless Light* (trans. Kilty), 396; see also Wallace, *Inner Kālacakra,* 158.

29. VP 5.120 (Bu vol. 3, VP ch. 5, 48a.1). Note that some presentations of these *thig-le* also array a parallel set of four in the lower half of the body: at the navel wheel (body *thig-le*), secret wheel (speech *thig-le*), center of the sexual organ (mind *thig-le*), and tip of the sexual organ (gnosis *thig-le*); for these, see Norsang Gyatso, *Ornament of Stainless Light* (trans. Kilty), 184, and Tenzin Gyatso and Jeffrey Hopkins, *Kalachakra Tantra,* 120.

30. OSL, 333; also see Kilty's translation of this passage in *Ornament of Stainless Light* (trans. Kilty), 397.

31. Though note here that Norsang Gyatso has the *thig-le* as being "transformed" into buddha-qualities, rather than being "purified."

32. Norsang Gyatso specifies its pure appearances as being "empty-forms" *(stong gzugs)*; see *Ornament of Stainless Light,* 334.

33. *sems mi gsal zhing mi rtog,* "minds that are unclear and nonconceptual" (see Norsang Gyatso, OSL, 333). This *thig-le* is responsible for nonconceptual minds, either ones that are confused (such as in deep sleep) or ones that are transcendent.

34. *gnas skabs bzhi.*

35. VP 5.120 (Bu vol. 3, VP ch. 5, 48a.1).

36. Just to suggest some of the variety here, a few of the more common classifications are:

Twofold groups: (1) conventional *thig-le (kun rdzob thig le)* and (2) ultimate *thig-le (don dam thig le)*; see the *Tantra of Unimpeded Sound,* 63.2. Note the similar Bön classification found in *Advice on the Six Lamps,* 281.3: (1) coarse bodily-constituent *thig-le (snyigs ma lus zungs kyi thig le),* and (2) vibrant mental *thig-le (dwangs ma sems kyi thig le).*

Threefold groups: (1) conventional *thig-le (kun rdzob thig le),* found in the right channel, (2) ultimate *thig-le (don dam thig le),* found in the central channel, and (3) natural *thig-le (rang bzhin thig le),* found in the left channel. See the *Garland of Precious Pearls Tantra,* 495.2.

Fourfold groups: (1) the excellent *thig-le* of the ground *(gzhi yi thig le bzang po),* (2) the excellent *thig-le* of the path *(lam gyi thig le bzang po),* (3) the peak of excellences *thig-le (bzang po rnams kyi rtse mo),* (4) the *thig-le* ornamented with excellences *(bzang po'i rgyan dang ldan pa);* see the *Tantra of the Blazing Lamps,* TB, 483.1.

Fivefold groups: In addition to the fivefold classification I discuss later in this chapter, MTP (262–263) mentions: (1) the excellent *thig-le* of the ground *(gzhi'i thig le bzang po),* (2) the excellent *thig-le* of the path *(lam gyi thig le bzang po),* (3) the excellent-excellent *thig-le (bzang po'i bzang po),* (4) the *thig-le* endowed with the eight excellences *(bzang po rgyan dang ldan pa'i thig le),* and (5) the *thig-le* of the excellent peak *(bzang po'i rtse mo'i thig le).*

Sixfold groups: (1) the all-good *thig-le (kun tu bzang po'i thig le),* (2) the *thig-le* of reality itself *(chos nyid kyi thig le),* (3) the *thig-le* of the expanse *(dbyings kyi thig le),* (4) the *thig-le* of the completely pure expanse *(dbyings rnam par dag pa'i thig le),* (5) the *thig-le* of primordial gnosis *(ye shes kyi thig le),* and (6) the *thig-le* of the great primordial gnosis *(ye shes chen po'i thig le);* see MTP 261. Note also the Bön work entitled *Esoteric Instructions on the Six Thig-le (Thig le drug pa'i man ngag),* found in the NR edition of the *bKa' rgyud skor bzhi;* these are the six lamps, with each lamp styled as a *thig-le.*

For a summary of various classifications of *thig-le* in the Seminal Heart tradition, see TDD chapter 5, an English translation of which can be found in David Germano, "Poetic Thought," 270ff.

37. See the above note on "twofold" classifications of *thig-le.*

38. See, for instance, Longchenpa's comments in TDD 5, translated in Germano, "Poetic Thought," 274.

39. *Rñiṅ ma'i rgyud bcu bdun* (New Delhi: Sanje Dorje, 1977), vol. 1, 63.2. Also see Germano's translation of this passage in "Poetic Thought," 274.

40. See chapter 3, question 3 of the tantra (TB edition, 481); also see the comments on this found on MTP, 260ff. The passage here is from TB, 483. The five *thig-le,* in order, are *gzhi gnas rang gi thig le, lus gnas rtsa yi thig le, kun rdzob rgyu yi thig le, don dam spros med thig le,* and *rang byung 'bras bu'i thig le.*

41. ZZNG, 403–404.

42. See KCT verse 4.195 for "garlands of *thig-le*" *(thig le'i phreng ba)* in Kālacakra day-yoga.

43. ZZNG, 403: *gzugs sku'i sa bon zhing khams kyi 'char gzhi.*

44. Bu vol. 1, VP ch. 1, 4b.3.

45. GN, 487–488: *de la thig dgod par byed pa ste/ don dam dang kun rdzob gnyis su byung la/ le 'dzin par byed pa ste/ kun rdzob kyis 'khor ba 'dzin la/ don dam gyis 'das pa 'dzin par byed pa'o/.*

46. *dgod par byed.*

47. Here again, it is important not to overemphasize the line between intellectualized sexuality and actual consort practice, especially as practitioners might denigrate sexual practices in one context but then engage in them in other contexts. Note, for instance, that Gyalwa Yeshé's biography of Yumo mentions Yumo receiving the Kālacakra initiation "using ten secret-mantra yoginī action-seals."

Translation 1

1. This is available at the Tibetan Buddhist Resource Center (TBRC) as part of the collection *Jo nang dpe rnying phyogs bsgrigs* (W00KG0638). (The title here is simply a modern title given to a collection of old manuscripts for purposes of distribution; it does not represent a traditional, organized collection or cycle of works.) Many thanks to Michael Sheehy for providing me with a copy of this.

2. This is contained in the collection *Yu mo'i gsal sgron rnam bzhi dang 'bro b'ai gsung sgros rgyas pa 'od zer phreng ba sogs,* which is part of the Jonang Publication Series (Jo nang dpe tshogs), series III, vol. 25 (Beijing: Mi rigs dpe skrun khang, 2010). The annotations here appear to reproduce the interlinear comments from the YM edition (which are often difficult to read in the manuscript).

3. The translation of KCT that Yumo used is quite similar to the KCT verses that are preserved in the commentary to *Stainless Light* called *Pad ma can* (D1350); this commentary, however, does not contain the complete text of KCT. Still, renderings of KCT verses that match Yumo's can occasionally be found there. Though this work is said to have been translated by Somanātha, the root verses from the *Kālacakra Tantra* that appear in it are rather different from the existing Somanātha-based translations of the tantra.

4. Throughout his four treatises, Yumo states that his good qualities and his ability to write authoritatively on the tantras are based on the kindness of an unnamed "Jetsün" (*rje btsun,* "foremost among the noble ones"). The epithet most probably refers to Yumo's principal teacher, 'Gro-mgon-gnam-la-rtsegs.

5. Reading from YM-SG; YM has "five bodies."

6. The "six parameters" *(mtha' drug)* is a set of six categories used for classifying tantric literature. These indicate whether a particular work (1) expresses itself through profound language or (2) does not; (3) uses terms that can be taken as they are (i.e., literally) or (4) does not (i.e., that uses terms symbolically); and expresses (5) the provisional meaning or (6) the definitive meaning. Yumo states the first parameter simply as *dgongs* (literally "intent"), though the term is usually seen as *dgongs skad* (literally "intent-language"). As Thurman has noted, works included in the first two parameters all "intend" to convey the ultimate meaning, so the sense is not really "intentional speech." Rather, the distinction is the notion that (parameter 1) students of greater ability are taught with profound, paradoxical, or mysterious language, whereas (parameter 2) students of lesser ability are taught with ordinary explanations. Thurman translates these as (1) "ulterior" statements and (2) "non-ulterior" or "ingenuous" statements. See Robert A. F. Thurman, "Vajra Hermeneutics," in *Buddhist Hermeneutics,* ed. Donald Lopez (Honolulu: University of Hawai'i Press, 1988), 137ff. For a traditional presentation of the six parameters, see the *Gnosis Vajra Compendium Tantra* (D0447, 284a.5).

7. That is, "secret mantra."

8. Both YM and YM-SG state that is from the *Supplement to the Kālacakra Tantra* (D0363); in fact, it is from the *Supplement to the Guhyasamāja Tantra* (D0443, 155b.3). The repetition of this error is one of several clues suggesting that YM and YM-SG are closely related. My reading of the passage is based on *The Guhyasamāja Commentary (dpal gsang ba 'dus pa'i rgyud kyi rgyud 'grel pa),* D1784, 316a.4.

9. In context, this refers to having understood the different classes of the Buddha's teaching, and then following the tantric path. An annotation in YM suggests it also refers to understanding the six yogas, after having obtained teachings on them.

10. This is from the *Nāmasaṃgīti* (D0360, 7b.1, verse 135). One of the main affinities between the Kālacakra tradition and the *Nāmasaṃgīti* is that the latter

appears to advocate a "gnosis body" *(jñānakāya, ye shes sku)* as being the final attainment of a buddha. See Wallace, *Inner Kālacakra,* 18.

11. This is verse II.69 from the *Five Stages* (D1802, 50b.7).

12. This is verse III.11 from the *Five Stages* (D1802, 52a.7). For this verse, I referred to Nāgabodhi's commentary *Garland of Jewels* (D1840, 117a.4).

13. Note how Yumo seems to hold up the Guhyasamāja "stage of self-blessing" as being at the pinnacle of tantric practice, i.e., equal with the Kālacakra yogas.

14. D0442, 97a.7.

15. *smig ma mkhan,* or *smyig ma mkhan.* I have not found this term in any lexicons (and it is misspelled in both YM and YM-SG). My translation is based on Newman ("Outer Wheel of Time," 263 n. 9), who translates a similar passage from the first chapter of VP.

16. This is verse III.12 from the *Five Stages* (D1802, 52b.1). For this verse, I referred to the *Garland of Jewels* commentary (D1840, 117a.6).

17. D1348, 10a.6.

18. D0417 (II.ii.49).

19. Snellgrove notes a passage from Bhadrapāda's *Hevajra* commentary, which explains that one cure for a burn is to rub oil on it, and keep it near a fire, so that fire is healed by fire. See David Snellgrove, *The Hevajra Tantra: A Critical Study* (London: Oxford University Press, 1959), vol. 1, 93 n. 1. A similar example appears in the section of the *Hevajra Tantra* just preceding Yumo's citation, which mentions how flatulence can be cured by eating beans.

20. D0443, 980.1.

21. D0443, 151b.1. The first quotation is from the section of the *Supplement* where questions are posed to the teacher. The answer is from the main body of the work, where the teacher gives his replies.

22. This phrase is from YM-SG; it is omitted in YM.

23. D0443, 151b.2.

24. Yumo's source for this is probably VP 1.2 (Bu vol. 1, VP ch. 1, 19b.3), where it is quoted as the word of "the Tathāgata." In the VP, the statement is used to indicate how the *Kālacakra Tantra* contains information (particularly about the "fourth" initiation) that helps to clarify cryptic passages in other tantras. Thus, one tantra can be understood by studying other tantras.

25. D0417, 2a.3 (I.i.6). This and the following quote are from the tantra's introductory scene, where Vajragarbha is asking his initial questions to the Teacher.

26. Both editions seem corrupt here; I translate somewhat loosely from YM-SG but emend the Tibetan *"shes"* to *"he"*: *rdo rje ni stong pa nyid shes ni bod pa nyid do/ thams cad skyob ni dgyes pa ste snying rje chen po'o/.*

27. D0417. Below is a rather complicated use of the term *gleng gzhi,* which is based on Yumo's reading of the *Hevajra Tantra.* The term *gleng gzhi* is most commonly used to refer to the "introductory scene" of a tantra, the scene at the beginning of a tantra where the stage is set, the characters are introduced, the basic questions of the tantra are posed, and so forth. However, *gleng gzhi* can also have the sense of "subject matter" (see TDCM's definition *gros mol gyi don gtso bo,* the "main topic of a discussion"), or can indicate "basis," the "basis of expression," or the "basic facts that impel a teaching."

The passages under discussion here are not from the introductory scene of the *Hevajra Tantra* but are from a chapter in the middle of the work (II.iii), the "Basis of All Tantras" or the "Basis of Explanation of All Tantras" *(rgyud thams cad kyi gleng gzhi).* The general idea of this chapter is that the "basis of all tantras," the basic subject matter that they seek to express, is union: two deities being united as one, or the unity of insight and compassion. To complicate matters, one way of describing that "basis" *(gleng gzhi)* is through referring to the two syllables E-VAM, the syllables that typically begin the "introductory scene" *(gleng gzhi)* of many tantras, in the phrase "Thus I have heard" *(evam mayā śrutam).* The essential point is that the first two syllables of a tantra can themselves be seen as indicating the basic teaching of the entire tantra: the union of insight and compassion (where E indicates insight or emptiness, and VAM indicates compassion).

28. D0417. II.iii, 53 in Snellgrove's edition.

29. Bu vol. 1, VP ch. 1, 37b.2 (commenting on KCT 1.1).

30. *dmigs pa med pa'i snying rje.* Literally compassion that does not "reference" or "objectify" any object, meaning that it is both nonconceptual and impartial. See Newman, "Outer Wheel of Time," 270, for a passage from VP explaining this term.

31. Note that Bu has Samāja *('dus pa)* instead of Māyajala *(sgyu 'phrul dra ba).*

32. *gtan la phab pa.*

33. *de ltar yin na nyan thos pa dag gi grub pa'i mtha' rnam pa gsum yod par 'dod pas rdul phra rab bsgom par thal lo/.* The difficult nature of this sentence is highlighted by the discrepancies between YM and YM-SG, and the annotations that appear in YM where a reader was working to understand. (YM-SG has *de ltar yin na nyan thos pa dag gis grub pa'i mtha'/ mtha' rnam pa gsum yod par 'dod la rdul phra rab bsgom par thal lo/*). Yumo does not detail what the "three tenets of the hearers" might be; annotations in YM specify them as "atomic particles, letters, and momentariness" *(rdul dang yi ge dang skad cig ma),* though this does little to clarify the matter. Typically discussions of the existence of atomic particles reference the tenets of the Vaibhāṣika, who are said to hold that all things are collections of irreducible atomic particles. Buddhist tenet literature often portrays Vaibhāṣikas as accepting ultimate truths as things that can bear analysis. Because mental analysis can go no further than those partless particles, they are said to be ultimate truths, and as such, ultimate truths are substantially existent *(rdzas yod).* See Jeffrey Hopkins, *Meditation on Emptiness* (London: Wisdom Publications, 1983), 337ff. For comments in *Stainless Light* on the Vaibhāṣika view, see VP 2.173.

34. The first noble truth, the truth of suffering *(sdug bsngal bden pa),* is often explained as having four aspects: the truths of (1) suffering *(sdug bsngal ba),* (2) impermanence *(mi rtag pa),* (3) being empty *(stong pa),* and (4) having no-self *(bdag med pa).* The assertion of a permanent or substantial existence would contradict these.

35. D3709, 43a.2. The last line here is literally "The remaining meditations are [for] that purpose" *(sgom pa lhag ma de don yin).* Jñānakīrti's comments suggest the connotation of "various" or "all other."

36. *gtan la phab pa'i stong pa nyid.*

37. *lam du 'gyur pa'i stong pa nyid bsgoms nas grol bar 'gyur ro/.* Yumo does not specify a source for this important quotation, nor does he clearly indicate its

beginning point. The passage appears to be a paraphrase of *Entry into Suchness* (D3709, 75a.5), though only the term "emptiness" appears there, not the critical phrase "emptiness that is a path" *(lam du 'gyur pa'i stong pa nyid):* "In the aim of engaging with the Great Seal, one does not contradict the path of meditation that is free of desire [i.e., ordinary non-tantric meditation]. As it is said: 'Liberation comes about through meditating on emptiness. The other meditations are all for the sake of that'" *(phyag rgya chen po la 'jug pa'i don du 'dod chags bral ba'i lam bsgom pa ni 'gal ba med de/ stong nyid bsgoms pas grol 'gyur te/ /bsgom pa lhag ma de don yin/ /zhes bshad pa yin no/ /).* Thus this might be read as Yumo adding his phrase "that is a path" as a comment onto the words of his source.

38. These are verses II.53–55 of Nāgārjuna's *Five Stages* (D1802, 50a.4); the *Five Stages* cites these as coming from the *Lalitavistara Sūtra* (D0095). These lines, however, do not appear in the extant version of that sūtra, and given its tantric content, the claim of its source is doubtful.

The passage presents a narrative that became popular beginning with the Yoga Tantras: the Buddha is urged to abandon a normative Buddhist practice and is given a tantric initiation that allows him to attain enlightenment. Yumo mentions the most famous of such passages just below (the *Tattvasaṃgraha,* D0479). A brief version also appears in Āryadeva's *Lamp Integrating the Practices;* see Wedemeyer's translation, 262. Wedemeyer mentions two more such passages: Ratnākaraśānti's commentary on Nāgārjuna's *Piṇḍīkṛtasādhana* (D1796, 1b.4–2b.4) and Khedrup Jé's version, found in Ferdinand D. Lessing and Alex Wayman, trans., *Mkhas Grub Rje's Fundamentals of the Buddhist Tantras* (The Hague: Mouton, 1968), 34–39.

39. I follow the *Garland of Jewels* commentary (D1840) here, which better reflects the Sanskrit with *mkha' dbyings gnas pa'i rgyal ba yis*. Yumo has *de tshe rgyal ba mkha' rdo rje* (as does Mimaki and Tomabechi's edition).

40. *'od gsal ba,* a reference to the most fundamental level of mind in the Guhyasamāja tradition.

41. This is a way of referring to Puṇḍarīka, the author of *Stainless Light.*

42. That is, it is merely an absence.

43. Yumo is rather cryptic here, and it is difficult to discern his meaning; some annotations in the YM edition attest to this, suggesting that an educated reader was struggling to make sense of this passage. Read straightforwardly, Yumo's words simply state, "A buddha's gnosis is a conventional truth" *(sangs rgyas kyi ye shes ni kun rdzob kyi bden pa ste).*

I suspect what is happening is that Yumo is referring to the Guhyasamāja stage of "self-blessing," which is also called "conventional truth" or "superficial reality" *(kun rdzob kyi bden pa).* As presented in chapter 6 of Āryadeva's *Lamp Integrating the Practices,* this is the stage where one attempts to transform one's body into a deity body that is devoid of atoms and produced "through mere gnosis." This would fit with Yumo's previous comments emphasizing the necessity for appearance and experience. See Wedemeyer's translation, *Āryadeva's Lamp that Integrates the Practices,* and also Yumo's citations on YM, 651 and 671.

However, the annotations in YM state that gnosis is conventional truth "from the perspective of conceptual thought" *(rtog pa'i [s]go nas).* I interpret this as suggesting that a buddha's gnosis is capable of taking a conceptual perspective on the world (i.e., seeing what ordinary beings see), but it understands that the objects it perceives are not intrinsically established. Further, Yumo seems to be saying that presentations of the ultimate as an "emptiness of inherent nature" are merely intellectual, and thus may be part of the buddha's "understanding" but not part of his "experience."

44. Again, Yumo's point is not entirely clear, so I have simply translated this literally. Should Yumo be discussing the Guhyasamāja stage of self-blessing, this might be "If something were to become [such an] object on that [stage of self-blessing], it would be unsuitable for it to be intrinsically established, because it is established as an object [composed] of gnosis."

An alternative reading could be formulated based on the annotations in YM, which say: "Buddha's conventionalities appear as false. But sentient beings' conventionalities have the characteristic of being deceptive" *(sangs rgyas kyi kun rdzob ni rdzun par snang pa yin la/ sems can kyi kun rdzob ni slu ba'i mtshan nyid do/)*. That is, buddhas are not isolated from conventionalities, but conventionalities appear to them as falsities, and thus are not properly "objects" of a buddha's gnosis.

45. D0419, 31a6.

46. Citation not located.

47. That is, if one had an inherent nature, then one's nature could not turn into that of a buddha.

48. Citation not located, though it does resemble MMK 24.14.

49. Citation not located.

50. *lam du 'gyur pa'i stong pa nyid.* Here Yumo is not as explicit about how this path-emptiness differs from the emptiness he deprecates as the "view." As he makes clear below, the path-emptiness is one that can become an object of the eyes.

51. These are verses V.26–28 from the *Five Stages* (D1802, 56b.1). The editions of Yumo's *Lamp* have several errors here, so I have relied on Dergé, as well as Mimaki and Tomabechi's edition; I have also used the *Garland of Jewels* commentary (D1840, 154a.1) particularly for verse 28.

52. According to PKṬYM, this verse provides synonyms for the "stage of communion" *(zung du 'jug pa'i rim pa),* the idea being that all these become integrated at that stage.

53. I.e., the stage of communion (PKṬYM, 155a.1).

54. According to PKṬYM, via realizing the stage of communion.

55. D1350, 79b.5. This is from the *Padminī-nāma-pañjikā (Padma can zhes bya ba'i dka 'grel),* D1350, a commentary attributed to Kālacakrapāda that explains the "difficult points" of *Stainless Light.* The title in Tibetan is literally *Lotus Endowed,* an epithet often used for the deity Avalokiteśvara, who is depicted holding a lotus (in the Kālacakra tradition, Puṇḍarīka, the author of *Stainless Light,* is thought to be an emanation of Avalokiteśvara). In Yumo's extensive citations from this work, he is almost exclusively interested in passages describing the Great Consort, the most excellent of women, who is well endowed with the "lotus" (i.e., *bhaga*) that leads to the attainment of unchanging bliss. In the context of Yumo's work, I thus translate the title as *Lotus Girl,* based on the usage of *padminī* as "excellent woman"; see Monier-Williams's entry for this term: "an excellent woman, a woman belonging to the first of the four classes into which the sex is divided." Such typologies of

women also feature in tantric classifications of consorts. See TDD, 214–215, for an example of such a classification, the members there being *dung can ma, glang sna can ma, pad+ma can, ri dwags can, ba glang can;* in this typology, the "lotus endowed" consort is one whose special ability is the production of bliss in the body of the yogi.

The passage here is commenting on an opening verse of praise in *Stainless Light* (Bu vol. 1, VP ch. 1, 2a.1). The verses briefly state the objects purified by different kinds of "gnosis": one's speech is purified by the "wishless gnosis," one's "mind" is purified by the "signless gnosis," and one's "gnosis" is purified by the "emptiness gnosis." This last statement is what is being commented on here; the root verse (according to PC) reads: "Purified by the 'emptiness gnosis,' / [Cognition becomes] completely pure, unchanging gnosis."

56. D1402, 136b.5. This is from Vajrapāṇi's commentary to the *Cakrasaṃvara Tantra (mngon par brjod pa 'bum pa las phyung pa nyung ba'i rgyud kyi bsdus pa'i don rnam par bshad pa).* The passage in Yumo is based on a different translation than the one in Dergé and also seems corrupt. Material in brackets is added based on Dergé.

The passage also needs more context to be understood clearly, so here I provide it with just a few more sentences from the text itself:

> Vajra-words like "Having all aspects, having no aspects" [express] the definitive meaning. Here, "Having all aspects, having no aspects" refers to the "unmoving," i.e., that which is seen via withdrawal [yoga]: things like pots, friezes, and so forth that appear in the manner of [the images that arise in] a mirror divination. "Having all aspects" refers to their being known through being seen via direct perception, which is free from conceptuality and unmistaken. "Having no aspects" refers to them as transcending atomic nature, [and thus being known] through that same freedom from conceptuality. Because they are objects realized by [both] covered and uncovered eyes, they are not form, but they are also not something that is other than form. They are not objects realized by the eyes, but they are also not objects that are realized without the eyes. In that way, "Having all aspects, having no aspects" [also] refers to the "moving," i.e., to the great [goddess] Prajñāpāramitā, emptiness endowed with all supreme aspects.

Here, "Having all aspects, having no aspects" *(rnam pa thams cad rnam pa med)* is from the *Nāmasaṃgiti* (D0360, 7b.7, verse 145). "Moving and unmoving" *(rgyu ma rgyu)* is a phrase sometimes used to refer to the visual forms that appear to a yogi "withdrawal yoga"; see this usage in a quote from the *Root Tantra,* which appears in *Stainless Light* 4.110 (Bu vol. 2, VP ch. 4, 45a.1). Note also the similarities between this passage and VP's comments on KCT 5.127 (Bu vol. 3, VP ch. 5, 52a.4).

57. Bu vol. 3, VP ch. 5, 54b.2 (commenting on KCT 5.127).

58. KCT 4.198 (Bu vol. 1, 96b.7). The rest of the *Lamp Illuminating Emptiness* is an extended commentary on this verse. In my translation here, I try to render the passage as closely as possible to the way that it appears in Yumo. The translation of the *Kālacakra Tantra* that Yumo worked from was very similar, perhaps identical, to that found in Kālacakrapāda's *Lotus Girl* (D1350, 191a.2). I have relied on that

commentary to resolve areas where the wording in YM and YM-SG seems to be mistaken, particularly the last line.

59. "Seal" here has the sense of a "stamp of authenticity," like the kind of unique seal or stamp held only by a king. Unchanging bliss and so forth are the authenticating features that arise from practicing sexual yoga with the "Great Seal," and which would not arise from union with lesser consorts.

60. Note that "root" tantra refers to the *Paramādibuddha-tantra.* The tantra is not extant, but tradition holds that the *Sekoddeśa (dbang mdor bstan pa)* was once part of it. This passage can be found there (D0361, verses 146–147, 19b.7). Note that this passage is also cited in chapter 2 of PC (p. 43b.4). Yumo's rendering has a few errors, so I read from text B in Orofino's edition, which is very close to Yumo's source. See also the VP on KCT 2.53 for comments similar to this verse.

61. Kālacakrapāda is the author of *The Lotus Girl* (D1350); the passage here can be found on 191a.2. The passage is commenting on KCT 4.198, the verse under discussion by Yumo. Underlined words in the passage are from the KCT verse. I rely on Dergé here to correct mistakes in Yumo.

62. *stong pa nyid kyi gzugs;* this is another way of saying "empty-form" *(stong gzugs)* and corresponds more closely to the normative Sanskrit *śūnyatābimba.* In later Tibetan literature, this form is less common than the simple *stong gzugs,* but it appears frequently here in Yumo.

63. D1350, 83a.6. This is commenting on a famous series of verses (also cited Yumo, on YM, 636) that are found at the beginning of *Stainless Light* (Bu vol. 1, VP ch. 1, 2a.7): "Having cast away the "action" seal, / And abandoned the "gnostic" seal, / Pure [bliss] arises from the Great Seal!" *(las kyi phyag rgya yongs dor zhing/ /ye shes phyag rgya rnam par spangs/ /phyag rgya che las yang dag skyes/ /).* Yumo here extracts Kālacakrapāda's comments on the third line, describing the Great Seal.

64. This is referring to *The Root Tantra.* The verses can be found in the *Sekoddeśa* (D0361, verses 21–22, 15b.6). Orofino's edition of the *Sekoddeśa* is quite helpful here, as Yumo's citation differs significantly from the two editions that she compares. I have based my translation on Yumo. The verses here are one of the classic locations in which the "fourth" initiation is discussed. The fourth initiation in Kālacakra is said to be experienced not by generating bliss with an "action" seal or a "gnostic" seal, but by experiencing the "unchanging" bliss with the Great Seal, who is an empty-form, endowed with all aspects. This is all quite difficult to discern in this passage, particularly because it is similar to the Rwa-chos-rab translation, which (as Orofino notes in her edition, 39ff.) seems to confuse "unchanging" or "unwavering" *(niḥspanda, mi g.yo ba)* with "similar to its cause" *(niṣyanda, rgyu 'thun pa).* Thus in the first verse (verse 21), what is rendered here as "similar cause" might be thought of as "unchanging." The 'Bro translation (which does not bear this confusion) reads much more simply: "From desire for the Great Seal / Arises the unmoving bliss. / This is the conferral of the 'great insight' initiation, / From which comes unwavering understanding." One way out of this would be to note that the "four joys" are occasionally referred to as types of "effect," and the first of these joys, associated with the navel region, is indeed referred to as "an effect similar

to its cause"; see Khedrup Norsang Gyatso's *Ornament of Stainless Light* (trans. Kilty), 375 and 669 n. 382, for mentions of this. It is possible, then, that readers like Yumo would understand this passage as referring in particular to that joy. Still, I tend to agree with Orofino's suggestion that this is simply a pervasive error. Note that Kilty's translation *Ornament of Stainless Light* (263) is also quite helpful on this passage, as it translates Naropa's comments.

65. Bu vol. 1, VP ch. 1, 2b.2 (this is in the initial praises that begin the VP).

66. Citation not located. What I have translated here as "ornaments" is *mtshan ma,* which I am taking as *vyañjana* ("sign," "badge," or "conceptual mark"). It might also be *nimitta,* suggesting that giving and so forth are simply "instrumental causes." Regardless, the point is that enlightenment ultimately comes from the *dharmadhātu,* not from activities like performing virtuous deeds. In Yumo's reading, *dharmadhātu (chos kyi dbyings)* is also a veiled reference to the Great Seal.

67. Yumo here is slowly building up a group of associations, in which he equates the meanings of "Great Seal" as "emptiness" and "Great Consort." Thus a host of key terms (Prajñāpāramitā, *dharmadhātu,* the mother of the buddhas, and so forth) are all suggested to refer to the visionary consort known as the Great Seal. An objector here suggests that "Great Seal" is simply a philosophical term referring to emptiness, the *dharmadhātu,* the abiding reality of things, and so forth. For Yumo, however, all these terms are code for the visionary Great Seal, an emptiness that has the ability to become the path, to be seen by the eyes.

68. This refers to the VP's lengthy comments on KCT 5.127; the citation here can be found on Bu vol. 3, VP ch. 5, 72b.5. Both YM and YM-SG seem confused on the last sentence, leading me to rely partially on Bu.

The term *dharmodaya (chos kyi 'byung gnas, or chos 'byung)* is literally "source of phenomena" but has the connotation of "vulva" (*mo mtshan;* see TDCM). It is also used as a technical tantric term, referring to a triangular diagram that is used to indicate the source of a maṇḍala or of a deity.

69. Bu vol. 1, VP ch. 1, 37a.5 (commenting on KCT 1.1). In the first line, I prefer Bu's *bud med dang* instead of YM and YM-SG's *bud med na.* Note also that in the closing line, Bu has the "emptiness of the ones with all aspects" *(rnam pa thams cad pa'i stong pa nyid)* instead of the "emptiness of all the omniscient ones" *(thams cad mkhyen pa'i stong pa nyid).*

70. *E* is the first syllable in *E-VAM* ("thus"), which is typically the first word in a sūtra or tantra, and thus the initial "source" of the teaching. *E* is often described as the feminine syllable (and thus having associations with insight and emptiness), while *VAM* is masculine (representing method, compassion, and so forth).

71. *Ye shes rdo rje kun las btus pa* (D0447, 284b.3). This is one of the main explanatory tantras related to the *Guhyasamāja Tantra.* YM and YM-SG are identical here, but both are slightly mistaken, so I read from Dergé. The context here is an explanation of the "six parameters" *(mtha' drug),* two of which are "conventional meaning" and "ultimate meaning." The tantra says that the term "lotus" is conventional, while its ultimate meanings are the following list of terms. YM and YM-SG mistakenly state that "lotus" is one of the definitive terms.

72. D0447, 283a.1. Again, I read from Dergé. Yumo is evidently just using this citation for the associations it makes between woman, lotus, and so forth. The passage is not talking about the Great Seal but is talking about one of the three levels

of mind *(rnam par shes pa gsum = snang ba gsum)* described in Guhyasamāja, called "luminance" *(snang ba).* It is said that this level of mind can result in the appearances of goddesses and so forth (while the level *snang ba mched pa,* for instance, results in the appearances of gods, vajras, and so forth).

73. This refers to a commentary on the *Cakrasaṃvara Tantra* attributed to Vajrapāṇi (D1402), which is one of the "three bodhisattva commentaries." The citation is from 81b.4. The context here does not directly reference the Great Seal; the commentary is discussing tantric synonyms, much like in the other sources Yumo quotes, and lists some synonyms for *bhaga* as a site where a tantric teaching might take place. The basis of the discussion is the famous opening line of the *Hevajra Tantra* saying that the Transcendent Victor was "dwelling in the *bhaga*" of his consort. "Basis" here refers to the *bhaga;* this is contrasted to the "based," which refers to bliss.

74. D1402, 81b.6. *The Vajrapāṇi Commentary* suggests that these are lines from the *Litany of Names of Mañjuśrī* (D0360), though they do not appear in the extant version of that work.

75. D0361, 15a.3 (verse 27). Orofino treats this and the following verses at length in her article "Divination with Mirrors." From her comparison of the two existing translations of the verses (p. 20), it is clear that the verses here in Yumo are related to the translation of Samantaśri rather than Somanātha.

76. D0361, 15a.6 (verses 32–34).

77. I.e., the officiant of the ceremony goes to the place that the young girl saw in the mirror, and then sees in reality what appeared in the mirror.

78. This is speculating on the nature of the image that the girl sees in the mirror. One way that the divination can go wrong is if the girl looks into the mirror and does not see a self-arisen image but just sees her own face. So, the idea is that if the image in the mirror were just an ordinary existent (rather than a miraculous appearance), it would just be an image of her face. If the image that appears was nonexistent, then it could be something random, like a rabbit with horns.

79. D0361, 20a.3 (verse 150).

80. *dPal phyag rgya chen po'i thig le zhes bya ba rnal 'byor ma chen mo'i rgyud kyi rgyal po'i mnga' bdag;* D0420, 89b.4.

81. Bu vol. 1, VP ch. 1, 2b.2.

82. D0420, 72b.2. I follow Dergé, as Yumo has some obvious errors and leaves out the second line.

83. I follow YM-SG for this sentence.

84. *dmigs pa dang bcas pa'i stong pa nyid.* Literally, "emptiness with reference points." Note how this contrasts with "compassion without reference points" *(dmigs pa med pa'i snying rje).* See *The Vajrapāṇi Commentary* (D1402, 124b.1) for a passage mentioning this dyad.

85. D1350, 213a.1. The passage here is commenting on KCT 5.112d, which briefly characterizes the transcendent initiations *('jig rten las 'das pa'i dbang)*; words in quotes represent root text from the KCT. The extract that Yumo provides is easier to understand if more of the passage is given: "[As I have just explained the worldly initiation, now] you might wonder, what is the transcendent initiation? This is expressed in [KCT 5.112d]: 'The transcendent initiation is desiring the excellent consort of the Supreme Lord of Conquerors.' Here, 'conquerors' refers to...."

Note that in Bu, KCT 5.112d has the more explicit "uniting with" instead of "desiring."

86. Here I have emended Yumo, which states that the verse is KCT 4.24. In fact, it is KCT 4.199 (Bu vol. 1, 97a.6). Yumo's citation also contains quite a few errors, so I have relied on the verse as it appears in *The Lotus Girl,* as this seems to be quite close to Yumo's source.

87. *ba thag.* I am unclear on the referent of this term; Yumo also uses it in his concluding verses on YM, 689. The YM-SG edition replaces *ba thag dang gtum mo* with *mthar thug gtum mo,* the "ultimate mystic fire."

88. *rtog pas ma rtags par mthong ba bzhin lam du shes par bya'o.*

89. This appears to be a variant of the passage appearing on Bu vol. 1, VP ch. 1, 5a.3 (in the initial praises and aphorisms that begin chapter 1 of the VP).

90. Bu vol. 1, VP ch. 1, 2a.7 (this is in the initial praises and aphorisms that begin chapter 1). I follow Bu for the third line of the first verse (reading *phyag rgya che las*) and for the third line of the second verse (reading *dbyings dag dang*). I keep Yumo's reading of the last two lines; he associates the gandharva city and the prognostic image with the Great Seal (by using the feminine *rang bzhin ma* instead of Bu's *rang bzhin can*). Bu seems to take them as referring to "bliss."

91. D0361, 15a.4 (verse 28). Yumo's source is very close to Orofino's Rwa edition. Orofino notes that in the third line "in the emptiness" should be "in the image" (with Tibetan translators reading *śūnye* instead of *bimbe*); see her "Divination with Mirrors," 619 n. 3, and her edition of the *Sekoddeśa,* 133 n. 28. I translate the passage as it appears in the Tibetan, adding interpolations based on how I think Yumo was using it in this context.

92. Bu vol. 1, VP ch. 1, 22a.5. Note also a similar discussion in *The Vajrapāṇi Commentary* (D1402, 125a.7). Bu annotates "experience of the desire [realm]" *('dod na spyod pa)* with "ejaculation produced through the two [sexual] organs"; "characteristic of the form existence" *(gzugs gyi srid pa'i mtshan nyid)* is annotated as "according to Vajrapāṇi, 'moving' bliss."

93. This is likely a reference to a brief work in the *dhāraṇi* section of the Kanguyr, a short prayer intended to bring worldly benefits: *Shis par brjod pa'i tshigs su bcad pa* (D1107). That prayer is taken from the *Lalitavistara Sūtra,* from the chapter dealing with the two merchants Trapuṣa and Bhallika (Ga-gon or Kha-mgon, and bZang-po), who are said to be the earliest lay disciples of the Buddha. Tradition says that the Buddha gave Trapuṣa and Bhallika eight of his hairs to venerate as relics, which would fit with Yumo's point here. For a translation of the story of these merchants, taken from the *Manorathapūranī,* see John Strong, *The Experience of Buddhism: Sources and Interpretations* (Belmont, CA: Wadsworth, 2002), 45ff. For more comments and references, see Strong's *Relics of the Buddha* (Princeton, NJ: Princeton University Press, 2004), 73ff.

94. D0418, 21a.1 (verse II.iv.41–47). Yumo's reference to the "latter part" *(dPal dgyes pa'i rdo rje [b]rtag pa phyi ma)* simply refers to the second part of the *Hevajra Tantra;* the tantra has two separate parts with their own chapter numbering and so is sometimes called the tantra "in two parts" *(brtag pa gnyis pa).*

95. The Sanskrit of this verse has *upabhujyate* ("to enjoy" or "to experience"). The verse thus has the sense that these are "experienced by means of this insight[-woman]."

96. The "Lord of the Maṇḍala" refers to Hevajra; Nairātmyā is Hevajra's consort.

97. *'khor ba na ma rig pa zhes bya ste.* Yumo makes several statements equating the Great Seal with "ignorance" *(ma rig pa)* in the saṃsāric perspective. His intention seems to be that the Great Seal is the source of the ordinary mind and the deceptive worlds it perceives, just as she is the Mother of the Buddhas. I suspect Yumo is also playing on the *ma* in *ma rig pa,* which can be a feminine particle, as well as a negative; that is, she is even the "mother" of ignorance, just as she is the mother of all the buddhas.

98. D0360, 3a.2 (verse 28). Yumo's suggestion is that the letter *A* from which Mañjuśrī arises is none other than the Great Seal.

99. *spros pas chog go.* This is a way of saying "I could go on, but I will just leave it here."

100. D0422, 128a.6. *The Jñānatilaka Tantra (dpal ye shes thig le rnal 'byor ma'i rgyud)* is a tantra in the Hevajra cycle; Jñānatilaka (Ye-shes thig-le) is the name of the buddha who speaks the tantra. Due to questionable wording in Yumo's passage, I relied on the passage from Dergé and also consulted the commentary *dPal ye shes thig le'i dka' 'grel* (D1203, 261a.6ff.).

"Goddess" refers to the interlocutor of the buddha Jñānatilaka, a goddess who is also identified as Prajñāpāramitā, and as the Great Seal. The reference to the navel wheel indicates a point in the mystic-fire practice, when the *thig-le* (thematized as the Great Seal herself) have risen up to the navel wheel, inducing joy that leads to insight. The reference to the realm of Brahma is then discussing her presence in the crown wheel. The commentary interprets these difficult lines by saying that the Great Seal is so-called because she dwells at the crown-wheel, "sealing" all beings, such that they all have the nature of the Buddha. The commentary does not specify what the reference of "countless" is; I have chosen "beings" based on its mention of sealing "all beings." Yumo's comments above suggest that he may take it as referring to all the countless appearances created by the 10 million world systems.

101. D0447, 283a5. Note that this passage is also cited in Āryadeva's *Lamp Integrating the Practices* (D1803, 87a.2), one of Yumo's favorite sources.

102. I.e., Yumo cites the above passage as a way of illustrating how the concept of "illusion" is a way of referring broadly to the Great Seal. The objector asks: In that passage, aren't the "illusions" simply referring to qualities of the tathāgatas, which are seen in the "*samādhi* of great bliss"?

103. Bu vol. 1, VP ch. 1, 4a.3 (this is in the praises and aphorisms that begin chapter 1).

104. PC (D1350, 91a.5) identifies the "eight prognostic images" *(pra ni rnam pa brgyad,* or, in Bu, *pra phab brgyad)* as "a reflection in a mirror, a dream, a city of gandharvas, a mirage, and so forth"; in its view the list seems to be simply an abbreviated version of the "twelve examples of illusion" given in the previous citation. The term might also refer to the eight media in which prognostic reflections can be seen: a mirrored dagger, a sword, one's thumb[nail], a lamp, the moon, the sun, [the surface of] water, and the eyes *(phur bu'i me long dang/ ral gri'am mthe bo dang/ mar me dang/ zla ba dang/ nyi ma dang/ chu dang/ thabs dang/ mig ste brgyad rnams la pra dbab pa 'jug par gsungs so/)*; for these, see Nāropa's comments on verses 29–30 of the *Sekoddeśa* (D1351, 362b.5).

Orofino (p. 615) notes how the Sanskrit *pratisenā* (prognostic image) is related to other "prati" words like *pratibhāsa* (reflection) and *pratibimba* (reflected image); this seems to be the case here, where it is little more than a synonym for "illusion" or "reflected image." The quote thus answers the objection that "illusion" might just refer to the common list of twelve, or to a particular meditative experience; in fact (Yumo suggests) the term refers to the Great Seal.

105. D1180, 10b.5. This refers to one of the "three bodhisattva commentaries," Vajragarbha's commentary to *The Hevajra Tantra.* The general context here is a discussion of the nature of the yoginīs in *The Hevajra Tantra,* Nairātmyā and so forth (10a.4). In particular, this section discusses how they should be regarded when they appear in the sky as objects of meditation (10b.3). Thus the passage really has a plural subject ("their reflection-like appearances…), but I use the singular to preserve Yumo's line of argument.

106. "Insight" *(shes rab)* is the feminine component of the dyad "method and insight." The letter *E* is the feminine component of the two syllables *E-VAM.*

107. D2224, 75b.5, lines 420–424. Yumo uses this title for what is today called Saraha's *Treasury of Dohā Verses (Do ha mdzod kyi glu).* For connections between Saraha and Kālacakra, see Wallace, *Inner Kālacakra,* 30, which notes a Jonang tradition, stated by Tāranātha, that views Saraha's own yogic practice as being based on Kālacakra's six yogas.

108. This passage is from Vajrapāṇi's commentary to *The Cakrasaṃvara Tantra* (D1402, 133a.1), which I read from Dergé rather than YM. The commentary here is discussing "withdrawal" and "concentration," the first of the Kālacakra completion stage yogas.

109. D1802, 646.4 (verses III.33–35). I read from Dergé and also consulted the *Garland of Jewels* commentary (D1840, 122b.2). The *Garland of Jewels* suggests these interpretations: being "chief" means to be the "chief" of the buddhas, i.e., Vajradhara. The line mentioning "seen and touched" actually refers to all the senses: "[from] seeing [through] touching."

110. This is verses III.26–27b from the *Five Stages* (D1802, 53a.1). I rely on the passage as it appears in Dergé and have made reference to the *Garland of Jewels* commentary (D1840, 120a.2). The comment about illusion and conventional truth has two meanings. First, it suggests how the characteristics of illusions (exemplified in the twelve examples of illusion) demonstrate the illusory-like quality of our ordinary existence. "Illusion" *(sgyu ma)* can also be taken as referring to the stage of self-blessing, also called the stage of "conventional truth," where one practices the illusion-like *samādhi* and attains an illusory body. Thus the line suggests how the illusory body attained through the stage of conventional truth is itself a profound type of illusion, or that becoming an illusion is a type of transcendence. As *Garland of Jewels* states, "other than attaining this body, there is no illusion-like *samādhi*" (120a.2).

For the final two cryptic lines, *Garland of Jewels* suggests that the first compares the illusory body to gandharvas, translucent beings that live in the sky, and are famously used to illustrate reflections and illusions (the *Garland* notes that they can cast away their bodies while still retaining their sense faculties, and then take on a new body). Because the illusory body can be perceived, but is not perceived with conceptual thought, it is not a concrete thing and is like a gandharva. Vajra Body, then, is (for *Garland of Jewels*) a reference to the Reality Body, the indestructible suchness from which the illusory Enjoyment Body arises.

111. D0420, 71a4.

112. "Post-attainment" refers to the state following meditation, when one begins to again re-encounter ordinary appearances. At that time, things appear to be concrete, but based on one's experience one does not believe in the concreteness, knowing that they are in fact illusory. "Yogas of activity" *(spyod lam gyi rnal 'byor)* refers to doing ordinary things like going, staying, standing up, and lying down.

113. I.e., they constitute the *samādhi* itself, not experiences that occur once the meditation is over. In the passage below, "conventional truth" is a synonym for this illusion-like *samādhi.*

114. D1803, 59b.7 (ch. 1). Here I have relied on Wedemeyer's study, especially for the critical Guhyasamāja term "radiances and prototypes," which Tibetans consistently mis-render as *rang bzhin gyis snang ba* (the term has the sense of *rang bzhin dang snang ba*). I use Wedemeyer's translation equivalents here. See Wedemeyer's discussion in *Āryadeva's Lamp that Integrates the Practices,* 95ff.

115. In Āryadeva's work, the illusion-like *samādhi (māyopama-samādhi, rgyu ma lta bu'i ting nge 'dzin)* is synonymous with the phase of Guhyasamāja completion stage practice called "self-blessing" *(svādhiṣṭhāna, bdag la byin gyis brlab pa),* or "[the stage of] conventional truth" *(saṃvṛti-satya, kun rdzob bden pa).* It is at this stage that one attempts to actually arise in a deity body, to "give rise to a deity [body composed] of mere gnosis" *(shes tsam gyis lha nyid du bskyed pa),* which is characterized by the twelve examples of illusion; (see Wedemeyer's discussion of CMP 6, in the introduction to his translation, p. 103ff., and his translation, p. 243ff.). Yumo likens this *samādhi* to the Kālacakra experience of having a vision of the Great Seal, who is still (in the most profound sense) "a mere appearance of one's mind" *(sems kyi snang ba tsam).* Yumo's objector thus raises two possible problems, suggesting that illusion-like *samādhi* has nothing to do with an experience of the illusory Great Seal, but might (1) refer to tantric practices where one attempts to arise in a deity body, but does so through conceptual means, or (2) refer to exoteric meditations, where one simply views things as being like illusions.

116. D1804, 110a.6 (verses 89–90).

117. Yumo here hints that Āryadeva's comments about gnosis *(ye shes)* appearing to itself in the context of Guhyasamāja are identical to the concept of the Great Seal, composed of mind, appearing to the mind of a yogi.

118. KCT 4.199 (Bu vol. 1, 97a.6). The passage here is rather corrupt and is even at variance with the same verse cited above on YM, 635. My translation is based on these two citations in Yumo but makes reference to PC, 468ff., where this translation of the verses is better preserved.

119. This is lines 371–372 from the *Treasury of Dohā Verses* (D2224, 75a.3).

120. *Ye shes grub pa.* This would seem to refer to the VP's long commentary on KCT 5.127 (called *mChog tu mi 'gyur pa'i ye shes grub pa*), but these verses do not appear there. I have not located them in any of Yumo's other sources, or in *dPal de kho na nyid ye shes grub pa* (D1551).

121. I.e., does she lead to liberation?

122. This is referring to the tantra *Ye shes thig le* (D0422), which Yumo also calls the "later supplement" *(phyi ma'i phyi ma)* to the tantra *Phyag rgya chen mo'i thig*

le. The citation is on 128a.2. Yumo's citation has one fewer line than the passage in Dergé and also has a few variant readings. For these reasons, I relied primarily on Dergé for the translation. I also consulted Jñānaparama's *Secret Reality (gsang ba'i de kho na nyid)* commentary (D1203, 260b.3).

123. The commentary suggests that this indicates that she embraces the buddhas, i.e., she is a pure ornament wrapped around them.

124. That is, the Great Seal is clearly said to be "like the sky," and above it was established that knowing things as "like the sky" is the cause of attaining liberation and omniscience.

125. KCT 5.116 (Bu vol. 1, 127b.3). Yumo cites this again below, on YM, 663. As the VP makes clear, the verse here is describing visionary experiences encountered in day-yoga. The opening word "There" refers to the vision of the "black line" *(re kha nag po)* arising from the central channel, in which the Omniscient Form *(thams cad mkhyen pa'i gzugs,* or *kun mkhyen gzugs)* appears.

126. Lokanātha is a way of referring to Puṇḍarīka, the author of *Stainless Light.* This is most probably referring to his comments on KCT 5.116, which say "it is not the mind of another" because "another's mind is not something that you can know [at this stage]" *(gshan gyi sems shes pa med pa'i phyir).* The point is that the visionary appearances being discussed here are seen using the "fleshy eye," while seeing (or seeing via) the minds of others is a higher attainment, a type of "seeing" performed with the "divine eye."

127. Bu vol. 3, VP ch. 5, 45a.7 (commenting on KCT 5.114). The VP here is explaining the name of the third initiation, the "insight-gnosis" *(shes rab ye shes)* initiation. Yumo's intends to use this citation to suggest how the Great Seal can appear "in the mind." His intent in citing the verse becomes more clear if just a little more context is added. To that end, following is KCT 5.114a, and the VP's comments on it (translated based on Bu):

(KCT): Insight *(shes rab)* and gnosis *(ye shes)* are the mind and its appearances in tenfold aspect.

(VP): Here, *insight and gnosis* are, respectively, the apprehending *mind and its* apprehended objects, the *tenfold* [appearances] of smoke and so forth, which are like *appearances* in a mirror, and like prognostic images. Those are "gnosis," the mind as an object of apprehension. That is the meaning [of this verse].

128. D0360, 5a.4 (verse 79). Wallace notes that the VP (commenting on KCT 4.133) uses this verse as "a theoretical basis for the Kālacakratantra practice of the stage of generation, more specifically, for the practice of meditation on the universal form *(viśva-rūpa)* of the empty and blissful Buddha that has many arms, legs, colors, and shapes"; see *Inner Kālacakra,* 20.

129. This is verse 156 of the *Sekoddeśa* (D0361, 20a.6).

130. The objection is that the passage seems to refer more to philosophical ideas than to a visionary goddess who is produced from your mind.

131. This is verse 158 from the *Sekoddeśa* (D0361, 20a.7). In the fourth line, I read *bsten* for *brten,* based on Orofino's two editions and Naropa's commentary (D1351, 286b.2).

132. This is from Saraha's *Treasury of Dohā Verses,* lines 403–406 (D2224, 75b.5).

133. D1348, 11a.2.

134. D1350, 93a.4. There are several errors in Yumo's citation, so I read from Dergé. The passage here is an analog of the *Stainless Light* comments on KCT 5.114, cited just above on YM, 648 (but note that Kālacakrapāda is not commenting directly on that verse here). The larger passage is a discussion of the meaning of "insight-gnosis," this being the name of the stage of the initiations that is famous for its sexual encounter between the initiate and a consort that was just united with the student's spiritual mentor. The initiation here is reinterpreted in visionary terms, providing a key example of how vision provides a way of dealing with some of the highly charged issues of sexual yoga.

The comments just before Yumo's extract help to clarify the passage: "What is 'insight' and what is 'gnosis'? I will explain this. Respectively, they are the apprehending mind, and the mind that is apprehended. Here, the apprehending mind is the one which apprehends the signs of smoke and so forth. The mind that is apprehended is the one that appears as those individual appearances of smoke and so forth. For instance, in a mirror.... "

135. D1350, 213a.4. This is *The Lotus Girl* commenting on KCT 5.113, one of the "easy to understand" verses that the VP does not explain. Note that Yumo's passage here is somewhat different than Dergé and also leaves out some fragments that appear in *The Lotus Girl* itself.

It is helpful to see the citation in its entirety, and in a slightly larger context. For that purpose, following are Kālacakrapāda's concluding comments on KCT 5.112d, and the entire passage on 5.113a that is cited in Yumo (underlined words are from KCT root verses). The verses are discussing how the Great Seal appears in the transcendent initiations *('jig rten las 'das dbang)*. According to KCT 5.112d, these initiations involve "desire for" (or "union with," according to Bu) the Great Seal. Note how Kālacakrapāda broadens this discussion and equates experiencing her in initiation with the experience of her during completion stage practices like withdrawal yoga.

(KCT 5.112d, from PC, 213a.1): The transcendent initiation is desiring the excellent consort of the Supreme Lord of Conquerors.

(PC's comments, beginning on 213a.2): "Desiring" her means, day and night, focusing on her with the mind. Through withdrawal [yoga] and so forth, the mind becomes of one taste with her. That is the transcendent initiation. You may wonder what that Great Seal is like. [This is explained in the verse beginning] "a mere manifestation of the mind."

(KCT 5.113, based on PC): She is a mere manifestation of mind, arisen from your mind, like a reflection in a mirror.

(PC's comments): Here, "a mere manifestation of mind" indicates that the form of the Great Seal, whose nature is emptiness, is simply a manifestation of your mind. It is not an external, concrete thing, on account of being a manifestation in your mind. So where does it come from? It is said to be "arisen from your mind." This means that it arises from your mind thanks to emptiness. This is like when your own face appears to you, as a reflection in a mirror.

136. This is from chapter 6 of *Lamp Integrating the Practices* (D1803, 84b.2). I read from Yumo's rendering here, but emend one critical error that occurs in both YM and YM-SG: in the last line, *sangs rgyas thams cad kyi rang bzhin* should clearly be *sangs rgyas thams cad kyi yid kyi rang bzhin.* (Yumo's point in selecting this passage is to support his discussion of bodies made of mind.)

The passage is discussing the Guhyasamāja completion stage practice called "self-blessing" or the "illusion-like *samādhi,*" where the yogi arises in an actual deity body, made of "mere gnosis." One of Yumo's projects throughout this work is to associate the stage of self-blessing with the visionary elements of the Kālacakra completion stage.

137. *rang gi sems yang dag pa ji lta ba bzhin du yongs su shes pa.* Āryadeva also uses this phrase in chapter 1 of his *Lamp* (D1803, 59b.7; the passage is also cited above on YM, 73). The idea is that a thorough knowledge of the three radiances *(snang ba)* and eighty prototypes *(rang bzhin)* allows one to mix the subtle levels of mind with wind energies, such that they give rise to a deity body.

138. The Sanskrit is more explicit here, stating that one takes on a deity body through the radiances of the three gnoses. See Wedemeyer's Sanskrit edition and his translation (p. 244).

139. *de bas na rang gi sems ni lam yin la/ de yang mig gi gzung yul du yod pa.* Note Yumo's implied point that visionary practice is hidden within all of the tantras.

140. Bu vol. 3, VP ch. 5, 89b.2 (commenting on KCT 5.127). This passage is poorly preserved in Yumo, though YM is better than YM-SG. I have translated it here based on Bu.

141. Citation not located. This passage is not contained in the *Sekoddeśa.*

142. D1350, 83b.6. Kālacakrapāda here is commenting on a verse from the beginning of *Stainless Light* (Bu vol. 1, VP ch. 1, 2b.1), which says that the unchanging bliss of the Great Seal *(phyag rgya chen po'i mi 'gyur bde)* is like a city of gandharvas and a prognostic image (i.e., it arises spontaneously and without conceptual thought).

143. This is verses III.23–24 from the *Five Stages* (D1802, 52b.6). Yumo's passage contains some minor errors, so I relied on Dergé and the commentary *Garland of Jewels* (D1840, 119b.6). The "illusory body" is the deity body or gnostic body that a yogi takes on at the Guhyasamāja stage of self-blessing. Here that deity body takes the form of Vajrasattva. What I translate as "resplendent" is *legs bris pa* (literally "well drawn" or "well fashioned"); in place of this, *Garland of Jewels* has *rab spros pa* ("completely elaborate"). The idea is that his image is completely endowed with all of his various characteristics (his major and minor marks and so forth), making him beautiful to behold.

144. Note how Yumo is here associating the Great Seal with the illusory body of the Guhyasamāja stage of self-blessing.

145. KCT 5.247 (Bu vol. 1, 146b.6). Yumo incorrectly states that this citation is from the "Methods of Accomplishment chapter of *The Condensed [Kālacakra] Tantra,*" referring to chapter 4. The verse itself is also in poor shape, beginning with *sems can* ("sentient being") rather than *sems tsam* ("merely mind"). The rest of the verse is full of questionable readings, so I have translated from Bu.

The verse is from a section of the KCT called "In Praise of the Great Five and Six Syllable Emptiness" *(yi ge lnga dang yi ge drug gi stong pa chen po dang thig-le stong pa la bstod pa).* As described in chapter 1, section 6 of *Stainless Light,* the "five syllable emptiness" is a group of five types of emptiness, each represented by a particular syllable, and thematized as the realization of one of the five gnoses *(ye shes lnga).* Each emptiness is related to one of the five aggregates, its realization "blocking" a particular aggregate, and thus preventing embodied existence in saṃsāra. The present verse is a praise of the fifth of those emptinesses, related to the "mirror-like gnosis"; this is the realization that either "blocks" the form aggregate or, in other contexts, is said to be the purified essence of the form aggregate. Collectively, the five emptinesses are said to be Vajrasattva himself (and who appears here as the object of homage).

The five emptinesses are a "male" classification of emptiness, its female counterpart being the "six emptinesses." *Stainless Light* makes frequent comments about the "union" of these, i.e., an integrated realization of all of them, constituting enlightenment. The converse of this seems to be that an ignorant experience (or perhaps an ordinary sexual "union") produces the ordinary world. This seems to be what Yumo is getting at here, that it is one's interpretive perspective, based one one's karmic heritage, that leads to the perception of the world as either transcendent or mundane. In this way, Vajrasattva (who is also thematized as the union of the five and six emptinesses) can be seen not just as a being who brings about the cessation of suffering but also as one who is a "producer of the three existences."

Unfortunately, VP hardly comments on this verse, indicating simply that it is a praise of the fifth of five emptinesses, and saying (Bu vol. 3, VP ch. 5, 146a.7) that there is no need to discuss it extensively, as the same topic is explained in chapter 1 of the VP. Khedrup Jé agrees (vol. nga, 608.3) that it does not need to be discussed and points the reader to the VP's comments on KCT 1.2 (Bu vol. 1, VP ch. 1, 54b.7), which is a discussion of the fifth emptiness. That passage provides many details of the five emptinesses but does not discuss a deity appearing in positive or negative form, conditioned by ignorance.

146. Both YM and YM-SG read "sentient being" *(sems can)* here; I emend this to "mere mind" *(sems tsam)* based on KCT 5.247; note that both YM and YM-SG have *sems can* (which is incorrect) in their rendering of KCT 5.247.

147. *stong pa nyid ma rig par snang pas.*

148. The question here asks: If instead of perceiving emptiness through the lens of ignorance (as above), what would happen if one were to perceive all empty things as arising from and pervaded by the Great Seal?

149. This portion of Yumo continues to be poorly preserved, and this short quote has not survived well. The quote can be found in PC (D1350, 100b.1) and Bu (vol. 1, VP ch. 1, 6a.3). The translation here is from PC, as it matches Yumo's citation in form. Bu reads: "The self-blessing is this: from emptiness, The three worlds come to be seen."

The Lotus Girl (D1350, 99b.5) indicates that the "hero stage" can refer to practices involving zombies and dwelling in charnel grounds, while the "stage of self-blessing" involves dwelling in places where one can receive the blessings of buddhas and bodhisattvas. It provides another, definitive interpretation of "self-blessing" in the passage that Yumo cites next.

Khedrup Jé's commentary *Illuminating Reality* (vol. kha, 293.2) is more helpful. He notes that the "hero stage" can refer to (completion stage) meditations on fierce deities, while the "stage of self-blessing" can refer to meditations on peaceful ones. However, ultimately speaking (says Khedrup Jé), the "hero stage" is a term referring to the completion stage practice of cutting off the 21,600 winds *(srog rlung)* in the body. The "self-blessing," then, refers to empty-form, i.e., to seeing the form of the

Great Seal in emptiness, through which one recognizes that the three worlds are essenceless and appear like images in a prognostic mirror.

150. D1350, 100b.2.

151. That is, one sees visionary appearances that are immaterial and yet appearing, and which thus are like everything in the external three worlds, which have no essence and yet appear. Through seeing those, one realizes that one's internal three realms (body, speech, and mind) have this same nature.

152. This is verses II.3.24–25b of the *Hevajra Tantra* (D0418, 17b.2).

153. The subject of the passage in the context of the *Hevajra Tantra* is "pure joy" *(dga' ba yang dag)* or "great bliss" *(bde ba chen po),* i.e., the bliss that, in the context of tantric initiation, arises when the student unites with the consort and experiences a moment in which all diversity disappears *(sna tshogs spangs ba'i skad cig).* The master points out to the student that this bliss (without emission) is a "great gnosis" *(ye shes chen po),* which leads to enlightenment (i.e., the birth of a buddha), just as ordinary bliss (with emission) leads to the birth of ordinary beings and the ordinary worlds that they perpetuate. Yumo is suggesting that this "bliss" or "great gnosis" is identical with the Great Seal. In contexts like this, the Great Seal is much more than a visionary consort, but is a gnosis that pervades the body and the world. Much like the dual functioning of sexual bliss, this gnosis can function to bring about either enlightenment or, as suggested above, the ordinary world. In this sense, it is "neither dual nor nondual."

154. I read this phrase based on YM-SG.

155. *sgyu ma'i gzugs kyis khyab.* This has the sense that everything "is" an illusory form. I.e., not only does the Great Seal pervade the world, her nature is that of the world. In visionary experience, that nature is put on display, and one is confronted with the fact that the animate and inanimate world is like a mirage, an illusion that functions and appears.

156. This is verses III.20–22 from the *Five Stages* (D1802, 52b.5). YM and YM-SG both leave out line 20b; I have included the line in the translation, as its omission is clearly an error. For this passage, I relied on the *Garland of Jewels* commentary (D1840, 119a.3) and used its rendering of 22c instead of Yumo or Dergé.

"In that way" refers to the previous verses, which describe how the illusion-like *samādhi* (aka the "stage of self-blessing") uses a process of combining wind with the "three consciousnesses," allowing the yogi to arise in a deity body called the "illusory body" *(sgyu ma'i lus)* or "gnostic body" *(ye shes kyi lus).* In this *samādhi,* one not only sees things like illusions but also takes on an illusion-like divine form. "All beings" being illusory suggests how ordinary beings are illusory in the general sense of all things being without inherent existence; beings with divine bodies are also illusory, in that they reside in "gnostic" or "illusory" bodies.

157. Citation not located. Yumo does not provide the name of his source here, and the passage does not appear in the *Five Stages* (the source of the previous quote).

158. *sGyu ma lta bu'i ting nge 'dzin kyi mdo* (D0130). Yumo's citation appears to be a summary of a passage beginning on 211b.3.

159. D1804, 111a.6 (verses 115–116). I read from Dergé to correct some obvious errors in Yumo. In verse 116c, the phrase "variegated reflections" *(sna tshogs gzugs brnyan)* is of interest to Yumo because of its resonance with the term "universal form" *(sna tshogs gzugs).*

160. *phyi'i khams gsum kyi skyon gyis gos pa med pa'i 'thad pa yang/ nang gi khams gsum rkyen [i.e., skyon] gyis ma gos pa'i phyir ro/.* That is, internally, the yogi maintains the standpoint of perceiving things as illusions. Here and in his ensuing comments, Yumo also seems to be suggesting how reflected images are less problematic than actual ones, in that their obvious unreality does not reinforce the mental afflictions in the way that concrete objects do.

161. D0368, 213b.5 (ch. 1).

162. This refers to *The Vajrapāṇi Commentary* (D1402). Unfortunately, these exact sentences do not appear in the Dergé edition. Yumo's citation bears some basic resemblance to the discussion beginning on 123b.7, which interprets the lines of the *Cakrasaṃvara Tantra* immediately preceding the ones that Yumo cites above; see in particular 124a.3 *(khams gsum pa ni ma lus pa/ /sangs rgyas gzugs su bsgom par bya/ /).* It is possible that Yumo is using this section, and its ensuing discussion of the four initiations, to interpret his Cakrasaṃvara citation. More likely, Yumo was working with a different translation, or the reference to *The Vajrapāṇi Commentary* is another of the many errors in this section.

163. Yumo is speaking cryptically here and is borrowing terminology from the *Kālacakra Tantra* passage just below. "Like the sun" refers to the gnostic seal, while "like lightning" refers to the Great Seal. Both appear with their features totally complete, but the visualized consort burns with a steady constancy, while the Great Seal appears in a sudden spontaneous flash.

164. *De nyid;* Yumo frequently uses "this one" to refer back to the topic indicated in the subhead. Here, it refers to the one "emanating rays like stainless lightning," i.e., the Great Seal.

165. KCT 5.73 (Bu vol. 1, 119b.5). This verse is also quoted in full on PC, 208a.6. In my translation, I read from Yumo, but based on PC read *gdong* for *stong* in 5.73b. I have also relied on Butön's notes to this verse (Bu vol. 1, 120a.1), which indicate that the one with "sunlike form" is the gnostic *mudrā*. He reads "vajras" in the last line as referring to the body, speech, mind, and gnosis vajras (which are ways of categorizing the completion stage); in other words, the Great Seal appears due to the practice of the six yogas.

166. KCT 5.246 (Bu vol. 1, 146b.4). Yumo's verse here is quite different from the version that appears in Bu. I translate from Yumo but am influenced by Bu and by Khedrup Jé (vol. lnga, 607.2). The verse is a praise of the third of the "five emptinesses," which is said to be the purified form of the element fire, to block the "feelings" aggregate, and to be symbolized by a *visarga*. For these five emptinesses, see the first chapter of *Stainless Light* (Bu vol. 1, VP ch. 1, 54a.7) and Newman's translation in "Outer Wheel of Time," 389ff.

167. I.e., what establishes that this language about "emanating rays" and "stainless lightning" is referring to the Great Seal?

168. This is referring to the Vajrapāṇi's commentary on the *Cakrasaṃvara Tantra* (D1402, 133b.2). Vajrapāṇi here is describing what is seen in the practice of the six yogas, during the branch of recollection *(rjes su dran pa).*

169. I have not located this citation in the tantra itself (D0494); Āryadeva quotes this passage on D1803, 85b.4, which is clearly Yumo's source. Note that Āryadeva has *thob par 'gyur* ("will be attained") instead of Yumo's *thong bar 'gyur* ("will be seen").

170. This is from chapter 6 of *Lamp Integrating the Practices* (D1803, 85b.4).

171. D1804, 221.7 (verse 118).

172. KCT 5.164 (Bu vol. 1, 135b.4). Note that the use of "original" body and "original" three worlds (*dang po'i lus,* and *dang po'i 'jig rten gsum*) is not reflected in Bu; I also read the third line based on Bu.

Note that Yumo and Butön disagree about the referent of this passage. For Yumo, it is describing the Great Seal: her bodily appearances in the sky, her speech, and her mind. In Butön's interpretation (Bu vol. 1, 135b.4), the verse is describing the characteristics and internal signs of someone who has made the attainment of the Great Seal *(phyag rgya chen po'i dngos grub),* so it is talking about the transformations of the yogi's body. For Butön, the passage would be: "Its atoms dissolved, [the yogi's] body becomes a vibrant clarity, like the sky, as its marks and so forth become totally complete. / The variety of the three worlds appears like a dream, vibrantly clear and free of obscurations. / [His] speech, never interrupted, is cast in all the different languages, and enters the minds of others. / [His] mind, full of profound bliss, unwavering, is always embraced by the innate [bliss]."

PC (D1350, 216b.4) reads the verse similarly and says it is describing "internal signs" of accomplishment, rather than an "external" manifestation as Yumo would have it: "Here, the yogi has attained the supreme and unchanging bliss, so his body passes beyond the atoms of earth and so forth. He attains a body that is luminous, and endowed with the thirty-two signs of a great being...."

173. *dang po'i gzugs.*

174. I.e., the major and minor marks of buddhahood.

175. KCT 5.156–158 (Bu vol. 1, 133b.6). I translate the verses as they appear in Yumo, using PC and Bu to correct obvious mistakes. *Stainless Light* does not comment on these difficult verses because they are "easy to understand." Being of lower intelligence, I have had to rely on Butön's interlineal comments, along with comments found in *The Lotus Girl* (D1350, 215a.3ff.), and comments by Khedrup Jé (vol. nga, 517ff.).

176. One way of reading these first three lines is as a suggestion that the Great Seal is operative in the maturation of a consort: being present as a dynamic emptiness in the protean elements of which she initially takes form, and being the force propelling her into becoming sentient, and finally into sexual maturity, the point at which she is able to experience (and give) bliss. Such a consort is thus a combination of emptiness and bliss.

177. *rdo rje'i go 'phang la gnas.* As PC and Bu make clear, this is an archaic way of referring to the "vajra words" of the fourth initiation, i.e., she is what is taught in the words of the fourth initiation.

178. Butön's annotations suggest that this verse describes the attainment of the six higher perceptions *(mngon shes drug),* which come about in correspondence to

the six great channels intentionally being blocked in yogic practice. As PC notes, the verse employs code language referring to the six channels, which is taken from the *Sekoddeśa* (verses 38ff.). Thus in the first line here, "body" refers to the upper left channel, the *lalanā;* so "through the force of the body" indicates that the higher perception of the divine eye comes about "through blocking the upper left channel." Similarly, "speech" refers to the lower left channel, the "urine" channel; "mind" refers to the upper central channel, the *avadhūtī;* "insight body" is the lower central channel, the "feces" channel; "insight speech" refers to the upper right channel, the *rasanā;* and "insight gnosis" (in the next verse) refers to the lower right channel, the "semen/blood" channel. For a discussion and diagram of these channels, see Orofino, "Ṣaḍaṅgayoga," 151ff.

179. Butön notes that "equal" bliss *(bde mnyam)* refers to things being of "equal taste" *(ro mnyam)* in the supreme and unchanging bliss. For him, "indestructible" is a reference to the sixth of the higher perceptions, the "apperception of the extinction of outflows" *(rang rig pa zag zad kyi mngon shes),* which means the knowledge of the exhaustion of the afflictions; his reason seems to be that this is a permanent condition, as the afflictions will not return.

180. That is, one's sense faculties all become divine through the practice of the above-described yogas, which involve the blocking of the six channels. Yumo's point in citing these verses is that such transformations of the sense faculties are the manifestation of the dynamics of the Great Seal, who pervades the body and thus gives it the ability to become divine.

181. D1350, 191a.4 (commenting on KCT 4.198).

182. D1350, 85a.6. This is commenting on a verse praising Viśvamātā ("Universal Mother" or "Mother of Variety"), which appears at the beginning of VP chapter 1 (Bu vol. 1, VP ch. 1, 2b.2). The passage that Yumo cites from *The Lotus Girl* is simply explaining Viśvamātā's name.

183. This is III.20d from the *Five Stages:* "Thus, in that way, all beings / Are explained here as being like illusions. / Resting in the illusion-like *samādhi* / Everything is seen to be like that [i.e., like illusions]."

184. This quote appears above on YM, 655–656. The meaning of the full quotation is that everything is an illusion, and in the illusory *samādhi* "all things are seen to be like that."

185. D1350, 191b.1 (commenting on KCT 4.198). The phrases "at night" and "of the eye sense-faculty and so forth" are not in Yumo but appear in the original text (Yumo starts his citation just after them). The passage is commenting on the phrase "not an object" from Yumo's main verse, KCT 4.198.

186. Literally, "free of objects" *(yul dang bral),* which means that the Great Seal is not composed of atoms and therefore does not "contain" objects or is not "composed" of objects.

187. VP 5.116 (Bu vol. 1, 127b.3). I read the second line here based on Bu.

188. The VP (Bu vol. 3, VP ch. 5, 46b.6) interprets this by saying that the visions here are presencings of one's own mind, seen with the fleshy eye of the tathāgatas. This fleshy eye is not capable of seeing others' minds, as that is a power reserved for the divine eye.

189. KCT 5.119 (Bu vol. 1, 127b.7). Yumo's point in citing the passage is that it suggests how with empty-forms the "aspects" and functions of a particular element

may be present (for instance, the heat of fire), but the physical atomic structure does not have to be present. The VP (Bu vol. 3, VP ch. 5, 47b.4) and Khedrup Jé (vol. nga, 236.4) both read the verse as describing empty-forms in general. Yumo is of course interested in the verse as it more specifically suggests the nature of the empty-form Great Seal, so the passage could be read as suggesting that "her" liquid dimension is not wet, and so forth.

The final line of the verse apparently has an error in Yumo. Both YM and YM-SG read "although endowed with all aspects, [these] are seen" *(rnam pa kun dang ldan yang mthong).* KCT 5.119 in Bu, the VP, and Khedrup Jé all have "although endowed with all aspects, [these] are not objects of sight" *(rnam pa thams cad pa yang blta bya min).* This is undoubtedly the intent, so I have corrected Yumo to "not seen," on the assumption that the negative *ma* has become confused with the first letter of *mthong*.

190. D1348, 13a.1.

191. D1350, 84b.4. This is commenting on a verse praising the Great Seal, located at the beginning of VP chapter 1 (Bu vol. 1, VP ch. 1, 2b.2), and also cited by Yumo above (YM, 633). Yumo's first extract here is commenting on the verse that praises Great Seal as being "beyond the nature of atomic particles"; the second extract deals with the line "having the nature of a prognostic image."

192. D1350, 167a.7. This section of *The Lotus Girl* is commenting on a verse found in the introductory section of VP chapter 4. The *Lotus Girl* passage here is focusing on VP's statements that the Reality Body is not permanent or impermanent, not singular or multiple, and not a thing or a non-thing (Bu vol. 2, VP ch. 4, 1a.7). This final characteristic is identical to the way that Yumo has just been describing the Great Seal. Along the same lines as Yumo, Butön's comments interpret "not a thing or a non-thing" as meaning that the Reality Body is not a "thing" because it transcends atomic structure, but is not a "non-thing" because it is present in emptiness. The feminine association that Yumo is looking for is found in the citation's final comment that the Reality Body "gives rise to" or "gives birth to" *(bskyed par mdzad pa)* the buddhas, a statement that is frequently applied to the Great Seal.

193. D0422. This appears to be from the passage on 128a.5, though the wording in the actual tantra is slightly different than here in Yumo: "You always dwell in the sky. / Conventionally, in the supreme of aspects.... " (The teacher here is addressing a group of goddesses, who are asking about their nature, thus "you" refers to a deity like the Great Seal.)

194. Lokanātha is a way of referring to Puṇḍarīka, the author of *Stainless Light*. The passage here is from *Stainless Light*'s comments on KCT 1.1d (Bu vol. 1, VP ch. 1, 48a.4).

195. This refers to the six Kālacakra completion stage yogas, which are often classified in the four groups of body-vajra, speech-vajra, mind-vajra, and gnosis-vajra.

196. *rkyen gyi don.* Bu here has *yid ches pa'i don* ("object of confidence"). Both *rkyen* and *yid ches* can translate the Sanskrit *pratyaya,* though the first is usually reserved for *pratyaya* meaning "condition," i.e., something that helps to ripen or bring about an effect; the latter is used for "belief, certainty, confidence."

197. Bu vol. 1, VP ch. 1, 58b.5. The passage here is expanding on the meaning of KCT 1.2d: "Teacher of gods and men! Please truly explain the maṇḍalas and initiations!"

198. This citation is from *The Tantra of Vairocana's Manifest Enlightenment* (D0494, 161b.5). Like the preceding quote, this one also deals with issues of the maṇḍala. The passage appears in chapter 2 of the tantra, which describes the construction of the maṇḍala and ritual initiation. The student Vajrapāṇi asks the teacher Vairocana why all of this ritual is necessary, given that the Buddha and the doctrine ultimately do not possess signs or concepts. Yumo extracts a portion of Vairocana's reply, which states that maṇḍalas and rituals are taught in order to aid beings, even though a buddha is devoid of the signs and concepts that such rituals involve.

199. D1348, 13a.1.

200. The last phrase here based on YM-SG.

201. D1350, 102b.1. I read this passage based on Dergé.

202. D0361, 20a.7 (verse 158cd of the *Sekoddeśa*). Yumo cites the full verse above (YM, 69): "Uniting with the daughter of a barren woman / In a dream indeed produces bliss. / So too, intimacy with the one / Who is a form arisen from the sky."

203. Yumo unfortunately does not specify a source for this important passage, although the first eight lines can be found in *The Vajra Heart Ornament Tantra* (D0451, 56a.5).

The whole passage, however, is cited (also without specifying a source) in Āryadeva's *Lamp* (D1803, 87b.1); it seems most likely that Yumo found it there. Note that the first eight lines also appear in Āryadeva's *Oral Instructions on the Enlightenment Stage* (D1806, 114b.2). A similar verse with the lamp-in-a-pot metaphor also appears in Āryadeva's *On Purifying Mental Obscurations* (D1804, 112b.1, verse 120). See also the related verse 5 of Nāgārjuna's *In Praise of Dharmadhātu* (D1118, 64a.1).

204. *dPal dam pa dang po'i rgyud.* Citation not located.

205. The objection here is that references to "seeing in the sky" should be understood as being either metaphorical or philosophical. Thus "sky" language is used simply to indicate how something is insubstantial or all-pervasive, it does not refer to an actual location *(gnas)* where something is seen, and certainly is not code language for *bhaga*, i.e., the "residence *(gnas)* of great bliss."

206. I.e., "sky" can refer to the Great Seal in her dimension as suchness or the *dharmadhātu* (the characteristic of all phenomena), but it can also refer to her as the *bhaga* (the residence of great bliss). See Yumo's comments above on YM, 630–631.

207. Bu vol. 1, VP ch. 1, 16a.4. This passage is from the second section of chapter 1 of *Stainless Light,* which describes the teacher, the retinue, the residence, and so forth of the *Paramādibuddha-tantra.* The *Paramādibuddha* is said to have begun (much like the famous beginning of the *Hevajra Tantra*) with a passage declaring that the discourse was delivered in the "residence of great bliss." The *Stainless Light* passage here interprets this comment, suggesting how it can mean "*dharmadhatu*" (i.e., the characteristic of all phenomena), or that it can have more overt sexual references like "source of phenomena," which is a tantric term for the female genitalia and womb (i.e., an actual location or residence).

208. *Ultimate Letters* is Yumo's way of referring to the *Treasury of Dohā Verses.* These four lines do not appear there in this exact form but are related to lines 175–178 (D2224, 72b.6).

209. See Yumo's comments on the phrase "in the sky" (YM, 645ff.).

210. *rang gis nyams su myong bar gyur pa'i bdag nyid.* "Entity" *(bdag nyid)* could also be rendered as "nature," "being," or even "self." Yumo seems to have picked up this phrasing from the tantra *Thig-le of the Great Seal*; just following the passage that Yumo extracts, the tantra says that the "bliss" just mentioned "continually abides as the nature of everything" *(thams cad bdag nyid rtag tu bzhugs).*

211. *lkog tu gyur pa'i blo'i yul las 'das pa ni nam mkha' ma yin te.* "Hidden objects" are those that cannot be perceived directly (e.g., by the senses), but that must be perceived indirectly, through the means of a sign; examples are emptiness and uncompounded space. Yumo's claim here is that the "path" is something that can be experienced in vision, that it is something that can be an object of the eyes.

212. D0420, 72a2. Note that in the actual tantra, seven lines appear between the first line of Yumo's extract and the remaining lines.

213. D0420, 67b.5.

214. *rlung mi shigs pa las rlung gi 'khor lo ma lus pa bskyed la.* Norsang Gyatso mentions that the indestructible wind *(rlung mi shigs pa)* is not a characteristic of the Kālacakra tradition, as it is not discussed in *Stainless Light* (indeed, Yumo's citation here is from a tantra in the Hevajra cycle). Yumo appears to suggest here that this indestructible wind can be thought of as the Great Seal, given that both of them are subtle dynamics that give rise to the world and its appearances *(snang ba).* See *Ornament of Stainless Light* (trans. Kilty), 196ff., where this wind is presented as a tiny, supreme, subtle wind located at the heart, responsible for the production of all phenomena: "This very subtle wind and its very subtle mind of clear light form the foundation of all phenomena of saṃsāra and are the special meditative foundations of the two forms of a buddha, with this wind being the special meditative foundation of the enjoyment body of a buddha." For a discussion of the role of wind in the formation of the body according to the Kālacakra tradition, see Wallace, *Inner Kālacakra,* 59ff.

215. That is, while retaining its subtle, singular nature, it gives rise to winds, beings, and so forth, which arise in the same way as reflections of a singular moon in multiple vessels of water.

216. This is KCT 5.113 (Bu vol. 1, 127a.2). The verse in Yumo is rather different from Bu, and even has some differences from PC, with which it normally accords. I translate from Yumo but use PC (D1350, 213a.3) to correct obvious errors, and I base my reading of the verse on its comments.

217. *The Lotus Girl* comments: "Here, via the six yogas, the radiance of gnosis *(ye shes kyi 'od zer)* rises up, and burns away the hosts of demons of subjects and objects."

218. *The Lotus Girl* comments: "Those light-rays of gnosis make the skandhas, which have the nature of demons, unobscured. Then, they make the bodhicitta drip from the forehead. As that bodhicitta goes downward, the four [joys, called] 'joy' and so forth are conferred. Then, when it returns upward from the tip of the vajra, there are the supreme and unchanging four effects, [called] 'similar to the cause' and so forth. This is said to be conveyed in a year of yoga." (The "four effects" are the effects produced by the bodhicitta passing through the navel, heart, throat, and crown wheels.)

219. *snyam du mos pa gang yin pa de lam ma yin par shes par bya'o.* The "path" emptiness, emptiness in its dimension of being the "abiding reality of phenomena," is a hidden phenomena, something that cannot be directly seen or dealt with but must be approached through a sign (or, as suggested below, an example). As such, Yumo suggests that it is something that you have conviction or even faith in, but do not directly encounter in experience. Yumo seems to have picked up this phrasing from the Āryadeva passage just below.

220. This is from chapter 6 of *Lamp Integrating the Practices* (D1803, 84b.6).

221. *snang ba tsam,* i.e., the phase from KCT 4.198 that Yumo is currently discussing. This is a critical comment, as it is one place where Yumo directly compares the Kālacakra six yogas with the Guhyasamāja stage of self-blessing. In the Kālacakra context, I translate *snang ba tsam* as "mere appearance," while in the Guhyasamāja context, I use Wedemeyer's translation "mere radiance."

222. This is from chapter 6 of Āryadeva's *Lamp* (D1803, 85a.1); it follows directly after Yumo's previous Āryadeva citation. The multiple meanings of *snang ba* ("appearance," "radiance," "shine forth," and so forth) become complicated in this passage. The term is important here, as it is the term under discussion from KCT 4.198: "mere appearance," though it has slightly different connotations in the Guhyasamāja context here. I use Wedemeyer's translation "three radiances" for the critical Guhyasamāja term *snang ba gsum,* to make it clear that it is a standard term in that tradition.

223. *thun mong du gyur pas yang ba.* Literally "because they are common, they are light" (with "light" meaning "not heavy," like air). I read this as indicating how the uncontactable mind, when mixed with wind, becomes able to appear. Note Wedemeyer's translation (p. 245), based on the Sanskrit, which would be a more accurate reflection of Āryadeva's actual work: "air is elemental, common, [and] light." The Sanskrit here would be *sādhāraṇa;* literally "common," Monier-Williams also gives "having or resting on the same support or basis." The Sanskrit, however, is rather different from the Tibetan translation.

224. "Conventional truth" or "superficial reality" *(kun rdzob kyi bden pa)* here is a synonym for the stage of self-blessing in Guhyasamāja. Yumo is referring to the presentations of this given in chapter 3 of Nāgārjuna's *Five Stages,* and chapter 6 of Āryadeva's *Lamp Integrating the Practices.*

225. I.e., if the Great Seal is a "mere appearance of the mind," then couldn't everyone see her, as everyone has a mind?

226. *stong pa'i gzugs brnyan.*

227. *rtog pa'i sems ma yin pa'i sems.*

228. This and Yumo's comment above are probably his paraphrase of the famous line from the 8,000-line sūtra (D0012, 3b.3) that states, "Mind is not mind, the nature of mind is radiant light" *('di ltar sems de ni sems ma mchis pa ste/ sems kyi rang bzhin ni 'od gsal ba lags so/).* This line is also cited in VP 1.3.

229. This is lines 373–378 from *The Treasury of Dohā Verses* (D2224, 75a.4).

230. *ka la ku ta.* As Saraha's thirteenth-century commentator bCom-ldan-rig-pa'i-ral-gri explains in his *Ornamental Flower for the Dohās* (trans. Schaeffer): "*Kālakūṭa,* or black fear, is the name of a poison which comes from the far ocean. Just as whoever takes it dies, in whomever co-emergence dawns all of their afflictive emotions and divisive concepts are slain." See Kurtis Rice Schaeffer, "Tales of the Great

Brahmin: Creative Traditions of the Buddhist Poet-Saint Saraha" (PhD diss., Harvard University, 2000), 325.

Thus the poison here is being used as a metaphor for the "innate," which Yumo would want to read as "innate bliss," i.e., the supreme nonconceptual bliss conveyed by union with the Great Seal. Yumo is interested in the passage because it suggests how a powerfully efficacious nonconceptual entity can be perceived when the ordinary "mind" becomes a "non-mind," or casts off the conceptuality that normally defines it.

231. This is similar to lines 381–386 from *The Treasury of Dohā Verses* (D2224); Yumo's source, however, is a translation that is quite different from Dergé.

232. Citation not located in D1350. The passage is related to a discussion at the beginning of PC, which states that the deity Kālacakra *is* a body composed of "an object of cognition" and "a cognition" related to a transcendent apperceptive mind. That discussion is explaining the opening line of *Stainless Light,* which describes Kālacakra as "a body in which cognition and the object of cognition are one" *(shes dang shes bya gcig pa'i sku).* Commenting on this line, *The Lotus Girl* (D1350, 76a.5) explains: "'Cognition' refers to an apprehending mind having an apperceptive nature. 'Object of cognition' refers to an apprehended mind having the nature of reality itself. Because those have the nature of Kālacakra, he is called 'a body in which cognition and the object of cognition are one.'"

In these contexts, "cognition" usually refers to the perceiving mind of the yogi or to Kālacakra himself. "Object of cognition" refers to the consort Viśvamātā, who is perceived as an object, but who is none other than the perceiving cognition itself. Such experiences are called "apperceptive" because they involve a mind perceiving itself. The emphasis in Yumo's citation is on "worldly," emphasizing the point made by Yumo above, that such visionary bodies do not appear to ordinary conceptual minds, and the fact that they are "appearances of the mind" does not mean that they are appearances of ordinary minds.

233. D1350, 102b.3.

234. This refers to the lengthy commentary on KCT 5.127, found in *Stainless Light.* The passage here can be found on Bu vol. 3, VP ch. 5, 73a.4. The bracketed reference to the Great Seal appears in Bu, but not in Yumo.

235. Bu vol. 2, VP ch. 2, 4a.3 (commenting on KCT 2.3).

236. This is lines 167–174 from *The Treasury of Dohā Verses* (D2224, 72b.5).

237. This is verses 27cd–28 from *On Purifying Mental Obscurations* (D1804, 108a.1).

238. D0447, 283a5. Yumo may have found this passage in Āryadeva's *Lamp* (D1803, 87a.1). Both Yumo and Āryadeva seem to want the sexual nature of the passage to be more oblique; in the tantra itself, the immediately preceding sentence is "The pure union of the vajra and the lotus is the method of pure 'mind' and 'that which comes from mind.'" Recall also that "mind" and "arisen from mind" are *sems* and *sems byung,* terms that are commonly used in exoteric contexts for "minds" and "mental factors."

239. *dPal dgyes pa rdo rje rtsa ba'i rgyud 'bum phrag lnga pa.* This is the large tantra that tradition holds as the source for the extant *Hevajra Tantra.* Some traditions suggest that an even larger version was the source of the 500,000. No such works have survived, and it is likely that Yumo found the passage quoted in another

exegetical work, perhaps from Vajragarbha's commentary. I have not located the passage; without context, the translation here should be considered preliminary, especially as YM and YM-SG disagree on the first line.

240. D0420, 71b.4.

241. D0420, 71a.7. This and the previous quote are from the "Chapter Explaining the Ultimate Meaning of the Term 'Self'" *(bdag sgra'i nges pa'i don zhes bya ba'i le'u).*

242. *bdag gi ming gis btags pa des As mtshon nas bshad pa de.* The letter *A* here refers to the first syllable of *A-ham* (Sanskrit for "I"). In the tantra itself, the larger passage is explaining both syllables of *A-ham* in order to suggest the ultimate meaning of "self" as a union of appearance and emptiness: *A* represents the appearing aspect, while *ham* is said to be without form (see D0420, 71b.2). Yumo is thus suggesting how the appearing dimension (i.e., the Great Seal) pervades all beings.

243. D0420, 71a.2.

244. Yumo is trying to make the case that the unnamed entity dwelling within everything mentioned in the above passages is in fact the Great Seal. He sees proof in this passage in the terms *bhaga* and *dharmadhātu,* which, as we learned earlier, are used as synonyms for the Great Seal.

245. D0422, 128a.2.

246. *ma dag pa'i dus na ma rig pa zhes brjod par 'gyur la.* The idea here seems to be that when Buddhists speak of something dwelling in all beings, they often speak of a "self," something that is only perceived to be there due to ignorance, and which perpetuates saṃsāric existence. The tantras, however (using strategies like explanations of the syllables *A* and *ham*), posit something pure dwelling within all beings, a pure "self," such as the Great Seal.

247. Bu vol. 1, VP ch. 1, 48a.5 (commenting on KCT 1.1d). I translate from Yumo here, though it differs from Bu. The ellipsis indicates a phrase that Yumo seems to have left out: "it is the innate joy" *(lhan cig skyes pa'i dka' ba dang).*

248. This is lines 323–326 from the *Treasury of Dohā Verses* (D2224, 74b.3).

249. *ci sems nyid 'od gsal ba nyid sems can la yod pa la ma rig pa zhes btags pa ma yin nam.* That is, aren't the above passages pointing to a lack of awareness of our nature, rather than indicating some entity like a Great Seal that dwells within us?

250. This exact passage does not appear in the Dergé edition (D0490), though it appears to be related to the verses on 53b.4. In the tantra itself, the subject of the passage is the goddess Prajñāpāramitā" *(shes rab kyi pha rol tu phyin ma).*

251. Here, Yumo seems to be using the "very nature of the mind" or the "mind-itself" *(sems nyid)* as a term for the Great Seal. His point is that, although the Great Seal may dwell within the ordinary mind and the elements of the physical body, this does not mean that she is the ordinary mind and body. Note that there is some confusion here between YM and YM-SG. YM has: *sems dang khams mtshungs pa min gyi/ sems nyid ni ma yin no/.* YM-SG has: *sems dang khams mtshungs pa yin gyi/ nyid ni ma yin no/.* Because the above passage discusses Prajñāpāramitā dwelling in the mind and the elements, I see no other way to read this passage but *sems dang khams mtshungs pa yin gyi/ sems nyid ni ma yin no/.*

252. The unspecified subject here is the complex of ideas surrounding the mind-itself, luminosity, Prajñāpāramitā, and the Great Seal.

253. The first lines six lines can be found on D0490, 53b.7; the remaining lines are not present.

254. *phyag rgya chen mo'i rgyu ma rig pa gnas pa la de skad ces brjod do.* "Causal agency" here is simply *rgyu* ("cause") but could also be read as "motion" to match "moving and unmoving" *(rgyu ba dang ni mi rgyu ba)* in the passage above. I suspect Yumo's intent is expressed in a similar verse near the beginning of the VP (Bu vol. 1, VP ch. 1, 5a.2): "Although fire always dwells in wood, it is not seen by means of cutting or splitting [the wood].... Similarly the luminosity of the mind is not seen by the means of conceptual meditations."

255. The name "sentient being" *(sems can)* is literally "mind possessor," in reference to the simple fact that they possess an ordinary mind *(sems)*. The question here asks: If all beings are in fact the residence of the Great Seal, then why wouldn't they be called "Great Seal possessors"? Or, less pedantically, if it is so obvious that the Great Seal dwells in all beings, why aren't all beings colloquially spoken of as her residence?

256. D1348, 24.2.

257. This passage does not appear in the Dergé edition of *Ornament of the Vajra Maṇḍala* (D0490); Yumo seems to have taken it from Āryadeva's *Lamp* (D1803, 72a.3), where it is also cited as being from *Ornament of the Vajra Maṇḍala.*

258. D0360, 3a.2 (verse 28).

259. D0360, 6a.7 (verse 110).

260. D0422, 122a.2. "Later-supplement" *(phyi ma'i phyi ma)* refers to the *Jñānatilaka Tantra (Ye shes thig le rnal 'byor ma'i rgyud).*

261. KCT 5.248 (Bu vol. 1, 146b.7). Here Yumo cites the title in a kind of diglossia, using the Tibetan for "wheel" *(dus)* and the Sanskrit for "time" *(cakra).* The VP identifies the "one and multiple, equal and unequal" language as being a reflection of Mādhyamika tenets *(dbu ma'i grub pa'i mtha')*; see Bu vol. 3, VP ch. 5, 146b.3.

262. *ma rig pa ni chos kyi rtsa ba yin pa'i phyir ro.* Yumo's point seems to be that Buddhist teachings all aim to overturn the ignorance that prevents us from seeing this.

263. D0361, 15a.6 (verses 32cd–33). Yumo here appears to read this passage slightly differently than it is usually interpreted. The full passage (which Yumo himself cites above on YM, 632) is "In a young girl's prognostic mirror, / A previously unseen thief is seen. / Having gone there, the officiant can see [him] / With his two ordinary eyes. / If [the girl] sees an existent form [in the mirror], / Why doesn't she see her own face? / If she sees a non-existent form, / Why isn't it the horns of a rabbit?" According to Nāropa's commentary (D1351, 263a.3), the passage describes a young girl *(gzhon nu ma)* whose eyes are blessed by mantras *(sngags)* so that she is able to see a prognostic image (of a previously unseen thief), which spontaneously arises in a mirror. The person who is the officiant *(sgrub pa po'i skyes bu)* of this prognostic ritual then goes to the place where the actual thief is, and sees what the young girl had told him about *(gzhon nu mas smras pa).*

Yumo cuts off the first two lines of verse, to elide mention of the "young girl," and his follow-up comments indicate that it is the "officiant" or "practitioner" *(sgrub pa po)* who is doing the seeing and non-seeing. I thus translate Yumo's follow-up comments to reflect how I think he wants the passage to be read.

264. He does not see his own face in the mirror, which responds to the objection about not seeing your own hand.

265. This one of several instances where YM and YM-SG have exactly opposite readings; here YM gives a positive sense ("not a cause to see"), and YM-SG gives a negative sense ("not a cause to not see"). I follow YM here: *rang la yod pa dang ye med pa mthong pa'i rgyur gyur pa ma yin no.* Such opposite readings of course tend to occur in difficult passages, where an editor may have been struggling to find the correct meaning. I understand Yumo's comment here as a response to the above objection that if something like the Great Seal were an intrinsic part of everyone, then she should be able to be seen, just as everyone with eyes can see their own hands. Yumo thus wants to suggest how it is plausible that something hidden within the person can come to be seen, and also how something obvious, like a body part, could not be seen. He thus turns to this passage, which (in the current context) suggests that a spiritually prepared practitioner can see extraordinary and ordinary appearances (the visionary thief and the actual thief), but in these acts of seeing still does not encounter something that is a part of him (his own face in the mirror). The follow-up question "How is this?" asks, "How is it that seeing can take place, when you are neither seeing something physical or immediately manifest, nor something illusory?"

266. Bu vol. 3, VP ch. 5, 47b.6 (commenting on KCT 5.119). Italics indicate root text (KCT 5.119). This discussion in the VP concludes with one final comment that seems helpful for interpreting Yumo's argument: "...the childish never see it. Why is this? It is due to the power of the demons of their afflictions."

267. Vajravārāhī is listed twice; her first mention is in Tibetan, while her name here is written in transliterated Sanskrit.

268. *de lta bu'i phyag rgya chen mo de ni sngon gyi dus na mthong bar 'gyur zhe na.* Because the following quotation is attributed simply to "the Buddha," the question appears simply to ask: "Is this Great Seal an authentic Buddhist teaching? Did practices related to seeing the Great Seal exist at the time of the Buddha?"

269. I have not located this precise passage, though it seems to be from the *Root Tantra.* Two passages similar to it appear in the first chapter of VP (Bu vol. 1, VP ch. 1, 19b.6, and 39a.3). Newman ("Outer Wheel of Time," 339 n. 29) has identified analogous passages in *The Hevajra Tantra, The Vajragarbha Commentary,* and the *Paramārthasaṃgraha.* The basic idea (which the VP indicates is found in "several tantras") is that if a yogi abandons conceptual deity-yoga type meditations, and practices completion stage type meditations for a single day, then the signs like smoke and so forth will arise. These signs provide confidence in the Buddha's words, proving that they are not false.

270. *rang gi rtog pa goms su 'jug pa'i phyir/ /'dod dang mya ngan 'jigs dang smyo/ /.* Yumo does not specify his source here, though it may be from the *Tshad ma rnam 'grel gyi rgyan* (D4221, 8a.4): *sngon mthong rjes su 'brang ba yis/ /rtogs pa don grub byed ma yin/ /'dod dang mya ngan 'jigs dang smyo/ /.* The sense here appears to be that conceptual meditations do not lead to quick appearance of the signs of smoke and so forth, but to the manifestation of negative emotions.

271. Yumo is quite terse here; he provides no source and introduces the passage simply with *'di skad du ston te.* This seems to indicate, "In explanations of

the opening phrase of most sūtras and tantras, 'At one time I heard this speech,' one finds the following explanations." What follows reads as a standard explanation of the first syllables of a sūtra or tantra *(E* = insight or emptiness, *vam* = compassion). This topic is often brought up in the Kālacakra context because the *Kālacakra Tantra* does not begin with this standard phrase, prompting the objection that it may thus not be an actual teaching of the Buddha. The typical Kālacakra response is to state that many terms and phrases can be used to express a single meaning, and thus a tantra does not have to begin with the stock phrase "At one time I heard this speech." This fits with Yumo's larger point here that there are many synonyms for the Great Seal, and that it is a concept that appears in many forms and can be experienced in multiple ways.

272. *yid la mi byed pa'i stong pa nyid.*

273. Based on YM-SG: *lhan cig skyes pa'i ye shes.* YM just reads "co-emergent" *(lhan cig skyes pa).*

274. In this line YM reads *rigs rgyud kyis,* and YM-SG reads *ring rgyud kyis;* I emend this to *rang rgyud kyis* (lit. "autonomously").

275. YM has: *zas gos 'phran tshegs gzhan la 'tshol byed pa'i.* I read this as *zas gos phran tshegs gzhan la 'tsho byed pa'i.*

276. Probably a reference to Yumo's principal teacher, 'Gro-mgon-gnam-la-rtsegs.

277. I read this line from YM-SG: *mtshon cha tshang par 'dzin pa yin,* i.e., I hold all of the secret weapons that protect one while progressing on the path. YM here has *mtshon cha tshangs par,* which would indicate "I hold the weapons, [just] as Brahma."

Translation 2

1. The first three are in editions of the *Collected Tantras of the Ancients (rNying ma rgyud 'bum):* (1) mTshams brag (TB), vol. 12 (na), 467–491; (2) gTing skyes (TK), vol. 9 (ta), 578–599; (3) sDe-dge (DG) vol. 4 (nga), 108b–117a. The A-'dzom-'brug-pa (AD) edition of the *Seventeen Tantras* was published in three volumes as *Rñiṅ ma'i rgyud bcu bdun* (New Delhi: Sanje Dorje, 1977). Note also that the tantra can be found in a manuscript edition of the *Collected Tantras* held by the British Library in London: the Rig-'dzin-tshe-dbang-nor-bu edition, vol. 10 (tha), 174a–182b; I have not had access to this edition.

2. The commentaries are in the "Lhasa" edition of the bKa' ma, sometimes called the "Exceedingly-Expanded Expanded Continuously Transmitted Precepts" *(bKa' ma rgyas pa shin tu rgyas pa),* referring to the fact that it more than doubles the size of the "Expanded Continuously Transmitted Precepts" published in 1982 by Dudjom Rinpoche.

The "Lhasa" edition was commissioned by the late Great Perfection master Khenpo Munsel (1916–1996) in 1993. The publication was compiled, managed, and edited by Tsering Gyamtso of Chamjor Monastery in Nyag-rong, working out of Chengdu, Sichuan. This treasure trove of rare works was printed in Lhasa in 110 volumes (the last volume being vol. *we*).

3. The commentary is found in vol. Be (105) of the above-mentioned edition of the *bKa' ma.* It is accompanied by a topical outline of the *Tantra of the Blazing Lamps,* called *A Summary of the Blazing Lamps (sGron ma 'bar ba'i don bsdus).*

4. By the editor's own admission, the current publication is a sort of pre-edition. A full re-editing, based on the original manuscripts, is in process but, like many such labors of love, is delayed for financial reasons. At the time of my visit with Tsering Gyatso in 2006, the manuscript was inaccessible. I am extremely grateful to him for providing me with an electronic edition of the commentary, based on the original manuscript and proofread; this has been an invaluable resource for my study here.

5. The title given here in the "language of India" *(rgya gar skad)* is based on DG and AD. In TB and TK, this title is either corrupt or in an Indian language other than standard Sanskrit (TB has *pu tsa sa ne gi ga ta rad na A lo ke dza la da dra*). It appears that the editors of DG and AD may have reconstructed the title, casting it into normative Sanskrit.

6. bCom-ldan-'das-dpal-snang-ba-rang-shar-ba.

7. Note that the organization of the tantra is slightly deceptive here, as the two introductory scenes and a brief summation of the tantra are included in chapter 1, a chapter that is technically dedicated to the "water lamp." The introductory scenes and the summary should be thought of as applying to the entire tantra, i.e., they are an introduction to and summation of all four chapters. Here, I have placed them within chapter 1 to preserve the way that the tantra has traditionally been organized.

8. The *Seventeen Tantras* follow a convention of having two introductory scenes: an "ordinary" one beginning with the formulaic line commonly translated "Thus I have heard at one time" *('di skad bdag gis bstan pa'i dus gcig na)*, and an "extraordinary" one beginning with the line "Thus I have taught..." *('di skad bdag gis bstan pa'i dus gcig na)*. These two scenes reinforce the basic scenario of the tantra, which is Dorjé Chang giving a lecture to himself. In this first introduction, Dorjé Chang is cast as an impersonal awareness, rising up from the ground and presencing to itself; this presencing—the ground seeing itself in a blaze of light—is the extraordinary way in which the core meaning of the tantra was first conveyed.

The remainder of the tantra presupposes that a portion of awareness did not recognize itself in the ground-presencing, and thus did not understand this initial teaching. In order to attain understanding, it has nowhere to turn but to itself, so Dorjé Chang (the student) is forced to ask Dorjé Chang (the Teacher) for a detailed explanation, using the convention of words.

9. I.e., the subjects explained in the *Tantra of the Blazing Lamps*.

10. This is a phoneticized rendering of what the commentary calls the "pith syllables that join the two introductory scenes" *(gleng gzhi gnyis kyi mtshams sbyar sgra don tshig)*. These are syllables that spontaneously resounded in the sky following the extraordinary introductory scene. Because they are not Tibetan (and thus would not properly be represented by Wylie transliteration), and because they vary considerably among the different editions of the tantra, I have simply given a basic phonetic rendering of them. While the first syllable (*sarba,* which is the Tibetan way of transliterating the Sansrkit *sarva,* "all") suggests that the syllables may be in an Indian language, Tibetan tantric literature frequently contains various kinds of "ḍākinī languages" *(dak yig)* and "code languages" *(brda yig),* which use characters that visually appear to be Tibetan but actually represent syllables and pronunciations

that are completely different than Tibetan. This brief passage would be an interesting subject for future research, especially given that the commentary MTP (p. 56ff.) treats it with more than forty pages of comments, the longest single section of the entire commentary.

11. *rgya che la dkyil yangs pa,* i.e., its vastness is not disorienting or barren, but still pervaded by the central core of its awareness.

12. The tantra simply reads *yongs su rdzogs pa* ("perfectly complete"), which MTP suggests refers to the teacher.

13. Several different names are used to distinguish Dorjé Chang the Teacher from Dorjé Chang in his guise as a student. In the context of this tantra, the *teacher* is referred to as Pure-Appearance Dorjé Chang (sNang-dag-rdo-rje-'chang), Dorjé Chang the Great, Teacher Dorjé Chang, Transcendent Victor Dorjé Chang, and Buddha Dorjé Chang. The *student* is referred to as Pure-Lineage Dorjé Chang or Pure-Continuum Dorjé Chang (rGyud-dag-rdo-rje-'chang), and Causal Dorjé Chang (rGyu-yi-rdo-rje-'chang).

14. MTP reads "flower" as referring to this tantra, perhaps based on the tantra's subtitle *Beautiful Precious Golden Flower*. An annotation in DG interprets it as referring to the "Reality Body and awareness" *(chos sku dang rig pa).*

15. The vocative *kye kye* is common at the beginning of tantric dialogues and appears frequently in this tantra. The student uses it as a sort of formal and excited salute when addressing the Teacher; the Teacher then uses it to express his happiness with the questions, and as a percussive wake-up call at the beginning of his speeches.

16. MTP, 121 lists these as distorted appearances, visionary appearances of primordial gnosis (such as the little-linked-lambs), and bardo appearances: *'khrul ba'i snang ba dang/ lta ba dngos byung gi ye shes dang/ chos nyid kyi bar ma do'i dang gsum gyi snang ba.*

17. The Teacher occasionally uses the vocative *kye ma* before addressing the student; this is similar to the vocative Hey! Hey! *(kye kye)*, but it carries the sense of wonder at the profundity of the questions, and a sense of urgency for the student to listen.

18. MTP, 125 explains these as (1) impure appearances, and (2) the naturally pure pure appearances of primordial gnosis *('khrul ba'i snang ba rang dag pa dag pa ye shes kyi shang ba gnyis ka).*

19. MTP, 126, explains these as (1) the eye consciousness *(dmig gi rnam shes)*, which apprehends forms, and (2) the unerring suchness of the eye *(mig gi de cho na nyid ma 'khrul pa)*, through which one's own awareness is perceived in vision.

20. That is, one sees the "factors of both cyclic existence and transcendence" *('khor ba dang nya ngan las 'das pa gnyis ka'i cha)*; see MTP, 127. This discussion revolves on a play on the common term "apprehending factor" *('dzin cha)*; as the term *cha* ("factor") can also mean "parts of a pair," the suggestion is that the "apprehending factor" of the eyes is twofold.

21. *ring ba'i rgyud.*

22. Due to this lamp functioning as the ordinary eye-consciousness, the raw data concerning the "external" world are gathered in; this gives rise to conceptual minds that interpret appearances as being other than the perceiver.

23. *bDag med sku,* i.e., the little linked-lambs.

24. MTP describes this as like when an honest man walks into a temple: he can appreciate the place and the objects that it contains but does not think of them as "mine."

25. I.e., water does not cling to anything and does not have any inherent shape.

26. MTP interprets this as meaning that during the development of the embryo, the water lamp matures the vibrant essence of all the sense faculties into a "pupil" *(a 'bras)* in the gateway of the eyes. This pupil is perhaps better thought of as the basic circular dark/light coloration of the eyes, which symbolizes the eyes' power to serve as the basis for cyclic existence and transcendence.

27. These are the eyes in their dimension of being unstained, like a lotus.

28. I.e., to apprehend the objects of all the sense faculties.

29. These are the coarse functions of the eyes, the powers that they derive from being formed by the ordinary elemental energies. The transcendent functions of the eyes are mentioned below as the powers derived from primordial gnosis (another way of saying "ultimate elemental energies"). This basic distinction of the eyes' "elements" and "gnosis" relates to an early stage in the body's development, where the development of the body is overseen by two tiny eyes, which direct the formation of its transcendent and mundane features.

30. MTP notes that "residence" *(gnas)* refers to the internal residence of awareness, i.e., the heart; "above" *(gong ma)* is the sky. Thus the transcendent functions of the eyes are to apprehend awareness within the body, and in the sky, during visionary experience.

31. Non-objects *(yul med)* refers to emptiness; MTP discusses this in terms of seeing the "eighteen emptinesses."

32. MTP only includes the above three lines in its explanation of the "residence," putting the below six lines near the end of the explanation of question 6. Note that TDD only cites the first three lines in its explanation of the "residence," but TCD includes all nine lines in its explanation.

33. The eyes being described here are not the ordinary eyes but the two tiny eyes that oversee the formation of the embryo. "Black and white" here suggests the basic dark/light features of an eye and is symbolic of these eyes' mundane and transcendent functions.

34. Note that this section is not commented on in MTP.

35. Though the query about "aspects" appears here in the statement of questions, it is not dealt with below, in the presentation of answers. Note also that this line appears only in TB (it is not in TK, DG, AD, or MTP).

36. MTP, 181 interprets this as meaning that this type of insight does not arise due to the words or esoteric instructions from others (such as lamas); rather, it is self-emergent.

37. MTP, 181 says that "others" here refers to other types of ordinary mind or impure cognition.

38. *skyed par byed pa'i rtsa bzhi.* According to MTP, this refers to the fact that the four channels (listed just below) give rise to the body *(lus)*, memory-driven thought *(dran pa)*, cognition *(shes pa)*, and the sense faculties *(dbang po).*

39. *lnga bzhi.* Literally "five/four," this is a shorthand way of referring to the five insights that reside in the four channels.

40. MTP, 205 interprets "four names" *(ming bzhi)* as referring to the body, the lamps, insight, and the three bodies. "Name" here may be playing off of the classic Buddhist concept of "name and form" *(ming dang gzugs)*, which is a way of referring to the five aggregates of which a person is composed. The person's form aggregate is the referent of "form," while the remaining nonphysical aggregates are called "name" or the "four names." In MTP's description, the "four names" also include the body and are potentials for sentient beings' physical and mental dimensions, which existed in the primordial ground, encapsulated in the ground's knowing dimension. The function of insight usually being to "distinguish" things, in this primordial context insight distinguishes the four names from each other, giving concrete structure to the person. MTP's comments on the passage are:

The "name" of the body *(lus kyi ming)* [arises] from the condensed pure quintessence of the elements *('byung ba'i dwangs ma 'dus pa)*. The "name" of the lamps *(sgron ma'i ming)* arises from the quintessence of primordial gnosis *(ye shes kyi dwangs ma)*. The "name" of insight *(shes rab kyi ming)* [arises] from the quintessence of cognitive energy *(shes pa'i dwangs ma)*. And the "name" of the three bodies *(sku gsum gyi ming)* [emerges] from the quintessence of awareness *(rig pa'i dwangs ma)*.

In the beginning, the primordial radiation composed of these four "names" became present as a natural flow from the ground, and in the end came to reside in the body. It exists [there] as insight, as the essence whose function is to distinguish everything: being and non-being, existence and non-existence, knowing and not-knowing, liberation and non-liberation, realization and non-realization, cyclic existence and transcendence, and so forth. Primordially it was present in the ground; it is not adventitious [and thus is] presently in the dimension of the body, residing and moving in the channels.

41. MTP interprets this by saying that when the mind comes under the control of primordial gnosis, the winds are stilled, such that they do not emerge from the gateways of the nostrils, the channels, or the crown of the head.

42. *de la sogs pa,* literally "that and so forth." MTP reads this as referring to beings who do not have the experiences listed above because their capacity for realization is the "lowest of the low." Even so, this insight will help them to answer basic questions about cyclic existence and transcendence, which will cause them to turn away from cyclic existence, develop faith in the Great Perfection, and eventually become enlightened.

43. MTP, 245 identifies this as the dharma eye *(chos kyi mig)*.

44. I.e., above in section 2.1.2.2, the Teacher made a brief statement about each of the four lamps, which the student claims not to have understood, and asks for further explanation.

45. MTP identifies *thig le'i sku* as the "empty body of the singular bindu" *(stong pa thig le nyag gcig gi sku)*.

46. MTP interprets this as meaning that whoever meditates on it will attain the four visions.

47. In its commentary on these lines, MTP (pp. 249–250) lists the four empowerments but does not detail how they might be related to the color red: "What is its color? Without having to confer them through activity or exertion, these four self-empowerments are perfectly complete within the ground: (1) the fabricated

empowerment whose conferral involves causes, (2) the unfabricated empowerment that is based on mere symbolic substances, (3) the extremely unfabricated empowerment that relies on signs, and (4) the completely unfabricated empowerment that relies on one's own condition. Thus, red is its predominant color, separating from the other [colors], and appearing clearly to oneself. This is not an adventitiously produced [appearance]. It is the presence of the primordial, natural, radiance of reality itself."

48. MTP suggests that this refers to the nature of the channels through which the *thig-le* move.

49. I.e., based on the use of bodily postures in yoga.

50. *stong pa nyid las rang log pa;* MTP reads this as meaning that it is not a static emptiness or vacuity.

51. *spros dang bsdu med par.* The tantra here seems to be imitating some of the language associated with the practice of "holding in" the *thig-le* in ordinary sexual yoga, as the phrase also suggests "without emitting or retaining." An annotation in MTP suggests this is describing a time when the karmic winds have ceased, such that the winds are neither coming nor going.

52. "Effort" refers to methods like manually stimulating the eye or the channels, described just below.

53. *srog chags rkun pa,* i.e., a cat *(byi la).*

54. MTP, 288 indicates that he understood these implicitly *(shugs gyis)* in the explanations of the other three lamps but did not fully grasp their details. These lines also suggest how Dorjé Chang's "misunderstanding" of Dorjé Chang is simply a ruse, an excuse for the tantra to be taught in words and thus benefit sentient beings.

55. I.e., corrals in the little linked-lambs.

56. MTP says this refers to not holding them back with wind-related yogas.

57. MTP interprets this line as "practicing constantly, they appear continuously."

58. MTP interprets this as an inseparable union with the buddhas.

59. MTP interprets this as the two branches of the preliminaries and the actual practice. The preliminaries are the "distinguishing" practices (colloquially called *ru shan*) of the first two lines, while the main practices involve the four visions, which are described obliquely in the following lines.

60. MTP interprets these lines as describing our sleep experiences, when awareness does not radiate into the sky in visions but rather remains internally radiant.

61. MTP, 316 notes that this is not the ordinary eye sense-faculty but rather the "suchness of the sense faculty, which is devoid of production or cessation."

62. MTP gives these as (1) the important point of the gateway, which is the eyes, (2) the important point of the objective sphere, which is the sky, (3) and the important point of awareness, which is the little linked-lambs.

63. In particular, from the space between the eyebrows (MTP, 318).

64. I.e., as the two sides that join to make a *na-ro;* see section 2.4.2.11 below.

65. *rang snang stong nyid.*

66. I.e., filled with rainbows.

67. The final two lines here appear in DG, AD, and TK. TB places them below at the end of section 2.4.5. TK also repeats them below. This section of MTP is lost, and MTP does not treat the lines below.

Translation 3A

1. *bKa' rgyud skor bzhi.* The collection is colloquially known as "the Zhang Zhung sNyan rGyud," although it does not contain all the works associated with this tradition. The title *Four Cycles* reflects the fact that the works in the collection are organized into the four categories "outer," "inner," "secret," and "ultra secret." The various editions of the collection are not always in agreement about which works belong in which categories. For a detailed review of editions, see Henk Blezer's "Brief Bibliographical Key to *Zhang Zhung Snyan Rgyud* Editions with Special Attention for Sources on the Early Lineage," *Revue d'Etudes Tibétaines 20* (2011): 135–203.

2. See Kværne's translation of this important catalog in "The Canon of the Tibetan Bönpos," *Indo-Iranian Journal 16* (1974): 18–56, 96–144. The catalog has become the conservative standard for which texts should be included in the canon, an issue that has taken on all the more importance given the destruction of the canon during the violence of the Chinese invasion. For descriptions of the extant edition of the *bKa'* section of the canon, and for issues surrounding the reconstruction of the *bKa' rten* section, see Martin, Kværne, and Nagano's catalog of the Kanjur, and Karmay and Nagano's catalog of the Katen texts.

3. The canon itself is divided into two main parts: (1) The "Word" *(bKa')*, which consists of works spoken by Buddhas, and (2) "That Based on the Word" *(bKa rten)*, which consists of treatises and commentaries. *Advice on the Six Lamps* appears in the first category; in Kværne's translation, it is listed under entry K 108. As a later, commentarial work, Drugyalwa's commentary is not listed in the catalog.

4. Samten Karmay, *A Catalogue of Bonpo Publications* (Tokyo: Toyo Bunko, 1977), 97.

5. Published by Professor Lokesh Chandra and Tenzin Namdak as *History and Doctrine of Bon-Po Niṣpanna Yoga* (New Delhi: International Academy of Indian Culture, 1968).

6. The title of the catalog is *bKa' rgyud skor bzhi'i dpe rtsis mu tig phreng ba.* A fragmentary copy of this catalog has been published previously. See p. 2a.6 for the mention of Shardza's authorship of the catalog at the time of the carving of the blocks, and for his editorial work *(zhib dag)* on the collection: *bka' rgyud skor bzhi'i par bkod pa'i dus na dpe rtsis bkod dgos kyi gsung gis bskul ba la brten nas skor bzhi'i bon rnams la zhib dag dang chab gcig tu shar rdza'i bya bral bkra shis rgyal mtshan gyis sbyar ba dge'o.*

7. The catalog also seems to have circulated separately. It does, however, appear that the catalog could be an intrinsic part of the Nyag-rong edition; at the very least, the Nyag-rong blocks were organized around a scheme similar to Shardza's catalog, as the numbers on the texts themselves follow the catalog. Two facts raise the suspicion that the catalog might have simply been attached to the Nyag-rong edition: first, the text titles as written in the catalog sometimes vary slightly from the renderings of the titles that appear on the title pages of the actual works; five of the items in the catalog are also missing from the printed text itself (which may simply indicate that the blocks or the print is incomplete).

8. This is the Snellgrove manuscript mentioned in Kværne's "Canon of the Tibetan Bönpos," K 108. Thanks to H.H. Menri Trizin for allowing me access to a copy of this manuscript.

9. *rDzogs pa chen po zhang zhung snyan rgyud bka' rgyud skor bzhi'i gsung pod,* ed. sNang-mtha'-bstan-'dzin-nyi-ma (n.p.: Zhang-Bod Educational and Cultural Texts, Zhang bod shes rig dpe tshogs, 2005). I refer to this edition with the abbreviation NTTZ. Thank you to Lopön Trinley Nyima for a copy of this.

10. See Daniel Martin, Per Kværne, and Yasuhiko Nagano, eds., *A Catalogue of the Bon Kanjur* (Osaka: National Museum of Ethnology, 2003), 2–3, for information on these editions. The editions are (1) the first edition, in 154 volumes (Chengdu: Ayong Rinpoche, 1985); (2) the second edition in 192 volumes (Sichuan: Ha-san-yon and bon-slob Nam-mkha' bstan-'dzin, 1987); and the third edition in 178 volumes (Chengdu [though listed as Lhasa]: Mongyal Lhasey Rinpoche and Shense Namkha Wangden, 1995).

11. Note that these commentaries are not in Nyima Tenzin's listing of the *bKa' rgyud skor bzhi*. It also seems notable that Uri's commentary is included in Snellgrove's Dolpo manuscript, while Drugyalwa's is not. Both commentaries are found in the Menri and Nyag-rong editions.

12. Uri Sogyal (U-ri-bsod-rgyal) is short for Uri Sonam Gyaltsen (U-ri-bsod-nams-rgyal-mtshan). The title of his commentary is *sGron ma'i 'grel pa nyi 'od rgyan* (ZZNG ba).

13. See his *brGyud pa'i bla ma'i rnam thar* (ZZNG ka), 66.5.

14. A biographical sketch of Drugyalwa is on BN, 98.4. For a biography in English, see Kværne's translation of a short biography from the *A khrid thun mtshams:* Per Kværne, "Bonpo Studies: The A Khrid System of Meditation, Part I," *Kailash 1*, no. 1 (1973): 41ff.

15. Karmay, *Arrow and the Spindle,* 119.

16. Karmay, *Arrow and the Spindle,* 119. Karmay also provides an interesting discussion of how the Dru family was brought to an end by being incorporated into the line of the Panchen Lamas, its properties becoming the possession of Tashi Lhunpo Monastery.

17. BN, 98.5.

18. Kværne, "A-Khrid System 1," 43.

19. *sGron ma drug gi dgongs don 'grel pa* (ZZNG ma).

20. Modern Bönpos have suggested to me that Uri is probably older, though I have not ascertained his exact dates (he is considered to be from the thirteenth century). His commentary also appears before Drugyalwa's in ZZNG collection, a pride of place that points toward it being older. It also seems relevant here that Drugyalwa's commentary does not appear in Snellgrove's Dolpo manuscript, though Uri's does.

21. There is, for instance, a whole world of Bön Prajñāpāramitā literature waiting to be explored. Individual texts being cast as both Bön and Nyingma works are also abundant. See, for instance, the ZZNG's own *rTags tshad gsal sgron che ba* (ZZNG sha) appearing in the Nyingma *Bi ma snying thig*, as Garab Dorje's *gSang ba chen po'i rtags kyi yi ge.*

Translation 3B

1. "Six Points on the Enlightened Mind" *(byang chub sems kyi gnad drug)* is an alternate way of referring to the lamps, but refers in particular to the brief descriptions of each of the lamps that appear below, at 2.1.3.3.2.

2. That is, Küntu Zangpo pervades everywhere and through everything, but this apparent diversity does not cause him to waver from his primordial state of enlightenment.

3. I.e., to the two forms.

4. *thug phrad 'bral med du 'tshal,* the idea being that Kūntu Zangpo is within you, such that you are always in contact with him, or that you constantly encounter each other.

5. Dra-bye, a location in northwestern Tibet said to be Gyerpungpa's main retreat site. For an investigation of this area, see John Vincent Bellezza, "A Preliminary Archaeological Survey of Da Rog mTsho," *Tibet Journal 25* (1999): 55–91.

6. *bcings tshad kyi sgrog las dkrol gnas/ mnyam pa'i thang la phyung ste.* This is a pithy phrase that appears in many of the histories of Gyerpungpa's encounters with his teacher. Literally, it says "having freed him from the full measure of the fetters that bound him, he sent him to the even plain." "Even plain" refers to his coming down from the heights of his arrogance, or being freed from the highs and lows of his ordinary mind. Another connotation is that of a horse being released from a hobble *(sgrog),* so that it can take its natural place roaming about the plains.

7. That is, all of his attainments and magical powers had still left him basically unchanged.

8. This sentence based on NR.

9. "Day" is included based on NR.

10. "Teacher" is based on NR.

11. *zab mo'i snying gtam tshig gsum khyod la bstan.* Literally, this is "I will teach you three words [of] profound heart-advice" (NR has *tshigs gsum,* "three verses"). There is no obvious threefold structure to the following advice. Drugyalwa interprets this line as meaning "three levels of advice"; his categories "internal, secret, and supremely secret" are three of the four classes of the ZZNG collection.

12. *spang gnyen ngo skal.* The idea here is that the 84,000 gateways, or teachings, of Bön each have a specific problem or "abandonment" that they can help overcome, those abandonments being the 84,000 afflictions. The number 84,000 is often used to mean "immeasurable," but is also said to be the number of breaths that a person takes in a single day. In this context, because ordinary mental states are said to be impelled by internal winds, each breath maintains one of the afflictions.

13. That is, they are like *ghee,* or clarified butter.

14. "Primordial Teacher" here refers to Küntu Zangpo, while "Sangdu" is gSang-ba-'dus-pa, the last teacher in this divine lineage, who (according to some sources) passes the teaching to the priests of the gods, nāgas, and humans, from whom it then came to the "hearing lineage" of men.

15. This sentence based on NR.

16. Lha-gshen-yongs-su-dag-pa, the first member of this lineage.

17. Based on NR. The Menri edition describes this not as the "long lineage" *(ring brgyud)*, but says "those were transmitted via *samādhi*" *(de dag ting 'dzin gyis brgyud la)*.

18. "Short" lineage refers to the teaching coming straight from Küntu Zangpo to Gyerpungpa, rather than the "longer" lineage that was passed from Küntu Zangpo through the mind transmission and down through the hearing transmission.

19. *don rgyud,* literally "meaning" or "significant" lineage. The term is used to refer to a lineage that transmits an essential meaning, in contrast to a lineage that transmits words *(tshig rgyud)*.

20. This sentence based on NR.

21. Based on the Menri root text: *snying po'i thog tu gang gis phebs pa min.* The Menri and NR editions of the commentary have *gnyen po* instead of *snying po,* suggesting that such teachings will not "become an antidote" to anything.

22. This is actually the concluding summation for the whole introductory section. Note also that the Menri edition states that there are three topics to this section; NR correctly states there are two.

23. *rgyal thebs*, which here has a meaning similar to *rgyal tshabs* ("regent"), i.e., someone who has the authority to act in place of the king.

24. See the homage, section 2.1.1, above.

25. I follow the root text here *(rang rig ye sangs rgyas)*; Drugyalwa has *rang rig ye shes sangs rgyas pa.*

26. *bon sku,* which is the Bön equivalent of the Dharma Body *(chos sku)*. Less literally, this would be the "Reality Body."

27. This last phrase glosses *'ubs kyi chub*. The colloquialism *'ubs kyi* means "collected together," and *chub* means "mastered" with the connotation of "enlightenment" *(byang chub)*. While a "buddha" *(sangs rgyas)* is perfection in its "expansive" *(rgyas)* form, the ground is here being characterized as a primordial, folded-in, unexpanded perfection, which then becomes spontaneously present through its own enlightened dynamics.

28. *cho 'phrul sna tshogs su g.yo.*

29. *byed pa*. Note that NR has *'byed pa* "divisions."

30. *bon dbyings*. This is the Bön equivalent of *chos dbyings (dharmadhātu)*. Less literally, it could be translated as "expanse of reality."

31. *shes rig rgyud kyi kun gzhi;* this is the ground in its "individuated" dimension, located at the heart of each particular being.

32. *ngo bo nyid kyi gzhi gcig.*

33. *'gal dog bri gang med.* The phrase *'bri gang med* can also mean that it never "decreases or increases," meaning that it does not have to become large to pervade a universe, or to become small to reside in a sesame seed.

34. *spyi spungs chen po.*

35. *bon nyid*. This is the Bön equivalent of *chos nyid (dharmatā)*. Less literally, it could be translated as "reality-itself."

36. This is a common formula for describing the ground: an "example" *(dpe)* expressing the nature of the ground is the sky or space *(nam mkha')*; the ultimate

"meaning" or "significance" *(don)* of the ground is that it is "reality itself" *(bon nyid)*; and the sign *(rtags)* through which the ground is realized is the "mind itself" *(sems nyid)*. (Note that, based on NR, I have reordered this sentence to make these correspondences more clear.)

37. *gnas pa don gyi kun gzhi.*

38. *rnam par shes rig rgyal po.*

39. *rig pa'i ye shes la yul can gyi shes pa zhes bya'o.* "Subjective" *(yul can)* is literally "object-possessor," a term commonly used to mean "subject," i.e., that which knows or "possesses" objects. Drugyalwa often uses the term in the sense of "source"; here the gnostic energy of awareness is being indicated as the source of the three visionary objects.

40. *grol ba'i gzhi.* This also has the sense of "the ground back to which they return," "the ground into which they disappear."

41. "Awareness" is based on the root text; Drugyalwa's commentary here actually reads "the gnostic energy of awareness" *(rig pa'i ye shes)*.

42. *bsam pa'i blo.* This plays off the term *blo'i sems* ("ordinary mind") in the root text.

43. The term *bön* here refers to objects of the mind; outside of Bön texts, the term *dharma (chos)* would be used.

44. Based on NR.

45. *yul can ma bu rtsal gsum rnam grangs.* "Source" here is *yul can;* literally "object possessor," the term commonly means "subject" (as opposed to "object"). Here it has the sense that the mother, son, and dynamic energy are the sources of the three bodies, the three poisons, and so forth, dependent on if they are properly recognized.

46. The Tibetan for these three is *gzhi, snying po,* and *cho 'prul.*

47. The unstated subject here would seem to be "the ground," as this is the conclusion of the section describing the ground.

48. The unstated referent of "that" would seem to "the ground." More particularly, Drugyalwa could be referring to "self-emergent primordial gnosis" *(rang byung ye shes)*, the dimension of awareness that shines forth as objects, and which contrasts to the perceiving dimension of awareness, termed "self-knowing primordial gnosis" *(rang rig ye shes)*.

49. Drugyalwa here distinguishes "memory" *(dran pa)* from "negative memory" or "wrong memory" *(log pa'i dran pa)*. The first would serve to bring about realization, through remembering or recognizing one's true nature. The latter refers to the memory-driven thought of the ordinary mind.

50. *lhag gir mthong.* Note that the root text in the ZZNG edition and Drugyalwa's follow-up comments here have the more common *lhag gis mthong.* This literally means "seen clearly," seen "evidently," but is being used here to evoke the accomplishment of "superior insight" or "higher seeing" (*lhag mthong)*.

51. I follow the root text here; Drugyalwa's rendering of the verse has "stainless" *(dri med)*.

52. *dmangs.* That is, just as it is inappropriate for a king to follow his people (rather than leading), so awareness does not follow after objects.

53. *yul gyi rig pa.* This does not refer to awareness as an object but to "awareness [that knows] the objects," awareness in its subjective dimension that perceives

awareness in its objective dimension; in other words, the self-knowing primordial gnosis *(rang rig ye shes).*

54. The "five bodies" *(sku lnga)* refers to the usual three buddha-bodies, plus (4) "the essential body" *(ngo bo nyid kyi sku)*, and (5) "the body of manifest enlightenment" *(mngon par byang chub sku).*

55. The "five deities" (*lha lnga)* is a set of five major deities in the Bön pantheon. Their names, along with the colors and directions normally associated with them, are (1) gShen-lha-'od-dkar (white, center), (2) Gar-gsas-btsan-po (green, north), (3) gNam-gsas-dbyings-rum (red, west); (4) rGod-gsas-khams-pa (blue, south); (5) gSas-rje-dbyings-rum (yellow, east).

56. *tshangs pa'i gsung dbyangs.* Here "brahmā's speech" is referring to superior, pure, or extraordinary speech.

57. *lhan skyes ma rig pa.*

58. *dran rig blo'i shes pa.*

59. *kun btag ma rig pa.*

60. This second line does not appear in Drugyalwa's commentary.

61. "Cognition" *(shes pa)* is based on the root text; the commentary here has "awareness" *(rig pa).*

62. *nyon mongs yid,* or (in the subject heading) *bdag 'dzin nyon mongs yid.*

63. NR is somewhat simpler: "Apprehending in that way, the apprehender apprehended itself as 'self' and the objects as 'other.'"

64. *'du byed las.*

65. *yid gzugs.*

66. The root text here has "strayed" *('khrul)*, while the commentary has "wandered" *('khyams).*

67. Uri's commentary (p. 316) more directly addresses the line from the root text. It describes how each type of consciousness is impelled toward its respective object due to the increase of karmic predispositions. This then causes straying (*'khrul ba)* into the "appearance" (*snang ba)* of one of the six types of beings. The eyes, for instance, are increasingly impelled toward visible form, due to growing karmic predispositions, and this ultimately results in beings straying into the hell realms. In the same way, the ears are related to the hungry ghost realm, the nose is related to the god and demigod realms, the tongue is related to the human realm, and the sense of touch is related to the animal realm. (Uri's outline does not refer to the mental consciousness.)

68. *lam rgyu lnga,* which is the same as the above "five paths of saṃsāra" *('khor ba'i lam lnga)*; these are five "paths" of rebirth, which correspond to the six types of beings, but with the gods and demigods counted as one.

69. "Mind" *(sems)* here is a way of referring to the ground *(gzhi)*, similar to the usage of "enlightened mind" *(byang chub sems)* as a synonym for the ground.

70. *nam mkha'i ngang*. The NR edition replaces this with "the light of space" (*nam mkha'i 'od)*, which matches the root verse.

71. Drugyalwa adds one significant word to the root verse here; he specifies that mind and winds emerge due to the "dynamic energy" *(rtsal)* of the relationship between the light of space *(nam mkha'i 'od)* and awareness. This provides a clear example of how the concept of *rtsal* is often seen as a dynamic energy that emerges from the relationship of two things.

72. The final six lines here do not appear in Drugyalwa's commentary.

73. Above, when Drugyalwa cites the root verses, he gives only a basic summary of the verses and interjects a few words of his own. I have reproduced the verses in full, based on the root text. Note also that the final six lines do not appear in the commentary at all. The discussions that Drugyalwa is pointing to begin on GDGG, 380.

74. I.e., as suggested by the following verses, the aggregates and poisons act as the cause and condition for action and the afflictions.

75. Drugyalwa's rendering of this line is slightly different from the root text, which reads "Come formative actions, and the various types of behavior."

76. "Formatives" *('du byed, saṃskāra)* are the fourth of the Buddhist "five aggregates," which are the five essential parts that make the mind and body of a person. In this context, "formatives" are a group of mental events *(sems byung)*, which are often enumerated in a list of forty-nine (these being derived from a larger group of fifty-one overall mental events, minus "feelings" and "discriminations" which are the second and third of the five aggregates). Some of the "formatives" are mental events like interest or mindfulness that are involved in ascertaining objects; some are "afflicted" mental events like ignorance, anger, jealousy, or laziness; other are virtuous mental events, like faith, equanimity, or nonviolence. Together, these determine how we react to objects and lead us to perform certain types of action (which Drugyalwa lists as virtuous, nonvirtuous, and neutral). As such, "formatives" are said to be the factors of mind that are responsible for the actual "planting" of karmic seeds in the ground, and for causing beings to take form in a particular birth. For the classifications of mental factors in the *abhidharma* context, see Louis de la Valée Poussin, *Abhidharmakoṣabhāṣyam of Vasubandhu*, translated from the French by Leo Pruden (Berkeley: Asian Humanities Press, 1988), vol. 1, 189ff. See also Hopkins, *Meditation on Emptiness,* 238ff.

77. The Menri edition identifies this as the conclusion to "the parting of cyclic existence and transcendence," but the conclusion to that section is above, at section 2.2.1.2.2.3. I thus follow NR here.

78. *rang chas su gnas,* which could also be read as "present as part of you."

79. *mkha' gsal nam mkha'i mthong rum.* Literally, "a radiant space" *(mkha' gsal)* that is "within the space-cavity" *(nam mkha'i mthong rum)*. This simply means "in a luminous space inside the chest cavity" (as is explained here, the chest and heart are related to the space element).

80. Each of the five main internal organs is said to be a "support" or "seat" *(rten)* for one of the five elements. This topic is discussed in more detail at GDGG, 381.

81. "Deep red tent" *(mchong gur smug po)* is literally "dark *mchong*[-colored] tent"; *mchong* is the name of a semiprecious stone (possibly sardonyx) that is dark red, orange, or brown, and striated with white. Because of its coloring, the stone is used as a metaphor for the heart. The "crystal roof," literally "crystal eaves" *(shel gyi kha bad can)*, refers to the fat that surrounds the heart. The metaphor here also evokes the iconic Tibetan image of a dark-colored tent topped with glittering snow.

82. *she thun rtsa 'dzin.* The term *she thun* is "heart" in the language of Zhang Zhung. This refers in particular to the channel that links the heart to the eyes.

83. This inner space is the "palace" where the "king of awareness" *(rig pa'i rgyal po)* dwells; the small cavity is also sometimes said to contain "the thumb-sized primordial gnosis" *(ye shes tshon gang)*, mentioned below at GDGG, 383.

84. *bon gyi sku,* which is the Bön equivalent of the Dharma Body *(chos sku).* Less literally, this would be the "Reality Body."

85. *khong gsal chen po;* this refers to an internal radiance, like a lamp inside a pot.

86. *khong shar chen po.*

87. The root text here reads "shine forth" *(shar)*; Drugyalwa's rendering of the root text replaces this with "related to" or "connected to" *('brel tshul).*

88. Uri is more explicit here, indicating that "body" refers to the parents' physical red/white contributions, which then come together with the memory-driven mind *(dran sems)* for the first time.

89. Light here represents the dimension of awareness that results in the formation of the body, as described just above.

90. *shes pa'i rtsal,* based on NR; the Menri edition has *gnas pa'i rtsal.*

91. This refers to the three main channels, the "trunk" from which all the other channels branch off. It also has the sense of the "trunk" or "core" of the physical body.

92. Note that Drugyalwa does not precisely follow these subject headings in his discussion below. The topical outline in the NR edition lays out this section more simply: "Second, how the channels and winds develop. This has two parts: (1) how the main channel-trunk develops, and (2) how its surrounding limbs develop."

93. The root text here is more specific: "that opens up the gateway of the heart-channel."

94. This refers to awareness exiting the body at the time of death. As Drugyalwa notes below, if awareness goes through the lower aperture, it results in a negative rebirth. In conversation, LTN explained that when someone is dying, if their lower half becomes cold first, it is said that their upper winds are still functioning and that awareness will exit through the top, resulting in a good birth. If their top half gets cold first, then their lower winds are still functioning, and consciousness will exit from below, resulting in a lower rebirth.

95. The root text here has "opens up" *(phyes)* rather than Drugyalwa's "defines" *(sel).*

96. *tshigs pa kha chen gyi them skas,* literally, the "staircase's large-mouthed joint."

97. This refers to the channel exiting the spinal column through the opening of the lowest vertebra.

98. The right and left channels split off from the central channel at the tailbone and then curve upward, so the shape is like the bottom part of the letter *cha* (ཆ).

99. *ag rtse'i khung bu,* or *ag tse'i khung bu.* This contrasts with the lower vertebra in that it has a small hole *(khung bu).* The sense here is that the right and left channels split off at the base of the spine, and then travel all the way up the spine, on the right and left of the central channel.

100. *lan cig rtse chung gi 'phar rtsa gnyis dang/ stod Ag rtse'i khung bu nas thon pa'o/.* LTN noted here that *rtse chung* can mean "neck" *(mjing pa),* which

helps to resolve this difficult sentence. NR has a more simplistic reading, saying that it is "the two superior channels and the trunk" *('phags rtsa gnyis dang stong po)* that exit the upper vertebra. See a similar reference in the *Tantra of the Blazing Lamps* (TB, 485), which mentions "The channel on the outer side of your neck / Which forcefully pulses and beats" *(rang gi mjing pa'i phyi rol rtsa/ /'phrig cing 'phar ba).*

101. Note that this is describing the ordinary right and left channels, not the special ones that lead from the heart to the eyes.

102. LTN noted here that the "smooth" and "rough" *('jam rtsub)* winds are those that respectively create (1) conditions conducive to realization or positive mental states, and (2) negativity. The "smooth" winds come in through the left nostril, while the "rough" ones come in through the right nostril; these come into play in some breathing practices, where the right nostril is blocked with the fingers, so that winds only come in through the left. Drugyalwa writes more on these winds at PK, 631.4ff.

103. *nyams rtogs 'od gsal gyi yon tan,* referring to visionary experiences.

104. *skyon gyi rtsal.*

105. *snyigs ma lus zungs kyi thig le,* "the solidified *thig-le* that are bodily constituents." This refers to the ordinary, conventional *thig-le* and contrasts with the "mental" *thig-le,* mentioned just below.

106. *yon tan gyi rtsal.*

107. *dwangs ma sems kyi thig-le.* These are the *thig-le* that contribute to the transcendent functioning of the body and are the equivalent to the "ultimate *thig-le*" *(don dam thig le)* in the *Tantra of the Blazing Lamps.*

108. *kun gzhi nam mkha'i rtsa.* Above it was noted that after the formation of the heart (the "seat" of the space element), the wind of the space element opened up these channels. The space element is generally thought of as the basic element from which all the other elements arise, and to which they return; in the same way, these channels are the basis of the development of the body and are the foundations that support all of our positive and negative mental experiences.

109. "Tent pole" here is *srog shing,* literally "life wood," referring to the main pole that holds open a tent.

110. The channels and winds are often organized in a hierarchy based on the metaphor of a tree; in descending order, the classifications are trunk *(sdong po),* branch *(yal ga),* limb *(yan lag),* and subsidiary limb *(nying lag).* This is summarized in chapter 5, at GDGG, 393.

111. This refers the five vital organs minus the heart, which has already formed.

112. *yan lag gi rlung.* This refers to the winds that (in the above hierarchy) are on the "limb" *(yan lag)* level, but has the added meaning that each is related to one of the limbs *(yan lag)* of the physical body, causing them to extend, filling them up like balloons.

113. *'byung ba nying lag gi lung.* These are the "winds" *(rlung)* related to the five "elements" or "elemental energies" *('byung ba).* They are "subsidiary limbs" in the sense of being lower in order than the "limbs" discussed above, and they also give rise to the subsidiary limbs of the body (the fingers, toes, and sense faculties).

114. *'byung ba dangs ma'i rlung;* in NR this is written *'byung lnga'i dangs pa'i rlung.* These are dimensions of the elemental winds that are "vibrant" in the sense

that they establish the energetic centers of perception, rather than establishing the solid, messy organs and vessels of the body.

115. This actually reads "the vibrant wind of the space-wind" *(mkha rlung gi dwangs ma'i rlung).* I have emended it to make it consistent with the rest of the list, and with Uri.

116. The root text here reads "radiation" *(gdangs)* rather than Drugyalwa's "vibrant quintessence" *(dwangs ma).*

117. *'byung lnga'i dwangs ma.* These are dimensions of the elements that are "vibrant" in the sense that they are responsible for creating the powers of perception; they contrast with the "solidified" or "coarse" dimensions of the elements that result in the substances (feces, urine, etc.) contained in the body's cavities.

118. I.e., the channel described just above that goes from the heart to the eyes. Note that this is not the special heart-to-eyes channel that is responsible for visionary experience.

119. *'byung ba snyigs ma'i rlung.* These contrast to the "vibrant" *(dwangs)* winds, discussed above.

120. Note that the root text omits this "five."

121. *nam mkha'i sems kyi bcud.* Literally this is "space's mind-essence"; I use the Sanskrit *citta* to convey how Drugyalwa seems to be resorting to euphemism.

122. *sha chen.* This term often appears as a tantric code word for "human flesh" but here is used as a euphemism for the contents of the stomach.

123. The root text has "shines" *(shar ba)* here, in place of Drugyalwa's "projects" *(dod pa).*

124. The name of this channel is given in the language of Zhang Zhung. Several different spellings occur: *rtsang ri pur langs* (GDGG), *tsang ri pur lang* (GDD), *tsang ri bur lang* (NR); the spelling in GDD is perhaps best. *Tsang ri* means "channel," and *pur lang* means "head," so this is simply the "head channel." It refers to the channel that runs from the heart to the eyes, not the central channel as a whole. From the heart, the eye channel is inside the central channel; the location described here is where it splits off, becoming independent.

125. I.e., the slender stem of the channel opens up as it approaches the eyes. Sometimes this is also said to be like the shape of a buffalo horn: a small tip that eventually opens wide at the site of the eyes. NR gives the spelling of the flower as *zar ma*, which would make it a "flax" flower.

126. It is important to note here that the eye sense-faculty is simply the gateway for this perception; it is not said to be what perceives the rays (or other visions). Traditional explanations emphasize that appearances like these rays can be perceived in the dark, or with the eyes closed, and so are not within the purview of the ordinary eye sense-faculty, as that is what processes exterior light.

127. "Canopy of the sky" translates the interesting word *mthong* (also spelled *mthongs*), which is used quite frequently in discussions of the lamps. *mThong* is also the common Tibetan verb for "to see," but it also can be used to mean "opening" or "cavity," referring specifically to the inner cavity of the chest, or the opening above us, i.e., the sky. Related to this latter sense, it can also simply mean "upward" as in *mthong la lta,* "to look upward."

128. The last term in the list is *bcud du shar ba'i snying po,* literally "the nucleus that shines forth as the essence." Essence *(bcud)* has the sense of "internal contents" or "vital contents," so this is the essential awareness at the heart shining outward.

129. The root text here has "appears directly, vividly, in the gateway of the sense-faculty" *(dbang po'i sgo la mngon sum du cer re shar).* Drugyalwa's rendering of the root verse is *dbang po'i mngon sum du cer re shar.*

130. *zang rtog ngan rtog.* Positive conceptual thoughts are those like studying religion, recalling religious instructions, and so forth; they are "positive" in the sense that, while they are still conceptual, they are at least morally beneficial.

131. Here I emend *spang zhing dor* to *blang zhing dor.* Note, however, that NR here has *ngan zhing dor,* which is similar to GDGG's *spang zhing dor.*

132. *rang chas su yod,* meaning that they are always present within you.

133. These topics refer to (1) a yogi being "introduced" to the nature of visions by a spiritual guide, who provides advice on how to interpret them; (2) "discovering" them *(dmar thag bcad pa)* means that you then definitively conclude what their nature is.

The term *dmar thag bcad* pa is common in Bön works, but it is quite difficult to convey the sense of the term in translation. Its components mean "red" *(dmar)* and "decision" or "resolution" *(thag bcad pa),* or even more literally "red" *(dmar)* "rope" *(thag)* "cutting" *(bcad pa),* where "cutting the rope" is the common Tibetan way of saying "to decide" or "to resolve." The term "red" here has the sense of something important, even something shocking. The idea is of encountering something critically important in such a way that one knows exactly what it is, and will not forget it. It is, for example, like opening up a body and seeing the red heart, pointing at it and saying, "That is the heart!" I use "discover" because it conveys the complex of suddenness, urgency, resolution, and relief that are inherent in the term. However, "discover" is problematic in that we do not typically think of a "discovery" as something that is preceded by an introduction, which is the case here. Wordier but more straightforward translations would be "making a critical determination" or "coming to a final resolution."

134. *bon sku,* the Bön correlate *chos sku (dharmakāya),* which could also be translated as "Reality Body."

135. Note that where Drugyalwa's rendering of the root text states that the "abiding nature" *(gnas lugs)* of the Reality Body is the universal ground; the root text states that the Reality Body's "residence" *(gnas)* is the universal ground.

136. *bon nyid,* the Bön correlate *chos nyid (dharmatā),* which could also be translated as "reality itself."

137. *bon dbyings,* the Bön correlate of *chos dbyings (dharmadhātu),* which could also be translated as "expanse of reality."

138. In place of Drugyalwa's "shining forth naturally" *(rang shar ba),* the root text here has "shining forth to itself" *(rang la shar ba).*

139. *snang ba chen po gsum,* the three "presencings" or "visions," which are (1) sound, (2) light, and (3) rays.

140. *snang ba'i rtsal lnga 'od lnga.* Note that NR has *snang ba'i rtsa ba 'od lnga,* "the root of appearances, the five lights." It is possible that there are some errors in this section based on the visual similarity between *rtsal* and *rtsa ba.* I have

simply translated literally from the Menri edition, as it and NR occasionally differ between *rtsal* and *rtsa ba.*

141. I.e., they are complete there in their potential form.

142. For the five bodies and five deities, see GDGG, 370.

143. For the buddhas of the five families, see GDGG, 394.

144. *srid pa.* The term in this context refers to the process of birth and death.

145. *khams.* This refers to a set of eighteen "spheres" or "constituents": the six objects, the six sense faculties, and the six consciousnesses.

146. *skye mched.* This refers to the six sense-powers and their six objects.

147. *ma 'dres yongs su rdzogs pa;* that is, while it knows holistically, it can still know individual, distinct things, its own unity not resulting in a homogeneity of experience.

148. I.e., while the Bön Body (or "Reality Body") is itself subtle and without form, it can be perceived through its "glow" *(gdangs)*, which takes the form of the five buddhas, who appear in the form of perceptible deities.

149. This could also indicate "the five demons [of] the five poisons."

150. *yi ge 'khor lo rdzogs pa'i zhing khams.* The "lettered retinue" refers to the retinue of buddhas represented as and emerging from seed syllables, and connotes how at this level the buddha has descended into the world of language and symbols.

151. *bon nyid,* the Bön equivalent of *chos nyid (dharmatā).* This could also be translated as the wheel of "reality itself."

152. The term "trunk" *(ldong po)* often refers to the three main channels but here refers just to the central channel. "Life channel" *(srog rtsa)* also refers to the central channel here; in other contexts it indicates one of the junctions of the heart (the aorta); the basic sense is of a vein or channel that, when cut, results in death.

153. The root text here has "natural shining forth" *(rang shar ba)* instead of Drugyalwa's "shining forth" *(shar ba).*

154. Shen *(gshen)* is a term that here means "priest" or "teacher" of Bön. The deities here are a common set of Shen from the Bön pantheon, called the "six subduing Shen" or "the six taming Shen" *('dul ba'i gshen drug)*, each of which is responsible for training beings in a particular realm. The deities are (1) Ye-gshen-tsug-phud, (2) lCe-rgyal-bar-ti, (3) gSang-ba-'dus-pa, (4) Ti-sangs-rang-zhi, (5) Mu-cho-ldem-drug, and (6) gSang-ba-ngang-ring. See Per Kværne, *The Tibetan Bon Religion: Iconography of a Living Tradition* (Boston: Shambhala Publications, 1996), 35.

155. In the Bön tradition, the buddhas of the five families are (1) Kun-snang-khyab-pa, (2) gSal-ba-rang-byung, (3) dGe-lha-gar-phyug, (4) Bye-brag-dngos-med, and (5) dGa'-ba-don-grub. Their consorts are simply named after the element associated with each family: (1) Sa-yi-lha-mo, (2) Chu-yi-lha-mo, (3) Me-yi-lha-mo, (4) rLung-gi-lha-mo, (5) Nam-mkha'i-lha-mo. See Jean Luc Achard, "Contribution Aux Nombrables de la Tradition Bon po," *Revue d'Etudes Tibétaines* 4 (October 2003): 111.

156. These are (1) Thang-ma-me-sgron, (2) Kha-ste-mu-ya, (3) gTsug-gshen-rgyal-ba, (4) sNang-ba-mdog-can, (5) Ba-rab-gling-bzhi, (6) Ba-rab-gling-rtsol, (7) Khri-rmang-rgyal-ba, and (8) lDe-bo gsung chen. See Achard, "Contribution Aux Nombrables," 123.

157. The "eight primordial ladies" *(ye lcam brgyad)*, or (in NR) "eight primordially purified ones" *(ye sangs brgyad)* are (1) Rig-pa'i-lha-mo, (2) sGra'i-lha-mo, (3) gTer-'dzin-lha-mo, (4) Gar-gyi-lha-mo, (5) sKu'i-lha-mo, (6) Thugs-rje'i-lha-mo, (7) sPos-kyi-lha-mo, and (8) sMan-gyi-lha-mo. See Achard, "Contribution Aux Nombrables," 123.

158. (1) dKar-mo-pad+ma'i-spyan, (2) dMar-mo-'bar-ma'i-ljags, (3) Ser-mo-thor-tshugs-can, and (4) sNgon-mo-chu-rkang-ma. See Achard, "Contribution Aux Nombrables," 102.

159. The five limbs minus the head, which is above.

160. These four are manifestations of Srid-pa'i-rgyal-mo: (1) Ne-slas-rgyal-mo, (2) Ting-nam-rgyal-mo, (3) Li-mun-rgyal-mo, and (4) Tshangs-stangs-rgyal-mo.

161. This refers to a group of six syllables *(yi ge drug)* that are related to the six realms of rebirth, and also associated with the body's six wheels (located at the crown, throat, heart, navel, secret area, and soles of the feet). In descending order, starting with the god-realm, the syllables are *A tha rni su tri du.*

162. "Lamps" here just refers to the eyes.

163. Emending *mdog bsgyur* to *mdog ma bsgyur*, based on NR, LTN, and NTTZ. The phrase literally means "without changing its color" and has the sense of leaving something alone, not messing with it or trying to touch it up.

164. Note that Drugyalwa's rendering of the root verse has reflections in "the mirror of cognition" *(rnam shes me long)*. I follow the root text here.

165. *sa ler gsal ba de'o.* Note that Drugyalwa's rendering of the root verse just has *gsal ba* here.

166. Here I omit a stray *shes pas,* based on NR.

167. Following Drugyalwa's outline, this would be referring mainly to the "essential awareness" *(ngo bo nyid kyi rig pa)* or "the Reality Body" *(bon sku)*, here characterized as primordial gnosis *(ye shes)*.

168. "Not stopping the flow of its river" *(chu rgyun ma bcad)* is simply a way of saying to not stop its continuity; "extend the rope" *(thag bsring)* means to "prolong" or "remain in."

169. A "false cave" *(rdzun phugs)* is something that you think will shelter or protect you but that does not really exist, a secure place or mindset that is ultimately fake.

170. Note that the root text here reads "are without exception are discovered" *(ma lus dmar thag bcad)*.

171. Both "mind" *(sems)* and "enlightened mind" *(byang chub sems)* here refer to the universal ground. "Liberated into its state" simply means that they dissolve back into it.

172. *'khrul snang.*

173. *bka' rgya,* literally "order-seal"; this is the command to keep these teachings secret from inappropriate students. Elsewhere Drugyalwa calls this an "order-seal of secrecy" *(gsang ba'i bka' rgya)*.

174. This is a play on the term "higher seeing," "superior seeing," or "special insight" *(lhag mthong, vipaśyanā)*. As Uri's commentary makes clear, the term in this context refers to the three appearances of sound, light, and rays.

175. *lcag ri mun pa.* This refers to the dark space that forms the boundary to our visual worlds. The term *lcag ri* can mean "iron mountains" (referring particularly to the encircling ring of iron mountains that form the outermost edge of a world

system) or can simply mean "fence." I use "iron mountains" here because it conveys both meanings and suggests the peaked shape of this boundary at the top of the visual sphere.

176. *yas kyi mig lpags*. This does not refer to the eyelids but to the fleshy brow that moves downward when you frown. By frowning, this comes downward and creates a black space at the top of the visual field.

177. The "queens of the eyes" *(mig gi rgyal mo)* simply refers to the eyeballs. "Clouds" refers to the cloudy appearance at the top of the visual field, seen when you roll your eyes upward.

178. The internal, external, and secret lamps forms a set of "three lamps" (also mentioned below at GDGG, 403). Drugyalwa also discusses these in PK, 627.4. The "three lamps" are (1) the externally existing lamp *(phyi srid pa'i sgron ma)*, referring to external sources of light like the moon or the sun (in the present context it appears to refer to the sky); (2) the internal lamp of the sense faculties *(nang dbang po'i sgron ma)*; and (3) the secret lamp of awareness *(gsang ba rig pa'i sgron ma)*.

179. "Visual canopy" here is *mthong rum*.

180. *mig lpags g.yogs pa'i nang du*. This suggests how dark-yogas are not always carried out in an elaborate dark-room, but can be performed simply by blocking the eyes, such as by wrapping the top part of the head in cloth to cover the eyes.

181. The root verse simply says "immeasurable" *(gzhal yas)*, a term that is often short for the "inestimable mansion" *(gzhal yas khang)* in which a deity lives. Here the term has a broader sense of the mansion, along with the main deity, retinue, and environment *(khor yug)*.

182. *grag stong*, which has the sense of "empty and yet resounding."

183. Uri's commentary on this verse is somewhat more straightforward, and I have used it to help interpret Drugyalwa's phrasing. Uri (ZZNG, 340) reads: "This is an introduction to sound. The 'conch lake' refers to the brain. From the center of the brain, the gateway of the empty-sound of Bön-itself emerges: a single channel that splits into two tips, and projects to the gateways of the ear sense-faculty. The 'half moons' *(zla gam)* are the ears. If the secret-channels of the ears are pressed with the fingers or the heel of the hand, the natural empty-sound of Bön-itself resounds continuously at the center of the brain, like thunder."

Future studies will hopefully focus more fully on sound-related practices in the Great Perfection. The suggestion here is that these follow the same basic model as visionary practices and are sometimes combined with visionary practices and sometimes practiced independently. The basic idea is that the ears are blocked (either manually or with an earplug like clay or *tsampa*), and the meditator focuses on the roaring sound within the head, which increases in intensity and sounds as if it is emerging from the center of the brain. As with photic practices, the aim is to identify the sound as the dynamic energy *(rtsal)* of awareness.

184. LTN explained that this could be, for instance, going to a river and listening to its sound, not analyzing it but just letting it be.

185. *nang brda thabs gzhan rkyen la ngo sprad*. This refers, for example, to using a physical technique to provide an introduction to sound: the method of pressing on the ears and listening to the sound inside your head, described above.

186. *dus gcig tu rtsal sbyong*. This refers to a practice that induces the experience of sound, light, and rays simultaneously. LTN explained that it involves placing your

hands on the sides of your head and using the fingers to stimulate various points around the head: (1) the sides of the neck are pressed with the thumbs, the pressure on these channels causing thought to subside; (2) the ears are blocked by the index fingers, leading to the production of internal sound; (3) the middle fingers press on the closed eyes, leading to the production of light and rays; (4) the ring fingers block the nostrils, stopping undue circulation of the winds as one breathes from the mouth; (5) the pinky fingers are not used. A depiction of a similar practice occurs in the famous Lukhang murals; see Baker and Laird, *Dalai Lama's Secret Temple*, 95.

187. Note that Drugyalwa's rendering of the root verse here actually reads "three rays" *(zer gsum)*. This "three" does not appear in the root text, or in the NR version of the commentary, so I have omitted it here.

188. Based on NR.

189. *snang la rang bzhin med par gsal la dngos po med par shar ro.* Note the similarity between this and Kālacakra's hallmark descriptions of the Great Seal.

190. For Drugyalwa, the three groups of verse here lay out the three basic visionary practices: dark-retreat, sky-gazing, and sun-gazing. Note that in this section Drugyalwa appears to make references to his own major work PK (617.3ff.). If so, this would establish that the present commentary was written after PK. I have noted these references below.

191. Note that Drugyalwa has "mind-fish" *(sems kyi nya mo)* instead of "goldfish" *(gser gyi nya mo)*. This appears to be an error, as the root text, the NR edition of Drugyalwa's commentary, and Uri all have "goldfish."

192. "General descriptions of the practice" *(spyir nyams su blang ba)* appears to be Drugyalwa referring to his own PK (p. 617.3), which contains a section by this same name.

193. The "mirrors" here are the eyes. Note that the root text and Uri both have "awareness" *(rig pa)* rather than "mind" *(sems)* in this line.

194. *nam mkha' gsum sbyor gyi lag len.* The "three skies" *(nam mkha' gsum)* are related to "the three lamps" *(sgron ma gsum;* see PK, 627.4) and "the three wheels" *('khor lo gsum;* see just below). In PK, Drugyalwa lists the three skies and correlates them with three emptinesses: (1) the externally existing sky *(phyi srid pa'i nam mkha')*, which is the ordinary empty space of the sky *(bar snang stong pa)*; (2) the internal sky of the sense faculties *(nang dbang po'i nam mkha')*, which is the empty channel-cavity *(rtsa'i sbubs stong pa)*; and (3) the secret symbolic sky *(gsang don rtags kyi nam mkha')*, which is the empty mind-itself *(sems nyid stong pa)*.

Drugyalwa discusses the "three skies" on PK, 622.3; a discussion of the "three wheels" follows. The "three lamps" appear in the present commentary, on GDGG, 399; see also on PK, 627.4.

195. Here, Drugyalwa appears to be pointing to his own discussion on PK, 621.2. "Meditative stabilization on the brilliant sky" *(snang gsal nam mkha'i ting 'dzin)* is a phrase that Drugyalwa uses to refer to sky-gazing *(nam mkha' Ar gtad)*, which he may have formulated based on the above root verse.

196. "Attentive mind" here is *dran pa sems,* though note that the root text and Uri both read *dran rig sems;* I am reading these variants as having the same essential meaning.

197. The "light wheels" *('od 'khor)* described here are "three skies" or "three lamps" (external, internal, and secret) cast in the form of "wheels"; they represent

the luminous circles of light produced by the lamps. LTN noted that "the internal wheel of the sense faculties" refers to, for instance, pressing the eyes, a practice that results in seeing circles of color, like the spots on a peacock feather. The external wheel refers to seeing external light, such as seeing rainbow colors in the exterior.

198. *sgron ma gsum sbyor gyi lag len.* See Drugyalwa's mention of the three lamps above at GDGG, 399; the first two of those lamps are identical to the "light-wheels" mentioned in this passage. See also Drugyalwa's PK, 627.4.

199. *rang gsal sgron ma'i ting nge 'dzin.* This is Drugyalwa's way of referring to the practice of sun-gazing; here he appears to be referring to his own discussion in PK, 624.5ff.

200. *rig pa'i snying po.*

201. *thig le'i nyag thag.*

202. I.e., due to the fluctuating quality of the vision, one doubts one's own abilities.

203. Uri describes this as the *thig-le* from the first vision increasing in size.

204. Note that this last line is omitted in the Menri edition of Drugyalwa's commentary. The line appears in the root text, as well as in the NR edition of Drugyalwa's commentary.

205. The "essence of awareness" *(rig pa'i ngo bo)* here refers to self-emergent primordial gnosis *(rang byung ye shes).*

206. I follow the NR edition here; the Menri edition reads "in every direction, internally and externally," but "internal and external" appears to contradict the topic of the paragraph, which is descriptions of external experiences.

207. Note that bronze *('khar ba)* is often made of five metals, so these bronze plates *('khar sder)* fit in with the imagery of circles containing multiples of five.

208. *dge sbyor.* Literally "virtuous activity," the term has the sense of a religious practice in which one has begun to have success.

209. The appearance of a lotus and wheel indicates the beginning of the manifestation of the buddhas of the five families, as these are the symbolic implements of the "lotus" and "wheel" families.

210. These are incomplete in the sense that some may not appear with their hand implements or distinctive features, which will become present as the visions progress.

211. I.e., this is not describing an event that happens at death, when the five psychophysical aggregates are "abandoned."

212. LTN noted that "three maṇḍalas" typically refers to (1) the external maṇḍala of earth *(phyi sa'i dkyil 'khor)*, where "earth" refers to substances like colored powders, which are used to create a representation of a maṇḍala; (2) the internal maṇḍala of the aggregates and constituents *(nang phung khams kyi dkyil 'khor)*, i.e., the body; and (3) the secret maṇḍala of awareness *(gsang ba rig pa'i dkyil 'khor).*

213. I.e., primordial gnosis (as both an "object" and a "subject") is stable here, and the fluctuations that characterized the earlier stages of vision are overcome.

214. *stong ba'i snang ba.* Drugyalwa's rendering of the root verse here differs slightly from the Menri edition of the root text, which reads, "The natural light of emptiness" or "Emptiness' own light" *(stong pa'i rang 'od).* Note that here, and in

the following lines about the "sound" and "rays" of emptiness, the Tibetan does not specify "emptiness" *(stong pa nyid)* but simply reads "empty" *(stong pa).*

215. Drugyalwa does not write out all the lines of the root text here but simply gives the first three and says "and so forth." My translation of the remaining lines is based on the Menri edition of the root text. However, Drugyalwa does appear to be working with a version of the root text that differs slightly from the Menri edition, and thus another option would be to supply the remaining lines from Uri's commentary (p. 342.6), as the first three lines there are identical to the ones in Drugyalwa's commentary.

216. "Thus" based on NR, which has *sprul pas* instead of *sprul zhing.* The presence of a buddhafield here indicates the Enjoyment Body, and the ability to manifest anywhere indicates the Emanation Body. These two, along with the Bön Body *(bon sku),* make up the "three bodies."

217. The "three grounds" here are the eleventh, twelfth, and thirteenth grounds, which are stages on the path to enlightenment where one actually becomes a buddha. These grounds are correlated to the attainment of the three buddha-bodies.

218. *rang chas su yod.* This has the sense of the three bodies existing "intrinsically" within the person. It does not carry the sense of "inherent existence," but simply suggests that everything necessary for enlightenment is complete within the person, that one does not need to look elsewhere for the three bodies.

219. Forceful method *(btsan thabs)* has the sense of a method that is abrupt, energetic, and produces quick results. As Drugyalwa notes here, this is not a path that takes eons but one that is accomplished right here in the present.

220. *rtogs thob dus mnyam du,* i.e., at the very moment the essential points are authentically realized, buddhahood will be attained.

221. Drugyalwa elaborates on this line a bit to clarify it. The actual root verse reads simply, "Like the jewel in the throat of the water dragon."

222. *lan gcig sgyu ma'i lus rnam rtog gi blo snang ba yul gyis sgrib g.yogs thams cad dang bral nas.* In Buddhist literature, the term "illusory body" *(sgyu ma'i lus)* takes on different meanings in different contexts. One common way that the term is used is to refer to the nonphysical body that is attained in the bardo. However, in this case the term simply refers to the ordinary, fleeting, illusion-like body that obscures and imprisons the mind during life. See the term used in this sense above on GDGG, 397.

223. Note that the Menri edition of Drugyalwa's commentary does not supply all the root text here, while the NR edition does.

224. Here, the body is referred to as *bzhi bsdus kyi phung po,* literally "the physical body composed of the four." The space element is left out of this particular configuration, as it is correlated with mind rather than the body.

225. *'brel ba yan lag lnga.* A channel runs from each of the five internal organs to one of the five limbs; this relationship is responsible for the limbs' initial development in the embryo and continued functioning in life. When one of the five organs loses its power, the limb to which it is connected also becomes weakened.

226. The first of this sentence is included based on NR.

227. The comment in parentheses is included based on NR.

228. The root text contains a small additional phrase specifying that this is advice "on how not to err" *(ma nor).* Note that this phrase does appear in the NR version of the commentary.

229. "Understood" is based on NR and NTTZ, which have *shes* instead of the Menri edition's *zles* (which is possibly an error for *zlos,* "to recite").

230. This refers to instructions that provide collections of "key points" or "nails" *(gzer bu),* such as the famous *Twenty-One Nails* found in the ZZNG.

231. For an essay on these metaphors, see David P. Jackson, "Birds in the Egg and Newborn Lion Cubs: Metaphors for the Potentialities and Limitations of 'All at Once' Enlightenment," in *Tibetan Studies: Proceedings of the 5th Seminar of the International Association for Tibetan Studies, Narita 1989*, ed. Ihara Shoren and Yamaguchi Zuiho (Narita: Naritasan Shinshoji, 1992), 95-114.

232. The "union of the sun and moon" *(nyi zla kha sbyor)* refers to the period when the moon is setting and the sun is rising at the same time, as if they are directly connected; this is used as a metaphor for buddhahood, where negative qualities disappear at the same time that enlightened qualities arise. "Dawn on the sixteenth day" *(bcu drug nam sangs pa)* refers to the morning after the full moon, the day when the moon is totally full and complete.

233. I read this phrase based on NR, which has *ji ltar sangs rgyas pa'i tshul ni.* The Menri edition reads *ji ltar rgyas pa'i tshul ni,* "As for how they are expanded *(rgyas)*.... " It is possible that the intent of the Menri edition is to explain the term "buddha" *(sangs rgyas)* by using the first sentence to explain *sangs,* and the present sentence to explain *rgyas.*

234. *bar do dang po,* the period of dying before the internal winds have ceased, referred to above as "the bardo of primordial gnosis."

235. *bon nyid 'od gsal gyi bar do.* The term *bon nyid* is the Bön equivalent of *chos nyid (dharmatā).* Less literally, this could be the "luminous bardo of reality-itself" or the "luminous reality-bardo."

236. Here Drugyalwa adds the word "internal" *(nang)* to the root text.

237. *stong pa'i rang sgra.*

238. This phrase is based on NR.

239. *ngo bo dang lhag mthong.* "Essence" here refers to the deepest nature of the mind, while "higher sights" refers to visionary experiences. This pair is sometimes used to indicate breakthrough and direct transcendence.

240. I.e., during life you recognized the three appearances as your mind, and now, here in the bardo, you recognize those same three appearances as your mind.

241. The references in this section to "introductions" refer to introductions that took place while one was alive, before entering the bardo.

242. Drugyalwa sometimes uses "subjective" *(yul can)* to mean "source"; the idea here is that enlightened body, speech, and mind have their source in the three visionary appearances.

243. Note that NR simply says "cause" *(rgyu)* rather than "cause and condition" *(rgyu rkyen).*

244. Note that the Menri edition of the root text has "seen" *(mthong)* instead of Drugyalwa's "realized" *(rtogs).*

245. "Three appearances" *(snang ba gsum)* is specified in the NR edition of Drugyalwa's commentary.

246. *rang du shar;* note that NR has "shine forth, naturally purified" *(rang sangs su shar).*

247. I.e., just by having heard them during life, even if they did not put them into practice.

248. Here I emend the Menri edition's *lha ma'i* to the NR edition's *lha mi'i.*

249. I.e., they will be able to practice it authentically in the next life.

250. In the Menri edition of the root text, this sentence begins with "Son of the family!" *(rigs kyi bu)*; the phrase is omitted here in Drugyalwa's commentary.

251. I.e., dwelling in the luminous bardo of Bön-itself" or "reality-itself" *(bon nyid 'od gsal bar do).*

252. *gnas lugs ngo mi shes.*

253. The Menri edition of the root text here has "the sun of awareness" *(rig pa'i nyi ma).*

254. "Extrinsic appearances" here is *gzhan snang,* which could also be translated as "appearances of other"; the idea here is that they are not seen as "self-presencings" *(rang snang)* or appearances of one's own mind. Note that Drugyalwa's rendering of the root verse differs slightly from the Menri edition of the root text; in place of Drugyalwa's "seen erroneously" *('khrul par mthong),* the root text has "seen as truly real" *(bden par mthong).*

255. *mthong snang.* Note, however, that the same term is used below referring to "roaring sounds" (which would not be visual).

256. *'char gzhi.*

257. *rmi lam bag chags kyi yid gzugs la brten pa.* The experiences that one has in a dream are not real but are appearances that result from one's karmic predispositions; similarly, this body seems to be real and physically present but is simply an appearance that results from karmic predispositions.

258. Note that where Drugyalwa has "via your karma" *(las kyis),* the Menri edition of the root text has "via mind" *(yid kyis).* "Mind" seems to make more sense here, given Drugyalwa's comments below about being able to travel to places simply by thinking about them.

259. Here you have the ability to go anywhere at will, except for entering a womb; you can walk through walls and so forth, but to enter a womb it must be one with which you have some karmic connection.

260. *las kyi rdzu 'phrul shugs kyis.*

261. The "fish" metaphor here is a traditional way of referring to the suffering and frustration one experiences at this point in the bardo.

262. I read from NR here, which has *sems can* ("sentient being"), rather than the Menri edition, which simply has *sems* ("mind").

263. *tsi chad,* following the Menri root text and Uri. There is some confusion about this word in Drugyalwa's commentary; the Menri edition replaces it with *sbyong tshad,* while NR has *bcings tsha.* The NR edition of the root text has *tshe chad.*

264. Note that "the appearances of" does not appear in the Menri edition of the root text.

265. The "mind" being realized here is the enlightened mind. Note that the line about "realizing the [enlightened] mind" is found in the root text but does not appear in the commentary or in Uri.

266. *sems med pa rnams*. Literally, this could be read as "those who have no mind," but the intent is "those for whom such a mind does not exist." It refers to not even recognizing the mere existence of the "mind," which here refers to the "enlightened mind" or the ground.

267. *rdzas med pa da lta nyid du mthong ba*. I.e., you see there is nothing in a place where you once mistakenly saw something.

268. In the Menri edition of the root text, this line begins with "Son of the family!" *(rigs kyi bu)*; the phrase is omitted here in Drugyalwa's commentary.

269. *rig pa dmar thag bcod pa,* literally "having made a critical *(dmar)* decision *(thag bcad)* regarding awareness," i.e., having come to a conclusive resolution about what awareness is and what it is not.

270. The verb here is rather difficult. The root text here has *snyems* (which typically means "arrogant," though TDCM notes that in older usage it can also mean "weak" or "humble," akin to the term *nyam chung*). The Menri edition of Drugyalwa's commentary glosses this as *mnga' bsnyems;* based on the passage below, I am reading this as *mnga' bsnyes* ("mastered").

271. The Menri edition of the root text specifies the full text-title here: *Advice on the Six Lamps (sgron ma drug gi gdams pa).*

272. I.e., it is an oral transmission that was never written down and buried as a treasure *(gter).*

273. *nang man ngag dmar khrid.* This is referring to the second of the four sections into which the ZZNG collection is divided. Note that the NR edition of Drugyalwa's commentary differs here, placing the commentary in the third section (called *gsang ba rig pa gcer mthong:* the "secret" cycle on the naked seeing of awareness).

274. NR contains a different colophon and also includes a concluding prayer that is not present in the Menri edition. The colophon provides a different picture of the origin of the text, stating: "The Venerable One from the Dru clan, Gyalwa Yungdrung, composed it as notes *(reg zig)*. I, Se-btsun-tshul-'od, respectfully requested it from 'Gro-mgon-shes-rab-rin-chen."

BIBLIOGRAPHY

Abbreviations

ABKB: *Abhidharmakośabhāsyaṃ (Chos mngon pa'i mdzod kyi bshad pa),* D4089.

BN: sPa-btsun-bstan-rgyal's *Biographies of the Lineage Lamas (brGyud pa'i bla ma'i rnam thar).*

Bu: *Collected Works of Butön.* I use this as my primary edition of the *Kālacakra Tantra* and *Stainless Light.*

D: The Dergé edition of the Tibetan canon.

DN: *Dīgha Nikāya.*

GDD: *Advice on the Six Lamps (sGron ma drug gi gdams pa);* this abbreviation refers to the Menri edition (New Delhi: International Academy of Indian Culture, 1968).

GDGG: Drugyalwa's *Commentary on the Intended Meaning of the Six Lamps (sGron ma drug gi dgongs don 'grel pa);* this abbreviation refers to the Menri edition (New Delhi: International Academy of Indian Culture, 1968).

GN: *Secret Tantra That Lights the Lamps (sGron ma snang byed 'bar ba'i gsang rgyud),* Vimalamitra's commentary to the *Tantra of Unimpeded Sound (sGra thal 'gyur).*

IOL: India Office Library.

KCT: *Kālacakra Tantra;* unless noted, citations refer to the edition in Butön's collected works.

LTN: Lopön Trinley Nyima, from Menri Monastery, oral conversation.

MMK: Nāgārjuna's *Prajñānāmamūlamadhyamakakārikā (dbu ma rtsa ba'i tshig le'ur byas pa shes rab ces bya ba),* D3824.

MN: *Majjhima Nikāya.*

MS: Manuscript edition of *bKa' rgyud skor bzhi* from Dolpo, collected by David Snellgrove.

MTP: *Mu tig phreng ba brgyus pa,* Vimalamitra's commentary to the *Tantra of the Blazing Lamps.*

NR: Blockprint edition of the *bKa' rgyud skor bzhi,* printed in Nyag-rong, and owned by Menri Monastery in Dolanji.

NTTZ: Published edition of the *bKa' rgyud skor bzhi,* edited by sNang-mtha-bstan-'dzin-nyi-ma.

OSL: Norsang Gyatso's *Phyi nang gzhan gsum gsal bar byed pa dri med 'od kyi rgyan (Ornament of Stainless Light).*

PC: *Padminī-nāma-pañjikā (Pan tsi ka pad ma can),* D1350.

PKṬYM: Muniśrībhadra's *Pañcakramaṭippaṇī Yogīmanoharā (rim pa lnga'i don mdor bshad pa rnal 'byor pa'i yid 'phrog ces bya ba),* D1813.

PK: Drugyalwa's *Phyag khrid.* Published in the collection *Sñan rgyud nam mkha' 'phrul mdzod draṅ ṅes skor źaṅ źuṅ sñan rgyud skor.* Dolanji: Tibetan Bonpo Monastic Centre, 1972. Drugyalwa's work is found in part 2 of this collection.

STNN: *Sangs rgyas kyi bstan rtsis ngo mtshar nor bu'i phreng ba,* by Nyi-ma-bstan-'dzin; translated by Per Kværne as "A Chronological Table of the Bon Po."

TB: The mTshams-brag edition of the *Seventeen Tantras.* Unless noted, citations to TB refer to the *Tantra of the Blazing Lamps (sGron ma 'bar ba'i rgyud).*

TCD: Longchenpa's *Theg mchog mdzod.*

TDCM: *Tshig mdzod chen mo.*

TDD: Longchenpa's *Tshig don mdzod.*

VP: *Vimalaprabhā;* unless noted, citations refer to the edition in Butön's collected works.

YM: Yumo's *sTong nyid gsal sgron,* found in *Jo nang dpe rnying phyogs bsgrigs* (TBRC W00KG0638).

YM-SG: The Sherab Gyaltsen edition of Yumo's *gSal sgron skor bzhi.*

ZZNG: *Zhang zhung snyan rgyud.* I use this abbreviation to refer specifically to the collection *bKa' rgyud skor bzhi.* Unless noted, these references are to the 1968 published edition, which reproduces blockprints from Menri Monastery. I also refer to this as "the Menri edition."

Buddhist and Bön Canonical Scriptures

Advice on the Six Lamps. sGron ma drug gi gdams pa. Published in *History and Doctrine of Bon-Po Niṣpanna Yoga,* 269–292. Reproduced by Professor Lokesh Chandra and Tenzin Namdak. New Delhi: International Academy of Indian Culture, 1968.

A Brief Explication of Initiations. dBang mdor bstan pa (Sekoddeśa). D0361.

Cakrasamvara Tantra. rGyud kyi rgyal po dpal bde mchog nyung ngu zhes bya ba (Tantrarāja-srī-laghusaṃbara-nāma). D0368.

Emanation of Blessings. See *Tantra of Vairocana's Manifest Enlightenment.*

Four Cycles of the Oral Transmission. bKa' rgyud skor bzhi. Published as *History and Doctrine of Bon-Po Niṣpanna Yoga.* Reproduced by Prof. Lokesh Chandra and Tenzin Namdak. New Delhi: International Academy of Indian Culture, 1968. For other editions of the *Four Cycles* collection, see the section "Bibliographic Information and Notes on Various Editions," at the start of the translation of *Advice on the Six Lamps.*

Garland of Precious Pearls Tantra. Mu tig rin po che phreng ba'i rgyud. See the A 'dzom 'brug pa edition of the *Seventeen Tantras,* published as *Rñiṅ ma'i rgyud bcu bdun,* vol. 2, pp. 417–537. New Delhi: Sanje Dorje, 1977.

Glorious Thig-le of the Great Seal Tantra. dPal phyag rgya chen po'i thig le zhes bya ba rnal 'byor ma chen mo'i rgyud kyi rgyal po'i mnga' bdag (Śri-mahāmudrā-tilakaṃ-nāma-yoginī-tantra-rājādhipati). D0420.

Gnosis Vajra Compendium Tantra. Ye shes rdo rje kun las btus pa zhes bya ba'i rgyud (Jñāna-vajra-samucchaya). D0447.

Guhyasamāja Tantra. De bzhin gshegs pa thams cad kyi sku gsung thugs kyi gsang chen gsang ba 'dus pa zhes bya ba brtag pa'i rgyal po chen po (Sarva-tathāgata-kyavākcittarahasyo guhyasamāja-nāma-mahā-kalparāja). D0442.

Hevajra Tantra. Kye'i rdo rje zhes bya ba rgyud kyi rgyal po (Hevajratantrarāja-nāma). D0417.

Jñānatilaka Tantra. dPal ye shes thig le rnal 'byor ma'i rgyud kyi rgyal po chen po mchog tu rmad du byung ba zhes bya ba (Śrī-jñānatilaka-yoginītantrarājā-paramamahādbhutam). D0422.

Kālacakra Tantra. mChog gi dang po'i sangs rgyas las phyung ba rgyud kyi rgyal po dpal dus kyi 'khor lo zhes bya ba (Paramādibuddhoddhṛta-śrīkālacakra-nāma-tantrarājā). D0362, D1346. Page numbers refer to the edition found in volume 1 of the collected works of Butön (Bu).

Litany of Names of Mañjuśrī. mTshan yang dag par brjod pa, 'Jam dpal ye shes sems dpa'i don dam pa'i mtshan yang dag par brjod pa (Nāmasaṃgiti, Mañjuśrī-jñāna-sattvasya-paramārtha-nāmasaṃgiti). D0360.

Perfection of Wisdom Sūtra in 25,000 Lines. Shes rab kyi pha rol tu phyin pa stong phrag nyi shu lnga pa (Pañcaviṃśatisāhasrikā-prajñāpāramitā). D0009

Perfection of Wisdom Sūtra in 8,000 Lines. 'Phags pa shes rab kyi pha rol tu phyin pa brgyad stong pa (Ārya-aṣṭasāhasrikā-prajñāpāramitā). D0012.

Supplement to the [Guhyasamāja] Tantra. rGyud phyi ma. D0443.

Supplement to the Kālacakra Tantra. dPal dus kyi 'khor lo'i rgyud phyi ma rgyud kyi snying po zhes bya ba (Śrī-Kālacakratantrottaratantra-hṛdaya-nāma). D0363.

Sūtra of the Illusion-like Samādhi. 'Phags pa sgyu ma lta bu'i ting nge 'dzin ces bya ba theg pa chen po'i mdo (Ārya-māyopamasamādhi-nāma-mahāyāna-sūtra). D0130.

Tantra of the Blazing Lamps. sGron ma 'bar ba'i rgyud. Found in various editions of *The Collected Tantras of the Ancients (rNying ma rgyud 'bum);* see in particular: (1) mTshams brag, vol. 12 (na), pp. 467–491; (2) gTing skyes, vol. 9 (ta), pp. 578–599; (3) sDe dge, vol. 4 (nga), pp. 108b–117a. See also the A 'dzom 'brug pa edition of the *Seventeen Tantras,* published as *Rñiṅ ma'i rgyud bcu bdun,* vol. 1, pp. 281–313. New Delhi: Sanje Dorje, 1977.

Tantra of Unimpeded Sound. sGra thal 'gyur. See the A 'dzom 'brug pa edition of the *Seventeen Tantras,* published as *Rñiṅ ma'i rgyud bcu bdun,* vol. 1, pp. 1–205. New Delhi: Sanje Dorje, 1977.

Tantra of Vairocana's Manifest Enlightenment. rNam par snang mdzad chen po mngon par rdzogs par byang chub pa rnam par sprul ba byin gyis rlob pa shin tu rgyas pa mdo sde'i dbang po rgyal po zhes bya ba'i chos kyi rnam grangs (Mahāvairocanābhisambodhi-vikurvatīadhiṣṭhāna-vaipulyasūtra-indrarājā). D0494.

Twenty-One Nails. gZer bu nyi shu rtsa gcig. Published in *History and Doctrine of Bon-Po Niṣpanna Yoga,* 503–519. Reproduced by Professor Lokesh Chandra and Tenzin Namdak. New Delhi: International Academy of Indian Culture, 1968.

Vajra Heart-Ornament Tantra. dPal rdo rje snying po rgyan gyi rgyud (Śrī-vajra-hṛdayālaṃkāra-tantra). D0451.
Vajra Maṇḍala Ornament Tantra. dPal rdo rje snying po rgyan ces bya ba'i rgyud kyi rgyal po chen po (Śrī-vajra-maṇḍalālaṃkara-tantra-nāma-mahātantrarājā). D0490.
Vajra Tent Tantra. Phags pa mkha' 'gro ma rdo rje gur zhes bya ba'i rgyud kyi rgyal po chen po'i brtag pa (Āryaḍākinī-vajrapañjara-mahātantrarāja-kalpa). D0419.

Buddhist and Bön Treatises, Commentaries, and Historical Works

ĀRYADEVA

Lamp Integrating the Practices. sPyod pa bsdus pa'i sgron ma (Caryāmelāpakapradīpa). D1803.
On Purifying Mental Obscurations. Sems kyi sgrib pa rnam par sbyong ba zhes bya ba'i rab tu byed pa (Cittāvaraṇa-viśodhana-nāma-prakaraṇa). D1804.
Oral Instructions on the Enlightenment Stage. mNgon par byang chub pa'i rim pa'i man ngag (Abhibodhikramopadeśa). D1806.

PATSÜN TENGYAL (SPA-BTSUN-BSTAN-RGYAL-SENG-GE-DPAL-BZANG)

Biographies of the Lineage Lamas (brGyud pa'i bla ma'i rnam thar) (BN), ZZNG pp. 1–130.

CANDRAKĪRI

Commentary on the "Supplement to [Nāgārjuna's] 'Treatise on the Middle Way.'" dBu ma la 'jug pa'i bshad pa (Madhyamakāvatārabhāṣya). D3862.

DRUGYALWA (BRU-SGOM-RGYAL-BA-G.YUNG-DRUNG)

A Commentary on the Intended Meaning of the Six Lamps. sGron ma drug gi dgongs don 'grel pa. Published in *History and Doctrine of Bon-Po Niṣpanna Yoga,* 355–422. Reproduced by Professor Lokesh Chandra and Tenzin Namdak. New Delhi: International Academy of Indian Culture, 1968.
Drugyalwa's Guidance [On the Practice of the Oral Tradition from Zhang Zhung]. Colloquially referred to as Drugyalwa's *phyag khrid,* or the *rgyal ba phyag khrid,* this is a manual that casts the ZZNG materials in practical terms. Published in the collection *Sñan rgyud nam mkha' 'phrul mdzod draṅ ṅes skor źaṅ źuṅ sñan rgyud skor.* Dolanji: Tibetan Bonpo Monastic Centre, 1972. Drugyalwa's work is found in part 2 of this collection.
A History of the Great Perfection's Oral Tradition from Zhang Zhung, Containing Biographies [of Its Lineage Holders]. rDzogs pa chen po zhang zhung snyan rgyud kyi lo rgyus rnam thar dang bcas pa. Published in the collection *Sñan rgyud nam mkha' 'phrul mdzod draṅ ṅes skor źaṅ źuṅ sñan rgyud skor,* 529ff. Dolanji: Tibetan Bonpo Monastic Centre, 1972.

GYALWA YESHÉ (RGYAL-BA-YE-SHES)

Biographies of the Glorious Kālacakra Lamas in the Lineage of the Jonang Tradition. dPal ldan dus kyi 'khor lo jo nang pa'i lugs kyi bla ma brgyud pa'i rnam thar. Beijing: Mi rigs dpe skrun khang, 2004.

GYERPUNGPA (GYER-SPUNGS-SNANG-BZHER-LOD-PO)

An Explanation of the Twenty-One Nails. gZer bu nyer gcig gi 'grel pa. Published in *History and Doctrine of Bon-Po Niṣpanna Yoga,* 521–581. Reproduced by Professor Lokesh Chandra and Tenzin Namdak. New Delhi: International Academy of Indian Culture, 1968. See 553ff. for a discussion of the four lamps.

JÑĀNAKIRTI

Entry into Suchness. De kho na nyid la 'jug pa zhes bya ba bde bar gshegs pa'i bka' ma lus pa mdor bsdus te bshad pa'i rab tu byed pa (Tattvāvatārākhyāsakala-sugatavāksaṃkṣipta-vyākhyā-prakaraṇa). D3709.

JÑĀNAPARAMA

Secret Reality: A Commentary on the Difficult Points of the Jñānatilaka Tantra. dPal ye shes thig le'i dka' 'grel gsang ba'i de kho na nyid ces bya ba (Śrī-Jñānatilaka-pañjikā-guhyatattva-nāma). D1203.

KĀLACAKRAPĀDA THE GREAT

Lotus Girl. Pan tsi ka pad ma can. Padma can zhes bya ba'i dka 'grel (Padminī-nāma-pañjikā). D1350.

KHEDRUP JÉ (MKHAS-GRUB-RJE, MKHAS-GRUB-DGE-LEGS-DPAL-BZANG)

Illuminating Reality: An Extensive Explanation of Stainless Light. dPal dus kyi 'khor lo'i 'grel chen dri med 'od kyi rgya cher bshad pa de kho na nyid snang bar byed pa. Published in *The Collected Works of the Lord mKhas-grub rJe dGe-legs-dpal-bzaṅ-po,* vols. 2–4 (kha-nga). New Delhi: Mongolian Lama Gurudeva, 1980.

KHEDRUP NORSANG GYATSO (MKHAS-GRUB-NOR-BZANG-RGYA-MTSHO)

Ornament of Stainless Light, Clarifying Outer, Inner, and Other Kālacakra. Phyi nang gzhan gsum gsal bar byed pa dri med 'od kyi rgyan. New Delhi: bod kyi gtsug lag zhib dpyod khang, 2004. Note Kilty's translation of this work, listed in the bibliography of English language sources.

LODRÖ DÖNYOD RINPOCHE (MKHAN-PO-BLO-GROS-DON-YOD)

A Cluster of Sapphires: An Ornament to the Religious History of Kālacakra. Dus 'khor chos 'byung rgyan indra nI la'i phra tshom; bDe bar gshegs pa'i ring lugs spyi dang bye brag rgyud thams cad kyi rgyal po dpal dus kyi 'khor lo'i chos skor gyi byung ba brjod pa thub bstan mdzes par byed pa'i rgyan indra nI la'i phra tshom. Darjeeling: Bokar Ngedon Chokhor Ling, 2005.

LONGCHENPA (KLONG-CHEN-RAB-'BYAMS-PA)

Treasury of Words and Meanings. Tshig don mdzod. Gangtok, Sikkim: Sherab Gyaltsen and Khyentse Labrang, 1983.

NĀGABODHI

Garland of Jewels: An Explanation of [Nāgārjuna's] Five Stages. Rim pa lnga pa'i bshad pa nor bu'i phreng ba zhes bya ba (Pañcakramaṭīkā-maṇimālā-nāma). D1840.

NĀGĀRJUNA

Five Stages. Rim pa lnga pa (Pañcakrama). D1802. Katsumi Mimaki and Tōru Tomabechi have published a helpful critical edition: *Pañcakrama: Sanskrit and Tibetan Texts Critically Edited with Verse Index and Facsimile Edition of the Sanskrit Manuscripts.* Tokyo: Centre for East Asian Cultural Studies for Unesco, the Toyo Bunko, 1994.

Fundamental Treatise on the Middle. dBu ma rtsa ba'i tshig le'ur byas pa shes rab ces bya ba (Prajñānāmamūlamadhyamakakārikā). D3824.

In Praise of the Dharmadhātu. Chos dbyings bstod pa (Dharmadhātustava). D1118.

NĀROPA

Commentary to "A Brief Explication of Initiations." dBang mdor bstan pa'i 'grel bshad don dam pa bsdus pa zhes bya ba (Paramārthasaṃgraha-nāma-sekoddeśaṭīkā). D1351.

NGAWANG LODRÖ DRAKPA (NGAG-DBANG-BLO-GROS-GRAGS-PA)

Moon Lamp: A Religious History of the Jonang School. Jo nang chos 'byung zla ba'i sgron me; dPal ldan jo nang pa'i chos 'byung rgyal ba'i chos tshul gsal byed zla ba'i sgron me. Krung go'i bod kyi shes rig dpe skrun khang, 1990.

PUṆḌARĪKA

Approaching the Ultimate. dPal don dam pa'i bsnyen pa (Śrī-paramārthasevā). D1348.

Stainless Light. bsDus pa'i rgyud kyi rgyal po dus kyi 'khor lo'i 'grel bshad rtsa ba'i rgyud kyi rjes su 'jug pa stong phrag bcu pa bcu gnyis pa dri ma med pa'i 'od ces bya ba (Vimalaprabhā-nāma-mūlatantrānusāriṇī-dvādaśasāhasrikā-laghu-kālacakratantrarājaṭīkā). D0845, D1347. Page numbers refer to the edition found in volumes 1–3 of the collected works of Butön (Bu).

SARAHA

Ultimate Letters. Don dam pa'i yi ge. An alternate title for the *Treasury of Dohā Verses (Do ha mdzod kyi glu).* D2224.

TĀRANĀTHA

Important Facts on the Origins of the Śrī Kālacakra Cycle. dPal dus kyi 'khor lo'i chos bskor kyi byung khungs nyer mkho. Collected works, vol. 2, text 1. A biographical sketch of Yumo is found on p. 16.

UNKNOWN

Amazing Histories of the Realizations of [Masters Following] the Transcendent Victor Kālacakra. bCom ldan 'das dpal dus kyi 'khor lo'i chos 'byung ngo mtshar rtogs brjod. An incomplete manuscript held in the Musée Guimet in Paris (no. 54588).

URI SONAM GYALTSEN (U-RI-BSOD-NAMS-RGYAL-MTSHAN)

Ornament of Sunlight: A Commentary on the [Six] Lamps. sGron ma'i 'grel pa nyi 'od rgyan. Published in *History and Doctrine of Bon-Po Nişpanna Yoga,* 293–354. Reproduced by Professor Lokesh Chandra and Tenzin Namdak. New Delhi: International Academy of Indian Culture, 1968.

VAJRAGARBHA

Vajragarbha Commentary. Kye'i rdo rje bsdus pa'i don gyi rgya cher 'grel pa (Hevajrapiṇḍārthaṭīkā). D1180. One of the "Three Bodhisattva Commentaries," this comments on *The Hevajra Tantra.*

VAJRAPĀNI

Vajrapāṇi Commentary. mNgon par brjod pa 'bum pa las phyung ba nyung ngu'i rgyud kyi bsdus pa'i don rnam par bshad pa zhes bya ba (Lakṣābhidhānāduddhṛita-laghu-tantra-piṇḍārtha-vivaraṇa-nāma). D1402. One of the "Three Bodhisattva Commentaries," this comments on the first 10.5 verses of *The Cakrasaṃvara Tantra.*

VIMALAMITRA (DRI-MED-SHES-GNYEN, MKHAS-PA-BYE-MA)

Secret Tantra That Lights the Lamps (sGron ma snang byed 'bar ba'i gsang rgyud). This is a lengthy commentary to one of the *Seventeen Tantras,* the *sGra thal 'gyur.* I have had access to two editions: a reproduction of a manuscript from Drepung Monastery, and the edition in the "Lhasa" edition of the Nyingma bKa' ma, published by Tsering Gyatso, vols. Ne and Pe.

Stringing a Garland of Pearls. Mu tig phreng ba brgyus pa. This is the commentary to the *Tantra of the Blazing Lamps (sGron ma 'bar ba'i rgyud).* From the "Lhasa" edition of the Nyingma bKa' ma, published by Tsering Gyatso, vol. Be (105), 15–325.

A Summary of the Tantra on the Blazing Lamps. sGron ma 'bar ba'i don bsdus. This is an outline *(sa bcad)* of the *Tantra of the Blazing Lamps (sGron ma 'bar ba'i rgyud).* From the "Lhasa" edition of the Nyingma bKa' ma, published by Tsering Gyatso, vol. Be (105), 5–14.

YUMO MIKYO DORJÉ (YU-MO-MI-BSKYOD-RDO-RJE)

Cycle of the Four Radiant Lamps. gSal sgron skor bzhi. Gangtok, Sikkim: Sherab Gyaltsen and Lama Dawa, 1983. Note that in this published edition the author is misidentified as A-wa-dhū-ti-pa-bsod-nams. The four texts can also be found in modern book format, published by the Jonang Foundation; they are contained in the collection *Yu mo'i gsal sgron rnam bzhi dang 'bro b'ai gsung sgros rgyas pa 'od zer phreng ba sogs,* which is part of the Jonang Publication Series (Jo nang dpe tshogs), series 3, vol. 25. Beijing: Mi rigs dpe skrun khang, 2010.

Lamp Illuminating Emptiness. sTong nyid gsal sgron. An independent manuscript of one of Yumo's above "four lamps." Included in *Jo nang dpe rnying phyogs bsgrigs,* TBRC W00KG0638.

Reference Works

Duff, Tony. *The Illuminator Tibetan-English Encyclopaedic Dictionary (Electronic Version)*. Kathmandu: Padma Karpo Translation Committee, 2000–2007.

Dung-dkar-blo-bzang-'phrin-las. *Bod rig pa'i tshig mdzod chen mo*. Beijing: Krung-go'i bod rig pa'i dpe skrun khang, 2002.

Ko-zhul-grags-pa-'byung-gnas and rGyal-ba-blo-bzang-mkhas-grub. *Gangs can mkhas grub rim byon ming mdzod*. Lanzhou: Kan su'u mi rigs dpe skrun khang, 1992.

Monier-Williams, Sir Monier. *A Sanskrit-English Dictionary*. London: Oxford University Press, 1899; Delhi: Motilal Banarsidass, 1990.

Zhang Yisun, ed. *Bod rgya tshig mdzod chen mo*. Beijing: Mi rigs dpe skrun khang, 1993.

Secondary Sources

Achard, Jean Luc. "Contribution Aux Nombrables de la Tradition Bon po: L'Appendice de bsTan 'dzin Rin chen rgyal mtshan à la Sphère de Cristal des Dieux et des Démons de Shar rdza rin po che." *Revue d'Etudes Tibétaines* 4 (October 2003): 78–146.

Allon, Mark. "The Oral Composition and Transmission of Early Buddhist Texts." In *Indian Insights: Buddhism, Brahmanism and Bhakti*, edited by Peter Connolly and Sue Hamilton, 39–61. London: Luzac Oriental, 1997.

Andrensen, Jensine. "Kālacakra: Textual and Ritual Perspectives." PhD diss., Harvard University, 1997.

Arnold, Edward A., ed. *As Long as Space Endures: Essays on the Kālacakra Tantra in Honor of H.H. the Dalai Lama*. Ithaca, NY: Snow Lion Publications, 2009.

Baker, Ian, and Thomas Laird. *The Dalai Lama's Secret Temple: Tantric Wall Paintings from Tibet*. New York: Thames & Hudson, 2000.

Bellezza, John Vincent. "A Preliminary Archaeological Survey of Da Rog mTsho." *Tibet Journal* 24, no. 1 (1999): 55–91.

Beyer, Stephen. "Notes on the Vision Quest in Early Mahāyāna." In *Prajñāpāramitā and Other Systems: Studies in Honor of Edward Conze*, edited by Lewis Lancaster, 329–340. Berkeley: University of California Press, 1977.

Bhikku Ñāṇamoli and Bhikku Bodhi, trans. *The Middle Length Discourses of the Buddha: A New Translation of the Majjhima Nikāya*. Boston: Wisdom Publications, 1995.

Blezer, Henk. "A Brief Bibliographical Key to *Zhang Zhung Snyan Rgyud* Editions with Special Attention for Sources on the Early Lineage." *Revue d'Etudes Tibétaines* 20 (2011): 135–203.

———. "'Light' on the Human Body: The Coarse Physical Body and Its Functions in the Aural Transmission from the Zhang Zhung on the Six Lamps." *Revue d'Etudes Tibétaines* 23 (2012): 117–168.

Brunnhölzl, Karl, trans. *In Praise of Dharmadhātu*, by Rangjung Dorje, Nāgārjuna and the Third Karmapa. Ithaca, NY: Snow Lion Publications, 2007. A translation of Nāgārjuna's *Dharmadhātustava*, with Rangjung Dorjé's commentary.

Burlingame, Eugene Watson, trans. *Buddhist Legends, Translated from the Original Pali Text of the Dhammapada Commentary*. Cambridge, MA: Harvard University Press, 1921.

Cech, Krystyna. "History, Teaching and Practice of Dialectics According to the Bon Tradition." *Tibet Journal* 11, no. 2 (1986): 3–28.

Chandra, Lokesh, and Raghu Vira. *Kālacakratantra and Other Texts*. New Delhi: International Academy of Indian Culture, 1966.

Dagkar, Namgyal Nyima. "The System of Education in Bonpo Monasteries from the Tenth Century Onwards." In *Tibetan Studies: Proceedings of the 6th Seminar of the International Association for Tibetan Studies, Fagernes 1992*, edited by Per Kværne, vol. 1, 137–143. Oslo: Institute for Comparative Research in Human Culture, 1994.

Dalton, Jacob P. "The Uses of the Dgongs Pa 'Dus Pa'i Mdo in the Development of the Rnying-Ma School of Tibetan Buddhism." PhD diss., University of Michigan, 2002.

———. *The Taming of the Demons: Violence and Liberation in Tibetan Buddhism*. New Haven, CT: Yale University Press, 2011.

Davidson, Ronald. *Indian Esoteric Buddhism: A Social History of the Tantric Movement*. New York: Columbia University Press, 2002.

———. "An Introduction to the Standards of Scriptural Authenticity in Indian Buddhism." In *Chinese Buddhist Apocrypha*, edited by Robert Buswell, 291–325. Honolulu: University of Hawai'i Press, 1990.

———. "The Litany of Names of Mañjuśrī." In *Tantric and Taoist Studies in Honor of R. A. Stein*, edited by Michael Strickman, 1–69. Brussels: Institut Belge des Hautes Études Chinoises, 1981.

———. "Masquerading as Pramāṇa: Esoteric Buddhism and Epistemological Nomenclature." In *Dharmakīrti's Thought and Its Impact on Indian and Tibetan Philosophy: Proceedings of the Third International Conference on Dharmakīrti and Pramāṇa,* edited by Shoryu Katsura, 25–35. Vienna: Österreichischen Akademie der Wissenschaften, 1999.

———. "Reframing Sahaja: Genre, Representation, Ritual and Lineage." *Journal of Indian Philosophy* 30 (2002): 45–83.

———. *Tibetan Renaissance: Tantric Buddhism in the Rebirth of Tibetan Culture*. New York: Columbia University Press, 2005.

de Körös, Csoma. "A Note on the Origin of the Kāla-Cakra and Ādi-Buddha Systems." *Journal of the Asiatic Society of Bengal* 2 (1833): 57–59.

Del Vico, Enrico, ed. *Kālacakra*. Rome: Editalia Edizioni d'Italia, 1996.

Demiéville, Paul. "The Mirror of the Mind." In *Sudden and Gradual: Approaches to Enlightenment in Chinese Thought,* edited by Peter N. Gregory, 13–40. Honolulu: University of Hawai'i Press, 1987.

Dhargyey, Geshe Ngawang. *A Commentary on the Kālacakra Tantra*. Translated by Gelong Jhampa Kelsang. Dharamsala: Library of Tibetan Works and Archives, 1985.

———. "An Introduction to and Outline of the Kālacakra Initiation." *Tibet Journal* 1, no. 1 (1975): 72–77.

———. "An Introduction to the Kālacakra Initiation." *Tibetan Bulletin* 4, no. 1 (1985): 12–14.

Dorje, Gyurme. "The Guhyagarbhatantra and Its XIVth Century Tibetan Commentary, Phyogs Bcu Mun Sel." University of London, 1987.
———, trans. *The Tibetan Book of the Dead: The Great Liberation by Hearing in the Intermediate States*. New York: Viking, 2006.
Dorje, Gyurme, and Matthew Kapstein. *The Nyingma School of Tibetan Buddhism*. Boston: Wisdom Publications, 1991.
Dreyfus, George. "Perception and Apperception in Tibetan Buddhist Epistemology." In *Tibetan Studies: Proceedings of the 7th Seminar of the International Association of Tibetan Studies, Graz 1995*, edited by Helmut Krasser, Michael Torsten Much, Ernst Steinkellner and Helmut Tauscher, 237–251. Wien: Verlag der Österreichischen Akademie der Wissenschaften, 1997.
———. *Recognizing Reality: Dharmakīrti's Philosophy and Its Tibetan Interpretations*. Albany: State University of New York Press, 1997.
Dunne, John D. *Foundations of Dharmakīrti's Philosophy*. Boston: Wisdom Publications, 2004.
Dyczkowski, Mark S. G. *The Doctrine of Vibration: An Analysis of the Doctrines and Practices of Kashmir Shaivism*. Albany: State University of New York Press, 1987.
Eckel, Malcolm David. *To See the Buddha: A Philosopher's Quest for the Meaning of Emptiness*. San Francisco: HarperCollins, 1992.
Ehrhard, Franz-Karl. "The 'Vision' of Rdzogs-Chen: A Text and Its Histories." In *Tibetan Studies: Proceedings of the 5th Seminar of the International Association for Tibetan Studies, Narita 1989*, edited by Ihara Shoren and Yamaguchi Zuiho, 47–57. Narita: Naritasan Shinshoji, 1992.
Eimer, Helmut, and David Germano, eds. *The Many Canons of Tibetan Buddhism*. Leiden: Brill, 2002.
Garfield, Jay L. *The Fundamental Wisdom of the Middle Way: Nāgārjuna's Mūlamadhyamakakārikā*. New York: Oxford University Press, 1995.
Garrett, Frances. *Embryology in the History of Tibetan Medicine: Becoming Human*. Abingdon: Routledge, 2008.
———. "Narratives of Embryology: Becoming Human in Tibetan Literature." PhD diss., University of Virginia, 2004.
Germano, David. "Architecture and Absence in the Secret Tantric History of the Great Perfection." *Journal of the International Association of Buddhist Studies* 17, no. 2 (1994): 203–335.
———. "The Elements, Insanity, and Lettered Subjectivity." In *Religions of Tibet in Practice*, edited by Donald Lopez, 313–334. Princeton, NJ: Princeton University Press, 1997.
———. "Food, Clothes, Dreams, and Karmic Propensities." In *Religions of Tibet in Practice*, edited by Donald Lopez, 293–312. Princeton, NJ: Princeton University Press, 1997.
———. "Mysticism and Rhetoric in the Great Perfection." Unpublished manuscript, 2006.
———. "Poetic Thought, the Intelligent Universe, and the Mystery of Self: The Tantric Synthesis of rDzogs Chen in Fourteenth Century Tibet." PhD diss., University of Wisconsin, 1992.

———. "Prophetic Histories of Buddhas, Ḍakinīs and Saints in Tibet." Unpublished manuscript, 1998.

———. "The Shifting Terrain of the Tantric Bodies of Buddhas and Buddhists from an Atiyoga Perspective." In *The Pandita and the Siddha: Tibetan Studies in Honor of E. Gene Smith,* edited by Ramon N. Prats, 50–84. Dharamshala: Amnye Machen Institute, 2007.

———. "The Secret Tibetan History of Buddhist Tantra in the Great Perfection." Unpublished manuscript, 1998.

———, trans. "The Treasury of Words and Meanings," by Longchenpa. Unpublished manuscript, 1998.

Germano, David, and William Waldron. "A Comparison of Ālaya-Vijñāna in Yogācāra and Dzogchen." In *Buddhist Thought and Applied Psychological Research: Transcending the Boundaries*, edited by D. K. Nauriyal, Michael S. Drummond, and Y. B. Lal, 36–68. New York: Routledge, 2006.

Gnoli, Raniero, and Giacomella Orofino, trans. *Nāropā: Iniziazione Kālacakra.* Milan: Adelphia Edizioni, 1994.

Gorvine, William M. "The Life of a Bönpo Luminary: Sainthood, Partisanship and Literary Representation in a 20th Century Tibetan Biography." PhD diss., University of Virginia, 2006.

Gregory, Peter N., trans. *Inquiry into the Origin of Humanity: An Annotated Translation of Tsung-Mi's Yüan Jen Lun with a Modern Commentary.* Honolulu: University of Hawai'i Press, 1995.

Griffiths, Paul. *On Being Buddha: The Classical Doctrine of Buddhahood.* Albany: State University of New York Press, 1994.

Grönbold, Günter. *The Yoga of Six Limbs.* Translated by Robert L Hütwohl. Santa Fe, NM: Spirit of the Sun Publications, 1996.

Guenther, Herbert. *From Reductionalism to Creativity: Rdzogs-Chen and the New Sciences of Mind.* Boston: Shambhala Press, 1989.

Gurung, B. C. *Bon in the Himalaya.* Kathmandu: Uma Gurung, 2003. A published edition of Gurung's dissertation at Tribhuvan University.

Gyatso, Janet. "Guru Chos-dbang's *gTer 'byung chen mo:* An Early Survey of the Treasure Tradition and Its Strategies in Discussing Bon Treasure." In *Tibetan Studies: Proceedings of the 6th Seminar of the International Association for Tibetan Studies, Fagernes 1992*, edited by Per Kværne, 275–287. Oslo: Institute for Comparative Research in Human Culture, 1994.

———. "Genre, Authorship, and Transmission in Visionary Buddhism: The Literary Traditions of Thang-stong rGyal-po." In *Tibetan Buddhism: Reason and Revelation*, edited by Steve Goodman and Ronald Davidson, 95–106. Albany: State University of New York Press, 1992.

———. "Healing Burns with Fire: The Facilitations of Experience in Tibetan Buddhism." *Journal of the American Academy of Religion* 67, no. 1 (1999): 113–147.

———, ed. *In the Mirror of Memory: Reflections on Mindfulness and Remembrance in Indian and Tibetan Buddhism.* Albany: State University of New York Press, 1992.

———. "The Logic of Legitimation in the Tibetan Treasure Tradition." *History of Religions* 33, no. 1 (1993): 97–134.

———. "Signs, Memory and History: A Tantric Buddhist Theory of Scriptural Transmission." *Journal of the International Association of Buddhist Studies* 9, no. 2 (1986): 7–35.

Gyatso, Khedrup Norsang. *The Ornament of Stainless Light: An Exposition of the Kālacakra Tantra.* Translated by Gavin Kilty. Boston: Wisdom Publications, 2004.

Gyatso, Tenzin, and Jeffrey Hopkins. *The Kālacakra Tantra: Rite of Initiation for the Stage of Generation.* London: Wisdom Publications, 1989.

Halkias, Georgios. "Transferring to the Land of Bliss: Among Texts and Practices of Sukhāvatī in Tibet." PhD diss., University of Oxford, 2006.

Harrison, Paul. "Buddhānusmṛti in the Pratyutpanna-Buddha-Saṃmukhāvasthita-Samādhi-Sūtra." *Journal of Indian Philosophy* 6 (1978): 35–57.

———. "Commemoration and Identification in Buddhānusmṛti." In *In the Mirror of Memory: Reflections on Mindfulness and Remembrance in Indian and Tibetan Buddhism*, edited by Janet Gyatso, 215–238. Albany: State University of New York Press, 1992.

———. *The Samādhi of Direct Encounter with the Buddhas of the Present: An Annotated English Translation of the Tibetan Version of the Pratyutpanna-Buddha-Saṃmukhāvasthita-Samādhi-Sūtra, with Several Appendices Relating to the History of the Text.* Tokyo: International Institute for Buddhist Studies, 1990.

Hartzell, James Francis. "Tantric Yoga: A Study of the Vedic Precursors, Historical Evolution, Literatures, Cultures, Doctrines, and Practices of the 11th Century Kaśmiri Śaivite and Buddhist Unexcelled Tantric Yogas." PhD diss., Columbia University, 1997.

Henning, Edward. "The Six Vajra-Yogas of Kālacakra." In *As Long as Space Endures: Essays on the Kālacakra Tantra in Honor of H.H. the Dalai Lama*, edited by Edward A. Arnold, 237–258. Ithaca, NY: Snow Lion Publications, 2009.

Hoffmann, Helmut. "Buddha's Preaching of the Kālacakra Tantra at the Stūpa of Dhānyakaṭaka." In *German Scholars on India: Contributions to Indian Studies,* edited by the Cultural Department of the Embassy of the Federal Republic of Germany, New Delhi, vol. 1, 136–140. Varanasi: Chowkhambha Sanskrit Series Office, 1973.

———. "Kālacakra Studies I: Manichaeism, Christianity and Islam in the Kālacakra Tantra." *Central Asiatic Journal* 13, no. 1 (1969): 52–73.

———. "Manichaeism and Islam in the Buddhist Kālacakra System." In *Proceedings of the IXth International Congress of the History of Religions 1958,* edited by the Congress Organizing Committee, 96–99. Tokyo: Maruzen, 1960.

Hopkins, Jeffrey. *Meditation on Emptiness.* London: Wisdom Publications, 1983.

———, trans. *Mountain Doctrine: Tibet's Fundamental Treatise on Other-Emptiness and the Buddha Matrix.* Ithaca, NY: Snow Lion Publications, 2006.

———. "Tantric Techniques." Unpublished manuscript, 2001.

Jackson, David P. "Birds in the Egg and Newborn Lion Cubs: Metaphors for the Potentialities and Limitations of 'All at Once' Enlightenment." In *Tibetan Studies: Proceedings of the 5th Seminar of the International Association for Tibetan Studies, Narita 1989,* edited by Ihara Shoren and Yamaguchi Zuiho, 95–114. Narita Naritasan Shinshoji, 1992.

Khamtrul Rinpoche. "A Geography and History of Shambhala." *Tibet Journal* 3, no. 3 (1978): 3–11.

Kalupahana, David J. *A History of Buddhist Philosophy: Continuities and Discontinuities*. Honolulu: University of Hawai'i Press, 1992.

Kapstein, Matthew, ed. *The Presence of Light: Divine Radiance and Religious Experience*. Chicago: University of Chicago Press, 2004.

———. "Rethinking Religious Experience: Seeing the Light in the History of Religions." In *The Presence of Light: Divine Radiance and Religious Experience*, edited by Matthew Kapstein, 265–300. Chicago: University of Chicago Press, 2004.

———. "The Strange Death of Pema the Demon Tamer." In *The Presence of Light: Divine Radiance and Religious Experience*, edited by Matthew Kapstein, 119–156. Chicago: University of Chicago Press, 2004.

Karmay, Samten. *The Arrow and the Spindle*. Kathmandu: Mandala Book Point, 1998.

———. *A Catalogue of Bonpo Publications*. Tokyo: Toyo Bunko, 1977.

———. "The Decree of the Khro-Chen King." *Acta Orientalia* 51 (1990): 141–159.

———. "A Discussion on the Doctrinal Position of Rdzog-Chen from the 10th to the 13th Centuries." *Journal Asiatique* 263 (1975): 147–156.

———. "A General Introduction to the History and Doctrines of Bon." *Memoirs of the Research Department of the Toyo Bunko* 33 (1975): 171–218.

———. *The Great Perfection: A Philosophical and Meditative Teaching of Tibetan Buddhism*. London: Brill, 1988.

———. *The Little Luminous Boy: The Oral Tradition from the Land of Zhang Zhung Depicted on Two Tibetan Paintings*. Bangkok: Orchid Press, 1998.

———. "rDzogs chen in Its Earliest Text: A Manuscript from Dunhuang." In *The Arrow and the Spindle,* 94–104. Kathmandu: Mandala Book Point, 1998.

———, trans. *The Treasury of Good Sayings: A Tibetan History of Bon*. London: Oxford University Press, 1972.

———. "Two Eighteenth Century Xylographic Editions of the Gzi Brjid." In *Indo-Tibetan Studies*, edited by Tadeusz Skorupski, 147–150. Tring: Institute of Buddhist Studies, 1990.

Karmay, Samten, and Yasuhiko Nagano, eds. *The Call of the Blue Cuckoo: An Anthology of Nine Bonpo Texts on Myths and Rituals*. Osaka: National Museum of Ethnology, 2002.

———, eds. *A Catalogue of the New Collection of Bonpo Katen Texts*. Osaka: National Museum of Ethnology, 2001.

———, eds. *A Catalogue of the New Collection of Bonpo Katen Texts—Indices*. Osaka: National Museum of Ethnology, 2001.

———, eds. *New Horizons in Bon Studies*. Bon Studies 2. Osaka: National Museum of Ethnology, 2000.

———, eds. *A Survey of Bonpo Monasteries and Temples in Tibet and the Himalaya*. Bon Studies 7. Osaka: National Museum of Ethnology, 2003.

Karmay, Samten, and Jeff Watt, eds. *Bon: The Magic Word*. New York: Rubin Museum of Art, 2007.

Kilty, Gavin, trans. *The Ornament of Stainless Light: An Exposition of the Kālacakra Tantra,* by Khedrup Norsang Gyatso. Boston: Wisdom Publications, 2004.

Kinnard, Jacob N. *Imaging Wisdom: Seeing and Knowing in the Art of Indian Buddhism*. Surrey: Curzon, 1999.

Kloetzli, Randy. *Buddhist Cosmology: From Single World System to Pure Land.* Delhi: Motilal Banarsidass, 1983.

Kongtrul, Jamgon. *Buddhist Ethics*. Translated by the International Translation Committee. Ithaca, NY: Snow Lion Publications, 1998.

———. *Myriad Worlds: Buddhist Cosmology in Abhidharma, Kālacakra and Dzog-Chen*. Translated by the International Translation Committee. Ithaca, NY: Snow Lion Publications, 1995.

Kroll, Paul W. "Body Gods and Inner Vision: The Scripture of the Yellow Court." In *Religions of China in Practice,* edited by Donald Lopez, 149–155. Princeton, NJ: Princeton University Press, 1996.

Kværne, Per. "Bonpo Studies: The A Khrid System of Meditation, Part I." *Kailash* 1, no. 1 (1973): 19–50.

———. "Bonpo Studies: The A Khrid System of Meditation, Part II." *Kailash* 1, no. 4 (1973): 247–332.

———. "The Canon of the Tibetan Bonpos." *Indo-Iranian Journal* 16 (1974): 18–56, 96–144.

———. "A Chronological Table of the Bon Po: The Bstan Rcis of Ñi Ma Bstan 'Jin." *Acta Orientalia* 33 (1971): 205–282.

———. "Dualism in Tibetan Cosmogonic Myths and the Question of Iranian Influence." In *Silver on Lapis: Tibetan Literary Culture and History*, edited by C. I. Beckwith. Bloomington, IN, 163–174: Tibet Society, 1987.

———. "The Great Perfection in the Tradition of the Bonpos." In *Early Ch'an in China and Tibet*, edited by Whalen Lai and Lewis Lancaster, 367–392. Berkeley: Berkeley Buddhist Studies Series, 1983.

———. "The Literature of Bon." In *Tibetan Literature: Studies in Genre*, edited by Jose Cabezon and Roger Jackson, 138–146. Ithaca, NY: Snow Lion Publications, 1996.

———. "A New Chronological Table of the Bon Religion: The Bstan-Rcis of Hor-Bcun Bstan-'Jin-Blo-Gros (1888–1975)." In *Tibetan Studies: Proceedings of the 4th Seminar of the International Association for Tibetan Studies, Schloss Hohenkammer, Munich 1985*, edited by H. Uebach and J. L. Panglung. Munich: Kommission für Zentralasiatische Studien Bayerische Akademie der Wissenschaften, 1988.

———. "On the Concept of Sahaja in Indian Buddhist Tantric Literature." *Temenos* 11 (1975): 89–135.

———. "The Study of Bon in the West: Past, Present, and Future." In *New Horizons in Bon Studies,* Bon Studies 2, edited by Samten Karmay and Yasuhiko Nagano, 7–20. Osaka: National Museum of Ethnology, 2000.

———. *Tibet Bon Religion: A Death Ritual of the Tibetan Bonpos*. Leiden: Brill, 1985.

———. *The Tibetan Bon Religion: Iconography of a Living Tradition*. Boston: Shambala Publications, 1996.

Kværne, Per and Thubten K. Rikey, trans. *The Stages of a-Khrid Meditation: Dzogchen Practice of the Bon Tradition*. Dharamsala: Library of Tibetan Works and Archives, 1996.

La Valée Poussin, Louis de (trans.). *Abhidharmakoṣabhāṣyam of Vasubandhu*. Translated from the French by Leo Pruden. Berkeley: Asian Humanities Press, 1988.

Larson, Gerald. *Classical Sāṃkhya: An Interpretation of Its History and Meaning*. Delhi: Moltilal Banarsidass, 1979.

Lessing, Ferdinand D., and Alex Wayman, trans. *Fundamentals of the Buddhist Tantras,* by Khedrup Jé. The Hague: Mouton, 1968.

Martin, Daniel. "The Emergence of Bon and the Tibetan Polemical Tradition." PhD diss., Indiana University, 1991.

———. "Human Body Good Thought (Mi Lus Bsam Legs) and the Revelation of the Secret Bonpo Mother Tantras." Master's thesis, Indiana University, 1986.

———. "Illusion Web: Locating the *Guhyagarbha Tantra* in Buddhist Intellectual History." In *Silver on Lapis: Tibetan Literary Culture and History*, edited by C. I. Beckwith, 175–209. Bloomington: Tibet Society, 1987.

———. *Mandala Cosmogony: Human Body Good Thought and the Revelation of the Secret Mother Tantras of Bon*. Wiesbaden: Harrassowitz Verlag, 1994.

———. "Pearls from Bones: Relics, Chortens, Tertons and the Signs of Saintly Death in Tibet." *Numen* 41 (1994): 273–324.

———. *Tibskrit Philology*. Edited by Alexander Cherniak. 2006. This is an electronic bibliographical reference that is freely circulated by Martin.

———. "Unearthing Bon Treasures: A Study of Tibetan Sources on the Earlier Years in the Life of Gshen-Chen-Klu-Dga'." *Journal of the American Oriental Society* 116.4 (1996): 619–644.

———. *Unearthing Bon Treasures: Life and Contested Legacy of a Tibetan Scripture Revealer, with a General Bibliography of Bon*. London: Brill, 2001.

Martin, Daniel, and Yael Bentor. *Tibetan Histories: A Bibliography of Tibetan-Language Historical Works*. London: Serindia Publications, 1997.

Martin, Daniel, Per Kværne, and Yasuhiko Nagano, eds. *A Catalogue of the Bon Kanjur*. Osaka: National Museum of Ethnology, 2003.

Matilal, Bimal Krisha. *Perception: An Essay on Classical Indian Theories of Knowledge*. Oxford: Clarendon Press, 1986.

McMahan, David. *Empty Vision: Metaphor and Visionary Imagery in Mahāyāna Buddhism*. New York: RoutledgeCurzon, 2002.

Miller, James. "Light." In *Daoism: A Beginner's Guide,* 114–130. Oxford: Oneworld Publications, 2003.

———. *The Way of Highest Clarity: Nature, Vision and Revelation in Medieval China*. Magdalena, NM: Three Pines Press, 2008.

Mullin, Glenn H., trans. *Bridging the Sutras and Tantras*. Ithaca, NY: Snow Lion Publications, 1982.

———. *The Practice of Kālacakra*. Ithaca, NY: Snow Lion Publications, 1991.

Namdak, Lopon Tenzin. *Bonpo Dzogchen Teachings According to Lopon Tenzin Namdak*. Kathmandu: Vajra Publications, 2006. Transcribed and edited, together with introduction and notes by John Myrdhin Reynolds.

———. *Heart Drops of Dharmakaya: Dzogchen Practice of the Bön Tradition*. Ithaca, NY: Snow Lion Publications, 1993.

———. *Shardza Tashi Gyaltsen: Kusum Rangshar, Oral Teachings by Lopon Tenzin Namdak Rinpoche*. Paris: Privately distributed transcript, 1999.

Namdak, Lopon Tenzin, and Tenzin Wangyal. *The Twenty-One Nails.* Vol. 2, *Oral Commentaries by Lopon Tenzin Namdak and Tenzin Wangyal Rinpoche.* Charlottesville, VA: Ligmincha Institute's Heartdrop Editions, 1996.

Narayan, Kirin. *Storytellers, Saints, and Scoundrels: Folk Narrative in Hindu Religious Teaching.* Philadelphia: University of Pennsylvania Press, 1989.

Newman, John. "Buddhist Sanskrit in the Kālacakra Tantra." *Journal of the International Association of Buddhist Studies* 11, no. 1 (1988): 123–140.

———. "Buddhist Siddhānta in the Kālacakra Tantra." *Wiener Zeitschrift für die Kunde Südasiens* 36 (1992): 227–234.

———. "Eschatology in the Wheel of Time Tantra." In *Buddhism in Practice*, edited by Donald Lopez, 284–289. Princeton, NJ: Princeton University Press, 1995.

———. "The Outer Wheel of Time: Vajrāyana Buddhist Cosmology in the Kālacakra Tantra." PhD diss., University of Wisconsin, 1987.

———. "The Paramādibuddha and Its Relation to the Early Kālacakra Literature." *Indo-Iranian Journal* 30 (1987): 93–102.

Norbu, Namkhai. *Drung, Deu, and Bön: Narrations, Symbolic Languages, and the Bön Tradition in Ancient Tibet.* Dharamsala: Library of Tibetan Works and Archives, 1995.

———. *The Mirror: Advice on Presence and Awareness.* Arcidosso, Italy: Shang Shung Editions, 1983.

Obeyesekere, Ranjini. "The Monk Cakkhupāla (Guardian of the Eyes)." In *Jewels of the Doctrine: Stories of the Saddharma Ratnāvaliya*, edited by Dharmasēna Thera, 9–35. Albany: State University of New York Press, 1991.

Orofino, Giacomella. "Apropos of Some Foreign Elements in the Kālacakratantra." In *Tibetan Studies: Proceedings of the 7th Seminar of the International Association of Tibetan Studies, Graz 1995*, edited by Helmut Krasser, Michael Torsten Much, Ernst Steinkellner, and Helmut Tauscher, 717–724. Wien: Verlag der Österreichischen Akademie der Wissenschaften, 1997.

———. "Divination with Mirrors: Observations on a Simile Found in the Kālacakra Literature." In *Tibetan Studies: Proceedings of the 6th Seminar of the International Association for Tibetan Studies, Fagernes 1992*, edited by Per Kværne, 612–628. Oslo: Institute for Comparative Research in Human Culture, 1994.

———, trans. *Naropa's Sekoddeśatika.* Milan: Adelphi, 1995.

———. "On the Ṣaḍaṅgayoga and the Realization of Ultimate Gnosis in the Kalacakratantra." *East and West* 46 (1996): 127–143.

———, ed. *Sekoddeśa: A Critical Edition of the Tibetan Translations.* Rome: Istituto Italiano per il Medio ed Estremeo Oriente, 1994.

———. "The State of the Art in the Study on the Zhang Zhung Language." *Annali, Istituto Universitario Orientale* 50, no. 1 (1990): 83–85.

Olivelle, Patrick, trans. *Upaniṣads.* New York: Oxford University Press, 1996.

Rinpoche, Patrul. *Words of My Perfect Teacher.* Translated by the Padmakara Translation Group. London: AltaMira Press, 1994.

Radhakrishnan, Sarvepalli, and Charles A Moore, eds. *A Sourcebook in Indian Philosophy.* Princeton, NJ: Princeton University Press, 1957.

Reynolds, John M. *The Oral Tradition from Zhang Zhung.* Kathmandu: Vajra Publications, 2005.

Reynolds, John M., and Lopon Tenzin Namdak. "The Instructions of Shardza Rinpoche for the Practice of Vision and the Dark Retreat." Unpublished manuscript, 1992.

Ricoeur, Paul. *The Symbolism of Evil.* Translated by Emerson Buchanan. Boston: Beacon Press, 1967.

Rinbochay, Lati, and Jeffrey Hopkins. *Death, Intermediate State and Rebirth.* Ithaca, NY: Snow Lion Publications, 1985.

Robinet, Isabelle. *Taoist Meditation: The Mao-Shan Tradition of Great Purity.* Albany: State University of New York Press, 1993.

Roerich, George N. (trans.). *The Blue Annals.* Delhi: Moltilal Banarsidass, 1996 (reprint of 1949).

———. "Studies in the Kālacakra I." *Journal of the "Urusvati" Himalayan Research Institute of the Roerich Museum* 2 (1932): 11–23.

Rossi, Donatella. *The Philosophical View of the Great Perfection in the Tibetan Bon Religion.* Ithaca, NY: Snow Lion Publications, 1999.

Ruegg, D. S. "The Jo Nan Pas: A School of Buddhist Ontologists According to the Grub Mtha' Sel Gyi Me Lon." *Journal of the American Oriental Society* 83, no. 1 (1963): 73–91.

Sanderson, Alexis. "The Doctrine of the Mālinīvijayottaratantra." In *Ritual and Speculation in Early Tantrism: Studies in Honour of André Padoux*, edited by Teun Goudriaan, 281–312. Albany: State University of New York Press, 1992.

———. "Purity and Power among the Brahmans of Kashmir." In *The Category of the Person: Anthropology, Philosophy, History*, edited by Michael Carrithers, Steven Collins, and Steven Lukes, 190-216. Cambridge: Cambridge University Press, 1985.

Schaeffer, Kurtis Rice. "Tales of the Great Brahmin: Creative Traditions of the Buddhist Poet-Saint Saraha." PhD diss., Harvard University, 2000.

Scheiddeger, Daniel. "Lamps in the Leaping Over." *Revue d'Etudes Tibétaines*, no. 8 (2005): 40–64.

Schopen, Gregory. *Bones, Stones, and Buddhist Monks: Collected Papers on the Archaeology, Epigraphy, and Texts of Monastic Buddhism in India.* Honolulu: University of Hawai'i Press, 1997.

———. *Buddhist Monks and Business Matters: Still More Papers on Monastic Buddhism in India.* Honolulu: University of Hawai'i Press, 2004.

Schwieger, P. "A Few Remarks on the Function of Vision for Tibetan Literature." Proceedings of the Eighth Seminar of the International Association for Tibetan Studies. Unpublished, Bloomington, Indiana, 1998.

Shakabpa, Tsepon W. D. *Tibet: A Political History.* Reprint, New York: Potala Publications, 1984.

Sharf, Robert. "Buddhist Modernism and the Rhetoric of Meditative Experience." *Numen* 42, no. 3 (1995): 228–283.

Shen, C. T. *The Five Eyes.* Taipei: Torch of Wisdom, 1976. Authored by "a shipping executive... with scientific training."

Singh, Jaideva, trans. *Spanda-Kārikās: The Divine Creative Pulsation,* by Vasugupta. Delhi: Moltilal Banarsidass, 1980.

———. *Vijñānabhairava or Divine Consciousness: A Treasury of 112 Types of Yoga.* Delhi: Moltilal Banarsidass, 1979.

Snellgrove, David. *The Hevajra Tantra: A Critical Study.* 2 vols. London: Oxford University Press, 1959.

———. *Indo-Tibetan Buddhism: Indian Buddhists and Their Tibetan Successors.* Boston: Shambhala Publications, 2002.

———. *The Nine Ways of Bon: Excerpts from Gzi-Brjid Edited and Translated.* Boulder, CO: Prajna Press, 1980.

Sopa, Geshe Lhundub, Roger Jackson, and John Newman. *The Wheel of Time: The Kālacakra in Context.* Madison, WI: Deer Park Books, 1985.

Stearns, Cyrus. *The Buddha from Dolpo: A Study of the Life and Thought of the Tibetan Master Dolpopa Sherab Gyaltsan.* Albany: State University of New York Press, 1999.

———. *Hermit of Go Cliffs: Timeless Instructions from a Tibetan Mystic.* Boston: Wisdom Publications, 2000.

———. "The Life and Tibetan Legacy of the Indian Mahāpaṇḍita Vibhūticandra." *Journal of the International Association of Buddhist Studies* 19, no. 1 (1996): 127–171.

Stevenson, Daniel B. "The Four Kinds of Samādhi in Early T'ien-T'ai Buddhism." In *Traditions of Meditation in Chinese Buddhism*, edited by Peter N. Gregory, 45–97. Honolulu: University of Hawai'i Press, 1986.

Strong, John. *The Experience of Buddhism: Sources and Interpretations.* Belmont, CA: Wadsworth, 2002.

———. *Relics of the Buddha.* Princeton, NJ: Princeton University Press, 2004.

Thondup, Tulku. *Buddha Mind: An Anthology of Longchen Rabjam's Writings on Dzogpa Chenpo.* Ithaca, NY: Snow Lion Publications, 1989.

———. *Hidden Teachings of Tibet: An Explanation of the Terma Tradition of the Nyingma School of Buddhism.* London: Wisdom Publications, 1986.

Thurman, Robert A. F. "Vajra Hermeneutics." In *Buddhist Hermeneutics*, edited by Donald Lopez, 119–148. Honolulu: University of Hawai'i Press, 1988.

Tomabechi, Tōru. "Étude Du Pañcakrama: Introduction Et Traduction Annotée." PhD diss., Université de Lausanne, 2006.

Turner, Victor. *Dramas, Fields, and Metaphors.* Ithaca, NY: Cornell University Press, 1974.

Vose, Kevin. "The Birth of Prāsaṅgika: A Buddhist Movement in India and Tibet." PhD diss., University of Virginia, 2005.

———. *Resurrecting Candrakīrti: Disputes in the Tibetan Creation of Prāsaṅgika.* Boston: Wisdom Publications, 2009.

Wallace, B. Alan, ed. *Buddhism and Science: Breaking New Ground.* New York: Columbia University Press, 2003.

Wallace, Vesna. "The Buddhist Tantric Medicine in the Kālacakratantra." *Pacific World,* n.s., no. 11 (1995): 155–174.

———. *The Inner Kālacakratantra: A Buddhist View of the Tantric Individual.* Oxford: Oxford University Press, 2001.

———. *The Kālacakratantra: The Chapter on the Individual Together with the Vimalaprabhā.* New York: American Institute of Buddhist Studies, 2004.

———. *The Kālacakratantra: The Chapter on the Sādhanā Together with the Vimalaprabhā Commentary*. New York: American Institute of Buddhist Studies, 2010.
———. "Medicine and Astrology in the Healing Arts of the Kālacakratantra." In *As Long as Space Endures: Essays on the Kālacakra Tantra in Honor of H.H. the Dalai Lama,* edited by Edward A. Arnold, 179–191. Ithaca, NY: Snow Lion Publications, 2009.
———. "The Six-Phased Yoga of the *Abbreviated Wheel of Time Tantra (Laghukālacakratantra)* According to Vajrapāṇi." In *Yoga in Practice*, edited by David Gordon White, 204–222. Princeton, NJ: Princeton University Press, 2012.
Wallace, Vesna, and Alan Wallace, trans. *A Guide to the Bodhisattva Way of Life,* by Śāntideva. Ithaca, NY: Snow Lion Publications, 1997.
Wangyal, Tenzin. *Nyam Gyü: The Experiential Transmission of Drugyalwa Yungdrung*. Landshut, Germany: Naldjor Institute, 1996.
———. *Wonders of the Natural Mind: The Essence of Dzogchen in the Native Bon Tradition of Tibet*. Barrytown, NY: Station Hill Press, 1993.
Wedemeyer, Christian. *Aryadeva's Lamp That Integrates the Practices*. New York: Columbia University Press, 2007.
———. "Vajrayana and Its Doubles: A Critical Historiography, Exposition, and Translation of the Tantric Works of Āryadeva." PhD diss., Columbia University, 1999.
White, David Gordon. *Sinister Yogis*. Chicago: University of Chicago Press, 2009.

Selected Works on Seeing and Blindness

Bexton, William H., et al. "Effects of Decreased Variation in the Sensory Environment." *Canadian Journal of Psychology* 8, no. 2 (1954): 70–76.
DeMott, D. W., and R. M. Boynton. "Sources of Entopic Stray Light." *Journal of the Optical Society of America* 48 (1958): 120–125.
Draaisma, Douwe. "Towards Dusk the Images Appear: Bonnet Syndrome." In *Disturbances of the Mind,* 11–39. Translated by Barbara Fasting. New York: Cambridge University Press, 2009.
Elkins, James. *How to Use Your Eyes*. New York: Routledge, 2000.
———. "A Multicultural Look at Space and Form." In "How the Visual Is Studied." Unpublished manuscript, 2006.
———. *The Object Stares Back: On the Nature of Seeing*. New York: Simon and Schuster, 1996.
———. *Visual Studies: A Skeptical Introduction*. New York: Routledge, 2003.
Feuerbach, Anselm von. *Kaspar Hauser: An Account of an Individual Kept in a Dungeon, Separated from All Communication with the World, from Early Childhood to About the Age of Seventeen*. 2nd ed. Translated by H. G. Linberg. Boston: Allen and Ticknor, 1833.
Fiser, Jozsef, Chiayu Chiu, and Michael Weliky. "Small Modulation of Ongoing Cortical Dynamics by Sensory Input During Natural Vision." *Nature* 431, no. 7008 (2004): 573–578.
Gold, Kenneth, and Peter V. Rabins. "Isolated Visual Hallucinations and the Charles Bonnet Syndrome: A Review of the Literature and Presentation of Six Cases." *Comprehensive Psychiatry* 30, no. 1 (1989): 90–98.

Gordon, Ian E. *Theories of Visual Perception*. New York: Psychology Press, 2004.
Gregory, Richard. *Concepts and Mechanisms of Perception*. New York: Scribner, 1974.
———. "Images of Mind in Brain." *Word and Image* 21 (2005): 120–123.
———, ed. *The Oxford Companion to the Mind*. 2nd ed. New York: Oxford University Press, 1987.
Hine, Robert. *Second Sight*. Berkeley: University of California Press, 1993. Hine's bibliography contains an extensive list of biographies, autobiographies, and narratives of blindness.
Horowitz, Mardi J. "The Imagery of Visual Hallucinations." *Journal of Nervous and Mental Disease* 138 (1964): 513–523.
Hull, John M. *Touching the Rock: An Experience of Blindness*. New York: Pantheon Books, 1990.
Lewis-Williams, J. D., and T. A. Dowson. "The Signs of All Times: Entoptic Phenomena in Upper Paleolithic Art." *Current Anthropology* 29, no. 2 (1988): 201–245.
Narayan, R. K., "A Breath of Lucifer." In *Under the Banyan Tree and Other Stories*, 102–116. Chennai: Indian Thought Publications, 2012 (Reprint).
O'Farrell, Lauren, Sandra Lewis, Amy McKenzie, and Lynda Jones. "Charles Bonnet Syndrome: A Review of the Literature." *Journal of Visual Impairment and Blindness* 104 (May 2010): 261–274.
Pascual-Leone, Alvaro, Lotfi B. Merabet, Denise Maguire, Aisling Warde, Karin Alterescu, and Robert Stickgold. "Visual Hallucinations During Prolonged Blindfolding in Sighted Subjects." *Journal of Neuro-Ophthalmology* 24 (2004): 109–113.
Pascual-Leone, Alvaro, Amir Amedi, Felipe Fregni, and Lofti B. Merabet. "The Plastic Human Brain Cortex." *Annual Review of Neuroscience* 28 (2005): 377–401.
Ramachandran, V. S. *A Brief Tour of Human Consciousness*. New York: Pi Press, 2004.
———. *Phantoms in the Brain: Probing the Mysteries of the Human Mind*. New York: William Morrow, 1998.
Ramachandran, V. S., E. L. Altschuler, and S. Hillyer. "Mirror Agnosia." *Proceedings of the Royal Society of London* 264 (1997): 645–647.
Ramachandran, V. S., and Richard Gregory. "Perceptual Filling in of Artificially Induced Scotomas in Human Vision." *Nature* 350, no. 6320 (1991): 699–702.
Ramachandran, V. S., and E. M. Hubbard. "Synaesthesia: A Window into Perception, Thought, and Language." *Journal of Consciousness Studies* 8 (2001): 3–34.
Riva, C. E., and B. Petrig. "Blue Field Entoptic Phenomenon and Blood Velocity in the Retinal Capillaries." *Journal of the Optical Society of America* 70, no. 10 (1980): 1234–1238.
Sacks, Oliver. *An Anthropologist on Mars: Seven Paradoxical Tales*. New York: Knopf, 1995. See especially "The Case of the Colorblind Painter" and "To See and Not See."
———. *The Island of the Colorblind*. New York: Knopf, 1997.
———. "The Mind's Eye: What the Blind See." *New Yorker* 79, no. 20 (2003): 48–59.
———. "The Prisoner's Cinema: Sensory Deprivation." In *Hallucinations*, 34–44. New York: Knopf, 2012.
———. "Silent Multitudes: Charles Bonnet Syndrome." In *Hallucinations*, 3–33. New York: Knopf, 2012.

Sanford, Charlotte, and Lester David. *Second Sight: A Miraculous Story of Vision Regained*. New York: M. Evans, 1979.

Senden, Marius von. *Space and Sight: The Perception of Space and Shape in the Congenitally Blind before and after Operation*. Translated from the German by Peter Lauchlan Heath. Glencoe, IL: Free Press, 1960.

Sinclair, S. H., M. Azar-Cavanagh, K. A. Soper, R. F. Tuma, and H. N. Mayrovitz. "Investigation of the Source of the Blue Field Entoptic Phenomenon." *Investigative Ophthalmology and Visual Science* 30, no. 4 (1989): 668–673.

Teunisse, R. J., et al. "Visual Hallucinations in Psychologically Normal People: Charles Bonnet's Syndrome." *Lancet* 347, no. 9004 (1996): 794–797.

Valvo, Alberto. *Sight Restoration after Long-Term Blindness: The Problems and Behavior Patterns of Visual Rehabilitation*. New York: American Foundation for the Blind, 1971.

Wells, H. G. "The Country of the Blind." In *Works of H. G. Wells*, 601–636. New York: Scribner's, 1925.

White, H. E., and P. Levatin. "Floaters in the Eye." *Scientific American* 206 (1962): 119–127.

SPELLING OF TIBETAN PERSONAL AND PLACE NAMES

All Good (kun-tu-bzang-po)
Ba-ri Lotsawa (ba-ri-lo-tsA-ba)
Butön (bu-ston)
Chapa Chökyi Seng-gé (phywa-pa-chos-kyi-seng-ge)
Dangma Lhüngyi Gyeltsen (ldang-ma-lhun-gyi-rgyal-mtshan)
Dergé (sde-dge)
Drenpa Namkha (dran-pa-nam-mkha)
Drepung ('bras-spungs)
Dro Gelong Sherap Drak ('bro-dge-slong-shes-rab-grags)
Drogön Namla-tsek ('gro-mgon-gnam-la-rtsegs; sgro-ston-gnam-la-rtsegs)
Druchen Gyalwa Yungdrung (bru-chen-rgyal-ba-g.yung-drung)
Druchen Namkha Yungdrung (bru-chen-nam-mkha'-g.yung-drung)
Drugyalwa (bru-rgyal-ba, bru-sgom-rgyal-ba-g.yung-drung)
Dzeng ('dzeng)
Gölo Zhönnupel ('gos-lo-gzhon-nu-dpal)
Gompa Tsüldrak (sgom-pa-tshul-grags)
Gyalwa Yeshé (rgyal-ba-ye-shes)
Gyerpung Nangzher Löpo (gyer-spungs-snang-bzher-lod-po)
Gyi-jo Dawé Özer (gyi-jo-zla-ba'i-'od-zer)
Hap Jo-sé Jampel (hab-jo-sras-'jam-dpal)
Jégom Nakpo (lce-sgom-nag-po)
Jetsün Seng-gé Wangchuk (lce-btsun-seng-ge-dbang-phyug)
Khedrup Jé (mkhas-grub-dge-legs-dpal-bzang)
Khedrup Norsang Gyatso (mkhas-grub-nor-bzang-rgya-mtsho)
Lang Darma (glang-dar-ma)
Loden Nyingpo (blo-ldan-snying-po)
Menri (sman-ri)
Meü Gong Dzö (rme'u-dgongs-mdzod)

Mt. Dönmo (don-mo-ri)
Ngödrup Drakpa (dngos-grub-grags-pa)
Ngog Lotsawa Loden Sherap (rngog-lo-tsA-ba-blo-ldan-shes-rab)
Nyang Tingdzin Zangpo (myang-ting-'dzin-bzang-po)
Öglun Gomchen Tashi Sherab ('og-blon-sgom-chen-bkra-shis-shes-rab)
Ölmo Lung-ring ('ol-mo-lung-ring)
Orgom Kündül ('or-sgom-kun-'dul)
Patsün Tengyal (spa-btsun-bstan-rgyal-seng-ge-dpal-bzang, spa-ston-bstan-rgyal-bzang-po)
Pönchen Tsenpo (dpon-chen-btsan-po)
Ra Chö-rap (rwa-chos-rab)
Relpachen (ral-pa-can)
Riwa Shertsul (ri-ba-sher-tshul)
Rong Tokmé Zhikpo (rong-rtog-med-zhig-po)
Samyé (bsam-yas)
Sangpu (gsang-phu)
Sangwa Düpa (gsang-ba-'dus-pa)
Sebön Trogyal (se-bon-khro-rgyal)
Shenchen Lu-ga (gshen-chen-klu-dga')
Shenrap Miwo (gshen-rab-mi-bo)
Sok Chenpo ('dul-'dzin-bla-ma-sog-chen-po)
Songtsen Gampo (srong-btsan-sgam-po)
Tapihritsa (ta-pi-hri-tsa)
Tāranātha (tA-ra-nA-tha)
Trigum Tsenpo (gri-gum-btsan-po)
Trisong Detsen (khri-srong-lde-btsan)
Tsang (gtsang)
Tsepung Dawa Gyaltsen (tshe-spungs-zla-ba-gyal-mtshan)
Uri Sogyal (u-ri-bsod-nam-rgyal-mtshan)
U-yuk ('u-yug)
Vimalamitra (bi-ma-la-mi-tra, mkhas-pa-bye-ma)
Yangtön Chenpo (yang-ston-chen-po)
Yeru Wensakha (g.yas-ru-dben-sa-kha)
Yumo Mikyo Dorjé (yu-mo-mi-bskyod-rdo-rje)
Zhang Zhung (zhang-zhung)
Zhangtön Tashi Dorjé (zhang-ston-bkra-shis-rdo-rje)

INDEX

action seal *(las kyi phyag rgya)*, 24, 133, 168–169, 174
Ādibuddha Tantra, 21, 26, 166, 169, 176–177, 186, 195
Advice on the Six Lamps, 10, 13, 60
  analysis of contents, 84
  commentaries on, 78
  editions of, 229
  English translation of, 234
  revelation of, 73, 77, 234, 266
afflicted mind *(nyon yid)*, 285, 287
Akaniṣṭha *('og min)*, 253, 312
All Good (Küntu Zangpo), 52–53, 59, 102, 115, 165, 187, 193, 265
  dwelling in the body, 312
  enlightenment of, 57, 85–86, 102, 240, 282
  etymology of, 266, 310
  source of Oral Tradition from Zhang Zhung, 72, 74, 76, 269
Approaching the Ultimate, 158, 176, 184, 186, 194
Āryadeva, 41, 173, 177, 180–181, 188, 191
Atiśa, 114
atomic particles *(rdul phra rab)*, in Kālacakra theory, 12, 24, 40, 42, 45, 98, 115, 120, 125–126, 160, 163, 167, 170, 173, 177, 182–186
awareness *(rig pa)*, 51–53, 55, 57, 64, 73, 83–87, 89, 92, 105, 116, 118, 136, 204–205, 210, 224, 234, 237, 246, 253, 255–256, 266, 276–277
  appearances as the "play" of, 56
  aspects of, 277
  contemplative introductions to, 316, 320, 322
  and doctrine of recognition, 56
  and enlightenment of All Good, 58
  and light, 126, 241
  presence in body, 297
  as singular component of universe, 56
  and the universal ground, 296
  and visionary experience, 57, 60–61, 65, 208

bardo *(bar do)*, 73, 82, 91, 198, 259, 332. *See also* lamp of the bardo period
  attaining liberation in, 336
  bardo of existence, 341
  bardo of primordial gnosis, 335
  karmic bardo of birth and death, 341
  luminous bardo of reality-itself, 337
  natural bardo of this life, 213
  perception of body during, 343
  reality bardo, 337
  referred to as a lamp, 332
  suffering during, 343
  visionary appearances during, 339, 342
Ba-ri Lotsawa, 79

bhaga, 48, 166, 173, 176, 192, 195–196
Blue Annals, 29
blue-field entoptic effect, 122
Bön, 10, 70
  11th century transformation, 70
  nine vehicles of, 71
  persecution of, 5, 70
  relationship with Nyingma and Sarma, 5
  third spread of doctrines, 70
  three Great Perfection traditions, 71
breakthrough *(khregs chod)*, 60
breath control yoga *(srog rtsol)*, 36
buddha eyes *(sangs rgyas kyi mig)*, 105, 107
buddha nature *(tathāgatagarbha)*, 101

Cakrasaṃvara Tantra, 25, 180
caṇḍālī flame, 37, 40, 89
  perception during recollection yoga, 38
  related to Great Seal, 38
Candrakīrti, 114
channels. *See* energy channels
Chapa Chökyi Seng-gé, 16
Charles Bonnet syndrome, 110
clear appearance *(gsal snang)*, 29
common ground *(spyi gzhi)*, 59, 147, 238, 273, 275
completion stage *(rdzogs rim)*, 29, 108. *See also* six limbed yoga
  consorts in, 39
  Guhyasamāja, 41
  Kālacakra, 31
  nonconceptual nature of, 31–32, 34, 168, 169
  relationship to generation stage in Kālacakra, 30
concentration yoga *(ting nge 'dzin)*, 40, 140
confusion *('khrul pa)*, 247, 250, 262, 296, 306, 342
consort *(phyag rgya)*, 44, 130
  Great Perfection critique of, 141
  in initiation ceremony, 131
  Kālacakra abandonment of, 39, 49, 132
  in Kālacakra generation stage, 30
  motion of *thig-le* associated with, 135
  physical, 39, 133
  purpose of lower consorts in Kālacakra, 169
  sacramental, 131
  visionary, 39, 49, 132
  visualized, 38, 132
crystal tube channel *(shel sbug can)*, 105, 213, 219
Cuckoo of Awareness, 52
Cycle of the Four Radiant Lamps, 8, 23
  editions of, 153
cyclic existence *('khor ba)*
  classifications of, 288
  and the eyes, 208
  and the Great Seal, 195
  parting from transcendence, 282
  relationship to ground, 85
  and visionary appearances, 191

Daoism, 17
dark room *(mun khang)*
  in Great Perfection, 61
  in Kālacakra, 33
Darok Lake, 77
daytime yoga *(nyin mo'i rnal 'byor)*, 33
death, 92
  attaining liberation at time of, 336
  contraction of elements, 260
  disintegration of body's elements, 260, 333
  importance of thoughts at time of, 336
  separation of body and mind at time of, 333
Deer Rock, 234, 266
dharma eyes *(chos kyi mig)*, 107
dharmadhātu, 101, 176
  synonym for the Great Seal, 165, 173, 181
direct perception *(mngon sum)*, 108, 116
direct transcendence *(thod rgal)*, 60
discovery *(dmar thag bcad pa)*, 90, 253, 315
divine eyes *(lha'i mig)*, 32–33, 107, 182–183

in Bön Great Perfection, 338, 343
divine pride *(lha'i nga rgyal)*, 29
Dorjé Chang (Skt. Vajradhara)
two versions of, in *Tantra of the Blazing Lamps*, 64
Draché Valley, 234, 266
Drenpa Namkha, 5
Drogön Namla-tsek, 28
Dru family, 231
Druchen Namkha Yungdrung, 79, 231
Drugom Gyalwa Yungdrung. *See* Drugyalwa
Drugyalwa, 10, 60, 72, 74, 78, 231
dynamic energy *(rtsal)*, 56, 83, 239, 253, 254, 277, 279–280, 283, 300–302, 318

earlier spread *(snga dar)*, 1
eight consciousnesses *(rnam shes tshogs brgyad)*, 86, 315
Emanation of Blessings, 185
embryology, 57, 88, 248, 300
emptiness *(stong pa nyid)*, 97
becoming visible, in Yumo, 48
as an object of experience, in Yumo, 43
as an object of meditation, in Yumo, 160
observable, 115
of other, 102
"path" emptiness in Yumo, 25, 43, 160
positive approaches to, 99
and seeing, 115
sexualized, 102
"view" emptiness in Yumo, 25, 43, 160
with all aspects, 98
empty form *(stong gzugs)*, 24, 34, 37, 45, 48, 98, 109, 115–116, 120, 125, 139, 164, 170–171, 174–175, 177–179, 182–183, 186, 189, 190–191, 196
mentioned in Drugyalwa's commentary, 325
empty seminal nuclei lamp *(thig le stong pa'i sgron ma)*, 66, 100, 206, 216
etymology of, 218
energy channels *(rtsa)*
of cyclic existence and transcendence, 302
enumerations of, 314
formation during development of body, 249, 301
four great channels, 219
heart-to-eyes channel, 105, 308
luminous, 104
role in process of dying, 334
subsidiary, 303
three primary, 88, 301
energy wheels *('khor lo)*
in formation of body, 249, 301
and four joys, 135, 140
and four *thig-le*, 139
in process of dying, 335
six, 314
in six yogas, 36–38
Enlightenment of Vairocana Tantra, 181
entoptic lights, 122
Entry into Suchness, 160
era of darkness *(mun pa'i bskal pa)*, 2
era of lamps *(sgron ma'i bskal pa)*, 1–2
E-VAM, 159
expanse *(dbyings)*, 61, 67, 222
inseparable from awareness, 61, 68
lighting up of, 68
and linked lambs, 62
outer and inner, 208
as one of "three spaces," 274
transformation into buddhafields, 62
visionary experience of, 225
eyes of insight *(shes rab kyi mig)*, 107

far-reaching-lasso water lamp *(rgyang zhags chu'i sgron ma)*, 64, 73, 89, 204, 206, 251, 307
etymology, 208
five bodies *(sku lnga)*, 284, 312
five buddha families *(rigs lnga)*, 313, 315
five channels *(rtsa lnga)*, 250
five deities *(lha lnga)*, 284, 312
five elements *('byung ba lnga)*, 127, 286
role in dying process, 333

five entrails *(nang khrol lnga)*, 250, 306
five eyes *(mig lnga)*, 105
related to emptiness, 109
related to Kālacakra six yogas, 109
five lights *('od lnga)*, 127, 226, 250–251, 295, 305, 309, 312
at time of death, 337
five objects *(yul lnga)*, 286
five primordial gnoses *(ye shes lnga)*, 313
five seats of the sense faculties *(dbang rten lnga)*, 250
five sense faculties *(dbang po lnga)*, 250, 305
Five Stages, 172
as a source in Yumo, 41
five thig-le *(thig le lnga)*, 136, 141
five visions *(snang ba lnga)*, 61, 258, 327
five vital organs *(don snying lnga)*, 250, 304
at time of death, 333
five winds *(rlung lnga)*, 301
fleshy eyes *(sha'i mig)*, 107
in Bön Great Perfection, 338
floaters, 122
form of emptiness *(stong pa nyid kyi gzugs). See* empty form
Four Cycles of the Oral Transmission, 73–74
editions of, 229
four flower goddesses *(me tog ma bzhi)*, 315
four thig-le *(thig le bzhi)*, 137
four visions *(snang ba bzhi)*, 59

Garab Dorjé, 51
gazes *(lta stangs)*, 33, 36, 124, 316, 322, 326
generation stage *(bskyed rim)*, 29
Kālacakra critique of, 31–32, 168
relationship to completion stage, 30
Glorious Thig-le of the Great Seal Tantra, 167
Gnosis Vajra Compendium Tantra, 166, 171, 191
gnostic energy of awareness *(rig pa'i ye shes)*, 276–277
gnostic seal *(ye shes phyag rgya)*, 38, 45, 168–169, 174
Great Perfection *(rdzogs chen)*, 9, 70
in renaissance period, 53
origin accounts, 51
three traditions in Bön, 71
Great Seal *(phyag rgya chen mo)*, 7, 44, 164, 171
as a consort, 168
desire for, 165
as dwelling in all beings, 191
and emptiness, 102, 115, 165
and empty form, 39, 175, 177
as an entity that is experienced, 187
identified with Prajñāpāramitā, 24
as pervading everything, 174, 195
as a sexual consort, 132
as singular and multiple, 194
as a source of bliss, 168, 170
as a source of light, 45
as source of world, 49
synonyms for, 44, 48, 196
union with, 45
various meanings of the term, 44
as a visionary appearance, 7, 24, 26, 39, 46, 185
ground *(gzhi)*, 56–57, 85, 272
ground-presencing *(gzhi snang)*, 58, 83
Guhyagarbha Tantra, 7, 52
Guhyasamāja Tantra, 25, 157
Guhyasamāja tradition
use in Yumo, 41–42
Guidance in the Letter A (a khrid), 71
Gurub Nangzher Löpo. *See* Gyerpungpa
Gyerpung Nangzher Löpo. *See* Gyerpungpa
Gyerpungpa, 73, 76, 234
enlightenment of, 346

heart (area of body), 86, 246, 295, 300
Hevajra Root-Tantra, 191
Hevajra Tantra, 3, 25, 42, 158, 170, 179
higher seeing *(lhag mthong)*, 8, 116, 256, 322

in visionary context, 90
higher sights *(lhag mthong)*, 261, 327
at time of death, 339
Highest Clarity (Shangqing), 17
Highest Yoga *(anuttara-yoga)*, 131

ignorance *(ma rig pa)*
co-emergent, 241, 285
completely reifying, 241, 286
and Great Seal, 170, 178, 193
illusion *(sgyu ma)*, 164, 171, 179, 322
analogies for, 171, 177, 191
illusion-like samādhi *(sgyu ma lta bu'i ting nge 'dzin)*, 162, 173, 179–180
inference *(rjes dpag)*, 108
initiation, 25, 90, 131, 140
introduction *(ngo sprod pa)*, 89–90, 252–253, 270, 311, 316, 322, 338
introductory scene *(gleng gzhi)*, 63, 159
ordinary and extraordinary, 64

jing ("essence" or "seminal essence"), 17
Jñānatilaka Tantra, 185, 192
Jonang, 27, 29, 102

Kadampa *(bka' gdams pa)*, 16
Kālacakra Root Tantra. See Ādibuddha Tantra
Kālacakra Tantra, 165, 174–175, 178, 182–184, 188, 195
critique of brahmins, 22
early history in Tibet, 23
history of, 21
as an "illuminating tantra," 25
and Islam, 21
Tibetan translations of, 23
verse 4.198 (root verse of Yumo's *Lamp*), 43, 163
views hidden in other tantras, 26
Kālacakrapāda, 7, 23, 98, 115, 163–164
Kawa Pal-dzeg, 55
Khedrup Norsang Gyatso, 40, 109, 139
Küntu Zangpo. *See* All Good

lamp *(sgron ma)*
metaphor for a buddha, 1
metaphor for *Advice on the Six Lamps*, 345, 347
metaphor for the eyes, 254
Lamp Illuminating Emptiness, 10, 24
analysis of contents, 42
editions of, 153
English translation of, 156
main arguments of, 24
problems with manuscripts, 154
style of, 25
Lamp Integrating the Practices, 173
as a source in Yumo, 41
lamp of the abiding ground *(gnas pa gzhi'i sgron ma)*, 73, 85, 236, 272, 316
lamp of the bardo period *(bar do dus kyi sgron ma)*, 73, 91, 259, 332
lamp of examples *(mtshon byed dpe yi sgron ma)*, 318
lamp of the fleshy heart *(tsi ta sha'i sgron ma)*, 73, 86, 246, 294
lamp that introduces the buddhafields *(zhing khams ngo sprod kyi sgron ma)*, 73, 89, 252, 310
lamp of the pure expanse *(dbyings rnam par dag pa'i sgron ma)*, 67, 206, 222–223
lamp of self-emergent insight *(shes rab rang byung gi sgron ma)*, 65, 206, 211–212
lamp of the signs of primordial gnosis *(ye shes rtags kyi sgron ma)*, 318
lamp of the smooth white channel *(dkar 'jam rtsa'i sgron ma)*, 73, 87, 248, 299
Lang Darma, 1
later dissemination *(phyi dar)*, 2
Later Hevajra Tantra, 175
Lhabön Yongsu Dakpa, 75
Litany of Names of Mañjuśrī, 120, 157, 170, 176, 194
little linked lambs *(lu gu rgyud)*, 61–62, 65–68
Longchenpa, 57, 60, 231
Lotus Girl, 7, 98, 115, 125, 163–164, 168, 176, 178–179, 183–184, 186, 189

Mañjuśrī Yaśas, 21
meditative concentration yoga *(bsam gtan)*, 35, 133, 137, 145
memory-driven mind *(dran pa'i blo)*, 283, 297
Menri Monastery, 71
mental factors *(sems byung)*
in Kālacakra visionary context, 47
mental form *(yid gzugs)*, 288
Meü Gong Dzö, 72
Mind Series *(sems sde)*, 52, 60, 72, 90
mind transmission of the nine Sugatas *(bder gshegs dgongs rgyud dgu)*, 235, 268
mirror divination, 98, 120, 163, 166–167, 169, 172, 177–178, 181, 185–186
monism, 55–56
mother and son, inseparability of *(ma bu dbyer med)*, 246
mother, son, and dynamic energy *(ma bu rtsal gsum)*, 83, 239, 280
contemplative introductions to, 316

Nāgārjuna, 41–42, 99, 101, 103, 113–114, 157–158, 160, 162, 172, 178–180, 183
naked seeing *(gcer mthong)*, 235, 251–252, 267, 270, 297, 308, 310–311
Nāmasaṃgiti, 42
Nāropa, 23, 38. *See also Ultimate Letters*
Ngödrup Drakpa, 72
Ngog Lotsawa, 16
nighttime yoga *(mtshan mo'i rnal 'byor)*, 33
Nyingma *(rnying ma)*, 10
during renaissance period, 4, 50
Great Perfection traditions, 51

observable emptiness *(dmigs pa dang bcas pa'i stong pa nyid)*, 43, 163, 168
Öglun Gomchen Tashi Sherab, 347
Ölmo Lung-ring, 5, 70
On Purifying Mental Obscurations, 173, 180, 182
Oral Tradition from Zhang Zhung *(zhang zhung snyan rgyud)*, 10, 71–72
connections with Seminal Heart, 72
experiential transmission *(nyams rgyud)*, 78
lineage, 74–75
long lineage, 76, 269
lower tradition *(smad lugs)*, 78
short lineage, 76, 269
transmission of the word *(bka' rgyud)*, 78
ultimate lineage, 269
upper tradition *(stod lugs)*, 78
oral transmission of the twenty-four men *(gang zag nyi shu rtsa bzhi'i snyan rgyud)*, 75, 235, 268
ordinary mind *(blo)*, 279
Orgom Kündül, 80
Ornament of Sunlight, 231
Ornament of the Vajra Maṇḍala Tantra, 193

path of emptiness, in Yumo. *See* emptiness
Patsün Tengyal, 74, 78, 80, 231
Perfection of Wisdom *(shes rab kyi pha rol tu phyin pa)* scriptures, 99, 162, 165, 189
on five eyes, 106–107
period of fragmentation *(sil pa'i dus)*, 2
phyag khrid (text by Drugyalwa), 379n19, 427n102, 432n178, 433n190, 433n192, 433nn194–195, 434nn198–199
play *(rol pa)*, 56
Pönchen Tsenpo, 79
Praise of Dharmadhātu, 101
Prajñāpāramitā (goddess), 102, 120, 127, 133, 145, 163–168, 170
Prajñāpāramitā (scriptures). *See* Perfection of Wisdom
pramāṇa, 3, 4, 16, 108, 121
Prāsaṅgika, 114
pratisenā. *See* mirror divination

primordial gnosis *(ye shes)*, 168, 196, 204–205, 209, 235, 246, 254–255, 270, 296, 318
prognostic mirror. *See* mirror divination

queens of the four times *(dus bzhi rgyal mo)*, 315

Ramachandran, V.S., 111
recognition *(ngo shes pa)*, 17, 48, 55–56, 58, 83, 84, 90–91, 253, 286, 296, 312, 331–332, 339
recollection yoga *(rjes dran)*, 37
Relpachen, 1
retention yoga *('dzin pa)*, 37
revealed literature, 12, 50, 53, 71, 74
Rong Tokmé Zhikpo, 81
Root Kālacakra Tantra. See Ādibuddha Tantra
rope/snake illusion, 340

Śaivism, 17, 52
Samantabhadra. *See* All Good
Śambhala, 21–22
Samyé Monastery, 1
Sangpu Monastery, 16
Sangwa Düpa (Guhyasamāja), deity in Bön, 75
Śāntideva, 28, 100, 114
Saraha, 174, 176, 189, 191
Sarma *(gsar ma)*, 4, 10, 23, 27, 42, 50–51, 92–93
self-blessing *(bdag la byin gyis brlab pa)*, 41–42, 157–158, 179, 188–189
Seminal Heart *(snying thig)*, 51, 53, 55
  connections with Oral Tradition from Zhang Zhung, 72–73, 81
seminal nuclei. *See thig-le*
sensory deprivation, 7, 12, 33, 65, 110, 121
Seventeen Tantras, 53, 60, 64
  editions of, 201
Shardza Tashi Gyaltsen, 230
Shen *(gshen)*
  eight primordial Shen, 315
  six subduing Shen, 315
Shenchen Lu-ga, 71
Shenrap Miwo, 70
single sphere *(thig le gcig)*, 274, 276, 278
singular essential ground *(ngo bo nyid kyi gzhi gcig)*, 274
singularity *(nyag gcig)*, 56
six consciousnesses *(rnam shes tshogs drug)*, 287–288, 314
six energy wheels *('khor lo drug)*, 315
six important points on the enlightened mind *(byang chub sems kyi gnad drug)*, 85, 235–236, 265, 269, 271, 311, 326
six parameters *(mtha' drug)*, 156, 177, 193, 199
six recollections *(rjes dran drug)*, 339
six superknowledges *(mngon shes drug)*, 261, 338
six-limbed yoga *(sbyor ba yang lag drug)*, 7, 43, 45, 49, 69, 98, 106, 137, 139, 164, 183
  body postures in, 124
  description of, 24, 31
  related to five eyes, 109
  role of *thig-le* in, 140
  in *Vajrapāṇi Commentary*, 31
sky-gazing, 13, 118–119
  in Great Perfection, 57
  in Kālacakra, 33
  in Perfection of Wisdom scriptures, 33
slender coil channel *(phra la 'khril ba)*, 105, 219
Sok Chenpo, 28
Somanātha, 4, 23, 28
Songtsen Gampo, 5
sound, in meditation practice 323
sound, light, and rays *(sgra 'od zer gsum)*, 83, 238–239, 243, 256, 258, 277, 279, 281–282, 284, 286, 289, 312, 324, 330
  at time of death, 337, 339, 342
spontaneity, 12, 24, 31, 34, 62, 69, 119, 132
stage of self-blessing *(bdag la byin gyis brlab pa'i rim pa)*. See self-blessing

Stainless Light, 38, 98, 108, 159, 163, 165, 168–169, 175, 177, 185, 190, 195
straying *('khrul pa)*, 58, 285, 293, 333, 342
Stringing a Garland of Pearls, 55, 60–63, 68, 201–202
Sucandra, 21
Supplement to the Guhyasamāja Tantra, 156
Sūtra of the Illusion-like Samādhi, 180

Tantra of the Adamantine Hero's Heart-Mirror, 58
Tantra of the Blazing Lamps, 10, 55, 104
  analysis of contents, 63
  editions of, 201
  English translation of, 204
  Tibetan commentary on, 55, 202
Tantra of the Primordial Buddha. See *Ādibuddha Tantra*
Tantra of Unimpeded Sound, 55, 142
Tapihritsa, 73, 76–77, 234, 267
ten signs *(rtags bcu)*, 34, 92, 137
thig-le, 61–62, 66, 134
  bodily, 249, 302
  etymology, 134
  four *thig-le*, 220
  in Kālacakra yogas, 35, 37, 137
  mental, 249, 303
  stacking during Kālacakra yogas, 40
  typology of, 135
  ultimate and conventional, 141
  visionary appearances of, 328
Thig-le of the Great Seal Tantra, 167, 171, 173, 187, 191, 195
three buddha bodies *(sku gsum)*, 252, 273, 284, 331
  at time of death, 340
  contemplative introductions to, 311
  discovery of, 315
three channels *(rtsa gsum)*, 303
three expressive energies *(rtsal gsum)*, 277
three gods that clear away poison *(dug sel lha gsum)*, 315
three great presencings *(snang ba chen po gsum)*, 83, 312
three lamps *(sgron ma gsum)*, 253, 316
three realms *(khams gsum)*, 180, 242, 288
thumb-sized primordial gnosis *(ye shes tshon gang)*, 82, 86, 301, 303
treasures *(gter)*, 5, 52–53, 71–72, 74, 77
Treasury of Words and Meanings, 57
Trigum Tsenpo, 70
Trisong Detsen, 51, 71, 76
tsang-ri bur-lang ("head channel"), 82, 89, 251, 308
Tsepung Dawa Gyaltsen, 76, 268

Ultimate Letters, 172, 174, 187, 193
universal form *(sna tshogs gzugs)*, 8, 125, 166, 176, 178–179, 182, 186, 189
universal ground *(kun gzhi)*, 273, 275, 294, 296
  at time of death, 342
  contemplative introductions to, 318
  ultimate abiding universal ground *(don gyi kun gzhi)*, 276
  universal ground of embodied knowing awareness *(shes rig rgyud kyi kun gzhi)*, 238, 274, 276, 278
universal ground consciousness *(kun gzhi rnam shes)*, 278
Uri Sogyal, 78, 231

Vajra Tent, 161
Vajradhara, 53
Vajragarbha Commentary, 3, 28
Vajrapāṇi, 51, 180–181
Vajrapāṇi Commentary, 31, 120, 163, 166, 172
Vajravārāhī, 196
view of emptiness, in Yumo. *See* emptiness
Vijñānabhairava, 17
Vimalamitra, 51, 55
vinaya, and restraint of the eyes, 65
vision, types of, 11
visionary "objects." *(snang ba'i yul)*, 276–277, 282–283, 285–286

visionary appearances
descriptions of, 323, 325, 327
nature of in Kālacakra, 34
visual "filling-in," 111
visualization, 6, 29
and sexual yoga, 132
association with conceptuality, 31
contrasted to vision, 11, 24, 39
in generation stage yogas, 29
Viśvamātā, 24, 44, 102, 127, 165, 196
as empty form image, 37
yoga as embracing Viśvamātā, 37

winds *(rlung)*, 88, 249
coarse *(snyigs ma)*, 305
role in development of body, 301
secondary, 249
smooth and coarse, 302
vibrant *(dwangs ma)*, 304
withdrawal yoga *(sor sdud)*, 32, 120, 133, 137, 145

Yangtön Chenpo, 78
Yeru Wensakha, 71, 79, 231
yogic postures *('dug stangs)*, 124
in Great Perfection, 61, 124
in Kālacakra, 33, 124
Yumo Mikyo Dorjé, 10
biography, 3, 27
early interest in Kālacakra, 23
magical abilities, 28, 29
writing style and methods, 26

Zhang Zhung, 5, 70
Zhangtön Tashi Dorjé, 54, 81

CPSIA information can be obtained at www.ICGtesting.com
Printed in the USA
BVOW04s1411081214

378284BV00001B/1/P

9 780199 982912